Windows 7: The Definitive Guide

William R. Stanek

O'REILLY®

Beijing · Cambridge · Farnham · Köln · Sebastopol · Taipei · Tokyo

Windows 7: The Definitive Guide
by William R. Stanek

Copyright © 2010 William Stanek. All rights reserved.
Printed in the United States of America.

Published by O'Reilly Media, Inc., 1005 Gravenstein Highway North, Sebastopol, CA 95472.

O'Reilly books may be purchased for educational, business, or sales promotional use. Online editions are also available for most titles (*http://my.safaribooksonline.com*). For more information, contact our corporate/institutional sales department: (800) 998-9938 or *corporate@oreilly.com*.

Editors: Brian Jepson and Laurel R. T. Ruma	**Cover Designer:** Karen Montgomery
Production Editor: Sumita Mukherji	**Interior Designer:** David Futato
Copyeditor: Nancy Kotary	**Illustrator:** Robert Romano
Production Services: Newgen North America	

Printing History:

October 2009:   First Edition.

ISBN: 978-0-596-80097-0

[C]   [4/10]

1259953106

Table of Contents

Preface xvii

Part I. Setting Up, Customizing, and Tuning Windows 7

1. Getting Started with Windows 7 3
Getting to Know Windows 7   3
Installing and Using Windows 7   7
    Logging On and Finalizing the Installation   8
    Performing Essential Configuration Tasks   9
    Reviewing and Activating Your Computer   15
Working with Windows 7   17
Logging On, Switching, Locking, Logging Off, and Shutting Down   21
    Logging On to Your Computer   21
    Switching Users   21
    Locking Your Computer   22
    Logging Off Your Computer   22
    Sleeping and Turning Off Your Computer   22

2. Optimizing Windows 7's Interface 25
Customizing Windows 7's Desktop   25
    Getting Around the Desktop   26
    Getting Around the Start Menu   29
    Getting Around the Taskbar   41
Using Desktop Gadgets   49
    Getting to Know Your Computer's Gadgets   50
Customizing Menus and the Control Panel   57
    Navigating and Customizing Your Computer's Menus   57
    Navigating and Customizing the Control Panel   60

3. Fine-Tuning Windows 7's Appearance and Performance **65**

Balancing Appearance and Performance   65
    Getting Your Windows Experience Index Score   66
    Understanding Your Windows Experience Index Score   67
    Improving Your Windows Experience Index Score   69
Understanding User Account Control and Its Impact on Performance   71
    User Accounts and Permissions   71
    Permission and Consent Prompting   72
    Elevation and the Secure Desktop   72
    Configuring and Tuning UAC   74
Understanding Windows 7 Personalization   75
    Personalization Settings   76
    User Experience Levels   78
Personalizing Windows 7   79
    Fine-Tuning Your Window Colors and Experience Level   80
    Choosing Your Desktop Background   82
    Choosing and Configuring Your Screensaver   85
    Choosing Your System Sounds   90
    Choosing Your Mouse Pointers   91
    Choosing and Managing Your Themes   93
    Configuring Your Monitors   94
Optimizing Performance   98
    Fine-Tuning Visual Effects   99
    Fine-Tuning Application Performance   101
    Fine-Tuning Virtual Memory   101
    Fine-Tuning Data Execution Prevention   104
    Using ReadyBoost to Enhance Performance   105

4. Installing, Configuring, and Maintaining Software **111**

Software Installation: What's Changed   111
Software Installation: What You Need to Know   113
    AutoPlay   113
    Autorun   114
    Application Setup   116
    Windows and 64-bit Programs   118
Installing and Running Your Software   119
    Installing Software   119
    Making Software Available to Others   120
    Using MS-DOS and 16-Bit Software with Windows 7   122
    Running Applications in Windows XP Mode   123
    Using Older Programs with Windows 7   123
Managing Software Once It's Installed   129
    Assigning Default Programs   129

Reconfiguring, Repairing, or Uninstalling Software   132
Viewing and Managing Currently Running Programs   134
Viewing and Managing Startup Programs   135
Adding and Removing Windows Features   137

5. Customizing Your Computer's Hardware Devices **141**
Hardware Installation: What's Changed   141
Which Type of Internal Device Is the Right Choice?   142
Which Type of External Device Is the Right Choice?   143
Hardware Installation: What You Need to Know   146
Where Does the Operating System Store Device Drivers?   146
How Does the Operating System Validate Device Drivers?   148
How Does the Operating System Obtain Driver Updates?   149
Learning About Your Computer's Hardware Devices   151
Viewing Installed Hardware   152
Getting to Know Your Computer's Hardware Devices   153
Viewing and Managing Device Information   161
Customizing Your Computer's Input Devices, Regional Settings, and Date/
Time   163
Optimizing Your Keyboard Settings   164
Optimizing Your Mouse Settings   167
Optimizing Your Audio Settings   169
Optimizing Your Computer's Regional and Language Settings   172
Optimizing Your Computer's Date and Time Settings   174
Installing and Managing Hardware   177
Getting Available but Unconfigured Hardware to Work   177
Installing New Hardware Devices   179
Installing and Maintaining Device Drivers   182
Rolling Back Device Drivers   184
Enabling, Disabling, Removing, and Uninstalling Hardware Devices   185
Troubleshooting Hardware   187

Part II.   Mastering Your Data and Digital Media

6. Exploring and Searching Your Computer **193**
Exploring Your Documents   193
Navigating Your Computer with the Address Bar   196
Accessing Locations on Your Computer   196
Using Selected Paths to Quickly Navigate Your Computer   198
Putting Windows Explorer to Work for You   203
Setting Folder Options   203
Optimizing Folder Views   206

Searching Your Computer 208
   Searching Your Computer: The Essentials 208
   Searching Your Computer: Search Options 210
   Searching Your Computer: Search Filters 213
   Searching Your Computer: Save Search Options 221
Indexing Your Computer for Faster Searches 223
   Adding or Removing Indexed Locations 223
   Specifying Files Types to Include or Exclude 226
   Optimizing File Properties for Indexing 229
   Resolving Indexing Problems 231

7. Navigating the Web with Internet Explorer 8 .... **233**
Getting Started with Internet Explorer 8 234
Getting Around the Web and Using Internet Explorer 8 238
   Navigating Web Page Addresses 238
   Searching the Web and Setting Search Providers 239
   Working with Internet Explorer Menus and Toolbars 242
   Using Caret Browsing and Other Features 244
   Configuring Web Pages as Home Pages 247
   Printing Web Pages Without Wasting Paper 248
   Understanding Status Bar Indicators 250
Protecting Your Computer While Browsing 251
   Viewing and Managing Add-Ons 251
   Understanding Web Address and Domain Restrictions 254
   Viewing and Managing Browsing History 255
   Blocking Pop-Ups 262
   Protecting Your Computer from Phishing 265
   Restricting Permissions Using Security Zones 265
   Setting Advanced Internet Options 275
   Troubleshooting Internet Explorer Problems 280

8. Creating Your Media Library with Windows Media Player **283**
Getting into Your Multimedia 283
   Configuring Windows Media Player for the First Use 284
   Navigating Windows Media Player Menus and Toolbars 287
Playing Your Media 297
   Playing Media Added to Your Library 298
   Playing Video DVDs Loaded into Your DVD Drive 301
   Playing Audio CDs Loaded into Your CD/DVD Drive 304
   Enhancing Your Playback 305
Building Your Media Library 309
   Adding Media Folders to Your Media Library 310
   Adding Media to Your Library When Played 311

Ripping Audio CDs into Your Media Library	312
Creating and Managing Playlists	320
Deleting Media and Playlists	321
Burning Audio CDs and Data CDs or DVDs	322
Syncing Your Media to MP3 Players and Other Devices	326

9. Capturing and Managing Your Digital Pictures and Videos **333**

Getting Started with Windows Live Photo Gallery	334
Accessing Key Features	336
Searching and Browsing Pictures and Videos	337
Organizing Your Gallery	339
Grouping and Sorting Your Gallery	339
Viewing Your Pictures and Videos	341
Viewing and Managing Ratings, Tags, and Captions	343
Identifying People in Your Pictures	346
Building Your Photo and Video Gallery	348
Adding or Removing Media Folders	348
Getting Your Digital Pictures	349
Getting Your Videos	350
Importing Digital Pictures from Cameras, Scanners, CDs, and DVDs	352
Importing Digital Videos from Cameras, CDs, and DVDs	356
Changing the Default AutoPlay Settings	356
Configuring Import Settings	358
Fixing Your Pictures	359
Sharing Your Photo and Video Gallery	366
Publishing Your Pictures	366
Printing Your Pictures	367
Emailing Your Pictures and Videos	369
Burning Data CDs and DVDs	370

10. Making Video DVDs and Movies **379**

Creating Video DVDs with Windows DVD Maker	380
Getting Started with Windows DVD Maker	380
Adding Your Pictures and Videos, and Setting the Play Order	383
Setting the DVD Burning and Playback Options	389
Customizing the DVD Menu	392
Customizing Your Picture Slideshow and Adding an Audio Soundtrack	395
Previewing and Finishing Your Video Project	397
Opening and Burning Saved Projects	400
Creating Movies with Windows Movie Maker	401
Getting Started with Windows Movie Maker	401
Creating Your Storyboard	404
Editing Your Storyboard	406

Creating an AutoMovie   409
Adding Effects to Your Video   412
Adding Transitions to Your Video   414
Adding Narration, Music, and Other Audio   416
Adding Titles, Credits, and Overlays   419
Setting Video Options   421
Previewing and Finishing Your Movie Project   422
Opening and Producing Saved Projects   427
Creating Movies with Windows Live Movie Maker   427
Getting Started with Windows Live Movie Maker   428
Creating and Editing Your Live Storyboard   430
Creating a Live AutoMovie   435
Adding Animations and Visual Effects to Your Live Video   436
Adding a Soundtrack to Your Live Video   438
Adding Text Overlays to Your Live Video   439
Previewing and Finishing Your Live Video Project   441
Opening and Producing Saved Projects   443

11. **Securing and Sharing Your Data** **445**
Securing Your Files   446
FAT Versus NTFS   446
File Attributes   446
NTFS Permissions   449
Controlling Access to Your Data   450
Basic Permissions   450
Special Permissions   453
Ownership Permissions   457
Inherited Permissions   459
Effective Permissions   460
Sharing Your Data   461
Enabling Sharing   461
Configuring Standard Folder Sharing   467
Accessing Shared Data   471
Accessing Shared Folders Offline   472
Working Offline and Syncing   474

12. **Setting Up Printers, Scanners, and Fax Machines** **477**
Installing Printers, Scanners, and Fax Machines   477
Installing Physically Attached Printers, Scanners, and Fax Machines   478
Installing Wireless and Bluetooth Printers   485
Installing Network-Attached Printers, Scanners, and Fax Machines   488
Sharing Printers, Scanners, and Fax Machines   491
Sharing Printers and Fax Machines   491

Connecting to Shared Printers and Fax Machines 493
Sharing and Connecting to Scanners 495
Configuring Printer, Scanner, and Fax Machine Properties 495
Changing Ports for Printers, Scanners, and Fax Machines 495
Changing Printer, Scanner, and Fax Machine Drivers 497
Setting Printer Scheduling, Prioritization, and Other Options 498
Managing Print, Fax, and Scan Jobs 501
Working with Print Jobs 501
Working with Printers 503
Working with Scanners and Fax Machines 504

13. Making the Most of Windows' Accessories **509**
Capturing Screens and Windows with the Snipping Tool 509
Creating Snips 509
Editing and Saving Your Snips 511
Setting Snipping Options 512
Creating Sticky Notes 513
Getting Your Computer to Listen 514
Getting Started with Speech Recognition 515
Configuring Speech Recognition for First Use 516
Using Speech Recognition for Dictation 519
Using Laptop and Tablet PC Extras 520
Navigating the Windows Mobility Center 521
Connecting to Projectors 523
Using Your Tablet PC Pen 526
Creating a Windows Journal 531
Making Your Computer More Accessible 535
Using the Ease of Access Center 535
Using the Magnifier 536
Using the On-Screen Keyboard 537
Using Narrator 538
Making the Keyboard Easier to Use 540

Part III.   Connecting and Networking

14. Setting Up Your Network **545**
Understanding Home and Small-Business Networks 545
Requirements for Building a Small Network 546
Installing Network Adapters in Your Computers 548
Installing Ethernet Routers, Hubs, and Switches 549
Setting Up a Wireless Router or Access Point 550
Mapping Your Networking Infrastructure 551

        Using the Network and Sharing Center   551
        Viewing the Network Map   557
        Viewing and Managing Your Network Connections   559
    Networking with TCP/IP   561
        Understanding IPv4   561
        Using Private IPv4 Addresses and Networking Protocols   563
        Understanding IPv6   564
        Configuring IPv4, IPv6, and Other Protocols   567
    Advanced Networking Concepts   571
        Introducing VPN   571
        Introducing IPSec   572
        Understanding the OSI Model   573
    Troubleshooting Common Problems on Small Networks   574
        Using the Network Diagnostics and Repair Option   574
        Checking Physical Connectivity   575
        Using the Command Line to Diagnose Network Problems   577
        Fixing Network Problems   580

15. **Protecting Your Computer with Windows Defender and Windows Firewall** **583**
    Navigating the Computer Security Maze   583
        Introducing Malware   584
        Understanding Antimalware Programs   586
        Understanding Computer Viruses   587
        Introducing Antivirus Programs   590
        Understanding Spyware   592
        Introducing Antispyware Programs   594
    Introducing Action Center   595
    Using Windows Defender   597
        Working with Windows Defender   597
        Configuring Windows Defender   598
        Scanning Your Computer for Spyware and Malware   607
        Using Windows Defender Tools   608
        Troubleshooting Windows Defender   610
    Working with the Windows Firewall   612
        Windows Firewall Features and Improvements   612
        Configuring Security for the Basic Windows Firewall   614
        Troubleshooting the Basic Windows Firewall   617
        Configuring Advanced Firewall Security   618
        Troubleshooting Advanced Firewall Problems   627

16. **Using Windows Live for Email, Calendars, and Contacts** **631**
    Getting Started with Windows Live   631
    Using Windows Live Mail   633

Getting to Know Windows Live Mail   634
Setting Up Windows Live Mail and Configuring Email Accounts   637
Creating, Sending, and Receiving Email   640
Protecting Yourself from Junk Email   643
Protecting Yourself from Phishing Links   645
Changing Windows Live Mail Security Settings   646
Using Windows Live Contacts   648
Getting to Know Windows Live Contacts   649
What's in a Live Contact?   650
Creating Live Contacts for Individuals   651
Importing and Exporting Contacts   653
Creating Contact Categories   653
Using Windows Live Calendar   655
Getting to Know Windows Live Calendar   655
Creating and Using Calendars   657
Sharing Your Calendars with Others   658
Synchronizing Google Calendar with Windows Live Calendar   662
Scheduling Appointments and Meetings   663
Viewing Agendas and Creating To-Do Lists   664

17. Mastering Dial-Up, Broadband, and On-the-Go Networking **669**
Configuring Dial-Up, Broadband, Wireless, and VPN   669
Creating Dial-Up Connections   672
Creating Broadband Connections   684
Creating VPN Connections   684
Configuring Proxy Settings   687
Enabling and Disabling Windows Firewall   689
Establishing Network Connections   691
Wireless Networking   692
Wireless Network Technologies   693
Wireless Network Devices   694
Installing and Configuring a Wireless Adapter   695
Connecting to and Managing Wireless Connections   696
Configuring Available and Preferred Wireless Networks   699
Setting Up a Wireless Router or Access Point   700

Part IV.   Managing and Supporting Windows 7

18. Managing User Accounts and Parental Controls **705**
Managing Access to Your Computer   706
Managing Your User Account   707
Changing Your Account Name   707

Changing Your Account Picture   708
Changing Your Account Type   709
Creating Your Password   710
Changing Your Password   710
Storing Your Password for Recovery   711
Recovering Your Password   712
Managing Other People's User Accounts   713
Creating User Accounts for Other People   713
Changing User Account Names for Other People   714
Changing the Account Picture for Other People   715
Changing the Account Type for Other People   716
Creating a Password for Other People's Accounts   717
Changing the Password on Other People's Accounts   718
Storing Another Person's Password for Recovery   719
Recovering Another Person's Password   720
Enabling Local User Accounts   720
Controlling the Way Account Passwords Are Used   721
Deleting Local User Accounts   722
Managing Access Permissions with Group Accounts   723
Creating Local Groups   723
Adding and Removing Local Group Members   726
Renaming Local User Accounts and Groups   726
Deleting Groups   726
Keeping Your Family Safe While Using Your Computer   727
Turning On Parental Controls   727
Selecting a Game Rating System   729
Configuring Time Restrictions   729
Configuring Game Restrictions   730
Configuring Application Restrictions   731
Configuring Additional Controls   733

19. **Managing Disks and Drives** **735**
Configuring Disks and Drives   735
Using Disk Management   736
Installing and Initializing New Disks   740
Converting a Basic Disk to a Dynamic Disk   741
Converting a Dynamic Disk to a Basic Disk   742
Preparing Disks for Use   743
Creating Mirrored, Spanned, or Striped Volumes   746
Adding a Mirror to an Existing Volume   748
Shrinking or Extending Volumes   749
Creating and Attaching Virtual Hard Disks   752
Formatting Volumes   753

Changing Drive Letters 754
Changing Volume Labels 755
Converting a Volume to NTFS 755
Deleting Volumes 756
Maintaining and Recovering Volumes 756
Troubleshooting Disk Problems 757
Breaking or Removing Mirroring 757
Resynchronizing and Repairing a Mirrored Set 758
Repairing a Mirrored System or Boot Volume 759
Using Compression and Encryption 760
Compressing Drives 760
Compressing Files and Folders 762
Encrypting Files and Folders 765

20. **Handling Routine Maintenance and Troubleshooting** **771**
Maintaining Your System Configuration 772
Configuring the Computer Name and Membership 772
Creating or Joining a Homegroup 776
Viewing Hardware Settings 777
Configuring User Profiles, Environment Variables, and Startup and
Recovery 779
Configuring Remote Access 785
General Maintenance Tools 789
Updating Your Computer 789
Cleaning Up Your Disk Drives 794
Checking Your Disks for Errors 797
Optimizing Disk Performance 799
Scheduling Maintenance Tasks 801
Getting Started with Task Scheduling 801
Creating Basic Tasks 803
Creating Advanced Tasks 806
Managing and Troubleshooting Tasks 807

21. **Getting Help and Handling Advanced Support Issues** **809**
Detecting and Resolving Computer Problems 809
Solving the Tough Problems Automatically (and Sometimes with a Little
Help) 810
Tracking Errors in the Event Logs 814
Resolving Problems with System Services 816
Creating Backups and Preparing for Problems 819
Configuring System Protection 820
Configuring Previous Versions 823
Scheduling and Managing Automated Backups 823

Recovering After a Crash or Other Problem   830
   Recovering Using Restore Points   831
   Restoring Previous Versions of Files   834
   Recovering Files from Backup   836
   Resolving Restart or Shutdown Issues   838
   Recovering from a Failed Resume   839
   Repairing a Computer to Enable Startup   840
   Recovering Your Computer Using Windows RE   843
   Safeguarding Your Computer from a Corrupted Windows RE   844
   Recovering Your Computer from Backup   845
   Reinstalling Windows 7   845
Getting Help and Giving Others Assistance   845
   Getting Help from Another Person   846
   Giving Other People Assistance   847
   Connecting to Your Computer Remotely   847
Troubleshooting Windows 7 Programs and Features   849
   Resolving Problems with Programs and Features   849
   Restoring the Windows 7 Boot Sector   853
   Changing Disc Close on Eject Settings   854
   Removing Disk Partitions During Installation   854

Part V. Advanced Tips and Techniques

22. Installing and Running Windows 7 859
Comparing Windows 7 Features and Versions   859
Installing Windows 7   862
   Performing a Clean Installation   863
   Performing an Upgrade Installation   864
Upgrading Your Windows 7 Edition   866

23. Exploring the Windows Boot Environment 867
Introducing the Windows 7 Boot Environment   867
Working with Boot Configuration Data   868
   Using the Startup and Recovery Dialog Box   869
   Using the System Configuration Utility   870
   Using the BCD Editor   871
Managing the BCD Data Store   876
   Changing the Default Operating System   876
   Changing the Default Timeout   877
   Enabling Physical Address Expansion   877
   Changing the Operating System Display Order   878
   Changing the Restart Boot Sequence   879

Managing the Boot Sector for Hard Disk Partitions 879
    Using the Boot Sector Configurator 879
    Installing a Previous Version of Windows on a Computer Running
    Windows 7 880

24. Using Group Policy with Windows 7 .... **883**
    Exploring Group Policy in Windows 7 883
        Introducing the Group Policy Client Service 884
        Using Multiple Local Group Policy Objects 884
        Enhancing Group Policy Application 885
        Improving Group Policy Management 885
        Editing Group Policy 888
    Working with Multiple Local Group Policy Objects 889
        Understanding Multiple Local Group Policy Object Usage 889
        Creating Multiple Local Group Policy Objects 891
        Deleting Local Group Policy Objects 892
    Updating Active Directory Group Policy Objects for Windows 7 894

25. Mastering Windows Media Center **895**
    Understanding Windows Media Center Requirements 895
    Selecting the Correct Hardware for Windows Media Center 896
        Video Cards 896
        Sound Cards 897
    Installing and Configuring Windows Media Center Using the Wizard 897
    Navigating Windows Media Center 901
        Adding Media to Your Libraries 902
        Working with Pictures + Videos 903
        Working with Music 911
        Working with Now Playing 914
        Working with Movies 915
        Working with Recorded TV 917
        Tracking Your Sports Players and Teams 919
        Working with the Extras Library 921
        Burning Discs 923
        Working with Tasks 924
    Fine-Tuning the Settings for Windows Media Center 924
        Configuring Window Behavior 925
        Configuring Visual and Sound Effects 926
        Configuring Parental Controls 927
        Configuring Automatic Download Options 930
        Configuring Optimization 931
        Using the About Windows Media Center Menu 931
        Viewing Privacy Information in Windows Media Center 932

Using Windows Media Center Setup   932
Troubleshooting Problems with Windows Media Center   936
    Troubleshooting with the Windows Media Center Setup Menu   936
    Troubleshooting Windows Media Center Networking Issues   937
    Troubleshooting TV Tuner and Video Capture Problems   938
    Troubleshooting Sound Problems   938

Index 941

Preface

As you've probably noticed, there's more than enough information about Windows 7 on the Web. There are tutorials, reference sites, discussion groups, and more to help make it easier to use Windows 7. However, the advantage to reading this book instead is that all of the information you need to learn Windows 7 is organized in one place and presented in a straightforward and orderly fashion. This book has everything you need to customize Windows 7, master your digital media, manage your data, and maintain your computer.

But wait, there's more: there are plenty of other Windows 7 books available. Other books introduce and simplify Windows 7, or provide quick starts or step-by-step guides, or promise to teach even dummies how to use Windows 7. In this book, I don't pretend anyone is a dummy and I don't just teach you the steps you need to follow; I teach you how features work, why they work the way they work, and how to customize them to meet your needs. You'll also learn why you may want to use certain features of the operating system and when to use other features to resolve any problems you are having. In addition, this book provides tips, suggestions, and examples of how to optimize your computer for performance, not just appearance. This book won't just teach you how to configure your computer—it'll teach you how to squeeze out every last bit of power, and how to make the most out of the features and programs included in Windows 7. It'll also teach you how to take advantage of the latest features.

Also, unlike many other books on the subject, this book doesn't focus on a specific user level. This isn't a lightweight beginner book or a book written exclusively for developers or administrators. Regardless of whether you are a beginner, power user, or seasoned professional, many of the concepts in this book will be valuable to you. And you'll be able to apply them to your computer regardless of which edition of Windows 7 you are using.

How This Book Is Organized

Rome wasn't built in a day, and this book wasn't intended to be read in a day, a week, or even 21 days. Ideally, you'll read this book at your own pace, a little each day as you work your way through all the features Windows 7 has to offer. This book is organized into 5 parts and 25 chapters. The chapters are arranged in a logical order, taking you from the simplest tasks to the more advanced ones. The tasks you'll perform the most and will get the most benefit from are right up front. The tasks you'll perform less often but will find extremely important for maintaining your computer come later.

In Part I, *Setting Up, Customizing, and Tuning Windows 7*, you'll find everything you need to set up, customize, and optimize Windows 7's core features:

Chapter 1, *Getting Started with Windows 7*
Provides details on getting started with Windows 7. You'll learn about the various editions of the product, upgrade options, starting and using Windows 7, and critical changes from earlier releases of Windows.

Chapter 2, *Optimizing Windows 7's Interface*
Focuses on optimizing the user interface in Windows 7. You'll also learn about key features, including full-screen previews, flip, flip 3D, and jump lists.

Chapter 3, *Fine-Tuning Windows 7's Appearance and Performance*
Provides tips and techniques for fine-tuning Windows 7's appearance and performance. You'll also learn how to personalize Windows 7.

Chapter 4, *Installing, Configuring, and Maintaining Software*
Discusses installing and configuring the software, and includes extensive details on how software installation has changed and the features you can use to manage the software once it's installed.

Chapter 5, *Customizing Your Computer's Hardware Devices*
Discusses installing and configuring hardware, and includes extensive details on how hardware installation has changed and the features you can use to manage hardware once it's installed.

Part II, *Mastering Your Data and Digital Media*, explores everything you need to know to take control of the data and media stored on your computer:

Chapter 6, *Exploring and Searching Your Computer*
Examines the changes and new features in Windows Explorer, including new navigation and search options. You'll also learn how to optimize the search features of the operating system.

Chapter 7, *Navigating the Web with Internet Explorer 8*
Discusses Internet Explorer, the browser included with Windows 7 editions. You'll learn tips and techniques for making the most of the powerful new features of the browser, and you'll learn how to protect your computer and your data while surfing the Web.

Chapter 8, *Creating Your Media Library with Windows Media Player*
Details how to use Windows Media Player to build a media library. You'll learn how to rip and burn audio CDs as well as data CDs and DVDs. You'll also learn how to make the most of your music, pictures, videos, and recorded TV shows.

Chapter 9, *Capturing and Managing Your Digital Pictures and Videos*
Shows you how to capture, organize, and manage digital pictures and digital videos using Windows Live Photo Gallery. You'll learn how to optimize and organize your collection, how to create slide shows, and how to burn CDs and DVDs to create copies of your pictures and videos.

Chapter 10, *Making Video DVDs and Movies*
Windows 7 includes built-in support for burning DVDs. This chapter explores the ins and outs of making video DVDs and movies using Windows DVD Maker and Windows Live Movie Maker.

Chapter 11, *Securing and Sharing Your Data*
Explains how to secure your data by setting access permissions, and how to share your data. As Windows 7 includes a completely new set of file sharing options, experienced users will want to read this chapter closely to learn about the new sharing options and how they are best used.

Chapter 12, *Setting Up Printers, Scanners, and Fax Machines*
Teaches you how to set up and configure printers, scanners, and fax machines.

Chapter 13, *Making the Most of Windows' Accessories*
Explores the wealth of accessories included with Windows 7, including the Snipping Tool, Windows Speech Recognition, Mobility Center, Sticky Notes, Windows Journal, and more.

Part III, *Connecting and Networking*, examines everything you need to know to get connected and network your computer:

Chapter 14, *Setting Up Your Network*
Describes how to set up a home or small-office network and how to configure Transmission Control Protocol/Internet Protocol (TCP/IP)—the primary networking protocol used by Windows 7.

Chapter 15, *Protecting Your Computer with Windows Defender and Windows Firewall*
Explores computer security and the features included in Windows 7 to protect your computer and your data while you are connected to the Internet. You'll learn about viruses, spyware, malware, and the programs used to protect your computer from them: Windows Defender and Windows Firewall.

Chapter 16, *Using Windows Live for Email, Calendars, and Contacts*
Explains how to use Windows Live desktop programs for e-mail, calendaring, and contacts.

Chapter 17, *Mastering Dial-Up, Broadband, and On-the-Go Networking*
Teaches you everything you need to know to master dial-up, broadband, and on-the-go networking.

In Part IV, *Managing and Supporting Windows 7*, you'll learn the techniques you can use to manage access to and support Windows 7:

Chapter 18, *Managing User Accounts and Parental Controls*
Focuses on user and group accounts, and discusses parental controls. Also discusses Windows Life Family Safety.

Chapter 19, *Managing Disks and Drives*
Provides tips for installing, partitioning, formatting, and mounting disks. You'll also learn about data compression and encryption.

Chapter 20, *Handling Routine Maintenance and Troubleshooting*
Provides a one-stop shop for everything you need to know to perform routine maintenance and begin troubleshooting.

Chapter 21, *Getting Help and Handling Advanced Support Issues*
Zeros in on advanced support issues to help you diagnose and resolve tough problems.

In Part V, *Advanced Tips and Techniques*, you'll learn about Windows 7's most advanced features:

Chapter 22, *Installing and Running Windows 7*
Although not everyone will need to install Windows 7 from scratch, this chapter tells you how to perform a standard installation and an upgrade installation.

Chapter 23, *Exploring the Windows Boot Environment*
Explores the new boot environment used by Windows 7. You'll learn about boot configuration data and how to view or edit it. You'll also learn how to manage the boot sector and install a previous version of Windows on a computer running Windows 7.

Chapter 24, *Using Group Policy with Windows 7*
Explains all about using Group Policy with Windows 7 and the important changes to Group Policy.

Chapter 25, *Mastering Windows Media Center*
Explores installing and configuring Windows Media Center. The chapter also provides a detailed guide to mastering Windows Media Center once you have it up and running. As you'll see, getting Windows Media Center to work can be a challenge—even for a seasoned professional.

Who Should Read This Book

Library Journal praised my last O'Reilly book, *Windows Vista: The Definitive Guide*, as the best of its kind on the market and recommended it above all other books. Over the past many weeks and months, I've endeavored to make this book worthy of that high praise as well—and I hope you agree.

As the author of over 100 books, I've always wanted to write the kind of how-to book that anyone — regardless of his or her skill level—could read from cover to cover and walk away with a wealth of knowledge about the subject at hand. O'Reilly is the first publisher to let me write a computer book for anyone and everyone in my own unique style, and the result is the book you hold in your hands. As the author of many other Windows books and a user of Windows since its earliest beginnings, I bring a unique perspective to this book—the kind of perspective you can gain only after working with a product for many, many years. I'm also a professionally trained writer, which means my approach is from the perspective of someone who is both deeply technical and an actual writer. In the past, readers have appreciated this rare combination and I hope find my approach refreshing as well.

Is this book for you? That depends:

- If you've seen Windows 7 and want to upgrade from an earlier release of Windows, this book is for you.
- If your home computer includes Windows 7 and you want to learn about the operating system, this book is for you.
- If you are using Windows 7 at work and you want to learn about the operating system, this book is for you.
- If you are an information manager and want to learn about Windows 7, this book is for you.
- If you are a developer or administrator and want to learn about Windows 7, this book is for you, but you'll probably want to have an administrators' book as well.

If you've never seen a computer before, but you've heard that Windows 7 is really neat, this book isn't for you. You'll need a more general book about computing before you are ready to use this book.

What You Need Before You Start

There are hundreds of books on the market that explain how to get started with computers, the Internet, and other technologies related to computers. This book isn't one of them. I'm assuming that if you're reading this book, you already have a working knowledge of computers and the Internet. If you don't have a computer at home, that's fine, but you should have previously used a computer at work or at a library. You should also have some knowledge of how operating systems work and how to use a browser to surf the Web. If you know what the Start button is and what Internet Explorer is, you're in good shape—please read on!

Conventions Used in This Book

Within this book, I'll use the following typographical conventions:

Italic
> Indicates URLs and introduces new terms.

`Constant-width`
> Indicates code terms, command-line text, and command-line options, and values that should be typed literally.

`Constant-width italic`
> Indicates variables and user-defined elements.

I'll also use the following elements:

> Notes, which provide additional information or highlight a specific point.

> Warnings, which provide details on potential problems.

Other Resources

No single magic bullet exists for learning everything you'll ever need to know about Windows 7. Although some books are offered as all-in-one guides, there's simply no way one book can do it all. With this in mind, I hope you'll use this book as it is intended to be used—as a comprehensive, but by no means exhaustive, guide. Plenty of other great Windows 7 books are available—and I've even written a few of them. So as you set out to learn and truly master Windows 7, I hope you'll keep this in mind.

Also, your current knowledge will largely determine your success with this or any other Windows 7 book. As you encounter new topics, take the time to practice what you've learned and read about. Seek out further information as necessary to get the practical, hands-on knowledge you need.

Throughout your studies, I recommend that you regularly visit Microsoft's Windows 7 site (*http://www.microsoft.com/windows7*) and Microsoft's support site (*http://support .microsoft.com*) to stay current with the latest changes in the operating system. To help you get the most out of this book, there's a corresponding website at *http://www.wil liamstanek.com/windows7*. This site contains information about Windows 7, updates to the book, and updated information about Windows 7.

How to Contact Us

The good folks at O'Reilly and I tested and verified the information in this book to the best of our ability, but you may find that features have changed (or even that we have made—gasp!—mistakes!). To make this book better, please let us know about any errors you find, as well as your suggestions for future editions, by writing to:

O'Reilly Media, Inc.
1005 Gravenstein Highway North
Sebastopol, CA 95472
800-998-9938 (in the U.S. or Canada)
707-829-0515 (international/local)
707-829-0104 (fax)

You can also send us messages electronically. To be put on the mailing list or request a catalog, send email to:

info@oreilly.com

There is a catalog page for this book, which lists errata, examples, or any additional information. You can access this page at:

http://www.oreilly.com/catalog/9780596528003

To ask technical questions or comment on the book, send email to:

bookquestions@oreilly.com

For more information about O'Reilly, please visit:

http://www.oreilly.com

For more information about the author, please visit:

http://www.williamstanek.com

You are welcome to send your thoughts to me at *williamstanek@aol.com*. If you contact me about features that you'd like to know more about, I'll try to either update my website or add the information to the next edition of the book. Thank you.

Using Code Examples

This book is here to help you get your job done. In general, you may use the code in this book in your programs and documentation. You do not need to contact us for permission unless you're reproducing a significant portion of the code. For example, writing a program that uses several chunks of code from this book does not require permission. Selling or distributing a CD-ROM of examples from O'Reilly books does require permission. Answering a question by citing this book and quoting example code does not require permission. Incorporating a significant amount of example code from this book into your product's documentation does require permission.

We appreciate, but do not require, attribution. An attribution usually includes the title, author, publisher, and ISBN. For example: "*Windows 7: The Definitive Guide* by William R. Stanek. Copyright 2010 O'Reilly Media, Inc., 978-0-596-80097-0."

If you feel your use of code examples falls outside fair use or the permission given above, feel free to contact us at *permissions@oreilly.com*.

Safari® Books Online

Safari Books Online is an on-demand digital library that lets you easily search over 7,500 technology and creative reference books and videos to find the answers you need quickly.

With a subscription, you can read any page and watch any video from our library online. Read books on your cell phone and mobile devices. Access new titles before they are available for print, and get exclusive access to manuscripts in development and post feedback for the authors. Copy and paste code samples, organize your favorites, download chapters, bookmark key sections, create notes, print out pages, and benefit from tons of other time-saving features.

O'Reilly Media has uploaded this book to the Safari Books Online service. To have full digital access to this book and others on similar topics from O'Reilly and other publishers, sign up for free at *http://my.safaribooksonline.com*.

Acknowledgments

Increasingly, I find myself trying to do things in fundamentally different ways than they've been done before. For this book, I had the crazy idea that I could get everything I've learned about Windows 7 over the past many years into a single volume that was not only clear and concise but also straightforward and easy to use, giving you, the reader, maximum value and maximum learning potential. With that in mind, I spent a great deal of time planning the approach I would take, and tapped into my previous experience writing many other Windows books before I wrote this one.

During the many long months of writing this book, I continued to refine that approach, focusing the content and zeroing in on everything I thought would be of value as you set out to learn and master Windows 7. I hope that as a result of all my hard work the book you hold in your hands is something unique. This isn't a 300-page introduction or a 1,500-page all-in-one reference. This is a relentlessly focused and comprehensive 950-page guide to what you truly need to know to master Windows 7 as a user.

Over the course of this project, I've worked with many different people at O'Reilly, but none were as helpful or instrumental to the writing process as my editors, Brian Jepson and Laurel Ruma. Not only did they believe in me, but they believed in and supported my vision for this project every step of the way. Whenever the inevitable obstacles arose during the writing, Brian was there to help and to ensure I had everything I needed to complete the writing. At crunch time, Laurel went above and beyond to help me complete the project. Others at O'Reilly that I've worked with during the project include Nancy Kotary. Nancy was the copyeditor for the book. She did a terrific job and was a pleasure to work with!

Hopefully, I haven't forgotten anyone, but if I have, it was an oversight. *Honest.* :-)

PART I

Setting Up, Customizing, and Tuning Windows 7

CHAPTER 1

Getting Started with Windows 7

I'll give you the bad news right up front: Windows 7 isn't what you think it is. Although Windows 7 *is* the latest release of the Windows operating system for personal computers, it *isn't* what it seems. Windows 7 does look a lot like its predecessors, albeit with a cleaner, more inviting interface. If you have a powerful computer, you might also be enjoying Windows 7's Aero Glass interface—or not. Regardless, you'd be hard-pressed not to notice all the eye candy Windows 7 presents, and this may lead you to believe that the operating system is little more than new veneer for the same old software. Nothing could be further from the truth—and in this chapter, I'll show you why. I'll start by helping you get to know Windows 7 and its various editions. After discussing how to start and use Windows 7, I will introduce some of the new ways in which you can work with this powerful operating system.

For the sake of this book, I'll assume that you are fairly familiar with the Windows operating system and have worked with Windows Vista, Windows XP, or an earlier release of Windows. If that description fits you, read this chapter to learn about the key changes in Windows 7 that will affect you the most. If you already have some experience with Windows 7, some of the material here may be familiar to you, but I recommend that you read the chapter anyway, because some of the subtler changes in the operating system have the biggest impact on your computer. Also, keep in mind that because I'm assuming prior experience with a Windows operating system, I won't discuss computing basics.

Getting to Know Windows 7

From top to bottom, Windows 7 is dramatically different from Windows XP and earlier versions of Windows. Though similar to Windows Vista, Windows 7 brings numerous important changes in both the interface and the underlying architecture. Continuing the trend started with Windows XP, Windows 7 offers separate home and business products. Unlike Windows XP, Windows 7 editions aren't organized by hardware type or processor architecture. Instead, Windows 7 comes in several distinctly different editions, including (in order from fewest features to most):

- Starter
- Home Basic
- Home Premium
- Professional
- Enterprise
- Ultimate

Each edition has a different set of features. Windows Starter Edition is a budget edition for casual users, as well as emerging markets. Windows 7 Home Basic and Home Premium are the standard editions for home users, and as such, they include various home entertainment features. Windows 7 Professional and Enterprise are the standard editions for business users, and as such, they include various business and management features. Windows 7 Ultimate is for those who want the best of both home and business features.

You can quickly determine which version of Windows 7 you are currently using by clicking Start→Control Panel→System and Security→System or by clicking Start, right-clicking on Computer, and choosing Properties. When working with the various Windows 7 editions, keep the following in mind:

- Windows XP had a separate edition for Media Center; Windows 7 includes Media Center as a standard feature. Both Home Premium and Ultimate include Media Center.
- Windows XP had a separate edition for Tablet PCs; Windows 7 includes support for Tablet PCs as a standard feature. Home Premium and higher editions all support Tablet PCs.
- Windows 7 Home Basic and Home Premium both include home entertainment features; only Windows 7 Professional, Enterprise, and Ultimate include the features necessary to join a Windows domain.
- Windows Home Basic supports many of the same features as Home Premium, but it doesn't support the Aero interface (which you'll learn about in Chapter 2).
- Windows Vista's Starter edition was available only to emerging markets, but computer manufacturers now have the option of installing the Windows 7 Starter edition on computers sold worldwide. Although the Start edition is extremely limited compared to other editions, if you've already bought a computer with the Starter edition, you'll be able to upgrade for a small fee.

If you purchased a new computer or you work in an office where a new computer was delivered to you, Windows 7 was probably installed for you, and you only had to turn on your computer and click a few buttons to get your computer up and running. Because of this, you probably didn't have much of a choice as to which version of Windows 7 was installed. Thanks to new Windows 7 features, your edition choices are more open than you may think, however, so don't skip ahead just yet.

If you are installing Windows 7 yourself or are upgrading your computer from an earlier version of Windows, you can pick which version to install and can install or upgrade to Windows 7, as discussed in Chapter 22 of this book. You can purchase an upgrade copy of Windows 7 for earlier releases of Windows. You can upgrade Windows Vista to a corresponding or better edition of Windows 7 by buying and installing an upgrade copy of Windows 7. Upgrade copies are available for Windows XP, but you can't upgrade in-place. Instead, you'll need to use Windows Easy Transfer to transfer your settings and files. Unfortunately, you'll need to reinstall your applications, because Windows Easy Transfer does not transfer programs. If you start Windows 7 Setup from within Windows XP, you'll be directed to run Windows Easy Transfer to back up your files and settings before you proceed.

With upgrade copies, you have two general upgrade options:

In-place upgrade
> With an in-place upgrade, you perform an upgrade installation of Windows 7 and retain your applications, files, and other settings as they were in the previous edition of Windows.

Clean install
> With a clean install, you replace your previous edition of Windows with Windows 7 and do not retain applications, files, and other settings. Although you must re-install all applications, you can retain files and other settings by running Windows Easy Transfer prior to installing Windows 7. After the installation is complete, you must run Windows Easy Transfer again to reload your files and settings.

As Table 1-1 shows, the version of Windows you are running largely determines your options for using upgrade copies of Windows 7. The in-place upgrade option means that a clean install option is also available, but not vice versa. For Windows XP, there will be upgrade pricing, but you will need to perform a clean install. For Windows 2000 and earlier versions, you must purchase and install a full (nonupgrade) copy of Windows 7.

Table 1-1. Using upgrade copies of Windows 7

Operating systems	Windows 7 editions					
	Starter	Home Basic	Home Premium	Professional	Enterprise	Ultimate
Windows 2000	Clean install	Clean install	Clean install	Clean install	Clean install	Clean install
Windows XP Home	Clean install	Clean install	Clean install	Clean install	Clean install	Clean install
Windows XP Professional	Clean install	Clean install	Clean install	Clean install	Clean install	Clean install
Windows XP Professional x64	Clean install	Clean install	Clean install	Clean install	Clean install	Clean install
Windows XP Media Center	Clean install	Clean install	Clean install	Clean install	Clean install	Clean install

Operating systems	Windows 7 editions					
	Starter	Home Basic	Home Premium	Professional	Enterprise	Ultimate
Windows XP Tablet PC	Clean install	Clean install	Clean install	Clean install	Clean install	Clean install
Windows Vista Home Basic	Clean install	In-place upgrade	In-place upgrade	Clean install	Clean install	In-place upgrade
Windows Vista Home Premium	Clean install	In-place upgrade	In-place upgrade	Clean install	Clean install	In-place upgrade
Windows Vista Business	Clean install	Clean install	Clean install	In-place upgrade	In-place upgrade	In-place upgrade
Windows Vista Enterprise	Clean install	Clean install	Clean install	In-place upgrade	In-place upgrade	In-place upgrade

Unlike Windows XP and earlier releases of Windows, your choices of Windows 7 editions don't end with the installation process. You can upgrade from the basic editions to the enhanced editions. To do this, you use a Windows Anytime Upgrade, as discussed in the section "Upgrading Your Windows 7 Edition" on page 866 of Chapter 22. Once you've completed the edition upgrade, your computer will have all the features and capabilities of the new edition.

Table 1-2 provides an overview of the differences between the various editions of Windows 7. You'll find a detailed list online at *http://www.williamstanek.com/windows7/*.

Table 1-2. Features differences between Windows 7 editions

Feature	Starter	Home Basic	Home Premium	Professional	Enterprise	Ultimate
Aero user interface			X	X	X	X
Accessibility settings	X	X	X	X	X	X
BitLocker Drive Encryption					X	X
Built-in diagnostics	X	X	X	X	X	X
Complete PC backup				X	X	X
Desktop deployment tools				X	X	X
DirectX Support	X	X	X	X	X	X
Dual-processor support (not counting processor cores)				X	X	X
Explorer windows	X	X	X	X	X	X
Encrypting File System				X	X	X
Fast resume and sleep	X	X	X	X	X	X
File and printer sharing connections		10	20	20	20	20

Feature	Starter	Home Basic	Home Premium	Professional	Enterprise	Ultimate
Internet Explorer	X	X	X	X	X	X
Network Access Protection Client				X	X	X
Network and Sharing Center	X	X	X	X	X	X
Parental controls	X	X	X			X
Policy-based quality of service for networking				X	X	X
Premier Support coverage				X	X	
Scheduled backups			X	X	X	X
Software Assurance availability				X	X	X
Speech recognition	X	X	X	X	X	X
Subsystem for Unix-based applications					X	X
SuperFetch	X	X	X	X	X	X
Sync Center		X	X	X	X	X
Tablet PC			X	X	X	X
User interface, multiple language installs					X	X
Volume licensing keys				X	X	
Virtual machine licenses (4)					X	X
Windows Defender	X	X	X	X	X	X
Windows Fax and Scan				X	X	X
Windows Firewall	X	X	X	X	X	X
Windows Gadgets		X	X	X	X	X
Windows Media Center			X			X
Windows Media Player	X	X	X	X	X	X
Windows ReadyBoost		X	X	X	X	X
Windows Update	X	X	X	X	X	X
Windows XP Mode				X	X	X
Wireless networking	X	X	X	X	X	X
Wireless network provisioning				X	X	X

Installing and Using Windows 7

Whether you are running the Starter, Home, Professional, Enterprise, or Ultimate edition of Windows 7, the core features of the operating system are the same. This means that on a home computer, an office workstation, or a mobile computer, you'll have the same standard set of features and you'll work with Windows 7 in the same way.

When you first start using Windows 7, you should do the following:

1. Log on and finalize the installation.
2. Perform essential configuration tasks.
3. Review your computer's configuration, upgrade hardware as necessary, and then activate the operating system.

I discuss these tasks in the following sections.

Logging On and Finalizing the Installation

Chapter 22 provides complete details for installing Windows 7. When you start Windows 7, you'll know it's a different kind of operating system from Windows XP and earlier versions of Windows. During installation, you are prompted to create a local machine account. This account is created as a computer administrator account. When the operating system starts, you can log on using this account.

After you install Windows 7 (or if you purchased a new computer with Windows 7 already installed), you'll have to complete a mini-setup the first time you start your computer. As part of the mini-setup, you'll need to finalize the operating system installation. The procedure you'll need to perform will be similar to the following:

1. When prompted, choose your country or region, your time and currency format, and your keyboard layout. Click Next.
2. Create a local machine account, which will be a computer administrator account. Enter a username. Click Next.
3. Type a computer name. Click Next.
4. Type and then confirm a password. Enter a password hint and then click Next.
5. Select a Windows Update option for the computer. Usually, you'll want to use the recommended settings to allow Windows 7 to automatically install all available updates and security tools as they become available. Choose Ask Me Later only if you want to disable Windows Update.
6. Setup displays the date and time settings. Make changes as necessary and then click Next.
7. If a network card was detected during setup, networking components were installed automatically. If you have a Wi-Fi card, you'll have to choose the wireless network to connect to. You'll also need to specify the location type for each detected network connection:
    a. Depending on the type of location and connection, click Home for a home network, Work for a network in a workplace, or Public Location for a public

network. Windows 7 will then configure the sharing settings as appropriate for this location.

    b. If there are multiple networks, you'll see a prompt for each network. You can configure each detected network in a different way.

8. Once you've configured all of your network adapters, Windows 7 will then prepare your desktop. When the operating system starts, you'll be able to log on.

As discussed in Chapters 21 and 23, Windows 7 includes a recovery environment that is built-in from the start. Most computer manufacturers will customize and extend this environment. Before you throw out or put aside the packaging that came with your computer, make a note of any special keys, such as Alt-F10, that you must press to reinstall the computer using the recovery image included on the computer's hard disk. Write this information down and put it someplace where you'll know to look for it in a year or two (or three or five). If your computer fails to start and normal recovery techniques don't work, you'll often be able to reinstall the computer using the manufacturer's recovery environment.

Normally, when you recover a computer using the manufacturer's recovery environment, the computer will be restored to the state it was in when the manufacturer shipped the computer to you. Therefore, if you choose to recover a computer in this way, you would lose all updates and changes you've made to your computer, including applications, documents, and system updates. Some computer manufacturers, like HP, include a backup and recovery tool that allows you to write updated system images to the custom recovery environment. If you make periodic updates to the stored system image using this tool, you may be able to recover the computer to a later state.

Performing Essential Configuration Tasks

Some aspects of Windows 7 are different depending on whether a computer is a member of a homegroup, workgroup, or domain. On a home network, your computer will operate in a homegroup or a workgroup configuration. On a business network, your computer will operate in a workgroup or a domain configuration.

Homegroups are loose associations of computers on home networks. When your computer is in a homegroup, you can share data with other computers on the home network using a password common to the all users in the homegroup. You set the homegroup password when you set up the homegroup and can modify the password as necessary at any time.

Workgroups are loose associations of computers where each computer is managed separately. Domains are collections of computers that you can manage collectively by means of domain controllers. Domain controllers are servers running Windows that manage access to the network and its resources.

Homegroups are available only when a computer running Windows 7 is connected to a home network. Workgroups and domains are available only when a computer

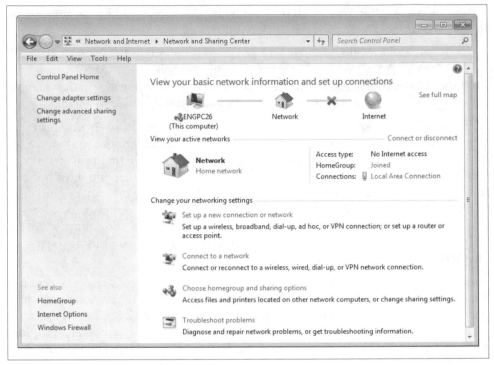

Figure 1-1. Review the network configuration

running Windows 7 is connected to a work network. You'll learn how to manage net-working and network connections in Chapters 14 and 17.

Changing your network location type

You can change the network location type for the network to which your computer currently is connected by following these steps:

1. Click Start→Control Panel. In Control Panel, click Network and Internet→Network and Sharing Center.

2. As shown in Figure 1-1, Network and Sharing Center shows the current networking configuration of your computer.

3. Under "View your active networks," locate the network you want to change, and click the link under it (it will be labeled Work Network, Home Network, or Public Network).

4. In the Set Network Location dialog box, choose Work Network, Home Network, or Public Network as appropriate and then click Close.

Connecting to the Internet

The Network and Sharing Center provides options for changing networking settings. Connecting your computer to the Internet is one of the essential tasks you may need to perform to finalize the initial setup of your computer. If your Internet connection wasn't set up automatically or you want to modify the default set up, click the "Set up a new connection or network option" in the Network and Sharing Center. Then click Connect to the Internet→Next. As Figure 1-2 shows, the Connect to the Internet option can help walk you through the configuration of an Internet connection in three specific scenarios.

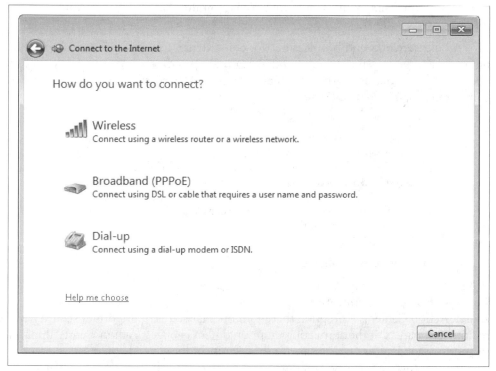

Figure 1-2. Connecting to the Internet

- If your computer has a wireless adapter and you need to connect to a wireless router or a wireless network, you can use the Wireless option to configure your connection. After you click an available wireless network, click Connect, then provide any required security and configuration information.

- If you are using DSL or a cable modem that requires a username and password, you can use the Broadband (PPPoE)—which stands for Point-to-Point Protocol over Ethernet—option to configure your connection. After you provide the required username and password, select the "Remember this password" checkbox and then click Connect. Keep in mind that you should rarely, if ever, connect your computer directly to your DSL or cable modem. Instead, purchase an inexpensive router with a hardware firewall, connect your computer to the router, and connect the router to your modem.

- If you are using a dial-up modem or ISDN, you can use the Dial-up option to configure your connection. Enter the dial-up phone number, provide the required username and password, and then select the "Remember this password" checkbox. Click Connect.

Keep in mind that if your computer is configured as part of a home or business network that is already connected to the Internet, you don't need to use the Connect to the Internet option—simply make sure that your computer has the proper configuration for its network adapter.

Most home networks and business networks use dynamically assigned network configurations. As this is the default configuration for Windows 7, you typically do not need to change your network settings as long as your computer's network adapter is connected properly to the network.

 If you use a wired network and your computer's network adapter isn't connected to the network via a network cable, connect the network cable now. Your computer will then configure its networking settings and should also detect that it is on a network. You'll then be prompted for the type of network. Once you've specified whether you are using a home, work, or public network, your computer will update its configuration for this network location.

Responding to Action Center notifications

When you log on to your computer, Windows normally displays an Action Center summary icon in the notification area. This icon has a flag with a red circle that has an X in it. Action Center is a program that monitors that status of important security and maintenance areas. If the status of a monitored item changes, Action Center updates the notification icon as appropriate for the severity of the alert. If you move the mouse pointer over this icon, you see a summary of all alerts. If you click this icon, Windows displays a popup dialog box with a summary listing of each alert or action item that needs your attention. Click an alert or action item link to open Internet Explorer and display a possible solution. Click the Open Action Center link to display the Action Center.

As Figure 1-3 shows, Action Center provides an overview of the computer's status and lists any issues that need to be resolved. You can view available solutions by clicking the View Problem Response button provided. For example, if a computer is experiencing a problem with its sound card and this problem can be resolved by installing a newer driver, clicking View Problem Response displays a More Information page. Here, this page provides more information about the problem and a link to download and

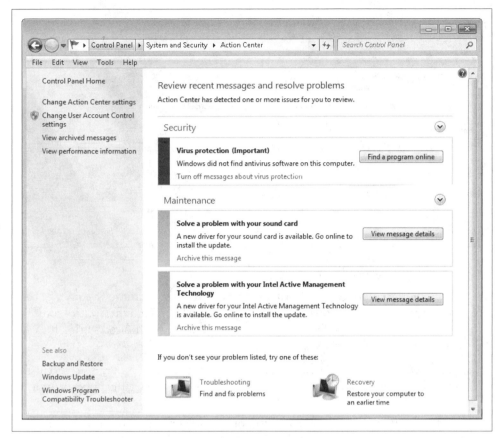

Figure 1-3. Review alerts and action items for your computer

install the latest driver, as shown in Figure 1-4. When you've resolved a problem, you can elect to archive the message for future reference by selecting the "Archive this message" checkbox before you click OK to close the More Information dialog box.

While you are working with the Action Center, you may want to choose the "View performance information" option (see Figure 1-3). Choosing this option displays the computer's performance rating and notifies you of whether there are any issues causing performance problems. The computer's base score is determined according to the worst performing component. For example, if the computer has little graphics memory, the computer will have a low score in this area and the base score will reflect this as well. To improve performance, upgrade the computer's graphics card (however, in some cases, obtaining updated drivers from your hardware vendor can provide a significant performance boost, especially if Windows has decided to use the built-in SVGA graphics driver for your system). To have Windows recheck the computer's performance, click "Re-Run the assessment" in the Performance Information and Tools window.

Figure 1-4. Get more information on a problem

After checking the computer's performance rating, you may want to modify the User Account Control settings. To do this, click the "Change User Account Control settings" option in Action Center. Use the slider provided to specify the desired setting for User Account Control and then click OK. You can:

- Select Always Notify to always notify the current user when programs try to install software or make changes to the computer and when the user changes Windows settings.

- Select Default to notify the current user only when programs try to make changes to the computer and *not* when the user changes Windows Settings.

- Select Notify Me Only When...(Do Not Dim My Desktop) to prevent User Account Control from switching to the secure desktop. Otherwise, this option works the same as Default.

- Select Never Notify to turn off all User Account Control notification prompts.

 Switching to the secure desktop enhances security, because the secure desktop restricts the programs and processes that have access to the desktop. This reduces the possibility that a malicious program or user could gain access to a process being elevated.

While working with Action Center, you may also want to reduce the number of alert window displays. You do this by turning alert messages on or off. Alert messages are divided into two categories:

Security

Security alerts that you can turn on or off include those related to Windows Update, Internet security settings, network firewall, spyware and related programs, User Account Control, and Virus programs.

Maintenance

Maintenance alerts you can turn on or off include those related to Windows Backup, checking for updates, and Windows troubleshooting. Quick links are provided to allow you to configure settings for the Customer Experience Improvement Program, problem reporting, and Windows Update.

To change the notification settings, click Change Action Center settings. Clear checkboxes for messages you don't want to see and select checkboxes for messages you do want to see. Save your settings by clicking OK.

Other setup tasks

Other essential tasks you may want to perform to initially set up your computer may include:

Transferring files and settings

You can use Windows Easy Transfer to transfer settings from one computer to another. Windows Easy Transfer transfers user accounts, files and folders, program settings, Internet settings, and email settings. For the transfer, you can use CDs, DVDs, USB flash drives, external hard drives, network folders, or a Windows Easy Transfer cable (which must be purchased separately). To start a transfer, click Start→All Programs→Accessories→Windows Easy Transfer.

Adding new users

You can configure user accounts for each person that will log on locally to the computer. To learn more about managing user account settings, see Chapter 18. For homegroup and workgroup computers, you can add users by clicking the "Add or remove user accounts option" in the Control Panel under User Accounts and Family Safety. For domain computers, you will manage user accounts in a slightly different way. See Chapter 18 for details.

Reviewing and Activating Your Computer

As Figure 1-5 shows, the System page in Control Panel (Start→Control Panel→System and Security→System) provides links for performing common tasks and a system overview in four basic areas.

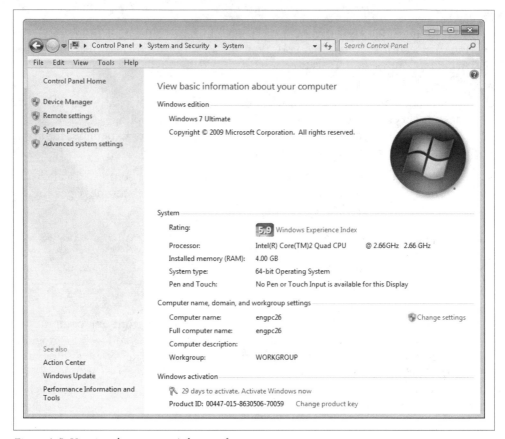

Figure 1-5. Viewing the computer's basic information

Windows edition

Lists the operating system edition and service packs. To protect your computer and optimize performance, you'll want to ensure that your computer is running the latest service pack. With Windows 7, you can install service packs and other product updates automatically as part of Windows Update. To learn more about Windows Update, see Chapter 20.

System

Lists the processor, total memory, and performance rating of your computer. Your computer's performance rating (the Windows Experience Index) was computed automatically during finalization of the installation. The Windows Experience Index is calculated based on the processor speed, total memory, graphics processor, and hard disk transfer rate. To learn more about updating your computer's performance rating and techniques for improving your computer's performance, see Chapter 3.

Computer name, domain, and workgroup settings
> Lists the computer name, description, domain, and workgroup details. All computers are members of either a workgroup or a domain, and this membership affects how you can configure the computer and the available options. To learn more about making your computer a member of a workgroup or domain, see Chapter 20.

Windows activation
> Lists the computer's product ID and activation status. If your computer is using a retail version of Windows 7, it must have a product key and you must activate the operating system using this product key. In Windows 7, the product key provided during installation is what determines the operating system version and features that are installed. When you upgrade your Windows 7 edition, you are essentially buying a new product key and telling Windows 7 to unlock and install the additional features of this edition. See Chapter 22 for details on upgrading Windows 7 editions.

Retail editions of Windows 7 use product keys. Windows 7 requires activation over the Internet. In the System console, activate the operating system by clicking "Activate Windows now" under "Windows activation" and then clicking "Activate Windows online now" in the Windows Activation dialog box. Your computer then checks your Internet connection and attempts to activate the operating system. If this process fails, you'll need to resolve any issues that are preventing your computer from connecting to the Internet and then click "Activate Windows online now" again.

Unlike with Windows XP, you can easily change your computer's product key with Windows 7. You may need to change your product key to comply with your license agreement. For example, you may already have a computer running on your network with the same single-computer product key you used when installing the copy you're trying to activate. In the System console, click "Change product key" under Windows Activation. In the Windows Activation window, shown in Figure 1-6, enter the product key. You do not need to enter the dashes in the product key. When you click Next, the product key will be validated. You'll then need to reactivate Windows 7 over the Internet.

Working with Windows 7

From startup to shutdown, Windows 7 is different from its predecessors—and these differences go far beyond the gadgets and other gizmos in Windows 7's highly designed interface, which I discuss in Chapter 2. If you want to truly know how Windows 7 works and what makes it tick, you need to dig under the hood.

Windows Vista was the first truly hardware-independent version of Windows, and Windows 7 continues this tradition. Unlike older releases of Windows, Windows 7 doesn't boot from a plain-text initialization file (which was limited and prone to tampering). Instead, the operating system uses the Windows Boot Manager and a more

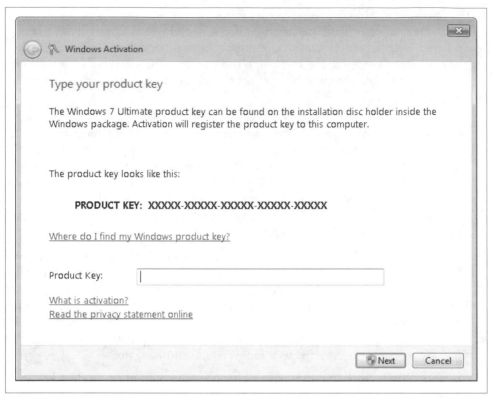

Figure 1-6. Changing your product key

robust configuration system to initialize and start the operating system. The Boot Manager is a key component of Windows 7's extensive boot environment. You'll learn all about the Boot Manager and the boot environment in Chapter 23; here's what you need to know right now:

- The boot environment dramatically changes the way the operating system starts. Microsoft created the boot environment to resolve several prickly problems related to boot integrity, operating system integrity, and firmware abstraction.

- The boot environment is loaded prior to the operating system, making it a preoperating system environment. As such, you can use the boot environment to validate the integrity of the startup process and the operating system itself before actually starting the operating system.

- The boot environment is created as an extensible abstraction layer. This means that the operating system can work with multiple types of firmware interfaces without requiring the operating system to be specifically written to work with these firmware interfaces. Rather than updating the operating system each time a new firmware interface is developed, the firmware interface developers can use the extensible boot environment to allow the operating system to communicate as necessary through the firmware interfaces.

Currently, Basic Input Output System (BIOS) and Extensible Firmware Interface (EFI) are the two prevalent firmware interfaces for computers. Firmware interface abstraction makes it possible for Windows 7 to work with BIOS-based and EFI-based computers in exactly the same way, and this is one of the primary reasons why Windows 7 achieves hardware independence.

The other secret ingredient for Windows 7's hardware independence is Windows Imaging Format (WIM). Microsoft distributes Windows 7 on media using WIM disk images. Here's what you need to know about WIM right now:

- Windows Image (*.wim*) files are used to deploy Windows 7. WIM uses compression and single-instance storage to dramatically reduce the size of image files. Using compression reduces the size of the image in much the same way as ZIP compression reduces the size of files. Using single-instance storage reduces the size of the image, because only one physical copy of a file is stored for each instance of that file in the disk image.

- Because WIM is hardware-independent, Microsoft can use a single binary for each supported architecture: one binary for 32-bit architectures and one binary for 64-bit architectures. If you work at a company that creates disk images of various computer configurations, you can use this technology to reduce the number of disk images you must maintain.

The final secret ingredient for Windows 7's hardware independence is modularization. Windows 7 uses modular component design so that each component of the operating system is defined as a separate independent unit or module. As modules can contain other modules, various major features of the operating system can be grouped together and described independently of other major features. Because modules are independent from one another, you can swap modules in or out to customize the operating system environment. Modularization has many benefits:

- Thanks to modularization, you can more easily add features to the operating system. Instead of having to go through a lengthy process for adding or removing components as with earlier releases of Windows, with Windows 7 you can easily turn features on or off. If you click Start→Control Panel→Programs→"Turn Windows features on or off," you can quickly and easily select features to add or remove using the Windows Features dialog box, shown in Figure 1-7.

- Thanks to modularization, Windows 7 is language-independent. Some languages are included with your version of Windows 7. Others you need to obtain separately and install. You can add or remove language packs as easily as you can Windows features. If you click Start→Control Panel→Change Display Language under Clock, Language, and Region, you can quickly and easily install and uninstall language packs. Click the Install/Uninstall Languages button to launch the Install or

Uninstall Display Languages Wizard, shown in Figure 1-8, and follow the prompts to add or remove language support. You'll need to insert the Windows 7 or language pack media when prompted.

Figure 1-7. Adding and removing features simply by turning them on and off

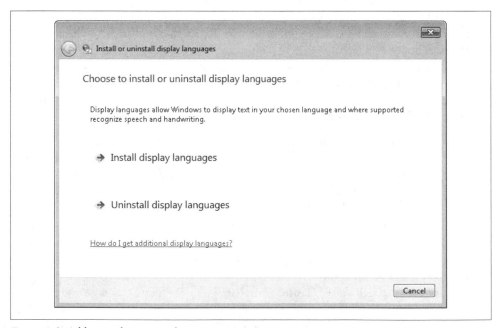

Figure 1-8. Adding and removing language support

Logging On, Switching, Locking, Logging Off, and Shutting Down

No tour of getting started with Windows 7 would be complete without discussing logging on, switching, locking, logging off, and shutting down. If you're an experienced Windows user, you may be tempted to skip this section, but please don't. Skim this section instead, because some of the changes aren't immediately obvious. Remember, some offices use workgroups, homegroups, or domains; some offices just buy computers, a cheap network access server, and never bother to futz with group or domain settings. Also, if you bring your personal computer into the office, it's not going to affect anything.

Logging On to Your Computer

Windows 7 displays the logon screen at startup. The way the startup screen works depends on whether you log into a domain (domains are common in large organizations):

- On most personal or small office computers, you'll see that all standard user and administrator accounts you've created on the computer are listed on the startup screen. To log on, click the account name (if you've only created one account, you'll see the password prompt right away). If the account is password-protected, you must click the account name, type the account password, and then click the arrow button.

- If you log into a domain, Windows 7 displays a blank startup screen after startup. You must press Ctrl-Alt-Delete to display the logon screen. By default, the last account to log on to the computer is listed in *Computer\username* or *domain\user name* format. To log on to this account, type the account password and then click the arrow button. To log on to a different account, click the Switch User button and then click "Log on as another user." Type the username and password, and then click the arrow button.

 When working at the office, you can specify the domain and the account name using the format *domain\username*, such as enigma\williams. If you want to log on to the local machine, type .*username*, where *username* is the name of the local account, such as .\williams.

Switching Users

If multiple people use your computer, you can easily switch users by pressing Ctrl-Alt-Delete and then clicking the Switch User button. When you do this, the logon screen is displayed, as with the Windows startup process (on a computer connected to a domain, a blank startup screen is displayed and you must press Ctrl-Alt-Delete again).

Another way to switch users is to click Start, hover over the arrow menu to the right of the Shut Down button, and click Switch User.

Locking Your Computer

You can lock your computer by pressing Windows-L (the Windows key is usually to the left of the space bar) or by pressing Ctrl-Alt-Delete and then clicking the Lock This Computer option. You can also lock the computer by clicking Start, hovering over the arrow menu to the right of the Shut Down button, and clicking the Lock option:

- On most personal or small office computers, a lock screen is displayed with the name of the user who locked the computer. If a password is required for that account, you'll also see a password prompt. Otherwise, you can click the account name or picture to log back on as that user.

- On computers connected to a domain, a lock screen is displayed with the name of the user who is logged on. If you want to log back on as the user, you must press Ctrl-Alt-Delete and then enter the user's password.

Logging Off Your Computer

When you are finished using your computer, you can log off or shut down. You can log off your computer by pressing Ctrl-Alt-Delete and then clicking the Log Off option. You can also log off by clicking Start, hovering over the arrow menu to the right of the Shut Down button, and then clicking Log Off.

 A running program may prevent logoff. If so, the Log Off dialog box is displayed and the programs currently running on the computer are listed. If one of the currently running programs is causing a problem with logging off, an explanation of the problem is displayed below the program name. You can then cancel the logoff or continue. Cancel the logoff if you want to save your work and exit a program. Continue logging off if you are sure you have saved your work.

Sleeping and Turning Off Your Computer

When it comes to turning off and shutting down, Windows 7 turns itself off and enters sleep mode by default. Entering sleep mode is not the same as shutting down. When entering sleep mode, the operating system automatically saves all work, turns off the display, and enters a low-power-consumption mode with the computer's fans and hard disks stopped. The state of the computer is maintained in the computer's memory. When the computer wakes from sleep mode, its state will be exactly like it was when you turned it off.

Whether and when your computer enters sleep mode is controlled by the Power plan and other power settings, as discussed in Chapter 2. To wake the computer from the sleep state, press a key on the computer's keyboard. Moving the mouse also wakes the computer.

 You can turn mobile computers off and on by closing and opening the lid. When you close the lid, the laptop enters the sleep state. When you open the lid, the laptop wakes up from the sleep state.

There are, however, a few gotchas with the power options and the sleep mode. The way the power options work depends on the following:

System hardware
> The computer hardware must support sleep mode. If the computer hardware doesn't support the sleep state, the computer can't use the sleep state.

System state
> The system must be in a valid state. If the computer has installed updates that require a reboot or you've installed programs that require a reboot, the computer can't use the sleep state.

System configuration
> Sleep mode must be enabled. If you've reconfigured the power options on the computer and set the power button and sleep buttons to alternative actions, the computer may not be able to enter sleep mode.

 When working with sleep mode, it is important to remember that the computer is still drawing power and that you should never install hardware inside the computer or connect devices to the computer when it is in the sleep state. The only exception is for external devices that use USB, IEEE 1394 (FireWire), and eSATA ports. You can connect USB, FireWire and eSATA devices without shutting down the computer. However, plugging in such a device may wake the computer back up.

Regardless of your computer's power button configuration, you can power it down completely by using the Shut Down or Hibernate option. Shutting down the computer and hibernating are the only ways to ensure that the power to the computer is turned off. To shut down your computer, click Start→Shut Down. You can also shut down your computer by pressing Ctrl-Alt-Delete and then clicking the red power button in the lower-right corner of the screen. As with standard sleep mode, a computer's ability to hibernate depends on its hardware, state, and configuration. If your computer is able to hibernate, you can put the computer in hibernation mode by clicking Start, clicking the "Shutdown options" button, and then selecting Hibernate. In hibernation mode, the state of the computer is saved to *Hiberfile.sys* and reloaded when you start the computer.

CHAPTER 2

Optimizing Windows 7's Interface

Everything that connects you—the user—to the computer is collectively referred to as the *user interface*. The basic elements of the user interface include the desktop, Start menu, taskbar, windows, dialog boxes, and wizards. These basic elements remain in Windows 7, and you'll be able to work with them in much the same way as you have previously. Continuing with the improvements introduced in Windows Vista, many other aspects of the user interface in Windows 7 have been revised. Because of the many changes, you'll find that you may have to learn new ways of performing common tasks, and you'll discover much that is new.

The user interface has two key aspects: appearance settings and user profile settings. Appearance settings determine the color schemes, screen resolution, and sizing for window text, buttons, and icons. User profile settings determine where user files are located and what interface preferences are used.

Like Windows XP and Windows Vista, Windows 7's default appearance settings work well. With the inclusion of automated screen sizing, screen resolution, and window sizing, appearance settings typically are optimized right at the start, making it easier to work with the operating system. Because a one-size-fits-all recipe would be very boring, Windows 7 gives you many choices for the appearance and behavior of your desktop, Start menu, taskbar, and other interface elements.

Your interface customizations are stored in your user profile. Because each user of your computer has a separate user profile, you are able to customize the desktop to meet your unique needs without affecting the interface settings of other users. This means your preferred settings will be remembered and restored each time you log on to your computer, and so will the preferred settings of any other users.

Customizing Windows 7's Desktop

The enhanced user interface in Windows 7 is visually stunning, and a key component in the interface is the desktop. As you'll discover in this section, you can work with the desktop and its related features in many new and exciting ways. If you're familiar with

Windows XP and Windows Vista, you may be tempted to skip this section, but don't—there are a lot of new features and new ways you can work with the desktop. As with Windows Vista, most editions of Windows 7 support Aero Glass to give your desktop special effects such as blending and transparency. However, the Windows 7 Starter and Home Basic editions do not support this feature.

Getting Around the Desktop

Figure 2-1 shows the Windows 7 desktop with the Aero Glass capabilities enabled. This desktop has standard features, but you can customize it with additional features as well. Standard desktop features include the Start menu, the taskbar, and the notification area.

Figure 2-1. Windows 7 desktop with Aero Glass

Programs or folders you open appear on the desktop in separate windows. You can arrange open program and folder windows on the desktop by right-clicking an empty area of the taskbar and then selecting one of the following viewing options:

Cascade Windows
> Arranges the open windows on the screen so that they overlap, with the title bar remaining visible

Show Windows Stacked
> Resizes the open windows and arranges them on top of each other, in one or more columns

Show Windows Side by Side
> Resizes the open windows and stacks them side by side

If you right-click an empty area of the taskbar and then select Show the Desktop, Windows 7 minimizes all open windows and displays the desktop. If you later right-click an empty area of the taskbar and select Show Open Windows, Windows 7 restores the minimized windows to their previous states.

In addition to opening program and folder windows, you can store files, folders, and shortcuts on the desktop. Any file or folder you save on the desktop appears on the desktop. Any file or folder you drag from a Windows Explorer window to the desktop stays on the desktop. You can add a shortcut to a file or folder to the desktop by following these steps:

1. Click Start and then click Computer.
2. Use the Windows Explorer window to locate the file or folder you want to add to the desktop.
3. Right-click the file or folder.
4. On the shortcut menu, point to Send To and then select Desktop (Create Shortcut).

You can add system icons to the desktop, too. By default, the only system icon on the desktop is the Recycle Bin. You can add or remove system icons by completing the following steps:

1. Right-click an empty area of the desktop and then select Personalize.
2. In the left pane of the Personalization window, click Change Desktop Icons under the Tasks heading.
3. Click Customize Desktop. This opens the Desktop Icon Settings dialog box, as shown in Figure 2-2.
4. Add or remove the Computer, Control Panel, Recycle Bin, Network, and User's Files icons by selecting or clearing the related checkboxes.
5. Click OK.

Once you've added an icon to the desktop, you can work with it using the techniques summarized in Table 2-1. If you no longer want an icon or shortcut on the desktop, right-click it and select Delete. When prompted, confirm the action by clicking Yes.

Figure 2-2. Adding and removing desktop icons

Table 2-1. Working with desktop icons

Desktop icon	Usage
Computer	Double-clicking the Computer icon opens a window from which you can access hard disk drives and devices with removable storage. Right-clicking the Computer icon and selecting Manage opens the Computer Management console. Right-clicking the Computer icon and selecting Map Network Drive allows you to connect to shared network folders. Right-clicking the Computer icon and selecting Properties displays the System page in Control Panel.
Control Panel	Double-clicking the Control Panel icon opens the Control Panel, which provides access to system configuration and management tools.
Network	Double-clicking the Network icon opens a window where you can access the computers and devices on your network. Right-clicking the Network icon and selecting Map Network Drive allows you to connect to shared network folders.
Recycle Bin	Double-clicking the Recycle Bin icon opens the Recycle Bin, which you can use to restore deleted items or permanently remove items. Right-clicking the Recycle Bin icon and selecting Empty Recycle Bin permanently removes all items in the Recycle Bin.
User's Files	Double-clicking the folder icon opens your user profile folder in Windows Explorer.

Getting Around the Start Menu

The Start button is the gateway to your computer's menu system. Clicking the Start button displays the Start menu. You can also display the Start menu by pressing Control-Esc or the Windows logo key on your keyboard.

The Start menu allows you to run programs, open folders, search your computer, get help, and more. As you can see in Figure 2-3, the Start menu in Windows 7 is organized differently than in Windows XP.

Figure 2-3. The Start menu in Windows 7

The Start menu has four key areas:

Programs list
> The programs list in the left pane displays recently used programs and programs that have been pinned to the Start menu. Click All Programs to see all the programs available to you, sorted in alphabetic order.

Search box
> The Search box in the lower portion of the left pane allows you to search your entire computer for files, folders, or programs.

Common folders and features
> The common folders and features (your username at the top, followed by Documents, Pictures, etc.) in the right pane provide quick access to the folders and features needed most often.

Shut down
> The Shut Down button is located in the lower portion of the right pane. Click the arrow to the right to access a menu with options to control the state of the computer (Switch user, Log off, Lock, Restart, Sleep, and Hibernate).

I discuss these Start menu features in the following sections.

Navigating and customizing the programs list

The Start menu's left pane displays recently used programs and programs that have been pinned to the Start menu. You can customize the programs list by pinning items to the Start menu and by changing the number of recently used programs to display.

Programs pinned to the Start menu are listed in the uppermost section of the programs list. Pinning programs to the Start menu provides quick access to your favorite programs. You can pin a program to the Start menu by following these steps:

1. Click the Start button.
2. Click All Programs and locate the program's menu entry.
3. Right-click the program's menu entry.
4. On the shortcut menu, select Pin to Start Menu.

If you no longer want a program to be pinned to the Start menu, you can unpin it by following these steps:

1. Click the Start button.
2. Right-click the program on the Start menu.
3. Select Unpin from Start Menu.

On the Start menu, recently used programs are listed in the lower portion of the programs list. You can remove a program from the recently used list by right-clicking it and then selecting "Remove from this list." This won't, however, prevent the program from being added to the list in the future.

You can customize the programs list by completing the following steps:

1. Right-click the Start button and then select Properties.
2. In the Taskbar and Start Menu Properties dialog box, the Start Menu tab is selected by default. Click Customize. Set the "Number of recent programs to display" option to the desired value.
3. Using small icons instead of large icons, you can display more programs on the list. Scroll down the list of options and clear Use Large Icons.
4. Click OK twice.

Navigating common folders and customizing the listed features

The Start menu's right pane provides access to commonly used folders and features. Though at first glance it may seem that this part of the Start menu is similar to the Start menu in Windows XP, this is deceiving, because there are major changes in the locations accessed by these buttons.

In Windows XP, your documents are stored by default in personal folders under *%SystemDrive%\Documents and Settings\%UserName%*. Your personal folder contains a *My Documents* folder, which in turn contains other folders, such as *My Pictures* and *My Music*. Windows XP also has additional folders, such as *Cookies*, *Local Settings*, *NetHood*, and *Printhood*.

 Windows 7 has many environment variables, which are used to refer to user-specific and system specific values. *%SystemDrive%* and *%User-Name%* refer to the SystemDrive and UserName environment variables, respectively. Often, I'll refer to environment variables using this syntax: *%VariableName%*. If you'd like to view the current value of any of these variables, click the Start menu, choose All Programs→Accessories→Command Prompt. Then type echo *%VariableName%*, such as echo *%SystemDrive%*, and then press Enter to see the value.

In Windows 7, some of these familiar folders don't exist. They are implemented as symbolic links that act as reparse points to another directory on the computer. Essentially, these symbolic links redirect programs from locations where these folders were stored in Windows XP and earlier versions of Windows to where the folders are stored currently. If you're ever curious about exactly how they work, open a command prompt and type **dir /al**. As the default directory for the command prompt is your user profile directory, you'll then see a list of the hidden symbolic links in your user profile directory. With the **dir** command, the /A option displays files and folders with specified attributes and the l specifies that you want to display symbolic links. Other names for symbolic links are reparse points and junctions.

In Windows 7, your documents are stored by default in personal folders under *%HomeDrive%\%HomePath%*. As Figure 2-4 shows, your personal folder contains the following folders:

AppData
> A hidden system folder for storing your application data

Contacts
> Contains your contacts for use in your mail programs

Desktop
> Contains your desktop configuration settings

Downloads
> Contains programs and data you've downloaded from the Internet

Favorites
> Contains your Internet favorites

Links
> Contains your Internet links

My Documents
> Contains your word processing documents

My Music
> Contains your music files

My Pictures
> Contains your pictures and digital images

My Videos
> Contains your video files

Saved Games
> Contains saved game data

Searches
> Contains your saved searches

 If you examine some of these folders from the Command Prompt, you'll see that they appear without the "My" prefix. For example, your *My Documents* folder is *%HomeDrive%\%HomePath%\Documents*.

In Windows 7, shared public documents are stored by default in public folders under *%Public%*. As Figure 2-5 shows, the public folder contains the following folders:

Desktop
> Contains the shared desktop configuration. Any public desktop items show up on all user desktops.

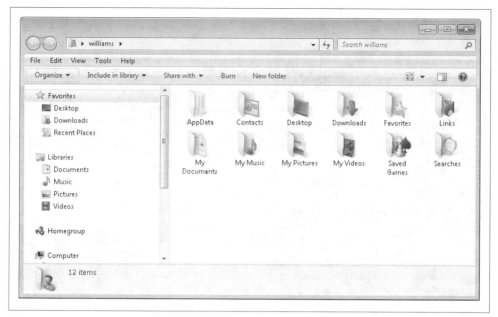

Figure 2-4. Navigating your personal folders

Downloads
    Contains shared, public programs and data downloaded from the Internet

Favorites
    Contains shared, public Internet favorites

Libraries
    Contains shared, public libraries

Public Documents
    Contains shared, public word processing documents

Public Music
    Contains shared, public music files

Public Pictures
    Contains shared, public pictures

Public Recorded TV
    Contains shared, public recorded television files

Public Videos
    Contains shared, public video files

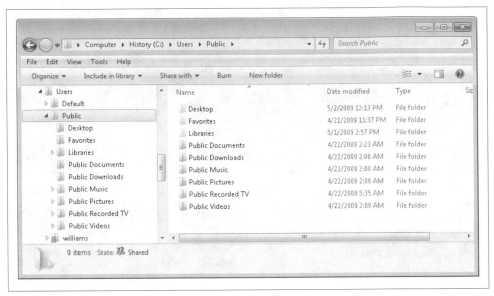

Figure 2-5. Navigating public folders

In addition to personal and public folders, Windows 7 uses libraries. As Figure 2-6 shows, a library is a combination of personal and public data grouped together and presented through a common view. The standard libraries include:

Documents
> Collects a user's My Documents data as well as Public Documents data

Music
> Collects a user's My Music data as well as Public Music data

Pictures
> Collects a user's My Pictures data as well as Public Pictures data

Videos
> Collects a user's My Videos data as well as Public Videos data

---

Getting a Better Understanding of Libraries

When you work with libraries, it is important to remember that they are only representations of collected data. Windows 7 creates merged views of files and folders that you add to libraries. As the libraries themselves do not contain any actual data, any action you take on a file or folder within a library is performed on the source file or folder. You can create new libraries to act as views to various collections of data as needed by right-clicking the Libraries node in Windows Explorer, pointing to New and then selecting Library.

If you're ever curious about how libraries really work, access the *%HomeDrive%\ %HomePath%\AppData\Roaming\Micrdosoft\Windows\Libraries* folder. In this folder,

---

you'll find the library definition files for your user profile. Each library definition file ends with the *.library-ms* extension and is formatted as an XML file that follows Microsoft's Library naming schema. If you view a library definition file, you'll find that it uses simple locations to define where contents in the library originate from. Folder and files are referenced by globally unique identifiers (GUIDs) and the serialized contents of a particular location are encrypted. Some properties of libraries are tracked in the registry, but these are primarily used only when you want to restore the original libraries, which you can do in Windows Explorer by right-clicking the Libraries node and selecting Restore Default Libraries.

Note also that the *%Public%\Libraries* folder also may have library definition files. For example, Windows Media Player and Windows Media Center both make use of the Recorded-TV library. As this library isn't a standard library in your user profile, it is represented in the *%Public%\Libraries* folder by the *Recorded-TV.library-ms* file.

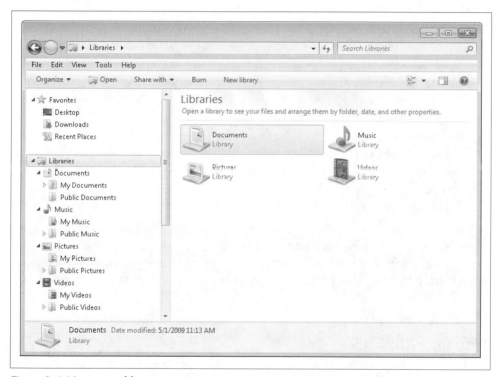

Figure 2-6. Navigating libraries

Knowing this, you can put the Start menu's common folder options into perspective. From top to bottom, the option buttons are as follows:

Current User
 Displayed as your logon name. Clicking this option opens your personal folder.

Documents

> Opens the Documents library, which contains the *My Documents* folder from your personal folder and the *Public Documents* folder.

Pictures

> Opens the Pictures library, which contains the *My Pictures* folder from your personal folder and the *Public Pictures* folder.

Music

> Opens the Music library, which contains the *My Music* folder from your personal folder and the *Public Music* folder.

Games

> Opens the *Microsoft Games* folder in Windows Explorer.

Computer

> Opens the Computer view in Windows Explorer. This allows you to access hard disk drives and devices with removable storage.

Control Panel

> Opens the Control Panel, which provides access to system configuration and management tools.

Devices and Printers

> Opens the Devices and Printers page in Control Panel, which provides access to devices, printers, and faxes you've configured for use.

Default Programs

> Displays the Default Programs page in the Control Panel. This lets you choose the programs that Windows 7 uses by default for documents, pictures, and more.

Help and Support

> Displays the Help and Support console. This lets you browse or search help topics.

You can add features to the Start menu's right pane using the Customize Start Menu dialog box. Right-click the Start button and then select Properties. In the Taskbar and Start Menu Properties dialog box, click the Customize button on the Start Menu tab. In the Customize Start Menu dialog box, select or clear options as appropriate and then click OK twice.

Features you can add include:

Administrative Tools

> Displays the Administrative Tools menu or window. This lets you access your computer's administrative tools.

Connect To

> Opens the Network and Sharing Center notification window. You also can open this window by clicking one of your network icons in the notification area.

Downloads

> Opens the *Downloads* folder in Windows Explorer.

Favorites
> Displays your favorite links as a menu. This lets you quickly access favorite locations.

Homegroup
> Opens the *Homegroup* folder in Windows Explorer so you can view files from other people on the network (as long as they've joined the homegroup).

Network
> Opens the Network Explorer. This allows you to browse the computers and devices on your network.

Recent Items
> Provides a menu view that lists recently opened files.

Run
> Displays the Run dialog box. This lets you run commands.

> Although you may have used the Run options previously, you'll find the Search box to be much easier to work with. Not only can you use the Search box to open and run commands quicker, but you can also run commands with fewer clicks.

Navigating the control buttons and customizing the power configuration

Below the common folder and feature buttons on the Start menu's right pane, you'll find your computer's Shut Down button. When you click the Shut Down Options button (the arrow to the right of "Shut down"), you have the following options:

Switch user
> Switches users so another user can log on

Log off
> Logs off the computer and ends your user session

Lock
> Locks the computer so that a logon screen is displayed

Restart
> Shuts down and then restarts the computer

Sleep
> Puts the computer in sleep mode, if possible given the system configuration and state

Hibernate
> Puts the computer in hibernate mode, if possible given the system configuration and state

As discussed in Chapter 1, your computer's power configuration determines how sleep mode works. Windows 7 has three power plans, which you can use to automatically manage the way your monitor, hard disks, and computer as a whole enter sleep or hibernation mode. Power plans also control other power settings. The standard power plans are:

Balanced
This plan uses a balanced approach to managing power and is the default.

High Performance
This plan optimizes the computer for performance by allowing it to consume as much power as needed.

Power Saver
This plan optimizes the computer to conserve power by allowing it to more quickly turn off the monitor, hard disks, and computer to conserve power.

Power plans have basic settings and advanced settings. The basic settings control when the display is turned off and when the computer enters sleep mode. On laptops, basic settings also control whether and how much the display is dimmed. The advanced settings control all other power configuration options. You can select a power plan to use with the Power Options utility in the Control Panel. Click Start→Control Panel. In the Control Panel, click System and Security→Power Options. Specify the power plan to use by selecting it under the Preferred Plans heading. Click "Change plan settings" to change the basic settings. From the basic settings, click "Change advanced power settings" to change the advanced settings.

You also can use power configuration settings to control the way in which the power button, the sleep button, and the "Password protection on wakeup" feature work. In the default configuration, pressing a computer's power button initiates a shutdown (pressing and holding the power button on most computers will shut the computer down instantly, which could cause you to lose data). Pressing a portable computer's sleep button or closing the lid puts it in sleep mode (on most modern computers, this puts the computer into a deep sleep in which it consumes very little power). By default, all power plans use the "Password protection on wakeup" feature to ensure that when your computer wakes up from sleep mode, no one can access your computer without first entering a password to unlock the screen.

You can configure power buttons and "Password protection on wakeup" options by following these steps:

1. Click Start→Control Panel.
2. In the Control Panel, click the System and Security link→Power Options.
3. In the left pane, click the "Choose what the power button does" link. This displays the "Define power buttons" page in the Control Panel, as shown in Figure 2-7.
4. Use the "When I press the power button" list to specify whether the computer should shut down, sleep, or hibernate when the power button is pressed. On a laptop, you'll have separate lists for when your computer is on battery and when your computer is plugged in.

5. Use the "When I press the sleep button" list to specify whether the computer should shut down, sleep, or hibernate when the sleep button is pressed. On a laptop, you'll have separate lists for when your computer is on battery and when your computer is plugged in.

6. On a laptop, use the "When I close the lid" list to specify the action to perform when you close the lid. You'll have separate lists for when your computer is on battery and when your computer is plugged in.

7. Use the "Password protection on wakeup" options to specify whether the computer requires a password on wakeup.

8. Click "Save changes."

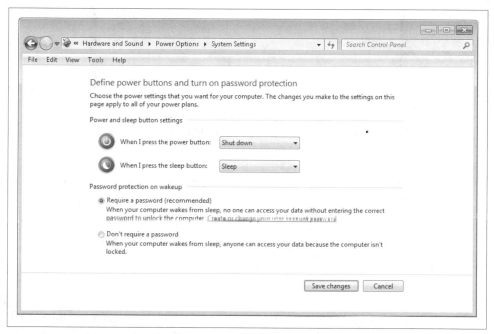

Figure 2-7. Configuring your computer's power buttons

Navigating the Search box

Below the Start menu's programs list in the left pane, you'll find the Search box. The Search box allows you to quickly search your computer or the Internet. You can work with the Search box using the following techniques:

- To use the Search box, click the Start button and type your search text (see Figure 2-8). Search results are displayed in the left pane of the Start menu. Click on a result to run a program or open a folder or file.

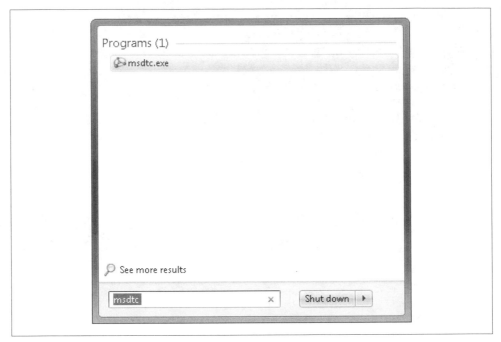

Figure 2-8. Searching your computer

- To clear the search results and return to the normal view, click the X button to the right of the Search box or press the Escape key.

 You don't need to click in the Search box before you begin typing. Just type your search text and you'll see any matching results.

Your computer uses the Windows Search service to perform the search. This service searches the entire computer using the search text you provided. As discussed in detail in Chapter 6, the Windows Search service matches the search text to words that appear in the title of any program, file, or folder and returns any matches found. For locations you've indexed, the Windows Search service also searches the contents of documents and file properties. You can customize the way search works by using the Indexing Options utility in the Control Panel, and by setting indexing options in the Folder Options utility in the Control Panel.

Getting Around the Taskbar

The taskbar in Windows 7 has several key features:

Start button
> Displays the Start menu, as previously discussed

Program buttons
> Provide access to pinned and running programs

Notification area
> Displays system notifications and the current time

Each area has feature enhancements. The sections that follow discuss the enhancements for the Quick Launch Toolbar, program buttons, and the notification area.

Navigating and customizing taskbar buttons

The taskbar displays buttons for open programs that allow you to switch between the applications you've opened or pinned to the taskbar. A new feature in Windows 7 is the ability to easily add any program to the taskbar. To customize the taskbar by adding programs, follow these steps:

1. Click the Start button.
2. Find the program you want to be able to quickly access in the menu.
3. Right-click the program's menu item.
4. On the shortcut menu, select Pin to Taskbar.

To remove a pinned program from the taskbar, right-click its icon and then select "Unpin this program from the taskbar." This removes the program's button from the taskbar.

In Windows 7, you can set the order of buttons for all opened and pinned programs. To do this, click the button on the taskbar and drag it to the desired position.

One of the more significant taskbar enhancements in Windows XP was the introduction of program grouping. Rather than display a button for each program, the taskbar groups similar buttons by default. Grouping buttons saves room on the taskbar and makes sure that in most cases you don't need to expand the taskbar to find the buttons for open programs. For example, if you open six different folders in Windows Explorer, these items would be grouped together under one taskbar button. Clicking the taskbar button would then display a popup dialog box with an entry for each window, allowing you to select the grouped window to open.

The way grouping and preview works depends on whether your computer supports Windows Aero Glass and whether you are using a theme that has Windows Aero Glass enabled:

- When you are using an Aero desktop theme, moving the mouse pointer over an open program's button on the taskbar displays a preview window with thumbnails for each open instance of the program. Moving the mouse pointer over a particular thumbnail preview brings the related window to the front of all the other windows. You can then switch to the window by clicking or close the window by moving the mouse pointer to the right and clicking the close button.

- When you are not using an Aero desktop theme, moving the mouse pointer over an open program's button on the taskbar displays a menu with icons and titles for each open instance of the program. Moving the mouse pointer over an item does not bring the related window to the front of all the other windows. However, you can still switch to the window by clicking in it or close the window by moving the mouse pointer to the right and clicking the close button.

You can customize taskbar behavior using the Taskbar Appearance options found on the Taskbar tab of the Taskbar and Start Menu Properties dialog box (see Figure 2-9). To display this dialog box with the Taskbar tab selected, right-click an open area of the taskbar and then select Properties. Once the dialog box is displayed, select or clear options as preferred and then click OK.

Figure 2-9. Customizing the taskbar

Table 2-2 details how you can use the options provided to customize taskbar behavior. By default, all the options are selected except Auto-Hide the Taskbar and Use Small Icons.

Table 2-2. Options for customizing the taskbar

Taskbar option	When selected	When not selected
Lock the taskbar	Locks the taskbar in place to prevent accidental moving or resizing.	Allows you to move the taskbar to dock it to other sides of the screen and to resize the taskbar to display fewer or more rows of buttons.
Auto-hide the taskbar	Allows the taskbar to automatically hide when you aren't using it and display only when you move the cursor over it.	Ensures that the taskbar is always displayed on the desktop (though not necessarily on top of other windows).
Use small icons	Reduces the size of program buttons, allowing more buttons to fit on the taskbar.	Uses large icons, which are easy to select and work with.
Use Aero Peek to preview the desktop	Enables the show desktop button at the end of the taskbar.	Hides the show desktop button at the end of the taskbar.
Taskbar option	**Used to**	**Options**
Taskbar location on screen	Set the location of the taskbar as bottom, left, right, or top.	Bottom, Left, Right, Top
Taskbar buttons	Specify whether taskbar buttons are always combined, combined only when the taskbar is full, or never combined.	Always combine, Combine when taskbar is full, Never combine

Windows 7 introduces several significant enhancements to the taskbar that are available only on a system that supports Aero. These enhancements are:

- Live thumbnails
- Windows Flip
- Windows Flip 3D
- Full-screen preview
- Peek and shake

When you move the mouse pointer over a taskbar button (and Show Windows Previews is enabled), Windows 7 displays a live thumbnail of the window, showing the content of that window. Figure 2-10 shows an example of a live thumbnail. If the content in the window is being updated, such as with a running process or active video playback, the thumbnail continuously updates to reflect the live state of the window. If the preview is for grouped taskbar buttons, Windows displays a thumbnail of the most recently started window and makes the thumbnail appear to include a group of windows. When you hover over the thumbnail, all of the grouped windows are displayed in a preview window.

Figure 2-10. A live thumbnail

When you press Alt-Tab, Windows 7 displays a flip view (Figure 2-11) containing live thumbnails of all open windows. Because the thumbnails are live views, they continuously update to reflect their current state regardless of the type of content. You can work with a flip view using the following techniques:

- Pressing Alt-Tab and then holding Alt keeps the flip view open.
- Pressing Tab while holding the Alt key allows you to cycle through the windows.
- Release the Alt key to select the current window and bring it to the front.
- Alternatively, select a window and bring it to the front by moving the mouse pointer over the thumbnail and clicking.

When you press the Windows logo key and the Tab key, Windows 7 displays a 3D flip view. This 3D flip view provides a skewed 3D view of all open windows. Because the 3D window views are live, the windows continuously update to reflect their current state regardless of the type of content. Figure 2-12 shows an example of a 3D flip view. You can work with a 3D flip view using the following techniques:

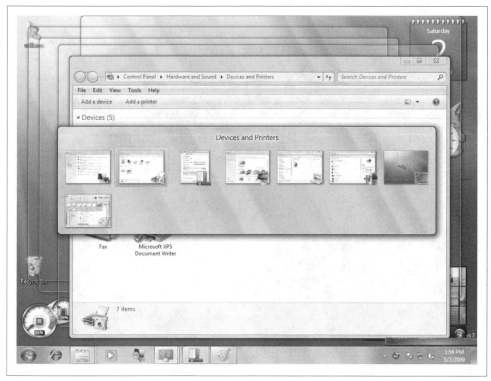

Figure 2-11. The flip view

- Pressing the Windows logo key and Tab and then holding the Windows logo key keeps the 3D flip view open.

- Pressing the Tab key while holding the Windows logo key allows you to cycle through the windows.

- Release the Windows logo key to select the current window and bring it to the front.

- Alternatively, select a window and bring it to the front by moving the mouse pointer over the thumbnail and clicking.

Windows 7 also adds jump lists. Figure 2-13 shows an example of a jump list. Jump lists are visible with or without Aero, and provide quick access to recently or frequently used files. Sometimes, you'll also have access to tasks that you can perform. To display a jump list for any program on the taskbar or Start menu, right-click the program button. You can then select a file to open or task to perform by clicking in the jump list.

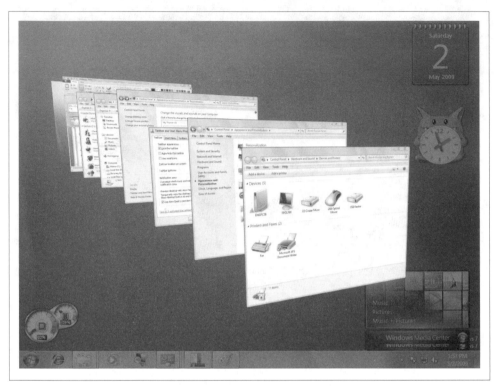

Figure 2-12. The 3D flip view

Figure 2-13. A jump list

By default, jump lists track up to 10 recent items. You can specify the maximum number of items to track using the Customize Start Menu dialog box. Right-click the Start button and then select Properties. In the Taskbar and Start Menu Properties dialog box, click the Customize button on the Start Menu tab. In the Customize Start Menu dialog box, specify the number of recent items to display in jump lists and then click OK twice.

Windows 7 provides new ways to work with windows as well. Using Snap, you can:

- Maximize a window by dragging it to the top of the screen. If you later drag the window away from the top of the screen, the window is resized to its original size.

- Drag the top or bottom border of window to expand it vertically. If you drag the window to the top or bottom of the screen, the window expands vertically to fill in the space between the bottom and the top of the screen. If you later drag the window away from the top of the screen, the window is resized to its original size.

Peek allows you to look past all your open windows and view the desktop. To peek at the desktop (Aero only), simply point to the right edge of the taskbar. When you do, open windows instantly turn transparent, revealing your desktop and any icons and gadgets it contains.

To focus on a single window and clear up the view (Aero only), click a pane of the window and give your mouse a shake. Every open window except that one is minimized. Shake the mouse again and all your windows are back.

Navigating and customizing the notification area

You'll find the notification area on the far-right side of the taskbar. As Figure 2-14 shows, the notification area has several key features:

- An options button (the up-pointing arrow) for accessing hidden notification icons, such as those used by programs you've installed. If you click the options button and then click the program icon, you'll open the program or display the program's notifications window. If you click the options button, then click and drag a program icon, you can move the icon to the notifications area or from the notifications area to the options window.

- An area for notification icons, such as those for the action center, network, power, volume, and clock controls.

Figure 2-14. Viewing system and program notifications

Notifications for programs and the operating system behave in different ways:

- Generally, if you move the pointer over a program notification icon and then click, you'll see a shortcut menu (provided one is available).
- Generally, if you move the pointer over a program notification icon and then double-click, you'll open the related program or window.
- Generally, if you move the pointer over a system notification icon, you'll see a tooltip that provides information about the notification.
- Generally, if you move the pointer over a system notification icon and click, you'll see a control window that provides information about the notification and allows you to configure the related feature.

You can use the system notification icons as summarized in Table 2-3.

Table 2-3. Working with system notification icons

System notification icon	Moving pointer over the icon	Clicking the icon
Action Center	Displays information about alert messages and system problems that you way want to try to resolve.	Displays a control window with links to the various alert messages. There's also a link for opening the Action Center.
Network	Displays the network to which you are connected and the current access configuration, such as Internet Access or Local Only.	Displays a control window with shortcut links for each connection. If there's no connection, use the Connect to a Network link to configure wireless network connections and the Open Network and Sharing Center link to manage your network configuration.
Volume	Shows the current system volume and speaker configuration.	Allows you to adjust the computer volume or mute the sound entirely. Click the Mixer link to display mixing options for application sound.
Clock	Displays the day of the week, date, and year.	Displays a calendar view of the current month and a clock depicting the current time. Browse other monthly calendars using the buttons provided. Click Change Date and Time Settings to modify the computer's date and time.

You can configure notification behavior by completing the following steps:

1. Right-click an open area of the taskbar, choose Properties, and then select Customize under the Notification area. Alternatively, click the "Notifications options" button and then click Customize.

2. On the Notification Area Icons page in Control Panel, shown in Figure 2-15, select the appropriate notification option for each program. Notification icons are listed by name and behavior. Click in the Behavior column to set the icon's behavior as "Show icon and notifications," "Only show notifications," or "Hide icon and notifications."

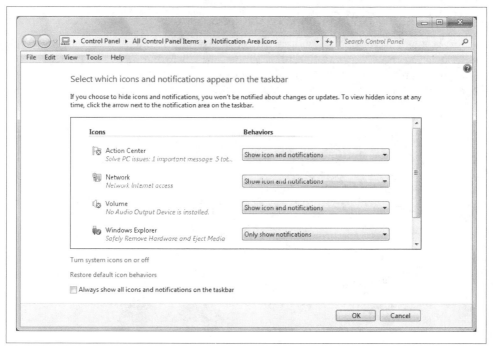

Figure 2-15. Customizing program and system notifications

You can show the icon and notifications, show only notifications, or hide the icon and notifications. Generally, you'll want to show the icon and notifications for important programs. However, if you find the notifications to be bothersome, you might want to show only the icon and notifications for action center and network.

3. To manage system icons, click "Turn system icons on or off" and then set the behavior for each icon to on or off as appropriate. Turning off a system icon removes the icon and turns off notifications. Click Customize notification icons to return to the previous page.

4. To always display program notification icons, select the "Always show all icons and notifications on the taskbar" checkbox.

5. Click OK.

Using Desktop Gadgets

Desktop gadgets are small applications designed to perform a very specific function, such as providing a desktop calendar or virtual notepad. Unlike in Windows Vista, you add gadgets directly to the desktop and no longer need a separate sidebar.

Getting to Know Your Computer's Gadgets

Windows has several default gadgets in most installations. You add gadgets to the desktop using the Gadget Gallery dialog box, shown in Figure 2-16. To access this dialog box, click Programs in Control Panel and then click Desktop Gadgets. Alternatively, click Start, point to All Programs, and then click Desktop Gadget Gallery.

Figure 2-16. Working with your computer's gadgets

The Gadget Gallery shows all the gadgets that are available on your computer. When multiple pages of gadgets are available, you can navigate the pages using the Previous and Next Page buttons provided in the upper-left corner of the window. You can also use the Search box to search for gadgets by name. As you type your search text, the list of gadgets is automatically filtered to include only those gadgets matching the search text you entered.

In the lower-left corner of the Gadget Gallery window, you'll find a Show details/Hide details button used to show or hide a Details pane. Clicking a gadget with the Show Details pane expanded displays the gadget details, which include the gadget name, version, and description. Clicking and dragging a gadget moves it to the desktop. Or, you can double-click the gadget to add it to the right-side of the desktop.

You can visit Microsoft's Gadget Gallery on the Internet by clicking either of the links provided. Some gadgets are updated automatically when new versions become available as part of the standard Windows Update process. Other gadgets you must update manually by downloading the desired gadget update.

You can work with gadgets in a variety of ways. You can move them around the desktop by clicking and dragging to move it to different locations on the desktop. You can display a gadget on top of all other windows by right-clicking the gadget and selecting Always on Top. Once you've moved the gadget to the top, right-clicking the gadget and selecting Always on Top a second time clears the setting and makes the gadget work like any other window—it can be brought to the front when in use or put to the back when not in use.

Every gadget has an opacity setting that controls whether you can see through it. Because the default opacity setting is 100 percent, you can't see through gadgets by default. If you want to be able to see through a gadget, right-click it, point to Opacity, and then select the desired opacity. The lower the opacity setting is, the more translucent the gadget will appear to be and the better you'll be able to see what's behind it. The higher the opacity setting is, the less translucent the gadget will appear to be and the less you'll be able to see what's behind it.

Now let's take a closer look at the gadgets you'll probably use the most.

 The Feed Headlines gadget displays data from selected Really Simple Syndication (RSS) feeds that have been configured in Internet Explorer. RSS feeds can contain news headlines, lists, and other information.

Using the Calendar gadget

Anyone who likes to keep a calendar on his or her desk to show the day of the week and day of the month will love the Calendar gadget. This gadget displays a desktop calendar that you can drag around the desktop.

You can work with the gadget in a variety of ways. As the leftmost view in Figure 2-17 shows, the current day and date are displayed by default. If you click the calendar, you can view the current month. You can view other months in the calendar using the right-facing and left-facing arrow buttons.

To display the day and date view for a particular entry, click it. The tab in the lower-left corner and the color of the view indicate that you are not viewing the current day and date. You can return to the current day and date view by clicking the tab in the lower-left corner of the calendar.

Figure 2-17. Navigating the Calendar gadget views

Using the Clock gadget

Anyone who likes wall clocks or dislikes the bland system clock will like the Clock gadget. This gadget displays an analog clock with hour and minute hands by default (see Figure 2-18). Moving the mouse pointer over the clock and clicking shows the digital time with hour, minutes, and seconds.

Figure 2-18. Working with the Clock gadget

The Clock gadget is one of several gadgets that have configurable properties:

- You can change the clock face to any one of the eight standard clock faces.
- The clock time zone you use can be different from that used by the computer clock.
- The clock can have a name, which is useful if you add more than one instance of the Clock gadget (which is handy if you want to see the time in multiple time zones simultaneously).
- The clock can have a second hand, though its movement can be rather distracting.

To change the time zone or modify other options, right-click the Clock gadget and then select Options. You can then use the dialog box shown in Figure 2-18 to set the clock options.

Using the CPU Meter gadget

Having problems with a slow or unresponsive computer, or like being able to see what's going on with your computer? If so, you might want to start using the CPU Meter gadget. This gadget displays the current percentage utilization of the computer's CPU and memory as a series of gauges (see Figure 2-19). The large gauge shows the CPU utilization; the small gauge shows the RAM utilization.

Figure 2-19. Working with the CPU Meter gadget

Similar to a tachometer in a car, the CPU and RAM gauges show high utilization in yellow and red. The gauges are handy if you are experiencing performance problems and are wondering what is happening with your computer.

Generally, if either gauge peaks into yellow or red usage, the computer may become sluggish and slow to respond because of the high utilization of its resources. If both gauges peak into yellow or red usage, or either gauge is at 98 percent utilization or higher, your computer may become extremely sluggish or unresponsive to your requests.

Windows 7 includes some great new features to resolve performance issues, which I will discuss in Chapter 3.

Using the Weather gadget

Anyone stuck in a cubicle without a window or wanting to know about the weather in some far-off place will like the Weather gadget. This gadget provides an overview of the weather at a particular location courtesy of the weather provider configured for your computer. The default weather provider is MSN. Using this gadget, you can tell at a glance whether it is sunny, cloudy, snowing, or raining (see Figure 2-20). You can also see the outside temperature.

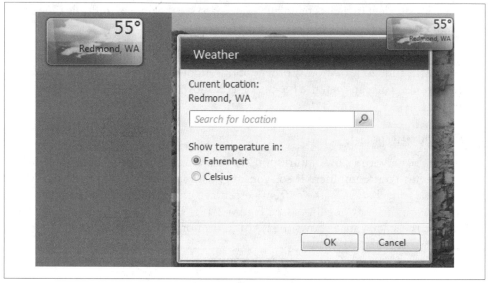

Figure 2-20. Using the Weather gadget

You can work with the gadget in several ways. You can set the location for which you want to view the weather, which is great if you are currently in Ohio but your heart and mind are in Colorado, where you're heading for vacation. You can also specify whether to display the temperature in degrees Fahrenheit or degrees Celsius.

To change the location of your weather reports or the way temperature is displayed, right-click the Weather gadget and then select Options. You can then use the dialog box shown in Figure 2-20 to set the weather options.

Using the Stock gadget

Anyone who tracks securities, companies, or indexes in the stock market will like the Stock gadget. This gadget provides an overview of the major stock market indexes by default (see Figure 2-21). In the United States, the major indexes are the Dow Jones Industrial Average ($INDU), the NASDAQ Composite Index ($COMPX), and the S&P 500 Index ($INX). Quotes are provided by the default quote provider with a 20-minute delay. The default quote provider is IDC Comstock.

You can work with the Stock gadget in several ways. By default, the Stock gadget displays details on three tracked stocks at a time, in a vertical column. The most recently tracked stocks are listed first. If you move the mouse pointer over the gadget, you'll see

Figure 2-21. Navigating the Stock gadget views

a control panel with several buttons. You can use the Scroll Up and Scroll Down buttons to navigate through the summary details for the stocks you are tracking.

You can change the position of a stock in the list by clicking its entry and dragging it slowly up or down. Using this technique, you can move a tracked stock from the bottom of the list to the top or from the top of the list to the bottom.

If you move the mouse pointer over a stock entry, a delete button is displayed in the upper-right corner. Click the delete button to stop tracking the stock.

All publicly traded securities, companies, and indexes have a stock symbol. If you want to add a security, company, or index, follow these steps:

1. Move the mouse pointer over the Stock gadget.
2. Click the "Add a stock symbol" button. This displays the second view of the Stock gadget, as shown in Figure 2-21.
3. In the Search box, enter the stock symbol for the security, company, or index you want to track and press Enter. If the stock is found, the stock is added to the list of tracked stock symbols, and you'll get quotes for it automatically.

If you want to view all of your tracked securities, companies, and indexes, move the mouse pointer over the Stock gadget and click the + button. To view a graph of the stock, move the mouse pointer over the stock entry and click. Be careful not to click the stock name, as this opens the stock's MSN page in Internet Explorer.

Using the Currency gadget

Anyone who converts money from one currency to another will like the Currency gadget. This gadget converts currency using the current market rate, allowing you to see at a glance how much your money is worth in another currency.

The default currency provider for this gadget is MSN Money. The Currency gadget is handy for anyone traveling to a foreign country or working in a country and getting paid in a currency other than the one to which he is accustomed.

As Figure 2-22 shows, the Currency gadget has two entries. The first entry sets the amount of a specific currency you want to convert and the second entry is the value in the specified currency. Using this feature you can, for example, convert 10 U.S. dollars into euros or 10 euros into U.S. dollars.

Figure 2-22. Using the Currency gadget

Using the Slide Show gadget

Users with pictures stored on the computer will like the Slide Show gadget. This gadget displays pictures from a selected folder as a continuous slide show where pictures rotate at a specified interval (see Figure 2-23).

Figure 2-23. Working with the Slide Show gadget

Moving the mouse pointer over the Slide Show gadget displays a control panel that allows you to pause the slide show or play the slide show. You can also navigate to the previous and next pictures using the Previous and Next buttons. The View button opens the currently displayed picture in Windows Live Photo Gallery. You'll learn more about Windows Live Photo Gallery in Chapter 9.

By default, pictures in your Pictures Library are displayed in the slide show. Right-click the Slide Show gadget and select Options, and you can modify the Folder setting to use any preferred folder by following these steps:

1. If you want to use your *My Pictures* folder, click in the Folder list and select *My Pictures*. To use another folder, click the Browse button to display the Browse for Folder dialog box. Use the Browse for Folder dialog box to locate and select the folder you want to use, and then click OK.

2. To include subfolders of the selected folder, select the Include Subfolders checkbox.

3. Click OK.

You can customize the way the slide show works by following these steps:

1. Open the Slide Show Options dialog box by right-clicking the Slide Show gadget and selecting Options.

2. Use the "Show each picture" list to set the duration to show each picture. You can set the duration using preset intervals, from five seconds to five minutes.

3. Use the "Transition between pictures" list to set the transition to use when changing to a new picture. If you don't want to use transitions, select None. Otherwise, select the desired transition, such as Fade.

4. By default, pictures are displayed in alphabetical order. To shuffle pictures rather than display them in order, select the "Shuffle pictures" checkbox.

5. Click OK.

Customizing Menus and the Control Panel

As you've seen, the desktop has many customizable features. You also can customize your computer's menus and Control Panel, and this section shows you how to do it.

Navigating and Customizing Your Computer's Menus

When you want to work with programs installed on a computer, you'll use the All Programs menu, as with earlier releases of Windows. When you click the Start button and then click All Programs, you'll see a list of programs installed on the computer, followed by a list of folders.

Depending on the system configuration, the programs you'll see include:

Default Programs
Opens the Default Programs dialog box, which you can use to configure default programs and features, as discussed in Chapter 4

Internet Explorer

Opens Internet Explorer, which you can use to browse the Web, as discussed in Chapter 7

Desktop Gadget Gallery

Opens the Gadget Gallery dialog box, which you can use to add gadgets to the desktop, as discussed earlier in this chapter

Windows DVD Maker

Opens Windows DVD Maker, which you can use to burn DVDs, as discussed in Chapters 9 and 10

Windows Media Center

Opens Windows Media Center, which you can use to manage home entertainment options for pictures, videos, movies, TV, and music, as discussed in Chapter 25

Windows Media Player

Opens Windows Media Player, which you can use to view pictures, play music, and play videos, as discussed in Chapter 8

Windows Update

Opens Windows Update, which you can use to keep your operating system up-to-date, as discussed in Chapter 20

The folders under the All Programs menu have also changed. The changes to the menu may take a while to get used to. Still, once you get used to the changes, navigating the menus will be fairly painless. The top-level folders are:

All Programs→Accessories

Provides access to the most commonly used accessories, including the Calculator, Command Prompt, Connect to a Network Projector, Connect to a Projector, Getting Started, Math Input Panel, Notepad, Paint, Remote Desktop Connection, Run, Snipping Tool, Sound Recorder, Sticky Notes, Sync Center, Windows Explorer, and WordPad.

Many of the standard accessories have been enhanced for Windows 7. For example, the Calculator now has Standard, Scientific, Programmer, and Statistics modes. Using predefined templates, you can perform unit conversion and date conversion. Using predefined worksheets, you can calculate mortgages, vehicle leases and fuel economy.

Out of all the accessories, my favorite is the Snipping Tool. You can use it to capture portions of a screen and then save, annotate, or share the captured snippet. By default, the Snipping Tool always captures portions of the screen to the clipboard, making snippets available in other programs as well.

All Programs→Accessories→Ease of Access

Provides access to the accessibility tools, such as the Ease of Access Center, Magnifier, Narrator, On-Screen Keyboard, and Windows Speech Recognition. The Ease of Access Center provides a central console for managing accessibility options.

Windows Speech Recognition is one of the most powerful new accessories. With the help of a microphone, this accessory allows you to train your computer to recognize your voice. You can then dictate and control your computer by voice.

All Programs→Accessories→System Tools

Provides access to commonly used system tools, such as Character Map, Disk Cleanup, Disk Defragmenter, System Information, System Restore, Task Scheduler and Windows Easy Transfer. Windows Easy Transfer replaces the Files and Settings Transfer Wizard in Windows XP.

Also includes Internet Explorer (No Add-ons), which is a protected version of Internet Explorer without browser extensions or other add-ons. You can use this version of Internet Explorer to protect your computer from potentially malicious websites and programs.

All Programs→Accessories→Windows PowerShell

Provides access to the graphical and command-line interface for Windows PowerShell. Windows PowerShell is installed by default in most installations.

All Programs→Games

Provides access to Microsoft games installed with the operating system. The available games depend on the edition of Windows 7 you are using.

All Programs→Maintenance

Provides access to maintenance tools, including the Backup and Restore, Create a System Repair Disc, Help and Support, and Windows Remote Assistance.

Note that Windows 7 includes Windows Recovery Environment (Windows RE) automatically. As long as you do not remove or damage the related recovery partition, you should be able to restore your computer as discussed in Chapter 21. As an extra precaution, you can create a system repair disc.

Also of note is that Windows 7 integrates Problem Reports and Solutions into the Action Center. The Action Center has many of the same options, and has been significantly enhanced.

All Programs→Startup

Lists programs that are set to start up automatically when you log on. This doesn't mean these are the only startup programs for your computer. You may configure other programs for automatic startup, as discussed in Chapter 4.

All Programs→Windows Live

Lists programs that are available when you install the Live Essentials applications on your computer. These applications are available for free download by visiting *http://www.windowslive.com/desktop* and include Windows Live Call, Windows Live Family Safety, Windows Live Mail, Windows Live Photo Gallery, and Windows Live Writer. Windows Live Mail combines the features of the Windows Mail, Windows Calendar, and Windows Contacts programs that are included with most editions of Windows Vista.

Windows 7 manages menus in different ways than Windows XP and earlier Windows releases. By default, menus are sorted alphabetically automatically as you add, change, or remove menus and menu items. Windows 7 highlights newly installed menus and programs, and opens submenus when you pause on them with the mouse pointer. Windows 7 also allows you to view shortcut menus and use drag-and-drop on the desktop and within menus.

You use the settings in the Customize Start Menu dialog box to control how Windows 7 manages its menus. Knowing this, you can customize your computer's menus by following these steps:

1. Right-click the Start button and select Properties. This opens the Taskbar and Start Menu Properties dialog box.

2. On the Start Menu tab, click Customize. This displays the Customize Start Menu dialog box.

3. Click the Use Default Settings button to restore the operating system default settings. Or use the following options to customize your menus:

   Enable context menus and dragging and dropping
   Select this option to allow shortcut menus to be displayed and to allow dragging and dropping. Clear this option to prevent shortcut menus from being displayed and to prevent dragging and dropping.

   Highlight newly installed programs
   Select this option to highlight menus and menu items for newly installed programs. Clear this option to disable newly installed program highlighting.

   Open submenus when I pause on them with the mouse pointer
   Select this option to open submenus when you pause on them with the mouse pointer. Clear this option to require clicking a submenu to expand it and view its contents.

   Sort all programs menu by name
   Select this option to sort the menu automatically by name. Clear this option to show newly installed menus and menu items last.

4. Click OK to save your settings.

Navigating and Customizing the Control Panel

Clicking the taskbar's Start button and then clicking Control Panel displays the Control Panel. You can also display the Control Panel in any Windows Explorer view by clicking the leftmost option button on the Address bar and selecting Control Panel. As with Windows XP, the Control Panel in Windows 7 has two views:

- Category Control Panel view, shown in Figure 2-24, is the default view and provides access to system utilities by category, utility, and key tasks. Category Control Panel view is also referred to as Control Panel. To access this view, select Category on the View By list.

- The All Control Panel Items view, shown in Figure 2-25, is an alternative view that provides access to all items in the Control Panel. Each Control Panel utility is listed separately by name. To access this view, select Large Icons or Small Icons on the View By list.

Figure 2-24. Using Category Control Panel view

Because the Category Control Panel view provides quick access to frequent tasks, it is the view you will use most often. With this view, the Control Panel opens as a console on which eight categories of utilities are listed. For each category, there's a top-level link and under this are several of the most frequently performed tasks for the category.

Clicking a category link provides a list of utilities in that category. For each utility listed within a category, there's a link to open the utility, and under this are several of the most frequently performed tasks for the utility. Table 2-4 lists the category associated with specific items; you can quickly find Control Panel items by referring to this table.

Table 2-4. Control Panel items by category

Category	Items found under this category
Appearance and Personalization	Desktop Gadgets, Display, Ease of Access Center, Folder Options, Fonts, Personalization, Taskbar and Start Menu
Clock, Language, and Region	Date and Time, Region and Language
Ease of Access	Ease of Access Center, Speech Recognition
Hardware and Sound	AutoPlay, Devices and Printers, Display, Power Options, Sound
Network and Internet	Homegroup, Internet Options, Network and Sharing Center
Programs	Default Programs, Desktop Gadgets, Programs and Features
System and Security	Action Center, Administrative Tools, Backup and Restore, BitLocker Drive Encryption, Power Options, System, Windows Firewall, Windows Update
User Accounts and Family Safety	Credential Manager, Parental Controls, User Accounts, Windows CardSpace

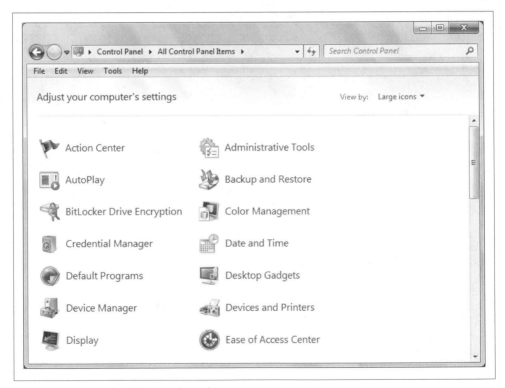

Figure 2-25. Using the All Control Panel Items view

In Category Control Panel view, all utilities and tasks run with a single click. The left pane of the console has a link to take you to the Control Panel home page, links for each category, and links for recently performed tasks. Not only is this very efficient, but it's also very easy to use.

Because menu options and Control Panel options open with a single click by default, you might want to configure your computer to use single-click to open items such as documents as well. This may help you avoid confusion as to whether you need to click or double-click. When you have single-click open configured, pointing to an item selects it.

You can configure single-click open by completing the following steps:

1. Click the Start button and then click Control Panel.
2. In the Control Panel, click Appearance and Personalization.
3. Under Folder Options, click Specify Single- or Double-click to Open.
4. In the Folder Options dialog box, select Single-Click to Open an Item (Point to Select) and then click OK.

Once you have everything set to open with a single click, hopefully you will find that working with the Control Panel and Windows Explorer is much more intuitive.

CHAPTER 3

Fine-Tuning Windows 7's Appearance and Performance

The appearance and performance of Windows 7 are closely tied together. You must often make a careful decision between the two to achieve a desired result. Because of this, fine-tuning Windows 7's appearance and performance is often a balancing act, especially if you want your computer to remain responsive under the widest circumstances possible.

Of the many interlinked appearance and performance features, the ones over which you have the most control are:

- Experience Index scoring
- Account controls
- Personalization settings
- Performance options

In this chapter, you'll learn how to fine-tune these features while maintaining the balance between appearance and performance.

Balancing Appearance and Performance

Because Windows 7 has a scalable user experience, there needed to be a way to determine the capabilities of a computer. The solution Microsoft developed was to capture a performance baseline based on specific performance metrics during installation of the operating system and after hardware or driver upgrades.

If you've upgraded a component that affects the Windows Experience Index, you can click "Re-run the assessment" to run the assessment again. If Windows decides that the current index information is out of date (as is likely to happen after upgrading hardware or installing a new driver), you'll have an option to Refresh Now. Changes to the computer's working environment can affect the index scores. Don't be surprised if your Windows Experience Index needs to be refreshed after setting Windows 7 up on a computer and installing new device drivers or hardware as may be required to complete the installation.

Getting Your Windows Experience Index Score

During installation, Windows 7 assigned your computer a Windows Experience Index. This index is a relative rating of your computer's capabilities with regard to its:

- Processor
- Physical memory (RAM)
- General graphics
- Gaming graphics
- Primary hard disk

The "general graphics" and "gaming graphics" component titles are misnomers; more appropriate titles would be "general graphics" and "multimedia graphics." Graphics is meant to reflect overall performance for Windows interfaces. Gaming graphics is meant to reflect performance for graphics-intensive applications, such as 3D business applications and 3D games.

To assign the Windows Experience Index, Windows 7 determines:

- The number of processors/processor cores installed on your computer and the processor type
- The number of calculations per second that your computer's processor can perform
- The total amount of physical memory installed on your computer
- The number of memory operations per second that your computer's memory can perform
- The total amount of graphics memory installed on your computer
- The relative performance of your computer's graphics adapter
- The data transfer rate of your computer's primary hard disk

These performance metrics help Windows 7 determine the relative performance of your computer. You can view your computer's Windows Experience Index and the related subscores by completing the following steps:

1. Click Start and then click Control Panel.
2. In the Control Panel, select System and Security.
3. Under the System heading, click Check the Windows Experience Index.
4. As shown in Figure 3-1, your computer's performance scores are listed by component in the Performance Information and Tools console.

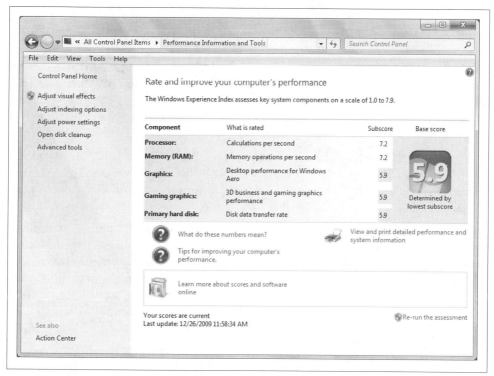

Figure 3-1. Viewing your computer's performance scores

Understanding Your Windows Experience Index Score

Your computer's base score is determined by the lowest subscore. The computer being rated in Figure 3-1 has a Windows Experience Index base score of 5.9. The base score can help you determine the type of software programs you can run on the computer. The base score also determines the level of performance Windows 7 delivers. Certain operating system features will work only when your computer meets the minimum base score requirements, and the use of certain other features, such as high display resolutions with Aero Glass or themes on multiple displays, will have a severe impact on your computer's performance.

Whether or not you use Aero is important. The Aero interface provides enhanced features including:

- Animated window closing and opening
- Live previews
- Smoother window dragging
- Transparent window frames

To use Aero, your computer's graphics card must support the Windows Display Driver Model (WDDM) and DirectX 9.0 or later. WDDM 1.0 and DirectX 9.0 were both released around the same time as Windows Vista. Both have been updated for Windows 7. Windows 7 display drivers that support WDDM 1.1 or later offer improved performance while also reducing the per-window memory usage by up to 50 percent. WDDM 1.1 supports DirectX 11. DirectX 11 offers enhancements and performance improvements over earlier versions.

Most current computers will have a base score of between three and five. The Windows Experience Index is designed to scale as computer technology advances. Thus, current computers have top scores in the 6s and 7s, and tomorrow's computers may have top scores in the 9s and 10s.

Table 3-1 provides an overview of what the base scores mean. If you want to improve your computer's base score, you can upgrade the hardware component responsible for the low score (most laptop computers cannot be upgraded in this way, however). For example, if gaming graphics is your lowest score, you could upgrade your graphics card to improve your rating. Don't do this, however, without first consulting the performance details to determine exactly how the component is configured currently.

Table 3-1. Understanding your computer's Windows Experience Index score

Base score	What the score means	Description of experience
1.0 to 1.9	Degraded user experience	You can use the computer for general computing, word processing, and music playback. The computer probably isn't suited for more advanced tasks, such as gaming or multimedia. The user experience will be severely limited.
2.0 to 2.9	Reduced user experience	You can use the computer for general computing, business applications, basic gaming, and basic multimedia. The computer probably isn't suited for more advanced tasks, such as multiplayer or 3D gaming and advanced multimedia. The user experience will be limited.
3.0 to 3.9	Basic user experience	You can use the computer for general computing, advanced business applications, expanded gaming, and expanded multimedia. The computer probably isn't suited for advanced gaming, such as multiplayer 3D gaming, or advanced multimedia, such as recording HDTV and playing HD video.
4.0 to 4.9	Full user experience	You can use the computer for advanced computing, advanced business applications, advanced gaming, and advanced multimedia. The computer can use all the new features of Windows 7 with full functionality. Aero Glass will display

Base score	What the score means	Description of experience
		higher resolutions while achieving good performance, and using themes on multiple monitors shouldn't affect performance.
5.0 to 5.9	Superior user experience	You can use the computer for the most demanding tasks, including those that are both graphics-intensive and processor-intensive. The computer can use all the features of Windows 7 with full functionality. Aero Glass will display higher resolutions while achieving good performance, and using themes on multiple monitors shouldn't impact performance.
6.0 to 6.9	Outstanding gaming and graphics experience	You can use the computer for 3D graphics and 3D applications, including those that are both graphics-intensive and processor-intensive. The computer should deliver an outstanding gaming experience and good frame rates for video playback at 1,280 × 1,024.
7.0 to 7.9	Excellent gaming and graphics experience	You can use the computer for 3D graphics and 3D applications, including those that are both highly graphics-intensive and highly processor-intensive. The computer should deliver an excellent gaming experience and excellent frame rates for video playback at high screen resolutions.

Improving Your Windows Experience Index Score

In the Performance Information and Tools console, you can view detailed performance and configuration information by clicking "View and print detailed performance and system information." As Figure 3-2 shows, the configured details are provided for each hardware component being tracked—you can print this information for future reference by clicking "Print this page." For many computers, gaming graphics will have the lowest subscore. By examining the details, you can see the key reason for this and typically, it is because the video card has a limited amount of dedicated graphics memory. In the example, the computer is listed as having 2,302 MB of graphics memory available. However, 1,790 MB is coming from shared system memory and only 512 MB is dedicated. During graphics-intensive gaming, this means the computer may borrow up to 1,790 MB of RAM from the available physical memory, leaving less physical memory available for applications and the operating system. For a better gaming experience, you'd want to upgrade to a graphics card with 1 GB or higher of dedicated memory. Alternatively, you could purchase a second graphics card for your computer, but there are several caveats to ensure proper operation. You'd want to check the computer to ensure a card slot is available and you'd want to ensure your computer can support two graphics cards. You'd want to check with the graphics card manufacturer to determine the proper configuration required to use the existing graphics card with another graphics card.

If your computer has no or low dedicated graphics memory, installing a new graphics card with 512 MB or more of dedicated RAM on the computer would increase substantially the graphics and gaming graphics subscores. You could then have Windows 7 recalculate the performance scores by clicking "Re-run the assessment." Windows 7 would then begin rating your computer by evaluating the performance of each tracked

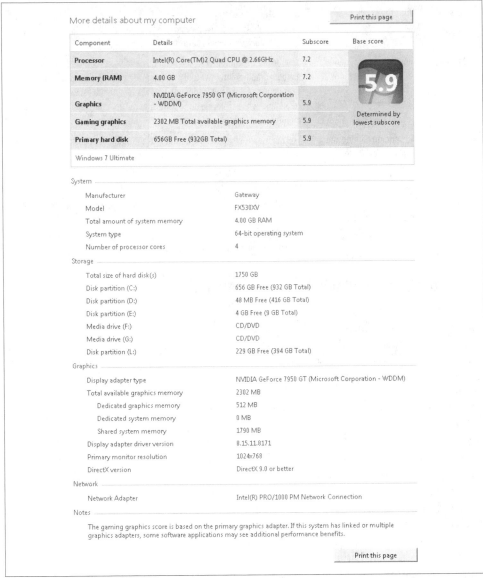

More details about my computer

Component	Details	Subscore	Base score
Processor	Intel(R) Core(TM)2 Quad CPU @ 2.66GHz	7.2	
Memory (RAM)	4.00 GB	7.2	**5.9**
Graphics	NVIDIA GeForce 7950 GT (Microsoft Corporation - WDDM)	5.9	
Gaming graphics	2302 MB Total available graphics memory	5.9	Determined by lowest subscore
Primary hard disk	656GB Free (932GB Total)	5.9	

Windows 7 Ultimate

System

Manufacturer	Gateway
Model	FX530XV
Total amount of system memory	4.00 GB RAM
System type	64-bit operating system
Number of processor cores	4

Storage

Total size of hard disk(s)	1750 GB
Disk partition (C:)	656 GB Free (932 GB Total)
Disk partition (D:)	48 MB Free (416 GB Total)
Disk partition (E:)	4 GB Free (9 GB Total)
Media drive (F:)	CD/DVD
Media drive (G:)	CD/DVD
Disk partition (L:)	229 GB Free (394 GB Total)

Graphics

Display adapter type	NVIDIA GeForce 7950 GT (Microsoft Corporation - WDDM)
Total available graphics memory	2302 MB
Dedicated graphics memory	512 MB
Dedicated system memory	0 MB
Shared system memory	1790 MB
Display adapter driver version	8.15.11.8171
Primary monitor resolution	1024x768
DirectX version	DirectX 9.0 or better

Network

Network Adapter	Intel(R) PRO/1000 PM Network Connection

Notes

The gaming graphics score is based on the primary graphics adapter. If this system has linked or multiple graphics adapters, some software applications may see additional performance benefits.

Print this page

Figure 3-2. Viewing your computer's configuration details

hardware component. When this process is completed, each component is listed with an appropriate subscore and the computer's new base score is listed in the Performance Information and Tools console. The rating process can take several minutes to complete.

The scores are meant to be helpful guidelines, and you can squeeze extra performance out of your computer in a variety of ways, but typically, this extra performance comes at a direct sacrifice to the way Windows 7 looks and behaves. For example, if your computer's base score is low because of graphics/gaming graphics, you can improve overall performance by turning off graphics-intensive features of the operating system, such as Aero Glass, visual effects, live previews, backgrounds, and themes. For more information on adjusting these features, see "Personalizing Windows 7" on page 79 and "Optimizing Performance" on page 98.

The detailed information tells you whether the display adapter supports WDDM and DirectX. In the Component list under Graphics, you'll see the display adapter type and the level of WDDM support. In the expanded list under Graphics, you'll see additional details, including the DirectX version supported.

Understanding User Account Control and Its Impact on Performance

User Account Control (UAC) is a collection of features designed to improve your computer's security and better protect it from malicious programs. UAC fundamentally changes the way Windows 7 works.

For Windows 7, there are significant changes to UAC as originally implemented in Windows Vista. You can now control exactly how UAC works. Before I discuss how to do this, let's first look at the way UAC works in a standard configuration.

User Accounts and Permissions

Windows 7 has two general types of user accounts:

- Standard user accounts
- Administrator user accounts

As I'll discuss in Chapter 18, standard users can perform any general computing tasks, such as starting programs, opening documents, and creating folders, as well as any support tasks that do not affect other users or the security of the computer. Administrators, on the other hand, have complete access to the computer and can make changes that affect other users and the security of the computer.

Unlike Windows XP and earlier releases of Windows, Windows 7 makes it easy to determine which tasks standard users can perform and which tasks administrators can perform. You may have noticed the multicolored shield icon, shown in Figure 3-3, next to certain options in Windows 7's windows, wizards, and dialog boxes. This is the Permissions icon. It indicates that the related option requires administrator permissions to run.

Figure 3-3. The Permissions icon, which indicates that the related option requires administrator permissions to run

Permission and Consent Prompting

In Windows 7, regardless of whether you are logged on as a standard user or as an administrator, you see a UAC prompt by default when programs try to make changes to your computer and when you try to run certain privileged applications. Computers can also be configured to prompt you whenever you make changes to Windows settings. The standard way the prompt works depends on whether you are logged on with a standard user account or with an administrator account.

If you are logged on with a standard user account, you are prompted to provide administrator credentials, as explained here and shown in Figure 3-4:

- On most personal or small office computers, the prompt lists each local computer Administrator account by name. To proceed, you must click an account, type the account's password, and then click OK.

- If you log into a domain, the prompt shows the logon domain and provides username and password boxes. To proceed, you must enter the name of an administrator account, type the account's password, and then click OK.

If you are logged on with an administrator account, you are prompted for consent to continue, as shown in Figure 3-5. The consent prompt works the same regardless of whether you are connected to a domain.

Elevation and the Secure Desktop

The process of getting a user's approval prior to running an application in administrator mode and prior to performing actions that change system-wide settings is known as *elevation*. Elevation enhances security by reducing the exposure and attack surfaces of the operating system. It does this by providing notification when you are about to perform an action that could affect system settings, such as installing an application, and eliminating the ability for malicious programs to invoke administrator privileges without your knowledge and consent.

Prior to elevation and display of the UAC prompt, Windows 7 does several things in the background. The key thing you should know is that by default Windows 7 switches to a secure, isolated desktop prior to displaying the prompt. The purpose of switching to the secure desktop is to prevent other processes or applications from providing the required permissions or consent. All other running programs and processes continue

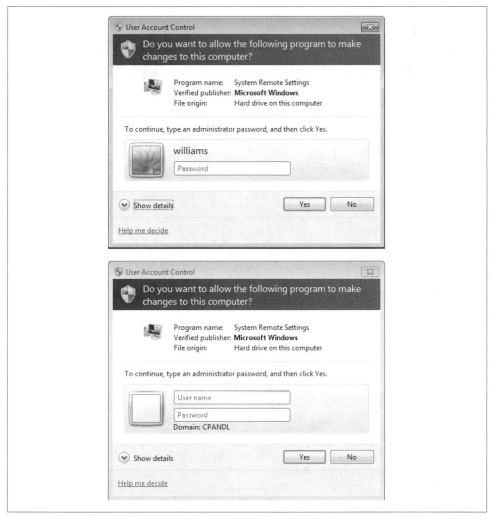

Figure 3-4. Providing the required credentials

to run on the interactive user desktop—only the prompt itself runs on the secure desktop.

Elevation, permission/consent prompts, and the secure desktop are the key aspects of UAC that affect you the most. As you can see, they have a measurable impact on the way Windows 7 works. Due to these UAC features:

- User accounts are not used in the same way as they are in Windows XP.
- Applications do not run in the same way as they do in Windows XP.
- Most configuration tasks are not performed in the same way as they are in Windows XP.

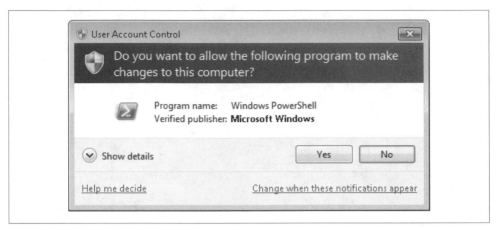

Figure 3-5. Providing consent to continue

Although these features have a far-reaching impact on the way you use Windows 7, they enhance security and provide your computer with better protection from malicious programs. If you use these features as they are intended to be used, your computer will be protected from many types of malicious programs.

Configuring and Tuning UAC

In Windows 7, UAC differentiates between changes to Windows settings and changes to the operating system made by programs and devices. Because of this, you can fine-tune the way UAC works so that you are notified about only particular types of changes. For example, most of the time you'll want to know only when programs are trying to install themselves or make changes to the operating system and won't want to be prompted every time you try to change Windows settings. In the revised UAC as implemented in Windows 7, you can now do this. You also can configure UAC so the secure desktop is not used. As I'll discuss in Chapter 18, you also can manage UAC through policy settings under Security Settings->Local Policies->Security Options.

On most personal or small office computers, you can fine-tune UAC by following these steps:

1. In Control Panel, click System and Security and then click the Change User Account Control Settings link under the Action Center heading.

2. On the User Account Control Settings page, shown in Figure 3-6, use the slider provided to choose when to be notified about changes to the computer. Your options and my recommendations (which differ somewhat from Microsoft's recommendations) are:

Always notify

Always notifies you when programs try to install software or make changes to the computer and when you change Windows settings. You should choose this option when a computer requires the highest security possible and you frequently install software and visit unfamiliar websites.

Default—notify me only when programs try to make changes to my computer

Notifies you only when programs try to make changes to the computer and not when you change Windows settings. You should choose this option when a computer requires high security and you want to reduce the number of notification prompts.

Notify me only when programs try to make changes to my computer (do not dim my desktop)

Works the same as Default but also prevents User Account Control from switching to the secure desktop. You should choose this option when you work in a trusted environment with familiar applications and do not visit unfamiliar websites. You may also want to use this option when it takes a long time for your computer to switch to the secure desktop.

Never notify

Turns off all User Account Control notification prompts. You should choose this option when security is not a priority and you work in a trusted environment.

3. Click OK. If you selected Never Notify, you will need to restart your computer for this change to take effect.

 Depending on the current configuration of UAC, you may be prompted for permissions or consent, as discussed previously. Because this is an inherent part of the user interface and a feature that you can enable or disable, I will not mention each time the prompt is displayed. Rather, I assume that you provide the permissions or consent as required.

On a computer that is logged into a domain, you may not be able to manage UAC using this technique. Though you may be able to configure individual UAC features through policy settings, these features will more than likely be set so that you cannot configure them.

Understanding Windows 7 Personalization

As you've seen, many factors can affect your computer's appearance and performance, including your hardware components and account controls. The way you achieve a balance between appearance and performance, however, is largely through the

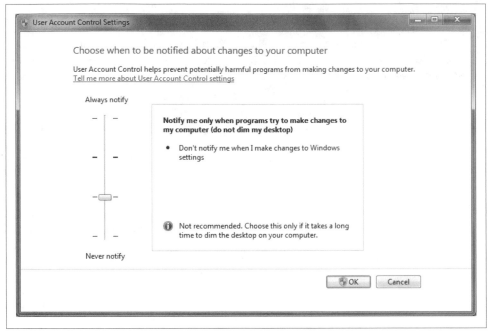

Figure 3-6. Fine-tuning UAC

trade-offs you make when applying personalization settings, and it is personalization settings that largely determine your experience.

Personalization Settings

In Windows 7, you can access personalization settings by clicking Start→Control Panel→Appearance and Personalization→Personalization or by right-clicking on the desktop and choosing Personalization. As Figure 3-7 shows, this displays the Personalization page in the Control Panel. The available personalization settings on the left side are:

Desktop Icons
Controls the default icons displayed on the desktop.

Mouse Pointers
Controls the mouse pointers used by Windows 7.

Account Picture
Sets the account picture that is displayed on the Start Menu.

Display
(This option appears in the bottom left.) Controls monitors used by Windows 7, their display resolutions, and their refresh rates. Also allows you to extend your desktop onto a second monitor.

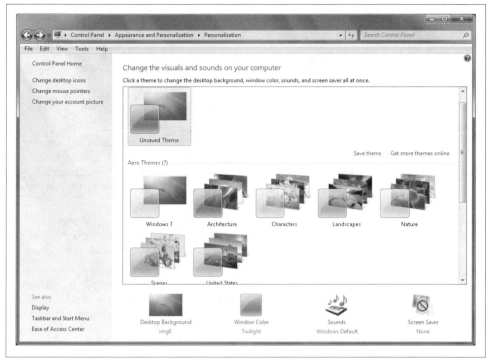

Figure 3-7. Viewing the personalization options

In the main portion of the window, you'll be able to access the following personalization settings:

Theme

Sets the theme used by Windows 7. A *theme* is a collection of appearance settings that includes the desktop background, sounds, and mouse pointers used by Windows 7. Changing themes and modifying certain aspects of a theme sets the user experience level and color scheme for your computer.

Desktop Background

Controls the desktop background colors and pictures used.

Window Color

Sets the color of window borders, the Start menu and the taskbar. With Aero themes, you can enable, adjust, and disable Windows transparency.

Sounds

Controls the system sounds used by Windows 7.

Screen Saver

Controls the screensaver and when it displays.

User Experience Levels

The user experience level is the foundation on which your personalization settings are based. Table 3-2 provides an overview of each user experience level.

Table 3-2. Understanding the user experience levels

User experience level	Can be used with	Provides
Windows Classic	Any Windows 7 edition; any Windows 7–capable computer	The look and feel of Windows 2000 while retaining the functionality improvements in Windows 7. You'll find a refined Start menu and streamlined Explorer windows, both with integrated search. You can switch to Windows Classic mode by selecting the Windows Classic theme in the Personalization control panel.
Windows Basic	Any Windows 7 edition; any Windows 7–capable computer	Adds slightly improved performance, gradients, and shading to the Windows Classic experience. You can switch to Windows Basic mode by selecting the Windows 7 Basic theme in the Personalization control panel.
Windows 7 Standard	Any Windows 7 edition; any Windows 7–capable computer	Adds improved performance and enhanced reliability to the Windows Standard experience. Supports the new Windows Display Driver Model (WDDM) to enable smooth window handling, increase stability, and reduce glitches, such as relics and slow screen refreshes while moving user interface elements. Supports Windows Flip.
Windows Aero	Windows 7 Home Premium edition or higher; any Windows 7–capable computer	Builds on the Windows 7 Basic experience. Adds Aero Glass, transparency for all windows, live preview, and Windows Flip 3D.

Each user experience level builds on and includes the features of the preceding level(s). If your computer has a low subscore for processor, physical memory, general graphics, gaming graphics, or any combination thereof, you may want to use the Windows Classic or Windows Basic experience level to improve your computer's performance. Figure 3-8 shows the look and feel of Windows Classic. Windows Classic and Windows Standard offer similar user experiences. Generally speaking, if you want to reduce the overhead associated with drawing gradients and shading, you can use the Windows Classic experience and you won't notice much difference.

If your computer has an average to high score for processor, physical memory, general graphics, gaming graphics, or any combination thereof, you may want to use the Windows 7 Standard or Windows Aero experience level to improve your computer's appearance. Windows 7 Basic and Windows Aero offer very similar user experiences. Figure 3-9 shows the look and feel of Windows 7 Basic.

Because of the previously listed feature differences among the various experience levels, you'll see related differences in the interface. A rather subtle change that you'll need to

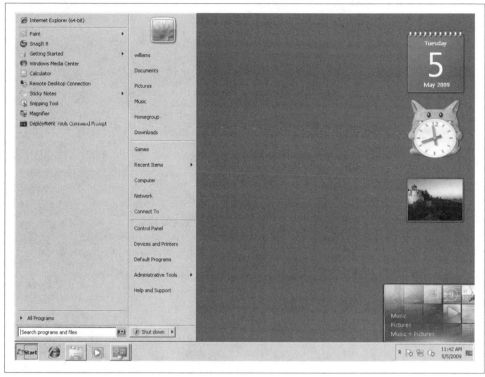

Figure 3-8. Viewing the classic experience level

watch out for has to do with the Window Color and Appearance page. Keep the following in mind:

- When you are using Windows Classic or Windows Basic, you can set the user experience level and color scheme, but you cannot mix colors or configure transparency settings. This is why clicking Windows Color and Appearance opens the Appearance Settings dialog box rather than the Windows Color and Appearance page in the Control Panel.

- When you are using Windows 7 Standard and Windows Aero, you can use the Windows Color and Appearance page in the Control Panel to change the color of windows, set color intensity, mix colors, and enable or disable transparency. To display the Appearance Settings dialog box so that you can set the user experience level and color scheme, you must click the "Advanced appearance settings" link.

Personalizing Windows 7

From fine-tuning your window colors and experience level to choosing your desktop backgrounds, screensavers, sounds, mouse pointers, themes, and display settings, you can personalize Windows 7 in many different ways. Navigating this maze of options

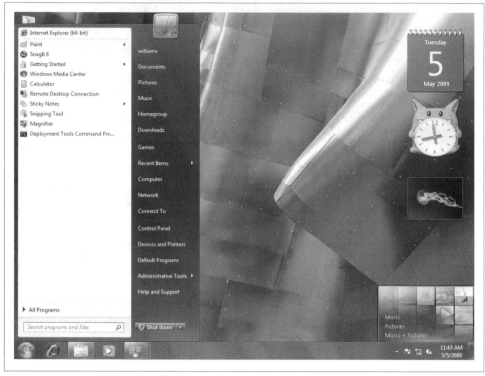

Figure 3-9. Viewing the enhanced experience level

can be tricky, especially when you want to achieve robust performance while maintaining a desired look and feel. Even experienced users often neglect the basics of this essential balancing act, so you may be tempted to skip this section. But don't.

Fine-Tuning Your Window Colors and Experience Level

Aero gives the user interface a highly polished, glassy look. When you use Aero, you can set the glass color, intensity, and transparency by selecting Window Color in the Personalization control panel. Several default colors are available, including twilight (blue), sky (light blue), ruby (red), pumpkin (orange), blush (pink), and white (frost). By selecting a color and then using the "Color intensity" slider, you can create softer or bolder colors. By enabling transparency, you make it possible to see through parts of windows, menus, and dialog boxes. You can also create the exact color you want using hue, saturation, and brightness color mixers. The one feature sorely missing is a way to enter numeric color values, which would allow you to use standard colors from color palettes.

Of these many Aero settings, the transparency setting is the biggest resource hog. If your computer has a low to middling score for its processor, physical memory, general graphics, or gaming graphics, you might want to disable this feature to achieve better performance.

The Power Saver power plan automatically disables transparency when running on batteries. For more information on power plans, see "Navigating the control buttons and customizing the power configuration" on page 37 in Chapter 2.

Optimizing Aero Glass

When you are using Windows Aero, you can configure the glass color, transparency, and intensity by completing the following steps:

1. Right-click an open area of the desktop and then select Personalize. On the Personalization page in the Control Panel, click Window Color.

2. As shown in Figure 3-10, select one of the base colors available. Do this to save time even if you want to use the color mixer.

3. To enable transparency, select the "Enable transparency" checkbox. To disable transparency, clear the "Enable transparency" checkbox.

4. Use the "Color intensity" slider to control the intensity of the color. Move the slider to the left to soften the color. Move the slider to the right to make the color bolder.

5. If you want to adjust the color, click the "Show color mixer" button and then use the hue, saturation, and brightness sliders to achieve the desired color.

6. Click OK to save your color settings.

Changing the experience level and appearance effects

By default, Windows 7 uses the highest experience level your computer is capable of. If you want to change the experience level, complete the following steps:

1. Right-click an open area of the desktop and then select Personalize.

2. Select a theme to use. This sets the base experience level. In most cases, you'll have several Windows Aero themes to choose from as well as several basic and high contrast themes. If you choose a theme other than a Windows Aero theme, you'll be using a reduced experience level.

3. Click Windows Color to fine-tune the color settings as discussed in the previous section. If you are using the Windows Classic or Windows Basic theme, you will not be able to mix colors or set transparency as described in that section.

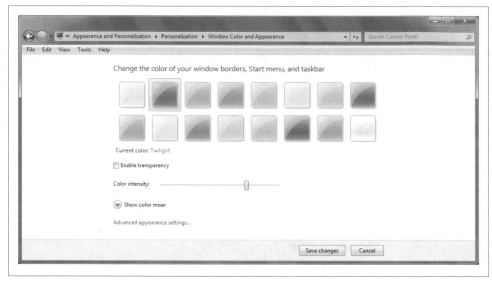

Figure 3-10. Setting the window color and appearance

Choosing Your Desktop Background

The Windows desktop can display a solid background color or a picture as Windows wallpaper. Windows 7 provides a fairly large set of ready-to-use background images that you can use as wallpaper.

On your computer's hard drive, these default background images are stored in sub-folders of the *%WinDir%\Web\Wallpaper* folder. The name of each subfolder sets the name of a category that appears when you are working with Windows desktop backgrounds.

You can create background images to use as Windows wallpaper as well. You must create these background images as *.bmp*, *.gif*, *.jpg*, *.jpeg*, *.dib*, or *.png* files. If you add images in these formats to name subfolders of the *%WinDir%\Web\Wallpaper* folder, the images will be available as part of the Windows wallpaper and organized into the named sets according to the subfolder names. If you do not have access to that folder, or if you would prefer to not make changes to that folder, you can also use pictures from your Pictures Library or specify a folder elsewhere.

Although working with images is discussed in Chapter 9, the key thing you need to know in terms of adding new wallpaper or even using your own images from a different location is that you should optimize every background image you use. If you don't do this, you risk affecting your computer's performance.

In case you're wondering why this may be so, let me tell you the cautionary tale of an experienced pro (me) who added a picture of his kids to the desktop background and suddenly found his computer's performance was moderately degraded. My digital camera takes high-resolution pictures—most do these days—and its pictures are about

4 MB in size, on average. By adding an unedited picture to the desktop background, I was forcing the operating system to swap in 4 MB of extra data every time the operating system displayed the desktop.

Now you may be thinking, "4 MB is no big deal; my computer has gigabytes of RAM." Well, the problem wasn't system memory (RAM) but graphics memory. Most computers use both dedicated and shared graphics memory. The dedicated memory on most computer video cards is relatively meager, in contrast to shared memory, which is part of RAM, so swapping in and out 4 MB is a big deal. Also, the image was sized at $3,072 \times 2,304$ pixels when the screen size I was using was $1,920 \times 1,200$ pixels. This means that not only did the graphics card have to manage this large picture, but also Windows 7 had to resize the image to fit on the screen.

The solution to the problem was fairly simple: I opened the image in my photo editor, resized it to $1,920 \times 1,200$ pixels, and saved the resized image with a new name to the *Pictures* folder in my profile. The resized image was 1 MB, and my computer was much happier.

If you examine the default images Windows 7 uses for wallpaper, you'll find that most are less than 2 MB in size. In fact, the Landscapes images, some of the most visually stunning wallpaper images, are the most highly optimized. You'll find that they are available at a standard screen ratio of $1,920 \times 1,200$.

You can set the background for the desktop by completing the following steps:

1. Right-click an open area of the desktop and then select Personalize.

2. On the Personalization page in the Control Panel, click Desktop Background. This displays the Desktop Background page, as shown in Figure 3-11.

3. Use the Picture Location pull-down menu to specify where to look for the picture you want to use, or click Browse to select a location. The default locations are as follows:

Windows Desktop Backgrounds
Displays the wallpaper images in the *%WinDir%\Web\Wallpaper* folder.

Pictures Library
Displays the images in your *Pictures* library, which is a combination of your *My Pictures* folder and the *Public Pictures* folder by default.

Top Rated Photos
Displays the top-rated pictures in your *Pictures* library. For more information about setting image ratings, see "Viewing and Managing Ratings, Tags, and Captions" on page 343 in Chapter 9.

Solid Colors
Allows you to choose from more than 50 background colors, or create your own background color by clicking More and then using the Color dialog box to select or mix your color.

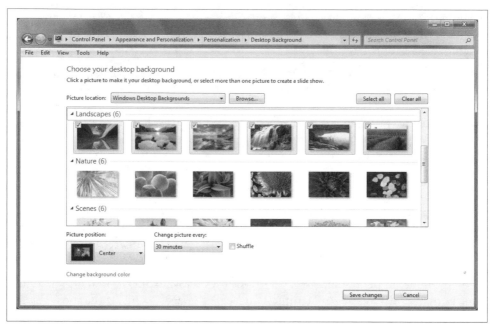

Figure 3-11. Choosing a desktop background

4. By default, when you select Windows Desktop Backgrounds, Pictures Library, or Top Rated Photos, all related images are selected automatically and the background will rotate between these images every 30 minutes by default. Using Shift-click, you can select multiple individual pictures. You also can select a category heading to select all images in a category. To deselect an image, clear the checkbox in its upper-left corner.

5. If you are using a background image, use the Picture position options to select a display option for the background. You have the following options:

Center

Centers the image on the desktop background. Any area that the image doesn't fill uses the current desktop background color. Click Change background color to set the background color.

Fill

Fills the desktop background with the image. Typically, the fill is accomplished by zooming in, which may result in the sides of the image being cropped.

Fit

Fits the image to the desktop background. Current proportions are maintained. This is a good option for photos and large images that you want to see without stretching or expanding.

Stretch

Stretches the image to fill the desktop background. The result is the current proportions are maintained as best as possible and then the height is stretched to fill any remaining gaps.

Tile

Repeats the image so that it covers the entire screen. This is a good option for small images and icons.

6. If you are using multiple background images, use the Change picture every list to specify how often Windows should change the background image, such as every 5 minutes, every 2 hours, or every 1 day. Normally, Windows goes through the images in order. To go through the images randomly, select the Shuffle checkbox.

7. When you are finished updating the background, click Save Changes.

Choosing and Configuring Your Screensaver

Screensavers turn on when a computer has been idle for a specified period. Originally, screensavers were designed to prevent image burn-in on CRT monitors by displaying a continually changing image. With today's monitors, burn-in is not much of a problem, but screensavers are still around because they offer a different benefit today: the ability to password-lock your computer automatically when the screensaver turns on.

 Windows 7 performs many housekeeping tasks in the background when the computer is idle. These housekeeping tasks extend to creating indexes, defragmenting hard disks, creating whole computer backups and system restore points, and more. Because of this, you should be more careful than ever when choosing a screensaver for your computer. So although you can install your fancy fish-tank screensaver with the sharks and stingrays, you may do so at the expense of your computer being able to efficiently perform background tasks while you are away from your desk rather than while you are sitting at your desk.

Selecting a screensaver

You can configure your screensaver by performing the following steps:

1. Right-click an open area of the desktop and then select Personalize.

2. Click the Screen Saver link to display the Screen Saver Settings dialog box, shown in Figure 3-12.

3. Use the Screen Saver listbox to select a screensaver. Although you can install additional screensavers, the standard screensavers are:

(None)

Turns off the screensaver.

Figure 3-12. Configuring the screensaver

3D Text

Displays the time or custom text as a 3D message against a black background.

Blank

Displays a blank screen (i.e., a screen with a black background and no text or images).

Bubbles

Displays multicolored bubbles floating across your desktop. The open windows and documents on the desktop remain visible.

Mystify

Displays arcing bands of lines in various geometric patterns against a black background.

Photos

Displays photos and videos from a selected folder as a slideshow.

Ribbons

> Displays ribbons of various thicknesses and changing lines against a black background.

(Other)

> If you've installed a screensaver program on your computer, you'll typically see options for the additional screensavers this program provides. Be careful with some of these, as they can require a substantial amount of system resources to maintain, preventing your computer from effectively performing background housekeeping tasks.

4. To password-protect the screensaver, select "On resume, display logon screen." Clear this option only if you do not want to use password protection.

5. Use the Wait box to specify how long the computer must be idle before the screensaver is activated. A reasonable value is between 10 and 15 minutes.

6. Click OK.

Customizing the 3D Text and Photos screensavers

Two of the standard screensavers deserve additional discussions: 3D Text and Photos. With these screensavers (and likely any custom screensavers you install), clicking Settings displays a dialog box that allows you to customize the screensaver. To customize the 3D Text screensaver, follow these steps:

1. In the Screen Saver Settings dialog box, select 3D Text as the screensaver and then click Settings. This displays the 3D Text Settings dialog box shown in Figure 3-13.

2. You can display the current time or a custom message as 3D text. To display the current time as 3D text, select Time. To display a custom message as 3D text, select Custom Text and then type your message.

3. Click Choose Font. Use the Font dialog box to set the font to use for the 3D text. The default font is Tahoma.

4. Use the Resolution slider to control the display resolution of the text. The higher the resolution, the more processing power required to draw and move the message.

5. Use the Size slider to control the size of the text.

6. Use the Rotation Speed slider to control the speed at which the text moves and rotates on the screen. The faster the rotation, the more processing power required to draw and move the message.

7. Use the Rotation Type listbox to select the type of rotation to use, such as spin or tumble. If you set the rotation type to None, you can turn off rotation and reduce the amount of processing power required to draw and move the message.

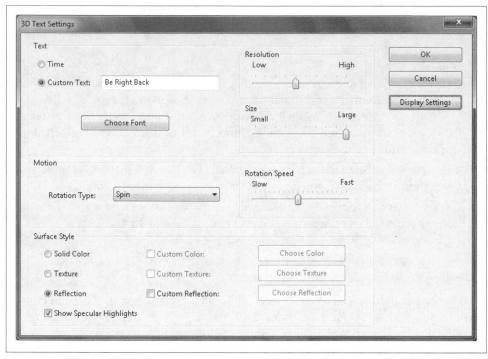

Figure 3-13. Configuring the 3D Text screensaver

8. Use the following Surface Style options to configure the way the 3D text looks:

Solid Color
> Displays the text in a solid color. Click Custom Color and then click Choose Color to display the Color dialog box. Choose the color to use and click OK.

Texture
> Displays the text with a textured surface. Click Custom Texture and then click Choose Texture to display the Choose Custom Texture dialog box. You can use any bitmap (*.bmp*) image as the texture. Once you find a *.bmp* image to use, click Open.

Reflection
> Displays the text with a reflective surface. Click Custom Reflection and then click Choose Reflection to display the Choose Custom Reflection dialog box. You can use any bitmap (*.bmp*) image as the texture. Once you find a *.bmp* image to use, click Open.

9. Click OK to save your settings and then click OK to use this screensaver.

The Photos screensaver is my favorite of all the screensavers. It displays a slideshow of photos. You can customize the Photos screensaver by following these steps:

Figure 3-14. Configuring the Photos screensaver

1. In the Screen Saver Settings dialog box, select Photos as the screensaver and then click Settings. This displays the Photos Screen Saver dialog box shown in Figure 3-14.

2. By default, this screensaver displays the images in your Pictures library, which is a combination of your My Pictures folder and the Public Pictures folder. If you want to use photos from a different folder, click Browse and then select the folder to use.

3. Use the options on the "Slide show speed" list to set the speed of the slideshow. The options are Slow, Medium, and Fast.

4. Normally, photos are displayed in alphanumeric order. If you want to shuffle the photos and display them in random order, select the "Shuffle pictures" checkbox.

5. Click Save and then click OK.

 If you've installed Windows Live Essentials (see "Getting Started with Windows Live Photo Gallery" on page 334 in Chapter 9) and selected Windows Live Photo Gallery, you'll also have the Windows Live Photo Gallery screensaver, which functions much like the Photos screensaver, but includes additional options such as a choice of transitions, and the ability to specify photos by tag or rating.

Choosing Your System Sounds

Windows 7 plays sounds in response to a wide variety of events, such as when you log on, when you open or close programs, or when you type an asterisk. Programs you install, such as America Online, can have their own sounds as well. You can configure all of these sounds and manage them collectively using sound schemes. A sound scheme is simply a set of sounds that you want to use together.

Windows 7 has two standard sound schemes: No Sounds, which turns off all program sounds except the Windows Startup sound played when you log on; and Windows Default, which is configured to use the standard Windows sounds. Other sound schemes available typically depend on the Windows 7 edition your computer is running and the extras you've installed. Some of the available sound schemes include Afternoon, Calligraphy, Characters, Cityscape, Delta, Festival, Garden, Heritage, Landscape, Quirky, Raga, Savanna, and Sonata.

Selecting a sound scheme

You can configure your system to use an existing sound scheme by completing the following steps:

1. Right-click an open area of the desktop and then select Personalize. (On Windows 7 Starter, select Control Panel→Hardware and Sound.)
2. Click the Sounds link to display the Sound dialog box with the Sounds tab selected, as shown in Figure 3-15. (On Windows 7 Starter, choose Change System Sounds under Sounds.)
3. Use the Sound Scheme listbox to choose the sound scheme to use.
4. Click OK to save your settings.

Customizing your sound scheme

You can configure your system to use a customized sound scheme by completing the following steps:

1. Right-click an open area of the desktop and then select Personalize. (On Windows 7 Starter, select Control Panel→Hardware and Sound.)
2. Click the Sounds link to display the Sound dialog box with the Sounds tab selected, as shown in Figure 3-15. (On Windows 7 Starter, choose Change System Sounds under Sounds.)
3. In the Program Events list, sounds are organized according to the program to which they relate and the related event that triggers the sound. To preview a sound for a particular event, select the event in the Program list and then click the Test button.
4. To change the sound for an event, select the event in the Program Events list and then use the Sounds list to choose an available sound. You can also click Browse

---

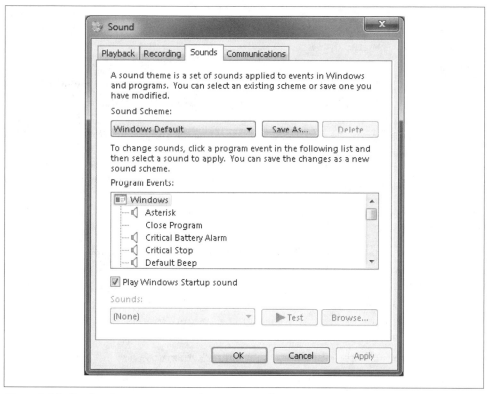

Figure 3-15. Configuring your computer's system sounds

to select other sounds available on the system. The sound files must be in Microsoft *.wav* format.

5. To save a changed sound scheme, click Save As, type a name for the scheme in the field provided, and then click OK.

6. Click OK to close the Sounds dialog box.

Choosing Your Mouse Pointers

In Windows, the innocuous mouse pointer has many faces, and each face tells something about the current way you are using the mouse pointer. The three types of mouse pointers you see the most are the Normal Select pointer, the Text Select pointer, and the Link Select pointer. You can configure the appearance of these and other types of mouse pointers and manage them collectively using pointer schemes. A *pointer scheme* is a set of mouse pointers that you want to use together.

Windows 7 has 12 standard pointer schemes. The schemes you'll use the most are:

(None)

This doesn't turn mouse pointers off. Instead, it uses nondescript pointers.

Windows Aero
> The standard pointers used with the Windows Aero experience. Also comes in large and extra-large options.

Windows Black
> Inverts the pointer colors so that black backgrounds are used instead of white backgrounds. Also comes in large and extra-large options.

Windows Standard
> The standard pointers used with the Windows Standard user experience. Also comes in large and extra-large options.

Selecting a mouse pointer scheme

You can configure your system to use an existing pointer scheme by completing the following steps:

1. Right-click an open area of the desktop and then select Personalize. (In Windows 7 Starter, select Control Panel→Hardware and Sound.)
2. In the left pane, click the Change Mouse Pointers link to display the Mouse Properties dialog box with the Pointers tab selected, as shown in Figure 3-16. (In Windows 7 Starter, select Mouse under Devices and Printers, then select the Pointers tab.)
3. Use the Scheme listbox to choose the pointer scheme to use.
4. Click OK to save your settings.

Customizing your mouse pointer scheme

You can configure your system to use a customized pointer scheme by completing the following steps:

1. Right-click an open area of the desktop and then select Personalize. (In Windows 7 Starter, select Control Panel→Hardware and Sound.)
2. Click the Mouse Pointers link to display the Mouse Properties dialog box with the Pointers tab selected, as shown in Figure 3-16. (In Windows 7 Starter, select Mouse under Devices and Printers, then select the Pointers tab.)
3. In the Customize list, pointers are organized according to their type. To change a pointer, select the pointer and then click Browse. This opens the Browse dialog box with the Cursors folder selected. Choose the cursor pointer to use and then click Open.
4. To save a changed pointer scheme, click Save As, type a name for the scheme in the field provided, and then click OK.
5. Click OK to close the Mouse Properties dialog box.

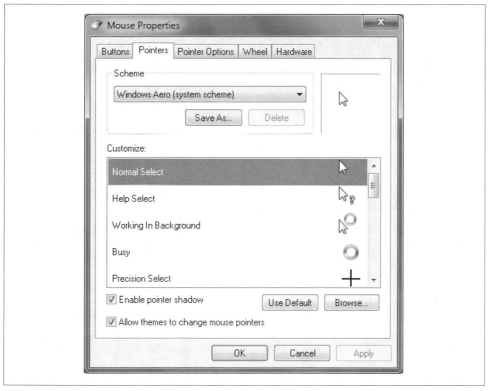

Figure 3-16. Configuring your computer's mouse pointers

Choosing and Managing Your Themes

Desktop themes are combinations of the visual and audio elements Windows 7 uses to set the appearance of menus, icons, backgrounds, screensavers, system sounds, and mouse pointers. The default themes your computer uses are based on the user experience level.

 To change the theme in Windows 7 Starter, open Control Panel→Appearance→Display→Change Color Scheme from the list of items to the left. You will be able to select from Windows 7 Basic, Windows Classic, and several high-contrast themes.

As you customize the backgrounds, screensavers, system sounds, and mouse pointers that your computer uses, you modify the default theme; you can then save these modified settings together as a new theme by following these steps:

1. Right-click an open area of the desktop and then select Personalize.

2. Click Save Theme. In the Save Theme As dialog box, enter a name for your custom theme and then click Save. Theme definition files end with the *.theme* file extension. Unless deleted in the future, the custom theme will appear as a My Themes option.

In addition to any custom themes you create, several default themes are available. You can apply a default or saved theme by completing these steps:

1. Right-click an open area of the desktop and then select Personalize.
2. Use the Theme list to select the theme you want to use. If you want to use a saved them from Microsoft's web site, click Get more themes online and then select the *.theme* file that contains the saved theme.

Configuring Your Monitors

Windows 7 automatically configures your monitor settings the first time you log on. Windows does this by choosing the best display settings for your monitor. The optimized settings include:

Screen resolution
Determines how much information is displayed on the screen, measured horizontally and vertically in pixels. Low resolutions, such as 640 × 480 or 800 × 600 pixels, fit fewer items on the screen but those items appear larger. High resolutions, such as 1,280 × 1,024 or 1,920 × 1,200, fit more items on the screen, but those items appear smaller. Clarity typically is determined by the dots per inch (dpi) being displayed. Generally, the higher the dpi, the better the text and on-screen elements will look. However, if you set the screen resolution too high, you might affect the supported refresh rate and color options, which could reduce clarity as well.

Refresh rate
Controls the frequency at which the screen is redrawn. To get the best possible display, you'll want to be sure you use as fast a refresh rate as possible. If the refresh rate is set too low, the screen can flicker, which can cause eyestrain and headaches. To reduce or eliminate flicker, you'll want the refresh rate to be at least 72 hz. On an LCD monitor, you should generally leave this at the default setting.

Color
Controls the number of color bits associated with each pixel. To get the best possible display, you'll want to use at least 32-bit color. With 24-bit color, you won't see most of Windows 7's visual effects. With 16-bit color, the edges of interface elements may appear to be jagged rather than smooth.

Your computer's video card and monitor together determine the screen resolution, refresh rates, and colors that you can use. Generally, you'll want to use the highest quality setting that is mutually supported. Most monitors have a base or native resolution, which is the resolution that the monitor was designed to display best.

Figure 3-17. Configuring the screen resolution and colors

Proper display depends on your computer using accurate information about your graphics card and monitor. Depending on which graphics card and monitor models Windows 7 thinks you have, different driver files are installed. These drivers determine which display resolutions, colors, and refresh rates are available and appropriate for the system. If the graphics card and monitor aren't detected and configured properly, Windows 7 won't be able to take advantage of their capabilities.

Your display settings can be less than optimal for many reasons. Sometimes Windows 7 doesn't detect the device, and a generic device driver is used. At other times, Windows 7 detects the wrong type of device, such as a different model, in which case the device will probably work but some features won't be available, or worse, incorrect (and incompatible) options will be available.

Setting the screen resolution and orientation

You can set the screen resolution and orientation by completing the following steps:

1. Right-click an open area of the desktop and then select Screen Resolution. This opens the Screen Resolution page in the Control Panel, as shown in Figure 3-17.

2. If you want to configure the second monitor on a system with multiple monitors or graphics cards, click 2 to select the second monitor.

3. Use the Resolution list to set the display size, such as 1,920 × 1,200 pixels.

4. Optionally, use the Orientation list to specify an alternate orientation for a monitor. The default orientation is landscape.

5. Click OK.

Setting the refresh rate and color quality

You can set the refresh rate and color quality for a monitor by completing the following steps:

1. Right-click an open area of the desktop and then select Screen Resolution.

2. If you want to configure the second monitor on a system with or graphics cards, click 2 to select the second monitor.

3. Click Advanced Settings. This opens a properties dialog box. Set the color quality or refresh rate using one of the following options:

   • On the Adapter tab, click "List all modes." The "List all modes" dialog box shows the color qualities and refresh rates supported by the selected monitor. Click OK.

   • On the Monitor tab, use the "Screen refresh rate" list to set the desired refresh rate. Use the Colors list to select a color quality, such as True Color (32 bit).

 If you clear the "Hide modes that this monitor cannot display" checkbox, Windows 7 will display refresh rates that exceed the capabilities of the monitor and graphics card. Select these additional hidden modes only when you know for sure that your monitor and graphics card support a particular mode, such as may be the case when you are using a generic driver. Keep in mind that running the computer at a higher refresh rate than it supports can damage the monitor and video adapter.

This checkbox may be disabled for certain displays, such as LCD monitors.

4. Click OK twice to save your settings.

Customizing multiple-monitor configurations

If multiple monitors are connected to your computer, you can designate one monitor as the primary and the other as the secondary monitor. You can also extend the desktop onto your second monitor. To configure options for multiple monitors, complete the following steps:

1. Right-click an open area of the desktop and then select Screen Resolution.

2. Select the monitor you want to work with. Monitor 1 is the primary monitor. Monitor 2 is the secondary monitor.

---

3. By default, the primary monitor is assumed to be on the left and the secondary monitor on the right. Because of this, when you move the mouse pointer off the right edge of the primary monitor, the mouse pointer appears on the left side of the secondary monitor. If you want the monitor on the right to be the primary monitor, you can reverse this order by clicking 2 and dragging to the left. Now when you move the mouse pointer off the left edge of the primary monitor, the mouse pointer appears on the right side of the secondary monitor.

4. To extend the desktop onto your secondary monitor's display, select the "Extend the desktop onto this monitor" checkbox.

5. Click OK.

Once you've configured your monitors, you'll find the pressing the Windows Key and P is a convenient way to quickly change the monitor configuration. After pressing Windows Key and P, you can:

- Select Computer Only to use only the main computer monitor or the built-in screen on a laptop.

- Select Duplicate to display the main computer monitor or the built-in screen on a laptop on a second monitor.

- Select Extend to extend the display across two monitors.

- Select Projector Only to display only on an external monitor or projector.

Setting the monitor or graphics card driver

If the monitor or graphics card shown in the Display Settings dialog box does not match the one you are using, you should visit your computer, monitor, or graphics card manufacturer's website and obtain the proper driver. Typically, you can do this by accessing the manufacturer's support page and entering the serial number or model of your computer, monitor, or graphics card. Most manufacturers maintain drivers for a number of years and provide updates for these drivers as they become available.

 In most cases, you'll either download a zipped file containing the drivers you need or an executable installer. To extract the files from a ZIP, you'll need to right-click the *.zip* file and then select Extract All. After you select a destination folder, click Extract.

You install monitor and graphics card drivers using separate procedures. To specify the monitor driver to use, follow these steps:

1. Right-click an open area of the desktop and then select Screen Resolution.

2. On a system with multiple monitors or graphics cards, click 2 to configure settings for the second monitor.

3. Click Advanced Settings. On the Monitor tab, click Properties.

4. In the Driver tab, click Update Driver. This starts the Update Driver Software Wizard.

5. Click "Browse my computer for driver software."

6. Click Browse to select a search location. Use the Browse for Folder dialog box to select the start folder for the search, and then click OK. Because Windows 7 searches all subfolders of the selected folder automatically, you can select the drive root path, such as C, to search an entire drive.

7. Click Next. Click Close when the driver installation is completed.

Most graphics drivers are installed using an executable installer. Run the installer and reboot if the installer asks you to do so. If you need to manually specify the graphics card driver to use, follow these steps:

1. Right-click an open area of the desktop and then select Screen Resolution.

2. On a system with multiple monitors or graphics cards, click 2 to configure settings for the second graphics card.

3. Click Advanced Settings. On the Adapter tab, click Properties.

4. In the Driver tab, click Update Driver. This starts the Update Driver Software Wizard.

5. Click "Browse my computer for driver software."

6. Click Browse to select a search location. Use the Browse for Folder dialog box to select the start folder for the search, and then click OK. Because Windows 7 searches all subfolders of the selected folder automatically, you can select the drive root path, such as C, to search an entire drive.

7. Click Next. Click Close when the driver installation is completed.

Optimizing Performance

In addition to the previously discussed features, you can fine-tune your computer's performance by setting these performance options:

- Visual effects
- Application performance
- Virtual memory
- Data Execution prevention
- ReadyBoost

The sections that follow discuss each performance option in turn.

Fine-Tuning Visual Effects

The Windows 7 interface has many graphical enhancements including visual effects for menus, toolbars, windows, and the taskbar. Because displaying these visual effects can require substantial system resources, Windows 7 lets you optimize the way visual effects are used. You can optimize for appearance or for performance. You can also customize the settings or let Windows 7 choose the best configuration.

The visual effects available are:

- Animate controls and elements inside windows
- Animate windows when minimizing and maximizing
- Animations in the taskbar and Start Menu
- Enable Aero Peek
- Enable desktop composition
- Enable transparent glass
- Fade or slide menus into view
- Fade or slide ToolTips into view
- Fade out menu items after clicking
- Save taskbar thumbnail previews
- Show shadows under mouse pointer
- Show shadows under windows
- Show thumbnails instead of icons
- Show translucent selection rectangle
- Show window contents while dragging
- Slide open combo boxes
- Smooth edges of screen fonts
- Smooth-scroll listboxes
- Use drop shadows for icon labels on the desktop
- Use visual styles on windows and buttons

You can configure Windows performance by completing the following steps:

1. In the Control Panel, click the System and Security category heading link.
2. Click System. In the left pane under See Also, click Performance Information and Tools.
3. In the left pane, click "Adjust visual effects." This opens the Performance Options dialog box shown in Figure 3-18.

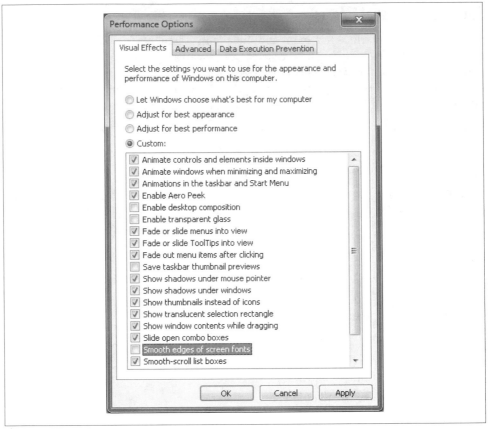

Figure 3-18. Optimizing visual effects

4. On the Visual Effects tab, you have the following options for controlling visual effects:

   Let Windows choose what's best for my computer
   Enables the operating system to choose the performance options based on the hardware configuration. For a newer computer, this option will probably be identical to the "Adjust for best appearance" option because of its hardware and performance capabilities.

   Adjust for best appearance
   Enables all visual effects for all graphical interfaces.

   Adjust for best performance
   Disables all visual effects.

   Custom
   Allows you to enable or disable the visual effects options individually.

5. Click OK to apply your settings.

Fine-Tuning Application Performance

Application performance determines the relative priority of applications being run by users and those being run by the operating system. Unlike earlier releases of Windows, Windows 7 does a much better job of prioritizing, and as a result, background processes and housekeeping tasks have less impact on performance. Because of this, the default configuration for application performance, which gives scheduling priority to applications you are running, is typically what you'll want to use. The only time you may want to change this behavior is if you are using a computer running Windows 7 as a server. For example, if you were using a computer as a printer server or web server, you would probably want to change the scheduling priority settings.

Control application performance by completing the following steps:

1. In the Control Panel, click the System and Security category heading link.
2. Click System. In the left pane under See Also, click Performance Information and Tools.
3. Under Tasks, click "Adjust visual effects." This opens the Performance Options dialog box.
4. On the Advanced tab, shown in Figure 3-19, select "Background services" to optimize performance for a computer you are using as a server. Otherwise, select Programs to optimize performance for a computer you use to run applications, such as Microsoft Word.
5. Click OK.

Fine-Tuning Virtual Memory

Your computer uses virtual memory to extend the amount of available RAM by writing physical memory (RAM) to disks through a process called *paging*. With paging, Windows 7 writes a set amount of RAM, such as 1,834 MB, to the disk as a paging file, where the operating system can access it from the disk when needed in place of physical memory.

Windows 7 writes paging files to disk drives as a file named *pagefile.sys*. Windows 7 creates an initial paging file automatically for the drive containing the operating system. By default, other drives don't have paging files, so you must create these paging files manually if you want to use them. However, in most instances, you won't need to put a paging file on multiple disks, as doing so won't necessarily boost performance.

As with many other aspects of performance, Windows 7 does a much better job than its predecessors do of automatically managing virtual memory. Typically, Windows 7 will allocate virtual memory at least as large as the total physical memory installed on the computer. This helps to ensure that paging files don't become fragmented, which can result in poor system performance.

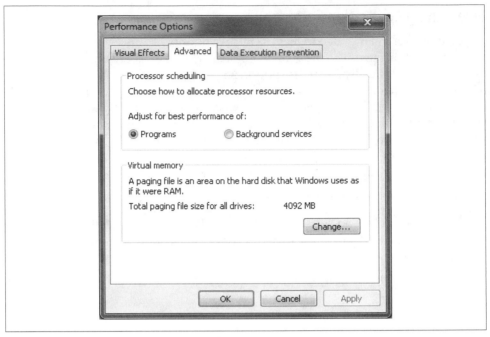

Figure 3-19. Setting the processor scheduling options

You can also manually manage virtual memory. If you do this, you'll typically want to use a fixed virtual memory size. You fix the size of the virtual memory by setting the initial size and the maximum size to the same value, and this in turn prevents fragmentation of the paging file.

In most cases, I recommend setting the total paging file size so that it's twice the physical RAM size on the system. For instance, on a computer with 1,024 MB of RAM, you would ensure that the "Total paging file size for each drive" setting is at least 2,048 MB.

If your computer has more than 4 GB of RAM, however, you'll probably want to set the paging file size so that it's approximately 1.5 times the size as the physical memory. For instance, on a computer with 6,144 MB of RAM, you would ensure that the "Total paging file size for each drive" setting is at least 9,216 MB.

To achieve optimal performance, you may want to consider using a fixed minimum of 1 times the RAM and a fixed maximum of either 2 times or 1.5 times the RAM. Fixing the size of the paging file in this way ensures that Windows allocates sufficient file space to the page file initially and doesn't need to repeatedly increase the size of the paging file as you start using programs on your computer.

You can manually configure virtual memory by completing the following steps:

1. In the Control Panel, click the System and Security category heading link.

2. Click System. In the left pane under See Also, click Performance Information and Tools.

3. Under Tasks, click "Adjust visual effects." This opens the Performance Options dialog box.

4. On the Advanced tab, click Change to display the Virtual Memory dialog box shown in Figure 3-20. The following information is provided:

   Drive [Volume Label] and Paging File Size (MB)
   Show the current configuration of virtual memory. The dialog box lists each volume with its associated paging file (if any). The paging file range shows the initial and maximum size values of the related paging file.

   Paging file size for each drive
   Provides information on the currently selected drive and enables you to set its paging file size. "Space available" indicates how much space is available on the drive.

   Total paging file size for all drives
   Provides a recommended size for virtual RAM on the system and shows the amount currently allocated.

5. By default, Windows 7 manages the paging file size for all drives. If you want to configure virtual memory manually, clear the "Automatically manage paging file size for all drives" checkbox.

6. In the Drive listbox, select the disk volume you want to work with.

7. Select "Custom size" and then enter an initial size and a maximum size.

8. Click Set to save the changes.

9. Repeat steps 6–8 for each disk volume you want to configure.

10. Click OK. If prompted to overwrite an existing *pagefile.sys* file, click Yes.

11. If you updated the settings for a paging file that is currently in use, you'll see a prompt explaining that you need to restart the system for the changes to take effect. Click OK.

12. Click OK twice to close the open dialog boxes. You'll see a prompt asking if you want to restart the system. Click Restart.

You can have Windows 7 automatically manage virtual memory by following these steps:

1. In the Control Panel, click the System and Security category heading link.

2. Click System. In the left pane under See Also, click Performance Information and Tools.

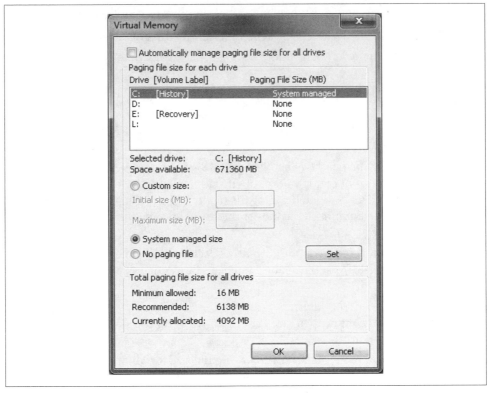

Figure 3-20. Configuring virtual memory

3. Under Tasks, click "Adjust visual effects." This opens the Performance Options dialog box.

4. On the Advanced tab, click Change to display the Virtual Memory dialog box shown in Figure 3-20.

5. Select the "Automatically manage paging file size for all drives" checkbox.

6. Click OK twice to close the open dialog boxes.

Fine-Tuning Data Execution Prevention

Data Execution Prevention (DEP) is a memory protection technology. Your computer uses DEP to mark all memory locations used by applications as nonexecutable unless the location explicitly contains executable code. If an application attempts to execute code from a memory page marked as nonexecutable, the processor can raise an exception and prevent it from executing. This behavior is designed to thwart a malicious program, such as a virus, from inserting itself into areas of memory. By allowing only specific areas of memory to run executable code, DEP protects your computer from many types of self-replicating viruses.

You can implement DEP via hardware or software. Hardware-based DEP is more robust because you can extend it to any program or service running on the computer. Software-based DEP is less robust because it typically works best when protecting Windows programs and services.

Windows 32-bit versions support DEP as implemented originally by Advanced Micro Devices Inc. (AMD) processors that provide the no-execute page-protection (NX) processor feature. Such processors support the related instructions and must be running in Physical Address Extension (PAE) mode. Windows 64-bit versions also support the NX processor feature but do not need to be running in PAE mode. And 64-bit computers natively support very large memory configurations.

You can determine whether your computer hardware supports DEP by completing the following steps:

1. In the Control Panel, click the System and Security category heading link.
2. Click System. In the left pane under See Also, click Performance Information and Tools.
3. Under Tasks, click "Adjust visual effects." This opens the Performance Options dialog box.
4. Click the Data Execution Prevention tab. As Figure 3-21 shows, the lower portion of this tab lists the DEP support available.

Once you've accessed the Data Execution Prevention tab, you can configure the way DEP works using these options:

Turn on DEP for essential Windows programs and services only
Enables DEP only for the operating system services, programs, and components. This is the default and recommended option for computers that support execution protection and are configured appropriately.

Turn on DEP for all programs except those I select
Enables DEP for the operating system, as well as all programs and services you are running.

Because some programs won't work with or will become unstable with software-based DEP, you may find that you have to add exceptions when you enable DEP for all programs. Click Add to specify programs that should run without execution protection. In this way, execution protection will work for all programs except those you have listed.

Using ReadyBoost to Enhance Performance

Windows 7 uses your computer's disk drives for paging files and system cache. Because reading from and writing to a disk is significantly slower than reading from and writing to physical memory (RAM), this can cause performance bottlenecks that make your

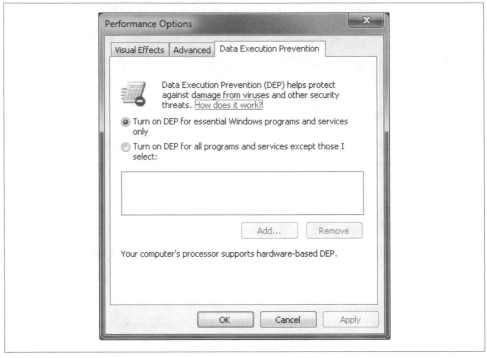

Figure 3-21. Viewing your computer's DEP configuration

computer seem sluggish or unresponsive. To reduce the performance impact related to reading and writing the system cache, Windows 7 introduces Windows ReadyBoost.

Windows ReadyBoost is a feature that lets you extend the disk-caching capabilities of the computer's main memory to a USB flash device. Using flash devices for caching allows the operating system to make random reads faster by caching data on the USB flash device instead of your computer's disk drives. Windows 7 can read flash devices up to 1,000 percent faster than physical disk drives, significantly boosting the overall performance of your computer.

The types of USB flash devices you can use with Windows ReadyBoost include:

- USB 2.0 flash drives
- Secure Digital (SD) cards
- CompactFlash cards

Further, these devices must be at least 256 MB or larger and have sufficiently fast flash memory. Because some flash devices have both slow and fast memory, you may find that Windows ReadyBoost can use only a portion of the memory on the device. You can reserve from 230 MB to 4,094 MB of flash memory for ReadyBoost. I recommend using from one to three times the installed RAM memory. On a system with more than 4 GB of memory, you will only be able to reserve a fractional amount as compared to the available memory. Currently, 4GB is the limit (but this limit may change as high performance USB flash drives and 64-bit computers become increasingly prevalent).

When Windows ReadyBoost is enabled, Windows 7 uses the USB flash device primarily for caching that uses random input/output and small, sequential input/output rather than large, sequential input/output. This is because the memory on USB flash devices is better suited to random I/O and small, sequential input/output than large, sequential I/O.

Because USB flash devices are meant to be portable, Windows 7 adds protections to prevent the sudden removal of a USB flash device from crashing the computer and to prevent reading of any sensitive data written to the flash device. To allow a USB flash device to be removed at any time, Windows 7 ensures that all data writes are made to the hard disk first and then copied to the flash device. This eliminates the potential for data loss when removing a flash device. To prevent reading of sensitive data, Windows 7 encrypts all data written to a flash device so that it can be used only with the computer on which it was originally written.

Enabling Windows ReadyBoost

You can enable Windows ReadyBoost by completing the following steps:

1. Insert a USB flash device into a USB 2.0 or higher port. If your computer has an SD, CompactFlash, or similar card slot, you can insert a supported flash device into that slot.

2. The AutoPlay dialog box should be displayed automatically.

 Windows 7 should display the AutoPlay dialog box automatically. If it doesn't, you've probably selected the "Always do this..." checkbox previously. You can clear a previous selection by clicking Start→Default Programs. On the Default Programs page in the Control Panel, click "Change AutoPlay settings." On the AutoPlay page, scroll down to the bottom of the page. Click "Reset all defaults" and then click Save. Remove the USB flash device and then reinsert it to display the AutoPlay dialog box.

3. If the flash memory performs at a sufficiently high speed, Windows 7 will display a "Speed up my computer" option in the AutoPlay dialog box. (If you always want to use the device with Windows ReadyBoost when inserted, select the "Always do this..." checkbox.) When you click "Speed up my system using Windows Ready-Boost," the device's Properties dialog box is opened to the ReadyBoost page, as shown in Figure 3-22. Do one of the following and then click OK:

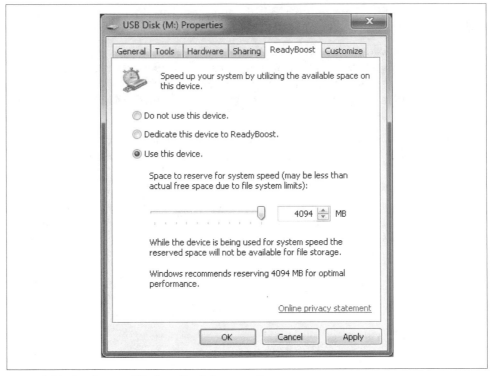

Figure 3-22. Configuring Windows ReadyBoost

- If you want the device to automatically reserve the maximum amount of space for ReadyBoost, select "Dedicate this device to ReadyBoost." Choosing this setting option doesn't prevent you from writing files to the device. It simply configures ReadyBoost to use as much space as can be reserved.

- If you want to use less space with ReadyBoost than the maximum possible, select "Use this device" and then use the "Space to reserve for system speed" slider or combo box to set the amount of space to use with ReadyBoost. If you reserve less than the total amount of space available, the free space can be used for files and data.

4. When you click OK, Windows 7 extends the computer's physical memory to the device.

If you previously inserted a flash device and declined to use Windows ReadyBoost, you can enable ReadyBoost by completing the following steps:

1. Click Start and then click Computer.

2. Right-click the USB flash device in the Devices with Removable Storage list and then choose Properties.

3. On the ReadyBoost tab, configure the options as discussed previously. For devices that don't support ReadyBoost, you cannot enable the device and the "Stop re-testing this device when I plug it in" option is selected by default. If you want Windows to retest the device, unselect this checkbox.

4. Click OK.

Configuring Windows ReadyBoost

Windows ReadyBoost does not have to use all available space on the USB flash device. You can also configure a specific amount of space to reserve for files and data. To do this, complete the following steps:

1. Click Start and then click Computer.
2. Right-click the USB flash device in the "Devices with removable storage" list and then choose Properties.
3. Click the ReadyBoost tab, as shown in Figure 3-22.
4. Use the "Space to reserve for system speed" slider or combo box to set the amount of space to use with ReadyBoost.
5. Click OK.

Ejecting a ReadyBoost device

You can safely remove a USB flash device that uses ReadyBoost at any time. Because Windows 7 writes to disk first and then copies data to the device, no data is lost and there is no negative impact on your computer. However, when you remove the device, your computer's performance level returns to its normal, nonboosted state. You can safely remove a USB flash device by completing these steps:

1. Click Start and then click Computer.
2. Right-click the USB flash device in the "Devices with removable storage" list and then choose Eject or Safely Remove.

CHAPTER 4

Installing, Configuring, and Maintaining Software

Most modern software and game programs have automated setup processes, making it easy to install and run your programs regardless of whether you are working with a 32-bit operating system or a 64-bit operating system. Resolving problems if automated setup fails or if a program does not run as expected is not so easy, however, which is why you need a strong understanding of how software installation works and the techniques you can use to diagnose and resolve any problems you encounter.

Software Installation: What's Changed

Compared to Windows XP and earlier releases of Windows, the processes of installing, configuring, and maintaining software and game programs are different in Windows 7. Primarily, this is because of changes to:

- The way accounts are used
- The way User Account Control (UAC) works
- The replacement of the Add/Remove Programs utility with the Uninstall or Change a Program control panel
- The way application access tokens are used
- The way applications write to the system locations

Unlike Windows XP and earlier releases of Windows, Windows 7 has only standard user accounts and administrator accounts. When you create a user in Windows 7, you choose one type of account or the other, removing the gray area between these two types of accounts that was previously available in the form of the Power Users group. In Windows 7, the Power Users group is included only for backward compatibility, and you should use it only when you need to resolve compatibility issues.

Access to Power Users and other groups is buried deep enough that you won't see it when you create a user in the Control Panel. You'll have to use the hidden User Accounts control panel (click Start, type lusrmgr.msc in the Search box, and then press Enter) in order to access the advanced group permissions needed to add a user to this group. You can also use the Computer Management administrative tool and select Local Users and Groups (not available on Windows 7 Starter).

In Windows 7, software installation, configuration, and maintenance are processes that require elevated privileges. Because of this, only administrators can install, configure, and maintain software. As discussed in Chapter 3, elevation is a feature of UAC. Because of UAC, Windows 7 is able to detect software installation. When Windows 7 detects a software-installation-related process, it prompts for permission or consent prior to allowing you to install, configure, or maintain software on your computer.

Windows 7 does not include an Add/Remove Programs utility (however, the Remove Programs functionality lives on in the Control Panel). Instead, it relies completely on the software and game programs themselves to provide the necessary installation features through a related setup or autorun program.

 Most programs created for Windows 95, Windows 98, Windows Me, Windows 2000, and Windows XP use *setup.exe* programs. Programs created for Windows Vista and later versions of Windows can use *autorun.exe* or other programs, such as *StartCD.exe*, particularly if those programs use current versions of Windows installers. For simplicity's sake, I'll refer to setup, autorun and similar programs as Setup programs.

Like Windows Vista, Windows 7 changes the way application access tokens are used and the way software programs write to system locations. These changes are so far-reaching that software not specifically designed to support this architecture is considered legacy software. This means there are two general categories of software that you can use with Windows 7:

- UAC-compliant applications
- Legacy applications

Any software written specifically for the revised architecture guidelines is considered a compliant application and can be certified as Windows-compliant. Applications written for Windows 7 have access tokens that describe the privileges required to run and perform tasks. UAC-compliant applications fall into two general categories:

Administrator user applications

If an application requires elevated privileges to run and perform tasks, it is considered an administrator user application. Administrator user applications can write to system locations of the registry and filesystem.

Standard user applications

If an application does not require elevated privileges to run and perform tasks, it is considered a standard user application. Standard user applications should write only to nonsystem locations of the registry and filesystem.

Any application written for Windows XP or an earlier version of Windows is considered a legacy application. Legacy applications run as standard user applications and in a special compatibility mode that provides virtualized views of file and registry locations. When a legacy application attempts to write a system location, Windows 7 gives the application a private copy of the file or registry value. Any changes are then written to the private copy, and this private copy is in turn stored in the user's profile data. If the application attempts to read or write to this system location again, it is given the private copy from the user's profile.

Software Installation: What You Need to Know

The more you understand about software installation, the better prepared you'll be to resolve problems you may encounter. Generally, the installation process starts when you trigger the AutoPlay or Autorun process. AutoPlay or Autorun in turn starts the software application's Setup program. Setup is a program responsible for managing the installation process. Part of the installation process involves validating your credentials and checking the software's compatibility with Windows 7.

AutoPlay

AutoPlay options determine how Windows 7 handles files on CDs, DVDs, and portable devices. You can configure separate AutoPlay options for each type of CD, DVD, and media your computer can handle.

With software and games, you have the following AutoPlay options (see Figure 4-1):

Install or run program

Uses the program's Autorun file to start installing or running the program automatically.

Open folder to view files using Windows Explorer

Opens Windows Explorer so that you can browse the CD or DVD.

Figure 4-1. Selecting the Autorun or Setup option to install or run a program

You can configure AutoPlay options by completing the following steps:

1. Click Start→Default Programs.

2. On the Default Programs page in the Control Panel, click Change AutoPlay settings.

3. As shown in Figure 4-2, use the lists under Media to set the default AutoPlay option to use for each type of media. The various AutoPlay options require Windows to determine the type of disc and media you've inserted. This can sometimes slow down the disc recognition process. "Ask me every time" is a safe choice, as it requires you to decide before any action is taken.

4. If you don't want to use AutoPlay, clear the "Use AutoPlay for all media and devices" checkbox. Keep in mind that this will disable AutoPlay for both media and devices.

5. Click Save to save your settings.

 Dislike AutoPlay for media but like AutoPlay for devices? Instead of disabling AutoPlay completely, set the default value for all media as "Take no action." This will allow you to still use AutoPlay with devices.

Autorun

When AutoPlay is enabled, Windows 7 checks for a file named *Autorun.inf* or a similar file, such as *StartCD.ini*, when you insert a CD or DVD into a CD or DVD drive. For software applications and games, this file identifies the Setup program and related installation parameters that should be used to install the software or game.

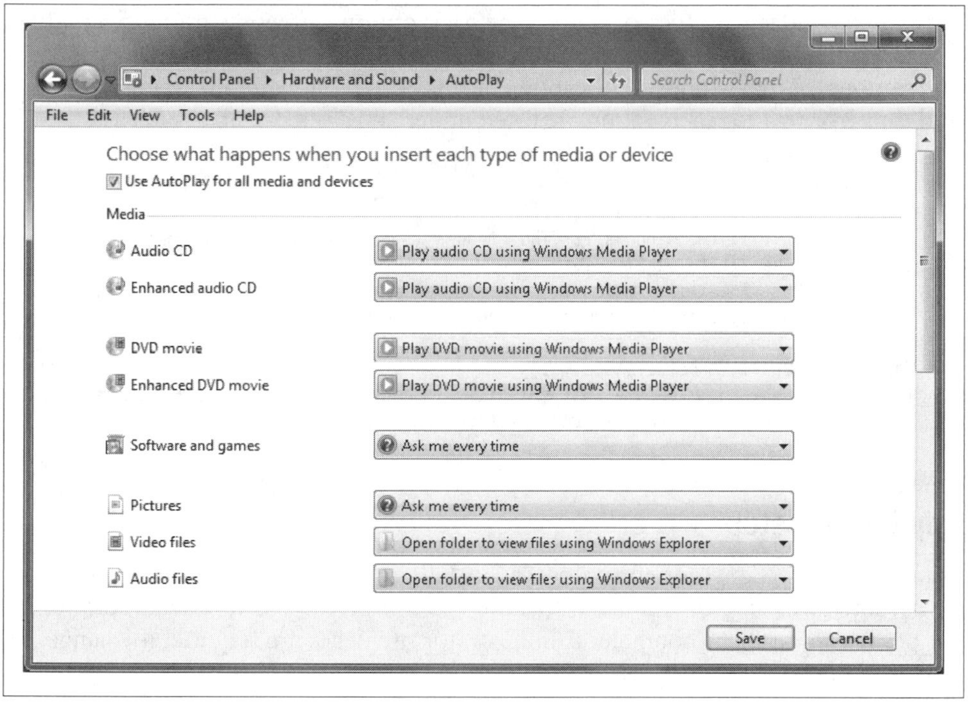

Figure 4-2. Setting AutoPlay defaults

Generally, *Autorun.inf*, *StartCD.ini*, and similar files are all text based. This means you can view their contents in any standard text editor, such as WordPad or Notepad. Most *Autorun.inf* files are similar to the following example:

```
[autorun]
OPEN=SETUP.EXE
ICON=SETUP.EXE,1
SHELL=OPEN
DisplayName=Microsoft Encarta 2007
```

When AutoPlay triggers this *Autorun.inf* file, Windows 7 opens a file named *Setup.exe* when the CD or DVD is inserted into the CD or DVD drive. Because *Setup.exe* is a program, Windows 7 runs this program. The *Autorun.inf* file also specifies an icon to use, and the program's display name. As long as AutoPlay is enabled, you can retrigger the default action by ejecting and then reinserting the installation media. You can also double-click on the drive's icon in Windows Explorer, but this will bypass the "Ask me every time" and go direct to an Autorun or AutoPlay action.

Although you'll usually find that an *Autorun.inf* file opens and then runs a Setup program, this isn't always the case. When AutoPlay triggers this *Autorun.inf* file, Windows 7 opens a file named *Default.htm* in Internet Explorer:

```
[autorun]
OPEN=Autorun\ShelExec default.htm
```

StartCD.ini and similar files expand on the basic options provided in *Autorun.inf* files. For example, *StartCD.ini* defines a window to display along with the graphics, text, and options for that window. The caption, display text, command to run, the run action and the error text for each option are listed under an [Option] entry, such as:

```
[Option1]
Caption=&TS Setup
DataText1=Install Windows TS.
DataText2=Install the Windows TS. The Windows TS contains a set of tools
to help you manage terminal services.
DataText3=Once the installation is complete, click Start, click All Programs,
click Windows TS, click Documentation and open the Windows TS User's Guide.
Cmd=msiexec.exe
CmdParameters=/i "%RootDir%\wts.msi"
ErrorSoln=Check to make sure that this file is accessible. If it is not accessible,
try opening the file from its original location.
Action=OPEN
```

Application Setup

With Windows 7, only administrators can install software. This means you must either install software using an account with administrator privileges, or provide administrator permissions when prompted. Administrator privileges are required to change, repair, and uninstall software as well.

Most software applications have a setup program that uses Windows Installer, InstallShield, or Wise Install. The job of the installer program is to track the installation process and make sure that the installation completes successfully. If the installation fails, the installer is also responsible for restoring your computer to its original state by reversing all the changes the Setup program has made. Although this works great in theory, you may still encounter problems, particularly when installing older programs. Older programs won't have and won't be able to use the features of the latest versions of installer programs, and as a result, they sometimes are unable to uninstall a program completely.

Because a partially uninstalled program can spell disaster for your computer, you should ensure your computer is configured to use System Restore as discussed in Chapter 21. Though the installers for most current programs automatically trigger a restore point creation before making any changes to your computer, the installers for older programs may not. You can manually create a restore point, as discussed in Chapter 21. This way, if you run into problems, you'll have an effective recovery strategy.

Before installing any software or game, you should do the following:

- Check whether it is compatible with Windows 7. You can determine compatibility in several ways. You can check the software packaging, which should specify whether the program is compatible or provide a Microsoft Windows 7 logo.

Alternatively, you can check the software developer's website for a list of compatible operating systems.

- Check the software developer's website for updates or patches for the program. If available, download the updates or patches prior to installing the software and then install them immediately after completing the software installation. Some software programs, such as Adobe Creative Suite and Microsoft Office, have automated update processes that you can use to check for updates after installing the software. In this case, after installation, run the software and then use the built-in update feature to check for updates or patches.

To avoid known compatibility issues with legacy applications, Windows 7 includes an automated detection feature known as the Program Compatibility Assistant. If the Program Compatibility Assistant detects a known compatibility issue when you install or run a legacy application, it notifies you about the problem and provides possible solutions for resolving the problem automatically. You can then allow the Program Compatibility Assistant to reconfigure the application for you. Although the Program Compatibility Assistant is helpful, it can't detect or avoid all compatibility issues. You may have to configure compatibility manually, as discussed in the section "Using Older Programs with Windows 7" on page 123.

 You should not use the Program Compatibility Assistant or the Program Compatibility Wizard to install older virus detection, backup, or system programs. These programs may attempt to modify your computer's filesystem in a way that is incompatible with Windows 7, and this could prevent Windows 7 from starting.

Diagnosing a problem you are having as a compatibility issue isn't always easy. For deeper compatibility issues, you may need to contact the software developer's technical support staff. Some issues even support staff may not be able to resolve without time to study the problem. Consider the following:

- When a computer manufacturer shipped computers with Windows XP, many recently purchased computers experienced infrequent "red screen" crashes. In contrast to blue screen crashes, which typically are related to operating system or hardware components, software drivers can cause a red screen crash. This problem was eventually pinpointed to an incompatibility between the firmware BIOS the computer was using and the software driver for certain graphics cards with a new 3D graphics feature. To resolve the problem, the computer's firmware BIOS and graphics card driver both needed to be updated.

- When a software manufacturer shipped a new version of its application suite, many recently purchased computers experienced problems starting and running the applications. After an automated update process had run, users were told their product licenses were invalid. This problem eventually was pinpointed to an incompatibility between the license-validation feature used by the application and a hard disk mirroring configuration being used by some customers. To resolve the problem, the software developers had to create an application patch that let the license-validation feature work with hard disks that were mirrored.

In both examples, the compatibility issues were the direct result of technological innovation. In the first example, graphics cards implementing new 3D graphics features caused an unforeseen incompatibility with the computer's firmware. In the second example, computers increasingly began shipping with mirrored hard disks, a feature that was previously used primarily on servers, and the license-validation feature was unable to recognize and validate the software applications across the mirrored disks.

Windows and 64-bit Programs

The future of computing is 64-bit, and we're in the midst of the changeover. To use 64-bit programs, you must install a 64-bit version of Windows.

Even if you don't foresee a need to run 64-bit applications, you may need the use the 64-bit version of Windows 7 to access all of the RAM in your computer. The 32-bit operating systems are, in theory, limited to 4 GB of RAM. In practice, this is generally closer to 3 GB, because some of the address space is reserved for other purposes.

A 64-bit operating system lets you go far beyond 4 GB, with its theoretical maximum memory measured in *billions* of gigabytes (but with significant practical limits, such as the number of memory slots in your computer and the maximum size of available memory modules).

For this reason, you'll find that computers sold with 4 GB or more of RAM invariably come with a 64-bit Windows operating system.

When you are working with a 64-bit operating system, keep the following in mind:

- Any 16-bit Windows applications will not install.
- The 64-bit programs will be installed by default in subfolders of the *Program Files* folder.
- The 32-bit programs will be installed by default in subfolders of the *Program Files (x86)* folder.
- Registry keys for 32-bit programs will be found in HKEY_LOCAL_MACHINE \SOFTWARE\Wow6432Node rather than HKEY_LOCAL_MACHINE \SOFTWARE.

Some programs may have both a 32-bit version and a 64-bit version. In most cases, you'll get better performance with the native 64-bit version of a program. If you encounter compatibility issues, you can run the 32-bit x86 version of the program instead. If you are running a program and don't know whether it is 32-bit or 64-bit, press

Ctrl-Alt-Delete to start Task Manager. On the Processes tab, 32-bit processes are identified with "*32" after the process name.

Installing and Running Your Software

Whether you are using your computer to create Word documents, view photos, or send email, you are running software that handles these tasks for you. Windows 7's job is to provide a framework for you to install, configure, and run your software.

Installing Software

Unlike Windows XP and earlier releases of Windows, Windows 7 doesn't provide a tool for adding, reconfiguring, or removing software. Instead, as mentioned earlier, it relies on the software itself to provide these features through a Setup program.

Most of the time installing and running your software using its Setup program is easy, and you can install your software from a CD or DVD by following these steps:

1. Insert the media disk into your computer's CD or DVD drive.
2. If Windows 7 displays the AutoPlay dialog box, click Run *Setup.exe* or a similar option under Install or Run Program. When Setup starts, follow the prompts to install the software, and skip the remaining steps.
3. If Windows 7 doesn't display the AutoPlay dialog box, click Start→Computer. In the Computer window, double-click the CD or DVD drive.
4. If Windows 7 detected the software's Setup program (using *Autorun.inf* or a similar file), you are then prompted for permission or consent to run the Setup program.
5. If Windows 7 doesn't detect the software's Setup program, the contents of the disc are displayed in Windows Explorer. Double-click the Setup program.
6. When the Setup program starts, follow the prompts to install the software.
7. Most software applications have a setup program that uses Windows Installer, InstallShield, or Wise Install. If the installation fails and the software has an installer, follow the prompts to allow the installer to restore your computer to its original state. Otherwise, exit Setup and then try rerunning the Setup program to either complete the installation or uninstall the program.

 In some cases, the Program Compatibility Assistant may not be able to determine whether the software installed properly, and may prompt you to tell it whether it installed correctly. If not, it will give you a chance to retry the installation using the compatibility mode settings that it thinks will work.

You can run installed software by selecting the software's menu option or double-clicking its desktop shortcut. If you run into problems installing or running the software, be sure to read the sections of this chapter titled "Making Software Available to Others", "Using MS-DOS and 16-Bit Software with Windows 7" on page 122, and "Using Older Programs with Windows 7" on page 123.

However, not all programs have distribution media discs. If you download a program from the Internet, it'll probably be in a ZIP or self-extracting executable file, and you can install the program by following these steps:

1. Start Windows Explorer.
2. Extract the program's setup files using one of the following techniques:
   - If the program is distributed in a *.zip* file, right-click the file and select Extract All. This displays the Extract Compressed (Zipped) Folders dialog box. Click Browse, select a destination folder, and then click OK. Click Extract.
   - If the program is distributed in a self-extracting executable file, double-click the *.exe* file to extract the setup files. You'll see one of several types of prompts. If you're prompted to run the file, click Run. If you're prompted to extract the program files or select a destination folder, click Browse, select a destination folder, and then click OK. Click Extract or OK as appropriate.
3. In Windows Explorer, browse the setup folders and find the Setup program. Double-click the Setup program to start the installation process.
4. When Setup starts, follow the prompts to install the software. If the installation fails and the software used an installer, follow the prompts to allow the installer to restore your computer to its original state. Otherwise, exit Setup and then try re-running Setup to either complete the installation or uninstall the program.

Making Software Available to Others

Most software programs written for Windows 2000 or later are made available automatically to all users on a computer. This occurs because the software writes to areas of the registry and filesystem available to all users, and because the software makes its program shortcuts available to all users. During installation, some software programs prompt you to choose whether you want to install the software for all users or only for the currently logged-on user. Other programs—typically older programs written for Windows 98 or earlier—install themselves only for the current user.

For software that requires per-user configurations, you can make the software available to multiple users by completing the following steps:

1. Log on to the computer using an account that should have access to the program.
2. Install the software using its Setup program.
3. Repeat this process for each user.

For software that doesn't require per-user configuration, you can make the software available to all users on your computer by completing the following steps:

1. Log on as the user who installed the program.

2. Click the Start menu and right-click All Programs. Choose Open from the menu that appears.

3. In the Programs folder, right-click the folder for the program group or the shortcut you want to work with. Then select Copy or Cut from the shortcut menu.

4. Click the Start menu and right-click All Programs. Choose Open All Users from the menu that appears.

5. In the Programs folder, right-click an open space and then select Paste. The program group or shortcut should now be available to all users of the computer.

6. Repeat steps 2–5 as necessary to copy all the related program groups and shortcuts for the software application.

 These instructions are very important in Windows XP mode. In Windows XP mode, the list of Windows XP applications that you can launch from Windows 7's Start menu is drawn from applications that have been installed for all users. Because Windows XP Mode is used for troublesome applications, it's not unusual to find that one of these applications is installed for the logged-in user rather than for all users.

You can make a program available only to you rather than to all users by completing these steps:

1. Log on using your account.

2. Click the Start menu and right-click All Programs. Choose Open All Users from the menu that appears.

3. In the Programs folder, right-click the folder for the program group or shortcut that you want to work with, and select Cut.

4. Click the Start menu and right-click All Programs. Choose Open from the menu that appears.

5. In the Programs folder, right-click an open space and then select Paste. The program group or shortcut should now be available only to the currently logged-on user.

6. Repeat steps 2–5 as necessary to copy all the related program groups and shortcuts for the software application.

 Moving the software's program group or shortcuts doesn't prevent other users from running the program—it simply hides the program from other users. They may still be able to start the software from Windows Explorer.

Using MS-DOS and 16-Bit Software with Windows 7

By default, only 32-bit versions of Windows 7 can run MS-DOS and 16-bit software. 32-bit Windows versions cannot run MS-DOS or 16-bit programs that require direct access to your computer's hardware or that require 16-bit drivers. 32-bit Windows versions can run only MS-DOS or 16-bit programs that don't require direct access to your computer's hardware and that don't require 16-bit drivers.

One way to reliably run 16-bit DOS applications on 64-bit versions of Windows is to install an open source emulator called DOSBox. DOSBox emulates the DOS shell and can be configured for an x86 computer of the appropriate vintage, making it perfect for those of us who grew up with a fondness for certain old-school DOS games and still need to play them, as well as those of us who are saddled with some seriously old code to run. Check it out at *http://www.dosbox.com*. With some effort, you can get 16-bit Windows running under DOSBox, but for running 16-bit Windows applications, you should use Windows XP Mode.

When you run an MS-DOS or 16-bit program, Windows 7 performs some compatibility tasks automatically. Under MS-DOS and 16-bit filesystems, filenames and directory names are restricted to eight characters with a three-character file extension, such as *Chapter3.txt*. This naming convention is often referred to as the 8.3 file-naming rule or the standard MS-DOS file-naming rule. MS-DOS and 16-bit folder paths are similarly restricted. On the other hand, the filesystems used with Windows 7 support long filenames of up to 255 characters. To help ensure that MS-DOS and 16-bit applications are compatible with your computer, Windows 7 translates between long and short filenames to ensure that your computer's filesystems are protected when an MS-DOS or 16-bit program modifies files and folders.

Windows 7 runs these MS-DOS and 16-bit programs using a virtual machine that mimics the 386-enhanced mode used by the original operating systems for which these programs were developed: Windows 3.0 and Windows 3.1. Unlike Windows XP and earlier Windows releases, Windows 7 runs multiple MS-DOS and 16-bit programs within a single virtual machine. Although each program is managed using a separate thread, all the programs share a common memory space. As a result, if one MS-DOS or 16-bit program fails, it usually means others running on the computer will fail as well.

By default, Windows 7 prevents one 16-bit or MS-DOS program from causing another to fail by running it in a separate memory space. Although running a program in a separate memory space uses additional memory, you'll usually find that the program is more responsive. Another added benefit is that you'll be able to run multiple instances of the program—as long as all the instances are running in separate memory spaces.

To configure a 16-bit or MS-DOS program to run in a separate memory space, complete the following steps:

1. Right-click the program's shortcut or menu option and then select Properties. This opens the program's Properties dialog box.

2. On the Shortcut tab, note the name of the program's executable file and then click the Open File Location button. This opens the folder in which the program's executable is stored in Windows Explorer.

3. Right-click the program's executable file and then select Properties.

4. On the Compatibility tab, you can now configure the desired compatibility settings.

5. Click OK to save the changes.

Running Applications in Windows XP Mode

Windows XP Mode lets you run older Windows XP software on your Windows 7 desktop. The feature comes as a separate download and works only with Windows 7 Professional, Enterprise, and Ultimate. Windows XP Mode also requires virtualization software such as Windows Virtual PC. Windows XP Mode and Windows Virtual PC are available for free on the Microsoft website. To download Windows XP Mode and the required software, visit the Windows Virtual PC website (*http://www.microsoft.com/windows/virtual-pc/default.aspx*).

The basic steps for installation are:

1. On the Virtual PC download page, select the type of Windows 7 you are running—either 32-bit or 64-bit—and then select the display language for Windows XP Mode, such as English.

2. Click the link provided to download Windows Virtual PC. Double-click the download to begin installation and then follow the prompts.

3. Click the link provided to download Windows XP Mode. Double-click the download to begin installation and then follow the prompts.

Microsoft has added features to Windows Virtual PC to make it easy to run many older Windows XP applications in Windows 7. You'll find it is fairly easy to set up Window XP Mode, and once you do, you can run Windows XP Mode applications with one click.

Using Older Programs with Windows 7

If you try to install a program with a known compatibility issue, Windows 7 warns you and opens the Program Compatibility Assistant to help you resolve the problem. Sometimes, however, a program won't install or will install but won't run, and you won't know why. To get the program to install or run, you'll need to adjust its compatibility settings, and Windows 7 provides two ways of doing this:

- Using the Program Compatibility Wizard to configure compatibility settings for you
- Editing a program's compatibility settings yourself

Although both techniques work the same way, the Program Compatibility Wizard is the only way you can change compatibility settings for programs that are on shared network drives, CD or DVD drives, or other types of removable media drives. The capability to work with various types of media allows the Program Compatibility Wizard to install programs that otherwise would not install.

Running the Program Compatibility Wizard

The Program Compatibility Wizard is similar to the Program Compatibility Assistant. The key differences between the two are:

- Windows 7 runs the Program Compatibility Assistant automatically when you try to install a program with a known compatibility issue.
- The Program Compatibility Wizard is a feature that you can use if you suspect a compatibility issue is preventing you from installing or running a program.

You can use the Program Compatibility Wizard for basic troubleshooting by completing the following steps:

1. On the Start menu, the desktop or Windows Explorer, right-click the program file or program shortcut and then select Troubleshoot Compatibility. This starts the Program Compatibility Wizard.

2. The wizard automatically tries to detect compatibility issues. Try to run the program using the recommended fixes. Click Try Recommended Settings, review the settings that will be applied, as shown in Figure 4-3, and then click Start the program.

3. After running the program, click Next and then do one of the following:
   - If the compatibility settings resolved the problem and you want to keep the settings, click "Yes, save these settings for this program."
   - If the compatibility settings didn't resolve the problem and you want to repeat this process from the beginning, click "No, try again using different settings" and continue with step 3 of the next procedure.
   - If the compatibility settings didn't resolve the problem and you'd like to check for an online solution, click "No, report the problem to Microsoft and check online for a solution."
   - If you want to discard the compatibility settings and exit the wizard, click Cancel.

Figure 4-3. Review the suggested compatibility settings and then test-run the program

You can use the Program Compatibility Wizard for advanced troubleshooting by completing the following steps:

1. On the Start menu, the desktop or Windows Explorer, right-click the program file or program shortcut and then select Troubleshoot Compatibility. This starts the Program Compatibility Wizard.

2. The wizard automatically tries to detect compatibility issues. Because you want to perform advanced troubleshooting, Click Troubleshoot Program after it completes its initial check of the program.

3. On the "What problems do you notice?" page (Figure 4-4), select options corresponding to the problems you've seen. The selections you make determine the wizard pages you see when you click Next and include the following:

    The program worked on earlier versions of Windows but won't install or run now
    When you select this option, you are prompted on one of the subsequent wizard pages to specify which version of Windows the program worked on previously. As your choice sets the compatibility mode, choose the operating system for which the program was designed. When running the program, Windows 7 will then simulate the environment for this operating system.

    The program opens but doesn't display correctly
    When you are trying to run a game, an educational program, or any other program that requires specific display settings, such as a program designed for Windows 98, you can select this option and then choose the type of display problem you are seeing. Your selections restrict the video display using 256

colors, 640 × 480 screen resolution, or both to help with programs that have problems running at higher screen resolutions and color depths. Your selections can also disable themes, desktop compositing, and display scaling of high dpi settings.

The program requires additional permissions

When you choose this option, the program will be configured to run with administrator privileges. Many programs developed for Windows XP and earlier versions of Windows need to run with elevated privileges to function properly. The program will then always attempt to run elevated privileges and prompt you for permission or consent as appropriate.

I don't see my problem listed

When you choose this option, the wizard will behave as if you had selected all three of the previous options.

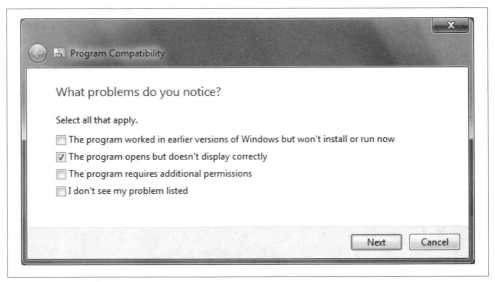

Figure 4-4. Specify the types of problems you've encountered while using the program

4. After you work your way through the wizard pages, review the compatibility settings that will be applied. Keep the following in mind if you need to specify display problems:

Error message saying the program needs to run in 256 colors

Selecting this option restricts your computer to 8-bit, 256-color video display when running the program. This setting is often required with games, multimedia, and educational software developed for Windows 95/Windows 98.

Program starts up in a small window (640 × 480 pixels) and won't switch to full screen
Selecting this option resizes the screen to 640 × 480 pixels when you run the program. This setting is often required with games, multimedia, and educational software developed for Windows 95/Windows 98.

Windows transparency isn't displayed properly
Selecting this option turns off desktop composition while running the program to prevent conflicts, such as those that may occur when your desktop background uses colors in one way and the program uses colors in another way. Use this option to correct problems with the display, particularly with the way the program uses colors.

Program does not display properly when large-scale font settings are selected
Selecting this option turns off scaling when your monitor uses a display setting with a high dpi. Use this option if the program's windows appear to be stretched and you want them to appear normally.

Window controls appear cut off, or the program changes visual themes when started
Selecting this option turns off themes and user experience settings while running the program to allow text on the program's menus and buttons to display without modification. Use this option if you have problems reading or accessing menus and buttons within the program and you want the program to use Windows 7 Basic experience settings.

5. If you don't want to apply these settings, click Cancel and repeat this procedure to select different options. If you want to test these settings, click "Start the program." The wizard will then run the program with the chosen compatibility settings.

6. After running the program, click Next and then do one of the following:

   • If the compatibility settings resolved the problem and you want to keep the settings, click "Yes, save these settings for this program."

   • If the compatibility settings didn't resolve the problem and you want to repeat this process from the beginning, click "No, try again using different settings and repeat this procedure starting with step 3."

   • If the compatibility settings didn't resolve the problem and you'd like to check for an online solution, click "No, report the problem to Microsoft and check online for a solution."

   • If you want to discard the compatibility settings and exit the wizard, click Cancel.

If your computer's display settings are reset, don't panic. You can restore the original display settings simply by exiting the program that is running in compatibility mode.

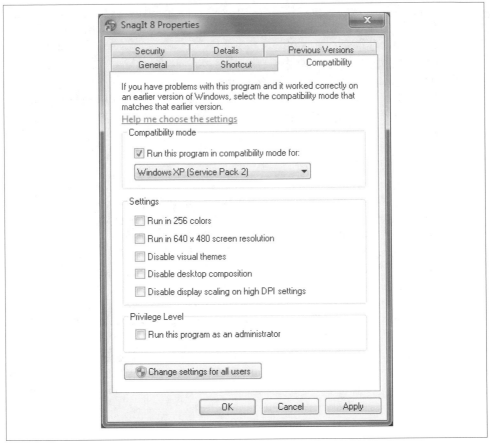

Figure 4-5. Choosing the compatibility options to enable

Setting compatibility options manually

Rather than using the Program Compatibility Wizard, you can manually configure compatibility settings. This is handy if you want to edit the settings after you configured them using the wizard. Complete the following steps:

1. Right-click the program's shortcut icon and then select Properties. Select the Compatibility tab, as shown in Figure 4-5. You cannot run programs that are part of the Windows 7 operating system in compatibility mode. Because of this, the options are unavailable for built-in programs.

2. By default, the compatibility options you select will apply only to the selected application shortcut. To apply the setting to all users on the computer and regardless of which shortcut is used to start the application, click "Change settings for all users" to display the Properties dialog box for the application's *.exe* file and then

select the compatibility settings that you want to use for all users who log on to the computer.

3. Select the "Run this program in compatibility mode for" checkbox and then use the selection menu to choose the operating system for which the program is designed.

4. Optionally, use the options in the Settings panel to restrict the video display settings for the program. Select 256 colors, 640 × 480 screen resolution, or both, as required.

5. Optionally, disable themes, desktop compositing, display scaling on high-dpi settings, or all three, as required.

6. Select the "Run as administrator" checkbox if the program requires elevated permissions to function correctly. Do not use this option for programs you do not trust.

7. Click OK. Double-click the shortcut to run the program and test the compatibility settings. If you still have problems running the program, you might need to modify the compatibility settings again, contact the software developer for an updated version, or try running it under Windows XP Mode (for more information on Windows XP Mode, see "Running Applications in Windows XP Mode" on page 123).

Managing Software Once It's Installed

Installing software is only one part of software management. Often after you install software, you'll need to make configuration changes to your computer or the software itself. You may want files of a certain type to open in the software when you click or double-click the files in Windows Explorer. You may need to reconfigure, repair, or uninstall the software. Alternatively, you may need to resolve problems with the way the software starts or runs. I discuss all of these tasks in the following sections.

Assigning Default Programs

When you install productivity applications, such as Microsoft Word or Adobe Photoshop, the installation process may configure your computer so that certain types of files automatically open in the application when you click or double-click them in Windows Explorer. The installation process may also configure your computer so that when you insert media containing music, video, or pictures, the media is opened and played automatically using a particular application.

Associating an application with particular file types and running an application for certain types of media are separate features. You make files with a specific extension or type open in a specific program by associating the file extension or type with the program. You make media on CDs, DVDs, or portable devices open and play in a particular program by making a program the default for AutoPlay.

You configure file associations and default programs either only for yourself or globally for all users of your computer. Your individual default settings override global default settings. For example, you might want Apple iTunes to be your default audio player, but the global default for all users could be set to use Windows Media Player.

Setting your default programs

You can configure your default programs by completing the following steps:

1. Click Start and then click Default Programs.
2. Click "Set your default programs."
3. As shown in Figure 4-6, select a program you want to work with from the Programs list.
4. If you want the program to be the default for all the file types and protocols it supports, click "Set this program as default" and click OK. Skip the remaining steps.
5. If you want the program to be the default for specific file types and protocols, click "Choose defaults for this program."
6. As shown in Figure 4-7, select the file extensions and protocols for which the program should be the default.
7. Click Save.

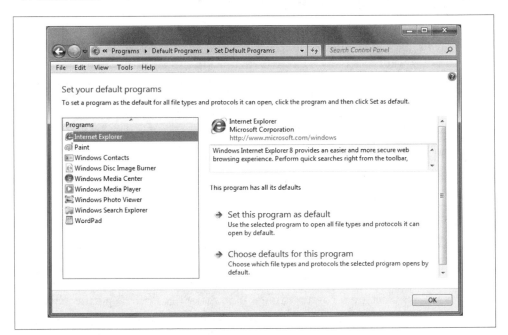

Figure 4-6. Selecting the program you want to work with

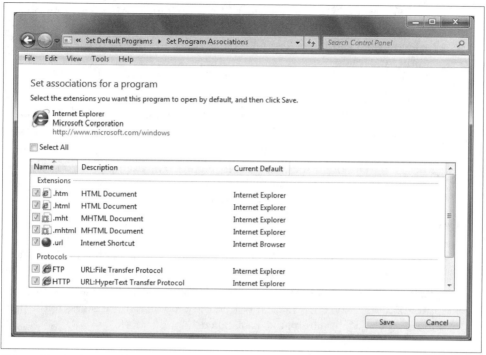

Figure 4-7. Configuring file extensions to associate with the program

Setting global default programs

You can configure global default programs—default programs for all the users of your computer—by completing the following steps:

1. Log on to your computer using an account with administrator privileges.

2. Click Start→Default Programs→Set Program Access and Computer Defaults.

3. Choose a configuration from one of the following options:

Computer Manufacturer

This option is available only if your computer came preinstalled with a customized version of Windows. This restores the manufacturer's original defaults for web browsing, sending and receiving email, playing media files, instant messaging, and Java Virtual Machine support, as well as whether you have access to other programs.

Microsoft Windows

Sets the currently installed Microsoft Windows programs as the defaults for web browsing, sending and receiving email, playing media files, instant messaging, and Java Virtual Machine support.

Enables access to other programs. If you've installed other programs, you can configure your computer to use the currently installed program for a particular task. For example, if you installed Microsoft Office, Microsoft Outlook is configured automatically for use as your default email program. To change this, you would click the "E-mail program" list and choose Windows Mail or another program.

Non-Microsoft

Sets the currently installed non–Microsoft Windows programs as the defaults for web browsing, sending and receiving email, playing media files, instant messaging, and Java Virtual Machine support.

Removes access to Microsoft Windows programs if you've configured non–Microsoft Windows programs as the defaults. For example, if you installed Mozilla as your web browser and set this as the default, the Non-Microsoft option removes access to Internet Explorer.

Custom

As shown in Figure 4-8, enables you to choose programs as the defaults for web browsing, sending and receiving email, playing media files, instant messaging, and Java Virtual Machine support.

Each program available to use as a default has a related "Enable access to this program" checkbox. If you clear this checkbox, you remove access to the program when a viable alternative is installed.

4. Click OK to save your settings.

Reconfiguring, Repairing, or Uninstalling Software

Once you install software, you can manage its installation using the Programs and Features page in the Control Panel. More than any other version of Windows, Windows 7 takes advantage of the features of the installer program used with your software. This means you'll have more configuration options than you otherwise would. For example, previously, most software allowed you to rerun Setup to uninstall the program but didn't necessarily allow you to rerun Setup to change or repair the software. Windows 7 surfaces these features to make it easier to manage your software.

You can use the Programs and Features page to reconfigure, repair, or uninstall software by following these steps:

1. Click Start→Control Panel→Uninstall a Program under Programs.

2. In the Name list, click the program you want to work with and then select one of the following options on the toolbar:
   • Change, to modify the program's configuration
   • Repair, to repair the program's installation
   • Uninstall, to uninstall the program
   • Uninstall/Change, to uninstall or change a program with an older installer program

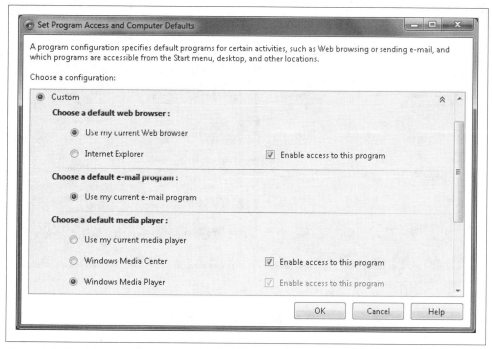

Figure 4-8. Choosing your computer's global defaults

If the uninstall process fails, you may be able to resolve the problem simply by rerunning the Uninstaller for the program. Occasionally, you may need to clean up after a failed uninstall. This may require removing program files and deleting remnants of the program in the Windows registry. A program called the Windows Installer Cleanup utility can help you clean up the registry. You'll find more information about the utility and the software for downloading online at the Microsoft Support website (*http://support.microsoft.com/kb/290301*).

Windows 7 will allow you to remove only programs that were installed with Windows-compatible setup programs. Programs designed for Windows 2000 and earlier releases of Windows may have a separate Uninstall utility. Some older programs work by copying their data files to a program folder; you would then uninstall the program by deleting the related folder.

After you uninstall a program, check the Program Files folder and other locations for data left behind either inadvertently or by design. Before deleting any remaining data, you should determine whether the files contain important data or custom user settings that could be used again if you reinstall the program.

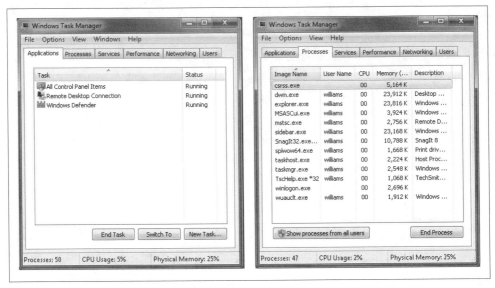

Figure 4-9. Accessing processes in Task Manager

Viewing and Managing Currently Running Programs

Task Manager is a handy tool for working with your computer's programs. You can start Task Manager by pressing Ctrl-Alt-Delete and then selecting Start Task Manager.

You can use Task Manager to view and manage your computer's currently running programs and processes. You can also use Task Manager to stop a program, which may be necessary, for instance, if a program is not responding and you want to quit the program.

As Figure 4-9 shows, Task Manager has two tabs for working with running programs:

Applications
> Lists applications you are currently running by name and status, such as Running or Not Responding. To exit a program, click the program in the Task list and then click End Task.

Processes
> Lists all programs and processes you are running on the computer by image name, your username, and resource usage. To stop a process, click the process and then click End Process.

By default, Task Manager's Processes tab shows only your running processes. To see running processes for all users, click "Show processes from all users" and provide consent or credentials if prompted. You'll then see all processes running on the computer. You will also be able to right-click a process and select from an extended list of management options, including:

Open File Location
   Opens the folder containing the executable file for the process in Windows Explorer

End Process
   Stops the process

End Process Tree
   Stops the process and all dependent processes

UAC Virtualization
   Allows you to modify UAC virtualization settings as may be necessary for debugging

Create Dump File
   Creates a memory dump file for the selected process

Properties
   Opens the Properties dialog box for the executable file

Viewing and Managing Startup Programs

Some software programs you install, such as antivirus or backup software, are configured as startup programs. As the name implies, startup programs run in the background and start automatically when you log on. You can view the currently configured startup programs using the System Configuration utility. The System Configuration utility also allows you to enable or disable startup programs.

Viewing your startup programs

You can open the System Configuration utility and view your startup programs by completing the following steps:

1. In Control Panel, click System and Security and then click Administrative Tools. On the Administrative Tools page, double-click System Configuration.

2. In the System Configuration utility, select the Startup tab, as shown in Figure 4-10.

Table 4-1 provides a summary of the configuration details for startup programs.

Table 4-1. Overview of configuration details for startup programs

Entry	Description
Command	Lists the complete file path to the executable file
Date Disabled	Lists the date and time that the startup program was disabled (if applicable)
Location	Lists the folder path where the startup program shortcut was created, or the Run key value in the registry
Manufacturer	Lists the company that published the software
Startup Item	Lists the application name that Windows 7 uses

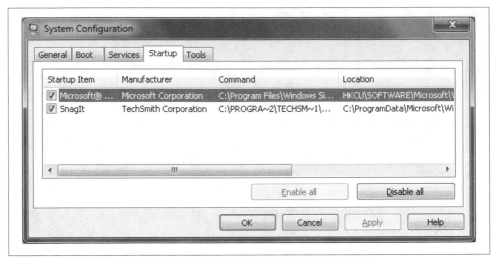

Figure 4-10. Viewing your startup programs

Enabling and disabling startup programs

While you are working with the System Configuration utility, you can configure your startup programs. You have several options for managing startup programs. You can:

Enable a specific startup program
> If you previously disabled a startup program, you can change this by enabling the program to run at startup. To do this, select the program's checkbox.

Disable a specific startup program
> If you don't want a program to start automatically when you log on, you can clear the related checkbox to disable it. A disabled startup program will no longer run on startup.

Enable all startup programs
> If you want all relevant programs to be started automatically, select Enable All.

Disable all startup programs
> If you don't want any relevant programs to be started automatically, select Disable All.

 If you no longer need a startup program or you want to prevent it from being enabled in the future, you can remove its shortcut from the location specified or look for an option in the program to disable automatic startup. Whenever you modify startup programs, you should restart your computer and determine whether there is any negative impact on your computer.

Adding and Removing Windows Features

In Windows XP and earlier versions of Windows, you use the Add/Remove Windows Components option of the Add or Remove Programs utility to add and remove operating system components. In Windows 7, operating system components are considered Windows features that can be turned on and off rather than added and removed.

Table 4-2 provides a complete list of available Windows features and their uses. The table also denotes the default on or off state for Windows 7 editions that support the feature.

Table 4-2. Windows features

Windows feature	Description	Default configuration
Games	Enables the games included with the operating systems. You can select the Games option to install all available games, or expand the Games node to select individual games. Games available include Chess Titans, FreeCell, Hearts, InkBall, Mahjong Titans, Minesweeper, Purble Place, Solitaire, and Spider Solitaire.	On
Indexing Service	Windows 7 uses the Windows Search service for content indexing and property caching of documents. If you are using your computer to provide web server services, you can enable Indexing Services for backward compatibility with search features used in your web pages.	Off
Internet Explorer 8	Windows 7 includes Internet Explorer 8. If you've installed a different browser, you can clear this option to uninstall Internet Explorer 8.	On
Internet Information Services	Windows 7 includes Internet Information Services 7. You can use this option and its related suboptions to configure FTP, web, and application services.	Off
Internet Information Services Hostable Web Core	Enables the hostable web core for Internet Information Services.	Off
Media Feature	Enables the core media features of Windows 7, as applicable for the operation system edition you are running. Can include Windows DVD Maker, Windows Media Center, and Windows Media Player.	On
Microsoft .NET Framework 3.5.1	Enables .NET Framework 3.5.1, which includes a comprehensive framework for client-server communications over a network. If you install applications that require the Windows Communication Foundation APIs, you can enable the related options.	Partial
Microsoft Message Queue (MSMQ) Server	Enables a server service that allows queuing for web applications.	Off
Print and Document Services	Enables network printing and document services. Use Internet Printing Client to enable your computer to use HTTP to connect to a web print server. Use LPD Print Service to enable your computer to work as a Line Printer Daemon and Remote Line Printer client. Use LPR Port Monitor to enable your computer to print to TCP/IP printers connected to a Unix server. Use Scan Management for managing scanned documents. Use Windows Fax and Scan to enable your computer to send, receive, and manage faxes, and to scan and manage documents.	On for Internet Printing Client and Windows Fax and Scan

Windows feature	Description	Default configuration
Remote Differential Compression	Enables your computer to transfer the differences between two objects over the network. This option is used primarily with Group Policy and domain configurations to reduce network bandwidth usage.	On
RIP Listener	Enables your computer to listen to route updates sent by routers that use Routing Information Protocol version 1 (RIPv1).	Off
Services for NFS	Enables your computer to participate in file sharing using the Network File Sharing (NFS) protocol. Use Client for NFS if your office or school network has NFS shares that you need to connect to.	Off
Simple Network Management Protocol (SNMP)	Enables Simple Network Management Protocol (SNMP) agents that monitor the activity of network devices and create reports of this activity. Use WMI SNMP Provider only if you are an administrator who uses SNMP administration tools for monitoring network activities.	Off
Simple TCPIP Services	Enables simple TCP/IP services, such as echo and daytime. These services may open your computer to attack and is not recommended for use with Windows 7.	Off
Subsystem for Unix-based Applications	Enables a compatibility subsystem for Unix-based applications and scripts.	Off
Tablet PC Optional Components	Enables optional components normally used with Tablet computers including the Input Panel, Snipping Tool, Sticky Notes, and Windows Journal.	On for Tablet PCs
Telnet Client	Enables your computer to connect to other computers using Telnet.	Off
Telnet Server	Enables your computer to receive Telnet connections from other computers. This service may open your computer to attack and is not recommended for use with Windows 7.	Off
TFTP Client	Enables your computer to connect to other computers using TFTP.	Off
Windows Gadget Platform	Enables desktop gadgets.	On
Windows Process Activation Service	Installs the .NET environment, configuration APIs, and process model for the Windows Process Activation Service.	Off
Windows Search	Enables content indexing, property caching, and search.	On
Windows TIFF IFilter	Enables tagging, indexing, and searching TIFF image files using optical character recognition (OCR).	Off
Windows Virtual PC	Enables Windows Virtual PC, a service that is necessary for Windows XP Mode (see "Running Applications in Windows XP Mode" on page 123).	On if you have installed Windows Virtual PC
XPS Services	Enables printing to XPS documents	On
XPS Viewer	Enables you to view and manage XPS documents	On

Figure 4-11. Turning Windows features on and off

You can turn Windows features on and off by following these steps:

1. Click Start→Control Panel→Programs.

2. Click "Turn Windows features on or off." This displays the Windows Features dialog box, as shown in Figure 4-11.

3. To turn features on, select feature checkboxes. To turn features off, clear feature checkboxes.

4. When you click OK, Windows 7 reconfigures components as appropriate for any changes you've made.

CHAPTER 5

Customizing Your Computer's Hardware Devices

One of the most frustrating aspects of working with computers is that just about every computer has different hardware devices. Even computers from the same manufacturer may have different motherboards, disk controllers, video cards, and network adapters. Like its predecessors, Windows 7 has an extensive list of compatible hardware devices and also supports Plug and Play. Helping you navigate your hardware options, understand how hardware installation works, optimize your hardware, and install new hardware is what this chapter is all about. As you'll learn, hardware has changed considerably in the past few years and there are many important new options.

Hardware Installation: What's Changed

Hardware installation hasn't changed much in Windows 7. What has changed significantly in the past few years is the array of options when it comes to hardware devices. Whether you are installing new hardware in your existing computer or getting acquainted with the types of hardware available for a computer you've recently purchased, it's important to consider your options carefully. All computers can use two types of hardware:

Internal hardware devices
> Internal hardware devices are devices you install inside your computer. Typically, you'll need to power down and unplug your computer (in the case of notebook computers, you'll also need to remove the battery), and then remove the computer case before you can install an internal device. Notebook computers generally have limited options when it comes to internal hardware devices.

External hardware devices
> External hardware devices are devices you connect to your computer. Because you don't have to open your computer's case to connect external devices, you typically

don't need to power down or unplug your computer before installing an external device.

The bulk of the message-board posts I see regarding hardware relate to the following:

- Which type of internal device is the right choice?
- Which type of external device is the right choice?

You'll find answers to these questions in the sections that follow.

Which Type of Internal Device Is the Right Choice?

When it comes to internal devices, the right type of device to use is typically the device your computer is designed to work with. Most current computers use internal devices with one of the following interfaces:

PATA

    Parallel ATA (PATA) devices were the standard in the home computer industry for many years. PATA includes technologies such as the older Enhanced Integrated Drive Electronics (EIDE) and the more recent AT Attachment/AT Attachment Packet Interface (ATA/ATAPI). Although PATA is still in wide use at the time of this writing, you may find that some newer computers don't have PATA I/O (input/output) ports. To add support for PATA devices, you can install a PCI Express PATA controller card. However, if your computer supports SATA (see following entry), it is generally a better choice, as SATA offers better speeds and a wider selection of drives available for purchase.

SATA

    Serial ATA (SATA) devices are becoming increasingly popular. As of the time this book was written, most motherboard manufacturers include SATA input ports on their boards. Because SATA cables are significantly smaller than PATA cables, this results in less clutter inside your computer and improved airflow, for better cooling. Though some older computer system motherboards don't have SATA I/O ports, you can install a PCI Express SATA controller card to add support for SATA drives.

SCSI

    You are unlikely to encounter SCSI (Small Computer System Interface) devices except on specialized computers such as servers or older computers that were high-end for their time. Before SATA and high-speed PATA, SCSI drives offered the best performance. The current generation of SCSI drives typically offer high reliability and very high rotational speeds (15,000 RPM, which is more than double the 7,200 RPM that tends to dominate the high end of SATA and PATA devices).

 Just because you can install a controller card in your computer doesn't mean you should. Before you install controller cards, you should determine the computer's bus speed and whether the system bus is capable of handling the additional load without becoming saturated.

You can use Windows 7 with both PATA and SATA hardware devices, and it doesn't really matter to the operating system which type of device you use. Your computer, on the other hand, must be configured specifically to work with PATA, SATA, or both. If you don't know whether your computer has PATA or SATA ports on the motherboard, you can look at the type of cables being used inside your computer. As Figure 5-1 shows, PATA cables and SATA cables are very different.

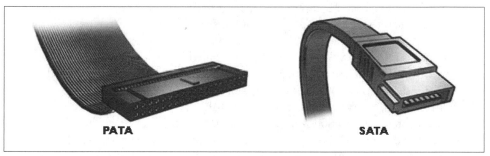

Figure 5-1. Comparing PATA and SATA cables

There are some feature differences between PATA and SATA that you should know about. Most PATA devices support a maximum data transfer rate of 100 Mb (megabits) per second and allow two devices to be connected per cable. Most PATA devices have a 10-pin jumper block, which configures whether the device is being used in a single device or Primary (Master)/Secondary (Slave) configuration. The pins on the jumper block are also used to configure cable selection settings.

Most SATA devices have a maximum data transfer rate of 150 or 300 Mb per second and allow only one device to be connected per cable. Most SATA devices have an 8-pin jumper block and there are no Primary (Master)/Secondary (Slave) configurations.

Which Type of External Device Is the Right Choice?

You connect external devices to your computer rather than installing them inside your computer. This makes external devices easier to install and means you can attach most external devices without having to reboot your computer. It's not so easy, however, to understand the various and similar-looking interfaces available with external devices. Most current computers use external devices with one of the following interfaces:

Universal Serial Bus (USB)
> USB 2.0 is the industry-standard peripheral connection for most Windows-based computers. This connection transfers data at a maximum rate of 480 Mb per second, with sustained data transfer rates usually from 10 to 30 Mb per second. The actual sustainable transfer rate depends on many factors, including the type of device, the data you are transferring, and the speed of your computer. Each USB controller on your computer has a fixed amount of bandwidth, which all devices

attached to the controller must share. If your computer's USB port is an earlier version—USB 1.0 or 1.1—you can use USB 2.0 devices, but the transfer rates will be significantly slower. To add support for USB 2.0 devices, you can install a PCI or PCI Express USB 2.0 controller card.

FireWire

FireWire, also called IEEE 1394, is a high-performance connection standard for most Windows-based computers. This interface uses a peer-to-peer architecture in which peripherals negotiate bus conflicts to determine which device can best control a data transfer. FireWire has several configurations, including FireWire 400 and FireWire 800. FireWire 400, also called IEEE 1394a, has maximum sustained transfer rates of up to 400 Mb per second and is suitable for hard drives, digital video, professional audio, high-end digital cameras, and home entertainment devices. FireWire 800, also called IEEE 1394b, has maximum sustained transfer rates of up to 800 Mb per second and is suitable for the high-speed connection and bandwidth required for multiple-stream, uncompressed digital video and high-resolution digital audio. To add support for FireWire devices, you can install a PCI or PCI Express FireWire controller card.

eSATA

External Serial ATA (eSATA) is an ultra-high-performance connection for super-fast, super-reliable data transfer to and from external mass storage devices. eSATA is up to three times faster than USB 2.0 and FireWire 400 and about 50 percent faster than FireWire 800. To add support for eSATA devices, you can install an eSATA controller card.

Although you can use Windows 7 with USB, FireWire, and eSATA hardware devices, your computer must be configured specifically to work with USB, FireWire, and eSATA. Many computers have USB, FireWire, or both ports that are accessible in the front of the computer as well as additional USB, FireWire, and eSATA ports accessible from the back of the computer. You'll also find that newer monitors have USB, FireWire, or both ports to which you can connect devices as well. Figure 5-2 shows the types of cable connectors and ports that are commonly used with USB and FireWire.

USB   FireWire 400 (IEEE 1394a)   FireWire 800 (IEEE 1394b)

Figure 5-2. Matching up USB and FireWire options

When working with USB, there are some important things to know. First, USB 1.0, 1.1, and 2.0 ports all look alike. To determine which types of USB ports your computer has, refer to the documentation that came with it. This documentation should list the types of USB ports and their locations. With an older computer, you will typically find USB 1.0 ports. Other computers may have a mixture of USB 1.1 and USB 2.0 ports. For example, your computer's high-end or professional-quality sound/video card may have a USB 2.0 port, while the rest of the USB ports on your computer are using USB 1.1.

Newer computers will typically have USB 2.0 ports. Newer LCD monitors will have USB 2.0 ports to which you can connect devices as well. When you have USB devices connected to a monitor, the monitor acts like a USB hub device. As with any USB hub device, all devices attached to the hub share the same bandwidth, and the total available bandwidth is determined by the speed of the USB input to which the hub is connected on your computer.

 If you don't know the version of your computer's USB ports and you don't have documentation for your computer, don't worry. I'll tell you about some tricks you can use to determine the USB version of your computer's ports a little later in this chapter, in the section "Viewing Installed Hardware" on page 152.

When working with FireWire, there are some important things to know as well. First, FireWire 400 and FireWire 800 ports and cables have different shapes, making it easy to tell the difference between them—if you know what you're looking for. If you look closely at FireWire 400 cables and ports, you'll see six pins or six connectors. If you look closely at FireWire 800 cables and ports, you'll see nine pins or nine connectors. Some older FireWire 400 cables and ports may have four pins and connectors. If so, the device you connect will not have bus power.

When you are purchasing an external device for your computer, you'll also want to consider how easy it is to connect the device to different systems. Although just about all Windows-based computers have USB 1.0 or higher ports, not all computers have FireWire or eSATA ports. Because of this, if you are purchasing an external device for use at home and at the office, you may want to get a device that supports USB. For a bit more money, you also may be able to get a device with a dual interface that supports USB 2.0 and FireWire 400, or a triple interface that supports USB 2.0, FireWire 400, and eSATA. A device with dual or triple interfaces will give you more options.

If you are purchasing a pocket-sized portable hard drive, keep in mind that most low-speed (5400 or 4200 RPM) USB drives can use the power supplied by a USB port without needing an external power supply. However, higher-speed (some 5400 and 7200 RPM) drives may not be able to spin up without more power.

If you encounter this problem, you may be able to use either an external power supply or a USB Y adapter to draw more power than is supplied by one USB port. FireWire supplies more power than USB, so if you are using a 6-pin FireWire 400 or a FireWire 800 cable to connect the drive, you should have plenty of power.

Hardware Installation: What You Need to Know

Each hardware device installed on your computer has an associated device driver. Drivers are specific to a particular architecture type. Drivers designed for 32-bit versions of Windows do not work on computers running 64-bit versions of Windows. If you are trying to install a hardware device that has only 32-bit drivers available, it won't work correctly on 64-bit versions of Windows.

The device driver tells the operating system how to use the *hardware abstraction layer* (HAL) to work with the related hardware device. The HAL in turn performs the low-level communications with the hardware device. When you install a hardware device through the operating system, you are essentially telling the operating system about the device driver it uses, and this is what allows the operating system to work with the device.

When you are installing hardware devices and working with device drivers, you need to know:

- Where the operating system stores device drivers
- How the operating system validates device drivers
- When the operating system checks for driver updates

You'll find answers to these questions in the sections that follow.

Where Does the Operating System Store Device Drivers?

Windows 7 has an extensive library of device drivers, which are maintained in the driver store. On 32-bit computers, you'll find the 32-bit driver store in the *%SystemRoot% \System32\DriverStore* folder. On 64-bit computers, you'll find the 64-bit driver store in the *%SystemRoot%\System32\DriverStore* folder and the 32-bit driver store in the *%SystemRoot%\SysWOW64\DriverStore* folder.

Within the driver store, you'll find subfolders with localized driver information for each language component configured on the system. For example, for localized U.S. English driver information, you'll find a subfolder called *en-US*.

The driver store also has a file repository containing nearly 10,000 files that support tens of thousands of different devices. The file repository is located in the *DriverStore \FileRepository* subfolder. The purpose of the file repository is to be the main storage location for device drivers. As you install updates and service packs for the operating system, you may also be updating or changing driver information files in the file repository.

Microsoft has certified every device driver in the driver store to be fully compatible with Windows 7. These drivers are also digitally signed by Microsoft to ensure their authenticity. When you install a Plug and Play hardware device, Windows 7 checks the driver store for a compatible device driver. If a device driver is found, Windows 7 automatically installs the device.

In the file repository, device drivers are organized by device class. In the various subfolders, you'll find *.inf* and *.sys* files for each device driver. You may also find *.pnf* and *.dll* files for drivers.

All device drivers have an associated Setup Information file, which ends with the *.inf* extension. The *.inf* file is a text file containing detailed configuration information about particular classes of devices or a related set of devices. As an example, the *msmouse.inf* file has driver information for logical serial mouse and logical PS/2 mouse devices from Microsoft (see Figure 5-3).

The driver information file specifies the basic configuration settings for the HAL and identifies any source or linked library files that the device should use. Source files have the *.sys* extension. Linked library files have the *.dll* extension. Some drivers also have associated component manifest (*.amx*) files. Component manifest files are written in eXtensible Markup Language (XML) and stored in the *Manifeststore* subfolder. They include details on the driver's digital signature and can include Plug and Play information used by the device to configure itself automatically.

All drivers installed on the operating system have a source *.sys* file in the *Drivers* subfolder. Within the *Drivers* folder, you'll find subfolders with localized driver source files for each language component configured on the system. For example, for localized U.S. English driver source files, you'll find a subfolder called *en-US*.

Following this, the key folders used with drivers on a computer localized for U.S. English are:

- *DriverStore*
- *DriverStore\en-US*
- *DriverStore\FileRepository*
- *Drivers*

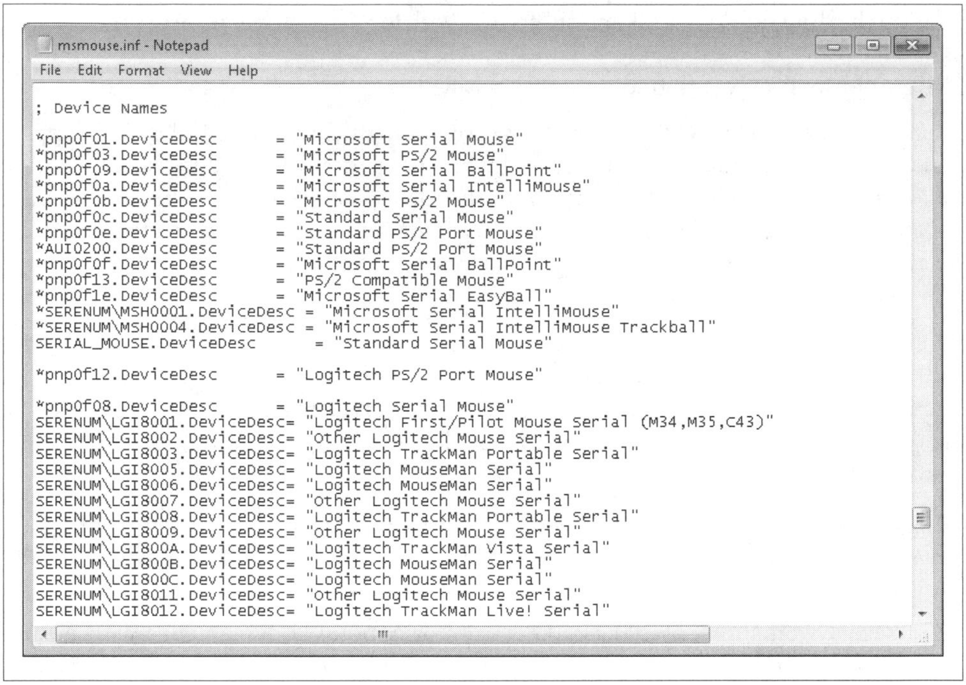

```
msmouse.inf - Notepad
File  Edit  Format  View  Help

; Device Names

*pnp0f01.DeviceDesc       = "Microsoft Serial Mouse"
*pnp0f03.DeviceDesc       = "Microsoft PS/2 Mouse"
*pnp0f09.DeviceDesc       = "Microsoft Serial BallPoint"
*pnp0f0a.DeviceDesc       = "Microsoft Serial IntelliMouse"
*pnp0f0b.DeviceDesc       = "Microsoft PS/2 Mouse"
*pnp0f0c.DeviceDesc       = "Standard Serial Mouse"
*pnp0f0e.DeviceDesc       = "Standard PS/2 Port Mouse"
*AUI0200.DeviceDesc       = "Standard PS/2 Port Mouse"
*pnp0f0f.DeviceDesc       = "Microsoft Serial BallPoint"
*pnp0f13.DeviceDesc       = "PS/2 Compatible Mouse"
*pnp0f1e.DeviceDesc       = "Microsoft Serial EasyBall"
*SERENUM\MSH0001.DeviceDesc = "Microsoft Serial IntelliMouse"
*SERENUM\MSH0004.DeviceDesc = "Microsoft Serial IntelliMouse Trackball"
SERIAL_MOUSE.DeviceDesc     = "Standard Serial Mouse"

*pnp0f12.DeviceDesc       = "Logitech PS/2 Port Mouse"

*pnp0f08.DeviceDesc       = "Logitech Serial Mouse"
SERENUM\LGI8001.DeviceDesc= "Logitech First/Pilot Mouse Serial (M34,M35,C43)"
SERENUM\LGI8002.DeviceDesc= "Other Logitech Mouse Serial"
SERENUM\LGI8003.DeviceDesc= "Logitech TrackMan Portable Serial"
SERENUM\LGI8005.DeviceDesc= "Logitech MouseMan Serial"
SERENUM\LGI8006.DeviceDesc= "Logitech MouseMan Serial"
SERENUM\LGI8007.DeviceDesc= "Other Logitech Mouse Serial"
SERENUM\LGI8008.DeviceDesc= "Logitech TrackMan Portable Serial"
SERENUM\LGI8009.DeviceDesc= "Other Logitech Mouse Serial"
SERENUM\LGI800A.DeviceDesc= "Logitech TrackMan Vista Serial"
SERENUM\LGI800B.DeviceDesc= "Logitech MouseMan Serial"
SERENUM\LGI800C.DeviceDesc= "Logitech MouseMan Serial"
SERENUM\LGI8011.DeviceDesc= "Other Logitech Mouse Serial"
SERENUM\LGI8012.DeviceDesc= "Logitech TrackMan Live! Serial"
```

Figure 5-3. Viewing the devices associated with the driver file

- *Drivers\en-US*
- *Manifeststore*

When you install a device driver, the driver is written to a subfolder of the *Drivers* folder and configuration settings are stored in the registry. The driver's *.inf* file is used to control the installation and write the registry settings. If the driver doesn't already exist in the driver store, it does not already have an *.inf* file or other related files on the system. In this case, the driver's *.inf* file and other related files are written to a subfolder of *DriverStore\FileRepository* when you install the device.

How Does the Operating System Validate Device Drivers?

Microsoft validates drivers using compatibility testing. Every device driver in the driver store is included because it passed extensive testing by the Windows Hardware Quality Lab. Once a device driver has been tested, Microsoft makes it possible to authenticate drivers by digitally signing them to prevent them from being tampered with. Because any changes to a signed driver void the digital signature, you can be sure that any device driver digitally signed by Microsoft is valid and authentic. Further, any device driver with a valid digital signature signed by Microsoft should not cause your system to crash or become unstable.

Drivers can also be digitally signed by their manufacturers. When a manufacturer digitally signs a driver, the manufacturer is giving proof of the driver's authenticity but not necessarily that it is 100 percent compatible with Windows 7. Still, as with drivers signed by Microsoft, any changes to a device driver signed by a manufacturer invalidate the digital signature, giving you a clear indication that a device driver has been tampered with.

Because unsigned drivers have been neither validated nor authenticated, they are much more likely than any other device driver or program you've installed to cause the operating system to freeze or your computer to crash. This is why Windows 7 warns you by default when you try to install a device with an unsigned device driver.

How Does the Operating System Obtain Driver Updates?

As you'll learn in Chapter 21, Windows 7 uses a feature called Windows Update to keep the operating system, its components and services, and related Microsoft software up to date. You can configure Windows Update to obtain updates for device drivers. If you do this, Windows 7 checks for driver updates as part of the normal update process.

Because Windows Update updates only device drivers included with the operating system, any devices you've installed that have their own device drivers are not necessarily updated in this way. Still, driver information files do contain information about particular classes of devices or related sets of devices, so it is possible that as manufacturers introduce new models of hardware devices, support for these newer devices will be added through the update process. This is one of the reasons that when you connect a new device, Windows 7 checks for a matching driver automatically using Windows Update.

As long as your computer is connected to the Internet when you install a new device, this check is automatic and transparent. If you don't want Windows 7 to check for drivers automatically, or you want Windows 7 to notify you before checking for drivers, you can change the default Windows Update Driver settings by completing the following steps:

1. Click Start and then click Control Panel→System and Security→System.
2. On the System page, click Change Settings under Computer Name, Domain, and Workgroup Settings. Or click Advanced System Settings in the left pane.
3. In the System Properties dialog box, click the Hardware tab→Device Installation Settings button.
4. As shown in Figure 5-4, select the desired update setting. The options available are:
   - Yes, do this automatically (recommended)
   - No, let me choose what to do
5. Click OK to save your settings.

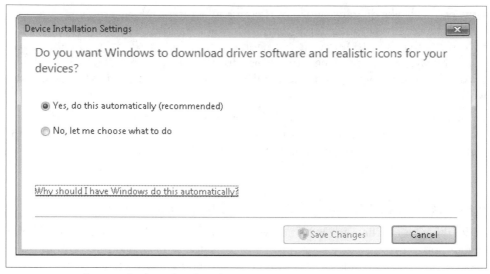

Figure 5-4. Configuring the desired update driver setting

Most of the time, you'll want to allow Windows to automatically download driver updates, as this will help ensure your hardware works properly. Keep in mind that even if Windows Update downloads driver updates, Windows won't necessarily install a driver update. Most driver updates will appear as optional updates that you'll need to install.

You can check for optional updates that are available by completing the following steps:

1. In the Control Panel, click System and Security→Windows Update.

 Before you install updated drivers, you should ensure that System Restore is enabled as discussed in Chapter 22. This will ensure that System Restore creates a restore point before Windows installs the driver. If you have a problem with your computer after installing the driver, you can recover your computer using the restore point.

2. On the Windows Update page, determine whether any optional updates are available. If optional updates are available, as shown in Figure 5-5, click the link provided.

3. On the Select updates to install page, review the available updates, select the checkbox for updates you want to install and then click OK. In the example shown in Figure 5-6, there was an optional update for the computer's graphics card.

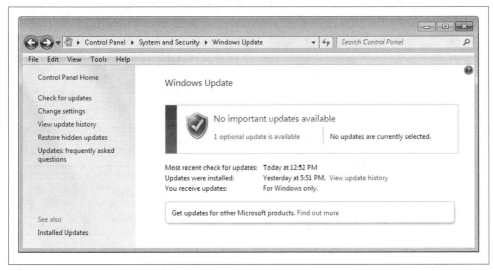

Figure 5-5. Checking for optional updates

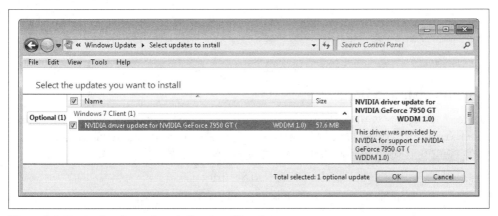

Figure 5-6. Reviewing the updates before installing them

Learning About Your Computer's Hardware Devices

Computers can have all sorts of hardware devices installed in and connected to them. Keeping track of all these components and their related device drivers without a little help would be nearly impossible, and that's where Device Manager comes in handy. You'll use Device Manager to learn about your computer's hardware components and the device drivers they use.

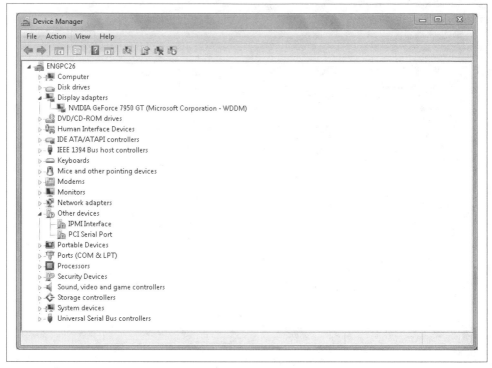

Figure 5-7. Reviewing your computer's hardware configuration

Viewing Installed Hardware

Device Manager is your window to the hardware components installed on your computer. You can access Device Manager and view all the hardware devices installed on your computer by completing the following steps:

1. In the Control Panel, click System and Security.
2. In the System section, click Device Manager.

As Figure 5-7 shows, Device Manager's default view shows the devices installed in or connected to your computer by device type. If you expand a device type node, such as DVD/CD-ROM devices, you'll see the actual hardware components that are installed. The device list shows warning symbols if there are problems with a device:

- A yellow warning symbol with an exclamation point indicates a problem with a device.
- A red *X* indicates a device that the user or administrator improperly installed or disabled for some reason.

The options on the View menu allow you to change the way devices are listed. The View menu options include:

Devices by type
> Displays devices by the type of device installed, such as disk drives or display adapters. This is the default view.

Devices by connection
> Displays devices by the type of connection. For example, you may see the base node for the computer as ACPI Multiprocessor PC or ACPI x86-based PC. ACPI stands for Advanced Configuration and Power Interface. ACPI defines which devices are present on a computer and what their capabilities are as to configuration and power management. If you expand the base node, you'll see the ACPI connections and a connection for the computer's hardware bus, such as PCI Bus. If you then expand the PCI Bus connection, you'll see all the hardware connected to the PCI bus.

Resources by type
> Displays the status of allocated resources by resource type and type of device using a resource. Resource types are direct memory access (DMA) channels, input/output (I/O) ports, interrupt requests (IRQ), and memory addresses.

Resources by connection
> Displays the status of all allocated resources by connection type rather than device type.

Show hidden devices
> Displays non–Plug and Play devices as well as devices that have been physically removed from the computer but haven't had their drivers uninstalled.

Getting to Know Your Computer's Hardware Devices

Because working with the various device types is straightforward but not always intuitive, let's look at the primary types of devices and how they are used. After reading this section, you'll know more about the ways you can work with and customize your computer's devices. Customizing your computer's keyboard, mouse, and audio settings is covered next.

Disk Drives

When you select Disk Drives in Device Manager, you'll see a list of the physical hard disks installed in the computer by type, such as USB or ATA. If you right-click a disk, select Properties, and then click the Policies tab, you'll see an important configuration option regarding the disk's write-caching optimization (see Figure 5-8). Removable disks, such as a USB disk, let you choose between quick removal and better performance. Because USB disks are easily unplugged, it is best to choose optimization for quick removal. Fixed disks, such as an ATA disk, let you specify write-caching settings, which generally should be left in their default configurations.

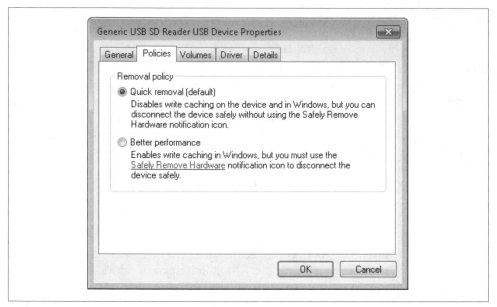

Figure 5-8. Viewing the disk driver settings for caching and safe removal

Display Adapters

When you select Display Adapters in Device Manager, you'll see a list of graphics cards (display adapters) installed in the computer by manufacturer and model, such as NVIDIA GeForce 7950 GT. If the device supports Windows Display Driver Model (WDDM), which is a requirement for Windows 7 Premium Ready computers, this should also be listed (in most cases).

DVD/CD-ROM Drives

When you select DVD/CD-ROM Drives in Device Manager, you'll see a list of the DVD/CD-ROM drives installed in the computer by manufacturer, type, and model. For DVD drives, if you want to know the type of read/write disks your computer supports, this is the place to check. The disk name may list DVD+RW if the DVD-ROM drive can burn to DVD+R discs, DVD-RW if the DVD-ROM drive can burn to DVD-R discs, or DVD+-RW if the DVD-ROM drive can burn to DVD+R and DVD-R discs.

 Most modern DVD drives support the whole range, so if you purchased your computer in the last few years, the computer likely will support both DVD-R and DVD+R. However, before you purchase a hundred-pack of one type of disc or the other, check other electronic devices you use to determine the types of discs they support. For instance, the TiVo unit I purchased with a DVD burner could burn only DVD-R discs.

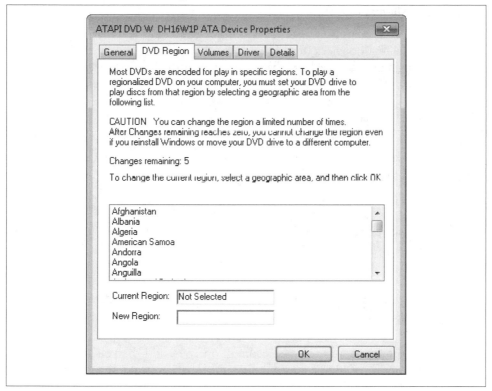

Figure 5-9. Viewing the encoded DVD region

Another tricky feature when burning DVD discs is the region code. Most DVDs are encoded to play in specific regions. In the United States, your DVD player is most likely set to work with Region 1–encoded discs. If you move to another country because of deployment, transfer, or whatever, you may find that you need to change the region code on your computer's DVD-ROM drive. You can do this by right-clicking the DVD-ROM drive in Device Manager, selecting Properties, and then clicking the DVD Region tab, as shown in Figure 5-9. On the DVD Region tab, select a country or geographic region and then click OK.

 You can change your DVD-ROM drive only a limited number of times, as per the "Changes remaining" value (see Figure 5-9). When the "Changes remaining" value reaches zero, you cannot change the region even if you reinstall Windows or move the DVD drive to a different computer.

Human Interface Devices

When you select Human Interface Devices in Device Manager, you'll see a list of the general-purpose input devices that are configured specifically as human interface devices, including mouse devices, trackballs, and keyboards. These devices are also listed under their specific device type.

IEEE 1394 bus host controllers

When you select "IEEE 1394 host controllers" in Device Manager, you'll see a list of the IEEE 1394 host controllers installed in your computer. You won't see this entry if your computer doesn't support IEEE 1394.

Imaging Devices

When you select Imaging Devices in Device Manager, you'll see a list of scanners, webcams, and other devices that can capture images.

Keyboards

When you select Keyboards in Device Manager, you'll see a list of the keyboards connected to the computer. Most keyboards have a power management setting that allows you to wake the computer by pressing a key. You can control this configuration by right-clicking the keyboard device, selecting Properties, and then clicking the Power Management tab. If you don't want to allow the device to wake the computer, clear the "Allow this device to wake the computer" checkbox.

Mice and other pointing devices

When you select "Mice and other pointing devices" in Device Manager, you'll see a list of the mouse, trackball, and other pointing devices connected to the computer. Most pointing devices have a power management setting that allows you to wake the computer by moving the device.

You can control the power management configuration by right-clicking the pointing device, selecting Properties, and then clicking the Power Management tab. If you don't want to allow the device to wake the computer, clear the "Allow this device to wake the computer" checkbox. Otherwise, this checkbox should be selected so that you can use the device to wake the computer.

 When I'm using power management options, I find it much more efficient to use only the keyboard to wake the computer. If you turn off the Wake the Computer setting for other input devices, this will prevent you from accidentally waking the computer by bumping the mouse or trackball.

Monitor

When you select Monitor in Device Manager, you'll see a list of the general type of monitor connected to your computer. If your computer's monitor has power management settings, you control these as discussed in Chapter 3.

Network Adapters

When you select Network Adapters in Device Manager, you'll see a list of the network adapters installed in or connected to your computer. Your computer's Ethernet card and wireless adapters will have an entry here.

Most network adapters have a power management feature that allows the operating system to turn them off to save power. Although you can also configure power management settings to wake the computer if the device becomes active, you should rarely do so, because this setting may cause the computer to periodically wake to refresh its network state. It may also cause a laptop to turn on when you don't want it to; this may allow someone to attempt to connect remotely to your computer when you think it is off and safe.

For network adapters, you can control the power management configuration by completing the following steps:

1. In Device Manager, right-click the network adapter, select Properties, and then click the Power Management tab, as shown in Figure 5-10.

2. If you want to allow the computer to turn off this device to save power, select the "Allow the computer to turn off this device to save power" checkbox. Otherwise, clear this option to ensure that the device isn't turned off to save power.

3. If you don't want to allow the device to wake the computer, clear the "Allow this device to wake the computer" checkbox. Otherwise, this checkbox should be selected so that you can use the device to wake the computer. The "magic packet" option causes the adapter to ignore all network messages except one that matches a specific pattern (hexadecimal FFFFFFFFFFFF).

4. Click OK.

 You'll find a wake-on-LAN configuration tool that support magic packets at *http://www.depicus.com/wake-on-lan/*.

Figure 5-10. Optimizing the power management settings as appropriate

 Sometimes when you are troubleshooting a networking problem, a Microsoft Knowledge Base article will tell you to change a specific property of your network adapter. You make this change on the Advanced tab in the network adapter's Properties dialog box.

Sound, video, and game controllers

When you select Sound, video, and game controllers in Device Manager, you'll see a list of the audio codecs, game ports, audio cards, audio drivers, video cards, video codecs, and video drivers installed in your computer by manufacturer, model, and type. By viewing the available devices, you can determine what type of sound and video cards are installed. If your computer has an integrated sound card, video card, or both, this is listed as part of the device name as well.

System devices

When you select System devices in Device Manager, you'll see a list of all the hardware components related to your computer's motherboard and system bus. If you want to determine whether your computer supports ACPI or has a PCI Express bus, this is the place to look.

If your computer seems to be losing track of time when you power it off, and you suspect there is an issue with your computer's CMOS clock (which runs on battery), System Devices is the place to look.

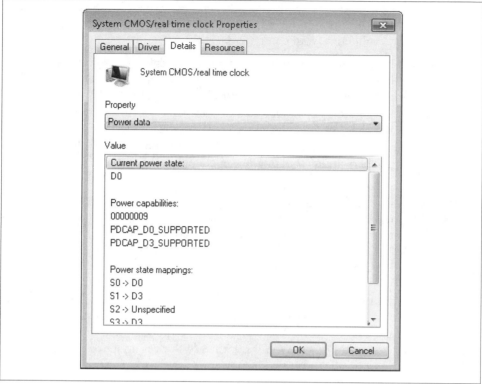

Figure 5-11. Checking the CMOS clock

Typically, a computer's CMOS battery will last 7 to 10 years or more. You can check your computer's CMOS clock by completing the following steps:

1. In Device Manager, expand System devices. Right-click "System CMOS/real time clock" and then select Properties.

2. On the Details tab, shown in Figure 5-11, select "Current power state," "Power data," or a similar power setting to determine the current power state of the CMOS clock.

3. If power settings information is provided, your clock is most likely working fine.

4. If you are unable to obtain this information when you select "Current power state," "Power data," or a similar power setting, you may need to replace the battery for the CMOS clock.

USB hubs and controllers

When you select Universal Serial Bus controllers in Device Manager, you'll see a list of all the USB devices installed in your computer, including controllers and hubs as well as some types of connected devices. Host controllers are listed by manufacturer, model, and type. The model and type details should also specify the USB version supported. For example, if you see entries for USB Universal Host Controller and USB2 Enhanced Host Controller, you'll know your computer has USB 1.0/1.1 ports and USB 2.0 ports.

A self-powered USB hub is a USB hub that supplies 5 volts DC to devices plugged into it. They can be built in to a computer or monitor, or be standalone devices with their own power supply. Most computers have multiple self-powered USB hubs and each of these hubs has a separate entry in Device Manager. Every device connected to a hub routes data through the USB controller associated with the hub. When you are working with a USB hub's Properties dialog box, you can determine the USB controller for a hub by checking the Location entry on the General tab (see Figure 5-12).

 Some USB hubs may be used by internal devices (such as Bluetooth or wireless network), and some USB hubs/controllers supported by your computer's chipset are not hooked up to anything. (Some PCs have header pins on their motherboard that you can connect an optional USB riser card to.) This is why you may see more hubs than USB ports.

Self-powered USB hubs include a Power Management tab. Once you've located the hub's controller, you can access the Properties dialog box for the controller. As shown in Figure 5-12, the total power available to the hub per port is listed under Hub Information. Under Attached Devices, you'll see a list of devices attached to the hub and whether there are any available ports. The power required for each attached device will also be listed.

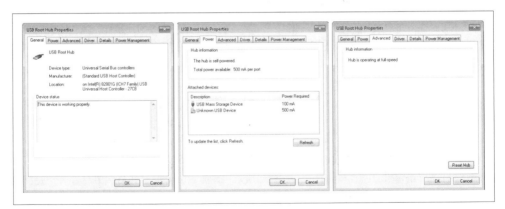

Figure 5-12. Checking properties for USB hubs

When you are working with the Power tab, note the power usage. A typical self-powered USB hub will have two ports with 500 mA available to each port. This amount of power allows you to connect a USB mouse, a USB keyboard, and most USB storage devices to your USB hubs. If the total power required is more than the hub can supply, you should connect one or more of the devices to a different USB hub.

Sometimes, you can inadvertently overload a hub, which will cause the connected devices to fail. If you suspect a problem with a hub, check the device status on General tab first. Next, review the Hub information on the Advanced tab to ensure that the hub is operating properly. If you suspect a problem with the hub, you can try to reset it by clicking Reset Hub.

Overloading the USB hub is usually a temporary condition that is remedied by resetting the hub or the computer. If you suspect a hub is no longer working, you may not need to worry. As most desktop computers have three to six (or more) USB hubs, you don't necessarily need to replace a failed USB hub (as most hubs are built into the motherboard, replacing the hub usually involves disabling it in the BIOS and installing a PCI-to-USB adapter card). Simply connecting the devices to USB ports that route through a different USB hub will solve the problem.

Most self-powered USB hubs have a power management feature that allows the operating system to turn them off to save power. You can configure related settings on the Power Management tab.

Each USB controller has a fixed amount of bandwidth that all attached devices must share. You can check the bandwidth being used by devices in the Properties dialog box for the USB controller. Click the Advanced tab as shown in Figure 5-13. When you connect multiple mass storage devices to ports attached to the same USB controller, you can sometimes saturate a USB controller. For example, my computer's main USB controller has ports for up to eight USB devices. Connecting multiple USB mass storage devices to this one USB controller wouldn't necessarily be a good idea, especially if I wanted to use the devices all at the same time.

By default, when you insert in a USB 2.0 device into a USB 1.0 or USB 1.1 port, your computer will tell you that the device could perform faster. If your computer has a mix of USB 1.0/1.1 and USB 2.0 ports, this message can help you find the faster USB 2.0 ports for your USB 2.0 devices. However, if you'd rather not see the related messages, you can turn the message off by clearing the "Tell me if my device can perform faster" checkbox on the Advanced tab of the corresponding controller's properties.

Viewing and Managing Device Information

Each hardware device installed in or connected to your computer has a driver file associated with it. You view and manage devices using Device Manager. If you right-click a device entry, you'll have device management options similar to the following:

Properties
    Displays the Properties dialog box for the device

Uninstall

Uninstalls the device and its drivers

Disable

Disables the device but doesn't uninstall it

Enable

Enables a device if it's disabled

Update Driver Software

Starts the Hardware Update Wizard, which you can use to update the device's driver

Scan for Hardware Changes

Checks the hardware configuration and determines whether there are any changes

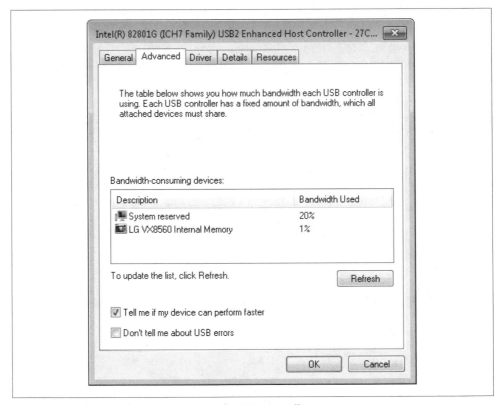

Figure 5-13. Checking the power usage on the USB controller

Using a device's properties information, you can view the location of its driver file and related details. Right-click the device you want to work with and then select Properties. In the Properties dialog box, click the Driver tab and then click Driver Details to display the Driver File Details dialog box.

Figure 5-14. Viewing the driver file details

As Figure 5-14 shows, the Driver File Details dialog box provides the following information:

Driver files
 Lists the full file path to all driver files used by the device.

Provider
 Lists the manufacturer of the driver.

File version
 Lists the version of the driver files.

Digital signer
 Lists whether and by whom the driver is signed. Drivers signed by Microsoft Windows are standard system drivers.

Customizing Your Computer's Input Devices, Regional Settings, and Date/Time

Of all the devices connected to your computer, the ones you use the most are the computer's keyboard and mouse. If you're like me, you may also use your computer audio devices about as often. Because you spend so much time working with these

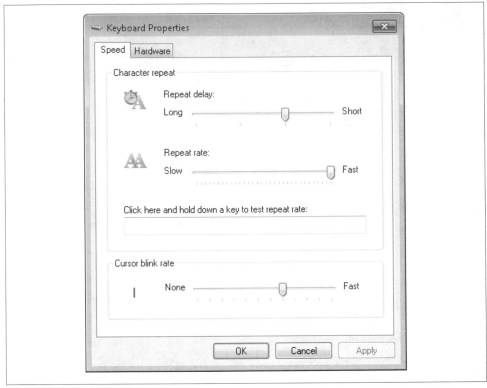

Figure 5-15. Configuring the keyboard settings

devices, you may want to customize their settings for the way you work, and this section will show you how.

Optimizing Your Keyboard Settings

Day in and day out, you probably tap away at your keyboard without giving much thought to the way it works. To get the most out of your computer, however, you really should take a few minutes to optimize your keyboard settings.

Configuring your computer's keyboard

You can view and configure your computer's keyboard settings by completing the following steps:

1. In the Control Panel, click Small Icons or Large Icons in the View By list and then click Keyboard. This displays the Keyboard Properties dialog box shown in Figure 5-15. (If you want to switch the Control Panel back to its default appearance, choose Category from the View by list.)

2. Use the "Repeat delay" slider to configure the delay for repeating characters when you hold down a key. There are four repeat delay intervals, with Long providing the longest repeat delay and Short providing the briefest repeat delay. If you are a novice typist or a person with a physical disability, you might want to set the repeat delay to Long to reduce the likelihood of accidentally repeating keys. If you work in data entry and frequently fill rows with the same character by pressing and holding a key, you may want to set the repeat delay to Short.

3. Use the "Repeat rate" slider to configure how quickly characters repeat when you hold down a key. The default repeat rate is Fast. If you have a problem with sticky keys or want to reduce the likelihood of excessively repeated characters, you can set a slower rate by moving the "Repeat rate" slider to the left.

4. Click in the field provided to test the repeat delay and repeat rate you've selected.

5. Use the "Cursor blink rate" slider to configure the rate at which the cursor blinks. If you find the blinking cursor annoying, set the cursor blink rate to None. If you sometimes have trouble finding the cursor, you may want to set the blink rate a little faster than normal to help you see it.

Configuring the device driver for your keyboard

All keyboards have device drivers that you can manage. To view or work with your keyboard's drivers, complete the following steps:

1. In the Control Panel, click Small Icons or Large Icons in the View By list and then click Keyboard.

2. On the Hardware tab, click Properties.

3. In the Keyboard Properties dialog box, click the Driver tab.

4. Using the buttons provided, you can view driver details, update drivers, roll back drivers, and uninstall drivers as necessary.

Configuring your programmable keyboard

If your computer has a programmable keyboard, such as the IntelliType keyboard from Microsoft, you'll find several additional tabs in the Keyboard Properties dialog box, including Key Settings and Zooming. You can use the options on these tabs to update the type of keyboard, reassign keys, and control zoom settings. You may need to install driver software from the keyboard manufacturer before you see this.

Updating the keyboard type. To update the type of IntelliType keyboard, complete the following steps:

1. In the Control Panel, click Small Icons or Large Icons in the View By list and then click Keyboard.

2. On the Key Settings tab, you'll see the model name of the keyboard as currently assigned in bold. Move the mouse pointer over the Update... entry to the right of the model name to display a clickable Update button.

3. When you click the Update button, the Update Keyboard dialog box is displayed.

4. Flip your keyboard over and read the keyboard model, such as Microsoft Natural Ergonomic Keyboard 800.

5. In the Keyboard Model list, select your keyboard model and then click OK twice.

Reassigning keys. To reassign keys on an IntelliType keyboard, complete the following steps:

1. In the Control Panel, click Small Icons or Large Icons in the View By list and then click Keyboard.

2. On the Key Settings tab, the current key assignments are listed by name and action, such as Starts America Online or Not Assigned. Click the key name you want to reassign and then click Edit.

3. You'll see one of several Reassign A Key dialog boxes. The simplest lets you choose a program to run. For primary programmable keys, such as Mail, you'll have several options:

    Start a program
        Choose this option and then use the selection list provided to choose a related program to start. For example, with Mail you might see options for America Online, Outlook, Windows Mail, and Hotmail.

    Choose from a list of commands
        Choose this option and then click Next. Select the command to perform, such as Copy (Ctrl-C), and then click Finish.

    Start a program, Web page, or file
        Choose this option and then click Next. Click Browse to select a program or file to open and then click OK. Or type a browser path to open a web page. Click Finish.

    Disable the user of this key
        Choose this option and then click Finish to disable the key.

4. Click OK.

Configuring the zoom key. To configure zooming on an IntelliType keyboard, complete the following steps:

1. In the Control Panel, click Small Icons or Large Icons in the View By list and then click Keyboard.

2. On the Zooming tab, use the Zooming slider to select a zooming speed.

3. To disable zooming, clear Enable Zooming. Otherwise, select this option to enable magnification using the zoom key.

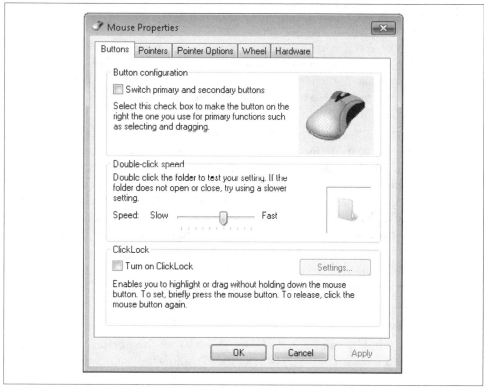

Figure 5-16. Configuring the mouse settings

4. To disable accelerated zooming, clear Enable Accelerated Zooming. Otherwise, select this option to enable faster zooming by pressing and holding the zoom key.

5. Click OK.

Optimizing Your Mouse Settings

You use the mouse pointer, trackball, or other input device every time you work with your computer, but have you taken the time to optimize the way it works? Probably not, because the mouse, like the keyboard, is another hardware component we tend to take for granted. Let's fix this by taking a few minutes to optimize your mouse.

Configuring your computer's mouse settings

You can optimize your computer's mouse settings by completing the following steps:

1. In the Control Panel, click Hardware and Sound and then click Mouse. This displays the Mouse Properties dialog box shown in Figure 5-16.

2. On the Buttons tab:

- If your mouse is on the left side of your keyboard rather than the right side, you're probably left-handed and may want to switch the primary and secondary mouse buttons by selecting "Switch primary and secondary buttons." With the buttons switched, the right button is for clicking and the left button displays the shortcut menu. As a result, wherever you are instructed to right-click something, you would actually need to left-click it.

- Use the "double-click speed" slider to adjust the way your computer recognizes a double-click. If you move the slider to the left, you increase the likelihood of your computer recognizing a double-click whether you double-click fast or slow. If you move the slider to the right, you decrease the likelihood that your computer will recognize double-clicks with longer pauses between clicks. Double-click the folder provided to test your settings. If the test folder doesn't open and close as expected, change the settings until you get the desired effect.

- Select "Turn on ClickLock" to select or drag without having to hold down the mouse button. With ClickLock on, briefly press the mouse button to set the lock, move the mouse without holding the button to drag, and then release the click lock by clicking the mouse button again.

3. Click the Pointer Options tab:

- On this tab, you can use the Motion slider to set the pointer speed. In most cases, you'll want a relatively fast pointer. To allow the pointer to zip across the screen, move the slider all the way to the right. To ensure that the pointer doesn't appear bouncy by increasing pointer precision, select "Enhance pointer precision." Enhancing pointer precision also lets you easily make small, precise pointer movements even when the pointer speed is set all the way to Fast.

- Select "Automatically move pointer to the default button…" to have the pointer automatically move to the default button in a dialog box.

- Select the "Display pointer trails" checkbox if you sometimes have trouble seeing the pointer, and then use the slider to adjust the length of the pointer trail. If you have trouble seeing the pointer sometimes and don't like pointer trails, select "Show location of pointer when I press the Ctrl key instead."

- Select "Hide pointer while typing" to hide the pointer (and get rid of an annoying distraction) while typing.

4. Click the Wheel tab:

- By default, most computers scroll three lines at a time when you move the mouse wheel one notch. You can use the "Vertical scrolling" options to set the number of lines to scroll, or select "One screen at a time" to configure the mouse wheel so that one notch scrolls a screen at a time.

- If you have a mouse wheel with a tilt feature, you can use this to scroll left and right a specified number of characters at a time. By default, the mouse horizontally scrolls three characters at a time. Enter a different Horizontal Scroll in the combo box provided, if desired.

5. Click OK to apply your settings.

Configuring the device driver for your mouse

All input devices, including mouse and trackball devices, have associated device drivers that you can manage. To view or work with your input device's driver, complete the following steps:

1. In the Control Panel, click Hardware and Sound and then click Mouse.
2. On the Hardware tab, click Properties.
3. In the Mouse Properties dialog box, click the Driver tab.
4. Using the buttons provided, you can view driver details, update drivers, roll back drivers, and uninstall drivers as necessary.

Optimizing Your Audio Settings

Most computers these days have sound cards as well as built-in, attached, or separately connected speakers. Your computer may also have an audio input device such as a microphone. Windows 7 handles sound a bit differently than its predecessors. In Windows 7, you can configure the computer's main volume and the volume for running applications separately. By default, the volume level for running applications is set relative to the main volume. Because of this, if you increase or decrease the main volume, the volume of running applications is increased or decreased as well relative to its initial value.

Controlling your computer's master volume and application volume

You can control the master volume and application volume for your computer using the following steps:

1. Click the Volume icon in the System Tray to display the Volume control.
2. With the Volume control displayed, you can adjust the main volume as necessary and the volume of running applications will be adjusted as well.
3. To adjust the volume for running applications, click Mixer and then use the Applications sliders to adjust the volume of running applications that have programmable audio input levels.

 The main volume must always be at least as high as the application volume. If you increase the volume of an application past the main volume level, you will increase the main volume as well.

Setting audio playback levels

For more advanced control of audio devices, you can use the Sound utility. In the Sound utility, playback and recording levels for sound are controlled separately. You can set the output levels for audio playback by completing the following steps:

1. In the Control Panel, click Hardware and Sound and then click Sound.

2. On the Playback tab, double-click the audio playback device you want to configure. This displays a Properties dialog box.

3. On the Levels tab, you can work with the main controls as follows:

   - Use the slider to set the desired playback volume.

   - To mute the device, click the sound button to the right of the slider. To unmute the device, click the sound button again.

   - To adjust the speaker balance, click the Balance button, drag the L and R sliders as appropriate to set the desired balance between the computer's left and right speakers, and then click OK.

4. Click OK to save the settings.

Setting up your speakers

To set up your speakers, complete the following steps:

1. In the Control Panel, click Hardware and Sound and then click Sound.

2. On the Playback tab, select the audio playback device you want to configure and then click Configure. This displays the Speaker Setup Wizard.

3. On the Choose Your Configuration page, use the "Audio channels" list to select the speaker setup that is most like your computer's configuration. You can use the options available as follows:

   Stereo
   >Select this option if your computer has one left speaker and one right speaker.

   Quadraphonic
   >Select this option if your computer has two pairs of speakers: front-left, front-right, rear-left, and rear-right.

   5.1 Surround
   >Select this option if your computer has surround sound with front-left, front-right, rear-left, rear-right, and center speakers.

   7.1 Surround
   >Select this option if your computer has surround sound with front-left, front-right, rear-left, rear-right, center, surround left, surround right and subwoofer speakers.

4. Test the configuration by clicking the Test button. Click any individual speaker depicted to test its playback. Click Next when you are ready to continue.

5. If you previously selected 5.1 Surround or 7.1 Surround, you'll see the Customize Your Configuration page next. As necessary, disable the center, subwoofer, rear speaker pair, or any combination thereof by clearing the related checkboxes. Click any speaker to test it. Click Next to continue.

6. On the Select Full-Range Speakers page, you can fine-tune the configuration. Select Front Left and Right to get more dynamic range out of your speakers (if this is supported). If you have speakers with limited dynamic range, clear the Front Left and Right, the Surround Speakers, or both checkboxes to reduce the dynamic range of the selected speakers.

7. Click Next and then click Finish.

Setting playback quality

To configure playback quality settings for your speakers, complete the following steps:

1. In the Control Panel, click Hardware and Sound and then click Sound.

2. On the Playback tab, double-click the audio playback device you want to configure. This displays a Properties dialog box.

3. On the Advanced tab, use the Default Format selection list to set the sample rate and bit depth to use. In most cases, the default setting is 16-bit, 44,100 Hz CD Quality sound, or 24-bit 48,000 Hz Studio Quality sound.

Setting audio recording levels

To set the input levels for audio recording, follow these steps:

1. In the Control Panel, click Hardware and Sound and then Sound.

2. On the Recording tab, double-click the audio recording device you want to configure. This displays a Properties dialog box.

3. On the Levels tab, use the slider provided to set the recording volume as appropriate. If a Balance button is provided, click the Balance button, drag the L and R sliders as appropriate to set the desired balance, and then click OK.

4. Some microphones have a MIC Boost option that is used to boost the microphone's input volume. On the Custom tab, select MIC Boost to boost the microphone volume.

5. Click OK to save your settings.

Setting audio recording quality

To configure the default recording quality, complete the following steps:

1. In the Control Panel, click Hardware and Sound and then click Sound.

2. On the Recording tab, double-click the audio recording device you want to configure. This displays a Properties dialog box.

3. On the Advanced tab, use the Default Format selection list to set the sample rate and bit depth to use. In most cases, the default setting is 2-channel, 16-bit, 44,100 Hz CD Quality sound or 24-bit 48,000 Hz Studio Quality sound.

4. Click OK to save your settings.

Optimizing Your Computer's Regional and Language Settings

In a global-connected world, you may often find yourself working in another country or working with a computer from another country. If this is the case, you may want to adjust the computer's regional settings, language settings, or both.

Regional settings control the default units of measurement, currency, and date formatting. By specifying that you are in a particular region of the world, you choose all the appropriate settings for that region. To configure regional settings, complete the following steps:

1. In the Control Panel, click Clock, Language, and Region and then click Region and Language.

2. On the Formats tab, use the "Format" list to select a country or region, as shown in Figure 5-17. The Examples area should now display the formatting standards for the selected region.

3. To customize these settings, use the Date and time formats to modify the time, and date settings for the region. If you want to modify currency and number settings, click Additional Settings. When you are finished, click OK to close the Customize Format dialog box.

4. Some software and services provide you with local information, such as news and weather. On the Location tab, you can use the selection list provided to set either the current location or the location for which you want to get local news and weather information.

5. On the Keyboards and Languages tab, click "Change keyboards." In the "Text services and input languages" dialog box, use the "Default input language" selection list to set the default input language to use with the keyboard.

6. If the computer has multiple input languages, a language bar is docked to the taskbar by default so that you can choose the input language. You can use the options on the Language Bar tab to control whether and how the language bar is displayed.

7. If the computer has multiple input languages, you can shift among input languages by pressing Left-Alt-Shift by default. On the Advanced Key Settings tab, you can set hot keys for switching among input languages and hot keys to switch to a specific input language as well. Under "Hot keys for input languages," select the desired Action, such as "To English (United States) – US," and then click Change Key Sequence. In the Change Key Sequence dialog box, select the Enable Key

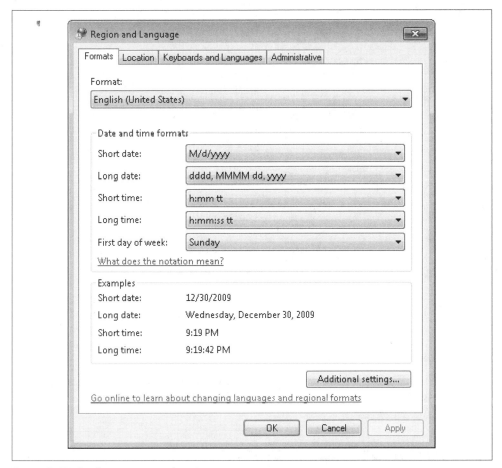

Figure 5-17. Configuring regional settings

Sequence checkbox, select the desired key sequence, such as Ctrl-0, and then click OK.

8. Click OK to save these settings.

You can easily change the display and input languages for Windows 7. Some languages are included with your versions of Windows 7. Other languages you need to purchase and install. To configure support for additional display and input languages, complete the following steps:

1. In the Control Panel, click Clock, Language, and Region and then click Region and Language.

2. On the Keyboards and Languages tab, click "Install/uninstall languages."

3. Click "Install display languages."

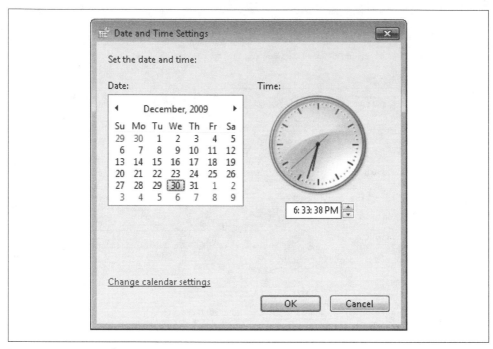

Figure 5-18. Setting the system time

4. To download and install languages using Windows Update, click Launch Windows Update. Otherwise, click Browse to locate the folder that contains the language files.

Optimizing Your Computer's Date and Time Settings

Your computer should always be set to the current date and time. If it isn't, you may have problems with misfiled documents or correspondence. Incorrect time settings could also cause you to miss appointments or meetings. When your computer is a member of a homegroup or domain, the computer's clock needs to be in sync in order to work properly.

Setting your computer's date and time

You can manually set your computer's date and time by completing the following steps:

1. On the desktop taskbar, click the clock in the System Tray and then click "Change date and time settings." This displays the Date and Time Settings dialog box.

2. To change the date and time, click "Change date and time." Use the options shown in Figure 5-18 to set the system date and time as appropriate, and then click OK.

3. To change the time zone, click Change Time Zone. Use the options shown in Figure 5-19 to set the time zone for the computer. Some time zones within the

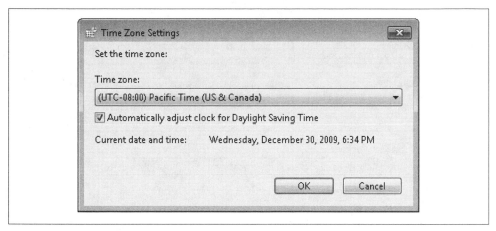

Figure 5-19. Configuring Daylight Saving Time

United States and abroad use Daylight Saving Time. If you select a time zone where this is applicable, you'll be able to select the "Automatically adjust clock for Daylight Saving Time" checkbox. Use Daylight Saving Time or clear this checkbox so that Daylight Saving Time is not used.

4. When you configure your computer to use Daylight Saving Time, the Date and Time dialog box tells you the date and time when Daylight Saving Time starts and ends, as well as how the clock will be adjusted. If you want to be reminded when the clock is changed, select the "Notify me when the clock changes" checkbox.

5. Click OK to save your settings.

Displaying time in additional time zones

You can configure your computer to display time in up to three time zones by completing the following steps:

1. On the desktop taskbar, click the clock in the System Tray and then click "Change date and time settings." This displays the Date and Time Settings dialog box.

2. Click the Additional Clocks tab, shown in Figure 5-20.

3. To configure a second clock, select the first "Show this clock" checkbox. Use the related selection list to choose the desired time zone and then type a display name for this time zone, such as `West Coast Time`.

4. To configure a third clock, select the second "Show this clock" checkbox. Use the related selection list to choose the desired time zone and then type a display name for this time zone, such as `Paris Time`.

5. Click OK to save your settings.

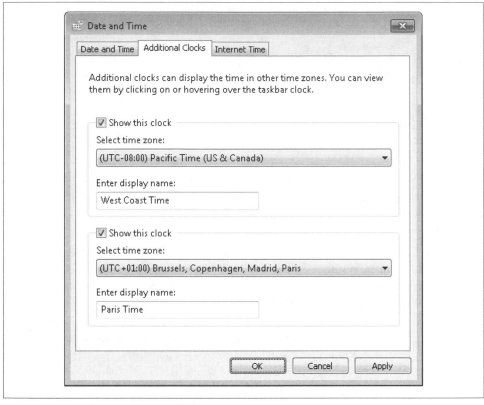

Figure 5-20. Displaying additional clocks

Once you've configured additional clocks, moving the pointer over the clock icon in the System Tray displays the time in each configured location. The computer's default system time is listed as Local Time.

Keeping your computer's clock synchronized

To keep system time in close synchronization with world time, you'll want to use Internet time. If your computer connects to a domain, Internet time is probably configured automatically by your organization's administrators.

On a personal or small office computer not connected to a domain, you can enable or disable Internet time by completing the following steps:

1. On the desktop taskbar, click the clock in the System Tray and then click "Change date and time settings." This displays the Date and Time Settings dialog box.
2. Select the Internet Time tab and then click "Change settings." This displays the Internet Time Settings dialog box, as shown in Figure 5-21.

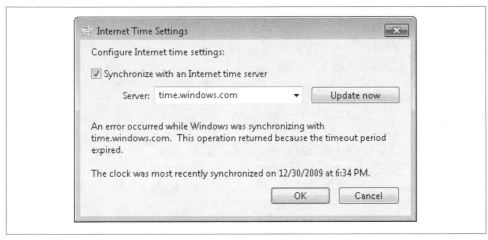

Figure 5-21. Configuring Internet time

3. To enable Internet time, select "Synchronize with an Internet time server" and then select the time server you want to use. Several default time servers are listed, including *time.windows.com* and *time.nist.gov*. You can select one of these or type in the fully qualified domain name of another time server to use.

4. To disable Internet time, clear the "Synchronize with an Internet time server" checkbox.

5. If an error message is shown, you can try to update and synchronize the computer time by clicking "Update now." While this technique can be used to correct minor deviations of time, it won't correct large deviations of time. Therefore, you may need to manually set the correct date before you can synchronize the time.

6. Click OK to save your settings.

Installing and Managing Hardware

When it comes to installing and managing hardware, Windows 7 is in many ways much smarter than Windows XP and earlier releases of Windows. As discussed previously, this is partly because the setup programs for hardware devices have gotten better and partly because Windows 7 itself has improved. A key new feature in Windows 7 that makes hardware installation and management easier is hardware diagnostics. Hardware diagnostics is a part of the top-to-bottom diagnostics framework discussed in Chapter 21.

Getting Available but Unconfigured Hardware to Work

Thanks to hardware diagnostics, Windows 7 automatically detects and tries to help you resolve issues with hardware components. If you installed Windows 7 on your

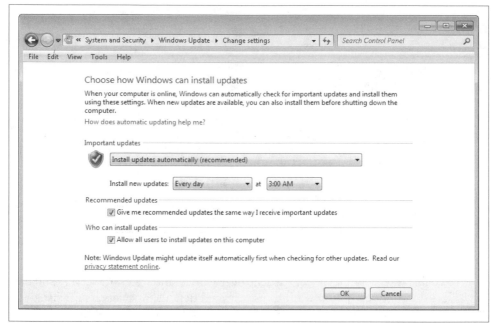

Figure 5-22. Configuring Windows update

computer, you may have found that certain hardware devices weren't automatically configured during installation. In many cases, hardware diagnostics will detect available but not configured hardware and then use the automatic update framework to retrieve required drivers the next time Windows Update runs.

The update process is subject to several caveats. You must enable Windows Update and configure it to allow retrieval of drivers and driver updates by completing the following steps:

1. In the Control Panel, click System and Security and then click Windows Update.

2. In Windows Update, click the "Change settings" link.

3. On the Important Updates list, select "Install updates automatically" as shown in Figure 5-22.

4. Under "Install new updates" select an install interval and time. If your computer is turned off at the designated install time, Windows will install the updates next time you turn on the computer.

5. To ensure you receive important updates, select "Give me recommended updates...."

6. To ensure anyone can install updates, select "Allow all users to install updates...."

7. Click OK.

When drivers become available, you must install them. Windows Update does not install drivers or driver updates automatically. To install downloaded drivers and driver updates, follow these steps:

1. In the Control Panel, click System and Security and then click Windows Update.
2. In Windows Update, click Check for Updates in the left pane and then click "View available updates."
3. If optional updates are available, click the link provided.
4. On the Select updates to install page, review the available updates, select the checkbox for updates you want to install and then click OK.
5. When you click OK, Windows 7 will create a restore point prior to installing device drivers, as long as System Restore is enabled. If necessary, you can use this restore point to recover the system, as discussed in Chapter 21.

Once you've installed the driver for a device, Windows 7 should both detect the hardware and install the device automatically. If Windows 7 detects the device but isn't able to install the device automatically, you may find a related solution in Action Center. Typically, Action Center will open automatically. This allows you to begin troubleshooting immediately.

In Figure 5-23, Windows has found updates for several device drivers that should resolve problems with the related hardware. In Action Center, expand the Maintenance panel to see available solutions for the detected problems. To view the solution for a problem, click View Message Details. Review the solution. Typically a link to download a required driver or other fix will be provided, as shown in Figure 5-24. You'll find that Action Center will help you resolve most post-installation problems with hardware devices.

Installing New Hardware Devices

Plug and Play is a technology that makes it possible for the operating system to detect the device type and automatically install a device using device drivers available on the computer or by prompting for required drivers. Most newer hardware devices are Plug and Play–compatible. This makes it much easier to install new hardware devices. With compatible internal devices, you typically will need to:

1. Run the device's setup program.
2. Shut down and unplug the computer.
3. Insert the device into the appropriate slot or connect it to the computer.
4. Restart the computer.
5. Let Windows 7 automatically detect and install the device.

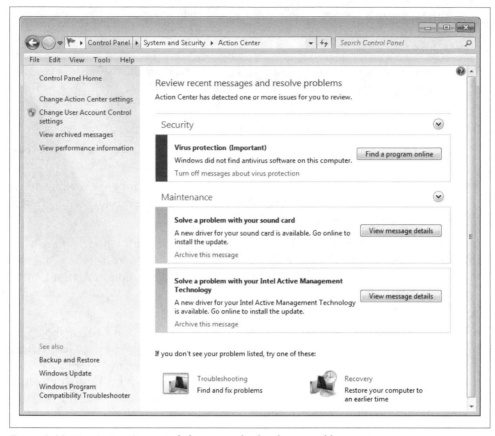

Figure 5-23. Use Action Center to help you resolve hardware problems

With compatible external USB, FireWire, or eSATA devices, you will typically need to:

1. Run the device's setup program.
2. Insert the device into the appropriate slot or connect it to the computer.
3. Let Windows 7 automatically detect and install the device.

However, not all devices have or need setup programs. For example, with USB flash devices, all you need to do is insert the device into the appropriate slot. Depending on the device, Windows 7 should automatically detect the new device, as shown in Figure 5-25, and then automatically install a built-in driver to support it. As shown in Figure 5-26, the Drive Software Installation component handles the installation task. The device should then run immediately without any problems.

The success of an automatic detection and installation depends on the device being Plug and Play–compatible and a device driver being available. Windows 7 includes many device drivers in a standard installation, and should be able to install any of these devices automatically. If driver updating is allowed through Windows Update,

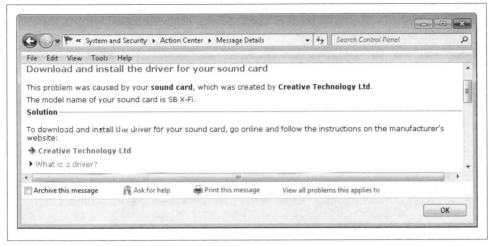

Figure 5-24. *Review the solution and follow the links provided to resolve the hardware problem*

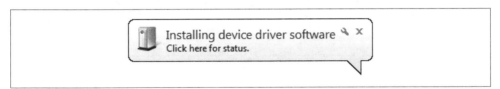

Figure 5-25. *Windows detects the device*

Windows 7 checks for drivers automatically using Windows Update either when you connect a new device or when it first detects the device. To control whether Windows 7 checks for drivers automatically using Windows Update, use the Device Installation Settings option on the System Properties Hardware tab (see "How Does the Operating System Obtain Driver Updates?" on page 149).

In some cases, Windows 7 might detect the new device but the Driver Software Installation component may run into problems installing the device. If this happens, you'll see errors similar to those shown in Figure 5-27. In this case, you should be redirected immediately to the Action Center. If there is a possible solution available, Windows 7 will display the solution as discussed previously.

If Windows 7 doesn't detect the device when you insert it, check the manufacturer's website for compatible installation software. Once you have installation software for the device, run it and then follow the prompts. The device should then be installed properly.

If Windows cannot install a device, there might be a problem with the device itself or a conflict with existing hardware. For additional details on troubleshooting, see the section "Troubleshooting Hardware" on page 187 in this chapter.

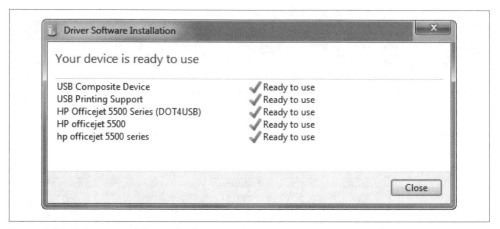

Figure 5-26. Driver software installation succeeds

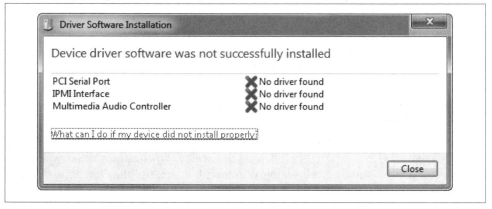

Figure 5-27. Driver software installation fails

Installing and Maintaining Device Drivers

Device drivers are the low-level workhorses of the operating system. They are responsible for making the appropriate calls to the HAL. Any inappropriate calls made by device drivers can cause systemwide problems that are difficult to trace back to the device drivers themselves. This can occur because when a device driver makes bad calls, these bad calls often cause other problems, such as service failures or improper read/write operations, which in turn can lead to fatal stop errors or data corruption.

Because device drivers are so important to proper system operation, it is crucial to periodically check for updates to your computer's drivers and apply driver updates as appropriate. Although Windows Update provides a way to check for updates to drivers included with the operating system, you can't rely exclusively on Windows Update. As discussed previously, you need to check the available updates periodically to see if there

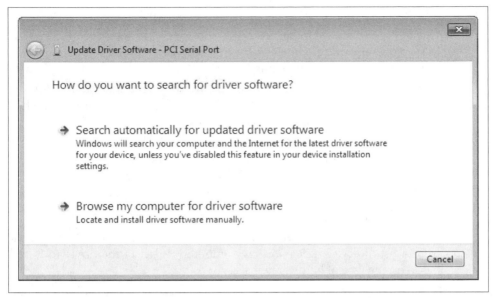

Figure 5-28. Updating the driver software

are optional updates for drivers that you may want to install. For other driver updates, you'll need to check the support pages at the website for your computer's manufacturer.

As driver updates become available, you'll need to determine whether you want to install the updates. If you've been having problems with a device or other system problems, you should probably install the driver updates. Keep in mind that in some cases, you may need to restart your computer to finalize the driver update. If you experience problems after installing or updating a driver, you roll back the driver to its previous version, as discussed in the next section, "Rolling Back Device Drivers" on page 184.

You can install and update device drivers using Device Manager. In the Control Panel, click System and Security and then click the Device Manager link under the System heading. In Device Manager, right-click the device you want to manage and then select Update Driver. This starts the Update Driver Software Wizard, as shown in Figure 5-28.

You can now search for the driver using one of the following techniques:

- Perform automatic search of Windows Update website and your computer:
  a. Click "Search automatically for updated driver software" to have Windows 7 search your computer and the Internet for the latest driver for the device.
  b. If Windows 7 finds a more recent driver than the one currently installed, it will install the driver. If Windows 7 does not find a more recent version of the driver, it will keep the current driver.
  c. Click Close.

- Perform search of your computer in locations you specify:

  a. Click "Browse my computer for driver software" and then click the Browse button if you want Windows 7 to search only your computer or if you want to locate the device driver manually.

  b. Use the Browse for Folder dialog box to select the start folder for the search and then click OK. All subfolders of the selected folder are searched automatically.

  c. Windows 7 will search the location you've specified for the latest driver for the device, and install the driver if found. If it does not find a more recent version of the driver, Windows 7 will keep the current driver.

  d. Click Close.

- Choose the driver to install:

  a. Click "Browse my computer for driver software" and then click "Let me pick from a list of device drivers on my computer" to select the driver to install based on the type of hardware device.

  b. Select the appropriate hardware type, such as Imaging devices or Printers, and then click Next.

  c. Scroll through the list of manufacturers to find the manufacturer of the device, and then choose the appropriate device in the right pane.

  d. If the manufacturer or device you want to use isn't listed, insert your device driver disk into the floppy drive or CD-ROM drive, and then click the Have Disk button. Follow the prompts. Afterward, select the appropriate device.

  e. After selecting a device driver through a search or a manual selection, click Next to continue.

  f. If the wizard can't find an appropriate driver, you'll need to obtain one and then repeat this procedure.

  g. Click Close.

Rolling Back Device Drivers

Sometimes you may find that installing a device or a device driver has the unintended consequence of causing your computer to fail to start up. If this occurs, don't panic. You should be able to recover your computer using the Last Known Good Configuration or Safe Mode, as discussed in Chapter 21. You will then need to roll back the device driver or recover the computer to a previous restore point. If this doesn't resolve the problem, you can use the Repair Your Computer option on the Advanced Boot menu to access the System Recovery options. System Recovery is also discussed in Chapter 21.

You may want to roll back a device driver for other reasons as well, such as when you are experiencing problems with the device or the device isn't working as you expected after updating the device driver. To roll back a device driver, follow these steps:

1. In the Control Panel, click System and Security and then click the Device Manager link under the System heading.

2. In Device Manager, right-click the device you want to manage and then select Properties. This opens the Properties dialog box for the device.

3. Click the Driver tab and then click "Roll back driver." When prompted to confirm the action, click Yes.

4. Click Close to close the driver's Properties dialog box.

 Keep in mind that if the driver file hasn't been updated, a backup driver file won't be available. Because of this, the "Roll back driver" button will be disabled and you will not be able to click it.

Enabling, Disabling, Removing, and Uninstalling Hardware Devices

The USB, FireWire, and eSATA devices you'll work with the most are the ones with removable storage, such as USB flash devices, digital cameras, and external disk drives. You may also have portable devices that can be connected to your computer, such as a smartphone. These USB, FireWire, and eSATA devices are meant to be portable and easily connected and disconnected. To disconnect and remove a device with removable storage or a portable device, complete the following steps:

1. Close any Command Prompts, PowerShell windows, or Windows Explorer views that are accessing data on the device.

2. Close any open document, picture, or other media file saved on the device.

3. Click Start and then click Computer. This displays the Computer console, a special view of Windows Explorer.

4. Under Devices with Removable Storage and Portable Devices, you'll see a list of devices you've connected to your computer, as shown in Figure 5-29. Do one of the following:

   • To disconnect a device with removable storage, right-click the device and then select Eject. If Windows thinks the device is still in use (and you've closed views and files accessing the device), click Continue when prompted to force Windows to remove the device.

   • To disconnect a portable device, such as a smartphone, you should use the options of the device itself or the device software to disconnect. For example, with my smartphone, I need to press End or CLR on the phone to disconnect from the computer. If your device presents itself to your computer as a storage device (for example, some smartphones make their memory cards appear as USB drives to your computer), eject the device as described in the preceding step before disabling the connection on the device.

5. Remove the device or disconnect its cable.

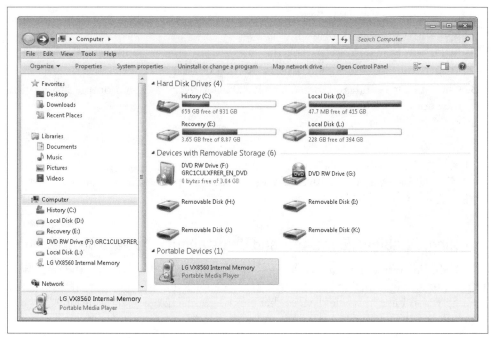

Figure 5-29. Viewing devices with removable and portable storage

You can reconnect the device later by plugging the device back in or connecting its cable to the appropriate port on your computer.

You can remove other devices that you no longer need as well. For printer devices connected via a serial or parallel port, you can simply disconnect the cable and then disable or remove the software printer associated with the hardware printer device, as discussed in Chapter 12.

For internal devices, you will need to shut down and unplug your computer, and then remove the device from the computer. When you restart the computer, Windows 7 should detect the configuration change and uninstall the drivers for the device.

In some cases, when you remove a device you'll need to tell Windows 7 this by uninstalling the device in the operating system. When you uninstall a device, Windows 7 removes the driver association for the device but doesn't prevent the device from being detected if it isn't physically removed.

If you want to prevent a device from being used but don't want to physically remove it, as may be the case for internal devices, you can disable the device. When you disable a device, Windows 7 prevents the device's drivers from loading and in this way blocks access to the device. Because a disabled device has no associated drivers, you can be sure that the disabled device isn't causing problems with your computer.

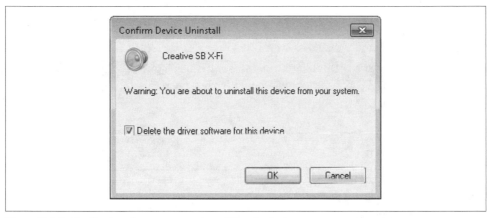

Figure 5-30. Confirming that you are uninstalling the device

You can uninstall a device through the operating system by completing the following steps:

1. In Device Manager, right-click the device you want to work with and then select Uninstall.

2. In the Confirm Device Uninstall dialog box, shown in Figure 5-30, select "Delete the driver software for this device" if you want to prevent Windows 7 from automatically reinstalling the device. This checkbox may not appear for all devices.

3. Click OK.

You can disable a device through the operating system by completing the following steps:

1. In Device Manager, right-click the device you want to work with and then select Disable.

2. When prompted to confirm the action, as shown in Figure 5-31, click Yes.

3. If you later want to enable a previously disabled device, you can do so by right-clicking the device in Device Manager and then selecting Enable.

Troubleshooting Hardware

Windows 7's comprehensive diagnostics framework can detect and diagnose automatically many common problems with hardware devices. When Windows diagnostics detects a problem, Windows 7 displays a Problem Reports and Solutions balloon telling you there is a problem. If you click this balloon, Windows 7 should open the Action Center, which can help you resolve the problem. While you are working with Action Center, you can use automated troubleshooting to help you resolve problems with your computer's hardware.

Figure 5-31. Confirming that you want to disable the device

To access Action Center and use automated troubleshooting, follow these steps:

1. In Control Panel, click System and Security and then click Action Center.

2. In Action Center, expand the Maintenance panel to see solutions to problem reports. If a solution for your problem isn't listed, scroll down and then click the Troubleshooting link.

3. Click the Hardware and Sound heading to access related troubleshooters.

4. Click a troubleshooter to have Windows diagnostics try to diagnose and resolve the problem automatically.

Although automated troubleshooting can resolve many types of problems, it won't resolve every problem. If you suspect that a device isn't working properly, you can check Device Manager to verify whether the device is working properly. For malfunctioning devices, you'll find an error status code and a suggested resolution for this error status code on the General tab of the device's Properties dialog box. In Device Manager, right-click the device you want to work with and then select Properties to view the error details.

You can resolve most hardware device problems by reinstalling the device driver. You can reinstall the driver for a device with a warning or error status by completing the following steps:

1. In the Control Panel, click System and Security and then click the Device Manager link under the System heading.

2. In Device Manager, right-click the device you want to work with and then select Properties.

3. On the Driver tab, click the Update Driver button.

4. Perform the driver reinstallation using one of the techniques discussed in "Installing and Maintaining Device Drivers" on page 182, earlier in this chapter.

You can also uninstall the drivers and let Windows 7 reinstall the current versions of the driver files from the driver store. To do this, right-click the device in Device Manager and then select Uninstall. In the Confirm Device Uninstall dialog box, click OK but do not select the "Delete the driver software for this device" checkbox. If reinstalling the device driver doesn't work, check to make sure the device is properly connected. You may need to disconnect and reconnect the device.

If you are still unable to get the device to work properly, visit the device manufacturer's website and check for alternative versions of the device driver. Sometimes an older version of a device driver is more stable than the latest version.

PART II

Mastering Your Data and Digital Media

CHAPTER 6

Exploring and Searching Your Computer

When it comes right down to it, regardless of what you use your computer for, its most important function is to make it possible for you to create and store documents, pictures, music, videos, and other files. Thanks to Windows 7's extensive interface enhancements, you have many options for working with your files and searching your computer. To get the most out of these features, you need to master Windows Explorer and Windows Search, which is exactly what this chapter is all about.

Exploring Your Documents

You might not have realized it before, but the Control Panel, My Computer, and My Network Places as used in Windows XP and earlier versions of Windows were simply different faces for Windows Explorer that allowed you to view and work with the features of your computer in different ways. Although these various faces for Windows Explorer weren't tightly integrated, Windows 7 corrects this, so that Windows Explorer behaves more like a console or browser shell—its many faces are now all well integrated, so that you always have similar functionality and features.

As you start working with Windows 7, you should know right away that Microsoft renamed My Computer and My Network Places as Computer and Network. One of the key reasons for this change was to simplify the naming and make them easier to reference.

As Figure 6-1 shows, Windows Explorer has:

- An Address bar for quickly navigating disks and folders
- A Search box for fast searches
- A menu bar for performing common tasks
- Options for organizing, sharing, and previewing folders and files

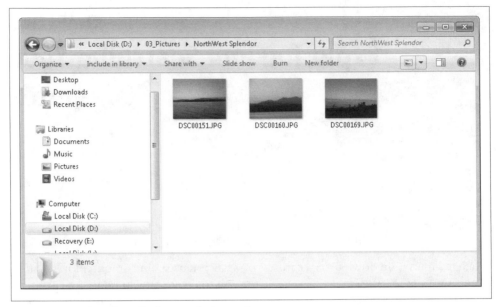

Figure 6-1. Use Windows Explorer to find your documents

As also shown in Figure 6-1, Windows Explorer organizes information according to a specific layout setting that includes several standard view panes, including a Navigation pane for making quick selections and a Results pane for viewing the folders and files stored in a selected location. Unlike summary details provided in Windows XP and earlier releases of Windows, the current version of Windows Explorer provides visual summaries of the types of content in your folders when you are working with certain views. A folder containing pictures will show a thumbnail graphic for some of those pictures stacked within the folder graphic. A folder containing documents will show a preview of those documents within the folder graphic.

When you select an item, you'll see details about that item in the Details pane. The details listed depend on the type of item.

For disk drives, you'll see a visual summary of space used. You'll also see drive designator, disk type, filesystem type, free space, and total size (Figure 6-2).

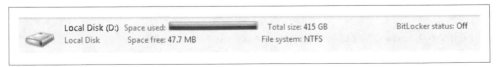

Figure 6-2. Summary for a disk drive

For devices with removable storage, you'll see similar information (Figure 6-3).

Figure 6-3. Summary for a removable storage device

For shortcuts, you'll see the folder name, creation date, last modified date, and size. If the shortcut is within a shared folder, you'll see details regarding how the related folder is shared (Figure 6-4).

Figure 6-4. Summary for a shortcut

For folders, you'll see the folder name and last modified date. If the folder is shared, you'll see details regarding how the folder is shared (Figure 6-5).

Figure 6-5. Summary for a folder

For pictures, you'll see filename, file type, the date the picture was taken, the picture's width and height dimensions, and file size. You'll also see tags and ratings associated with the picture (Figure 6-6).

Figure 6-6. Summary for a picture

For music and audio books in Windows Media Player–supported formats, you'll see album cover, filename, file type, and size. You'll also see the artists' names, album name, genre, play time (length), and rating (Figure 6-7).

Figure 6-7. Summary for an audio file

For movies and videos in Windows Media Player–supported formats, you'll see a preview of the first frame, filename, date modified, date created, and size (Figure 6-8).

Figure 6-8. Summary for a video file

Navigating Your Computer with the Address Bar

The ubiquitous Address bar appears at the top of Windows Explorer and all its related views. Because you see the Address bar so much, you may take it for granted and not get the most out of its new features. Let's fix that by taking a closer look at what the Address bar offers.

Accessing Locations on Your Computer

The Address bar displays your current location as a series of links separated by arrows. This allows you to determine the current location on your computer, or on your network. File and folder locations aren't the only types of locations you can navigate using these features. You can also navigate Control Panel categories and network devices.

In the example shown in Figure 6-9, the location is:

```
Computer→Local Disk (C:)→Users→williams
```

Figure 6-9. The address path, which lists the current location

This tells you that the absolute path followed to get to the current location is *C:\Users \williams*.

In some cases, you might also see a relative or abbreviated path, such as when you follow a shortcut or browse to a path that cannot be fully depicted on the Address bar. As shown in Figure 6-10, a relative or abbreviated path is indicated by the left-pointing double-angle character (<<). In this example, the location is:

```
« mypictures→Summer Vacation→Islands of Adventure
```

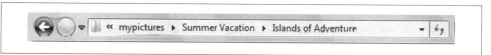

Figure 6-10. The address path providing a relative location

This tells you that the relative or abbreviated path of the current location is *mypictures \Summer Vacation\Islands of Adventure*.

When you are working with network paths in the Network view of Windows Explorer, as shown in Figure 6-11, you'll have quick access to network locations and shared resources on remote servers. Click the Network entry in the path to display a list of remote computers and network resources. Click the name of a remote computer or network resource to list its shared resources.

Figure 6-11. Working with network resources

Here are the features of the Address bar, from left to right:

Forward/Back buttons
> The Forward and Back buttons allow you to navigate locations you've already visited. Similar to when you are browsing the Web, the locations you've visited are stored in a location history, and you can browse the location history by clicking the Forward and Back buttons.

Recent Pages button
> The Recent Pages button provides a drop-down list of recently accessed locations. You can jump to a recently accessed location quickly by clicking the Recent Pages button and then clicking the desired location. Because the recently accessed locations are limited to the current session, only locations you've accessed since opening the current Windows Explorer window are listed.

Address Path button
> The Address Path button shows the absolute or relative path you are currently accessing and provides options for working with this path. As discussed next, the Address path includes a Location Indicator icon, a Path Selection list button, Location Path entries, and a Previous Locations button.

Refresh button

> The Refresh button refreshes the view. Clicking the Refresh button displays any updates to contents in the selected location.

Out of all these features, the one you'll work with the most is the Address path. The Address path has four key components, from left to right:

Location Indicator icon

> The Location Indicator icon depicts the type of resource you are currently accessing. You'll see different icons, including those for disk drives, folders, virtual folders, and so on. Clicking the Location Indicator icon shows the actual path or location, such as *C:\Users\Williams\Pictures*. To restore the original view, press Esc. You can double-click the icon to view the same drop-down list provided by the Previous Locations button.

Path Selection list button

> The Path Selection list button provides access to the available base locations. Selecting a base location allows you to quickly access a key Windows Explorer view, such as Control Panel, Computer, or Desktop.

Location Path entries

> The Location Path shows the absolute or relative path to the current location. You can access a folder anywhere along the path that's displayed by clicking the link for that folder. You can access a subfolder of any folder displayed by clicking the arrow to the right of the folder. This displays a list of all folders in the selected folder, and you can access one of these folders by clicking it.

Previous Locations button

> This provides a drop-down list of locations you've accessed, which can include file locations, network drive locations, and web addresses. Unlike the Recent Pages button, the locations listed can include locations opened in previous Windows Explorer sessions. You can jump to a recently accessed location quickly by clicking the Previous Locations button and then clicking the desired location.

Using Selected Paths to Quickly Navigate Your Computer

Base locations accessible via the Path Selection list button are important, because they allow you to access key locations on your computer with the click of a button. Clicking the Path Selection list button is the easiest way to access and navigate base locations. If you are participating in a homegroup, you'll be able to access computers in the homegroup by selecting the related option. Other base locations available include:

Current user (displayed as the user name)

> Selecting this base location accesses your personal folder in Windows Explorer (see Figure 6-12). Depending on your selection, the taskbar may be updated to include these additional options: Open, for opening a selected folder or file; Share with, for sharing a selected folder or file; Burn, for burning a selected folder or file to CD

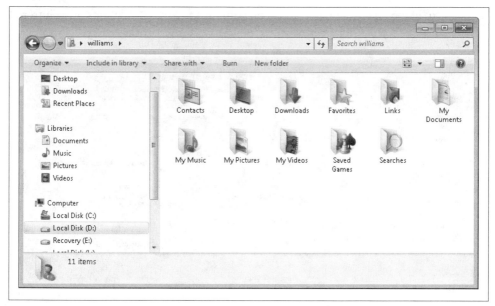

Figure 6-12. Accessing your documents, pictures, and other files

or DVD; and Include in library, for adding a selected folder or file to your library. When you select a file, you may also see Print, E-mail, Slide Show, and Preview options.

Computer

Selecting this base location accesses your computer's hard disk drives and devices with removable storage (see Figure 6-13). Depending on your selection, the taskbar may be updated to include these options: "System properties," for accessing the System console in the Control Panel; "Uninstall or change a program," for opening the Installed Programs console in the Control Panel; "Map network drive," for mapping a shared folder on a computer; and Properties, for accessing a selected item's Properties dialog box.

Control Panel

Selecting this base location accesses the Control Panel in Windows Explorer (see Figure 6-14). You can then work with Control Panel options using Category, Large Icons, or Small Icons view. The Control Panel doesn't have a menu bar, but it does have an Address bar and Search box. Using the Search box, you can quickly find Control Panel tools and task links.

Desktop

Selecting this base location accesses the desktop in Windows Explorer (see Figure 6-15). This allows you to view and work with all the shortcuts, files, and folders stored on the desktop. When you select files or folders, you'll have the same options as when you are working with your personal folder or any other folder. Use this view to help you clean up the clutter on your desktop or to find items on a cluttered desktop.

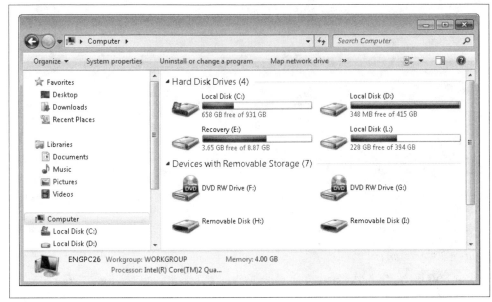

Figure 6-13. Accessing disk drives and devices with removable storage

Figure 6-14. Accessing the Control Panel

Figure 6-15. Accessing items stored on the desktop

Network

Selecting this base location accesses the base page for the computers and devices on your network (see Figure 6-16). Depending on your selection, the taskbar may be updated to include these additional options: Search Active Directory, for when you are at the office and want to find available resources; Network and Sharing Center, for configuring network sharing and printing options; "Add a printer," for adding a printer; and "Add a wireless device," for adding a wireless device.

Libraries

Selecting this base location accesses the base page for libraries on your computer (see Figure 6-17). A library is a combination of personal and public data grouped together and presented through a common view. Depending on your selection, the taskbar may be updated to include these additional options: Open, for opening the selected folder or file; Share with, for configuring sharing options for your computer; Burn, for burning a selected folder or file to CD or DVD; and New library, for creating a custom library.

Recycle Bin

Selecting this base location accesses the Recycle Bin in Windows Explorer (see Figure 6-18). Depending on your selection, the taskbar may be updated to include these options: "Empty the Recycle Bin," for permanently deleting all Recycle Bin items; "Restore all items," for restoring all Recycle Bin items to their original locations; and "Restore this item," for restoring a selected item to its original location.

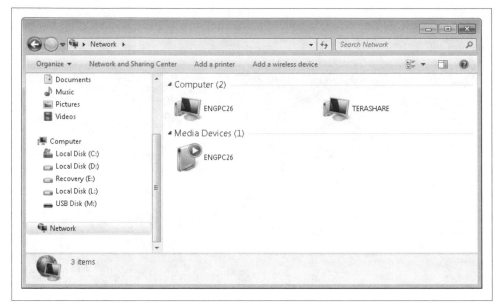

Figure 6-16. Accessing computers and devices on your network

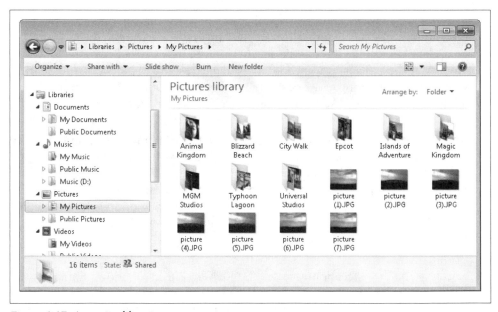

Figure 6-17. Accessing libraries on your computer

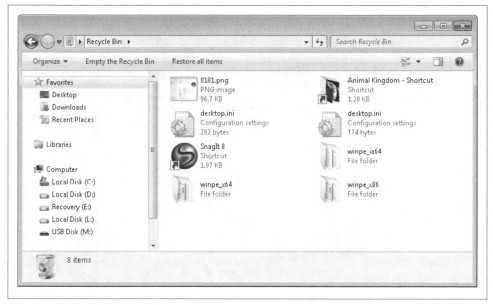

Figure 6-18. Accessing deleted items on your computer

Putting Windows Explorer to Work for You

Now that you know the essential for navigating your computer with Windows Explorer, let's look at how you can make Windows Explorer work for you. I'll start by discussing ways you can customize Windows Explorer and then I'll provide specific tips and techniques to optimize folder views.

Setting Folder Options

Day in and day out, you use Windows Explorer and its various views to navigate your computer's files and folders. Unfortunately, Explorer's default settings are configured for general use and not specifically for the way you work. Isn't it about time you customized Windows Explorer for the way you prefer to work? Not only will this save you time, but it will also make Windows Explorer easier to work with.

You control the way Windows Explorer works using the Folder Options dialog box. To access this dialog box, open Windows Explorer, click Organize, and then click "Folder and search options." As Figure 6-19 shows, most of the options you'll want to work with are on the View tab. Review Table 6-1 to see how each option works and then choose the settings that work best for you.

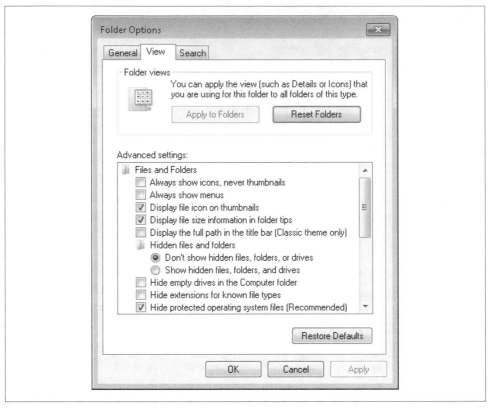

Figure 6-19. Configuring Windows Explorer using View tab options

Table 6-1. Configuration options for Windows Explorer

Setting	When selected	When not selected
Always show icons, never thumbnails	Windows Explorer shows large thumbnail images of the actual content for pictures and other types of files. When folders have many pictures, this option can slow down the display as Windows Explorer has to create the thumbnail representation of each image.	Windows Explorer does not create thumbnails. Instead, Windows Explorer shows the standard file and folder icons.
Always show menus	Windows Explorer always shows the menu bar, providing quick access to the menus. (You can also toggle this option by clicking Organize, pointing to Layout and then selecting Menu Bar.)	Windows Explorer hides the menu bar and you must elect to display it by pressing the Alt key.
Display file icon on thumbnails	Windows Explorer adds file icons to thumbnails it displays.	Windows Explorer displays thumbnails without file icons.

Setting	When selected	When not selected
Display file size information in folder tips	Windows Explorer displays a tool tip showing the creation date and time, the size of the folder, and a partial list of files when you move the mouse pointer over a folder name or folder icon.	Windows Explorer displays a tool tip showing the creation date and time when you move the mouse pointer over a folder name or folder icon.
Display the full path in the title bar	When you press Alt-Tab to access the flip view, Windows displays the actual file path instead of the folder name when you move the mouse pointer over a Windows Explorer window. If you are using the Windows Classic theme (see Chapter 3), this will display the actual file path instead of the folder name in the title bar.	When you press Alt-Tab to access the flip view, Windows displays the folder name when you move the mouse pointer over a Windows Explorer window. If you are using the Windows Classic theme, this will display the folder name in the title bar.
Hidden files and folders	Windows Explorer displays hidden files, folders, or drives.	Windows Explorer does not display hidden files, folders, or drives.
Hide empty drives in the computer folder	Windows Explorer displays information about empty drives in the Computer window.	Windows Explorer does not display information about empty drives in the Computer window.
Hide file extensions for known file types	Windows Explorer does not display file extensions for known file types.	Windows Explorer displays file extensions for known file types.
Hide protected operating system files	Windows Explorer does not display operating system files.	Windows Explorer displays operating system files.
Launch folder windows in a separate process	Windows runs each instance of Windows Explorer in a separate process. Though this requires more memory and generally slows down the process of opening new windows, it also means that each instance is independent of the other. Thus, if one instance crashes or hangs, it generally will not affect other instances of Windows Explorer.	Windows runs all instances of Windows Explorer in the same process. Though this saves memory and generally speeds up the process of opening new windows, it also means that all instances of Windows Explorer are dependent on each other. As a result, if one instance crashes, they all crash, and if one instance is in a pending or wait state, all instances could become locked.
Show drive letters	Windows Explorer displays drive letters as part of the information on the Locations bar.	Windows Explorer does not display drive letters as part of the information on the Locations bar.
Show encrypted or compressed NTFS files in color	Windows Explorer lists encrypted files and compressed files using different colors. Normally, encrypted files are displayed with green text and compressed files are displayed using blue text.	Windows Explorer does not distinguish between encrypted, compressed, and normal files.
Show pop-up description for folder and desktop items	Windows Explorer shows tool tips with additional information about a file or folder when you move the mouse over the file or folder.	Windows Explorer does not show tool tips with additional information about a file or folder when you move the mouse over the file or folder.
Show preview handlers in Preview pane	When the Preview pane is visible, Windows Explorer displays previews of selected files and folders.	When the Preview pane is visible, Windows Explorer does not display previews of selected files and folders.

Setting	When selected	When not selected
Use checkboxes to select items	Windows Explorer displays checkboxes that you can use to select files.	Windows Explorer allows you to select files, folders, and other items using only the standard selection techniques such as click, Shift-Click and Ctrl-Click.
Use Sharing Wizard	Windows Explorer uses the File Sharing wizard for configuring file sharing, as discussed in Chapter 11.	Windows Explorer uses the advanced file sharing options. When you try to share files, you'll need to click Advanced Sharing on the Sharing tab so that you can configure permissions, caching and connections settings separately.
When typing into a list view, automatically type into the Search box	When you are working with the list view and press a letter key, Windows Explorer enters the text you type into the Search box.	When you are working with the list view and press a letter key, Windows Explorer selects the first file or folder with that letter.

Optimizing Folder Views

Windows Explorer uses view templates to determine what each folder looks like in the Contents pane. The predefined templates include the following:

General Items
> For folders that contain a mix of file types including documents, pictures, and other folders.

Documents
> For folders that contain mostly documents.

Music
> For folders that contain mostly digital music. When you are working with music, the Music pane provides the Play, Play All, and Burn options.

Pictures
> For folders that contain mostly pictures. By default, each picture is displayed with a thumbnail that you can use for quick browsing. When you are working with pictures, the Picture pane provides Preview, Slide Show, Print, and Burn options.

Videos
> For folders that contain mostly videos. When you are working with videos, the Video pane provides Play, Play All, and Burn options.

Folder view settings you use are seen by all users who access the system, either locally or remotely. The default view for most folders is Documents. If you have write permissions on a folder, you can customize the folder view. You can even apply a favorite view to all folders of that type on the system as well.

You can configure custom views for folders by following these steps:

1. In Windows Explorer, right-click the folder you want to customize, and then select Properties.

2. Click the Customize tab, as shown in Figure 6-20.

3. On the "Optimize this folder for" list, choose the template you want to use, such as Pictures. To apply the view to subfolders of this folder, choose "Also apply this template to all subfolders."

4. Optionally, customize the folder preview. By default, a folder shows a folder icon with thumbnails for the first few files as a folder preview. If you want, you can set a specific background picture or other file that will be used instead of the thumbnails. Click Choose File, and then use the Browse dialog box to select the picture or other file you want to use as part of the folder's preview.

5. Click OK.

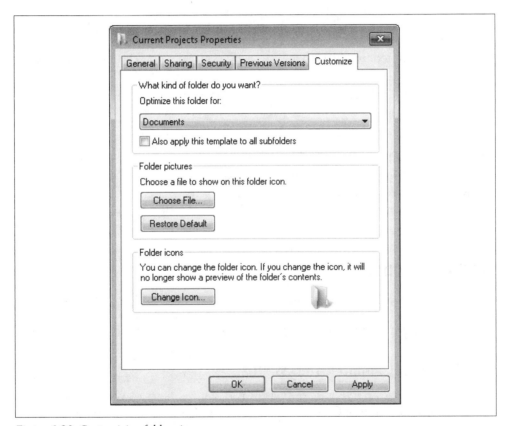

Figure 6-20. Customizing folder views

You also can apply a custom view to all the folders of a particular type on the system or restore the default view to the folders. To apply a custom view to all the folders of a particular type, complete the following steps:

1. In Windows Explorer, select the folder you want to work with. Use the options of the View list or View menu to configure the folder view that you want to use, such as Large Icons.

2. Click Organize and then click Folder And Search Options.

3. In the Folder Options dialog box, select the View tab.

4. To apply the current folder view to all folders of this type, click Apply To Folders.

5. To restore all folders of this type to their default view, click Reset Folders.

6. Click OK.

Sometimes you'll want all folders—regardless of type—to use the same default view. To do this, follow these steps:

1. In Windows Explorer, right-click the folder you want to work with, and then select Properties.

2. Select the Customize tab. Under Optimize This Folder For, choose General Items. Click OK.

3. In Windows Explorer, select the folder. Use the options on the View list or View menu to configure the folder view that you want to use, such as Large Icons.

4. Click Organize and then click Folder and Search Options.

5. In the Folder Options dialog box, select the View tab.

6. To apply the current folder view to all folders of this type, click Apply To Folders.

7. Repeat this procedure four times, once each for the Documents, Pictures, Music, and Videos templates. In step 2, choose Documents, Pictures, Music, or Videos as appropriate.

Searching Your Computer

In the section "Navigating the Search box" on page 39 of Chapter 2, I discussed using the Start menu Search box. The Search box in Windows Explorer is similar. However, there are some important differences and many additional advanced options.

Searching Your Computer: The Essentials

The Search box, shown in Figure 6-21, is provided in all views of Windows Explorer. This means you can search Control Panel, Network, Computer, Desktop, Public, and Recycle Bin locations.

Figure 6-21. The Search box, for searching for files and folders

The way the Windows Search service performs a search depends on where you are searching. A general search works like this: the Windows Search service matches the search text to words that appear in the title of any file or file folder, the properties of any indexed file or folder, and the contents of indexed documents. The automatic indexing of selected files and folders is a key feature of Windows 7 that improves the search results and helps to speed up the search process.

With Windows Explorer, you must click in the Search box prior to typing your search text. This means a basic search requires two steps:

1. In Windows Explorer, access the start location for your search.
2. Click in the Search box and then enter the search text.

 As discussed previously in Table 6-1, the "When typing into a list view" option controls whether you have to click in the search box before entering search text. By default, you must click in the search box. If you enable "Automatically type into the Search Box," any text you type into a list view is entered automatically in the Search box.

The Windows Search service is the operating system feature that performs the search. Once the Windows Search service completes a search in the selected location, it automatically begins another search if you enter additional search text or if you change the search text. You can stop a search in progress at any time by clicking the Stop button—the red X on the right side of the Address bar. You can repeat a search by clicking the Refresh button.

With the Computer view of Windows Explorer, you can use the Search box to search your entire computer, including all disk drives and all devices with removable storage. To do this, follow these steps:

1. Click Start and then click Computer.
2. Click in the Search box and then enter the search text.

With other views of Windows Explorer, the Windows Search service does not perform a whole computer search. Instead, it searches only the selected location and its subnodes. This means if you were to search the *C:\Documents* folder, the Windows Search service would search *C:\Documents* and all its subfolders. It would not search other folders or other locations.

As Figure 6-22 shows, results are returned to the Results pane in Windows Explorer and the Address bar is updated to reflect that you are viewing search results. The search results themselves are displayed in Content view by default. In this view, search results are listed by name, date modified, size, authors, and tags. If you click the Location Indicator icon on the left side of the address path, you'll see the actual search text passed

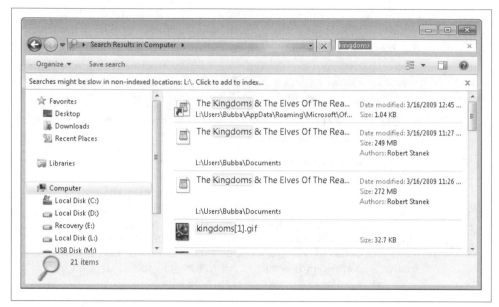

Figure 6-22. The Windows Search service, which returns results matching the search text

to the Windows Search service. See "Searching Your Computer: Save Search Options" on page 221, for details on saving searches so that you can run them again in the future.

As you've seen, the basics of searching for files and folders are fairly straightforward. To improve your search results, however, you need to use the advanced search options and features built into Windows 7. These additional advanced features include:

- Search options, for fine-tuning the search results
- The Search pane, for filtering search results
- Indexing options, for managing which files and folders are indexed
- Save Search, for saving advanced search criteria for future searches

I discuss these advanced search features in the following sections.

Searching Your Computer: Search Options

Search options control the way the Windows Search service searches your computer. By default, Windows Search searches indexed locations and nonindexed locations in different ways:

- In indexed locations, the Windows Search service searches filenames and contents. This means that it will look for matches to your search text in filenames and folder names, file properties and folder properties, and the actual textual contents of files.

- In nonindexed locations, the Windows Search service searches filenames only. This means it will look for matches to your search text only in filenames and folder names. It will not look for matches to your search text in file and folder properties, or in the actual textual contents of files.

By default, Windows Search searches subfolders of a selected location and allows partial matches. Thanks to partial matching, the Windows Search service matches your search text to part of a word or phrase rather than to whole words only. This allows you to search for *picture* and get matching results for *pictures*, *pictured*, *my picture*, *my pictures*, and so on.

You can customize the search options for your computer by completing the following steps:

1. In Windows Explorer, click Organize on the menu bar and then click "Folder and search options." Finally, select the Search tab in the Folder Options dialog box.

2. As shown in Figure 6-23, you can then use the Search tab options in the Folder Options dialog box to configure search options. To restore the default search options, discussed previously, click Restore Defaults, click OK, and then skip the remaining steps.

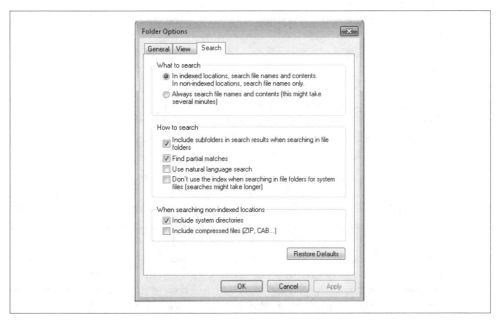

Figure 6-23. Configuring the search options

3. On the "What to search" panel, select the options that best describe what you want to be searched. To have the Windows Search service always search filenames and contents, select "Always search file names and contents." To have the Windows Search service search contents only for indexed locations, select "In indexed locations."

> If you select the "Always search" option, you force the Windows Search service to ignore whether a folder is indexed when searching. This does not mean that indexes won't be used, however. When indexes are available, the Windows Search service will use them. When indexes aren't available, the Windows Search service will not be able to use indexes to speed up the search process, and this can result in extremely slow searches.

4. On the "How to search" panel, use the following options to configure how searches work:

Include subfolders in search results
> When selected, the Windows Search service searches the selected location and all subfolders underneath it. This lets you search entire drives or complete folder structures. When not selected, the Windows Search service searches only the selected location and does not search their subfolders.

Find partial matches
> When selected, the Windows Search service returns results for partial matches as well as whole-word matches. When not selected, the Windows Search service performs whole-word searches only.

Use natural language search
> When selected, the Windows Search service allows you to enter search text as a question you might ask someone else. For example, you could enter the question, "Where is the Music folder?" and the Windows Search service would know that you are looking for a folder named *Music* or folders containing music. When not selected, the Windows Search service uses all the text you enter for matching, as discussed previously.

Don't use the index when searching in file folders for system files
> When selected, the Windows Search service ignores indexes when searching in file folders for system files. This forces the Windows Search service to examine the current state of system files, but it can be extremely slow. When not selected, the Windows Search service uses indexes to speed up the search process if indexes are available. Normally, system files are not indexed as they aren't searched very often by most users and for this reason you'll want to bypass the index when you are searching for system files. However, if you are an advanced user or administrator and have indexed system files, you'll want to use the index when searching (in most cases).

5. On the "When searching non-indexed locations" panel, specify whether the Windows Search service includes system locations, compressed files, or both when searching nonindexed locations.

6. Click OK to save your search options.

Searching Your Computer: Search Filters

Sometimes you won't know the exact name of a resource you are looking for. Instead, you may know only part of the name, the approximate size of the file, the general type of file, or when you last modified the file. In these cases, you can use the Search pane to narrow your results using search filters.

Windows Explorer supports several important search filters for files:

Datemodified:
> Filters the search results according the date files and folders were last modified.

Size:
> Filters the search results according to file and folder size.

Kind:
> Filters the search results according to general kind of file, such as all document files.

Type:
> Filters the search results according to specific type of file, such as a *.wma* file.

Filtering Your Searches

You can use just about any indexable property associated with a file or folder as a filter in your searches. The basic syntax is *PropertyName:* where *PropertyName* is the property name entered without spaces followed by a colon, such as `Datecreated:`. Incidentally, you can use Datecreated: in the exact same way as DateModified:. For example, you could use `Datecreated:Last week` as your search filter.

Some other ones you may want to use include Rating: and Dimensions:. Rating: allows you to search on the star rating you assigned to media files. Use the value `Rating:1 star`, `Rating:2 stars`, `Rating:3 stars`, `Rating:4 stars`, `Rating:5 stars` or `Rating:Unrated`.

`Dimensions:` allows you to search on the width and height dimensions of pictures. You can use the value `Dimensions:="1024 x 768"`, `Dimensions:="1152 x 864"`, `Dimensions:="1536 x 2048"`, `Dimensions:="2048 x 1536"`, `Dimensions:="Unspecified"` or whatever custom dimension you used. In addition to the equals (=) operator, which provides an exact match, you can use less than, greater than, less than or equal to, greater than or equal to, or not equals: <, >, <=, >=, <>.

With pictures from a digital camera, you can even use Cameramodel: as a search filter. For example, you could search for all the pictures you've taken with your Sony Cybershot camera by entering `Cameramodel:=cybershot`.

To find properties that you may be able to filter on, right-click different types of media files and select Properties. In the Details pane, you'll see a list of all the properties for that type of file. Keep in mind that indexing options control what types of files are indexed. For more information, see "Indexing Your Computer for Faster Searches" on page 223.

You can use search filters with or without keywords. If you want to begin a search with a keyword and then filter the results, you type the keyword or phrase, click in the search window and then select or enter the filter prefix. If you want to begin a search without a keyword, click in the search window and then select or enter the filter prefix.

In the sections that follow, I'll examine each search filter. Although I won't combine search filters in the examples, you can combine multiple search parameters in a single search. For example, you could search using the date modified, size, and type filters. Searches that combine multiple filters and are difficult to recreate are the ones you'll want to save for later reuse. See "Searching Your Computer: Save Search Options" on page 221 for details.

Searching on a date or range of dates

When you are working with the Datemodified: filter you can select a date or date range to search. Any file with a last modification date matching your parameters is returned in the search results.

You can work with the calendar in a variety of ways. As Figure 6-24 shows, the current day and date are displayed by default. The calendar has the following views:

Month
> The month view is the default. While working with the month view, you can view other months in the calendar using the right-facing and left-facing arrow buttons. Click and drag in the calendar to select a series of dates, such as the 9th through the 15th days of the month.

Year
> The year view lists the months in a year. You can access the year view from the month view by clicking the month and year entry at the top of the calendar. While working with the year view, you can view other years in the calendar using the right-facing and left-facing arrow buttons. Click and drag in the calendar to select a series of months.

Decade
> The decade view lists the years in a 10-year period. You can access the decade view from the month view by clicking twice at the top of the calendar. While working with the decade view, you can view other decades in the calendar using the right-facing and left-facing arrow buttons. Click and drag in the calendar to select a series of years.

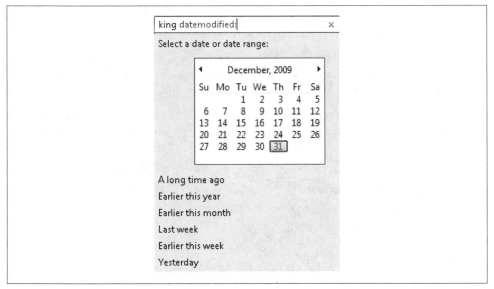

Figure 6-24. Searching on the last modification date

Century

> The century view lists the 10-year periods in a particular century. You can access the century view from the month view by clicking three times at the top of the calendar. While working with the century view, you can view other centuries in the calendar using the right-facing and left-facing arrow buttons. Click and drag in the calendar to select a series of decades.

Why this is important is because it can help you quickly find exactly what you are looking for. For example, if you know you created the photos you are looking for in the 1990s, you can quickly search on related dates by following these steps:

1. Open Windows Explorer to the top-level folder from which you want to start searching. If you want to search the entire computer, select Computer as your location.

2. Click in the Search box. Optionally, type a keyword or phrase to search on.

3. Select Datemodified:.

4. In the Search pane, click the top of the calendar three times, click the left arrow button and then click 1990–1999.

5. Press Enter to begin your search.

The Datemodified: filter accepts shorthand entries as well. Using a shorthand entry, you can directly input the date search. The basic syntax varies by locality. For U.S. English, the syntax is:

```
Datemodified: Mm/Dd/Yyyy
```

or:

```
Datemodified: Mm/Dd/Yyyy .. Mm/Dd/Yyyy
```

where *Mm* is a one- or two-digit value for the month, *Dd* is a one- or two-digit value for the day of the month, and *Yyyy* is a four-digit value for the year. Knowing this, you could create a search from 1/1/2005 to 12/31/2005 by following these steps:

1. Open Windows Explorer to the top-level folder from which you want to start searching. If you want to search the entire computer, select Computer as your location.
2. Click in the Search box. Optionally, type a keyword or phrase to search on.
3. Select or type `Datemodified:`.
4. Type `1/1/2005 .. 12/31/2005`.
5. Press Enter to begin your search.

The calendar also has preset buttons for:

A long time ago
  Search for files and folders created prior to the current year.

Earlier this year
  Search for files and folders created earlier in the current year.

Earlier this month
  Search for files and folders created earlier in the current month.

Last week
  Search for files and folders created in the previous week.

Earlier this week
  Search for files and folders created earlier in the current week.

Yesterday
  Search for files and folders created yesterday.

You can search using the preset values by following these steps:

1. Open Windows Explorer to the top-level folder from which you want to start searching. If you want to search the entire computer, select Computer as your location.
2. Click in the Search box. Optionally, type a keyword or phrase to search on.
3. Select or type `Datemodified:`.
4. Type the preset label or click the preset button in the Search pane.
5. Press Enter to begin your search.

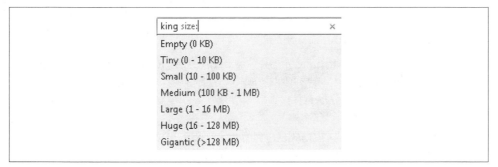

Figure 6-25. Searching on the approximate file size

Searching on an approximate file size

When you are working with the Size: filter, you can specify an approximate file size. Any file with an approximate file size matching your parameters is returned in the search results. As Figure 6-25 shows, the available options are:

Empty
    Allows you to search for empty files.

Tiny
    Allows you to search for files of 0 to 10 kilobytes.

Small
    Allows you to search for files of 10 to 100 kilobytes.

Medium
    Allows you to search for files of 100 kilobytes to 1 megabyte.

Large
    Allows you to search for files of 1 megabyte to 16 megabytes.

Huge
    Allows you to search for files of 16 megabyte to 128 megabytes.

Gigantic
    Allows you to search for files over 128 megabytes.

By typing the preset label or clicking the preset button in the Search pane, you can quickly find files that meet specific size criteria. For example, if you know the file you are looking for is small and has the keyword "report," you could search for it by following these steps:

1. Open Windows Explorer to the top-level folder from which you want to start searching. If you want to search the entire computer, select Computer as your location.

2. Click in the Search box. Type report.

3. Select or type Size:.

4. Click or type `Small`.

5. Press Enter to begin your search.

The Size: filter accepts shorthand entries as well. Using a shorthand entry, you can directly input the size parameters for the search. The basic syntax is:

```
size: SmallestSize .. LargestSize
   SmallestSize.. LargestSize
```

where *SmallestSize* is the smallest file size that meets your parameters and *LargestSize* is the largest file size that meets your parameters. Use kb to specify a size in kilobytes, mb to specify a size in megabytes, and gb to specify a size in gigabytes. Knowing this, you could create a search for files between 500 KB and 100 MB by following these steps:

1. Open Windows Explorer to the top-level folder from which you want to start searching. If you want to search the entire computer, select Computer as your location.

2. Click in the Search box. Optionally, type a keyword or phrase to search on.

3. Select or type `Size:`.

4. Type `500kb .. 100mb`.

5. Press Enter to begin your search.

You also can use the greater than (>) and less than (<) symbols in your searches. For example, to search for files less than 1 MB in size, you would type `Size:<1mb` and then press Enter to begin your search. To search for files greater than 1 MB in size, you would type `Size:>1mb` and then press Enter to begin your search.

Searching for a specific kind or type of file

When you are working with libraries and certain other folders, the Kind: and Type: filters are available when you click in the Search box. These filters are also available when you are working with other folders but you must enter the filter prefix, such as Kind: or Type: to access the filter's options.

Any file with a kind of type that matches your parameters is returned in the search results. The kinds of files you can search for include:

Calendar
 Filters the search results so that only calendar items are included in the search results.

Communication
 Filters the search results so that only calendar, email, contact, and instant message items are included in the search results.

Contact
> Filters the search results so that only contact items are included in the search results.

Document
> Filters the search results so that only document files are included in the search results.

E-mail
> Filters the search results so that only email messages are included in the search results.

Feed
> Filters the search results so that only messages from RSS feeds are included in the search results.

Folder
> Filters the search results so that only folders are included in the search results.

Game
> Filters the search results so that only game data and other game files are included in the search results.

Instant Message
> Filters the search results so that only instant messages are included in the search results.

Journal
> Filters the search results so that only journal entries are included in the search results.

Link
> Filters the search results so that only links are included in the search results.

Movie
> Filters the search results so that only movie files are included in the search results.

Music
> Filters the search results so that only music files are included in the search results.

Note
> Filters the search results so that only note files are included in the search results.

Picture
> Filters the search results so that only pictures are included in the search results.

Program
> Filters the search results so that program files are included in the search results.

Recorded TV
> Filters the search results so that recorded television programs are included in the search results.

Saved Search
> Filters the search results so that saved searches are included in the search results.

Task
> Filters the search results so that tasks are included in the search results.

Video
> Filters the search results so that video files are included in the search results.

Web History
> Filters the search results so that items from your web history are included in the search results.

By typing the Kind: prefix, an equals sign, and the kind label in the Search pane, you can quickly find files of a particular kind. For example, if you know the file you are looking for is a document file and the file name includes the keyword "report," you could search for it by following these steps:

1. Open Windows Explorer to the top-level folder from which you want to start searching. If you want to search the entire computer, select Computer as your location.

2. Click in the Search box. Type `report`.

3. Select or type `Kind:`.

4. Click Document in the list provided or type `=Document`.

5. Press Enter to begin your search.

The Type: filter allows you to search for a specific type of file by its file type label or file extension. For example, you can search for files with the type "MP3 Format Sound" or files with the *.mp3* file extension. By typing the Type: prefix, an equal sign and the type label in the Search pane, you can quickly find files of a particular type. For example, if you know the file you are looking for is a *.doc* file and the filename includes the keyword "report," you could search for it by following these steps:

1. Open Windows Explorer to the top-level folder from which you want to start searching. If you want to search the entire computer, select Computer as your location.

2. Click in the Search box. Type `report`.

3. Select or type `Type:`.

4. Type `=.doc`.

5. Press Enter to begin your search.

The Type: filter also accepts three special flags:

"Directory"
> Filters the search results for directories only.

"File Folder"
Filters the search results for file folders only.

"Compressed (zipped) Folder"
Filters the search results for compressed (zipped) folders only.

Generally speaking, if you don't use one of these special flags, any search you perform with a filter matches only files. In contrast, searches on keywords are matched only against both files and folders.

Following this, you could search for a directory with report as part of its name by following these steps:

1. Open Windows Explorer to the top-level folder from which you want to start searching. If you want to search the entire computer, select Computer as your location.

2. Click in the Search box. Type `report`.

3. Select or type `Type:`.

4. Type `="Directory"`.

5. Press Enter to begin your search.

 Want to know a secret? A little-known fact is that these same search filters are available with Windows Explorer, the Start menu, and other search boxes in Windows 7. To use these filters with other Search boxes, simply type the filter prefixes, labels and search parameters to use. For example, if you click Start and then type `kind:=music` into the Search box, you'll see a list of all the music on your computer. If you have a lot of music, you'll then need to click See All Results to get an expanded view of the search results.

Searching Your Computer: Save Search Options

Whenever you perform a search, Windows 7 updates the menu bar in Windows Explorer to include a Save Search button. Clicking this button allows you to save your search criteria so that you can rapidly perform an identical search in the future. Windows 7 saves your search criteria as a search folder.

Search folders have a blue icon with a magnifying glass. As Figure 6-26 shows, searches are listed according to the search filters you used in the Searches folder under the Saved Search heading. You can work with search folders in the same way you work with regular folders. This means you can:

- Use Ctrl-X to cut and Ctrl-V to paste a search folder in a new location.
- Use Ctrl-C to copy and Ctrl-V to paste to create copies of search folders.
- Use Delete to remove search folders.

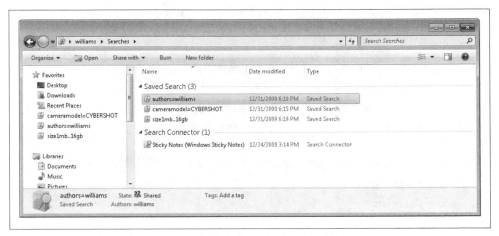

Figure 6-26. Saved searches are stored by default in the Searches folder

When you open or double-click a search folder, the Windows Search service either retrieves the cached results of your previous search or performs a new search using the search criteria. The result is a list of matching files and folders that appear to be in the selected folder. The folder actually does not contain any files or folders, however. A search folder's only actual (physical) content is the associated search string.

You can create a search folder by completing the following steps:

1. Perform a search as discussed previously.
2. Click Save Search on the menu bar.
3. In the Save As dialog box, accept the default name for the search folder or type a new name.
4. Click Save to create the search folder. Searches are saved with the *.search-ms* file extension.

Search folders you create are stored by default in your Saved Searches folder within your profile. You can access saved searches at any time by clicking Start, clicking your user name on the Start menu, and then double-clicking Searches.

You can run a search again by accessing Saved Searches and then opening or double-clicking the search folder. Although you cannot edit search folders to update the search criteria, you can delete a search folder, configure the desired search criteria, and then save the new search using the old search folder name.

Indexing Your Computer for Faster Searches

In addition to performing searches, the Windows Search service is also responsible for indexing your computer. You tell the Windows Search service about locations that should be indexed by designating them as searched locations. Once you've designated a folder as an indexed location, the Windows Search service is notified that it needs to update the related index whenever you modify the contents of the folder.

You can manage the indexing of your computer's files and folders in several ways. You can:

- Add or remove indexed locations.
- Specify file types to include or exclude.
- Optimize file properties for indexing.
- Rebuild indexes if you suspect problems.

The sections that follow discuss these indexing options.

Adding or Removing Indexed Locations

The Windows Search services indexes the following locations by default:

Internet Explorer feeds and history
> This means that if you are using Internet Explorer, your RSS feed messages and browser history will be indexed for fast searching.

Microsoft Office Outlook
> This means that if you installed Microsoft Office Outlook, your mail saved on your computer will be indexed for fast searching.

Offline files
> This means that if you configured offline files, as discussed in Chapter 11, all offline file folders will be indexed for fast searching.

Start menu
> This means that the Start menu and all related menu options are indexed for fast searching.

Users
> This means that your personal folders and the personal folders of others who log on to your computer are indexed for fast searching.

Libraries
> This means that anything that is stored in a Library (including Libraries you have created and folders you have added to a Library) is indexed for fast searching. For more information on Libraries, see "Navigating common folders and customizing the listed features" on page 31 in Chapter 2.

Figure 6-27. Reviewing the current indexed locations

 Your computer includes application data folders within user profiles. These data folders, saved in the *%SystemDrive%\Users\%UserName% \AppData* folders, are excluded from indexing by default. This is the desired setting in most cases, as you don't want to index folders or files associated with application data.

The fastest and easiest way to index folders is to just add the folder to a Library.

You can add or remove indexed locations by completing the following steps:

1. Click Start and then click Control Panel. In the Control Panel, click Large Icons or Small Icons on the View By list (to return to the original view, click the View by list and select Category). Finally, click Indexing Options.

2. As shown in Figure 6-27, the Indexing Options dialog box provides an overview of indexing on your computer, which includes the total number of items indexed

and the current indexing state. The currently indexed locations are listed under Included Locations.

3. In the Indexing Options dialog box, click Modify.

4. In the Indexed Locations dialog box, click Show All Locations (it's at the bottom of the dialog box).

5. In the Indexed Locations dialog box, shown in Figure 6-28, select locations to index, or clear checkboxes for locations you no longer want to index. The locations you can index include offline file folders, Microsoft Office Outlook, hard disk drives, and devices with removable storage. If a node can be expanded, you'll see an open triangle to the left of the location name. Click this to expand the location. For example, you could expand Local Disk (C:) to select a folder on the C: drive.

 Some system folders are excluded from indexing and are displayed dimmed to prevent them from being selected. If you enable indexing of the entire system drive, those system folders are excluded automatically.

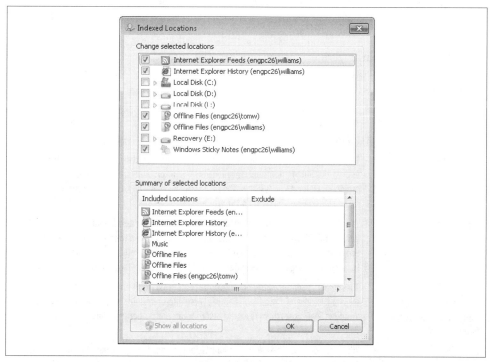

Figure 6-28. Modifying the indexed locations

6. When you click OK to save your changes, the Windows Search service index adds locations and removes indexes for removed locations.

Specifying Files Types to Include or Exclude

From previous discussions, you know that the Windows Search service is designed to index:

- Filenames and folder names
- File and folder properties
- File and folder contents

What you don't know is *how* the Windows Search service determines which types of files and folders to index. It does so according to the file extension.

File extensions and file types go hand in hand. File type associations determine what type of data is stored in a file and how the file should be handled when opened. When you open most types of files, a helper application handles the display of the file. For example, when you open a document file with the *.doc* extension, Microsoft Office Word is used to display the document.

The Windows Search service uses the information that it knows about file types and file extensions to help it index files more efficiently. More specifically, Windows 7 assigns a file filter to each file extension, and this filter determines exactly how files with a particular extension are indexed.

Table 6-2 provides an overview of the standard file filters. As you install additional applications on your computer, additional file filters may be installed as well to improve indexing of related application files.

Table 6-2. File filters used by the Windows Search service

Filter name	Filter description
File Properties filter	This filter is used with binary files, media files and other nontext-based file formats. As the name implies, this filter retrieves only the filename and file properties. It does not filter the contents of a file, but it is extremely useful when searching for image files, which are rich with metadata such as file size, camera type, and more.
HTML filter	This filter is designed to work with files formatted using Hypertext Markup Language (HTML). Because this filter recognizes HTML markup tags, you can use it to extract filenames, file properties, and file contents. Because this filter also understands <META> tags, you can also use it to extract meta tag properties within the <HEAD> </HEAD> tags of an HTML file.
Microsoft Office Document filter, Microsoft Office Filter, Office Open XML Format filters	These filters are designed to work with documents in Microsoft Office, including the documents for Word, Excel, and PowerPoint. Because these filters recognize Office document formats, Windows Search uses them to extract text contents and properties unique to Office.
MIME filter	This filter is designed to work with email attachments formatted using the Multipurpose Internet Mail Extension (MIME) file format. For messages containing attachments, this filter helps the Windows Search service identify the associated file type so that the attachment's contents can be indexed appropriately.

Filter name	Filter description
Plain Text filter	This filter is designed to improve indexing of plain-text files and file types not registered for use with specific applications. It filters filenames, file properties, and file contents. This is the default filter, and it is not able to recognize any document formats. It handles files as a sequence of ASCII or Unicode characters.
XML filter	This filter is designed to work with files formatted using the eXtensible Markup Language (XML). Because this filter recognizes XML markup tags, you can use it to extract filenames, file properties, and file contents.

You can specify file types that the Windows Search service should include or exclude when indexing files by completing the following steps:

1. Click Start and then click Control Panel. In the Control Panel, click Large Icons or Small Icons on the View By list (to return to the original view, click the View by list and select Category). Finally, click Indexing Options.

2. In the Indexing Options dialog box, click Advanced to display the Advanced Options dialog box shown in Figure 6-29.

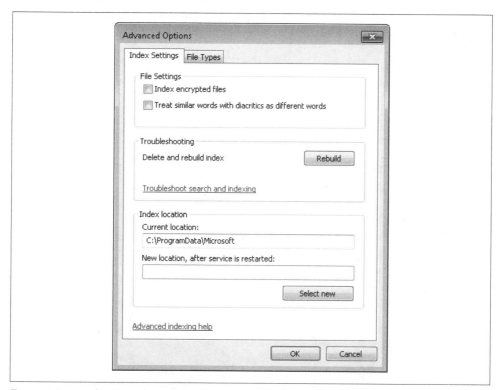

Figure 6-29. Configuring advanced index settings

3. On the Index Settings tab, select the "Index encrypted files" checkbox if you want the Windows Search service to index files that have been encrypted. Selecting or clearing this option will cause the Windows Search service to completely rebuild the indexes on your computer.

4. If you want to improve indexing of non-English characters, select the "Treat similar words with diacritics as different words" checkbox. A diacritic is a mark above or below a letter that indicates a change in the way it is pronounced or stressed.

 If you select "Treat similar words with diacritics as different words," you'll see a warning prompt stating that the Windows Search service will completely rebuild the indexes for indexed locations on your computer. The Windows Search service needs to rebuild the indexes completely to include previously ignored or substituted characters.

5. On the File Types tab, shown in Figure 6-30, each file extension and filter association is listed. If a file extension is selected, the Windows Search service includes files of this type when indexing. If a file extension is not selected, the Windows Search service excludes files of this type when indexing. Select or clear file extensions as appropriate.

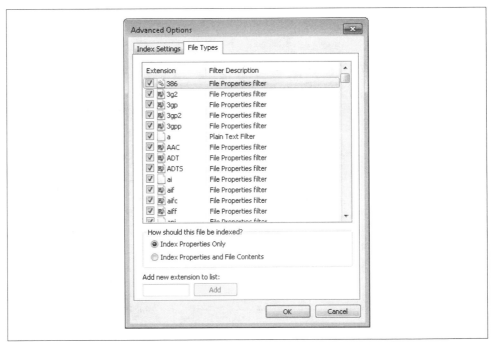

Figure 6-30. Controlling the types of files that are indexed

6. When you install new applications, those applications may register new filters with the Windows Search service and configure related file extensions to use these filters. This is the best way to add indexing functionality. If you want to add support for a particular file extension, type the file extension in the text box provided and then click Add.

7. To change the way files with a particular extension are indexed, select the file extension and then click either Index Properties Only or Index Properties and File Contents.

 Change the way indexing works for a file extension only when you are sure the indexing configuration you've chosen works. Generally speaking, you can always stop indexing the contents of a particular file type but rarely can you index the contents of a file type that isn't already being indexed. Trying to index the contents of a nontext-based file type can cause indexing problems.

8. Click OK to save your settings.

Optimizing File Properties for Indexing

As with file contents, the Windows Search Service indexes file properties to display search results of indexed files and folders faster. All files have properties associated with them and the type of file determines what the related properties are. Document files can have properties such as:

- Title
- Subject
- Tags
- Rating
- Categories
- Comments
- Authors
- Last Saved By
- Company
- Manager
- Data Last Saved

Photos and other types of image files can have special properties in addition to standard document properties, such as:

- Dimensions
- Width

- Height
- Horizontal Resolution
- Vertical Resolution
- Bit Depth
- Camera Maker
- Camera Model
- Exposure Time
- ISO Speed
- Focal Length

Music and other types of audio files can have special properties in addition to standard document properties, such as:

- Artists
- Album Artist
- Album
- Year
- Genre
- Length
- Bit Rate
- Producers
- Publisher

You can view and configure a file's properties by completing the following steps:

1. Right-click the file and then select Properties.
2. In the Properties dialog box, click the Details tab.
3. Click a property's entry to select it for editing, and then type the desired property value. Separate multiple values with a semicolon. For example, if you want to add tags to a file, you would click the Tags property, type the first tag, type a semicolon, type the second tag, and so on.
4. Click OK.

Although additional properties can be useful, sometimes you won't want this information to be saved with a file. For example, if you are publishing a file to a website or sending a file to someone as an attachment, you might not want this additional and possibly sensitive information to be associated with the file. You can remove extended properties from a file by completing the following steps:

1. Right-click the file and then select Properties.
2. In the Properties dialog box, click the Details tab.

3. Click the Remove Properties and Personal Information link.

4. Do one of the following:

   - In the Remove Properties dialog box, select "Create a copy with all possible properties removed" to create a clean copy of the file. When you click OK, the copy is created with the same filename as the previously selected file, and the suffix - *Copy* is added.

   - In the Remove Properties dialog box, select "Remove the following properties from this file" to clean properties from the original file without creating a copy. Either select properties to remove or all Select All to remove all extended properties. When you click OK, the selected extended properties are removed on the original file.

Resolving Indexing Problems

In order for you to perform searches, the Windows Search service must be running. It must also be running to index files. If you suspect you are experiencing a problem with searching or indexing, you should check the status of the Windows Search service. For details on how to work with and troubleshoot services, see Chapter 21.

Other problems you may experience with searching and indexing have to do with:

Corrupt indexes
> An indicator of a corrupt index is when your searches do not return the expected results or new documents are not being indexed properly.

Improper index settings
> An indicator of improper index settings is when your searches fail or the Windows Search service generates bad file errors in the event logs.

Index location running out of space
> An indicator of the index location running out of space is when indexing of new documents fails and there are out-of-disk-space reports in the event logs for the Windows Search service.

The Windows Search service does a good job of correcting some problems with indexes automatically. For other types of problems, you'll find error reports in the form of Windows events in the system event logs. You can correct most problems with searching and indexing by completing the following steps:

1. Click Start and then click Control Panel. In the Control Panel, click Large Icons or Small Icons on the View By list (to return to the original view, click the View by list and select Category). Finally, click Indexing Options.

2. In the Indexing Options dialog box, click Advanced to display the Advanced Options dialog box shown previously in Figure 6-29.

3. If you suspect your computer's indexes are corrupt, click Rebuild. Windows 7 rebuilds the indexes on your computer by stopping, clearing out indexes, and then starting the Windows Search service. Indexes also may be rebuilt whenever you restart your computer.

4. By default, the Windows Search service creates indexes in the *%SystemDrive% \ProgramData\Microsoft* folder. If the *%SystemDrive%* folder is low on disk space or if you want to try to balance the workload by using other hard disk drives, you may want to change the index location. To do this, click Select New on the Index Location panel. In the Browse for Folder dialog box, select the disk drive and folder in which the index should be stored and then click OK. The next time you restart your computer or the Window Search service, indexes will be created in the new location.

5. Click OK. In the Indexing Options dialog box, you can track the status of reindexing files by watching the number of indexed items increase. The indexing status will indicate whether indexing is complete or in progress.

CHAPTER 7

Navigating the Web with Internet Explorer 8

Back in the late 1990s, Internet Explorer became the top choice for browsing the Web by offering innovative features and being the best of its class. While other browsers from those heady, fast-paced days of the World Wide Web's early evolution have all but disappeared, Internet Explorer has continued. It now dominates the web browser market, but for a while it lost something special. Namely, it lost some of the cutting-edge innovation that made it the leader in the first place. With version 7, Internet Explorer regained its place as a cutting-edge web browser with innovations worthy of applause—and version 8 is even better.

Windows 7 includes Internet Explorer 8 as the default program for accessing web pages. Internet Explorer 8 is also available as a free download for anyone using Windows XP or later versions of Windows. Version 8 features a streamlined interface that increases the viewing area for web pages, tabbed browsing for easier navigation when you are viewing multiple web pages, and an extensive security shield that is designed to safeguard the integrity of your computer and protect your personal information.

Whether you are a novice or a pro, you'll find that Internet Explorer 8 is easy to work with and that it offers many possibilities for customization and optimization. Before you race off to customize and optimize Internet Explorer 8, however, you should take a few minutes to get to know its new interface, as discussed in the first part of this chapter. You'll then be better prepared for the advanced discussion in the second part of this chapter, in which I cover key features and techniques you can use to work with the browser.

Getting Started with Internet Explorer 8

Generally, Internet Explorer 8 is installed by default with all versions of the Windows 7 operating system that are for sale in the United States. In Europe and elsewhere, there are versions of the Windows 7 operating system that do not include this browser. Additionally, as Internet Explorer 8 is a feature of the operating system that can be turned on or off, your computer may have this feature disabled, depending on who configured it. If you find that Internet Explorer 8 is unavailable, you should first check Windows Features to see whether the feature is turned off by clicking Start→Control Panel→Programs→Turn Windows Features On Or Off. If the option for Internet Explorer 8 is not selected, select it and then click OK to make the browser available. If you do not have an option for Internet Explorer 8, you can download and install the browser by visiting *http://www.microsoft.com/downloads*.

You can start Internet Explorer 8 by selecting Internet Explorer on the Start menu or by clicking Internet Explorer on the taskbar. When you are browsing the Internet, Internet Explorer 8 runs in an enhanced security mode, called Protected Mode, by default. You can also start Internet Explorer 8 in a locked-down mode, called No Add-ons Mode, by clicking Start→All Programs→Accessories→System Tools→Internet Explorer (No Add-ons). In this special, locked-down mode, Internet Explorer runs without ActiveX controls or browser extensions.

 On 64-bit systems, you'll have a 32-bit version and a 64-bit version of Internet Explorer 8. The 32-bit version is the default and is started when you click the Internet Explorer icon on the task bar. You can start the 64-bit version by clicking Start→All Programs→Internet Explorer (64-bit). The 64-bit version is not the default, as of the time of this writing, because 64-bit versions of add-ons for Internet Explorer may not be available. Because the "bitness" of add-ons generally must be the same as the bitness of Internet Explorer, you need to use the 32-bit version of Internet Explorer to use 32-bit add-ons.

With Internet Explorer 8, Microsoft shows that it has clearly been listening to customers and watching the competition. As you can see in Figure 7-1, Internet Explorer 8 maximizes web page display while reducing the toolbar size, uses tabs instead of separate windows, and features an integrated Web Search box.

Tabbed browsing is the enhancement that has the most significant impact on the way you browse the Web. With tabbed browsing, you can open new browser pages in a separate tab rather than in a separate window. In this way, tabbed browsing helps you organize web pages so that you can easily navigate among them simply by clicking tabs. Although Internet Explorer still allows you to open new windows by pressing Ctrl-N or selecting Page→New Window, you may not need to do this and may instead want to open a new tab.

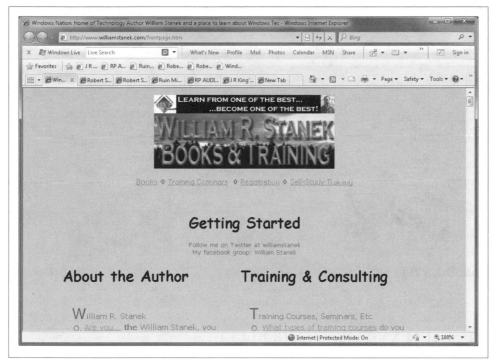

Figure 7-1. Getting to know Internet Explorer 8

Each Internet Explorer window can have up to eight pages open on separate tabs. You can open a page in a new tab in several ways. You can hold the Ctrl key while clicking a link to open the referenced page in a new tab. You can display a new tab by pressing Ctrl-T and then typing the desired web page address in the Address field. As Internet Explorer always displays the New Tab button to the right of the last tab in the line of available tabs, you can also click this button and then type the desired web page address in the Address field.

Internet Explorer gives you several options for working with tabs. You can change the order of tabs by clicking a tab and dragging it to the left or right until you reach the desired position. You can close a tab by right-clicking it and selecting Close. You can close all tabs except the current tab by right-clicking the tab and selecting "Close other tabs."

Whenever there are at least two tabs in use, a Quick Tabs preview and Tabs List button are added to the toolbar to the left of the tabs. Pressing Ctrl-Q or clicking the Quick Tabs button displays a thumbnail preview of all tabbed pages, as shown in Figure 7-2 (you must have at least two tabs open to see the Quick Tabs button or for Ctrl-Q to have any effect). To access one of the tabbed pages, you simply click the page's thumbnail. The Tabs List page displays a list of open web pages. To access one of these pages, you click its entry in the list.

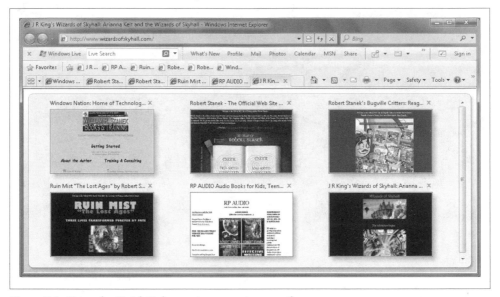

Figure 7-2. Using the Quick Tabs preview to navigate easily

Another feature that you'll find especially helpful is the Favorites Center. You can access the Favorites Center by clicking the Favorites Center button on the toolbar, by pressing Alt-C or by pressing Ctrl-I. With the Favorites Center, shown in Figure 7-3, you finally have a single location to view and access the following:

Favorites

Lists your favorite web pages. The Favorites view has a master favorites list that, by default, is organized in the order in which you add pages. You can rearrange page entries by clicking them and dragging them up or down in the list. You can organize favorites into folders as well for easy navigation and quick access. Simply click a folder to display the related list of favorites.

Feeds

Lists Really Simple Syndication (RSS) feeds to which you've subscribed. RSS feeds can contain news headlines, lists, and other information provided by businesses or individuals.

History

Lists pages you've accessed by date and site. You'll find entries for the current day, day of the week, past week, and so on. If you click a date entry, you'll see folders for each site accessed on that date. Clicking a site entry shows the pages visited at the site. Clicking a page entry opens the page for viewing.

In addition to the Favorites Center, Internet Explorer 8 has a Favorites bar. The Favorites bar is a new toolbar that you can display or hide by clicking Tools→Toolbars→Favorites Bar. When you click the Add to Favorites Bar button, they

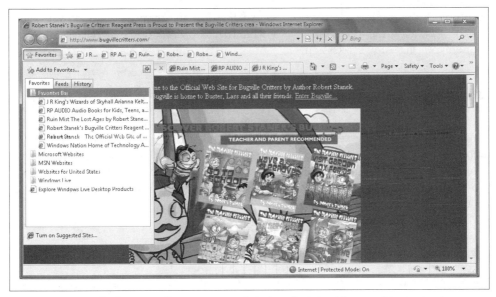

Figure 7-3. Using the Favorites Center to access favorites, feeds, and browser history

automatically appear on the Favorites bar for easy access. Clicking a favorite opens the page on the current tab. If you right-click a favorite, you can open the page in a new tab or a new window.

Though Internet Explorer's locked-down mode improves security and helps to safeguard your computer, nothing changes about the way Internet Explorer maintains the browsing history, temporary files, cookies, user data, or passwords. However, there is a way to prevent Internet Explorer from recording any information, including information about searches, pages you visited, and your user data and passwords. To do this, you need to open an InPrivate browsing session. You can start a private session by opening a new tab and selecting Browse with InPrivate on the page that appears or by selecting Browse with InPrivate on the Safety menu. When you are in a private session, you can be sure none of your information is tracked. To end the private session, just close the InPrivate browser window.

Whenever you work with Internet Explorer 8, you can enter about:tabs in the browser address field to open the Tabs page. The Tabs page provides additional options including:

Reopen closed tabs
Allows you to view tabs that you closed since starting Internet Explorer.

Browse with InPrivate
Allows you to open an InPrivate window for Internet Explorer.

Use An Accelerator
Allows you to open a web service with text that you've copied from a web page.

If Internet Explorer closed unexpectedly, such as if your computer loses power, you'll see the Tabs page the next time you start Internet Explorer and will have the option to reopen your last browser session.

Getting Around the Web and Using Internet Explorer 8

Tabbed browsing, Quick Tabs, and the Favorites Center are just a few of the more obvious ways Internet Explorer has changed. Some of the subtler changes in Internet Explorer have to do with the toolbars and related options. As Figure 7-4 shows, Internet Explorer 8 has a Title bar, Address bar, Menu bar, Standard toolbar, Favorites bar, Command bar, and Status bar. The sections that follow discuss tips and techniques for working with these toolbars.

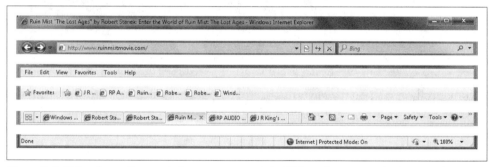

Figure 7-4. Using the toolbars to help you get around the Web and customize Internet Explorer

Navigating Web Page Addresses

Although in earlier releases you could move the Title bar and Address bar, you can no longer do so in Internet Explorer 8. In Internet Explorer 8, the Title bar and Address bar are fixed in place. The only time the Title bar and Address bar are not displayed is when you are in full-screen mode. You can turn full-screen mode on and off by pressing F11.

The Title bar shows the title of the current web page, followed by a description of the browser or a custom title if the browser Title bar has been customized through Group Policy settings. In Group Policy, you'll find the Browser Title policy setting for customizing the Title bar under *User Configuration\Windows Settings\Internet Explorer Maintenance\Browser User Interface* (see Figure 7-5).

Figure 7-5. The Title bar in Internet Explorer

The Title bar is but one of many aspects of Internet Explorer that you can customize through Group Policy. You'll find more information on working with Group Policy in Chapter 24.

The Address bar features Forward and Back buttons, an Address box, a Path History button, Compatibility View, Refresh and Stop buttons, and a Web Search box (see Figure 7-6).

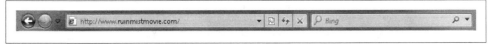

Figure 7-6. The Address bar in Internet Explorer

You can work with the Address box in a variety of ways. To open a page in the currently selected tab, click in the Address box, type the web address, and then press Enter. Alternatively, you can press Alt-D to select the Address box (highlighting the web address of the currently displayed page) without having to move the mouse and click. You can then type the desired web address and press Enter.

At the far-right side of the Address box is the Address History button, which depicts a down arrow. Clicking this button shows a menu with three sections: pages you've visited by typing into the address bar, other pages from your browsing history, and a selection of sites from your favorites. You can then navigate to an address by selecting it. Alternatively, you can display the address history by pressing F4, use the up and down arrow keys to select an address, and then press Enter to browse to this address.

 Another handy shortcut for working with web addresses is to type only the name of the website you want to visit, and then press Ctrl-Enter to add the *http://www.* to the beginning and the *.com* to the end of the name. For example, if you entered yahoo, you could press Ctrl-Enter to create the address *http://www.yahoo.com* and go directly to that address.

Searching the Web and Setting Search Providers

Internet Explorer 8 integrates a search feature directly into the browser window. To search the Web using the default search provider, click in the Web Search box, type your search text, and then press Enter or click the Search button. If you hold Alt while pressing Enter, you'll open the search in a new tab. To help you save time, Internet Explorer 8 also offers relevant search suggestions as you type words into the search box. You can click a suggestion at any time to execute a search without having to type an entire word or phrase.

Figure 7-7. Configuring additional search providers as alternatives

On most configurations of Internet Explorer 8, the default search provider is Bing. Bing is a search service provided by Microsoft, and not surprisingly, it has the most extensive search listings I've found anywhere—Google and Yahoo! included.

Search services and search suggestions are separate features. You can add search providers to Internet Explorer 8 by following these steps:

1. In Internet Explorer 8, click the Search Options button to the right of the Search button.

2. On the shortcut menu, select Find More Providers.

3. On the Add Search Providers to Internet Explorer 8 page, you'll find a list of search providers. Click the search provider you want to add. This displays the Add Search Provider dialog box shown in Figure 7-7.

 Add search providers only from sites you trust. Just because a site is listed as a provider, it doesn't mean the site is trustworthy or reliable. It simply means the site has built-in search facilities and the site owner sent Microsoft a provider file that can use those built-in search facilities.

4. To make the search provider your default for web searches, select the "Make this my default search provider" checkbox.

5. To use search suggestions from the provider, select the "Use Search Suggestions From This Provider" checkbox.

6. Click Add Provider.

You can have only one default search provider. If you make a particular provider your default, you'll use this provider any time you type search text and then press Enter or click the Search button. To use an alternative search provider, click in the Web Search

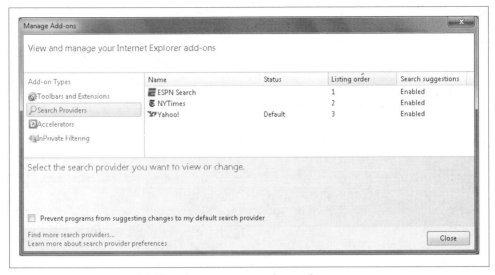

Figure 7-8. *Setting a new default and removing a search provider*

box, click the icon for the alternate provider and then type your search text. You also can click the Search options button, click the alternate provider and then type your search text.

When you have configured multiple search providers, you can make a provider your default or remove a provider by completing the following steps:

1. In Internet Explorer 8, click the Search Options button to the right of the Search button.

2. On the shortcut menu, select Manage Search Providers.

3. In the Manage Search Providers dialog box, shown in Figure 7-8, you'll find a list of search providers you've configured for use.

4. You can now:

   • Change the listing order of a provider by clicking the provider and then clicking "Move up" or "Move down" as appropriate.

   • Disable search suggestions for a selected provider by clicking "Disable suggestions."

   • Enable search suggestions for a selected provider by clicking "Enable suggestions."

   • Make a provider the default by clicking the provider in the Search Providers list and then clicking "Set as default."

   • Remove a provider by clicking the provider in the Search Providers list and then clicking Remove.

Working with Internet Explorer Menus and Toolbars

The Menu bar features the menus used in early versions of Internet Explorer. You'll find the File, Edit, View, Favorites, Tools, and Help menus (see Figure 7-9).

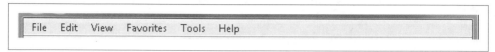

Figure 7-9. The Menu bar in Internet Explorer

In Internet Explorer 8, you can work with the Menu bar in several different ways. You can display the Menu bar by pressing the Alt key and then hide the Menu bar by pressing the Alt key again. You can turn on and lock the Menu bar by selecting Menu Bar on the Tools menu. Once you turn on and lock the Menu bar, you can no longer hide it by pressing the Alt key until you unlock it.

The Standard toolbar is the main toolbar in Internet Explorer 8. The Standard toolbar has a fixed position. The only time the Standard toolbar is not displayed is when you are in full-screen mode. In previous editions of Internet Explorer, the Standard toolbar included the standard commands. In Internet Explorer, the standard commands are displayed on the Command bar, which splits the space with the Standard toolbar when it is being displayed. You can display a shortcut menu with hidden options by clicking the Expand (>>) button on the far-right side of the combined Standard/Command toolbar (see Figure 7-10).

Figure 7-10. The Standard and Command toolbars in Internet Explorer

On the Standard toolbar, to the right of the New Tab button or on the Expand shortcut menu, you'll find the following options:

Home
> Displays the page or pages you've configured for access when you start Internet Explorer or click the Home button.

Home Options
> (The small menu to the right of the Home button that depicts a down arrow.) Displays a shortcut menu that allows you to select and manage home pages.

Feeds
> Displays RSS feeds detected on the current page. This makes it possible to get updates about a page through RSS.

Feeds Options
> (The small menu to the right of the Feeds button that depicts a down arrow.) Displays a shortcut menu that allows you to select options for RSS feeds.

Email
> Allows you to email a page to someone.

Print
> Displays the Print dialog box, which allows you to print the current page.

Print Options
> (The small menu to the right of the Print button that depicts a down arrow.) Displays a shortcut menu that allows you to select printing options, including Print Preview and Page Setup.

Page
> Displays a menu for managing windows and pages.

Safety
> Displays a menu for deleting the browser history, managing InPrivate browsing and configuring SmartScreen filters. Malicious websites use hidden forms and other phishing tactics to steal information you've previously entered into form fields, and SmartScreen filters help to stop this from happening.

Tools
> Displays a menu for customizing the Internet Explorer interface and configuring standard options.

Help
> Displays a menu with help options.

You can use the options on the Page menu to edit, view, and save pages. Two important options that make it easier to view web pages and their contents are Text Size and Zoom.

The Text Size submenu provides options that let you resize the text in a web page relative to its original font size. You can use the Text Size options to resize text on a page by clicking Page, clicking Text Size, and then selecting the desired text size, such as Medium or Larger.

The Zoom submenu provides options that let you enlarge or shrink an entire web page and all its contents, including both images and text. You can quickly increase magnification by simultaneously pressing the Ctrl key and the + (plus sign) key on your numeric keypad. You can quickly decrease magnification by simultaneously pressing the Ctrl key and the – (minus sign) key on your numeric keypad. Press Ctrl-0 to return to the original magnification. If you click Page and then click Zoom, you can select a desired zoom setting, such as 50 percent or 200 percent.

The Tools menu on the Standard toolbar provides access to Internet Explorer's safety and security features as well as other features. The options include:

Diagnose Connection Problems
> Starts network diagnostics for helping you determine the possible cause of connection and access problems.

Manage Add-ons

Provides options for viewing and managing browser add-ons installed on your computer.

Pop-up Blocker

Provides options for managing the way pop-up blocking works. You can also enable and disable pop-up blocking.

Compatibility View

Displays the current website as viewed in Internet Explorer 7, which may correct display problems with a website that hasn't been updated for Internet Explorer 8. Each time you access the site in the future, it will be displayed in compatibility view automatically. To exit compatibility view, select this option again while viewing a website. If you access a website with compatibility problems, a Compatibility View button may be displayed on the toolbar as well.

Work Offline

Configures Internet Explorer to work offline. When you are working offline, Internet Explorer attempts to retrieve pages you access from its offline browsing cache. If a page is available for offline browsing, Internet Explorer displays the page. Otherwise, Internet Explorer displays an error message.

Internet Options

Provides options for configuring Internet Explorer's settings. You can use the related dialog box to configure settings for security, privacy, content, connections, programs, and more.

Suggested Sites

Allows you to enable or disable suggested sites. Suggested Sites is an online service that uses your browsing history to suggest other websites you may be interested in. You can view suggested sites by clicking Suggested Sites on the Favorites bar or clicking "See suggested sites" while viewing the Favorites Center.

 When you turn on Suggested Sites, your browsing history is sent to Microsoft. Microsoft saves the history, compares it to lists of related websites and then subsequently uses this comparison to suggest other similar sites. If you don't want your browsing history to be sent to Microsoft, do not use this feature.

Using Caret Browsing and Other Features

Internet Explorer 8 includes many new and enhanced features, which I'll discuss throughout this chapter. Here are some features you'll want to know more about right now:

Caret Browsing

Normally, you use the mouse to select text and move around within a web page. When Caret Browsing is enabled, as per the default configuration of Internet

Explorer 8, you can use the navigation keys on your keyboard, including Home, End, Page Up, Page Down, and the arrow keys, to select text and move around within a web page. This makes it easier to select, copy, and paste text to another document without having to use a mouse.

With Caret Browsing on, you can move up, down, left and right on the Web page by pressing and holding the arrow keys. To select text, move the cursor to the beginning of the text, hold down the Shift key and move the arrow keys until the text you want is selected. With text selected, you can copy by pressing Ctrl-C and paste by pressing Ctrl-V. To turn on Caret Browsing, press F7.

Cross-site scripting filters

Many safety features are built into Internet Explorer 8. One of these features, called the cross-site scripting filter, is designed to limit reflection attacks. A reflection attack occurs when a website adds scripting elements to otherwise legitimate requests to another website, often in an attempt to gain access to privileged information. To prevent reflection, the cross-site scripting filter identifies potentially malicious script embedded in web addresses and prevents it from executing. Internet Explorer 8 also includes the SmartScreen filter, which replaces the standard phishing filter in Internet Explorer 7.

Compatibility View

The component in Internet Explorer that renders pages from markup has been modified to more closely support industry standards for page layout, including compliance with Cascading Style Sheets (CSS) 2.1. CSS 2.1 is a simple mechanism for adding style, such as fonts, colors, spacing, and positioning, to web documents. Internet Explorer also provides forward-looking support for CSS 3.0. However, enforcing compliance with these and other standards can change the way pages display in the browser, which is where Compatibility View comes in.

The Compatibility View feature automatically detects compatibility issues in web pages and displays the page as it would have been viewed in Internet Explorer 7. This can correct display problems with a website that hasn't been updated for Internet Explorer 8. Each time you access the site in the future, it will be displayed in Compatibility View automatically. To manually enter Compatibility View, select Tools→Compatibility View.

If you access a website with the potential to have compatibility problems, a Compatibility View button will be displayed on the toolbar as well. If you are having trouble viewing the page, click the button to enter Compatibility View.

To exit compatibility view, click the button or select Tools→Compatibility View while viewing a website.

Automatic Crash Recovery

Automatic Crash Recovery can help to prevent the loss of work in case the browser crashes or hangs. Over 70 percent of all Internet Explorer crashes and hangs are caused by browser extensions, such as ActiveX controls, Browser Helper Objects, and toolbars. To prevent problems from extensions, Internet Explorer isolates the user interface frame from the browser tab set by keeping them in separate processes. By isolating extension code in the tab process, Internet Explorer protects the integrity of the browser and limits many failures to the tab that was responsible. Automatic recovery is then invoked, restoring the tab's current page, back and forward history, session cookies, and form data.

When a crash or hang is successfully recovered, Internet Explorer notifies you by displaying a caption bubble on the tab. If a failure cannot be prevented from crashing both the tab and the frame processes, or an unexpected shutdown occurs, such as when your computer loses power, Internet Explorer can restore your last tab set. When you next start Internet Explorer, you'll see a dialog box stating "Your last browsing session closed unexpectedly." Click "Restore your last session" to reopen all tabs that were open when your browser closed.

Suggested Sites

Suggested Sites is an online service that uses your browsing history to suggest other websites you may be interested in. You can view suggested sites by clicking Suggested Sites on the Favorites bar or clicking See Suggested Sites while viewing the Favorites Center.

When you turn on Suggested Sites, your browsing history is sent to Microsoft. Microsoft saves the history, compares it to lists of related websites and then subsequently uses this comparison to suggest other similar sites. If you don't want your browsing history to be sent to Microsoft, do not use this feature.

Web Slices

Internet Explorer 8 also supports web slices. A web slice is a portion of a web page that you can subscribe to. Web Slices behave just like RSS feeds. You can subscribe to get updates and be notified of changes. When Internet Explorer discovers suitable content on a page, the Feeds button on the Command toolbar changes from the orange RSS icon to the green Web Slice icon. When you click the button, Internet Explorer 8 offers to subscribe to the web page, and is it detects changes in the web Slice, it notifies you of updates. You can preview these updates directly from the Favorites bar and click through to the website.

If a page has both Web Slice content and an RSS feed, you can still subscribe to the RSS feed. Click the Feed Options button to the right of the Web Slice button and select the desired feed.

Download parallelization

To support faster downloads, Internet Explorer supports up to six connections per web server instead of two, and also improves performance by allowing parallelization of downloads. This also ensures that a request is not blocked to a web server if two connections already exist.

Figure 7-11. Adding or changing your home page

Configuring Web Pages as Home Pages

One of my favorite features in Internet Explorer 8 is the ability to have up to eight home pages. When you configure a web page as a home page, Internet Explorer opens the page whenever you start a new browser session or click the Home button. If you have more than one home page configured, Internet Explorer opens each page in a separate tab.

The Home Options button to the right of the Home button allows you to display and select from a list of home pages that you've configured. You can also use the options it provides to add, change, or remove home pages. You can add or change home pages by completing the following steps:

1. In Internet Explorer 8, click the Home Options button to the right of the Home button.
2. On the shortcut menu, select Add or Change Home Page. This displays the Add or Change Home Page dialog box shown in Figure 7-11.
3. Choose one of the following options and then click Yes to save your settings:

   Use this webpage as your only home page
   Removes any previously configured home pages and sets the currently selected web page as your only home page.

   Add this webpage to your home page tabs
   Adds the currently selected web page to the bottom of your home page tabs.

 You can have up to eight home pages only. If you try to add a new home page and already have eight home pages, you'll see a warning prompt stating that you've already selected the maximum number of supported home pages. To add the web page as a home page, you'll need to remove at least one of the other home pages.

Use the current tab set as your home page
> Configures all the web pages you've opened in the current tab set as your home pages. Internet Explorer adds the pages in the order in which the tabs are open currently. You will not be able to change the order later.

 Being able to add the current tab set as your home page can save you a great deal of time. To use this feature to your best advantage, open in separate tabs up to eight web pages that you visit frequently. To get the pages in the desired order, click and drag the related tabs into the desired positions. Once you have all the pages open and in the desired order, select Add or Change Home Page and then choose "Use current tab set as your home page."

You can remove home pages by completing the following steps:

1. In Internet Explorer 8, click the Home Options button to the right of the Home button.
2. On the shortcut menu, click Remove. This displays a new shortcut menu.
3. Click a page to remove it or click Remove All to remove all pages.
4. When prompted to confirm the action, click Yes.

Printing Web Pages Without Wasting Paper

Another of my favorite new features in Internet Explorer 8 is the new printing engine. Unlike earlier releases of Internet Explorer, the default printing option is to shrink the selected page to fit your default printer settings—this feature alone is extremely helpful. If you select the Print Options button to the right of the Print button and then select Print Preview, you can customize the print layout using the dialog box shown in Figure 7-12.

 In Print Preview, four Adjust Margin guides are provided—one each for the left, right, top, and bottom margins. Not only do these guides show you visually where the margins are located, but you can also click a margin guide and drag left/right or up/down.

Table 7-1 summarizes the Print Preview options by listing the buttons on the top and bottom rows from left to right. The most important new option is the Change Print Size button, which lets you set the print size as a percentage of the actual page size. You can click the Change Print Size button and then select Shrink to Fit to ensure that a page prints properly.

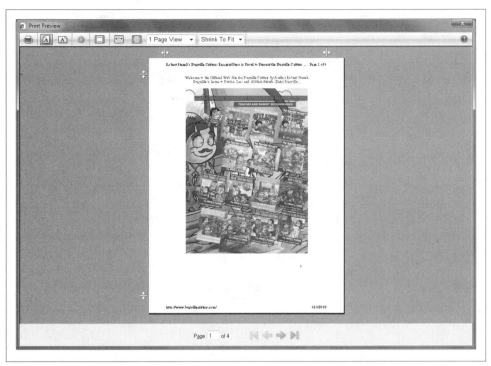

Figure 7-12. Using Print Preview to help you configure printing options

Table 7-1. Print Preview options in Internet Explorer

Location/Option	Press to select	Description
Top row		
Print Document	Alt-P	Prints the document with the current settings.
Portrait	Alt-O	Changes the print orientation to portrait.
Landscape	Alt-L	Changes the print orientation to landscape.
Page Setup	Alt-U	Displays the Page Setup dialog box for configuring page size, paper source, headers, footers, and margins.
Turn Headers and Footers On or Off	Alt-E	Turns on or off the printing of headers and footers. You'll see headers and footers in the preview if they are turned on currently.
View Full Width	Alt-W	Resizes the page width so that it fills the preview window.
View Full Page	Alt-1	Resizes the print preview so that the full page is shown.
Show Multiple Pages	Alt-N	Allows you to select the number of print pages to preview simultaneously.
Change Print Size	Alt-S	Allows you to change the print size of the page. Use the print preview to determine how the web page will print. To ensure that the page prints properly with the margins you've selected, choose Shrink to Fit.

Bottom row		
Current Page	Alt-A	Allows you to specify which print page you want to preview.
First Page	Alt-Home	Allows you to view the first printed page.
Previous Page	Alt-left arrow	Allows you to go to the previous page in the print preview.
Next Page	Alt-right arrow	Allows you to go to the next page in the print preview.
Last Page	Alt-End	Allows you to view the last printed page.

Understanding Status Bar Indicators

The Status bar shows web addresses in links as well as the load progress and error status of the current page. When you are working with Internet Explorer 8, don't overlook important changes to the Status bar. On the right side of the Status bar, you'll find an InPrivate filtering indicator, an Internet security indicator, and a view magnifier (see Figure 7-13).

Figure 7-13. The Status bar in Internet Explorer

The filtering status indicator specifies the filtering status as it relates to the currently accessed site or page. When you are accessing a website that contains content from another provider, such as a news article, a map or an advertisement, some information about your visit is sent to the provider. As you visit other websites that contains content from the same provider, the provider can build a profile of your web browsing patterns. If you don't want information about your visit shared with a provider, you can block your information from being shared. However, this could cause some of the content on websites you visit to be unavailable. To manage filtering, click the filtering icon and then:

- Select Off to turn filtering off and allow your information to be shared.
- Select Automatically Block to turn filtering on and prevent your information from being shared.
- Select Choose Content to Block to be able to selectively block information sharing.
- Select Settings to configure the filtering state and other options.

When you've enabled blocking either selectively or completely, moving the pointer over the filtering status indicator displays a tooltip that specifies whether any content is being blocked.

The Internet security indicator specifies the current security zone and mode that Internet Explorer is using. Internet Explorer has separate security zones for Internet, Local Intranet, Trusted Sites, and Restricted Sites. When accessing sites in the Internet zone, Internet Explorer uses Protected Mode by default.

The View Magnifier icon shows the current Zoom setting. If you click the option button to the right of this icon, you can use Zoom settings to shrink or expand the textual and graphical contents of a web page. Shrink the page by selecting a zoom size smaller than 100 percent. Expand the page by selecting a zoom size larger than 100 percent.

Protecting Your Computer While Browsing

When you are browsing the Internet, Internet Explorer 8 runs in Protected Mode. This isolates it from other applications in the operating system and prevents add-ons from writing content in any location beyond temporary Internet file folders without explicit user consent. By isolating Internet Explorer from other applications and restricting write locations, Windows 7 prevents many types of malicious software from exploiting vulnerabilities on your computer. Protected Mode also restricts the way domains, web addresses, and security zones are used.

Protected Mode is a key component in Internet Explorer's comprehensive safety and security suite, but many other safety and security features work together to protect your computer from malicious software. These additional security features include a pop-up blocker and a phishing filter. They also include privacy and content settings.

Viewing and Managing Add-Ons

Protected Mode limits the ActiveX controls and other add-ons that can run in Internet Explorer. Protected Mode also gives you better control over the add-ons that are installed and used. Internet Explorer organizes add-ons into four broad categories:

- Toolbars and extensions
- Search providers
- Accelerators
- InPrivate filtering

As I've already talked about search providers and filtering, I'll focus on toolbars, extensions, and accelerators. You manage these and other add-ons using the dialog box shown in Figure 7-14. To access this dialog box, click Tools→Manage Add-ons while working with Internet Explorer.

Configuring toolbars and extensions

When you select Toolbars and Extensions as the add-on type in the Manage Add-ons dialog box, you can view and manage add-ons, in these unique categories:

All add-ons
Lists all the add-ons that Internet Explorer has used since you installed Windows or the latest version of Internet Explorer.

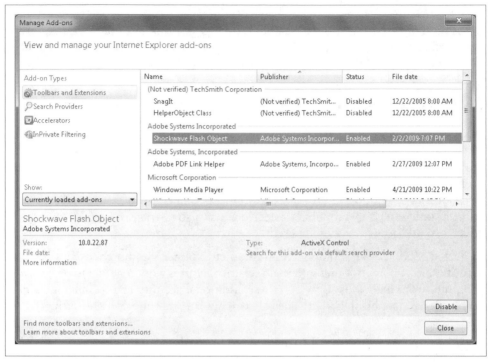

Figure 7-14. Viewing and managing browser add-ons

Currently loaded add-ons
    Lists the add-ons that Internet Explorer is currently using.

Run without permission
    Lists the add-ons configured for use on your computer.

Downloaded controls
    Lists the add-ons you've downloaded from the Internet and configured for use.

In the "Run without permission" list, you'll find default add-ons that are included with Internet Explorer or that you've downloaded through updates from Microsoft, as well as add-ons that you have installed and granted permission to run. For example, if you downloaded the ActiveX control for Flash and granted run permission to this control, you'll see it on the "Run without permission" list and the "Downloaded controls" list. Although you can enable or disable any ActiveX controls and other add-ons, you can delete only ActiveX controls and other add-ons that you've downloaded.

Disabling and enabling add-ons is easy. Click the add-on you want to work with. To disable the add-on, click "Disable" to prevent the add-on from running in Internet Explorer. To enable the add-on, click "Enable" to allow the add-on to run in Internet Explorer.

To remove an add-on, select the add-on by clicking it and then click the "More information" link. In the More Information dialog box, click Remove. When prompted to confirm that you want to delete the add-on, click Yes. If the add-on has an entry in the Uninstall a Program control panel, you should use that to remove it. This makes it more likely that you will remove all trace of it.

Rather than disabling or deleting an add-on you've installed, such as the Adobe Shockwave Flash Object, you can specify the websites on which the control can run. To do this, select the add-on by clicking it and then click the "More information" link. In the More Information dialog box, you can configure the add-on so it can run on all sites or only specific sites. To allow the add-on to run on all sites when enabled, click "Allow on all sites." To allow the add on to run only on specified sites, click "Remove all sites." Next, to allow the add-on to run, you'll need to enable it and then when you visit websites, you'll need to allow it to run when prompted. This will allow the add-on to run whenever you visit the website.

Configuring accelerators

Accelerators are a new feature in Internet Explorer 8 that help you quickly perform routine tasks without having to navigate to other websites. To use accelerators, you highlight text on any web page and then click the blue accelerator icon that appears above your selection. You can then select one of the installed accelerators to perform a specific task, such as:

- Blog with Windows Live
- E-mail with Windows Live
- Map with Bing
- Search with Bing
- Translate with Bing

While you are working with the accelerator shortcut menu, you can click All Accelerators to view additional accelerators that may be available. If you click All Accelerators→Find More Accelerators, you'll open the Accelerators gallery in a new tab and be able to browse for additional accelerators to install.

When you select "Accelerators" as the add-on type in the Manage Add-ons dialog box, you can view and manage accelerators, as shown in Figure 7-15.

Each type of accelerator you can install has a specific category. For example, the Blog with Windows Live accelerator is in the Blog category. For each category, you can specify a default accelerator to use in the Manage Add-ons dialog box. Click the accelerator in the name list and then click "Set as default." To stop using an accelerator as the default, simply select another default for the related category. Alternatively, you can click the accelerator in the name list and then click "Remove as default."

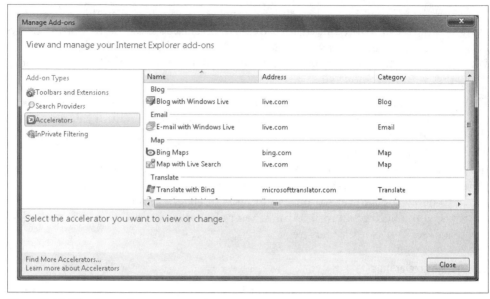

Figure 7-15. Viewing and managing accelerators

Disabling and enabling accelerators is easy. Click the accelerator you want to work with. To disable the accelerator, click Disable to prevent the accelerator from running in Internet Explorer. To enable the accelerator, click Enable to allow the accelerator to run in Internet Explorer.

To remove an accelerator, select the accelerator by clicking it and then click Remove. When prompted to confirm that you want to delete the accelerator, click Yes.

Understanding Web Address and Domain Restrictions

In Internet Explorer, the component responsible for parsing web addresses and determining domain name and location components is the Universal Resource Locator (URL) handler. URLs are simply the formal names of web addresses and other types of addresses that you can use to universally locate resources on the Internet. While the URL handler is extracting the domain name and location components from a web address, it performs several checks to ensure the validity of the web address and prevent possible URL-parsing exploitations, such as URLs that attempt to run commands or URLs that perform suspect actions.

As part of its standard features, Internet Explorer 8 supports both standard English domain names and internationalized domain names. English domain names are domain names represented using the letters A–Z, the numerals 0–9, and the hyphen. Internationalized domain names, also referred to as IDNs, are domain names represented using native language characters.

Unfortunately, as sometimes happens when features are introduced, Internet Explorer's support for internationalized domain names makes it possible to create lookalike domain names for popular and trusted sites. For example, someone might create a site at *http://www.micrósoft.com*, and if you didn't look really closely at the domain name, you could be fooled into believing you were accessing *http://www.microsoft.com*.

To help ensure that international characters aren't used to make a site seem like something it isn't, Internet Explorer implements international domain name antispoofing. International domain name antispoofing is designed to warn you against sites that could otherwise appear as known, trusted sites. Thanks to this feature, you'd receive a warning notification about possible spoofing if you clicked on a lookalike link.

Viewing and Managing Browsing History

As you browse the Web, Internet Explorer stores information about the pages you visit, the content of those pages, the information that websites collect from you, and the information you provide while at websites. This information is collectively referred to as your *browsing history*. Your browsing history includes:

Temporary Internet files
Temporary Internet files are copies of web pages, images, and other related files.

Browser cookies
Browser cookies store information about you collected by the websites you visit.

History list
The history list stores a list of websites and pages you've visited according to the date accessed and the web address.

Form data
Form data consists of information you've typed into online forms.

Passwords
Passwords consist of passwords you've used when you signed into websites that use forms-based authentication.

Internet Explorer stores copies of this information to improve your browsing experience. If you visit the same site or page later, Internet Explorer can use the data it has stored in its browser cache on your computer rather than having to reload the page and its contents over the Web. This data can also be used to reauthenticate you on websites that require authentication and to provide information for automatically completing web forms.

Configuring temporary Internet file storage

With temporary Internet files, Internet Explorer can use copies of web pages, images, and other related files rather than having to download these files. This allows you to view pages faster on subsequent visits. You can control the way Internet Explorer stores copies of temporary Internet files by completing the following steps.

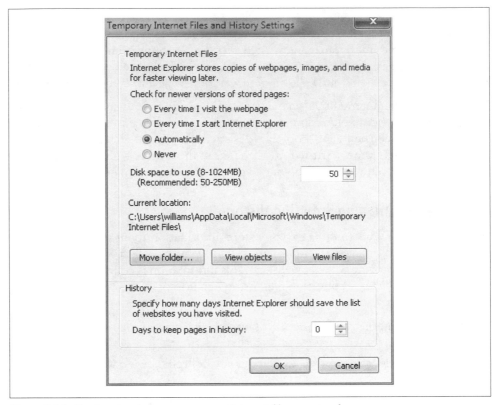

Figure 7-16. Configuring the way temporary Internet files are stored

1. In Internet Explorer, click Tools→Internet Options. This displays the Internet Options dialog box.

2. On the General tab, click Settings under Browsing History. This displays the Temporary Internet Files and History Settings dialog box, as shown in Figure 7-16.

3. Configure how Internet Explorer uses stored data using the following "Check for newer versions of stored pages" options:

Every time I visit the webpage
> Select this option if you want Internet Explorer to check for a newer version every time you access a page. With this option selected, Internet Explorer will use a newer version when available and the cached version of the page otherwise.

Every time I start Internet Explorer
> Select this option if you want Internet Explorer to check for a newer version the first time you access a page during a browser session. With this option selected, Internet Explorer will use a newer version when available and the cached version of the page otherwise.

Automatically

Select this option if you want Internet Explorer to check for a newer version the first time you access a page during a browser session, and to check for changes to images in a page according to the frequency with which they are changed. With this option selected, Internet Explorer will use a newer version when available and the cached version of the page otherwise. Internet Explorer will also check for newer images less frequently when images are changed infrequently.

Never

Select this option if you want Internet Explorer to always use a cached version of a page if available. With this option selected, Internet Explorer will download a page only the first time you access it and will use the cached version of the page otherwise.

4. Use the "Disk space to use" combo box to set the amount of disk space reserved for temporary Internet files. The recommended space to reserve is from 50 MB to 250 MB; the default value is based on the amount of free space available.

5. By default, your temporary Internet files are stored in your user profile. If you want to move the folder used for temporary Internet files to a different location, click "Move folder" and then use the Browse for Folder dialog box to select the new location. Generally speaking, you'll want to move the temporary Internet files only if your primary disk is running low on space and you have another disk available.

6. Click OK to save your settings.

Configuring the history list

With the history list, Internet Explorer stores information about the date you accessed a site and the pages you visited while at the site. You can control the way Internet Explorer creates and uses the history list by completing the following steps:

1. In Internet Explorer, click Tools→Internet Options. This displays the Internet Options dialog box.

2. On the General tab, click Settings under Browsing History. This displays the Temporary Internet Files and History Settings dialog box shown in Figure 7-16.

3. By default, Internet Explorer saves 20 days' worth of information regarding websites and web pages you've accessed. If you don't want Internet Explorer to create a history list, you can set the "Days to keep pages in history" box to 0. Otherwise, set the "Days to keep pages in history" box to the desired number of days to retain the browser history.

4. Click OK to save your settings.

Configuring AutoComplete settings for forms and passwords

AutoComplete settings control whether and how Internet Explorer stores web addresses, form data, and passwords. As you type web addresses in the Address bar, these addresses are listed according to the text you enter, allowing you to select an address in the history list. With form data, Internet Explorer stores the text you entered into online forms. When you fill out similar form fields later, Internet Explorer displays the data you previously provided so that you can select it rather than having to retype it.

With passwords, Internet Explorer stores the passwords you used when you signed into websites that use forms-based authentication. When you visit a site again, Internet Explorer can use the password to reauthenticate you or provide the password for you after you enter your username.

You can control the way AutoComplete works by completing the following steps:

1. In Internet Explorer, click Tools→Internet Options. This displays the Internet Options dialog box.

2. On the Content tab, click Settings under AutoComplete. This displays the Auto-Complete Settings dialog box shown in Figure 7-17.

3. Use the following options to configure how AutoComplete works, and then click OK to save your settings:

   Address bar
   > Select this option to save AutoComplete data for web addresses.

   Browsing history
   > Select this option to include web addresses from the browsing history.

   Favorites
   > Select this option to include web addresses from your favorites lists.

   Feeds
   > Select this option to include web addresses from your RSS feeds.

   Use Windows Search for better results
   > Select this option to use Windows Search results to enhance AutoComplete's results.

   Forms
   > Select this option to save AutoComplete data for form fields.

   User names and passwords on forms
   > Select this option to save AutoComplete data for usernames and passwords you enter.

   Ask me before saving passwords
   > Select this option to prompt you before saving a password. If you don't select this option, passwords are saved automatically.

Figure 7-17. Specifying the AutoComplete settings to use

Configuring the use of browser cookies

Internet Explorer stores in browser cookies the information about you that is collected by the websites you visit. Websites use cookies for a variety of reasons, such as tracking your preferences and storing information about items you've added to a shopping cart. When you access the same site later, the site can use the information stored in the cookie to enhance your browsing experience or obtain any necessary information about you.

Internet Explorer allows sites to store cookies on your computer based on where those sites are located. For sites on your local network and sites you've specifically designated as trusted, Internet Explorer accepts all cookies regardless of your privacy settings. For sites you've specifically designated as restricted, Internet Explorer blocks all cookies regardless of your privacy settings. When you are accessing sites on the public Internet that are configured as neither trusted sites nor restricted sites, you can manage the way cookies are used on the Privacy tab of the Internet Properties dialog box.

Internet Explorer relies on a website's compact privacy policy to determine how the site uses cookies. The World Wide Web Consortium (W3C) has defined an official recommendation regarding web privacy, called the Platform for Privacy Preferences Project (P3P). P3P enables websites to report their privacy practices in policy statements. Internet Explorer relies on what the site reports and cannot determine whether cookies are used as reported.

When working with cookies, the two important terms to understand are *explicit consent* and *implicit consent*. Explicit consent means you have specifically opted to allow a site to collect personal information, such as when you accept a site's rules during signup. Implicit consent means you haven't opted out or told the site you don't want personal information to be collected. On the Privacy tab, use the Settings slider to specify how cookies should be used. Privacy settings available include:

Block All Cookies
> Blocks all new cookies and ensures that websites cannot read any existing cookies. Because Allow exceptions are ignored while this setting is selected, any sites you've configured as Allow exceptions are blocked as well.

High
> Blocks all cookies from sites that do not have a declared privacy policy regarding consent. It also blocks all cookies with a declared privacy policy stating that cookies gather information that could be used to contact you without your explicit consent.

Medium High
> Blocks cookies from sites other than the one you are viewing if they do not have a declared privacy policy statement regarding consent. It blocks cookies from other sites with a declared privacy policy stating that cookies gather information that could be used to contact you without your explicit consent. It also blocks cookies from the current site if there is a declared privacy policy statement specifying that cookies gather information that could be used to contact you without your implicit consent.

Medium
> The default privacy setting. Blocks cookies from sites other than the one you are viewing that do not have a declared privacy policy regarding consent. It restricts cookies from the current site and blocks cookies from other sites that have a declared privacy policy stating that cookies gather information that could be used to contact you without your implicit consent.

Low
> Blocks cookies from sites other than the one you are viewing that do not have a declared privacy policy regarding consent. It restricts cookies from other sites that have a declared privacy policy stating that cookies gather information that could be used to contact you without your implied consent.

Accept All Cookies
> Accepts all new cookies and allows websites to read existing cookies. Because Block exceptions are ignored while this setting is selected, any sites you've configured as Block exceptions are allowed as well.

You can configure Internet Explorer's cookie settings by completing the following steps:

1. In Internet Explorer, click Tools→Internet Options. This displays the Internet Options dialog box.
2. On the Privacy tab, shown in Figure 7-18, use the Settings slider to set the desired privacy level for cookies.

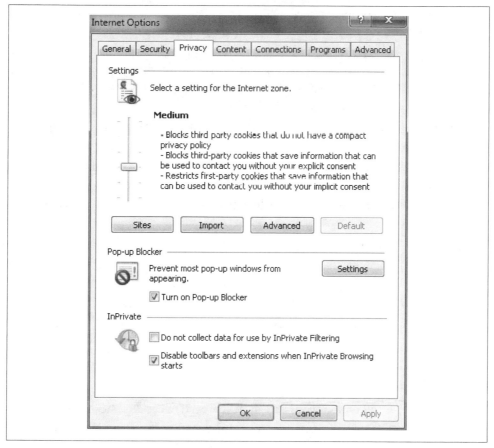

Figure 7-18. Configuring cookie settings for the Internet zone

3. To make an exception for a site rather than raise or lower your privacy setting, click the Sites button. Type the address of the website in the field provided, and then click Allow or Block as appropriate. If you click Allow, cookies for the site will always be accepted. If you click Block, cookies for the site will always be blocked.

 You cannot make exceptions when you use the Block All Cookies or Allow All Cookies setting. With these settings, all cookies are always either blocked or allowed.

Clearing your browsing history

Occasionally, you may want to clear your browsing history. You may want to do this to prevent malicious individuals from getting your information or to maintain your privacy regarding websites and pages you've visited. You may also want to do this if you are experiencing problems accessing a particular site or page, or to ensure that you are accessing the most recent version of a website or page.

Although Internet Explorer makes it appear you can clear out the browsing history while the application is running, you need to close all Internet Explorer windows to fully clear out the browsing history. You also can configure Internet Explorer to clear out the history when you exit the browser and close all open windows.

To automatically clear the history when you exit Internet Explorer, complete these steps:

1. In Internet Explorer, click Tools→Internet Options. This displays the Internet Options dialog box.

2. On the General tab, select the "Delete browsing history on exit" checkbox and then click OK.

To clear out your browsing history, complete these steps:

1. Close all Internet Explorer windows. Click Start→Control Panel→Network and Internet→Internet Options.

2. On the General tab, click Delete under Browsing History. This displays the Delete Browsing History dialog box shown in Figure 7-19. Note that the dialog box has two sections. The first checkbox is for preserving data; all the others are for removing data.

3. If you want to preserve cookies and other temporary files for websites listed in the Favorites Center, select the "Preserve Favorites website data" checkbox. Otherwise, to ensure all temporary data can be removed, clear this checkbox.

4. Specify the individual types of temporary Internet files to remove by selecting their checkboxes.

5. Click Delete to clear out the specified types of temporary Internet files.

Blocking Pop-Ups

Some web pages contain pop-ups. A *pop-up* is a subwindow that is displayed when you access a web page. Sometimes pop-ups appear on top of the browser window; other times they appear under the browser window. Because most pop-ups contain ads or are otherwise unwanted content, Internet Explorer blocks most types of pop-ups it recognizes by default in all security zones, except the Local Intranet zone. This means Internet Explorer uses the Pop-up Blocker when you are browsing sites on the public Internet, trusted sites, and restricted sites, but does not use the Pop-up Blocker when you access sites on your local network.

By default, when a pop-up is blocked, Internet Explorer displays a message on the Information bar stating this. If you click the Information bar and select Temporarily Allow Pop-ups, Internet Explorer will allow pop-ups from the site until you navigate

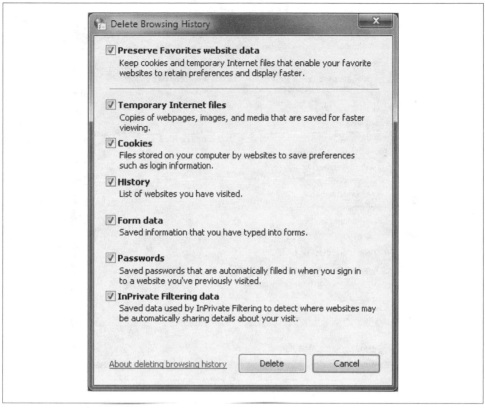

Figure 7-19. Deleting your browsing history

away from the page. Alternatively, if you click the Information bar and select Always Allow Pop-ups from This Site, Internet Explorer will configure the site as an Allowed Site, and all pop-ups for the site will then be displayed.

You can enable or disable pop-up blocking by completing the following steps:

1. In Internet Explorer, click Tools→Internet Options. This displays the Internet Options dialog box.

2. On the Privacy tab, select the Turn on Pop-up Blocker checkbox to enable the Pop-up Blocker, or clear the Turn on Pop-up Blocker checkbox to disable the Pop-up Blocker.

With pop-up blocking enabled, you can configure the way the Pop-up Blocker works by completing the following steps:

1. In Internet Explorer, click Tools→Internet Options. This displays the Internet Options dialog box.

Figure 7-20. Configuring Pop-up Blocker settings

2. On the Privacy tab, select Settings under Pop-up Blocker. This displays the Pop-up Blocker Settings dialog box shown in Figure 7-20.

3. You can use these options to add or remove allowed sites:

   Add
   > To allow a site's pop-ups to be displayed, type the address of the site in the field provided, such as *www.msn.com*, and then click Add. This site is then permitted to use pop-ups regardless of Internet Explorer settings.

   Remove
   > To remove a site that is currently allowed to display pop-ups, click the site address and then click Remove.

   Remove All
   > To remove all sites that are currently allowed to display pop-ups, click Remove All. When prompted to confirm the action, click Yes.

4. To stop playing a sound when a pop-up is blocked, clear "Play a sound when a pop-up is blocked."

5. To stop displaying an information message in the browser when a pop-up is blocked, clear "Show Information Bar when a pop-up is blocked."

6. By default, most types of automatic pop-ups are blocked when the Pop-up Blocker is enabled. You can use the following options of the Blocking Level list to control the types of pop-ups that are blocked:

   High: Block all pop-ups (Ctrl-Alt to override)
   > With this setting, Internet Explorer tries to block all pop-ups. To temporarily override this setting, press Ctrl-Alt while clicking a link to open a page and its related pop-up.

   Medium: Block most automatic pop-ups
   > With this setting, Internet Explorer tries to block pop-ups most commonly used to display ads or other unwanted content. Some types of pop-ups are allowed. To override this setting temporarily, press Ctrl-Alt while clicking a link to open a page and its related pop-up.

   Low: Allow pop-ups from secure sites
   > With standard (HTTP) connections, Internet Explorer attempts to block pop-ups most commonly used to display ads or other unwanted content. With secure (HTTPS) connections, Internet Explorer allows pop-ups.

7. Click Close and then click OK to save your settings.

Protecting Your Computer from Phishing

Phishing is a technique whereby a site attempts to trick you into giving them personal information by impersonating your bank or other trusted establishment that you have a relationship with. Internet Explorer 8 includes SmartScreen filter, which is a phishing filter that is designed to warn you about potential phishing sites and known phishing sites. The warning is displayed on the Status bar as discussed previously.

SmartScreen filter is active by default for all security zones, except the Local Intranet zone. This means Internet Explorer uses the phishing filter when you are browsing sites on the public Internet, trusted sites, and restricted sites, but does not use the phishing filter when you access sites on your local network.

The phishing filter is always on by default. In Internet Explorer, you can turn off this feature by clicking Safety→SmartScreen Filter→Turn Off SmartScreen Filter. You can then manually check sites if desired by using the Check This Website option. If you suspect a site is collecting personal information without your knowledge or consent, you can report the site by using the Report Unsafe Website option. Keep in mind that you may have granted implied consent to a site when you signed up to use a site, or when you downloaded and installed a particular browser add-on or related Internet software.

Restricting Permissions Using Security Zones

Security levels and zones are important parts of Internet Explorer's security features. You can display security options for Internet Explorer by clicking Tools→Internet

Options, and then clicking the Security tab in the Internet Options dialog box, as shown in Figure 7-21. The standard levels of security that you can use are:

High
> Appropriate for sites that might contain harmful content. With this security level, Internet Explorer runs with maximum safeguards and with less-secure features disabled.

Medium-high
> Appropriate for most public Internet sites. With this security level, Internet Explorer prompts you prior to downloading all potentially unsafe types of content and disables downloading of unsigned ActiveX controls.

Medium
> Appropriate only for trusted sites. With this security level, Internet Explorer prompts you prior to downloading most potentially unsafe contents and disables downloading of unsigned ActiveX controls.

Medium-low
> Appropriate only for sites on your internal network. With this security level, Internet Explorer disables downloading of unsigned ActiveX controls but downloads and runs most types of content without prompting. This option is available only for the "Local intranet" and "Trusted sites" zones.

Low
> Appropriate only for sites you know are trustworthy, such as secure internal sites. With this security level, Internet Explorer uses minimal safeguards, and downloads and runs most types of content without prompts. This option is available only for the "Local intranet" and "Trusted sites" zones.

Internet Explorer 8 uses security zones to help you restrict permissions according to where websites are located and what you know about them. Each security zone is assigned a default security level. From most trusted to least trusted, the security zones are:

Local intranet
> This zone is used to configure security settings for sites on your local network. The default security level is Medium-low.

 Unlike early releases of Windows, Windows 7 (and Vista) can automatically detect when websites are on your local network. Windows 7 does this by checking the network address of the website and comparing it to the network address of your computer. Windows 7 also considers sites bypassed by the proxy server and network paths, such as Universal Naming Convention (UNC) paths, as being on the local network.

Figure 7-21. Managing the overall security on a per-zone basis

Trusted sites

> This zone is used to configure security settings for sites that you explicitly trust and that are considered to be free of content that could damage or harm your computer. The default security level is Medium.

Internet

> This zone is used to configure security settings for sites on the public Internet, and is used for all sites not placed in other zones. The default security level is Medium-high.

Restricted sites

> This zone is used to configure security settings for sites that could potentially damage your computer. The default security level is High.

When you are working with the "Local intranet," "Trusted sites," and "Restricted sites" zones, you can specify the web addresses of sites that should be associated with these zones. With the "Local intranet" zone, you can also control the way Windows 7 detects sites on the local network.

Setting the security level for a zone

One way to modify the security level for a zone is to assign a new security level. With the "Local intranet" and "Trusted sites" zones, you can assign any desired security level. With the Internet zone, the only allowed security levels are Medium, Medium-high, and High. With the Restricted zone, the only allowed security level is High. You can also enable or disable Protected Mode on a per-zone basis. Protected Mode is enabled by default for all zones except the "Trusted sites" zone.

To configure the security level for a particular zone, follow these steps:

1. In Internet Explorer, click Tools→Internet Options. This displays the Internet Options dialog box.
2. On the Security tab, click the zone you want to work with.
3. To change the security level, move the "Security level for this zone" slider up or down to the desired level.
4. To enable Protected Mode for the zone, select the Enable Protected Mode checkbox. To disable Protected Mode for the zone, clear the Enable Protected Mode checkbox. Any changes you make to the Protected Mode settings require that you restart Internet Explorer for the changes to take effect.
5. To restore the default security settings for the selected zone, click the "Default level" button.
6. Click OK to save your settings.

To reset security for all zones, follow these steps:

1. In Internet Explorer, click Tools→Internet Options. This displays the Internet Options dialog box.
2. On the Security tab, click the "Reset all zones to default level" button and then click OK to save your settings.

Setting a custom security level for a zone

In addition to being able to assign a specific security level for a zone, you can also set a custom level by configuring the individual security settings summarized in Table 7-2. Generally, you want to set a custom level only to resolve a specific problem you are experiencing and should otherwise rely on the predefined security levels to achieve the desired results. To resolve a problem with a specific site, you might want to consider adding it to a different zone temporarily rather than changing settings for all Internet sites. For example, you could add a site to the Trust Site zone temporarily to see if this resolves a problem.

You can configure a custom security level for a particular zone by completing these steps:

1. In Internet Explorer, click Tools→Internet Options. This displays the Internet Options dialog box.
2. On the Security tab, click the zone you want to work with.
3. Click the "Custom level" button to display the Security Settings dialog box.
4. Use the individual security settings to specify how you want to handle potentially risky actions, files, programs, and downloads. With most settings your options may include:

   Prompt
   Click Prompt to be prompted for approval before proceeding.

   Disable
   Click Disable to skip prompting and automatically refuse the action or download.

   Enable
   Click Enable to skip prompting and automatically accept the action or download.

5. Click OK to save your settings.

Table 7-2. Internet Explorer security settings and their meanings

Security category/setting	Description
.NET Framework	
Loose XAML	Controls the use of Extensible Application Markup Language (XAML) documents that are formatted loosely (rather than strictly) according to their Document Type Definitions (DTDs).
XAML Browser Applications	Controls the use of XAML browser applications for viewing XAML documents within Internet Explorer.
XPS Documents	Controls the use of XML Paper Specification (XPS) formatted documents.
.NET Framework-reliant components	
Permissions for components with manifests	Controls how .NET Framework components with manifests are used. They are either disabled completely or run in High Safety mode.
Run components not signed with Authenticode	Controls the use of .NET Framework components that are not digitally signed.
Run components signed with Authenticode	Controls the use of .NET Framework components that are digitally signed.
ActiveX controls and plug-ins	
Allow previously unused ActiveX controls to run without prompt	Controls whether new ActiveX controls can run without first prompting for permission.
Allow scriptlets	Controls the use of scriptlets in web pages.

ActiveX controls and plug-ins

Automatic prompting for ActiveX controls	Controls whether you are automatically prompted each time before using ActiveX controls.
Binary and script behaviors	Controls the direct execution of binary executables and scripts, such as when you click links to an executable or script.
Display video and animation on a web page that does not use external media player	Controls whether embedded video and animation play in Internet Explorer.
Download signed ActiveX controls	Controls the downloading of signed ActiveX controls.
Download unsigned ActiveX controls	Controls the downloading of unsigned ActiveX controls.
Initialize and script ActiveX controls not marked as safe for scripting	Controls whether ActiveX controls not marked as safe for scripting can be modified or scripted based on the contents of a web page.
Only allow approved domains to use ActiveX without prompt	Controls whether installed ActiveX controls can run on a domain other than the one you installed it from.
Run ActiveX controls and plug-ins	Controls whether ActiveX controls and browser plug-ins run in Internet Explorer.
Script ActiveX controls marked for safe scripting	Controls whether ActiveX controls marked for safe scripting can be modified or scripted based on the contents of a web page. If you change this setting, you must restart Internet Explorer for the change to be applied.

Downloads

Automatic prompting for file downloads	Controls whether Internet Explorer prompts you for file downloads.
File download	Controls whether Internet Explorer downloads files.
Font download	Controls whether Internet Explorer downloads fonts.

Enable .NET Framework setup

Enable .NET Framework setup	Controls whether .NET Framework setup is launched when you visit a site that contains .NET content.

Miscellaneous

Access data sources across domains	Controls whether scripts and other elements in a page can access data sources from other domains.
Allow META refresh	Controls whether automatic refresh or redirection of a page is allowed using the HTML META tag.
Allow scripting of Microsoft web browser control	Controls whether a web page can script the browser control directly.
Allow script-initiated windows without size or position constraints	Controls whether a script in a web page can open a window without size or position details.

Miscellaneous

Allow web pages to use restricted protocols for active content	Controls whether a web page can use restricted protocols with scripts and other types of active content.
Allow websites to open windows without Address or Status bar	Controls whether a script in a web page can open a window without an Address or Status bar.
Display mixed content	Controls whether a web page can display content from both secure and unsecure sources.
Don't prompt for client certificate selection when no certificates or only one certificate exists	Controls whether Internet Explorer prompts you to select a client certificate when there is only one or no certificate available.
Drag and drop or copy and paste files	Controls whether Internet Explorer allows you to use drag and drop or copy and paste with web pages.
Include local directory path when uploading to a server	Controls whether Internet Explorer includes the full local directory path when you upload files to a remote server.
Installation of desktop items	Controls whether Internet Explorer allows items to be installed on the desktop.
Launching applications and unsafe files	Controls whether Internet Explorer allows other applications to be started and whether it allows unsafe files to be opened.
Launching programs and files in an IFRAME	Controls whether Internet Explorer allows other applications and files to be opened in an IFRAME.
Navigate windows and frames across different domains	Controls whether Internet Explorer allows windows and frames to come from multiple domains.
Open files based on content, not file extension	Controls whether Internet Explorer opens files based on the Multipurpose Internet Mail Extension (MIME) type or based on the file extension.
Submit nonencrypted form data	Controls whether Internet Explorer can submit nonencrypted (plain-text) form data to a website.
Use Pop-up Blocker	Controls whether the Pop-up Blocker is enabled or disabled.
Use SmartScreen Filter	Controls whether the phishing filter is enabled or disabled.
User data persistence	Controls whether user data such as browsing history is included in a web page that has been saved to disk.
Websites in less privileged content zone can navigate into this zone	Controls whether websites in a zone with a lower security level can redirect to websites in a zone with a higher security level.

Scripting

Active scripting	Controls whether Active scripting of web pages is allowed.
Allow programmatic clipboard access	Controls whether a script or other element in a web page can read what is copied to your computer's clipboard.
Allow Status bar updates via script	Controls whether a script or other element in a web page can update the Status bar.

Scripting	
Allow websites to prompt for information using scripted windows	Controls whether a script or other element in a web page can display a prompt.
Enable XSS filter	Controls whether cross-site scripting filtering is enabled. When enabled the filter tries to limit cross-site scripting attacks which occur when a website adds JavaScript to otherwise legitimate requests to another website, often in an attempt to gain access to privileged information.
Scripting of Java applets	Controls whether a script or other element in a web page can script Java applets.
User authentication	
Logon	Controls the way user authentication works when you need to log on to a website. The options are Anonymous Logon, Automatic Logon Only in Intranet Zone, Automatic Logon with Current User Name and Password, and Prompt for User Name and Password.

Configuring local intranet detection and sites

Windows 7 automatically detects sites on the local network according to their network address. If you experience problems with sites not being detected properly, you may want to disable automatic detection settings and allow only specifically included types of sites to be considered local sites. In addition to or instead of doing this, you can specifically identify a site as being on the local network.

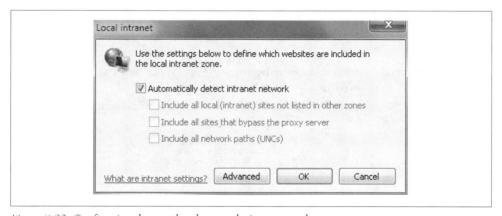

Figure 7-22. Configuring the way local network sites are used

To configure local intranet detection, specify local sites, or both, complete the following steps:

1. In Internet Explorer, click Tools→Internet Options. This displays the Internet Options dialog box.
2. On the Security tab, click the "Local intranet" zone and then click the Sites button. This displays the "Local intranet" dialog box, as shown in Figure 7-22.

3. If Windows 7 is unable to detect sites on the local network automatically, you may need to manually configure the intranet zone settings. To do this, clear "Automatically detect intranet network" and then specify sites to include. You can include local (intranet) sites not listed in other zones, sites that bypass the proxy server, and network paths (UNCs) by selecting the related checkboxes. To exclude a type of resource, clear the related checkbox.

4. To specify additional sites for the "Local intranet" zone or require secure verification using Hypertext Transfer Protocol Secure (HTTPS) for all sites in the "Local intranet" zone, click the Advanced button. This displays a new "Local intranet" dialog box with the following options:

   Add
   > To add a site to the "Local intranet" zone, type the web address for a site, then click Add.

   Remove
   > To remove a site from the "Local intranet" zone, click the web address, then click Remove.

   Require server verification (https:) for all sites in this zone
   > To require secure verification for all sites in this zone using HTTPS, select this checkbox.

5. Click OK twice.

Configuring trusted sites

If you find that the normal security settings are too restrictive for a site that you explicitly trust and know to be free of content that could damage your computer, you can designate the site as a trusted site by completing these steps:

1. In Internet Explorer, click Tools→Internet Options. This displays the Internet Options dialog box.

2. On the Security tab, click the "Trusted sites" zone and then click the Sites button. This displays the "Trusted sites" dialog box, as shown in Figure 7-23.

3. To add a site to the "Trusted sites" zone, type the web address for the site and then click Add.

4. To remove a site from the "Trusted sites" zone, click the web address and then click Remove.

5. To require secure verification for all sites in this zone using HTTPS, select the "Require server verification (https:) for all sites in this zone" checkbox.

6. Click OK to save your settings.

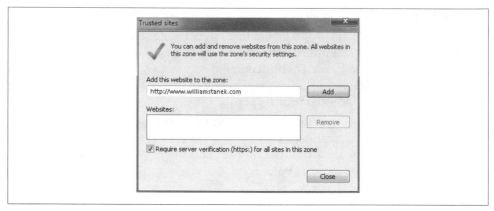

Figure 7-23. Configuring trusted sites and related options

Configuring restricted sites

If you find a site that has offensive content or content that could damage your computer, you can designate the site as a restricted site by completing the following steps:

1. In Internet Explorer, click Tools→Internet Options. This displays the Internet Options dialog box.

2. On the Security tab, click the "Restricted sites" zone and then click the Sites button. This displays the "Restricted sites" dialog box, as shown in Figure 7-24.

3. To add a site to the "Restricted sites" zone, type the web address for the site, then click Add.

4. To remove a site from the "Restricted sites" zone, click the web address, then click Remove.

5. Click OK to save your settings.

Figure 7-24. Configuring restricted sites

Keep in mind that designating a site as a restricted site doesn't stop you or anyone else from accessing the site. Instead, it establishes a higher level of security for the site.

Setting Advanced Internet Options

In the Internet Options dialog box, you'll find a wide variety of advanced settings on the Advanced tab. These advanced options allow you to fine-tune the way Internet Explorer works. Some advanced options can be set through other settings in the Internet Options dialog box, but they are provided on the Advanced tab so that you have a central location for managing settings.

Advanced settings are organized into several categories. The main categories are:

Accessibility
Settings designed to improve ease of access

Browsing
Settings that control the general way browsing works in Internet Explorer as well as the way web pages are displayed

HTTP 1.1
Settings that control whether and how Internet Explorer uses HTTP 1.1

International
Settings that control whether and how Internet Explorer displays and sends international domain names

Multimedia
Settings that control how Internet Explorer works with pictures, sounds, animations, and ClearType text

Printing
Settings that control whether Internet Explorer prints background colors and images on web pages

Security
Settings that control the way Internet Explorer uses various security and authentication technologies

Table 7-3 lists all the advanced options and details how they are used. Generally, you want to change advanced settings only to resolve a specific issue with the way Internet Explorer displays or accesses web pages. Otherwise, you should rely on the predefined settings. In Table 7-3, a setting is followed by a plus sign (+) if it is enabled by default and an asterisk (*) if you must restart Internet Explorer for a setting change to take effect.

You can configure advanced options by completing these steps:

1. In Internet Explorer, click Tools→Internet Options. This displays the Internet Options dialog box.
2. On the Advanced tab, select or clear individual advanced options to control the way Internet Explorer displays or accesses web pages. With most settings, select them to enable the setting and clear them to disable the setting.
3. Click OK to save your settings.

Some changes to advanced options may cause Internet Explorer to work differently than expected. If you experience unintended consequences because you have changed advanced options, you can restore the default configuration for advanced options by completing these steps:

1. In Internet Explorer, click Tools→Internet Options. This displays the Internet Options dialog box.
2. On the Advanced tab, click "Restore advanced settings."

Table 7-3. Internet Explorer advanced options and their meanings[a]

Category/setting	Description
accessibility	
Always expand ALT text for images	Specifies whether the image size should expand to fit all of the alternate text when the Show Pictures checkbox is cleared.
Enable Caret Browsing for new windows and tabs	Controls whether Caret Browsing is enabled. With Caret Browsing on, you can move up, down, left, and right on the web page by pressing and holding the arrow keys. To select text, move the cursor to the beginning of the text, hold down the Shift key and move the arrow keys until the text you want is selected. With text selected, you can copy by pressing Ctrl-C and paste by pressing Ctrl-V.
Move system caret with focus/selection changes	Specifies whether to move the system caret whenever the focus or selection changes. Some accessibility aids, such as screen readers and screen magnifiers, use the system caret to determine which area of the screen to read or magnify.
Reset text size to medium for new windows and tabs+*	Specifies whether Internet Explorer resets the text size to Medium for new windows and tabs.
Reset text size to medium while zooming+*	Specifies whether Internet Explorer resets the text size to Medium while zooming.
Reset zoom level for new windows and tabs	Specifies whether Internet Explorer resets the zoom level when you open new windows and tabs.
Browsing	
Automatically recover from page layout errors with Compatibility View+	Specifies whether Internet Explorer tries to detect and correct compatibility issues automatically.
Close unused folders in History and Favorites+*	Specifies that when you open a folder in the Favorites bar, History bar, or Organize Favorites window, any folders opened previously will close.
Disable script debugging (Internet Explorer)+	Specifies whether you want to turn off your script debugger, if one is installed. Website developers use script debuggers to test programs and scripts on their web pages.

Browsing

Disable script debugging (Other)+	Specifies whether you want to turn off your script debugger, if one is installed. Website developers use script debuggers to test programs and scripts on their web pages.
Display a notification about every script error	Specifies whether to display the actual script errors when a page does not appear properly due to problems with its scripting. This feature is off by default, but it is useful to developers when testing web pages.
Display Accelerator button on selection+	Specifies whether the Accelerator button is displayed when you select text on a web page. This button provides quick access to Accelerators that are available in the browser.
Enable automatic crash recovery+*	Specifies whether crash recovery is enabled. Automatic Crash Recovery can help to prevent the loss of work in case the browser crashes or hangs.
Enable FTP folder view (outside of Internet Explorer)+	Specifies whether to show FTP sites in folder view, which is similar to browsing folders in Windows Explorer. This feature might not work with certain types of proxy connections. If you clear this checkbox, FTP sites will display their contents in an HTML-based layout.
Enable page transitions+*	Specifies whether, as you move from one web page to another, Internet Explorer fades out the page you are leaving and fades in the page to which you are going.
Enable suggested sites	Specifies whether support for suggested sites is enabled. Suggested Sites is an online service that uses your browsing history to suggest other websites you may be interested in.
Enable third-party browser extensions+*	Specifies whether you want to enable features you installed for use with Internet Explorer that companies other than Microsoft may have created.
Enable visual styles on buttons and controls in webpages+	Specifies that you want the controls in web pages to use Windows display settings.
Enable websites to use the search pane*	Specifies whether websites can use the Search pane in Internet Explorer.
Force offscreen compositing even under Terminal Server*	Specifies that you want to force off-screen compositing even if you are running Terminal Server. This will eliminate the flashing you see with the compositing normally used by Internet Explorer running under Terminal Server; however, choosing this option might severely decrease the performance of Internet Explorer running under Terminal Server.
Notify when downloads complete+	Specifies whether to display a message at the end of a file download, to indicate that the download is complete.
Reuse windows for launching shortcuts (when tabbed browsing is off)+	Specifies that when you click a web link in an Internet-aware program, such as Office Outlook, and an Internet Explorer process is already open, the web page is launched within that instance of Internet Explorer instead of starting a new process.
Show friendly HTTP error messages+	Specifies whether, when there's a problem connecting with an Internet server, to provide a detailed description with hints on how to correct the problem. If you clear this checkbox, you will see just the error code and the name of the error.
Underline Links	Specifies how you want links on web pages underlined. The options are Always, Hover, and Never. To underline all links, click Always. To not underline links, click Never. To underline a link when your mouse pointer is over the link, click Hover.
Use inline AutoComplete (outside of Internet Explorer)	Specifies whether you want Internet Explorer to use the SmartScreen filter prior to completing entries when you type web addresses in. The web address you enter will be checked against a list of reported unsafe websites.

Browsing

Use most recent order when switching tabs with Ctrl-Tab	Specifies whether you want to view tabs in order of the most recently viewed tab when pressing Ctrl-Tab.
Use Passive FTP (for firewall and DSL modem compatibility)+	Specifies whether to use passive FTP, which does not require an FTP server to open a separate, direct connection to a port on your computer. Some network configurations will work only with passive mode turned on, and others will work only with passive mode turned off. This feature allows you to select which mode to use for compatibility with your network settings. Most network configurations will support both modes. The passive FTP mode allows FTP to work even if your computer cannot be contacted directly from outside your network (such as if your computer is connected to a firewalled router on a home or office network).
Use smooth scrolling+	Specifies whether a special type of scrolling is used to display content at a predefined speed.

HTTP 1.1 settings

Use HTTP 1.1+	Specifies whether to attempt to use the HTTP 1.1 protocol when connecting to websites. Some older web servers still use HTTP 1.0, so if you are having difficulties connecting to a website, you might want to clear this checkbox.
Use HTTP 1.1 through proxy connections+	Specifies whether to attempt to use the HTTP 1.1 protocol when connecting to websites by using a proxy server. Some older web servers still use HTTP 1.0, so if you are having difficulties connecting to a website through a proxy connection, you might want to clear this checkbox.

International

Always show encoded addresses*	Specifies how to display Internet addresses that contain UTF-8-encoded characters, which is used by some non-U.S. domain names. If you enable this option, these addresses will be displayed in an encoded format (starting with xn--) and will make it impossible for you to visit websites with these characters. For more information, see "Understanding Web Address and Domain Restrictions" on page 254 earlier in this chapter.
Send IDN server names+*	Specifies whether international domain names are sent to sites on the public Internet using UTF-8 encoding.
Send IDN server names for Intranet addresses*	Specifies whether international domain names are sent to sites on the local network using UTF-8 encoding.
Send UTF-8 URLs+*	Specifies whether to use UTF-8 encoding when exchanging web addresses that contain characters from any language.
Show Information Bar for encoded addresses+*	Specifies whether web addresses are displayed on the Information bar using UTF-8 encoding.
Use UTF-8 for mailto links*	Specifies whether mailto links in web pages use UTF-8 encoding rather than ASCII encoding.

Multimedia

Always use ClearType for HTML*	Specifies whether ClearType is used for text in web pages.
Enable automatic image resizing+	Specifies that you want Internet Explorer to resize large images automatically so that they fit in the browser window.
Play animations in webpages +*	Specifies whether animated images can play when pages are displayed.
Play sounds in webpages+	Specifies whether music and other sounds can play when pages are displayed.

Multimedia

Show image download placeholders	Specifies whether placeholders should be drawn for images while they are downloading. This allows items in the page to be positioned where they would appear when the images are fully downloaded. This option is ignored if the Show Pictures checkbox is cleared, as placeholders are always shown when Show Pictures is disabled.
Show pictures+	Specifies whether images should be included when pages are displayed. When this checkbox is cleared, you can still display an individual image by right-clicking the icon that represents the graphic and then clicking Show Picture.
Smart image dithering+	Specifies whether you want Internet Explorer to smooth images so that they appear less jagged when displayed.

Printing

Print background colors and images	Specifies whether you want Internet Explorer to print background colors and images when you print a web page. Selecting this checkbox might cause your printer to use a lot of ink.

Search from the Address bar

Search from the Address bar	Specifies whether and where search results are displayed. The default option is to display the results in the main window.

Security

Allow active content from CDs to run on My Computer*	Specifies whether active content (such as ActiveX controls) from CDs opens automatically in Internet Explorer.
Allow active content to run in files on My Computer*	Specifies whether active content (such as ActiveX controls) from files on your computer opens automatically in Internet Explorer.
Allow software to run or install even if the signature is invalid	Specifies whether software with an invalid digital signature can run or install.
Check for publisher's certificate revocation+	Specifies whether you want Internet Explorer to check a software publisher's certificate to see if it has been revoked before accepting it as valid.
Check for server certificate revocation+*	Specifies whether you want Internet Explorer to check an Internet site's certificate to see if it has been revoked before accepting it as valid.
Check for signatures on downloaded programs+	Specifies that you want Internet Explorer to verify the integrity of programs you download. When you download programs, a dialog box will appear providing the information that Internet Explorer finds during the check.
Do not save encrypted pages to disk	Specifies whether secure, encrypted web pages are saved in your Temporary Internet Files folder. As these pages may contain sensitive personal information, you may not want to save encrypted pages on a shared computer.
Empty Temporary Internet Files folder when browser is closed	Specifies whether to clear the Temporary Internet Files folder when you close the browser.
Enable DOM storage+	Controls whether DOM storage is enabled. DOM storage is a method for storing and retrieving strings of key-value pairs. Data can be maintained in memory until the tab that created it is closed, or stored on the local machine. This allows web developers to cache text on your computer in a similar fashion to using cookies.

Security	
Enable Integrated Windows Authentication+*	Specifies that you want to turn on Integrated Windows Authentication.
Enable memory protection to help mitigate online attacks	Specifies whether you want to enable memory protection to help protect your computer against online attacks. You can select this option only if your computer supports it.
Enable native XMLHTTP support+	Specifies whether support for XML HTTP is enabled.
Enable SmartScreen Filter	Specifies whether support for the phishing filter is enabled.
Use SSL 2.0	Specifies whether you want to send and receive secured information through Secure Sockets Layer Level 2 (SSL 2.0), the standard protocol for secure transmissions. All secure websites support this protocol.
Use SSL 3.0+	Specifies whether you want to send and receive secured information through Secured Sockets Layer Level 3 (SSL 3.0), a protocol that is intended to be more secure than SSL 2.0. Some websites might not support this protocol.
Use TLS 1.0+	Specifies whether to send and receive secured information through Transport Layer Security (TLS), an open security standard similar to SSL 3.0. Some websites might not support this protocol.
Use TLS 1.1	Specifies whether to send and receive secured information through TLS 1.1.
Use TLS 1.2	Specifies whether to send and receive secured information through TLS 1.2.
Warn about certificate address mismatch+*	Specifies whether Internet Explorer should warn you if the address (URL) in a website's security certificate is not valid.
Warn if changing between secure and not secure mode	Specifies whether Internet Explorer should warn you if you are clicking links or submitting forms between Internet sites that are secure and sites that are not secure.
Warn if POST submittal is redirected to a zone that does not permit posts+	Specifies whether to warn you when information you enter on a web-based form is being sent to a website in a zone other than the one you are currently viewing.

[a] + indicates that a setting is enabled by default; * indicates that you must restart Internet Explorer for a setting change to take effect.

Troubleshooting Internet Explorer Problems

Internet Explorer has several built-in features for helping you resolve problems you may experience. If you are having problems accessing a web page or connecting to the Internet, you can initiate network diagnostics by selecting Diagnose Connection Problems on the Tools menu. As shown in Figure 7-25, Windows Network Diagnostics will then attempt to identify the problem. If the problem can be repaired automatically, you'll see a list of possible solutions. Click the solution to apply it.

Sometimes a problem you are experiencing may be related to:

- The toolbars and add-ons you've installed
- The way you've configured the browsing history

- The security settings or security levels you've applied
- The advanced options you've configured for use
- The search providers and home pages you've configured for use

Figure 7-25. Using network diagnostics to identify problems

Rather than trying to troubleshoot each individual configuration area, Internet Explorer gives you a simple solution for resetting all Internet Explorer settings. The only settings not reset to their original default states are personal settings, such as those for home pages, search providers and accelerators, as well as settings enforced through Group Policy.

You can reset all Internet Explorer settings by completing the following steps:

1. In Internet Explorer, click Tools→Internet Options. This displays the Internet Options dialog box.
2. On the Advanced tab, click Reset under Reset Internet Explorer Settings.
3. When the warning dialog box shown in Figure 7-26 is displayed, click Reset. Optionally, select the "Delete personal settings" checkbox before clicking Reset to delete personal settings, including home pages, search providers, and accelerators. Note that this step will not delete favorites or feeds.
4. Click Close and then click OK. Close all Internet Explorer windows and restart Internet Explorer.

When you exit all Internet Explorer windows and then restart Internet Explorer, all your Internet Explorer settings will be reset, and this should resolve any problems you're experiencing due to Internet Explorer configuration.

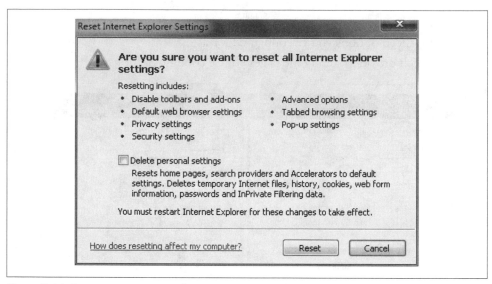

Figure 7-26. Resetting Internet Explorer settings to resolve problems related to Internet Explorer configuration

CHAPTER 8

Creating Your Media Library with Windows Media Player

To tell the truth, I was never been a big fan of Windows Media Player. It always seemed to me that the developers at Microsoft were more interested in the device's custom visual designs and background visualizations than what mattered most: creating an excellent media player that works like a media player should. That has changed, starting with Windows Media Player 11, and now—with Windows Media Player 12—Microsoft has made the player even better by reducing the focus on custom visual designs (known as *skins*), streamlining the bloated menus, tightening up the interface, and completely reorganizing the media library. The result is a media player that:

- Makes it easy to organize and find your media
- Supports all media types: music, pictures, videos, recorded TV, and other media
- Provides professional enhancements for music and video playback

So much has changed in Windows Media Player 12 that (like Windows 7 itself) it seems more like a new program than the same old media player to which we've grown accustomed. Because of this, don't try to rip or burn CDs without first reading this chapter in its entirety. And whatever you do, don't give away your original CDs and DVDs just yet, because you're still going to need them. Also, right up front, you should know that Windows Media Player 12 can play audio and video files formatted for use with Apple iTunes and Apple iPod (as long as the files are not rights-management protected).

Getting into Your Multimedia

Before you can get started with Windows Media Player 12, you're going to need to configure the player for first use. Afterward, you'll want to familiarize yourself with the interface and the supported media formats.

Windows Media Player Not Always Installed

Generally, Windows Media Player 12 is installed by default with Home Premium and Ultimate editions of the Windows 7 operating system that are for sale in the United States. In Europe and elsewhere, these editions of the Windows 7 operating system may not include this media player. Additionally, as Windows Media Player is a feature of the operating system that can be turned on or off, your computer may have this feature disabled, depending on who configured it. If you find that Windows Media Player is not available, you should first check Windows Features to see whether the feature is turned off by clicking Start→Control Panel→Programs→"Turn Windows features on or off." In the Windows Features dialog box, expand the Media Features node by double-clicking it. If you the option for Windows Media Player is not selected, select it and then click OK to make the media player available. If you do not have an option for Windows Media Player, you can download and install the media player by visiting *http://download.microsoft.com*.

Configuring Windows Media Player for the First Use

With Windows Media Player 12, navigating your media library is easier than ever—if you master the subtle changes in the interface. When you first start Windows Media Player by clicking Start→All Programs→Windows Media Player, you'll have to specify how Windows Media Player should be configured. As Figure 8-1 shows, you have two choices.

Figure 8-1. Choosing the initial settings for Windows Media Player

Recommended settings

Configures the default settings you'll want to use most often. If you want to change the settings later, click Organize and then select options. In the Options dialog box, select the Privacy tab. You'll have similar options as with step 2 of the Custom Settings procedure.

Custom settings

Allows you to configure the settings to use. This gives you more control over the way Windows Media Player obtains and stores media information.

You can configure Windows Media Player to use express settings by clicking "Recommended settings" and then clicking Finish. With express settings, Windows Media Player is configured as your default music and video player. Windows Media Player can download CD and DVD information from the Internet, obtain media usage rights automatically, and send anonymous usage information to Microsoft for the Customer Experience Improvement Program.

You can configure Windows Media Player to use custom settings by completing the following steps:

1. Select Custom Settings and then click Next. This displays the Select Privacy Options page shown in Figure 8-2.

Figure 8-2. Choosing your privacy options

2. Use the following settings to configure your privacy settings and then click Next:

Display media information from the Internet

Select this option to allow Windows Media Player to try to obtain media information for the CDs and DVDs that you play. With music CDs, this allows Windows Media Player to retrieve the full details about the CD, including the album cover, album title, album artist, and song titles for each track. To obtain the media information, Windows Media Player sends the CD or DVD identifier to a database operated by your default online store or a Windows Media database, such as the one at *http://fai.music.metaservices.microsoft.com*. The online store or Windows Media database then sends the information back to your computer, where the information is stored. If your computer is offline, Windows Media Player stores the request for media information so that it can try to obtain the media information the next time you connect your computer to the Internet.

Update music files by retrieving media information from the Internet

Select this option to allow Windows Media Player to update music files by retrieving media information from the Internet. Windows Media Player can automatically obtain and update missing media information for music files that are added to or stored in your library, as long as the information is available. Choosing this setting will cause Windows Media Player to modify your music files by updating their metadata (when the information is available).

Download usage rights automatically when I play or sync a file

Select this option to allow Windows Media Player to acquire usage rights automatically for protected content when a file requires them. Usage rights allow you to use protected Windows Media-based files in a specific way. With a *play right*, you have the right to play the file. With a *burn right*, you have the right to burn the file to an audio CD. With a *sync right*, you have the right to sync the file to a portable device, such as an MP3 player. You cannot play, burn, or sync protected content if you do not have a license. In some cases, you may be required to pay for the license. In other cases, you may be required to complete a form before the content provider will issue the license to you.

Send unique Player ID to content providers

Select this option to allow Windows Media Player to send its unique identifier to web servers. The identifier identifies the player connection to a server and does not contain any personally identifiable information about you. Web servers typically use the identifier to monitor your connection, gather statistics, and provide access to content.

Cookies

Click this button to configure how cookies are used on your computer. Windows Media Player uses the cookie settings in Internet Explorer to communicate with other computers when playing streaming content and to communicate with the web sites that provide content to the player. Cookies also enable content providers to provide personalized services from their web sites. See "Configuring the use of browser cookies" on page 259 in Chapter 7 for more information on cookies.

I want to help make Microsoft software and services even better by sending Player usage data to Microsoft

Select this option to send Microsoft anonymous information about the way you use Windows Media Player. Microsoft uses this information to improve future versions of Windows Media Player. Anonymous information about your hardware configuration and how you use related services is also sent to Microsoft.

Store and display a list of recently/frequently played: (Music, Pictures, Video, Playlists)

Select this option to allow Windows Media Player to save lists of your most recently played files. These lists are used to allow you to navigate using the Forward and Back buttons and other similar options for music, pictures, video, and playlists.

3. On the Select the Default Music and Video Player page, you can set Windows Media Player as the default music and video player and then click Next. Or, you can choose the file types that Windows Media Player will play. In this case, when you click Next, the Set Program Associations dialog box is displayed, as shown in Figure 8-3. You will then need to:

   a. Select checkboxes for file types for which Windows Media Player should be the default.

   b. Clear checkboxes for file types for which Windows Media Player should not be the default.

   c. Click Save to save your settings.

4. On the Choose an Online Store page, you can choose the online store that you want to use or elect to set up a store later. Click Finish to complete the initial setup.

Navigating Windows Media Player Menus and Toolbars

Windows Media Player 12 has a streamlined interface. Not only does this make working with Windows Media Player 12 more intuitive, but you'll also find that it is easier to organize your media. As Figure 8-4 shows, Microsoft gave Windows Media Player a complete makeover that includes:

A combined Navigation and Address toolbar

Provides browser-like Back and Forward buttons that let you navigate to pages you've viewed previously and allows you to navigate through the media available on your computer as well as these Quick Access buttons: Play, Burn, and Sync.

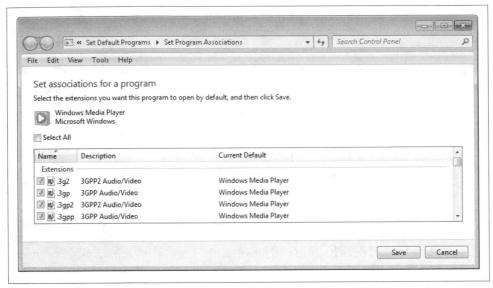

Figure 8-3. Selecting the file extensions that should be opened in Windows Media Player

An Options toolbar

Provides Organize, Stream, Create Playlist and View options as well as a Search box.

A Controls toolbar

Provides basic controls for playing whatever is selected currently and playing. The buttons are "Turn shuffle on/off," "Turn repeat on/off," "Stop," "Previous," "Play/Pause," "Next," "Mute," "Volume control," and "Switch to Now Playing."

Figure 8-4. Using Windows Media Player 12 to view and manage your music, videos, pictures, and more

Using the combined Navigation and Address toolbar

Like Windows Explorer, the Navigation toolbar includes Forward and Back buttons that allow you to access locations you've previously viewed. Clicking a Quick Access button on the Navigation toolbar allows you to access the main areas of Windows Media Player. You can:

- Click the Library address path to view and manage your media.
- Click Play to play media selected on your computer or a CD or DVD.
- Click Burn to create audio CDs and to create data discs on CD or DVD.
- Click Sync to synchronize your media to and from a portable device.

If you click a Play, Burn, or Sync, a related list will appear on the right. Clicking one of these buttons a second time closes the list. Although a mini toolbar at the top of each list will provide several options, you'll need to click the options button at the right of the toolbar to see all available options.

As Figure 8-5 shows, Windows Media Player 12 has an address path similar to the one used in Windows Explorer. When you click Library on the Navigation toolbar, the Address toolbar displays your current location as a series of links separated by arrows. This allows you to determine at a glance the current location within your media library.

Figure 8-5. The Navigation and Address toolbars in Windows Media Player 12

In the example shown in Figure 8-5, the location is:

    Library→Music→Album→Afterglow

The path portion of the toolbar has three key components. From left to right, they are:

Media Type selector (in Figure 8-5, to the left of Library)
> This option button allows you to select the media library or media loaded on the computer's CD or DVD drives.

Select a Category button (in Figure 8-5, to the left of Music)
> This button provides access to the available media locations within your library. Selecting a media location allows you to access the primary view for that particular type of media within your library.

View entries (in Figure 8-5, to the left of Album)
> This button provides access to the views for the selected media category. For example, with the Music category, the views include Artist, Album, and Genre.

Media locations accessible via the Select a Category button are important because they allow you to access the last media locations you were working with for a particular media type. Clicking the Select a Category button is the easiest way to access and navigate media locations. For example, if you select Library as the media type, Videos as the category, and Genre as the view, you'll see a list of videos available on your computer by genre.

Using the Options toolbar

The Organize menu on the Options toolbar provides customization options. If you select the Customize Navigation pane option, you can customize the way the Navigation pane is organized. If you select the Layout option, you can:

- Show/Hide the List pane
- Show/Hide columns for the selected view
- Show/Hide the classic menu bar

The Stream menu allows you to configure access and streaming options. You can:

- Allow Internet access to your media by selecting "Allow Internet access to home media." This lets you stream music, pictures, and videos from your computer to a computer outside your home (not available in all editions of Windows 7).
- Allow remote control of the media player by selecting "Allow remote control of my player." This lets other computers and devices push music, pictures, and videos to your media player.
- Turn on media streaming by selecting "Turn on media streaming." This allows you to send music, pictures, and videos to other computers and devices on your network.

The Create Playlist button allows you to create a new playlist. If you click the option menu to the right of the button, you can choose either a regular Playlist (which you add music to manually) or an Auto Playlist (a smart playlist that includes music based on criteria that you specify in the dialog that appears). After selecting this option, type the name of the playlist and then press Enter. Click the playlist to display the list for editing and viewing in the main window. To add files to the playlist, drag and drop them from your library on to the playlist name. Double-click the playlist to begin playing it.

To the left of the Search box, you'll find the View Options button. View options allow you to switch among the following views:

Icon view
Shows thumbnail icons for album covers or pictures without details.

Expanded Tile/Tile view
Shows thumbnail icons for album covers or pictures with details.

Details view
Shows details without thumbnail icons.

In most cases, you'll want to use Expanded Tile or Tile view, as they give you a preview of the album cover or picture and all the related details. For each media type, you can customize the details listed in the related views by completing the following steps:

1. Using the Select a Media Category list, select the media category you want to work with, such as Music.
2. Click Organize→Layout and then click Choose Columns.
3. Select the columns to view. Clear the columns to hide.
4. Click OK to save your settings.

Using the Search box

The Options toolbar also includes a Search box. You can use the Search box to quickly search for the media information associated with the currently selected type of media. The Search feature matches complete or partial words included in the media information.

You can search your media by completing the following steps:

1. Click in the Search box.
2. Type your search text.

Windows Media Player returns matches as you type. Click the Clear button to clear the search results.

Using the Navigation Pane

Regardless of which type of media you are working with, the primary navigation options in the Navigation pane are the same. The only options that change are those associated with the Library node. Library node options change based on the type of media selected. Figure 8-6 shows an example of the primary navigation options in the Navigation pane on my computer.

Your options will be slightly different depending on your default online store, the CD/DVD drives configured for your computer, and the devices you've connected. If your computer has multiple CD/DVD drives, you'll have an entry for each drive. If you've connected multiple devices with removable storage, you'll have an entry for each device. To customize the Navigation pane, click Organize→Customize Navigation Pane. You can then choose the subnodes for playlists, music, videos, pictures, and more.

Navigating your music library

Windows Media Player 12 supports playing music and sound files in the most popular formats. With Music, the primary views are:

Artist
 Lists your music by artist, number of songs, length, and rating.

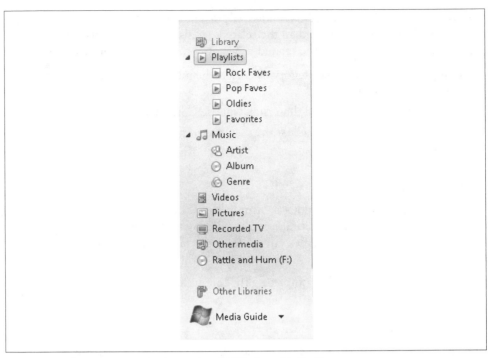

Figure 8-6. The primary navigation options in Windows Media Player

Album
> Lists your music by album, without song details.

All music
> Lists your music by artist and album name, with details for each song.

Genre
> Lists your music organized into stacks by genre, such as alternative, country, pop, and rock.

Year
> Lists your music organized into stacks by year recorded.

Rating
> Lists your music organized into stacks by its rating.

Figure 8-7 shows the Album view. If you select Music→Library node, all the primary views are available selection. Additional views for contributing artist, composer, parental ratings, online stores, and folders are also available.

Most music companies record audio CDs using audio encoding, and Windows Media Player reads these files in CD audio (*.cda*) format. When you copy music from audio CDs (the process is called *ripping*), Windows Media Player stores the files on your hard disk using the default audio format and bit rate. The default audio format is Windows Media Audio (*.wma*), and the default bit rate is 128 kilobits per second (Kbps). You

Figure 8-7. Working with music in Windows Media Player in the Album view

can increase or decrease the default bit rate as appropriate. To get the best quality, you should increase the bit rate to 192 Kbps, which increases the size of the ripped files on your hard drive. For more information, see "Ripping Audio CDs into Your Media Library" on page 312, later in this chapter.

Table 8-1 provides an overview of the audio formats that Windows Media Player 12 supports. Some audio formats can be used for both audio and video. These formats, listed in Table 8-3, include professional and surround-sound formats that Windows Media Player can create and play.

Table 8-1. Audio formats supported by Windows Media Player 12

File type	File extensions
3GPP2 audio	*.3g2, .3gp, .3gp2, .3gpp*
Advanced Audio Coding	*.aac*
ADTS audio	*.adt, .adts*
AIFF sound	*.aif, .aifc, .aiff*
AU sound	*.au, .snd*
AVI video	*.avi*
CD audio track	*.cda*
MIDI audio	*.mid, .midi, .rmi*
MOD audio	*.mod*

File type	File extensions
MP2 audio	.mp2
MP3 audio	.mp3, .m3u
MP4 audio	.m4a
Real Media audio	.rmi
WAV audio	.wav
Windows Media Audio	.wma
Windows Media Audio shortcut	.wax

Navigating your picture library

Windows Media Player 12 supports viewing digital pictures from scanners and cameras. With pictures, as shown in Figure 8-8, the primary views are:

All Pictures
Shows all your pictures by date taken and filename.

Tags
Shows all your pictures organized into stacks by tag.

Date Taken
Shows all your pictures organized into stacks by date taken.

Rating
Shows all your pictures organized into stacks by rating.

Folder
Shows all your pictures organized into stacks according to the folder in which they are stored on your hard drive.

Table 8-2 provides an overview of the picture formats Windows Media Player 12 supports. Because Windows Media Player is meant to be used with digital cameras and scanners and not with web images, it does not support some older file formats, such as GIF.

Table 8-2. Picture formats supported by Windows Media Player 12

File type	File extensions
Bitmap image	.bmp
JPEG image	.jpg, .jpeg, .jfif
PNG image	.png
TIFF image	.tif, .tiff
Word Perfect image	.wpg

Figure 8-8. Working with pictures in Windows Media Player

You'll find that viewing pictures in Windows Media Player is similar to viewing pictures in Windows Live Photo Gallery. The two applications do in fact share subcomponents. However, Windows Media Player provides only basic features for viewing pictures and playing slide shows. Windows Live Photo Gallery, on the other hand, has extended viewing, editing, and slideshow features.

Navigating your video library

Windows Media Player 12 supports playing videos with or without audio in the most popular formats. With Videos, shown in Figure 8-9, the primary views include:

All Video
>   Lists all your videos organized by letter of the alphabet and title.

Actors
>   Lists all your videos organized into stacks by the actors who star in them.

Genre
>   Lists all your videos organized into stacks by genre, such as drama and action.

Rating
>   Lists all your videos organized into stacks by rating.

If you select the Video→Library node, all the primary views are available for selection. Additional views for parental ratings, online stores, and folders are also available.

Figure 8-9. Working with videos in Windows Media Player

Table 8-3 provides an overview of the video formats Windows Media Player 12 supports. Windows Media Player 12 supports a professional audio and video with audio format that allows you to use immersive surround sound if your computer has a multichannel or high-resolution audio card. It also supports other related formats, which are listed in the table as well.

Table 8-3. Video formats supported by Windows Media Player 12

File format/type	File extensions
Video formats	
AVCHD video	*.m2t, .m2ts, .mts*
DVD video	*.mpa, .m1v, .m2v, .mp2, .mp2v, .mpv2, .vob*
MPEG 1 and MPEG 2 video	*.m2t, .m2ts, .mpe, .mpeg, .mpg, .mts, .ts, .tts*
MPEG-4 video	*.m4v, .mp4, .mp4v*
QuickTime video	*.mov*
Audio/Video format	
3GPP2 Audio/Video	*.3g2, .3gp, .3gp2, .3gpp*
Windows Media Audio/Video Professional	*.asf, .wm, .wmv*
Recorded TV format	
Microsoft Digital Video Recorder	*.dvr-ms, .wtv*

Additional supported formats	
Windows Media Audio/Video playlist	.asx, .wpl, .wmx, .wvx
Windows Media Player Skin File	.wms
Windows Media Player Skin Package	.wmz
Windows Media Download Package	.wmd
Windows Media Library	.wmdb

Navigating your recorded TV library

Windows Media Center records live TV in the Microsoft Digital Video Recorder (DVR-MS) format. You can play back recorded TV in Windows Media Center or in Windows Media Player. With recorded TV, shown in Figure 8-10, the primary views include:

All TV
    Lists all your recorded TV shows organized by date recorded.

Series
    Lists all your recorded TV shows organized into stacks by show/series.

Genre
    Lists all your recorded TV shows organized into stacks by genre, such as mystery, drama, and action.

Actors
    Lists all your recorded TV shows organized into stacks by the actors who star in them.

Rating
    Lists all your recorded TV shows organized into stacks by rating.

If you select Recorded→Library node, all the primary views are available for selection. Additional views for parental ratings, online stores, and folders are also available.

Playing Your Media

Once you've configured Windows Media Player 12, you can use it to play any audio or video file on your computer. If Windows Media Player is the default player for this type of file, you can launch the player and play the file simply by double-clicking it. With other types of supported files, you can right-click the file, select Open With, and then choose Windows Media Player as the program you want to use to open the file. Although you can open and play media files using either of these techniques, doing so isn't the best or most constructive use of Windows Media Player. Instead, follow the techniques outlined in the sections that follow to get the most out of the player features built into Windows Media Player.

Figure 8-10. Working with recorded TV in Windows Media Player

Playing Media Added to Your Library

With media added to your library, you can select media to play simply by double-clicking an audio track, picture file, or video file. The way the media is presented and played depends on the type of media.

With an audio track, the related album or audio book starts playing, beginning with the audio track you selected and continuing according to the order of the tracks, or autoshuffling if you've turned on the autoshuffle feature. If you click the "Switch to Now Playing" option in the lower-right corner of the window, you'll open the album in the Now Playing window. As shown in Figure 8-11, the Now Playing window provides a streamlined control bar with buttons for "Stop," "Previous," "Play/Pause," "Next," "Mute," and "Volume control." In the upper-right corner, you'll find the "Switch to Library" option.

With a picture file, the related picture folder starts playing in the Now Playing window, beginning with the picture you selected and continuing with a slideshow according to the order of the pictures, or autoshuffling if you've turned on the autoshuffle feature. As shown in Figure 8-12, the Now Playing window provides a full control bar with buttons for "Turn shuffle on/off," "Turn repeat on/off," "Stop," "Previous," "Play," "Next," "Mute," "Volume control," and "View full screen." In the upper-right corner, you'll find the "Switch to Library" option.

Figure 8-11. Playing your music

Figure 8-12. Playing your pictures

You can play music while you are viewing a slideshow. Simply start playing an album or other audio before you start the slideshow. When you are playing music or other audio, you can use the mute and volume control options.

With video or recorded TV files, the related video or TV folder starts playing in the Now Playing window. The Now Playing window (Figure 8-13) provides a streamlined control bar with buttons for "Stop," "Previous," "Play," "Next," "Mute," "Volume control," and "View full screen." In the upper-right corner, you'll find the "Switch to Library" option.

Figure 8-13. Playing your videos

After you've selected the media you want to play, you can control playback using the Controls toolbar. The Controls toolbar has two slightly different configurations: standard controls and streamlined controls.

When working with music in Windows Media Player, the main window allows you to select easily from among the available tracks or files, and the standard controls from left to right are:

Turn Shuffle On/Off
Toggles the shuffle feature on or off. When shuffle is on, Windows Media Player will play items in the current playlist or selection in random order rather than in sequence.

Turn Repeat On/Off
Toggles the repeat feature on or off. When repeat is on, Windows Media Player will play the current playlist or selection in its entirety and then play it again.

Pause
Pauses playing or displaying the current file.

Previous
Goes to the previous file. If you click and hold this button, you can rewind.

Play
Plays the current file.

Next
> Goes to the next file. If you click and hold this button, you can fast-forward.

Mute
> Mutes the sound.

Volume Control
> Adjusts the sound level.

Switch to Now Playing
> Displays the Now Playing window.

With music, videos and recorder TV, the Now Playing window shows a progress indicator that graphically depicts how much of an audio or video track has played. To the right of the album or movie cover, Windows Media Player shows descriptive text that rotates among the album or movie title, the artists or actors, and the name of the current track.

Here are some handy shortcuts for working with the media player:

- Ctrl-1 switches to the library in Windows Media Player.
- Ctrl-2 switches to the custom skin for the mini player.
- Ctrl-3 switches to the Now Playing window.
- Ctrl-B goes to the previous song.
- Ctrl-F goes to the next song.
- Ctrl-P starts or pauses playback.
- Ctrl-S stops playback.
- F7 mutes the sound.
- F8 decreases the playback volume.
- F9 increases the playback volume.

Playing Video DVDs Loaded into Your DVD Drive

As discussed in Chapter 4, your computer's AutoPlay options control what happens when you insert a movie into your DVD drive. AutoPlay can be set to play the movie using Windows Media Player, open the drive folder in Windows Explorer or take no action. However, when Windows Media Player is open and running in the foreground, Windows Media Player takes over and plays the movie automatically by default. If the movie doesn't begin playing automatically, you can play the movie by double-clicking its entry in the Navigation pane. Alternatively, you can right-click the movie's entry in the Navigation pane and then select Play.

Windows Media Player starts playing the introductory materials, and then you'll see the DVD Start screen, which you can use to play the video, access specific episodes or chapters, view bonus material, or select an alternative language.

Figure 8-14. Playing a movie

 Windows Media Player uses media information from the Windows Media database to display the movie title and information about the movie. If you aren't connected to the Internet and the required information wasn't previously downloaded into the Windows Media Player cache, you'll see the title "Unknown DVD."

When working with video DVDs, you'll see the modified Controls toolbar shown in Figure 8-14. Here, the first three buttons of the standard Controls toolbar are replaced with these two buttons:

DVD menu

Displays the DVD menu for selecting special features, getting DVD information, setting the video playback size, or viewing the video in full-screen mode.

Stop button

Stops playing the video. As with a DVD player, if you then click Play, play resumes from the beginning.

Clicking the View Full Screen button or Full Screen option on the DVD menu displays the video in full-screen mode. You can exit this mode clicking the Exit Full-Screen Mode button or by pressing the Esc key. When a movie first starts to play, you can skip the introductory materials by selecting the first movie track in the main window or by selecting the Root Menu option on the DVD menu.

On the DVD menu, you'll see a Special Features submenu that can include these submenus:

Audio
> Use this menu to choose an alternative language soundtrack. For example, with my *Crouching Tiger, Hidden Dragon* movie, I could listen to the movie in Chinese (Taiwan), English (United States), or French (France).

Captions
> Use this menu to turn closed captioning on or off. You may also be able to select the language for closed captioning.

Camera Angles
> Use this menu to choose the camera angle for viewing.

On the DVD menu, you'll also see a Set Video Size menu that you can use to set the default video size. By default, Windows Media Player is configured to fit the video to the player and then to resize the video if you resize the player. You can turn off either or both of these options. You can also set a relative playback size within the window of 50 percent, 100 percent, or 200 percent.

All commercially produced DVDs are encoded with a unique code, similar to a bar code. Windows Media Player reads this code and sends it to a Windows Media database to obtain information about the DVD. This information is then stored in the Windows Media Player cache so that it is available the next time you play the DVD. If Windows Media Player doesn't download the DVD information automatically or you've recently connected your computer to the Internet, select "Get DVD information" on the DVD menu to retrieve the DVD information.

When you are working with the main window in Windows Media Player, you can get the DVD information by completing the following steps:

1. Right click the DVD entry in the Navigation pane and then select "Find album info." You'll then see the "Find DVD information" dialog box shown in Figure 8-15.

2. In the "Find DVD information" dialog box, the information about the DVD should be displayed automatically. If it isn't, click Search and follow the prompts to select the correct DVD.

3. Once you have the right DVD information, you can customize any of the text entries associated with the DVD by clicking Edit, modifying the text entries as appropriate, and then clicking Next.

4. Click Finish to save the DVD information to the Windows Media Player cache.

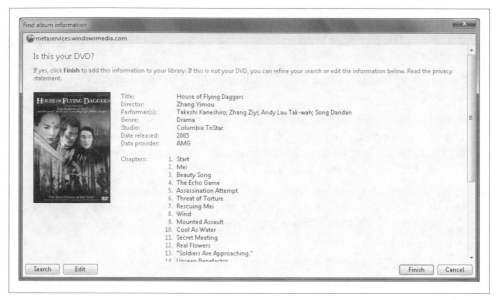

Figure 8-15. Getting movie information

Playing Audio CDs Loaded into Your CD/DVD Drive

Normally, your computer's AutoPlay options control what happens when you insert an audio CD into your DVD drive. However, when Windows Media Player is open and running in the foreground, Windows Media Player takes over and plays the audio CD automatically by default. If the audio CD doesn't begin playing automatically, you can play the audio CD by double-clicking its entry in the Navigation pane. Alternatively, you can right-click the audio CD's entry in the Navigation pane and then select Play.

Windows Media Player starts playing the audio CD with Track 1, except when the shuffle feature is on. When the shuffle feature is on, Windows Media Player randomly selects the songs to play.

As with video DVDs, all commercially produced music CDs have a unique set of attributes (length of the tracks, total play time, etc.). Windows Media Player turns this information into a code and sends it to a Windows Media database to display the album art, album title, artist, and song titles. This information is then stored in the Windows Media Player cache so that it is available the next time you play the music CD.

If you aren't connected to the Internet and the required information wasn't previously downloaded into the Windows Media Player cache, you'll see the title "Unknown CD." You can force Windows Media Player to refresh the media information by right-clicking the audio CD entry in the Navigation pane and selecting "Update album info." If the album information isn't available, you can right-click the audio CD entry in the

Figure 8-16. Using visualizations

Navigation pane and select "Find album info" to search for the correct information. Once you have the right album information, you can customize any of the text entries associated with the album as necessary before saving the information to the Windows Media Player cache.

When working with audio CDs, you'll see the standard Controls toolbar. In the Now Playing window, you can display visualizations. You can choose from among the many different types of visualizations available by right-clicking in the window, pointing to Visualizations, and then selecting a desired visualization on the Alchemy, Bars and Waves, or Battery submenu (Figure 8-16). Some of the visualizations are soothing, such as Battery→Event Horizon and Bars and Waves→Ocean Mist. Other visualizations are frenetic, such as Alchemy→Random and Bars and Waves→Scope.

To display the album art or audio book cover rather than a visualization, right-click in the Now Playing window, point to Visualizations, and then select Album Art. You can turn off visualizations by right-clicking in the Now Playing window, pointing to Visualizations, and then selecting No Visualization.

Enhancing Your Playback

Windows Media Player 12 includes several controls for enhancing audio and video playback. When you are working with Now Playing, you can display these controls by right-clicking in the Now Playing window, pointing to Enhancements, and then selecting the custom control you want to use to enhance the playback. Once custom controls are displayed, you can navigate among them using the Forward and Back buttons to the left of the control name. You can close the controls by clicking the Close button (the red button with the X in the upper-right corner of the control window).

The "Crossfading and auto volume leveling" control

When you are playing music, you can cross-fade audio tracks and reduce volume differences between songs using the "Crossfading and auto volume leveling" control, shown in Figure 8-17. Cross-fading gives you a smooth, gradual transition between songs on your playlist. When you turn on cross-fading, the volume at the end of a song fades out by gradually decreasing and the volume of the next song fades in and gradually increases. To enable and configure cross-fading, click "Turn on Crossfading" and then move the slider to select the amount of overlap time you want between the song ending and the song starting (if any).

If your songs play at different volume levels, you can have Windows Media Player normalize the volume for you so that you don't have to adjust it manually when a new song starts. To do so, click "Turn on Auto Volume Leveling." Both of these features work only with audio files that are in Windows Media or MP3 format and contain volume-leveling information. This information is added automatically when you rip audio into your media library.

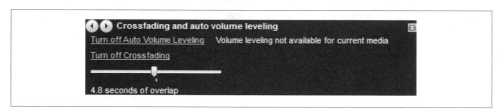

Figure 8-17. The "Crossfading and auto volume leveling" control

The "Graphic equalizer" control

The "Graphic equalizer" control, shown in Figure 8-18, helps you equalize audio playback for specific types of audio. To use the graphic equalizer, follow these steps:

1. If the graphic equalizer is turned off, click "Turn on" to enable Windows Media Player to equalize your audio playback.
2. The third link provided is for the Select Preset list. Clicking this option allows you to choose preset equalizer settings for Rock, Rap, Grunge, Metal, Dance, Techno, Country, Jazz, Acoustic, Folk, New Age, Classical, Blues, Oldies, and more.
3. After you select a preset, you can modify individual equalizer bands by using the sliders provided. To control how the sliders move in relation to one another, click one of the slider option buttons to the left of the equalizer.

Your changes are automatically saved to the Custom preset. To revert to the default settings, click Reset.

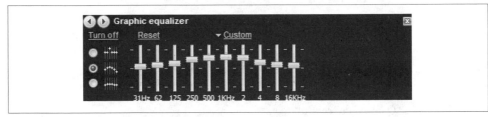

Figure 8-18. The "Graphic equalizer" control

The "Play speed settings" control

The "Play speed settings" control, shown in Figure 8-19, allows you to slow down or speed up playback. For example, you might want to slow down an instructional video or audio so that you can follow along more closely, or you might want to skip through a boring video presentation by using a faster playback speed.

Figure 8-19. The "Play speed settings" control

Playback speed is set to a numeric value where a play speed of 1.0 is the normal speed, anything less than 1.0 is a slower speed, and anything greater than 1.0 is a faster speed. To set the play speed, you can click the Slow, Normal, and Fast links. Or you can move the Play Speed slider to the desired play speed.

> With some videos, you can move forward or backward one frame at a time using the Next Frame and Previous Frame buttons. These buttons are displayed below the "Play speed" slider.

The "Quiet mode" control

You can use the "Quiet mode" control, shown in Figure 8-20, to reduce the difference between the loudest and softest sounds in a song. This feature works only with audio files that are in Windows Media Audio Pro or Windows Media Audio Lossless format. These formats contain volume-leveling information that is added automatically when you rip audio into your media library using either of these formats.

To enable and configure Quiet Mode, click the "Turn on" link and then specify the desired difference between loud and soft sounds by clicking either "Medium difference"

Figure 8-20. The "Quiet mode" control

or "Little difference." With "Medium difference," you'll get loud sounds that range up to 12 decibels (dB) above the average and soft sounds that range up to 12 dB below the average, so there'll be a smaller difference between loud and soft sounds as compared to when you are using a full dynamic range. With "Little difference," you'll get loud sounds that range up to 6 dB above the average and soft sounds that range up to 6 dB below the average, so there'll be the smallest difference between loud and soft sounds as compared to when you are using a full dynamic range.

The "SRS WOW effects" control

You can use the "SRS WOW effects" control, shown in Figure 8-21, to optimize bass, stereo, and other audio effects. SRS audio is a sound-enhancing technology, created by SRS Labs, Inc., to create high-quality immersive audio. You can turn on SRS WOW effects by completing the following steps:

1. Click the "Turn on" link.
2. Optimize the sound output for your speakers by clicking the Speakers link until it lists the appropriate type of speakers. The options are "Normal speakers," "Large speakers," and "Headphones."
3. Use the TruBass slider to specify the level of bass enhancement. Moving the slider to 0 turns off TruBass. The default setting is 50, for normal bass enhancement.
4. Use the WOW Effect slider to specify the stereo effect. Moving the slider to 0 turns off WOW Effect. The default setting is 50, for normal stereo effect.

 Because other audio settings on your computer can affect the volume and audio effects in Windows Media Player, you may find that you need to adjust the audio settings in Windows 7 rather than in Windows Media Player.

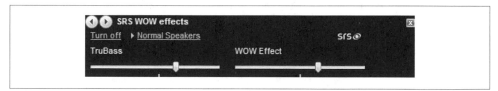

Figure 8-21. The "SRS WOW effects" control

The "Video settings" control

The "Video settings" control, shown in Figure 8-22, helps you control video playback. You can set hue, saturation, brightness, and contrast using the sliders provided. To reset these values to their default state, click the Reset link. By default, Windows Media Player is configured to fit the video to the player window on resize, allowing Windows Media Player to adjust the video size automatically if you change the size of the player window. Using the "Select video zoom settings" list, you can fit the player to the video on start or set a relative playback size within the window of 50 percent, 100 percent, or 200 percent.

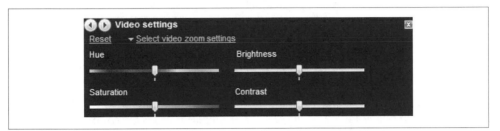

Figure 8-22. The "Video settings" control

The "Dolby Digital settings" control

You can control the way Dolby Digital sound is used in Windows Media Player by using the "Dolby Digital settings" control, shown in Figure 8-23. You can set Normal sound to reduce the audio range for a quieter listening experience, Night sound to increase dialog while reducing other sounds, or Theater sound to increase the dynamic range for all sounds. These settings only apply to content encoding with Dolby Digital.

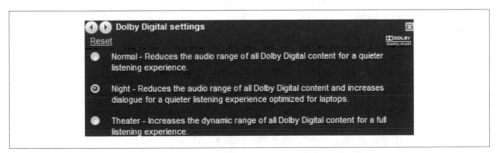

Figure 8-23. The "Dolby Digital settings" control

Building Your Media Library

Windows Media Player is designed to help you create and organize a media library. Your media library contains any folders you've added that contain media files, audio CDs you've ripped, and TV shows you've recorded. Within your library, your media is organized by category with separate areas for music, pictures, video, recorded TV, and other media and subcategories for artists, albums, songs, genre, year created, and so on. Windows Media Player adds all the media information automatically for audio CDs, movie DVDs, and recorded TV when your computer is connected to the Internet.

Because Windows Media Player handles most of the heavy lifting for you, building your media library is easy. All you need to do is add folders containing media files to your library, copy your audio CDs to your library, and let Windows Media Player handle the details. Using the built-in audio CD and data CD/DVD features, getting your media out of your library is just as easy. You can save copies of your music and other audio files to audio CDs, and you can save copies of your media to data CDs and DVDs. If you have an MP3 player or other device with removable storage, you can sync your media library to your device as well.

Adding Media Folders to Your Media Library

The easiest way to add media to your library is simply to move the media files to the appropriate personal folder. To add music or other audio to your library, simply copy or move the audio files to your *Music* folder. To add digital pictures to your library, simply copy or move the digital pictures to your *Pictures* folder. To add videos or re-corded TV to your library, simply copy or move the video or TV files to your *Videos* folder.

Wondering how this works? Well, when you start Windows Media Player, the player checks your *Music*, *Pictures*, and *Videos* folders as well as the related public folders for any audio, picture, or video files that have been added, and then updates your media library to reflect these changes automatically.

 It is important to note that you can add non-copy-protected audio and video files formatted for use with Apple iTunes and Apple iPod. Windows Media Player 12 is able to play these files now because it natively supports the formats these devices use.

You can also use Windows 7's new Library feature to have Windows Media Player add media from and monitor other folders by completing the following steps:

1. In the Navigation pane, right-click the type of media you want to work with and then select the related Manage Library option. For example, if you want to add music, you right-click Music and then select Manage Music Library to open the Music Library Locations dialog box shown in Figure 8-24.

2. In the Library Locations dialog box, the related personal folder and public folder for the type of media you are working with are selected by default under "Library Locations." This is why the player monitors your *Music*, *Pictures*, and *Videos* folders as well as the related public folders.

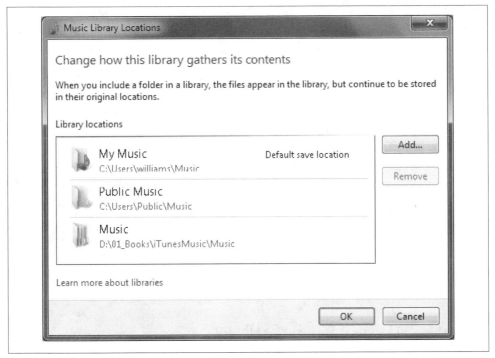

Figure 8-24. The Library Locations dialog box

 You can monitor files stored in another user's personal folders only if that person has shared the folder with you. For more information on folder sharing, see Chapter 11.

3. To monitor additional folders, click Add. In the Include Folder In... dialog box, select the folder to monitor and then click Include Folder.

4. To stop monitoring a folder, select the folder in the Library Locations list and then click Remove. Removing the folder tells Windows Media Player to stop monitoring the folder. The folder still exists on your disk drive.

5. When you click OK, Windows Media Player will search your computer and add or remove media as appropriate. In the lower-right corner of the Windows Media Player window, you'll see an "Updating media library" entry. When the update is complete, you'll briefly see an "Update complete" entry.

Adding Media to Your Library When Played

By default, when you play an audio or video file on your computer or on a removable storage device, Windows Media Player adds the audio or video file to your library. However, Windows Media Player adds audio or video that you play from shared media or folders on other computers only when you elect to do so. Additionally, Windows

Media Player does not automatically add files that you play from removable media, such as a CD or DVD. You use ripping settings to configure the way Windows Media Player works with removable media.

You can change the way Windows Media Player handles files you play by completing the following steps:

1. Click Organize and then click Options. This displays the Options dialog box.

2. In the Options dialog box, select the Player tab.

3. When you play media files that are stored on your computer or on a removable storage device, they are added automatically to Windows Media Player. If you don't want this to happen, clear the "Add local media files to library when played" checkbox. Otherwise, select this checkbox to automatically add local files that you play to your library.

4. When you play media files that are stored on other computers, they are not added automatically to Windows Media Player. If you want to add these files to your library, select the "Add remote media files to library when played" checkbox.

5. Click OK to save your settings.

Ripping Audio CDs into Your Media Library

With ripping, you copy tracks on audio CDs to your computer and store them as files. Before you start ripping audio CDs, you should:

- Learn about the audio formats that are available and then select a default audio format that best fits your quality needs and the type of audio CDs you work with the most.

- Configure the default ripping settings to specify how music is ripped and where music you've ripped is stored.

Choosing audio formats for ripping CDs

When you rip audio CDs, the audio codec in Windows Media Player works behind the scenes to convert the encoded audio from the audio CD to a standard file format that you can play. The audio encoding formats available are:

- Windows Media Audio
- Windows Media Audio with Variable Bit Rate
- Windows Media Audio Pro
- Windows Media Audio Lossless
- MP3 audio
- WAV audio

The sections that follow discuss how each audio format is used.

Windows Media Audio. The audio codec in Windows Media Player 12 is capable of ripping and playing audio files in Windows Media Audio format. Windows Media Audio is the default format and the default bit rate is 128 Kbps. You'll find that this audio format is best used with stereo recordings.

Though other audio formats and bit rates are available, you may be surprised to learn that Windows Media Audio encoding is one of the most efficient audio encoding techniques available. With Windows Media Audio, the audio codec samples audio at 44.1 or 48 kilohertz (kHz) using 16 bits. This offers quality sound at these bit rates:

48 Kbps
> With audio encoding at 48 Kbps, you get the smallest file sizes possible at a direct cost to sound quality. This encoding uses about 22 MB per CD.

64 Kbps
> With audio encoding at 64 Kbps, you get smaller file sizes and a small increase in sound quality. This encoding uses about 28 MB per CD.

96 Kbps
> With audio encoding at 96 Kbps, you get average file sizes and a modest increase in sound quality. This encoding uses about 42 MB per CD.

128 Kbps
> With audio encoding at 128 Kbps, you get large file sizes and a large increase in sound quality. This encoding uses about 56 MB per CD.

160 Kbps
> With audio encoding at 160 Kbps, you get larger file sizes and a larger increase in sound quality. This encoding uses about 69 MB per CD.

192 Kbps
> With audio encoding at 192 Kbps, you get the largest file sizes and the largest increase in sound quality. This encoding uses about 86 MB per CD.

Windows Media Audio with Variable Bit Rate. The audio codec in Windows Media Player 12 is capable of ripping and playing audio files in the Windows Media Audio with Variable Bit Rate format. This format is best used when you want to get the highest quality with stereo recordings.

Windows Media Audio with Variable Bit Rate enables you to record stereo and even higher-quality audio at smaller file sizes by automatically varying the encoding bit rate according to the complexity of the audio data. With Variable Bit Rate, the audio codec in Windows Media Player increases the bit rate to capture complex sections of the audio data and decreases the bit rate to maximize the compression of less complex sections. The result is compact, high-quality compression at these bit rates:

40 to 75 Kbps
> With variable audio encoding at 40 to 75 Kbps, you get the smallest file sizes possible at a direct cost to sound quality. This encoding uses about 18 to 33 MB per CD.

50 to 95 Kbps

With variable audio encoding at 50 to 95 Kbps, you get smaller file sizes and a modest increase in sound quality. This encoding uses about 22 to 42 MB per CD.

85 to 145 Kbps

With variable audio encoding at 85 to 145 Kbps, you get average file sizes and a large increase in sound quality. This encoding uses about 37 to 63 MB per CD.

135 to 215 Kbps

With variable audio encoding at 135 to 215 Kbps, you get large file sizes and a substantial increase in sound quality. This encoding uses about 59 to 94 MB per CD.

240 to 355 Kbps

With variable audio encoding at 240 to 355 Kbps, you get the largest file sizes and the highest sound quality possible without using lossless encoding. This encoding uses about 105 to 155 MB per CD.

Windows Media Audio Pro. The audio codec in Windows Media Player 12 is capable of ripping and playing audio files in Windows Media Audio Pro. This format is best used when you want to record audio in 5.1 or higher channel surround sound. If you record audio in this format but play it back on a computer that doesn't have a sound card that supports surround sound, the multiple channels of audio are combined into two-channel stereo audio, ensuring that you always get the best playback experience.

Windows Media Audio Pro enables you to immerse yourself in multichannel surround sound at the same bit rate as stereo MP3 files. Windows Media Audio Pro also offers dynamic range control. During encoding, the maximum and average audio amplitudes are recorded as part of the encoding process. Using the Quiet Mode feature, you can configure playing to use full dynamic range, a medium difference range up to 12 dB above the average, or a minimal difference range up to 6 dB above the average.

With Windows Media Audio Pro, the audio codec samples audio at 44.1 or 48 kHz using 16 bits with stereo capabilities at 32 to 96 Kbps, and 20 bits with 5.1-channel surround at 128 to 256 Kbps. Although Windows Media Player cannot encode at higher rates, the player can play back at 48 kHz using 24 bits with 5.1- or 7.1-channel surround at rates up to 768 Kbps.

File sizes for Windows Media Audio Pro are similar to those for Windows Media Audio, with one exception. With Windows Media Audio Pro, you can rip audio at 32 Kbps, which uses about 14 MB per CD but offers low quality for music. However, you can use this low bit rate with spoken-word audio, such as a voice broadcast or audio book that contains no music, to achieve superior quality and highly compressed file sizes. At the supported stereo and higher rates, Windows Media Audio Pro offers a 1.5:1 to 2:1 compression savings over Dolby Digital 2.0, Dolby Digital 5.1, and DTS 5.1 surround sound.

Windows Media Audio Lossless. Windows Media Audio Lossless enables you to create a bit-for-bit duplicate of the original audio tracks so that no data is lost. You can use this format for archiving audio CD masters and preserving them exactly as they were created. With this audio format, the audio codec in Windows Media Player still performs compression, but this compression is mathematically lossless.

Because the audio codec increases the bit rate to capture complex sections of the audio data and decreases the bit rate to maximize the compression of less complex sections, Windows Media Audio Lossless offers a 2:1 to 3:1 compression savings over the original audio format. Thus, the variable, lossless rate of between 470 and 940 Kbps uses about 206 to 411 MB per CD.

Like Windows Media Pro, Windows Media Audio Lossless offers dynamic range control. During encoding, the maximum and average audio amplitudes are recorded as part of the encoding process. Using the Quiet Mode feature, you can configure playing to use full dynamic range, a medium difference range up to 12 dB above the average, or a minimal difference range up to 6 dB above the average.

MP3 audio. The audio codec in Windows Media Player 12 is capable of ripping and playing audio files in MP3 format. The Moving Picture Experts Group (MPEG) created standards for video and audio compression. MPEG-1, MPEG-2, MPEG-3, and MPEG-4 are standards for audio and video compression. MP3 (short for MPEG-1 layer 3) is the standard for audio compression. MP3 is popular on the Internet, but you may be surprised to learn that Windows Media Audio and related formats are actually the most commonly used audio formats in the world at the time of this writing.

With MP3, the audio codec samples at these bit rates:

128 Kbps
With audio encoding at 128 Kbps, you get the smallest file sizes possible at a direct cost to sound quality. This encoding uses about 57 MB per CD.

192 Kbps
With audio encoding at 192 Kbps, you get average file sizes and a large increase in sound quality. This encoding uses about 86 MB per CD.

256 Kbps
With audio encoding at 256 Kbps, you get large file sizes and a substantial increase in sound quality. This encoding uses about 115 MB per CD.

320 Kbps
With audio encoding at 320 Kbps, you get the largest file sizes and the highest sound quality possible with MP3 encoding. This encoding uses about 144 MB per CD.

MP3 is best used when you want to be able to directly copy files to an MP3 player. However, keep in mind that some devices called MP3 players aren't solely MP3 players. For example, the Apple iPod is happy to play MP3 files, but music purchased through iTunes generally uses MPEG-4 encoding and saves audio files with the *.m4a* extension. Most modern so-called MP3 can play a variety of formats beyond MP3.

WAV audio. The audio codec in Windows Media Player 12 is capable of ripping and playing audio files in Microsoft WAV format. As WAV is lossless, you can use this format to create a bit-for-bit duplicate of the original audio tracks so that no data is lost. Unlike the Windows Media Audio Lossless format, however, the audio codec does not compress the audio data. Because there is no compression, WAV audio uses about 600 MB per CD. WAV is best used when you want to create archive masters that are the same size on disk as the original audio CD.

Configuring the default rip settings

You can configure the default rip settings by completing the following steps:

1. Click Organize and then click Options. This displays the Options dialog box.
2. In the Options dialog box, select the Rip Music tab, as shown in Figure 8-25.
3. Ripped files are automatically added to your media library and stored in the default folder for ripped music. The default folder for ripped music is your personal *Music* folder. You can change the Ripped music folder by clicking Change under "Rip music to this location." In the Browse for Folder dialog box, choose a storage folder for your music and then click OK.
4. Ripped audio files are named numerically according to the track number, followed by a space and the song title (if data is available). You can change the default naming scheme by following these steps:
   a. Click File Name under "Rip music to this location."
   b. In the File Name Options dialog box, select the details you want to include in the filename, including the artist, album, track number, song title, genre, and bit rate.
   c. Select an item and then click Move Up or Move Down to arrange the detail order.
   d. Use the Separator list to specify the separator used between each detail item. You can choose a space, dash, dot, or underline.
   e. Use the preview text to double-check the filename, and then click OK to save your filename options.

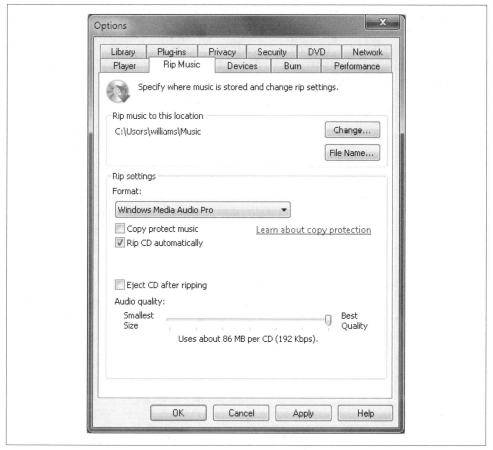

Figure 8-25. Configuring the default rip settings

Because Windows Media Player stores all available metadata about a song in the ripped file, don't feel that you have to add all the available fields to the filenames. No matter what you choose for the filenames, Windows Media Player will display everything it knows about a track (assuming that it can retrieve information about the CD it was ripped from).

5. For ripping, Windows Media Audio is the default format and the default bit rate is 128 Kbps. Use the Format list to select the desired format. Use the "Audio quality" slider to set the default bit rate.

6. By default, music you rip is not copy-protected. If you copy-protect the tracks you rip by selecting the "Copy protect music" checkbox, usage rights are required to play, burn, or sync the files.

7. By default, Windows Media Player does not rip an audio CD when you insert it and then select the Rip tab. If you always want to rip audio CDs (that aren't already in your library) when you insert them, select "Rip CD automatically." If you would rather start the rip process yourself, clear the "Rip CD automatically" checkbox to turn off automatic ripping.

8. If you want to open the CD/DVD tray after ripping an audio CD, select the "Eject CD after ripping" checkbox.

9. Click OK to save your settings.

Ripping audio CDs

Once you've configured the default rip settings, ripping an audio CD is easy. With automatic ripping, Windows Media Player rips the audio CD as soon as you insert it, and you don't have to do anything. With manual ripping, you must insert the audio CD, right-click the audio CD entry in the Navigation pane and then select "Rip CD to library."

With any of these options, you should connect to the Internet before Windows Media Player begins ripping the audio CD. This ensures that Windows Media Player can get the media information and name the ripped files as appropriate for the filename settings you've configured.

Figure 8-26. Viewing the progress of the rip

As shown in Figure 8-26, you can view the progress of the rip by selecting the audio CD in the Navigation pane. You can control the rip in a couple of ways:

- As Windows Media Player rips the audio CD, you can clear the checkboxes next to any songs that you don't want to rip.
- You can stop the rip process by right-clicking the audio CD entry in the Navigation pane and selecting "Stop rip."

 If your computer has multiple CD/DVD drives, you can rip multiple CDs simultaneously. Simply insert the audio CDs you want to rip and then start ripping. You can use the entries in the Navigation pane to manage the rip process for each audio CD you are ripping. You'll find one entry for each CD/DVD drive.

After you've ripped an audio CD, you can select and play the ripped audio in your media library. If you weren't connected to the Internet when you ripped the audio CD, you'll see a warning prompt when the player finishes ripping the audio CD. You can still add the media information. You can also edit the media information as necessary.

To get the media information for an audio CD, follow these steps:

1. Connect to the Internet.
2. Click Music in the Navigation pane and then click Album.
3. Right-click the album and then select "Find album info."
4. In the "Find album information" dialog box, shown in Figure 8-27, information about the album that best matches and other matches should be displayed automatically. If it isn't, click Search.
5. Click the album that is the correct match for your album and then click Next.
6. Once you have the right album information, you can customize any of the text entries associated with the album by clicking Edit and modifying the text entries as appropriate.
7. Click Finish to save the album information to the Windows Media Player cache.

If you already have the media information for an audio CD but want to check for updates or corrections, you can do so by completing these steps:

1. Connect to the Internet.
2. Click Music in the Navigation pane and then click Album.
3. Right-click the album and then select Update Album Info.

 With either technique, you will be prevented from getting media information if the "Update music files by retrieving media info from the Internet" option is not selected. To resolve this problem, click Organize and then click Options. This displays the Options dialog box. On the Privacy tab, select the "Update music files by retrieving media info from the Internet" checkbox and then click OK.

Figure 8-27. Finding album information in the Windows Media database

Creating and Managing Playlists

Both the Navigation pane and Play pane have features for working with playlists. A *playlist* is a list of media files that you want to play together. Although you can mix and match media types as you see fit, you'll usually want to have separate playlists for pictures, music, and videos.

Creating and using playlists

At the far right of the Address toolbar is the Play button. Click this button to display your current playlist, where you can drag items to the list to add them. Click this button again to close the current playlist view. You can work with playlists in a variety of ways:

- To add an album, a stack, or an individual item as the only item on the current playlist, right-click it and select Play.
- To add an album, a stack, or an individual item to the current playlist, right-click it, point to Add To, and then select Play List.
- To add an album, a stack, or an individual item to an existing playlist, right-click it, point to Add To, and then select the playlist to which it should be added.
- To add an album, a stack, or an individual item to a new playlist, right-click it and then select Add To and then select Additional Playlists. In the Add To Playlist dialog box, click Create Playlist. Type the name of the playlist and then press Enter.

Using the Play pane, you can create a playlist by completing these steps:

1. If the Play pane is not displayed, click the Play button.
2. If you don't want to use any items on the list currently, click "Clear list."
3. Drag and drop files onto the list.
4. To change the order of individual items on the list, click an item and then drag up or down as appropriate.
5. To change the order of a group of files on the list, select the items and then drag up or down as appropriate.
6. To create and save the list, click "Save list."
7. Type the name of the playlist and then press Enter.

Using the Navigation pane, you can play items in a playlist by clicking the playlist and then pressing the Play button on the Controls toolbar. Alternatively, you can right-click the playlist and then select Play.

Editing playlists

Using the Navigation pane, you can edit a playlist by completing these steps:

1. If the Play pane is not displayed, click the Play button.
2. In the Play pane, you'll see left and right arrow buttons for accessing the previous list and next list respectively. Click the "Previous list" button until the playlist you want to work with is displayed.
3. Drag and drop files onto the list.
4. To change the order of individual items on the list, click an item and then drag up or down as appropriate.
5. To change the order of a group of files on the list, select the items and then drag up or down as appropriate.
6. To save your changes, click "Save list."

Deleting Media and Playlists

You can easily delete an album, a playlist, or other media items from your media library by right-clicking the item and selecting Delete. By default, when you delete items, you'll see the dialog box shown in Figure 8-28, and you can specify whether to delete the selected item from the library only, or from the library and your computer.

This dialog box also has a "Don't show this message again" checkbox. If you select this option, the default action you select will always be used when you delete items and you won't see this warning prompt again. You can still control the way deleting items works, however. To do this, click Organize and then select Options. On the Library tab, clear the "Delete files from my computer when deleted from library" checkbox if you want

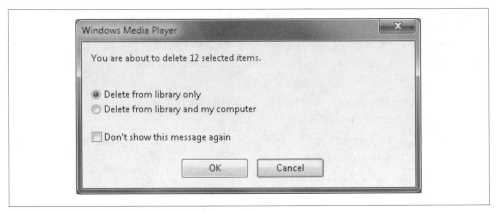

Figure 8-28. Specifying the deletion technique

to delete items only from the library. Otherwise, select this checkbox to delete items from the library and your computer.

Burning Audio CDs and Data CDs or DVDs

Windows Media Player makes it easy to create your own custom CDs and DVDs. You can burn audio CDs as well as data CDs or DVDs. An audio CD is a CD that you can play in a standard CD player. A data CD or DVD is a disc that stores a copy of your media. With some CD players, you may be able to play a data CD with Windows Media Audio (WMA), MP3, or WAV files.

To burn CDs or DVDs, your computer must have a readable/writable CD or DVD drive. If you aren't sure whether your computer has a readable/writable CD or DVD drive, you should look at the faceplate on the drive tray. A readable/writable CD or DVD drive should have a large RW logo to indicate this, and under this logo it should state the supported format or formats. A CD burner can support CD-R, CD-RW, or both disc types. A DVD burner can support DVD-R, DVD+R, or both disc types. Most DVD burners also support CD-R, CD-RW, or both disc types.

Burning an audio CD

You can burn audio CDs in a standard audio format that can be used in most computers and CD players that play CD-R and CD-RW discs. Any audio files in your media library can be burned onto an audio CD, as can any audio files on your computer but not in your library, as long as they are in a format supported by Windows Media Player. A standard CD-R and CD-RW disc can hold almost 80 minutes of audio.

Figure 8-29. Burning an audio CD to create a custom mix up to 80 minutes in length

 When burning audio CDs, it is important to keep in mind that Windows Media Player inserts two seconds between each song if you've cleared the "Burn CD without gaps" option. This option is selected by default in most configurations of Windows Media Player. To check the status of this option, click Burn options on the Burn tab and then select More burn options.

You can burn an audio CD by completing the following steps:

1. If the Burn pane is not displayed, click the Burn button.

2. Insert a blank CD-R or CD-RW disc into your CD/DVD burner. As shown in Figure 8-29, you'll see details about the CD drive in the Burn pane. By default, the disc type should be set as Audio CD. If it isn't, click the Burn Options button and then select Audio CD.

3. If your computer has multiple disc burners and the burner you want to use is not the one selected, choose the one you want to use by clicking the Next Drive link in the Burn pane.

 Although you can rip multiple CDs at a time, you can burn discs to only one burner drive at a time.

4. Add albums or songs from your media library by clicking and dragging them from the Details pane to the Burn pane to create a list of files to burn. If you need to clear the list before beginning to build your burn list, click "Clear list."

5. Windows Media Player calculates how many minutes and seconds of empty space remain on the disc after you add each song to the burn list, as long as you are working with songs in your media library. To add a song that is on your computer but not in your library, right-click the file and then click Add to Burn List, or drag the file to the Burn pane.

6. If Windows Media Player is unable to determine the duration of songs added from files on your computer, it may not be able to calculate accurately how many songs can fit on the CD. To resolve this, right-click a song on the burn list and select Play to help Windows Media Player determine the correct duration of the song.

7. If you select more files than can fit on one disc, Windows Media Player can burn all of the files to multiple discs. Or you can create a data disc instead of an audio disc to fit more files on the disc. However, many CD players cannot play music burned to a data disc.

8. It is possible that the last song will not fit even if the total time exactly matches the CD length. This can occur if you've configured Windows Media Player to insert two second gaps between songs when burning. If you want to burn only one disc in this session, remove files from the list until they all fit on one disc: right-click a file you want to remove, and then click Remove from List. Removing files from the burn list will not delete the files from your media library.

9. In the burn list, drag files up or down to arrange them in the order you want them to appear on the disc. If you have chosen to burn more than one disc at once, make sure that files will be burned to the disc you want.

10. Click Start Burn. If you are burning multiple discs, insert a blank disc when the first one has finished burning, and then click Start Burn. Repeat this step until you have finished burning all of the discs. As a disc is burned, you can check its progress in the burn list.

Burning a data CD or DVD

Burning data CDs and DVDs is different from burning audio CDs. Data CDs can store up to 700 MB of data. Single-sided single-layered data DVDs can store up to 4.7 GB of data. Your computer may also be able to burn double-sided single-layered or single-sided dual-layered DVDs that can store up to 8.5 GB of data, or double-sided dual-layered DVDs that can store up to 17.1 GB of data. Some DVD burners will let you burn to any format supported, and others can burn in only a specific format. Windows Media Player supports burning data discs to CD-R, CD-RW, DVD-R, DVD-RW, DVD +R, DVD+RW, and dual-layered DVD+R discs. Other formats are not supported, including DVD-RAM, DVD-Audio, and DVD-Video.

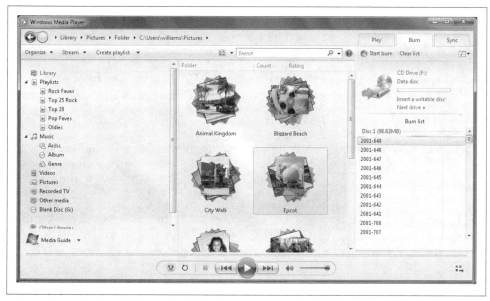

Figure 8-30. Burning a data CD or DVD to create copies of your media or to play in newer CD and DVD players

With data CDs and DVDs, you can burn any files in your library as well as any files on your computer. You can burn files in any format to create copies of your data. You can then use your data disc with your computer or other people's computers. On the other hand, if you burn the same type of media file, you can create discs that many newer CD and DVD players can read. If you create a data CD with albums and songs in WMA, MP3, or WAV format, any newer CD player that supports these formats can read and play the disc. Because data CDs can hold many more songs than audio CDs, you can create amazing customized CDs. If you create a data CD with pictures in JPEG format, any newer DVD player that supports this format can read and play the disc as a slide-show. Because data DVDs can hold an enormous number of JPEG images, you can create photo-album slideshows that run for hours.

Burn a data CD or DVD by completing the following steps:

1. If the Burn pane is not displayed, click the Burn button.
2. Click the Burn Options button and then click Data CD or DVD.
3. Insert a blank disc into your CD/DVD burner. As shown in Figure 8-30, you'll see details about the CD or DVD drive in the List pane. If your computer has multiple disc burners and the burner you want to use is not the one selected, choose the one you want to use by clicking the Next Drive link in the List pane.

Although you can rip multiple CDs at a time, you can burn discs to only one burner drive at a time.

4. Add pictures, albums, songs, videos, recorded TV, or other files from your media library by clicking and dragging them from the Details pane to the Burn pane to create a list of files to burn. If you need to clear the Burn pane before beginning to build your burn list, click "Clear list."

5. To add a file that is on your computer but not in your library, right-click the file and then click Add to Burn List, or drag the file to the Burn pane. If you select more files than can fit on one disc, Windows Media Player can burn all of the files to multiple discs.

6. If you want to burn only one disc in this session, remove files from the list until they all fit on one disc: right-click a file you want to remove, and then click Remove from List. Removing files from the burn list will not delete the files from your media library.

7. In the burn list, drag files up or down to arrange them in the order you want them to appear on the disc. If you have chosen to burn more than one disc at once, make sure that files will be burned to the disc you want.

8. Click Start Burn. If you are burning multiple discs, insert a blank disc when the first one has finished burning, and then click Start Burn. Repeat this step until you have finished burning all of the discs. As a disc is burned, you can check its progress in the burn list.

Syncing Your Media to MP3 Players and Other Devices

Windows Media Player allows you to sync your media easily to MP3 players and other devices with removable storage. To get started, you'll need to set up the device for syncing and then either manually sync your media or configure automatic syncing. If the files you select for syncing aren't in formats the device can use, Windows Media Player will automatically convert the files to formats the device supports. Note that some devices, such as iPods, may not work with Windows Media Player.

Setting up a device for syncing

Configure an MP3 player or other device for syncing by completing the following steps:

1. Turn on your device and connect it to the computer.

2. Check the device to determine whether you need to select a specific syncing option. For example, you may need to specify that you want to sync music or that you want to sync data.

3. Start Windows Media Player. If the player is already open and you are viewing the Now Playing window, click the "Switch to Library" button.

4. On the Device Setup page, Windows Media Player assigns the device a default name. You can modify this name.

5. The first time you use the device Windows Media Player selects a sync method that works best for the device, depending on the device's storage capacity and the size of your media library. Do one of the following:

   - If the device's storage capacity is less than 4 GB or your entire library won't fit on the device, the device is set up for manual sync. When you click Finish, you'll need to select the files and playlists that sync with the device using the Sync pane. Once you've specified the files to sync, you can edit the sync settings to configure automatic syncing of these files.

   - If the device's storage capacity is greater than 4 GB and your entire library will fit on the device, the device is set up for automatic sync. When you click Finish, your entire library is synced with the device. Your device will sync automatically whenever you connect it to your computer and Windows Media Player is running. However, by editing the sync settings you can selectively sync with the device and don't have to sync your entire library with the device.

To modify the sync settings after setting up a device, complete the following steps:

1. Turn on your device and connect it to the computer.

2. Check the device to determine whether you need to select a specific syncing option. For example, you may need to specify that you want to sync music or that you want to sync data.

3. Start Windows Media Player. If the player is already open and you are viewing the Now Playing window, click the "Switch to Library" button.

4. If the Sync pane is not displayed, click the Sync button. The Sync pane shows the name of the device and the amount of available space, as shown in Figure 8-31. In this example, the default name of the device was LG VX8560 Internal Memory and the device had 846 MB of free space.

5. Click the Sync Options button and then click Set up Sync.

6. On the Device Setup page, select the "Sync this device automatically" checkbox to enable automatic syncing. Clear this checkbox to use manual syncing.

Syncing a device manually

To choose the files and playlists that are synced manually, complete the following steps:

1. Turn on your device and connect it to the computer.

2. Check the device to determine whether you need to select a specific syncing option. For example, you may need to specify that you want to sync music or that you want to sync data.

Figure 8-31. Reviewing the device details and setting a device name

3. Start Windows Media Player. If the player is already open and you are viewing the Now Playing window, click the "Switch to Library" button.

4. If the Sync pane is not displayed, click the Sync button. The Sync pane shows the name of the device and the amount of available space.

5. On the Sync pane, create a list of items you want to add to the device by dragging items to the sync list. You can add albums, songs or any other files the device supports to the list. As you add items to the playlist, note the amount of free space remaining.

6. When you've configured your sync list, click Start Sync to start the sync. Similar to when ripping audio CDs, you'll see the sync progress. To see the sync results in the main pane, click the link provided.

7. Repeat this procedure whenever you want to update the device manually in the future.

 While a device is syncing, you can stop the sync by clicking Stop Sync, but you won't be able to resume the sync by clicking the Start Sync button. Instead, you'll need to view the sync results by clicking the re-sults provided and then in the main pane you'll see the status of each file. Files with a status of "Synced to device" were successfully synced. Files with a status of "Stopped" were not synced to the device. To add files there weren't synced back to the sync list, right-click the file and then select Add to Sync List. Using Ctrl-click or Shift-click, you can select multiple stopped files at one time and then when you right-click and select Add to Sync List, they'll all be added to the Sync list.

Syncing files automatically

Automatic syncing doesn't have to be all or nothing. You can selectively sync files even if a device is configured for automatic sync. To configure selective automatic sync, complete the following steps:

1. Turn on your device and connect it to the computer.

2. Check the device to determine if you need to select a specific syncing option. For example, you may need to specify that you want to sync music or that you want to sync data.

3. Start Windows Media Player. If the player is already open and you are viewing the Now Playing window, click the "Switch to Library" button.

4. If the Sync pane is not displayed, click the Sync button. Click the Sync Options button and then click Set up Sync. This displays the Device Setup page.

5. In the Device Setup page, select the "Sync this device automatically" checkbox, as shown in Figure 8-32.

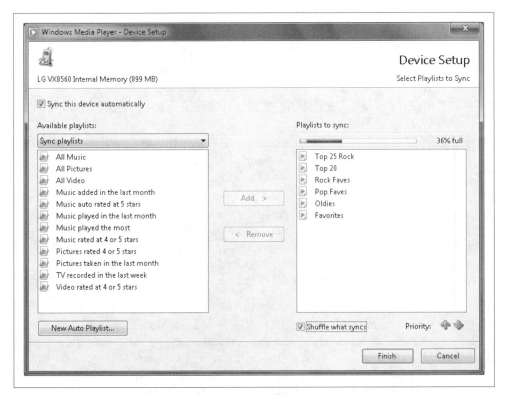

Figure 8-32. Selecting the playlists to sync automatically

6. On the "Available playlists" list, Personal Playlists is selected by default and all your personal playlists are configured for syncing.

7. If you select Sync Playlists on the "Available playlists" list, you can configure any of the following lists for syncing:

   - All Music
   - All Pictures
   - All Video
   - Music added in the Last Month
   - Music Auto Rated 5 Stars
   - Music Played in the Last Month
   - Music Rated 4 or 5 Stars
   - Pictures Rated 4 or 5 Stars
   - Pictures Taken in the Last Month
   - TV Recorded in the Last Week
   - Video Rated at 4 or 5 Stars

8. You can manage the list of playlists to sync in several different ways. You can:

   - Add a list that isn't selected by clicking it and then clicking Add.
   - Remove a selected list by clicking it and then clicking Remove.
   - Change the priority of a list by clicking it and then clicking the Up Priority or Down Priority button.

9. If you have selected more media items than can fit on the device, you can select the "Shuffle what syncs" checkbox to shuffle the priority order each time you sync. This way you'll get different playlists each time.

10. When you click Finish, Windows Media Player will automatically sync with the device. As shown in Figure 8-33, you'll see the sync progress in the main pane. Any files that require conversion prior to syncing will be listed as "Conversion required." Files being converted are listed as Converting, with a progress bar showing the percent complete. Files being synced are listed as Syncing, with a progress bar showing the percent complete. Files that have been synced are listed as "Synced to device."

Each time you connect the device in the future, Windows Media Player will automatically sync with the device as well. To change the automatic sync configuration, repeat this procedure. To stop automatic sync, click the Sync Options button, point to the device on the shortcut menu, select End Sync Partnership, and then click Yes when prompted to confirm. You will then need to add or remove files manually.

Figure 8-33. Viewing sync progress

CHAPTER 9

Capturing and Managing Your Digital Pictures and Videos

Windows XP and earlier releases of Windows include the Windows Picture and Fax Viewer for viewing digital pictures, performing basic editing, and playing slideshows using a series of pictures. Although Windows 7 includes several programs for working with pictures including Windows Photo Viewer and Windows Media Player, you'll likely want to get a more full-featured program to work with your digital pictures, and this is where Windows Live Photo Gallery comes in handy. With Windows Live Photo Gallery, you can:

- View digital pictures and videos in any supported formats.
- Organize digital pictures and videos by tags, date taken, ratings, and folders.
- Touch up digital pictures by adjusting exposure and color, cropping, rotating, and so on.
- Print optimized versions of digital pictures at full-page or preset sizes.
- Play slideshows using a series of digital pictures.
- Burn CDs and DVDs to create copies of your pictures and videos.
- Publish to an online album or blog.

Because Microsoft designed Windows Live Photo Gallery to coexist with Windows Media Player, you can use the same pictures and videos as those you're using with Windows Media Player. Any changes you make to picture and video properties in Windows Live Photo Gallery will be reflected in Windows Media Player when the media information updates, which typically happens automatically. The same is true for Windows Live Photo Gallery. If you make changes to picture and video properties in Windows Media Player, the changes will be reflected in Windows Live Photo Gallery when the media information updates.

Getting Started with Windows Live Photo Gallery

Windows Live Photo Gallery (Figure 9-1) is one of several free programs available as part of the Windows Live Essentials program from Microsoft. Other free programs available include Windows Live Mail, Windows Live Messenger, and Windows Live Writer. To get Windows Live Photo Gallery and other programs, all you need to do is visit *http://www.windowslive.com*. After you sign up for the program and sign in, you'll be able to click the Download Now button or a similar option and then follow the prompts to download and run the Windows Live Setup program. When Setup starts, select the programs you want to install and then click Install. That's it! Once you install the Windows Live programs, they are available by clicking Start→All Programs→Windows Live and then selecting the program that you want to run.

If you've never worked with live web-enabled programs before, you'll notice some important changes when working with the Windows Live Essentials programs. When you install the Windows Live Essentials programs, your computer is configured to use an enhanced version of Windows Update called Microsoft Update (if this isn't already installed). Microsoft Update checks for updates to Microsoft programs as well as Windows and this helps ensure the Windows Live Essentials programs can be updated automatically and in much the same way as Windows itself. For more information on working with Windows Update and Microsoft Update, see Chapter 20.

Because these programs are completely web based, they are updated out of band from Windows and from other Microsoft programs, like Office. This means that Microsoft can more easily deploy new versions of the programs. New versions of Windows Live Essentials programs typically aren't installed automatically and instead may appear as optional updates in Windows Update that you need to select and then install. You would need to check Windows Update periodically for these types of updates. That said, if you know there are new versions of the programs, you can download and install the new versions manually simply by repeating the download process you used to install the programs in the first place. When you start the download process and Setup starts, Setup will tell you if there are new versions that can be installed. You can then select the new versions to install or cancel the install if there aren't new versions available.

Windows Live Photo Gallery allows you to view, edit, organize, and share pictures and videos. You start Windows Live Photo Gallery by clicking Start→All Programs→Windows Live→Windows Live Photo Gallery. The first time you start Windows Live Photo Gallery you are prompted to sign in to Windows Live and then prompted to use the program as the default for supported file types. As Figure 9-1 shows, the main window has these key elements:

Navigation toolbar

Provides browser-like Back and Next buttons that let you navigate to pages you've viewed previously. It also has these Quick Access buttons: File, Fix, Info, Publish, E-Mail, Print, Make, Slide Show, and Extras.

Navigation Pane

Provides quick access for organizing and displaying pictures and videos by type, folders, date taken, and tags.

Preview/work area

Displays thumbnail previews of pictures and videos when you select a particular category or type, and provides the main work area for when you are performing tasks such as fixing pictures.

Controls toolbar

Provides basic controls for manipulating a selected picture or video. You can rotate pictures clockwise or counterclockwise, delete selected items, begin and navigate a picture slideshow, view details or thumbnails, and change the default display size.

Figure 9-1. Using Windows Live Photo Gallery to view and manage your digital pictures and videos

 The controls toolbar lists the total number of items in Windows Live Photo Gallery as well as the total number of items you've selected. By default, Windows Live Photo Gallery uses only your *My Pictures* and *My Videos* folders as well as *Public Pictures* and *Public Videos* folders. See the section "Building Your Photo and Video Gallery" on page 348, later in this chapter, for details on adding pictures and videos to your library.

Accessing Key Features

As Figure 9-2 shows, the Navigation toolbar includes Forward and Back buttons that allow you to access locations you've previously viewed. Clicking a Quick Access button on the Navigation toolbar allows you to access the main areas of Windows Live Photo Gallery.

Figure 9-2. The toolbars in Windows Live Photo Gallery

You can use the Navigation toolbar's Quick Access buttons as follows:

File
> Allows you to add folders, import images from cameras, video cameras, and elsewhere, and to manipulate existing files.

Fix
> Allows you to edit a selected picture using Auto Adjust, Adjust Exposure, Adjust Color, Straighten Photo, Crop Photo, Adjust Detail, Fix Red Eye, and Black and White Effects options.

Info
> Displays an Information pane for a selected picture or video that provides details about the related file.

Publish
> Allows you to publish selected pictures or videos to online albums, including a personal, group, or event album on the Windows Live service.

E-Mail
> Allows you to email selected pictures and videos.

Print
> Allows you to print selected pictures. You can also order prints from Kodak and other companies.

Make
> Provides additional options for working with pictures and videos. The Create Panoramic Photo option merges two or more pictures together to create a combined, panoramic image. The Make a Movie option opens the selected pictures and videos in Windows Live Movie Maker so that you can make a movie. The Burn a DVD and Burn a Data CD options allow you to create a DVD video using Windows DVD Maker. Note that only computers running Windows 7 Home Premium or Windows 7 Ultimate have Windows DVD Maker.

Make a Movie
> Opens the selected pictures and videos in Windows Live Movie Maker so that you can make a movie.

Slide Show
> Plays a slideshow of the currently listed or currently selected pictures. You can also play a slideshow by pressing F12 or Alt-S. To stop the slideshow, press the Esc key.

Extras
> Allows you to download additional photo tools that are available as add-ins. Also allows you to open selected pictures or videos in another program, such as Windows Media Center or Paint.

On the far right side of the Navigation toolbar, you'll find the Sign In option that allows you to sign in to the Windows Live service. When you are signed in, clicking your user id displays options that allow you to sign out, view photos you've published in your personal albums online, or access your Windows Live account. You do not need to be logged in to Windows Live to use Windows Live Photo Gallery. You need to sign in to the service only if you want to use the connected-online features, such as publishing pictures to an online album.

Searching and Browsing Pictures and Videos

The Navigation pane, shown as a separate panel on the left side of Windows Live Photo Gallery, and the Quick Search box, shown in the top-right corner of Windows Live Photo Gallery, provide quick access for organizing and displaying pictures and videos by type, tags, date, ratings, and folders. As Figure 9-3 shows, the Navigation Pane includes several top-level categories and subcategories. Selecting a category or subcategory displays related pictures, videos, or both.

You can use the Navigation pane categories as follows:

All Photos and Videos
> Under the All Photos and Videos category are subcategories for My Pictures, My Videos, Public Pictures and Public Videos. These subcategories allow you to quickly return a list of all personal or public pictures as well as all personal or public videos in folders that Windows Live Photo Gallery can use.

Date Taken
> Use Date Taken to navigate through pictures and videos according to the year, month, and date they were created.

People Tags
> Under the People Tags categories, you'll find a list of all the people tags you've used with pictures and videos. People tags are keywords that aid in searching and organizing your media according to contacts in your address book. You use people tags to identify friends, family, and others in your pictures and videos. Clicking "Add a New Tag" allows you to create a new people tag to be used as a keyword. You can drag one or more pictures or videos to a named tag category to add the tag to those items. You can use the Face Detection feature to identify a person's

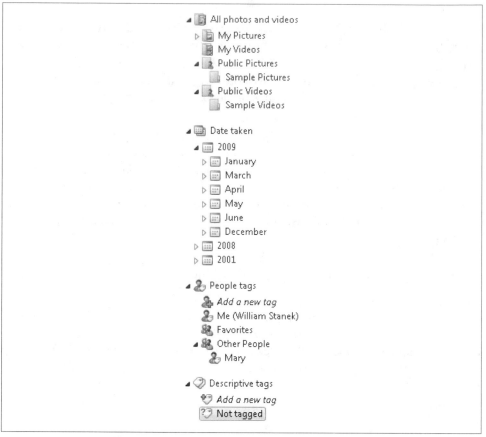

Figure 9-3. The Navigation Pane

face in a picture and associate a people tag with the person's face (see "Identifying People in Your Pictures" on page 346, later in this chapter).

Descriptive Tags

Under the Descriptive Tags categories, you'll find a list of all the descriptive tags you've used with pictures and videos. Descriptive tags are keywords that aid in searching and organizing your media. The way you use descriptive tags is up to you. You could use descriptive tags to specify where the picture was taken, what the picture shows, and more. Clicking "Add a New Tag" allows you to create a new descriptive tag to be used as a keyword. Clicking "Not Tagged" displays all pictures and videos that you haven't tagged. You can drag one or more pictures or videos from the Not Tagged category to a named tag category to add the tag to those items.

The people tags and descriptive tags you use are added to the properties of your pictures and videos. If you right-click a picture or video and then select Properties, you can manage people tags using the People property and descriptive tags using the Tags property. Although both properties are listed under the Description heading, the People property exists only if you've added a people tag to a picture or video. Note that you can select multiple pictures and videos for editing.

Like many other Windows programs, Windows Live Photo Gallery has a Search box. You can use the Search box to quickly search for pictures and videos. The Search feature matches complete or partial words in the media information associated with pictures and videos. This allows you to search on filename, tags, and other information associated with pictures and videos.

You can search your media by completing the following steps:

1. Click in the Search box.
2. Type your search text.

Windows Live Photo Gallery returns matches as you type. Click the Clear button to clear the search results.

Organizing Your Gallery

Microsoft designed Windows Live Photo Gallery to help you create and organize a picture and video gallery. Your gallery automatically contains pictures in your personal Pictures folder, videos in your personal *Videos* folder, shared pictures in your computer's *Public Pictures* folder, and shared videos in your computer's *Public Videos* folder. Your gallery can also include other folders that you've added as well as pictures and videos from cameras. Within your gallery, your pictures and videos are grouped and sorted automatically so that you can browse them by tags, date taken, ratings, folders, and more.

Grouping and Sorting Your Gallery

As Figure 9-4 shows, the work area of Windows Live Photo Gallery includes Arrange By, Sort Direction, and Filter By options. You can use the Arrange By button to display the grouping options.

Figure 9-4. Options for viewing and grouping thumbnails

Figure 9-5. Arranging pictures and videos by rating

The Arrange By options control how Windows Live Photo Gallery groups related sets of pictures and videos in the All Pictures, All Pictures→My Pictures, All Pictures→My Videos, and any other views you select. By default, pictures and videos are automatically grouped, which typically means they're grouped by month and year taken if your gallery includes media taken over several years, or day and month taken if your gallery includes media taken only in a particular year. The grouping options are similar to those you can select by browsing the Navigation pane. You can group pictures and videos by name, date, rating, type, descriptive tag, and people tag.

By default, groups are organized in ascending order, which means that with time-related groupings the newest groups are listed first. You can also organize groups in descending order, which means that with time-related groupings the oldest groups are listed first. Figure 9-5 shows pictures arranged in descending order according to their rating.

The Sort Direction options control how Windows Live Photo Gallery sorts pictures and videos within grouped sets. By default, pictures and videos are sorted in ascending order according to the date taken. You can also sort within groups by filename, date modified, rating, descriptive tag, and people tag.

The Filter By options control whether Windows Live Photo Gallery filters pictures and videos according to their rating. By default, all pictures and videos are shown regardless of their rating. If you want to filter by rating, select the star rating and then specify a

Figure 9-6. Previewing a picture by hovering over it

constraint. The star rating goes from 1 to 5 stars. The constraints are: "and higher," "and lower," and "only." For example, you could show pictures and videos rated 3 stars and higher by selecting 3 stars and then clicking "And higher." Or you show only pictures and videos rated 5 stars by selecting 5 stars and then clicking "Only."

Viewing Your Pictures and Videos

Windows Live Photo Gallery provides several ways to view your pictures and videos. If you move the pointer over a picture for several seconds, you'll see a close-up preview such as the one shown in Figure 9-6. With videos, you'll see a preview of the first frame of the video.

You can open a picture for viewing or play a video by double-clicking it. The picture or video will then fill the work area. If the Info pane is displayed, you can close it by clicking the Close Info pane button. This will give you more area for viewing pictures and videos.

When viewing pictures, the Controls toolbar is displayed in the lower portion of the main window, as shown in Figure 9-7.

Figure 9-7. Controls for pictures

From left to right, the controls on the toolbar are:

Previous

Moves to the previous picture or video. You can also view the previous picture by pressing the left arrow key on your keyboard.

Next

Moves to the next picture or video. You can also view the next picture by pressing the right arrow key on your keyboard.

Rotate Counterclockwise

Rotates the selected picture counterclockwise. You can also rotate a picture counterclockwise by pressing the Ctrl key and the comma (,) key.

Rotate Clockwise

Rotate the selected picture clockwise. You can also rotate a picture clockwise by pressing the Ctrl key and the period (.) key.

Delete

Deletes the selected picture. You can also delete a picture by pressing the Delete key. Deleting a picture will remove it from the gallery and your computer.

Play Slide Show

Plays a slideshow of the currently listed pictures. You can also play a slideshow by pressing F12 or Alt-S. To stop the slideshow, press the Esc key.

 Picture slideshows start with the picture you are viewing and continue through all pictures in the currently selected node in the Navigation pane. With this in mind, you can play slideshows of all pictures taken during a specific year, month, or date by clicking the related Date Taken node, clicking the first picture, and then starting a slideshow by clicking the Play Slide Show button. You can play slideshows of all pictures with a particular tag or rating by selecting the tag or rating, double-clicking the first picture, and then starting the slideshow by clicking the Play Slide Show button.

Actual Size/Fit to Window

Lets you view the picture at its actual size or fit it to the window size. You can also press Ctrl-0 to switch between actual size and window size.

Zoom in

Increases magnification by zooming in. You can also zoom in by pressing -.

Zoom in or out

Increases or decreases magnification by zooming in or out.

Zoom out

Decreases magnification by zooming out. You can also zoom out by pressing =.

When viewing videos, Windows Live Photo Gallery displays the Controls toolbar in the lower portion of the main window, as shown in Figure 9-8.

Figure 9-8. Controls for videos

From left to right, the selectable controls on the toolbar are:

Timeline

Tracks the video timeline and the current frame position within the video. If you click and drag the Current Frame button that moves along the timeline slider, you can fast-forward or rewind through a video. If you click a specific part of the timeline, you can go to that time in the video.

Previous

Moves to the previous video or picture. You can also view the previous video or picture by pressing the left arrow key on your keyboard.

Play/Pause

Plays or pauses the video. You can also play or pause the video by pressing Ctrl-Space.

Next

Moves to the next picture or video. You can also view the next picture by pressing the right arrow key on your keyboard.

Delete

Deletes the selected video. You can also delete a video by pressing the Delete key. Deleting a video will remove it from the gallery and your computer.

Play Slideshow

Plays a slideshow of pictures. If you click this button when viewing a video, you'll see a slideshow of any pictures in the current selection you made before playing the video.

Viewing and Managing Ratings, Tags, and Captions

In Gallery view (when not viewing an individual picture or video), on the Controls toolbar, in the lower-right corner of the main window, you'll find the View Details/ View Thumbnails button. This button allows you to switch between the Details view and the Thumbnails view. You also can switch between these views by pressing Ctrl-0.

To get more details about pictures and videos, display the Thumbnails view. As Figure 9-9 shows, you'll see the following:

- Filename and file extension
- Date taken or created
- File size
- Image size or video runtime

Figure 9-9. Getting basic details about pictures and videos

- Rating
- Caption

With the Details view, you can add ratings and captions to individual pictures and videos. To add a rating, move the pointer over the star rating until the desired rating is highlighted, and then click. To add or edit a caption, click Add Caption or click the existing caption, type the desired caption, and then press Enter or click another area of the window.

Another way to get more detailed information about pictures and videos is to turn on the Info pane by clicking the Info button on the toolbar. The Info pane is also shown in Figure 9-10.

With the Info pane, you can do things that you can't do with the Details view. You can:

- Add the same rating to multiple items by clicking the pictures and videos you want to rate, moving the pointer over the star rating in the Info pane until the desired rating is highlighted, and then clicking.

- Add or edit the captions for multiple items by clicking the pictures and videos you want to work with, clicking the Add Caption text in the Info pane, typing the desired caption, and then pressing Enter or clicking another area of the window.

- Add the same tag to multiple items by clicking the pictures and videos you want to work with, clicking the Add People Tags text or the Add Descriptive Tags text, typing the desired tag, and then pressing Enter.

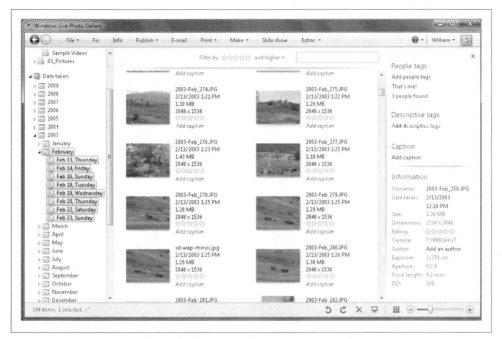

Figure 9-10. Getting more detailed information about pictures and videos

- Assign a tag that is used with some of your selected pictures or videos by right-clicking the tag to assign and then selecting Assign to All. Such tags will appear with a number in parentheses, such as `vacation(3)`, which indicates how many of the pictures have that tag assigned.

- Remove a tag from multiple items by clicking the pictures and videos you want to work with, right-clicking the tag to remove, and then selecting Remove Tag.

- Remove a caption from multiple items by clicking the pictures and videos you want to work with, clicking the caption to highlight its text, pressing Delete, and then pressing Enter or clicking another area of the window.

All these techniques help you provide additional information for your pictures and videos. You can also use tags and ratings to help you view and organize your pictures and videos in different ways. Once you've assigned tags, you can click the People Tags or Descriptive Tags node in the Navigation pane to see a list of all the tags you've assigned. Then, by clicking a tag, you can view all the pictures and videos with that tag.

Once you've assigned ratings, you can filter by the rating to see:

- Only pictures with that rating
- Pictures with that rating or higher
- Picture with that rating or lower

Identifying People in Your Pictures

Adding people tags to your pictures can make it easy to sort and find pictures of friends, family, and others. You can add people tags with or without face detection. Without face detection, the people tag works like a descriptive tag. With face detection, the people tag identifies the people in your pictures by their face. By moving the mouse over a person's face, you then can view the name of each person in a picture. By selecting the person's name under People's tags, you can highlight their face in the picture.

 At the time of this writing, Windows Live Photo Gallery does not include actual facial recognition. The face detection feature can find faces but you still need to tell the program who is who.

Face detection is a feature that can be turned on or off. In Gallery view (when not viewing an individual picture or video), click File→Options, select or clear the Enable Face Detection checkbox and click OK. You can use the face detection feature to identify the faces of people in your pictures.

When the Info pane is displayed or you've opened a picture for viewing by double-clicking it, face detection automatically identifies the faces in pictures you select. Under the People Tags heading, Photo Gallery will specify how many people were found in the picture. In the example shown in Figure 9-11, Photo Gallery has detected one person in the picture. The way you identify the person depends on how you are viewing the picture. If you are working with the main window, you can identify the person by clicking the "1 person found" link, typing the person's name and then pressing Enter. If you've opened the picture for viewing, you can identify the person by clicking the person's name under the People Tags heading or by clicking the "Identify" link under the People Tags heading, typing the person's name and then pressing Enter.

 When you are logged in to the Windows Live service, you can identify the faces of Windows Live contacts in your pictures. Under the People Tags heading, expand the group that contains the contact that you want to add. Drag the photo to the contact and then double-click the photo. In the Info pane, click Locate next to the people tag you just added and then click the face of the person in the picture.

You identify a person in a picture with multiple people in a slightly different way. You can:

- Click the person's face to display the Tag Someone dialog box.
- Move the mouse over the Identify link to highlight the person's face in the picture and then click to display the Tag Someone dialog box.

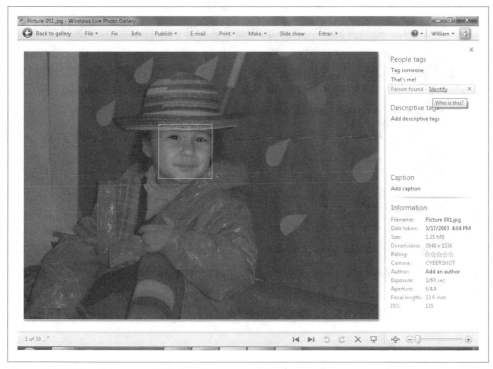

Figure 9-11. Identifying a person's face

You identify a person using the Tag Someone dialog box either by clicking the person's name or using the search feature. If the person isn't listed yet, type the person's name, click Add New Person, and then press Enter.

Although face detection works fairly well, it won't always detect every person in your pictures. Face detection can fail for a variety of reasons, such as if the person's face is only partially seen or if the face is very small in the frame. To resolve this, move over the person's face and do one of the following:

- If Photo Gallery detects the face, the face will be highlighted when you move the mouse pointer over it. You'll be able to specify who the person is by clicking the person's name under the People Tags heading or by clicking the corresponding "Identify" link under the People Tags heading, typing the person's name and then pressing Enter.

- If Photo Gallery doesn't detect the face, you'll be able to specify who the person is by clicking the person's face or by clicking Tag Someone under the People Tags heading. As shown in Figure 9-12, Photo Gallery then displays a face selection box and the Tag Someone dialog box. You can click and drag the face selection box to any location in the picture. You can resize the box by moving to a corner, clicking and dragging to make the box bigger or smaller. After you've sized and positioned the box, you can select the person's name in the Tag Someone dialog box either

Figure 9-12. Tagging someone

by clicking the name or using the search feature. If the person isn't listed yet, type the person's name, click Add New Person, and then press Enter.

Building Your Photo and Video Gallery

As you've seen, Windows Live Photo Gallery handles most of the important organization tasks for you, and this makes adding to your gallery easy. All you need to do is add picture and video folders for Windows Live Photo Gallery to monitor, or copy pictures and videos to folders that it already monitors. You can also get pictures and videos from cameras. Using the built-in print, email, and burn features, getting your media out of your gallery is just as easy. You can print copies of your pictures and videos, save copies of your media to data CDs and DVDs, and email pictures and videos to friends.

Adding or Removing Media Folders

Whenever you start Windows Live Photo Gallery, it checks your *My Pictures* and *My Videos* folders for any picture or video files that have been added and then updates your gallery to reflect these changes automatically. Because of this, the easiest way to add media to your gallery is simply to move the media files to the appropriate folder. To add digital pictures to your library, simply copy or move the digital pictures to your

My Pictures folder. To add videos to your library, simply copy or move the videos to your *My Videos* folder.

Windows Live Photo Gallery also monitors the *Public Pictures* and *Public Videos* folders. Therefore, if you have pictures or videos that you'd like to share with others who use your computer, you can put the shared pictures and videos in these folders.

You can have Windows Live Photo Gallery add media from and monitor other folders in exactly the same way by completing the following steps:

1. Right-click the "All photos and video" category in the Navigation pane, and then select Include a Folder in the Gallery. This displays the Include a Folder in the Gallery dialog box.

2. In the Include a Folder in the Gallery dialog box, select the folder containing pictures, videos, or both that you'd like to add, and then click OK.

As long as you have appropriate permissions to access the folder, Windows Live Photo Gallery will then begin adding pictures and videos from the folder to your gallery. How long this takes depends on how many pictures and videos you are adding. While adding media, the application may run more slowly than usual.

You can remove a folder that you added if you no longer want to include a folder's items in your gallery. To do this, right-click the folder and then select Remove from the Gallery. When prompted, confirm that you want to remove the folder from the gallery by clicking Yes. Removing the folder from the gallery tells Windows Live Photo Gallery to stop monitoring the folder. It doesn't delete the folder or its contents from your computer.

Getting Your Digital Pictures

One way of using a digital picture camera with your computer is to connect the camera directly. After you run your digital camera's Setup program (if any), you can connect most digital cameras directly to your computer using a USB or FireWire cable. With your camera turned on, you then access the digital pictures on it as you would any other device with removable storage. In Windows Live Photo Gallery, you can also select the Import from Camera or Scanner option on the File menu to import digital pictures directly.

Rather than connecting your camera directly, you can purchase a memory-card reader that plugs into a USB slot on your computer. Once you've connected the card reader to your computer, you simply insert the memory card. As with a direct camera connection, you then access your digital pictures as you would any other device with removable storage. Because most digital cameras use memory sticks, computers and monitors increasingly are being shipped with built-in memory card slots. You simply insert your memory card into the slot that works with the type of memory card you have.

Table 9-1 provides an overview of the picture formats Windows Live Photo Gallery supports. Windows Live Photo Gallery is meant to be used with digital cameras and video cameras and not with web images. Because of this, it does not support some older file formats, such as GIF.

Table 9-1. Picture formats supported by Windows Live Photo Gallery

File type	File extensions
Bitmap image	*.bmp, .dib*
HD photo	*.wdp*
Icon image	*.ico*
JPEG image	*.jpe, .jpeg, .jpg, .jfif*
PNG image	*.png*
TIFF image	*.tif, .tiff*

You'll find that viewing pictures in Windows Live Photo Gallery is similar to viewing pictures in Windows Media Player. The two applications do in fact share subcomponents. However, Windows Media Player provides only basic features for viewing pictures and playing slideshows. Windows Live Photo Gallery, on the other hand, has extended viewing, editing, and slideshow features.

Getting Your Videos

When it comes to video cameras, getting videos to your computer requires a mixed bag of tricks. This is because, unlike digital picture cameras, you can capture video from both analog video cameras and digital video cameras.

Capturing video from analog video cameras

An analog-only video camera records video to tape and outputs video using an analog signal. To capture video from a video camera that only supports analog output, you will need to have a video capture card that can support analog input (usually the yellow, red, and white cables). You can find many video and TV capture cards on the market, but many of these are designed primarily for capturing a digital television signal, so be sure to obtain a video capture card that supports this older analog input.

You'll need to install the video capture program that came with your video capture card before capturing video.

An A/V cable for an older video camera will have a connection jack on one end that plugs into your video camera and mono or stereo audio and video connectors on the other end of the plug. You plug the audio and video connectors into the audio and video jacks on your video capture card. If your video capture card has stereo inputs, you'll need a Y connector cable that passes the mono audio into left and right stereo channels.

An A/V cable for a newer video camera will have a connection jack on one end that plugs into your video camera and stereo audio and video connectors on the other end of the plug. You plug the audio and video connectors into the left audio, right audio, and video capture jacks on your video card. If your video capture card has mono input for audio, you'll need a Y connector cable that passes the left and right stereo channels into the mono input channel.

To capture video, you'll need to turn your camera on and then start the video capture program. After you rewind the tape to the beginning or position the tape at the desired start point, press Play on the video camera and then begin to capture the video. When you are finished capturing, you'll need to save the video using a format that Windows Live Photo Gallery supports.

 MiniDV and similar video cameras have tapes but store data digitally. To capture video from a video camera that uses tapes to store data digitally and that supports digital output, see the following section, "Getting video from digital video cameras or cell phones" on page 351. If your camera has a FireWire or USB connection, it most likely records in a digital format and you don't need to use analog inputs to capture the video. However, some digital video cameras have USB connections that transfer only still images taken with the camera. When in doubt, check the manual that came with the camera or consult the manufacturer's website.

Getting video from digital video cameras or cell phones

Digital video cameras store data digitally on a tape, data disc, memory card, or hard disk drive. Table 9-2 provides an overview of the digital video formats Windows Live Photo Gallery supports.

Table 9-2. Video formats supported by Windows Live Photo Gallery

Video formats	File extensions
3GPP2 audio/video	*.3g2, .3gp, .3gp2, .3gpp*
AVCHD video	*.m2t, .m2ts, .mts*
DVD video	*.mpa, .m1v, .m2v, .mp2, .mp2v, .mpv2*
MPEG 1 and MPEG 2 video	*.mpe, .mpeg, .mpg, .ts, .tts*
MPEG-4 video	*.m4v, .mp4, .mp4v*
Windows Media Audio/Video Professional	*.asf, .wm, .wmv*

As with digital picture cameras, one way of using a digital video camera with your computer is to connect the camera directly. After you run your digital camera's Setup program, you can connect most digital video cameras directly to your computer using a USB or FireWire cable. With the camera turned on, you then access the digital media on your camera as you would any other device with removable storage or a CD/DVD drive. Most digital video cameras can take digital pictures as well as digital videos.

If your digital video camera uses data discs in a size and format that your computer's CD/DVD drive can read, you have it easy. All you need to do is insert the data disc into the CD/DVD drive and then you can work with your media as you would any other data disc. In Windows Live Photo Gallery, you can also select the Import from Camera or Scanner option on the File menu to import digital videos and pictures directly.

If your digital video camera uses memory sticks, you can purchase a memory card reader that plugs into a USB slot on your computer. Once you've connected the card reader to your computer, you simply insert the memory card and access your digital media as you would any other device with removable storage. Because most digital cameras use memory sticks, computers and monitors increasingly are being shipped with built-in memory card slots. You simply insert the memory card into the slot that works with the type of memory card you have.

Importing Digital Pictures from Cameras, Scanners, CDs, and DVDs

You can import digital pictures into your gallery and automatically name your imported items by completing the following steps:

1. Connect your camera or video camera to your computer, insert a data CD or DVD containing pictures into your CD/DVD drive, or connect your memory card reader to your computer with a memory stick inserted.

2. You'll usually see an AutoPlay dialog box similar to the one shown in Figure 9-13. If you don't, click Start→Computer, right-click the device and then select Open AutoPlay.

3. In the AutoPlay dialog box, click "View pictures using Windows Live Photo Gallery." If you always want to import pictures into Photo Gallery when you connect this camera or insert this type of memory card, select the "Always do this for pictures" checkbox and click "View pictures using Windows Live Photo Gallery." Then, the next time you import pictures, you'll bypass the AutoPlay dialog box and go straight to the View Pictures dialog box.

 If you don't want to rotate or edit pictures prior to importing them, you can bypass the view part of the import process by selecting "Import Pictures and Videos using Windows Live Photo Gallery" instead of selecting "View Pictures and Videos using Windows Live Photo Gallery." You'll then start the import process with step 7.

Figure 9-13. Selecting an AutoPlay option

4. As shown in Figure 9-14, your pictures are open for importing in Windows Live Photo Gallery. You'll see the first picture in the group of pictures being imported. The current image number and the total number of images available for import are listed in the lower-left corner of the window.

Figure 9-14. Previewing images available for importing

5. Using the controls on the toolbar, you can preview and perform basic manipulation of each image available for importing. If the image needs to be rotated prior to importing, you can rotate the image. If you want to permanently remove it from the camera, you can delete it. If you want to preview all images before importing, you can view a slideshow.

6. Using the menu bar and menu options, you can make copies of an image, view image properties, fix an image in Editing mode and more. Editing mode allows you to adjust exposure and color, straighten or crop a picture, fix red-eye, add effects and more. One of the coolest editing features is Adjust Detail, which you can use to sharpen an image or reduce noise. In Figure 9-15, an out-of-focus image was brought into focus by clicking Adjust Detail and then clicking Analyze. When you are fixing an image, you'll stay in the Editing mode until you close the Editing pane by clicking the Close Edit Pane button.

7. When you are ready to begin importing, click Import to Gallery. In the Import Photos and Videos dialog box, you can:

Review, organize, and group items to import
Items are grouped automatically by date. Use the Adjust Group slider to change the amount of time between groups. For each unique grouping, you can specify whether items in the group are imported by selecting or clearing the Select All Items in This Group checkbox. You also can assign each group a name and tags. By default, the subfolders in which pictures are stored are named by date or by the group name. By default, the filenames for pictures are the same as their original file names on the device. Tags are added to each picture in the group.

Import all new items now
All new items are selected for importing. Items are grouped automatically by date. By default, the subfolders in which pictures are stored are named by date or by the name you assign. By default, the filenames for pictures are the same as their original filenames on the device. Your tags are added to every picture.

More options
Allows you to manage the import options, as discussed in "Configuring Import Settings" on page 358, later in this chapter.

8. When you click Import, Import Photos and Videos will begin importing the selected pictures. As shown in Figure 9-16, you'll see the progress of the import process. You'll also have the option of selecting the Erase After Importing checkbox to remove all pictures you are importing from the device or memory stick.

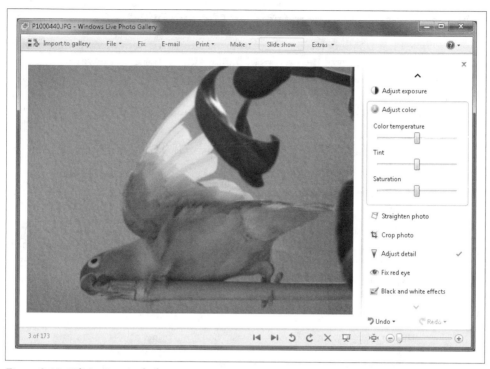

Figure 9-15. Editing images before importing

Figure 9-16. View the import progress

Importing Digital Videos from Cameras, CDs, and DVDs

Windows Live Photo Gallery has one set of import settings for both pictures and videos, and handles the importing of most types of digital videos in the same way as pictures. If you want to import digital videos using the same basic technique as pictures, follow the steps discussed in the previous section titled "Importing Digital Pictures from Cameras, Scanners, CDs, and DVDs" on page 352. You'll then be able to preview and delete your videos prior to importing them.

You also can import digital videos into your gallery and automatically name your imported items by completing the following steps:

1. Connect your camera, video camera, or memory storage device to your computer or insert a data CD or DVD containing pictures into your CD/DVD drive.

2. You'll usually see an AutoPlay dialog box similar to the one shown previously in Figure 9-13. In the AutoPlay dialog box, you'll want to click "Import pictures and videos using Windows" to begin the import process. If you don't see the AutoPlay dialog box, click Start→Computer, right-click the device and then select Open AutoPlay.

 If you always want to import videos when you connect this camera or insert this type of memory card, select the "Always do this for video files" checkbox and then click "Import pictures and videos." The next time you import videos, you'll bypass the AutoPlay dialog box and go straight to the Import Pictures and Videos dialog box.

3. After the Import Videos Wizard determines how many videos are available for importing, you'll see the Importing Pictures and Videos dialog box, shown in Figure 9-17.

4. In the "Tag these pictures" text box, enter a tag for the videos you are importing. Click Import Settings to manage the import options as discussed in "Configuring Import Settings" on page 358.

5. Click Import to import the videos into a subfolder of your default videos folder. By default, the subfolder is named with the date imported and videos retain their original filename.

Changing the Default AutoPlay Settings

AutoPlay settings are designed to make your life easier by remembering your preferred choices for various types of media and then performing related actions for you automatically. Sometimes, though, the AutoPlay settings won't perform the desired action and you'll want to reset them so that the AutoPlay dialog box is displayed.

Figure 9-17. Importing videos

You can reset the AutoPlay settings by completing the following steps:

1. In the Windows Live Photo Gallery main view, click File and then select Options. This displays the Windows Live Photo Gallery Options dialog box.

 If the File menu doesn't have an Options item, it's because you aren't in the main view. Click the Back to Gallery button and then repeat this step.

2. On the Import tab, click the "Change default AutoPlay options" link. This displays the AutoPlay page in the Control Panel, as shown in Figure 9-18.

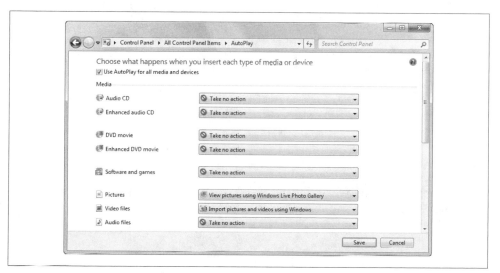

Figure 9-18. Enabling and configuring AutoPlay

3. Make sure the "Use AutoPlay for all media and devices" checkbox is selected.

4. To ensure that the AutoPlay dialog box is displayed, set the AutoPlay options for Pictures and Video Files to "Ask me every time." Alternatively, if you want to begin importing immediately every time you connect a device, select "Import Pictures and Videos using Windows Live Photo Gallery" for Pictures and "Import Pictures and Videos Using Windows" for Video Files.

5. Click Save to save your settings.

Configuring Import Settings

The import settings in Windows Live Photo Gallery control how digital pictures and digital videos are imported. You can set separate default settings by completing the following steps:

1. In the Windows Live Photo Gallery main view, click File and then select Options.

 If the File menu doesn't have an Options item, it's because you aren't in the main view. Click the Back to Gallery button and then repeat this step.

2. In the Windows Live Photo Gallery Options dialog box, click the Import tab, as shown in Figure 9-19. This is the same dialog you will see if you click More Options from the Import Photos and Videos dialog.

Figure 9-19. Setting the default import options

3. On the "Settings for" list, select Cameras, Video Cameras, Album Download, or CD and DVDs as appropriate.

4. The "Import to" list shows the default import location. If you want to set a different default import location, click Browse and then use the Browse for Folder dialog box to select the folder to use. This folder should be one that is monitored by Windows Live Photo Gallery or a subfolder of a monitored folder.

5. Use the Folder Name list options to specify the naming scheme of the folder created for storing the imported items. You can set this to:

   • Date Imported + Name

   • Date Taken + Name

   • Date Taken Range + Name

   • Name + Date Imported

   • Name + Date Taken

   • Name + Date Taken Range

   • Name

   • (None)

6. Use the "File name" list options to specify the default naming scheme for imported pictures and videos. You can select "Name," "Original file name," "Original file name (preserve folders)," "Name + Date Taken," or "Date Taken + Name." If you don't use the original filename, filenames will include a sequential numeric suffix, such as *Halloween 001.jpg*, *Halloween 002.jpg*, and so on.

7. If you don't want to keep the pictures or videos on your camera or memory stick after importing, select the "Delete files from device after importing" checkbox. Because pictures or videos are erased only when the import completes successfully, you don't have to worry about accidentally deleting pictures or videos that didn't get imported.

8. If your camera has a sensor that can detect whether you took a picture horizontally or vertically, Windows Live Photo Gallery can use the related information to automatically rotate pictures that would otherwise appear to be sideways on your computer. To enable automatic rotation, select the "Rotate photos during import" checkbox.

9. To ensure that pictures are opened in Windows Live Photo Gallery after importing, select the "Open Windows Live Photo Gallery after importing files" checkbox.

10. Click OK to save your settings.

Fixing Your Pictures

Windows Live Photo Gallery has built-in features for fixing pictures. In any picture-related view, you can click the Rotate Clockwise or Rotate Counterclockwise button on the Controls toolbar to rotate pictures to the proper orientation. If you select multiple pictures with the same orientation problem, you can rotate them all to the proper orientation at the same time by clicking the Rotate Clockwise or Rotate Counterclockwise button.

 If a picture has the read-only attribute, you won't be able to edit it. To resolve this issue while working with Photo Gallery, click File and then click Properties. In the picture's Properties dialog box, clear the Read-only checkbox and then click OK.

If you don't have appropriate permission, you won't be able to edit pictures, either. You can resolve this by modifying the security permissions of the folder in which the pictures are stored or by modifying the security permissions of the picture you are trying to edit. While working with Photo Gallery, if you can't edit a picture due to security permissions, you can resolve this by clicking File and then clicking Properties to open the picture's Properties dialog box. Use the options on the Security tab to add the appropriate permissions for your user account and then click OK.

If you do not have administrative privileges, you won't be able to change the permissions. Consider copying the file and making your changes to that copy instead.

Editing picture color, brightness, and contrast

You can perform additional editing of individual pictures by completing these steps:

1. In Windows Live Photo Gallery, double-click the picture you want to edit. If the Edit pane is not already displayed, click the Fix button on the toolbar.

2. As Figure 9-20 shows, the picture is then displayed in view mode with the Edit pane.

Figure 9-20. Editing picture color, brightness, and contrast

3. If the color and exposure setting in your picture don't look right, you can correct or enhance the picture automatically by clicking Auto Adjust.

4. If the brightness and contrast still don't look right, you can adjust them independently by clicking Adjust Exposure and then using the Brightness, Contrast, Shadows and Highlights sliders to achieve the desired results.

5. After you've adjusted the exposure either automatically or manually, you can use the black-and-white sliders in the histogram to shift the highlight and shadow levels.

 A histogram illustrates how pixels in a picture are distributed by graphing the number of pixels at each color intensity level. This helps to depict the tonal range of the picture and show whether the picture contains enough detail to make a good correction.

Detail in the shadows is shown in the left part of the histogram, detail in midtones is shown in the middle, and detail in highlights is shown on the right. An underexposed picture has a lot of detail in the shadows. An overexposed picture has a lot of detail in highlights. A properly exposed picture has full tonality with detail concentrated in the midtones.

6. If the colors still don't look right, you can adjust them by clicking Adjust Color. You can then use these color settings to adjust the color:

Color Temperature
> Use this slider to adjust the overall tone of the picture. Move the slider to the left to make the colors appear cooler (bluer). Move the slider to the right to make the colors appear warmer (redder).

Tint
> Use this slider to adjust the predominant color in the picture by adding or removing green. Move the slider to the right to remove green. Move the slider to the left to add green.

Saturation
> Use this slider to make the colors in the picture more or less vivid. Move the slider to the left to make the colors less vivid. Move the slider to the right to make the colors more vivid.

7. Click the Back to Gallery button to save the changes to the picture automatically. If you don't want to save your changes, press Ctrl-Shift-Z before clicking the Back to Gallery button.

Straightening and cropping pictures

Sometimes the person taking a picture didn't hold the camera straight. Correcting this by hand isn't very easy. Don't worry: Photo Gallery can help you straighten and crop any picture easily. To straighten or crop a picture, follow these steps:

1. In Windows Live Photo Gallery, double-click the picture you want to edit. If the Edit pane is not already displayed, click the Fix button on the toolbar.

2. The picture is then displayed in view mode with the Edit pane. To straighten the picture, do one of the following:

   - To straighten the picture by cropping and rotating to the left, move the Straighten Photo slider to the left.

   - To straighten the picture by cropping and rotating to the right, move the Straighten Photo slider to the right.

3. To crop the photo, click Crop Photo to display the options shown in Figure 9-21. Photo gallery then displays a frame selection box. You can click and drag the frame selection box to any location in the picture. You can resize the box by moving to a corner or edge, clicking and dragging to reshape the box. After you've sized and positioned the box, click Apply to save your changes.

4. Click the "Back to gallery" button to save the changes to the picture automatically. If you don't want to save your changes, press Ctrl-Shift-Z before clicking the "Back to gallery" button.

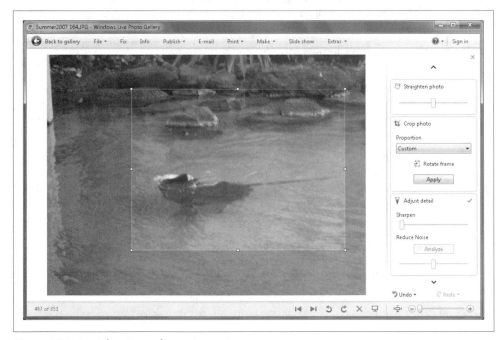

Figure 9-21. Straightening and cropping a picture

Sharpening, reducing noise and bringing pictures into focus

Although Windows Live Photo Gallery has many excellent editing features, my favorites are those for adjusting detail. Not only can you sharpen pictures and reduce noise, but often you also can bring slightly out of focus pictures into focus. To do this, you are going to have Photo Gallery focus on a portion of the picture and then attempt to sharpen the picture or reduce noise automatically or manually. With automatic adjustment, Photo Gallery will analyze the center of focus and use the results of the analysis to determine how to make appropriate corrections.

To adjust the detail in a picture, follow these steps:

1. In Windows Live Photo Gallery, double-click the picture you want to edit. If the Edit pane is not already displayed, click the Fix button on the toolbar. The picture is then displayed in view mode with the Edit pane.

2. When you click Adjust Detail, Photo Gallery displays the image at actual size. Typically, this makes it look like you've zoomed in on the picture.

3. Mouse the mouse pointer over the picture. Click and drag until the item you want to focus on is in view.

4. If the picture is out of focus or blurry, you can try to correct the problem automatically by clicking Analyze. After Photo Gallery analyzes and corrects the picture, move the mouse pointer over the picture, click and drag the scroll around and to review the results. If you want to fit the picture to the window, click the Fit to Window button or press Ctrl-0.

5. As necessary, use the Sharpen slider to sharpen the details in the picture and the Reduce Noise slider to reduce noise in the picture. Review the results by fitting the picture to the window and zooming in to check details as appropriate.

6. Click the "Back to gallery" button to save the changes to the picture automatically. If you don't want to save your changes, press Ctrl-Shift-Z before clicking the Back to Gallery button.

Fixing red-eye

Camera flash can sometimes make it look like people in your pictures have red highlights in their eyes. To try to fix red-eye, follow these steps:

1. In Windows Live Photo Gallery, double-click the picture you want to edit. If the Edit pane is not already displayed, click the Fix button on the toolbar. The picture is then displayed in view mode with the Edit pane.

2. Use the Zoom slider to zoom in on the picture. You'll want the face of the person with red-eye to be very large in the frame. Press and hold the Alt key and then click and drag until you see the problem you want to correct.

3. Drag the mouse pointer to draw a rectangle around the eye you want to fix. Be careful to only select one eye at a time and then only select the eye itself. If you aren't careful, you may fill parts of the picture with blue shaded areas. If you make a mistake, press Ctrl-Z to undo the change.

4. Click the "Back to gallery" button to save the changes to the picture automatically. If you don't want to save your changes, press Ctrl-Shift-Z before clicking the "Back to gallery" button.

Using undo and redo while fixing pictures

While you are fixing your picture, you can use the Undo button to undo any changes you don't like and the Redo button to redo changes you previously undid. Multiple undo and redo changes are saved, allowing you to step backward and forward through changes. You can also undo and redo specific changes.

To undo a specific change or changes, follow these steps:

1. Click the option button to the right of the Undo button. This displays a shortcut menu with a list of Undo changes, as shown in Figure 9-22.
2. The most recent change is listed first and in bold. To undo this change, click it or press Ctrl-Z.
3. To undo a specific change, click the change you want to undo in the list. This will undo every change that occurred after that change as well.
4. To undo all changes, click Undo All or press Ctrl-Shift-Z.

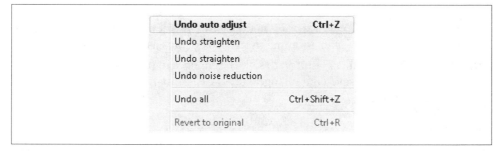

Figure 9-22. Choosing an undo option

To redo a specific change or changes, follow these steps:

1. Click the option button to the right of the Redo button. This displays a shortcut menu with a list of Redo changes, as shown in Figure 9-23.
2. The most recent change is listed first and in bold. To redo this change, click it or press Ctrl-Y.
3. To redo a specific change, click the change you want to redo in the list.
4. To redo all changes, click Redo All or press Ctrl-Shift-Y.

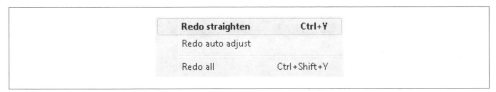

Redo straighten	Ctrl+Y
Redo auto adjust	
Redo all	Ctrl+Shift+Y

Figure 9-23. Choosing a redo option

Restoring the original version of a picture

Whenever you edit a picture using the Edit pane, Windows Live Photo Gallery automatically saves a copy of the original picture. If you're unhappy with the results, follow these steps to restore the original picture at any time (prior to automated deletion of the original):

1. In Windows Live Photo Gallery, click the picture you want to restore and then click the Fix button on the toolbar.
2. The Undo button is changed to a Revert button. To revert to the original version of the picture, click the Revert button or press Ctrl-R.
3. Confirm the action when prompted by clicking Revert again.
4. Click the Back to Gallery button.

Controlling when the original versions of pictures are deleted

When you fix a picture in Windows Live Photo Gallery, Windows saves a copy of the original in case you later want to undo the changes. By default, these copies are never erased, but over time, you may find that they are using up space on your disk drive. To free up this space, you can have Windows automatically delete originals after a specified period. To do this, complete the following steps:

1. In the Windows Live Photo Gallery main view, click File and then select Options. This displays the Windows Live Photo Gallery Options dialog box, as shown in Figure 9-24.
2. On the General tab, use the "Move originals to Recycle Bin after" list to specify whether and when originals are moved to the Recycle Bin. To save originals indefinitely, select Never. To save originals for a specific amount of time and then delete them, select the desired retention time, such as "One week" or "One month."
3. Click OK to save your settings.

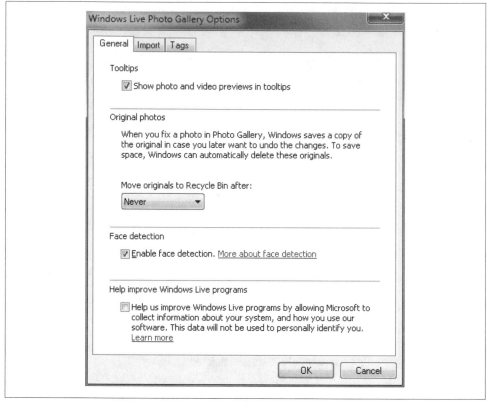

Figure 9-24. Specifying when, if ever, copies of originals should be moved to the Recycle Bin

Sharing Your Photo and Video Gallery

Using the built-in publish, print, email, and burn features, getting your media out of your gallery is just as easy as getting it into your gallery. You can publish pictures to online albums, print copies of your pictures and videos, save copies of your media to data CDs and DVDs, and email pictures and videos to friends.

Publishing Your Pictures

When you are signed in to the Windows Live service you have a variety of options for publishing your pictures online. To get started, select the picture or pictures you want to publish, click Publish and then do one of the following:

- Click Online Album to publish the selected picture or pictures to a personal album in your account online at the Windows Live website.

- Click Group Album to share the selected picture or pictures with a Windows Live group in which you are a member.
- Click Event Album to share the selected picture or pictures on an event page you or someone you know is hosting.
- Click More Services and then click Publish On Flickr to publish to your Flick account, providing you are a member of the service.

Printing Your Pictures

Windows Live Photo Gallery features a smart printing feature that allows you to print enhanced, high-quality pictures. You can print multiple pictures at a time by selecting them before you start printing. You can then print pictures at full-page size, or you can combine pictures and print them at these smaller sizes:

- 4 × 6 with two pictures per page
- 5 × 7 with two pictures per page
- 8 × 10 with one picture per page
- 3.5 × 5 with four pictures per page
- Wallet size with nine pictures per page
- Contact sheet with 35 pictures per page

When you're printing pictures, keep the following in mind:

- If you're printing at a size larger than the original picture size, you may get a blurry picture. For the best results, print pictures using a size equal to or smaller than the original picture size.
- If you're printing to regular paper or paper not designed for photos, you won't get the best results. For the best quality, print pictures on premium photo paper. With premium glossy or matte paper, you'll usually want to print to the shiniest side.

In Windows Live Photo Gallery, you can print pictures by completing the following steps:

1. Select the pictures you want to print.
2. Click the Print button on the toolbar and then select Print.
3. In the Print Pictures dialog box, shown in Figure 9-25, use the Printer list to select the printer you want to use.
4. Use the "Paper size" list to select the paper size you want to use, such as Letter or Legal. To use a size not listed, choose More and then click the size you want to use, or click "User defined size" at the bottom of the list.
5. Use the Quality list to select the print quality, such as 600 × 600 dots per inch (dpi). In most cases, you'll want to print using the highest dpi setting that the printer supports.

6. In the left pane, select the picture size, such as 4 × 6 in.

7. Select the "Fit picture to frame" checkbox to have Windows enlarge the picture to fit the exact size you've selected. If you want the picture to print at its original proportions, clear this checkbox, but keep in mind that you may have gaps because the digital picture isn't proportioned exactly to the dimensions you selected.

8. Use the "Preview next print page" and "Preview previous print page" buttons to review how the pictures will print.

 By default, the pictures are enhanced and sharpened before printing and the Print Pictures dialog box hides options that may not be compatible with your printer. To change these print settings, click the Options link.

9. Click Print to print your pictures.

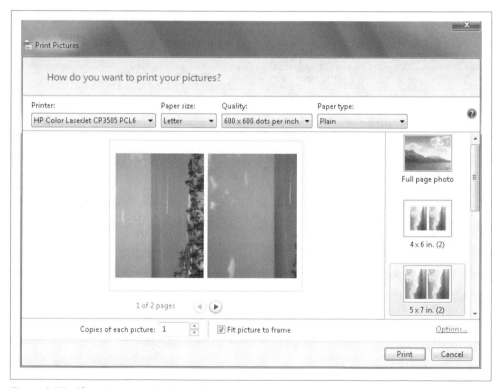

Figure 9-25. Choosing your printing options

Emailing Your Pictures and Videos

Windows Live Photo Gallery makes it easy to send copies of pictures and videos to your friends as attachments to an email message. With pictures, it'll even show you the estimated size of the attached pictures and let you resize pictures automatically so that they have smaller file sizes.

Emailing pictures

In Windows Live Photo Gallery, you can email pictures to your friends by selecting the pictures you want to email and then clicking the Email button. If you are using an email program other than Windows Live Mail, the pictures are attached to your email message. If Windows Live Mail is your default email program, Windows Live Mail opens and displays the New Message dialog box. Windows Live Mail has two email modes. In regular email mode, the pictures are attached to your email message as with other email programs.

In photo email mode, your pictures are inserted into the body of the message and you have a variety of editing options, as shown in Figure 9-26. You can add matting, wood frames and other effects. You can autocorrect, change to black and white instead of color, and rotate pictures. Although photos are normally inserted using a medium size, you can select a new size as well. Windows Live Mail will then resize the pictures if you've changed the picture size. After you complete the To, Cc, Subject, and message body fields as appropriate, you can send the message with your pictures attached by clicking Send.

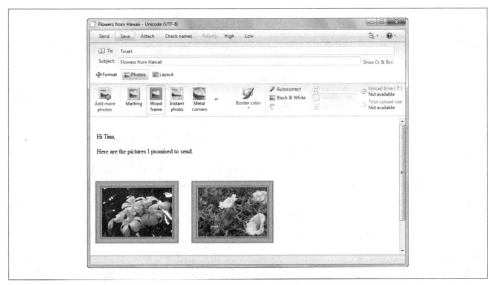

Figure 9-26. Using Windows Live Mail in photo email mode

Emailing videos

In Windows Live Photo Gallery, you can email videos to your friends by completing the following steps:

1. Select the videos you want to email and then click the Email button.

2. Windows opens a new email message in your default mail program and attaches the videos to this message.

3. After you complete the To, Cc, Subject, and message body fields as appropriate, you can send the message with your videos attached by clicking Send.

Burning Data CDs and DVDs

Windows Live Photo Gallery has built-in CD and DVD burning features. You can use these features to create archive copies and to share pictures and videos with others. Before you burn data CDs and DVDs, you should familiarize yourself with the disc types and disc filesystem options that are available.

 You don't necessarily have to use Windows Live Photo Gallery to burn data CDs and DVDs. Anytime you insert a blank CD or DVD, Windows 7 shows a Burn button on the Windows Explorer toolbar. Clicking this button starts the Burn a Disc Wizard, and you can burn discs in much the same way as discussed in this section.

Navigating the available types of data discs

With data CDs and DVDs, you can burn any files in your gallery to create a data disc. As discussed in Chapter 8, if you create a data DVD with pictures in JPEG format, any DVD player that supports this format can read and play the disc as a slideshow. An alternative to this is to make a movie as a DVD-Video using your pictures. You will then be able to play the DVD in just about any DVD player, providing that you use a standard type of DVD disc. Because data DVDs can hold an enormous number of JPEG images, you can create photo-album slideshows that run for hours.

When you are working with data CDs and DVDs, you need to keep in mind that computer and home or car CD and DVD players are different. Your computer DVD player typically is designed to read commercially produced CD-ROMs and DVD-ROMs as well as computer-burned CDs and DVDs in specific formats. To make matters worse, different Windows programs may have varying support for different disc types. Case in point: Windows Live Photo Gallery supports a similar but different set of disc types than Windows Media Player.

Although Windows Live Photo Gallery won't burn audio CDs, it does give you more burning options for data discs than Windows Media Player does. Windows Live Photo Gallery supports burning data CDs to CD-R, CD+R, and CD-RW. Windows Live

Photo Gallery supports burning data DVDs to DVD-R, DVD-RW, DVD+R, DVD+RW, and DVD-RAM. DVDs can be either single-sided and single-layered or single-sided and dual-layered. DVD-Audio and DVD-Video aren't supported for data disc burns, but you can make a movie as a DVD-Video, as discussed in Chapter 10.

Many CD/DVD burners support multiple disc types. Of the many types of writable discs, not all discs can be formatted with a filesystem and used in the same way. To help you choose the right disc for the task, Table 9-3 provides some tips and advice.

Table 9-3. Navigating CD and DVD options

Disc type	How used	Compatible with
CD-R, CD+R, DVD-R, DVD+R	These disc types are recordable. Data cannot be deleted once recorded.	Compatible with many computers and some CD/DVD players.
CD-RW, DVD-RW, DVD+RW	These disc types are re-recordable. Data can be deleted after it is recorded, and you can write data to the disc many times.	Compatible with many computers and some CD/DVD players.
DVD-RAM	These disc types are re-recordable. Data can be deleted after it is recorded, and you can write data to the disc many times.	Compatible with fewer computers and CD/DVD players.

Navigating data disc filesystem options

Most Windows programs create data discs using a mastered approach and discs are written in the appropriate filesystem format automatically. With a mastered approach, you select a collection of files that you want to copy to a disc and then burn all the files at once. When you are burning large collections of files, this is a convenient approach with the added bonus of compatibility with any computer or device that supports the type of data disc you are using.

When you burn files to data discs using mastering, you burn files in a session. In many CD/DVD burning programs, you have the option of leaving a session open to allow you to add files later, and then you close the session when you are done adding files. By closing the session, you finalize the disc and allow it to be read on other computers and devices. Otherwise, while a session is open, the disc can be read only on your computer. Windows Live Photo Gallery uses the built-in CD/DVD burn feature of Windows 7. Instead of opening a session, Windows 7 creates a burn list and copies files you want to burn to a temporary folder. Once you've collected all the files you want to burn, you can open a burn session, write the files, and then close the burn session. Once the burn session is closed, you can no longer add to the disc.

With Windows Live Photo Gallery, you can create data discs with what Windows 7 calls a "live filesystem." A data disc with a live filesystem works like any other type of removable storage, such as a USB flash key or a removable disc drive. You can copy files to the disc immediately without having to burn them, simply by copying and pasting files or by dragging and dropping files. If the disc is re-recordable, you can remove files simply by selecting them and deleting them. If you eject the disc, you can insert it into your CD/DVD drive later and continue to use it like removable storage. The major drawback, however, is that home and car CD/DVD players cannot read data discs with a live filesystem—only computers can.

Technically, data discs with a live filesystem are formatted using the Universal Disc Format (UDF) rather than the standard CD File System (CDFS). Although UDF has been around for a long time, you might not have heard of it before, because although Windows has supported UDF since Windows 98, you needed to purchase a separate CD/DVD burner program to actually create and use UDF. That is no longer the case with Windows 7.

At the time I wrote this book, UDF versions included the following:

UDF 1.5
> This format is compatible with Windows 2000 and later versions of Windows. It might not be compatible with Windows 98 or Apple computers.

UDF 2.0
> This format is compatible with Windows XP and later versions of Windows. It might not be compatible with Windows 98, Windows 2000, or Apple computers.

UDF 2.01
> This is the default format, and it includes a major bug fix that you'll want to take advantage of in most cases. This format is compatible with Windows XP and later versions of Windows. It might not be compatible with Windows 98, Windows 2000, or Apple computers.

UDF 2.5
> This format is optimized for Windows Vista and later versions of Windows. It might not be compatible with earlier versions of Windows or Apple computers.

As Windows 7 uses UDF 2.01 by default, this means data CDs you burn with a live filesystem will be compatible with Windows XP, Windows Vista, and later versions of Windows.

Burning data disc masters

You can burn a mastered disc by completing the following steps:

1. In Windows Live Photo Gallery, select one or more of the pictures and videos you want to burn to disc.
2. Click Make and then click Burn a Data CD. Windows Live Photo Gallery will then open the tray on your default CD/DVD burner.
3. Insert a blank disc into your CD/DVD burner and then close the tray. You can insert a CD or DVD.
4. In the Burn a Disc Wizard, type a disc title, select With a CD/DVD Player, as shown in Figure 9-27.

Figure 9-27. Creating a mastered data disc

5. When you click Next, the data disc is opened in Windows Explorer, as shown in Figure 9-28. The "Files Ready to Be Written to the Disc" pane shows the pictures and videos you've selected. This is your burn list. Don't close this window.

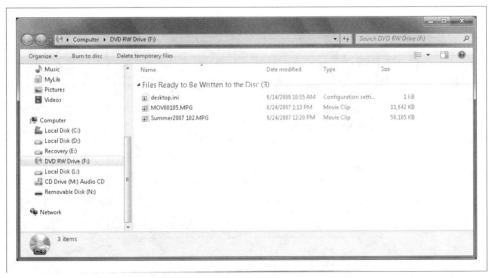

Figure 9-28. Adding files to the burn list

Files on the burn list are copied from their original location and written as temporary files to a temporary folder. This temporary folder is created in your personal profile. Copies of these files are created to be sure that all the files are in one place and that you have appropriate permissions to access the files before trying to burn the disc.

6. To add more pictures and videos, select them in Windows Live Photo Gallery, click Make, and then select Burn a Data CD. If you try to add any pictures or videos that are already added to the burn list, you'll see the Copy File dialog box shown in Figure 9-29. Before you click "Copy and Replace," "Don't Copy," or "Copy, but keep both files" as appropriate, you might want to select the "Do this for the next ... conflicts" checkbox to perform the same action for all duplicate copies.

7. To add files that are on your computer but are not in your gallery, drag the files to the burn list in Windows Explorer. You can add any type of file using this technique; not just pictures or videos.

8. If you want to remove a picture or video from the burn list, click it and then click "Delete temporary files." When prompted to confirm the action, click Yes. The related temporary file is then moved from the burn list to the Recycle Bin. The original version of the picture or video will still exist in its original location.

Figure 9-29. Resolving conflicts by selecting an appropriate option

9. Once you've added all the files you want to burn, access the burn list in Windows Explorer. Click an open area within the burn list and then press Ctrl-A and then on the status bar click the Show More Details link. Note the total size of all selected files, and remove files as necessary so that all the files fit on one disc. Unlike Windows Media Player, the Burn to Disc Wizard will not burn files to multiple discs.

 If you are unsure of the total capacity of a disc, simply look at another disc of the same type. The capacity is written on the disc. Most data CDs can hold up to 700 MB of data. Most single-sided single-layered DVDs can hold up to 4.7 GB of data.

10. When you are ready to continue, click Burn to Disc. In the Burn to Disc Wizard, the disc title is set using the title you provided previously, and the recording speed is set to the maximum speed supported by the CD/DVD drive.

11. When you click Next, Windows 7 will add the files you selected to a disc image and then write the files to your data disc. When finished burning the disc, Windows 7 will automatically eject the disc. By default, the temporary files are deleted and you can click Finish to exit the Burn to Disc dialog box. If you want to burn the same files to another disc, select the "Yes, burn these files to another disc" checkbox before clicking Finish.

Keep the following in mind when working with the Burn to Disc Wizard:

- If an error occurs while burning, you'll see a burn error message. As shown in Figure 9-30, you'll have the option of trying again with a different disc, deleting the temporary files that have not burned, or saving all the temporary files and trying to burn them later. If you try again, make sure you select a slower burn speed. Although your CD/DVD drive may be able to burn at a high speed, the disc itself may not be rated for burning at the speed you've selected.

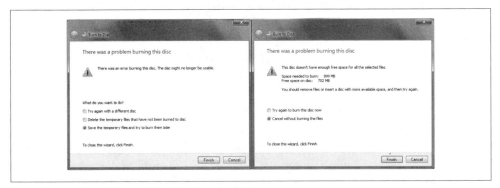

Figure 9-30. Specifying what you want to do if a burn error occurs

Generally, if you see a burn error, only a portion of your files will be written to the disc. If the burn session is still open, you can try to burn to the disc again. However, in some cases, you may find that you have to use a new blank disc.

- If you miscalculated the capacity of your data disc, you'll see a free space error and will have to click Cancel or Finish. Both actions exit the Burn to Disc Wizard. Don't worry; you don't have to start over. When you click Cancel or Finish, you'll see the Windows Explorer window with the files you are trying to burn. Remove files to reduce the total size of the data and then click Burn to Disc.

 Rather than deleting items, you can change the type of disc you're working with. If you inserted a CD but want to use a DVD instead, simply eject the CD and insert a DVD. You'll then see the Burn to Disc Wizard.

Burning a data disc with a live filesystem

You can burn a data disc with a live filesystem by completing the following steps:

1. In Windows Live Photo Gallery, select one or more of the pictures and videos you want to burn to disc.

2. Click Make and then click Burn a Data CD. Windows Live Photo Gallery will then open the tray on your default CD/DVD burner.

3. Insert a blank disc into your CD/DVD burner and then close the tray. You can insert a CD or DVD.

4. In the Burn a Disc Wizard, type a disc title, select Like a USB Flash Drive, as shown in Figure 9-31.

5. By default, Windows 7 burns live discs using UDF version 2.01. When you click Next, Windows 7 formats the data disc and then copies the selected pictures and videos to the disc.

6. Click Start and then click Computer. In the Computer window, right-click the CD/DVD drive you were working with and then select Open. The data disc is opened in Windows Explorer.

7. Because you are working with a live disc, there is no burn list. You can now work with the disc as follows:

   - To add files that are on your computer but not in your gallery, drag the files to the burn list in Windows Explorer. You can add any type of file using this technique; not just pictures or videos.

   - To add pictures and videos in your gallery, select the pictures and videos in Windows Live Photo Gallery, click Make, and then click Burn a Data CD. The files will be copied to the live data disc.

- To remove a picture or video from the disc, click it and then press Delete, or right-click it and then select Delete. With *rewritable* (RW) discs, the file is removed and the space is freed for other files. With *recordable* (R) discs, the file is marked as deleted but actually still exists on the disc. Because of this, the space used by the deleted file is still allocated and cannot be used by other files.

Figure 9-31. Selected files, copied to the disc

While the disc is inserted, Windows 7 will maintain an open burn session for the disc. If you eject the live data disc, Windows 7 will close the burn session so that you can use the disc with other computers. From then on, whenever you insert the disc, you'll be able to add or remove files using Windows Explorer, Windows Live Photo Gallery, and other Windows programs. Windows 7 will open another burn session only if you modify the disc's contents. As before, you can close the session by ejecting the disc.

 You can also close a burn session by right-clicking the CD/DVD drive in the Computer window and selecting "Close session."

CHAPTER 10
Making Video DVDs and Movies

Windows 7 includes built-in support for burning DVDs. As you've seen in earlier chapters, you can use these features to create data DVDs in Windows Media Player and Windows Live Photo Gallery. If you are running the Windows 7 Home Premium or Ultimate edition, you can also use these features to create video and movie DVDs using Windows DVD Maker and Windows Movie Maker.

The differences between Windows DVD Maker and Windows Movie Maker mostly have to do with your level of involvement and the level of customization you want. With Windows DVD Maker, your video DVDs can have digital-picture slideshows with soundtracks, and digital videos that include their own soundtracks. When you add pictures and videos, Windows DVD Maker handles most of the background tasks for you so that you can produce video DVDs with minimal fuss. In fact, you can design a full-featured video DVD complete with title, menu, soundtrack, pan and zoom motion for your picture slideshows, and notes—all in just a few minutes.

If you want more than the essentials, you will need to use Windows Movie Maker. With Windows Movie Maker, you have full control over every aspect of movie production. You can create movies using digital pictures and videos. To create professional-looking movies, you can add titles, effects, transitions, and credits. Your movies can also have soundtracks that combine narration, music, and other types of audio. A finished movie, however, is not a finished DVD production. Therefore, after you produce your movie, you'll have to use Windows DVD Maker to create a finished DVD production.

So there you have it—two ways to create video DVDs with two different approaches. One allows you to produce finished DVDs. The other is a movie maker with enough added production capabilities to please even the most ardent recreational video producer.

Beyond this, Microsoft also offers Windows Live Movie Maker as part of Windows Live Essentials. You can think of Windows Live Movie Maker as an evolving product that is a streamlined version of Windows Movie Maker. Windows Live Movie Maker is primarily designed for making web videos.

Creating Video DVDs with Windows DVD Maker

Windows DVD Maker helps you create videos and complete DVDs with minimal fuss. That's why it's my favorite of the two video makers available for Windows 7.

Getting Started with Windows DVD Maker

You can start and use Windows DVD Maker in several ways. When you are working with Windows Live Photo Gallery (see Chapter 9), you can select the initial pictures and videos you want to work with and then click Burn→Video DVD to open Windows DVD Maker with these items selected. Otherwise, you can start Windows DVD Maker by clicking Start→All Programs→Windows DVD Maker.

As Table 10-1 shows, Windows DVD Maker works with a wide variety of image, sound, and video formats. This list is different from the formats supported by Windows Live Photo Gallery and Windows Media Maker. The most notable changes are that Windows DVD Maker supports GIF images but does not support the AIFF or AU sound format. Also of note is that Windows DVD Maker supports the Microsoft Digital Video Recorder format, allowing you to create video DVDs with recorded TV.

Table 10-1. File formats supported by Windows DVD Maker

File format/type	File extensions
Bitmap image	*.bmp*
DIB image	*.dib*
GIF image	*.gif*
JPEG image	*.jpg, .jpe, .jpeg, .jfif*
PNG image	*.png*
TIFF image	*.tif, .tiff*
WordPerfect image	*.wdp*
Windows Meta File	*.wmf, .emf*
Sound formats	
MP3 audio	*.mp2, .mp3*
WAV audio	*.wav*
Windows Media Audio	*.wma*
Video formats	
AVI video	*.avi*
DVD video	*.mpa, .m1v, .mp2v, .mpv2*
MPEG 1 and MPEG 2 video	*.mpe, .mpeg, .mpg*
Audio/Video format	
Windows Media Audio/Video Professional	*.asf, .wm, .wmv*

File format/type	File extensions
Recorded TV format	
Microsoft Digital Video Recorder	*.dvr-ms, .wtv*

When working with digital pictures, digital videos, and sounds, it is also important to note that Windows DVD Maker works with files that are already in the proper formats, and doesn't include features for converting formats. Additionally, all the files you want to use must be on your computer's disk drive, on a data disc you've inserted into your CD/DVD drive, or on a device with removable storage connected to your computer. Although Windows DVD Maker can read music and other sound files from a data disc, it doesn't include features for ripping raw CD audio files from audio discs.

When you start working with Windows DVD Maker, you may notice that the program works more like an extended wizard than a standalone program, and that's because it's designed to help you through the steps involved in video production. The first time you start Windows DVD Maker, you'll see the page shown in Figure 10-1. This page introduces Windows DVD Maker. If you clear the checkbox before you click "Choose Photos and Videos" to continue, you won't see this page again unless you are using a new user account.

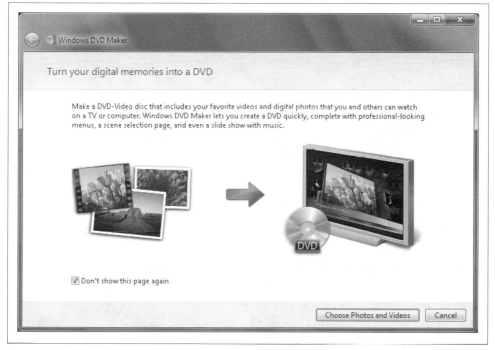

Figure 10-1. Getting started with Windows DVD Maker

Figure 10-2. The "Add pictures and video to the DVD" page

Windows DVD Maker has two main pages. The first page you see in Windows DVD Maker is the "Add pictures and video to the DVD" page shown in Figure 10-2. You'll use this page to add items, set the play order, and configure the DVD burning and playback options.

When you click Next, you'll see the "Ready to burn disc" page, which is shown in Figure 10-3. On this page, you can customize the DVD menu style and text, as well as set up your picture slideshow and add an audio soundtrack. You can also preview and burn your video from this page.

Using the options provided on these two pages, you create video DVDs by following a series of prescribed steps. The basic steps are as follows:

1. Add your pictures and videos, and then set the play order.
2. Set the DVD burning and playback options.
3. Customize the DVD menu style and text.
4. Set up your picture slideshow and add an audio soundtrack.
5. Preview and save your video project.
6. Burn your video.

Figure 10-3. The "Ready to burn DVD" page

I discuss tasks related to each step in the following sections.

Adding Your Pictures and Videos, and Setting the Play Order

With Windows DVD Maker, you can create video DVDs that include and combine pictures, videos, and recorded TV. Windows DVD Maker works with these different media types in different ways. Digital videos and recorded TV shows you select are added as individual items on the burn list. Pictures you select are added to a *Slide show* folder. Each video DVD can have up to 998 videos or recorded TV shows but only one *Slide show* folder. The *Slide show* folder is handled as a media item separate from videos and recorded TV, and can itself hold up to 999 pictures.

Selecting pictures and videos for your DVD

Windows DVD Maker gives you several ways to select the pictures and videos to include in your video. My favorite way is to select all the pictures and videos I want to use in Windows Live Photo Gallery first and then add the selected items automatically to Windows DVD Maker. One way to do this is to click the first picture or video to add,

Figure 10-4. Selecting pictures in Windows Live Photo Gallery

hold the Ctrl key, and then select each additional picture or video to add individually. When you are done selecting items, you release the Ctrl key, and then click Make→Burn a DVD in Windows Live Photo Gallery. Unfortunately, once you've selected an initial list in Windows Live Photo Gallery and accessed Windows DVD Maker, you can't go back to Windows Live Photo Gallery and select an additional set of pictures and videos to add. This means you'll have to select all the pictures and videos first to make the most out of this shortcut.

Sometimes, though, you want to add hundreds of items to a video, and it isn't always practical to select each item individually in Windows Live Photo Gallery before starting Windows DVD Maker. Here's one handy workaround I've come up with:

1. In Windows Live Photo Gallery, turn on the Info pane by clicking the Info button.

    Only one instance of Windows DVD Maker can be open at a time. Because of this, you must start Windows Live Photo Gallery and then click Make→Burn a DVD to open Windows DVD Maker.

2. Select one or more items that you want to add to the video DVD.

3. In the Info pane, click Add Descriptive Tags, type a unique name that identifies the video you are creating, such as Stanek Family DVD Volume 4, and then press Enter (see Figure 10-4).

4. Repeat steps 2 and 3 until you've added this tag to all the pictures and videos for the video DVD. You don't have to type the tag each time, however. Instead, when you click Add Descriptive Tags, select the tag in the list provided, and then press Enter.

5. In the Navigation pane, select Descriptive Tags to view the list of tags associated with your pictures and videos, and then click the tag you're using for the video.

6. In the work area, select all the items for the video by clicking the first item in the list, holding the Shift key, and then clicking the last item in the list. Alternatively, you can press Ctrl-A.

7. Click Make and then click Burn a DVD to open Windows DVD Maker with these items selected.

I often find myself creating video DVDs related to specific dates on which I took pictures and videos. With that in mind, here's another handy workaround I've come up with:

1. In Windows Live Photo Gallery, right-click Date Taken and then select Expand All. If you don't see an Expand All option, right-click Date Taken and then select Collapse and then right-click Date Taken again and then select Expand All.

2. In the Navigation pane, click the node for the first year, month, or date to include in the video.

3. While holding the Ctrl key, click the next node to include in the video and repeat this step until you've selected all the pictures and videos for the video.

4. Release the Ctrl key.

5. In the work area, select all the related items by clicking the first item in the list, holding the Shift key, and then clicking the last item in the list. Alternatively, you can press Ctrl-A.

6. Click Make and then click Burn a DVD to open Windows DVD Maker with these items selected.

7. In Windows DVD Maker, the total runtime of all selected items is shown in the lower-left corner of the main window.

In Windows DVD Maker, you can select the items to add to your video by completing the following steps:

1. On the "Add pictures and video to the DVD" page, click the "Add items" button on the toolbar.

2. As shown in Figure 10-5, use the "Add Items to DVD" dialog box to browse to a folder containing pictures or videos you want to add.

3. Select the items to add using one of the following techniques:

   • Select an individual item by clicking it.

   • Select a series of items by clicking the first item, pressing and holding the Shift key, clicking the last item, and then releasing Shift.

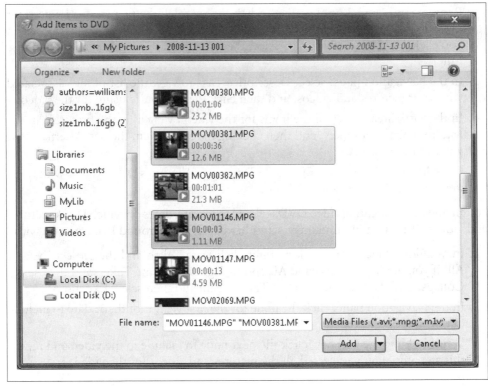

Figure 10-5. Selecting items to add

- Select multiple items individually by clicking the first item, pressing and holding the Ctrl key, clicking each additional item in turn, and then releasing Ctrl.

4. Click Add.

As Figure 10-6 shows, Windows DVD Maker lists the runtime of all selected items as a portion of the total running time possible in the lower-left corner of the main window. This runtime may change if you modify the slideshow properties. Most single-sided DVDs can have a total running time of up to 150 minutes. Most single-sided double-layered DVDs can have a total running time of up to 300 minutes.

If you want your video to play on home DVD players, ensure wide compatibility for your video by using a single-sided single-layered DVD rather than a single-sided double-layered DVD. In addition, if your DVD burner supports multiple formats, the type of disc you use will determine the format. DVD-R and DVD+R have the widest support, with DVD-RW and DVD+RW close behind in terms of support.

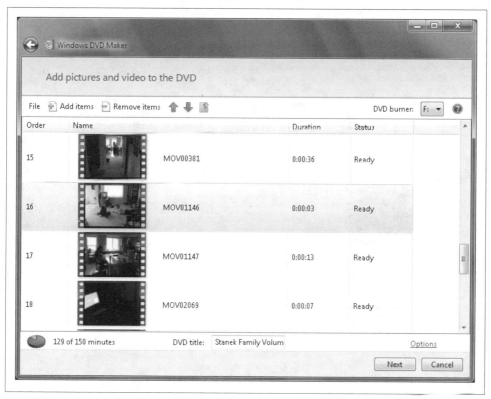

Order	Name	Duration	Status
15	MOV00381	0:00:36	Ready
16	MOV01146	0:00:03	Ready
17	MOV01147	0:00:13	Ready
18	MOV02069	0:00:07	Ready

Add pictures and video to the DVD

File   Add items   Remove items

Windows DVD Maker

DVD burner: F:

129 of 150 minutes   DVD title: Stanek Family Volum   Options

Next   Cancel

Figure 10-6. Checking the video runtime

Setting the play order

In Windows DVD Maker, the listing order sets the order in which items are played (see Figure 10-7). The first item on the list plays first, the second item plays second, and so on. You can control an item's play order using the Move Up and Move Down buttons. Click an item you want to move and then click the Move Up or Move Down button until the item is in the desired position on the playlist. You can also drag and drop items to reorder them. When setting the play order, note the duration and status of each item.

On video DVDs that include both digital pictures and digital videos, I've found that it's often best to have the picture slideshow first. One of the reasons for this is that you can sync the slideshow to a music soundtrack, and this helps to keep the audience engaged. Additionally, if you show the live video first, it seems anticlimactic for you then to start showing a slideshow—even if that slideshow does have a cool soundtrack. After all, it is hard for digital pictures to compete with live action.

Figure 10-7. Setting the play order of your picture slideshow and videos

Pictures in the *Slide show* folder also have a play order. If you double-click the *Slide show* folder, you can then view and set the play order for pictures, as shown in Figure 10-8. You can control the play order of pictures in the slideshow using the Move Up and Move Down buttons. Click a picture you want to move and then click the Move Up or Move Down button until the picture is in the desired position on the playlist. When you are done working with pictures, you can click the parent folder button to go back to the main burn list. This button is displayed as a folder icon and an up arrow.

 If your pictures span a period of months or years rather than hours or days you may want to ensure that the pictures are viewed in the order that they were taken. This seems to be one of the best approaches. But there's one interesting effect when you're doing a tribute to an individual, and that is to work from the present to the past, especially if you have pictures that go through the person's life from the present to when he was a child. Alternatively, you can go from a person's childhood to the present, but it is sort of fun to slip back slowly into past memories.

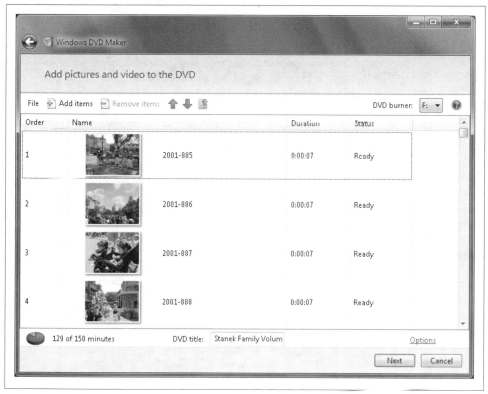

Figure 10-8. Setting the play order of pictures

By default, each picture in the slideshow is displayed for seven seconds. You'll be able to change this setting and sync the slideshow length with your soundtrack later. See the section "Customizing Your Picture Slideshow and Adding an Audio Soundtrack" on page 395, later in this chapter, for details.

Setting the DVD Burning and Playback Options

Windows DVD Maker allows you to add a DVD menu to your videos, to encode your videos using an aspect ratio for widescreen or standard screen, and to format your videos using either NTSC or PAL video format. In Windows DVD Maker, you can set these and other options by completing the following steps:

1. On the "Add pictures and video to the DVD" page, the "DVD burner" list shows which drive will be used for burning the DVD. If your computer has multiple DVD burners, select the disc you want to use.

2. Use the "DVD title" text box to set the working title for the DVD.

3. The Options link is in the lower-right corner. Click this link to display the Options dialog box shown in Figure 10-9.

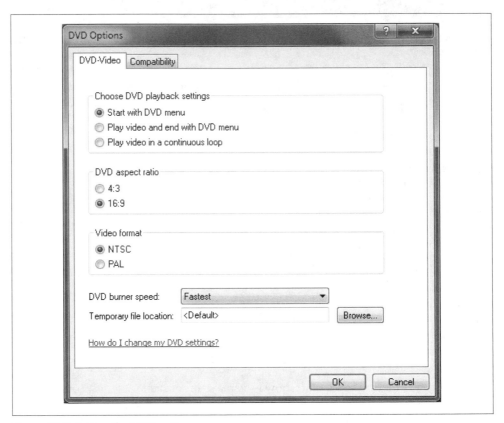

Figure 10-9. Setting the DVD options

4. Under "Choose DVD playback settings," choose how you want the DVD to play by selecting one of the following options:
   - If you want the DVD menu to display when the disc is inserted in a DVD player, click Start with DVD Menu.
   - If you want the video to play immediately when the disc is inserted in a DVD player and show the menu at the end, click "Play video and end with DVD menu."
5. If you want the video to play automatically and loop continuously, click "Play video in a continuous loop." With this setting, you will see the menu only if you choose the Menu option using the remote control for your DVD player.

6. Under "DVD aspect ratio," choose the DVD aspect ratio. The aspect ratio is expressed as the relation of the video width to the video height. For widescreen, choose 16:9 as the aspect ratio. For standard (full) screen, choose 4:3 as the aspect ratio.

When deciding which aspect ratio to choose, consider who will be playing your video and the type of screen she has. Although all monitors and TVs can play videos recorded in either aspect ratio, your video will look best when using the native format supported by the monitor or TV. A widescreen video will look best on a widescreen monitor or TV. A standard video will look best on a standard monitor or TV.

7. Under "Video format," select either NTSC or PAL. If you are unsure of which format to use, don't change the default format, because this is set based on the Regional and Language Options in the Control Panel. You will need to change the format only when you plan to share your video DVD with a friend who lives in another country or region.

Video signals are broadcast using a standard format. NTSC is the standard format in North America and Japan. PAL is the standard format for most of Europe. Though there are other broadcast standards, such as SECAM used in France and variations of PAL used in some European countries, NTSC and PAL are the standard formats in widest use.

8. The "DVD burner speed" list is set by default to Fastest, allowing you to encode the DVD at the fastest speed your DVD burner supports. The rated speed of the DVDs you are using will largely determine your success when burning at faster speeds. If you experience problems when burning DVDs at the fastest speed supported, try using a slower setting or discs rated for a higher burn speed. On some DVDs, the top-rated burn speed is imprinted clearly as part of the label. On other DVDs, you may have to look closely at the packaging or the small-print lettering on the DVD itself.

9. By default, Windows DVD Maker creates a working version of the DVD in a temporary folder within your profile. Because your profile is stored on the system drive, which is typically the *C:* drive, this drive must have at least 5 GB of available disk space when you are creating a single-sided single-layered DVD, and 10 GB of available disk space when you are creating a single-sided double-layered DVD. If you want to choose a folder on another drive for the temporary files, click Browse and then use the Browse for Folder dialog box to select the new folder to use.

10. Click OK to save your settings.

Figure 10-10. Choosing the menu style

Customizing the DVD Menu

Video DVDs can include a menu that is displayed either at the start of the video or at the end of the video. The primary options on this menu are as follows:

Play
 Plays the video from the start.

Scenes
 Displays a scenes selection page, allowing you to navigate to a particular part of the video.

Notes
 Displays a notes page if you've added notes to the video.

You can customize the menu and the related menu pages on the "Ready to burn DVD" page. From the "Add pictures and video to the DVD" page, you can display the "Ready to burn disc" page, which is shown in Figure 10-10, by clicking Next.

On the "Ready to burn disc" page, you can use the options on the Menu Styles list to choose a menu style, such as Highlights or Video Wall. When you select a style, Windows DVD Maker displays a large preview of that style in the main work area.

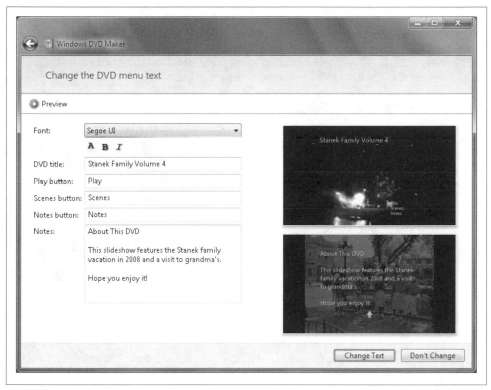

Figure 10-11. Customizing the DVD menu text

After you've selected a menu style, you can customize the menu text by completing the following steps:

1. Click the "Menu text" button on the toolbar. This displays the "Change the DVD menu text" page, shown in Figure 10-11.

2. Each menu style has default font settings. If you want to change the font used for menu text, click the Font list and select the font you want to use.

3. To change the font color, click the Font Color button (it shows the letter A), choose a color in the Color dialog box, and then click OK.

4. Most menu text is displayed in bold but not italic by default. To toggle bold and italic on and off, click the related buttons.

5. If you didn't already set the disc title, type in the text box provided.

6. By default, the text for the Play, Scenes, and Notes buttons says Play, Scenes, and Notes, respectively. If you want to make this text more descriptive, enter the text you'd like to use in the fields provided. For example, you may want to use Play Video, View Scenes, and Display Notes instead of the default text.

Figure 10-12. Customizing the DVD menu style

7. The Notes button is displayed only when you type notes for the DVD. If you want to add notes to the DVD, enter the notes in the text box provided. As shown in the example, you may want to preface your notes with a heading, such as the one shown, leave a blank space, and then type the main text of your note.

8. When you are finished customizing the menu text, click Change Text to save your changes and return to the "Ready to burn" page.

After you've customized the menu text, you can customize the menu style by completing the following steps:

1. Click the "Customize menu" button on the toolbar. This displays the "Customize the disc menu style" page, shown in Figure 10-12.

2. The Font options on this page are the same as those on the "Change the DVD menu text" page. If you've already set the font options, you don't need to again.

3. Each menu style has two key characteristics: a background and one or more cut frames in the foreground. With some menu styles, you can specify a picture or video to display in the background and a picture or video to display in the cut frames. Click the Browse button to the right of the "Background video" text box

to set the background video. Click the Browse button to the right of the "Foreground video" text box to set the foreground video for the cut frames.

4. To play an audio file whenever the DVD menu is accessed, click the Browse button to the right of the "Menu audio" text box. Use the "Add audio to the menu" dialog box to select the audio file to play, and then click Add. When choosing an audio file, keep in mind that only a 5- to 10-second clip of the selected audio file is played, and this clip comes from the beginning of the audio file.

5. On the scenes page in the finished DVD, scene buttons show a preview of scenes to which you can navigate in the video. Each menu style has a default button style, but you can choose your own button style using the options on the "Scenes button styles" list. If you'd like to save your menu style as a custom style you can use in another project, click "Save as a new style."

6. When you are finished customizing the menu style, click Change Style to save your changes and return to the "Ready to burn" page.

Customizing Your Picture Slideshow and Adding an Audio Soundtrack

After you configure the DVD menu for the video, the next step is to customize the slideshow and add an audio soundtrack by completing these steps:

1. Only video DVDs that have digital pictures have slideshows. If your DVD has pictures, click the "Slide show" button on the "Ready to burn" page. This displays the "Change your slide show settings" page shown in Figure 10-13.

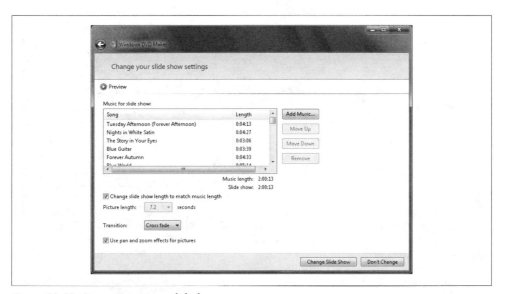

Figure 10-13. Customizing your slideshow

2. By default, each picture is set to display for seven seconds. Use the "Picture length" list to select the desired display time, such as five seconds. When you make changes to the picture length, note the corresponding change in the running time for the slideshow.

3. Use the Transition list to specify whether and how transitions are used to move from one picture to the next in the slideshow. After you select a transition, click Preview and then play the video to see what the transition will look like.

4. To give your pictures the effect of live motion, select the "Use pan and zoom effects for pictures" checkbox. Some of the transitions work best when panning and zooming is turned off. Others work best when panning and zooming is turned on. As an example, cross-fade works well with pan and zoom turned on, while inset works best with pan and zoom turned off.

5. If you want your slideshow to have a soundtrack, click Add Music. This displays the Add Music to Slide Show dialog box shown in Figure 10-14.

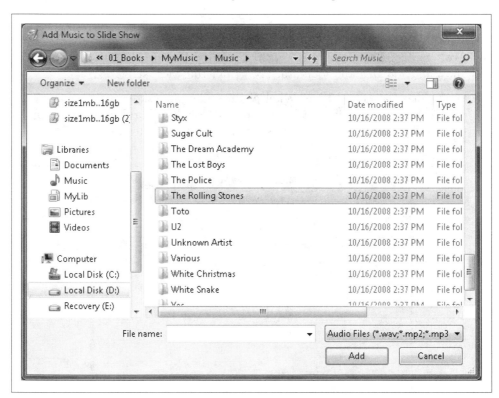

Figure 10-14. Adding your music

6. Because your Music library is the default location for your music, the Add Music to Slide Show dialog box accesses this folder by default. In your *Music* folder or any other default folder for music, you'll see your music organized by artist. If you double-click the folder for an artist, you'll find either the related album or subfolders for each album when multiple albums by one artist are stored on your computer.

7. Once you've worked your way through the folders and subfolders for artists and albums, you'll see a list of songs. You can select songs to add to the DVD using any of the following techniques:

   • Select an individual song by clicking it.

   • Select a series of songs by clicking the first song, pressing and holding the Shift key, clicking the last song, and then releasing Shift.

   • Select multiple songs individually by clicking the first song, pressing and holding the Ctrl key, clicking each additional song in turn, and then releasing Ctrl.

8. Click Add to close the Add Music to Slide Show dialog box and add your selected songs to the "Music for slide show" list. You can repeat steps 5–7 to add songs by other artists or from other albums. Each time you add songs, note the music length and the slideshow running time. When the music length is within a few minutes of the slideshow running time, you can select the "Change slide show length to match music length" checkbox to sync the soundtrack and the slideshow running times.

9. When you are finished customizing the slideshow, click Change Slide Show to save your changes and return to the "Ready to burn" page.

Previewing and Finishing Your Video Project

After you've customized the DVD menu and slideshow, you can click Preview to get a preview of what the finished DVD will look like (see Figure 10-15). You can always choose a different menu style and different customization options if you aren't pleased with the results. Keep in mind, however, that the way the DVD looks on your screen probably won't match what the DVD will look like when it's finished. This is because processing and fully encoding a DVD requires a great deal of processing power, and Windows DVD Maker doesn't fully process or encode the DVD to generate the preview.

When you are ready to continue, you can save your video as a Windows DVD Maker Project. Project files are saved with the file extension *.msdvd*. Unlike your video, which may be multiple gigabytes in size, project files are relatively small. They contain the settings for the DVD menu, menu text, and slideshow. They also contain a file manifest that has the file paths to all the items included in the video.

Figure 10-15. Previewing your DVD

You can save as a project file and then burn your DVD by following these steps:

1. Click File and then select Save As.

2. In the Save Project dialog box, shown in Figure 10-16, type a descriptive name for your video and then click Save.

 By default, your project is saved in your personal *Videos* folder. If you don't want to use this folder, click the Browse for Folders button to expand the dialog box and include additional folder browsing features. You can then select a folder in which to save your project.

3. Click Burn. If you haven't already done so, insert a blank disc into your DVD player when prompted. Windows DVD Maker will begin to encode your DVD. As shown in Figure 10-17, you'll see a Burning dialog box that tracks the progress of the encoding process. Encoding and burning your DVD can take several hours. During this time, you shouldn't perform other tasks on the computer that might cause burn problems, such as trying to rip or play a CD or DVD on a different drive.

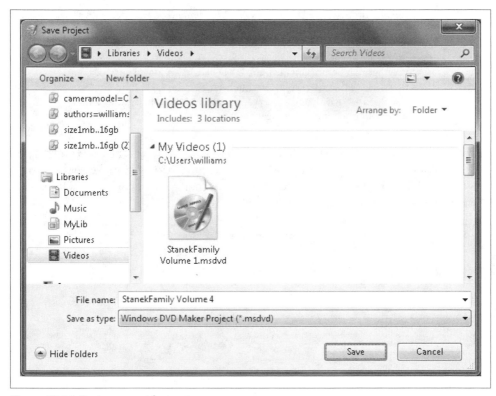

Figure 10-16. Saving your video project

Figure 10-17. Creating your DVD video

The total time required to burn a DVD will depend on the speed of your DVD burner as well as the speed of your computer's CPU and the amount of RAM on your computer. If you haven't already used Ready-Boost with a USB flash device, as discussed in Chapter 3, you may want to configure it before you burn the DVD because it may give your computer a needed boost. On a computer with a 2.66 GHz dual-core processor, 3 GB of RAM, and a 8x DVD burner, I found that burning a DVD took about one minute per gigabyte of data.

4. When encoding is complete, Windows DVD Maker will eject the DVD and display the "Your disc is ready" message, as shown in Figure 10-18. To make another copy, insert a blank DVD and then click "Make another copy of this disc." Otherwise, click Close to return to the Windows DVD Maker main window.

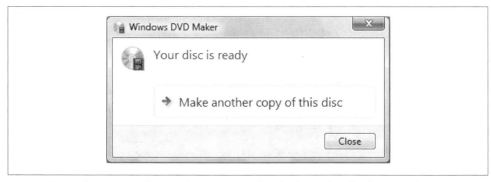

Figure 10-18. The message that Windows DVD Maker displays when the disc is ready

Opening and Burning Saved Projects

You can open saved projects using the Search box on the Start menu. Click Start and then type `video` into the Search box to see a list of all videos and related video project files. Double-click the *.msdvd* project file you want to open. Windows 7 will then start Windows DVD Maker and open the selected project file for editing.

In Windows DVD Maker, you can open saved projects by completing the following steps:

1. On the "Add pictures and video to the DVD" page, click File and then click Open Project File. This displays the Open Project dialog box.

2. In the Open Project dialog box, the last folder location you used for saving project files is opened by default. If this isn't the folder you want to use, browse to the folder containing the saved project file.

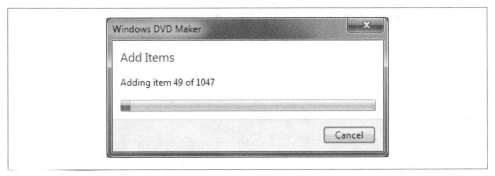

Figure 10-19. Opening a saved project

3. Click the project file and click Open. Windows DVD Maker will then read the project file and begin adding the items it references. As shown in Figure 10-19, the progress of this import process is tracked in the Add Items dialog box.

4. When Windows DVD Maker finishes adding items, review the order of videos and pictures, check to make sure the DVD burner you want to use is selected, and then click Next.

5. On the "Ready to burn" page, you'll see a preview of the DVD menu. You can make any necessary changes and then click Burn to start burning the DVD.

6. If you haven't already inserted a DVD, you'll be prompted to insert one. As before, the DVD burning process may take several hours.

Creating Movies with Windows Movie Maker

After you've created a few video DVDs in Windows DVD Maker, you may want to do a bit more in terms of production. This is where Windows Movie Maker comes into the picture. With Windows Movie Maker, you produce the video every step of the way, from beginning title to end credits.

Getting Started with Windows Movie Maker

Windows Movie Maker 6.0 is included with Windows Vista. When you've upgraded to Windows 7 from Windows Vista, you can start and use Windows Movie Maker in several ways. When you are working with Windows Live Photo Gallery, you can select the initial pictures and videos you want to work with, click Make and then click Make a Movie to open Windows Movie Maker with these items selected. Otherwise, you can start Windows Movie Maker by clicking Start→All Programs→Windows Movie Maker.

As Table 10-2 shows, Windows Movie Maker works with a wide variety of image, sound, and video formats. This list is different from the formats supported by Windows DVD Maker. The key change is that Windows Movie Maker supports AIFF and AU sound formats, and Windows DVD Maker does not.

Table 10-2. File formats supported by Windows Movie Maker

File format/type	File extensions
Bitmap image	*.bmp*
DIB image	*.dib*
GIF image	*.gif*
JPEG image	*.jpg, .jpe, .jpeg, .jfif*
PNG image	*.png*
TIFF image	*.tif, .tiff*
Word Perfect image	*.wdp*
Windows Meta File	*.wmf, .emf*
Sound formats	
AIFF sound	*.aif, .aifc, .aiff*
AU sound	*.au, .snd*
MP3 audio	*.mp3, .m3u*
WAV audio	*.wav*
Windows Media Audio	*.wma*
Video formats	
AVI video	*.avi*
DVD video	*.mpa, .m1v, .m2v, .mp2, .mp2v, .mpv2, .mp2v*
MPEG 1 and MPEG 2 video	*.mpe, .mpeg, .mpg*
Audio/Video format	
Windows Media Audio/Video Professional	*.asf, .wm, .wmv*
Recorded TV format	
Microsoft Digital Video Recorder	*.dvr-ms*

As with Windows DVD Maker, Windows Movie Maker works with files that are already in the proper formats and doesn't include features for converting formats. Unlike Windows DVD Maker, however, Windows Movie Maker includes features for importing video and audio from digital video cameras. Windows Movie Maker doesn't include features for ripping raw CD audio files from audio discs. However, you can use any existing audio, video, or pictures on your computer's disk drive, a data disc you've inserted into your CD/DVD drive, or a device with removable storage connected to your computer. You can also add narration using a microphone. The same narration features allow you to record input from other sources as well.

When you start working with Windows Movie Maker, shown in Figure 10-20, you'll see that it has these key features.

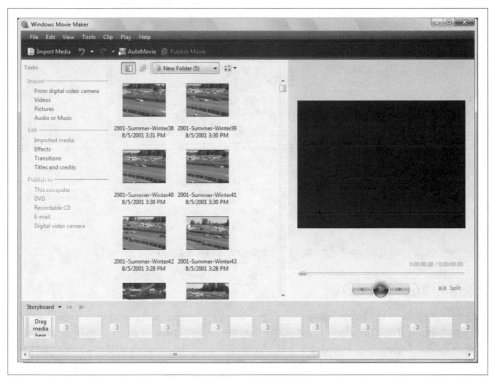

Figure 10-20. Getting started with Windows Movie Maker

A Tasks pane
    Lists the common tasks that you may need to perform when making a movie.

A Collection pane
    Provides options for listing effects and transitions as well as collection folders for media you've imported into Windows Movie Maker.

A Preview pane
    Allows you to preview the video.

A work area
    Allows you to manage the media items you've added to the video.

Using the options provided in the main window, you create movies by following a series of prescribed steps. The basic steps are as follows:

1. Create your storyboard.
2. Edit the storyboard.
3. Add effects and transitions.
4. Add narration, music, and other audio.
5. Add titles, credits, and overlays.

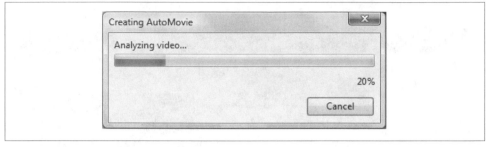

Figure 10-21. Creating an AutoMovie

6. Set the video options.

7. Preview and save your video project.

8. Publish your movie.

I discuss tasks related to each step in the sections that follow.

Creating Your Storyboard

In Windows Movie Maker, each video you are producing is created as a video project with a storyboard. The storyboard provides a representation of each media item you've added to the video in the order the items are played. In this way, the storyboard not only serves as an outline for the presentation, but it also lets you visualize the project in a way you otherwise would not be able to. At a glance, you can see the work from start to finish, and this is extremely important in the way you conceptualize the project.

As you add media items to your video, you build the storyboard and set the play order for each item you are including. To your storyboard, you can add titles, credits, effects, and transitions. Unlike Windows DVD Maker, Windows Movie Maker doesn't put pictures into a separate folder. Instead, all media items are added to the same storyboard, and that storyboard can have many thousands of media items.

As with Windows DVD Maker, you can select all the pictures and videos you want to use in Windows Live Photo Gallery first, and then add the selected items automatically to Windows Movie Maker. After you use the same tricks discussed previously, click Make and then click Make a Movie to open Windows Movie Maker with these media items. Windows Movie Maker will then analyze the media items and create a movie for you automatically using these media items (see Figure 10-21). Your AutoMovie will have a title frame, automatic fade settings for each media item, automatic transition settings between media items, and an end credits frame. This will save you considerable time in terms of finalizing your movie.

In Windows Movie Maker, you can select the items to add to your video by completing the following steps:

1. On the Task pane, click the appropriate Import option.

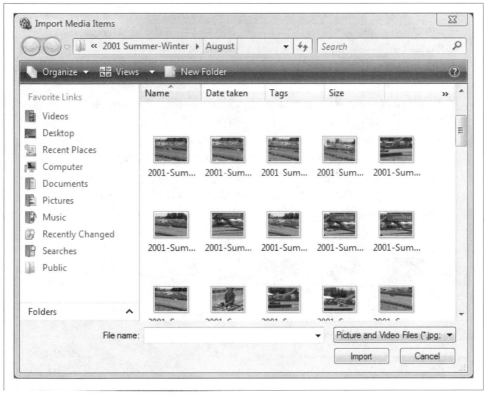

Figure 10-22. Importing pictures and videos

2. As shown in Figure 10-22, use the Import Media Items dialog box to browse to a folder containing pictures or videos you want to add.

3. Select the items to add using one of the following techniques:

   • Select an individual item by clicking it.

   • Select a series of items by clicking the first item, pressing and holding the Shift key, clicking the last item, and then releasing Shift.

   • Select multiple items individually by clicking the first item, pressing and holding the Ctrl key, clicking each additional item in turn, and then releasing Ctrl.

4. When you click Import, Windows Movie Maker adds the items to a Collections folder and then displays the items in this folder in the Collections pane. As shown in Figure 10-23, any item you select in the Collections pane is displayed in the Preview pane.

5. At this point, the items are not added to the storyboard. You can add items to the storyboard using these techniques:

- To arrange items in a specific order before selecting them, right-click in the Collections pane, point to Arrange Icons By, and then select the desired arrangement, such as Date Taken, File Name, or Name and Date.

- To add an item to the storyboard, click it and drag it to the desired location in the storyboard. When you drag the item to the storyboard, you'll see a position pointer that indicates where the item will be added.

- To place an item on a part of the storyboard not displayed, click and drag the item to the left or right edge of the storyboard.

- To select multiple items, use the previously discussed Shift and Ctrl techniques and then drag those items to a desired location in the storyboard.

- To select and then add all items to the end of the storyboard, right-click in the Collections pane and then click Select All. Right-click again and then select Add to Storyboard. Alternatively, press Ctrl-A and then press Ctrl-D.

Figure 10-23. Selecting pictures or videos to preview them

Editing Your Storyboard

As you add media items to the storyboard, Windows Movie Maker lists the runtime of the video as the second time entry in the preview area. This runtime may change if you modify the transitions and effects applied. Most single-sided DVDs can have a total

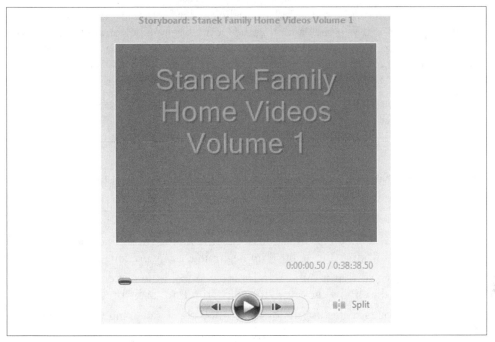

Figure 10-24. Using the Preview controls to manage playback

running time of up to 150 minutes. Most single-sided double-layered DVDs can have a total running time of up to 300 minutes.

After you add items, you can fine-tune the play order. To change the play order of an item or a group of items, select the item or items and then drag left or right until you reach the desired position. To remove an item, right-click it and then select Remove. Removing an item removes it from the storyboard but does not delete it from your computer.

While you are optimizing the play order, you may want to preview the video. As Figure 10-24 shows, the Preview pane provides the following button controls:

Play/Pause
    If you click the Play button, the video plays from the current position in the storyboard. Clicking the Play button again pauses playback.

Previous Frame
    Rewinds to the previous frame of the video.

Next Frame
    Advances to the next frame of the video.

Split
    Splits a video clip you are playing into two clips at the current position.

Above the button controls, you'll find a Timeline slider for previewing your video and managing playback. If you click and drag the Current Frame button on the end of the Timeline slider, you can fast-forward or rewind through a video. If you click a specific part of the timeline, you can go to that time in the video.

 On the left side of the Storyboard pane, you'll find Play/Pause buttons as well as a Rewind Storyboard button. Clicking the Rewind Storyboard button moves to and selects the first storyboard in your video.

Anytime you are working with video clips, you have several editing options. When you are playing video clips, you can:

- Click the Split button to split the video into two clips at the current position.
- Trim the video so that it only includes footage from the current position to the end of the clip by clicking Clip→Clip Trim Beginning, or by pressing I.
- Trim the video so that it only includes footage from the current position to the beginning of the clip by clicking Clip→Clip Trim End, or by pressing O.
- Clear trim points to restore the original video clip by clicking Clip→Clear Trim Points.
- Combine video clips you previously split by selecting the videos and then clicking Clip→Combine, or by pressing N.

While you are fixing your storyboard, you can use the Undo button to undo any changes you don't like, or the redo button to redo changes you previously undid. Multiple undo and redo changes are saved, allowing you to step backward and forward through changes. You can also undo and redo specific changes.

To undo a specific change or changes, follow these steps:

1. Click the option button to the right of the Undo button. This displays a shortcut menu with a list of Undo changes, as shown in Figure 10-25.
2. The most recent change is listed first. To undo this change, click it.
3. You can also undo multiple actions, but only in the exact order in which they were performed. To undo multiple actions, drag down until all the actions you want to undo are selected, and then click the shortcut menu.

To redo a specific change or changes, follow these steps:

1. Click the option button to the right of the Redo button. This displays a shortcut menu with a list of Redo changes, as shown in Figure 10-26.
2. The most recent change is listed first. To redo this change, click it.

Figure 10-25. Selecting the changes to undo

Figure 10-26. Selecting the changes to redo

3. You can also redo multiple actions, but only in the exact order in which they were performed. To redo multiple actions, drag down until all the actions you want to redo are selected, and then click the shortcut menu.

By default, each picture in the slideshow is displayed for 5 seconds, and transitions last 1.25 seconds. You'll be able to change this setting later. See "Setting Video Options" on page 421 for details.

Creating an AutoMovie

After you finish creating and editing your storyboard, you are ready to move on to the next phase of video production, which involves adding effects, transitions, titles, credits, and a soundtrack. While you can perform each of these tasks manually, you can also have Windows Movie Maker perform them for you automatically using the AutoMovie feature. Not only is this a great timesaver, but it also allows you to see firsthand how various approaches to video production work.

To create an AutoMovie, complete the following steps:

1. In Windows Movie Maker, click the AutoMovie button on the toolbar.
2. As shown in Figure 10-27, you can now select one of the following AutoMovie editing styles:

   Fade and Reveal
   Applies fade and reveal transitions throughout the video.

Flip and Slide
> Applies flip, slide, reveal, and page curl transitions throughout the video.

Highlights Movie
> Adds cut and fade transitions throughout the video, and inserts title and credit frames.

Music Video
> Attempts to sync the video to music you select. This works best if the selected music is as long in duration as the video.

Old Movie
> Applies the film age effect to media items.

Sports Highlights
> Selects video clips showing action, and inserts title and credit frames.

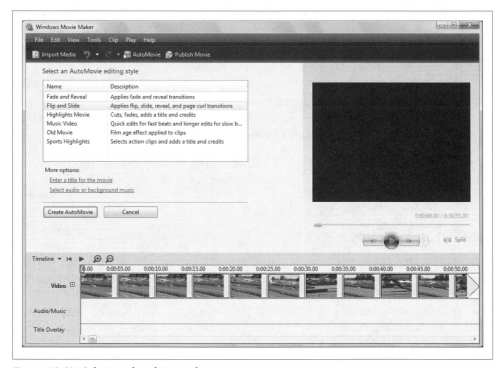

Figure 10-27. Selecting the editing style

3. Click the "Enter a title for the movie" link and then type the title text, as shown in Figure 10-28.

4. Click the "Select audio or background music" link to display the "Add audio or background music" page shown in Figure 10-29.

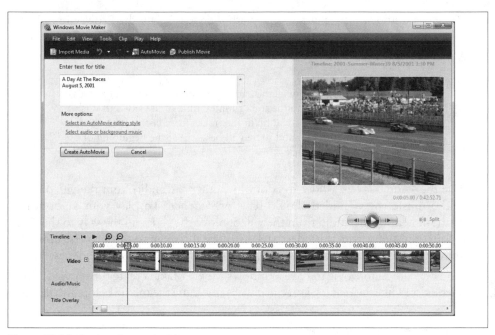

Figure 10-28. Setting the movie title

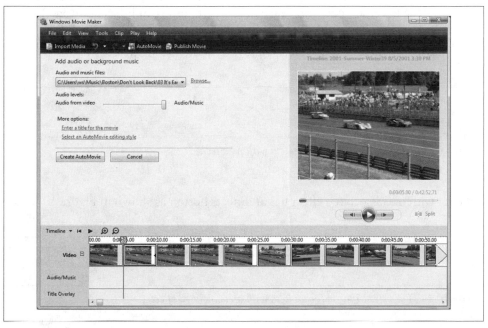

Figure 10-29. Setting the audio options

5. To select audio or music files to play with the video, click the Browse link. In the Open dialog box, select the first audio file you want to use in the video and then click Open. Repeat this process to select each additional audio file to include.

 The total running time of all the audio files you select should be at least as much as or more than the total running time of the video. If it isn't, Windows Movie Maker will fill in the tracks from last to first, starting at the end of the video, and there will be a gap at the beginning of the video with no soundtrack.

6. Use the "Audio levels" slider to control whether the audio from the video or the audio/music you've added should have precedence. To play your audio/music without hearing the audio from the video, move the slider all the way to the right. To mix the audio from the video back in, move the slider to the left. The more you move the slider to the left, the more prevalent the audio from the video will be.

7. Click Create AutoMovie to have Windows Movie Maker create the movie for you. If you don't like the results, you can always fine-tune the movie before finalizing it.

Adding Effects to Your Video

Your videos can have effects that are used when a media item is first displayed. You can add the same effect to multiple items, and a single item can have multiple effects as well. In the lower-left corner of the item's storyboard is an Effects button. The appearance of this button tells you whether an item has effects associated with it.

An item with no effects has an Effects button as shown in Figure 10-30.

Figure 10-30. The Effects button for an item with no effects

An item with one associated effect has an Effects button as shown in Figure 10-31.

Figure 10-31. The Effects button for an item with an associated effect

An item with multiple associated effects has an Effects button as shown in Figure 10-32.

Figure 10-32. The Effects button for an item with multiple associated effects

You can add effects to media items by completing the following steps:

1. In Windows Movie Maker, click Effects in the Tasks pane to display the available effects in the Collections pane, as shown in Figure 10-33.
2. To see how an effect works, click it and press the Play button in the Preview pane.
3. To use an effect, click it and then drag it to the item to which the effect should be added. Alternatively, click the effect, press Ctrl-C, click the item to which the effect should be added, and then press Ctrl-V.
4. Repeat this process to add multiple effects to the same item.

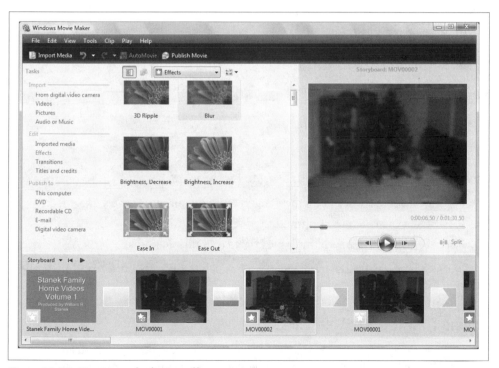

Figure 10-33. Viewing and selecting effects

Another way to manage multiple effects applied to the same item is to follow these steps:

1. Right-click the item's Effects button in the storyboard and then select Effects.
2. Use the Add or Remove Effects dialog box, shown in Figure 10-34, to manage the effects associated with the selected item:
   - To add an effect, select it in the "Available effects" list and then click Add.
   - To remove an effect, select it in the "Displayed effects" list and then click Remove.
   - To change the order of displayed effects, click an effect and then use the Move Up or Move Down button to position it.
3. Click OK.

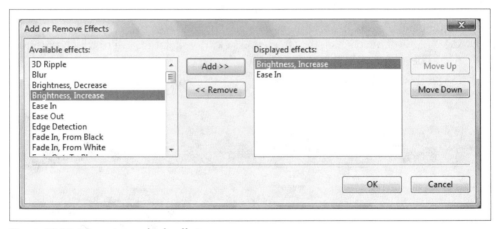

Figure 10-34. Managing multiple effects

To add the same effect to multiple items, follow these steps:

1. On the storyboard, select all the items that you want to use the same effect.
2. Right-click the effect to apply and then select Add to Storyboard.
3. Repeat this process to add multiple effects to multiple items.

To remove all effects from a media item, right-click the Effects button and then select Remove Effects.

Adding Transitions to Your Video

Your videos can have transitions that are used when moving between media items. You can use only one transition between media items. For example, you can transition by slowly revealing the new media item or by sweeping in, but not by using both techniques.

As shown in Figure 10-35, you'll find a transition board to the right of each media item. If a current transition is applied, the transition board will show a summary graphic. If no current transition is applied, the transition board will be dimmed.

Figure 10-35. Using transitions

You can add transitions to media items by completing the following steps:

1. In Windows Movie Maker, click Transitions in the Tasks pane to display the available transitions in the Collections pane, as shown in Figure 10-36.

2. To see how a transition works, click it and then press Play in the Preview pane.

3. To use a transition, click it and then drag it to the item to which the transition should be added. Alternatively, click the transition, press Ctrl-C, click the item to which the transition should be added, and then press Ctrl-V.

Figure 10-36. Viewing and selecting transitions

To add the same transition to multiple transition boards, follow these steps:

1. On the storyboard, select all the transition boards that you want to use the same transition.

2. Right-click the transition to apply and then select Add to Storyboard.

To remove a transition from a transition board, right-click the transition board and then select Remove.

Adding Narration, Music, and Other Audio

You can add narration, music, and other audio to your videos. To add narration, you will need a sound card with a microphone jack and a microphone. You will then need to connect the microphone to the microphone jack on your computer. Once you do this, you can narrate the video by completing these steps:

1. In Windows Movie Maker, display the timeline instead of the storyboard by clicking View and then selecting Timeline. Alternatively, you can press Ctrl-T to toggle between the storyboard and the timeline.

2. Click Tools→Narrate Timeline to display the Narrate Timeline pane, as shown in Figure 10-37.

3. Click the "Show options" link to display the additional options for narration.

4. To mute your computer's speakers, click the "Mute speakers" checkbox.

5. On the "Audio device" list, select the microphone or audio source you are using as the audio input device.

6. On the timeline, click a media item to set the start position of the narration. If you want to insert the narration starting at the beginning of the video, click the first media item.

7. Click Start Narration to begin recording and then speak into your microphone. As you narrate, the timeline moves to show you the current position in the video. Note also that the "Narration captured" value shows you the total length of your narration.

8. Click Stop Narration to stop recording your narration.

9. You can then play back the video to see and hear the results.

 You can record input from other audio sources using the Line In jack on your computer's audio card. After you connect an audio cable from the alternative audio source to your computer's Line In jack, select Line In as the audio source in the "Audio device" list. When you start playback on the alternative audio source and then click the Start Narration button, the audio from the alternative source is recorded and inserted into your movie. To stop recording audio from the alternative source, click the Stop Narration button.

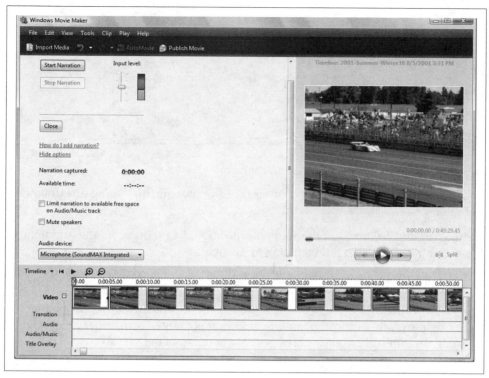

Figure 10-37. Narrating your movie

To add music or other audio to your video, complete the following steps:

1. In Windows Movie Maker, display the timeline instead of the storyboard by clicking View and then selecting Timeline. Alternatively, you can press Ctrl-T to toggle between the storyboard and the timeline.

2. If the Collections pane isn't displayed, display it by clicking View→Collections.

3. On the standard toolbar, click Import Media. Use the Import Media Items dialog box to select one or more audio files to work with, and then click Import. The audio files will be added to the Collections pane.

4. On the timeline, click a media item to set the start position for the music you are adding. If you want to insert the music starting at the beginning of the video, click the first media item.

5. Right-click the audio file you want to insert at the current position, and then select Add to Timeline.

6. In the timeline, scroll left and right to check the placement of the audio file. You can also click Play to play the video from the current position.

7. Repeat steps 4–6 to add other audio files to the video.

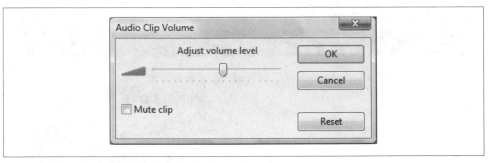

Figure 10-38. Adjusting the volume level of an audio clip

You can manage audio files you inserted into the timeline using the following techniques:

- To trim the beginning of the audio file, position the pointer over the beginning of the audio clip, click, and then drag to the right.
- To trim the ending of the audio file, position the pointer over the end of the audio clip, click, and then drag to the left.
- To move an audio clip to a different position in the timeline, move the pointer left or right over the audio clip until the selection pointer is displayed. Click and then drag the audio file to the desired position in the timeline.

If the playback volume of the audio is too soft or too loud, you should right-click the entry for the audio in the timeline and then select Volume. In the Adjust Clip Volume dialog box, shown in Figure 10-38, use the "Adjust volume level" slider to adjust the volume of the audio clip, and then click OK.

 While you are editing the video, you might sometimes want to mute an audio track temporarily. In the Adjust Clip Volume dialog box, you can mute the audio volume completely by selecting the "Mute clip" checkbox.

By default, the audio levels are set to mix the audio from the video clip and the audio/music you've added at equal levels of volume. You can control whether the audio from video clips or the audio/music you've added should have precedence by clicking Tools and then clicking Audio Levels. This displays the Audio Levels dialog box shown in Figure 10-39.

To play your audio/music without hearing the audio from the video, move the slider all the way to the right. To mix the audio from the video back in, move the slider to the left. The more you move the slider to the left, the more prevalent the audio from the video will be. When you are finished setting the volume levels, click the Close button in the Audio Levels dialog box.

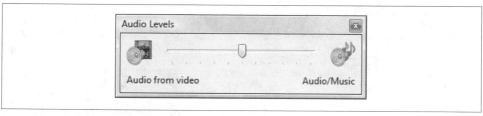

Figure 10-39. Setting the balance between audio from video and audio/music

Adding Titles, Credits, and Overlays

Your videos can have title frames, credits, and title overlays. You can add title frames at the beginning of the video or before a selected clip. You can add credits to the end of the video. Title overlays are title frames displayed over the top of a selected media item.

You can add titles to your video by completing these steps:

1. In Windows Movie Maker, click Tools and then click Titles and Credits.

2. In the Titles pane, click one of the following links:
    - Title at the Beginning
    - Title Before the Selected Clip
    - Title on the Selected Clip

3. If you are inserting a title before or on a clip, select the clip to use in the timeline.

4. As shown in Figure 10-40, enter the primary title in the first text box provided and any subtitle in the second text box provided.

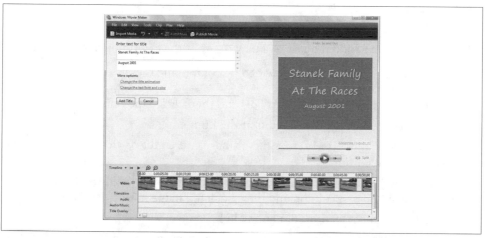

Figure 10-40. Adding a title to the movie

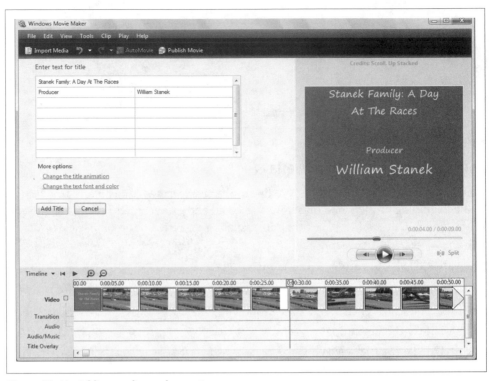

Figure 10-41. Adding credits to the movie

5. Click the "Change the title animation" link.

6. Choose the title animation. Different animations are provided for one-line titles and two-line titles. Use a two-line title animation if you entered a subtitle.

7. Click the "Change the text font and color" link.

8. Use the options provided to set the title font and color.

9. Click Add Title to add the title to a new frame at the beginning of the video.

You can add credits to the end of the video by completing these steps:

1. In Windows Movie Maker, click Tools and then click Titles and Credits.

2. In the Titles pane, click the "Credits at the End" link.

3. As shown in Figure 10-41, enter the primary end credit or video title in the first text box provided.

4. In the subsequent rows, you can enter video credits by role/title and name. Enter a role/title in the first column and the associated name in the second column.

5. Click the "Change the title animation" link.

6. Choose the credits animation. Different animations are provided for credits than for titles.

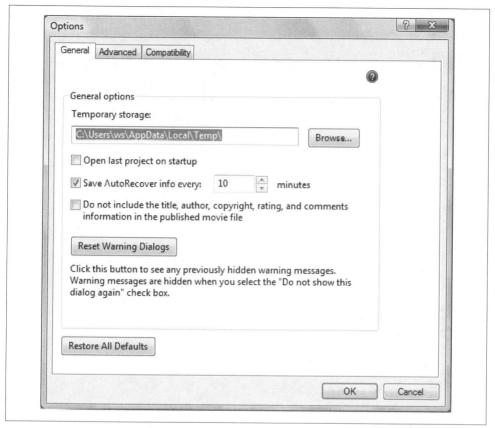

Figure 10-42. Setting the save and recovery options

7. Click the "Change the text font and color" link.

8. Use the options provided to set the title font and color.

9. Click Add Title to add the credits to a new frame at the end of the video.

Setting Video Options

Windows Movie Maker allows you to encode your video using an aspect ratio for widescreen or standard screen, and to format your video using either NTSC or PAL video format. In Windows Movie Maker, you can set these and other options by completing the following steps:

1. Click Tools and then click Options to display the Options dialog box shown in Figure 10-42.

2. By default, Windows Movie Maker creates a working version of the DVD in a temporary folder within your profile. Because your profile is stored on the system drive, which typically is the *C:* drive, this drive must have at least 5 GB of available

disk space when you are creating a single-sided single-layered DVD, and 10 GB of available disk space when you are creating a single-sided double-layered DVD. If you want to choose a folder on another drive for the temporary files, click Browse and then use the Browse for Folder dialog box to select the new folder to use.

3. By default, AutoRecover data for your video project is saved every 10 minutes. Similar to Microsoft Office applications, such as Word, this allows you to recover to the last saved position should something unexpected happen while you are making your movie. If Windows Movie Maker freezes or the power goes out, the last saved position will be loaded automatically the next time you restart Windows Movie Maker. If you want to use a different AutoRecover interval, enter the desired interval in the text box provided, such as five minutes.

4. Click the Advanced tab, as shown in Figure 10-43.

5. By default, pictures are displayed for 5 seconds and transitions are displayed for 1.25 seconds. You can change the display time for pictures by entering a new display time in the "Picture duration" text box. You can change the display time for transitions by entering a new display time in the "Transition duration" text box.

When deciding on the duration of pictures and transitions, keep in mind the prospective audience and the tempo of your music. If your music has a relatively fast beat, you may want to use a shorter display duration. If your music has a slower beat, you might want to use a longer display duration. In most cases, you'll want pictures to be displayed for between 3 and 10 seconds, with transitions of 1 to 1.5 seconds.

6. Under "Video format," select either NTSC or PAL as the video format. If you are unsure of which format to use, don't change the default format, because this is set based on the Regional and Language Options in the Control Panel. You will need to change the format only when you plan to share your video with a friend who lives in another country or region.

7. Under "Aspect ratio," choose the aspect ratio. The aspect ratio is expressed as the relation of the video width to the video height. For widescreen, choose 16:9 as the aspect ratio. For standard (full) screen, choose 4:3 as the aspect ratio.

8. Click OK to save your settings.

Previewing and Finishing Your Movie Project

When you are finished fine-tuning your movie, you'll want to preview it to ensure that the movie is exactly as you want it to be. You can preview the movie at full-screen size by clicking View and then selecting Full Screen. Alternatively, press Alt-Enter. To exit full-screen preview mode, press the Esc key. You can also preview at alternative display

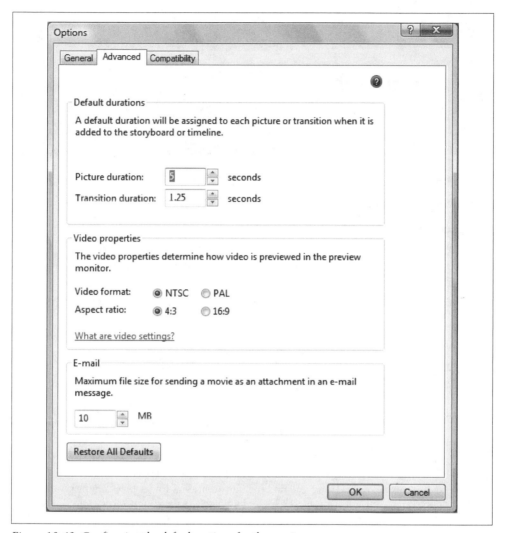

Figure 10-43. Configuring the default options for the movie

sizes by clicking View, pointing to Preview Monitor Size, and then selecting the desired display size.

When you are ready to continue, you can save your video as a Windows Movie Maker Project. Project files are saved with the file extension *.mswmm*. Although Windows Movie Maker Project files can run multiple megabytes in size, they are still considerably smaller than your final movie file.

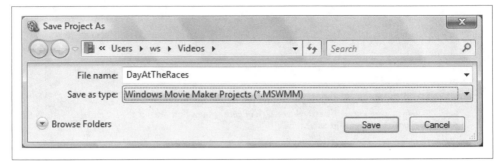

Figure 10-44. Saving your movie project

You can save as a project file by completing the following steps:

1. Click File and then select Save As.

2. In the Save Project As dialog box, shown in Figure 10-44, the last folder location you used for saving project files is opened by default. If this isn't the folder you want to use, browse to the folder you want to use.

3. Type a descriptive name for your video and then click Save.

Although you can use spaces in the video name, I've chosen not to use spaces in the example to make it easier to work with the file. With this project name, if you were to click Start and then type dayat into the Search box, you'd see this project file in the Files list and could then double-click the filename to open the movie in Windows Movie Maker. Of course, you could also click Start and then type mswmm into the Search box to see a list of all movie project files.

By default, your project is saved in your personal *My Videos* folder. If you don't want to use this folder, click the Browse for Folders button to expand the dialog box and include additional folder browsing features. You can then select a folder in which to save your project.

After you save your project, you can publish your movie. Publishing your movie creates the finished video file. In most cases, you'll want to publish the movie to your computer or to a DVD. If you publish the movie to your computer, you'll select the encoding settings as shown in Table 10-3.

Table 10-3. Movie encoding settings for Windows Movie Maker

File type	File extension	Aspect ratio	Bit rate	Display size	Frames per second
DV-Video	.avi	4:3	28.6 Mbps	720 × 480	30
Windows Media Portable Device	.wmv	4:3	1.0 Mbps	640 × 480	30
Windows Media DVD Quality	.wmv	4:3	3.0 Mbps	720 × 480	30

File type	File extension	Aspect ratio	Bit rate	Display size	Frames per second
Windows Media DVD Widescreen Quality	.wmv	16:9	3.0 Mbps	720 × 480	30
Windows Media HD 720p	.wmv	16:9	5.9 Mbps	1,280 × 720	30
Windows Media HD for Xbox 360	.wmv	16:9	6.9 Mbps	1,280 × 720	30
Windows Media HD 1080p	.wmv	16:9	7.8 Mbps	1,440 × 1,080	30
Windows Media Low Bandwidth	.wmv	4:3	117 Kbps	320 × 240	15
Windows Media VHS Quality	.wmv	4:3	1.0 Mbps	640 × 480	30

To publish your movie to a video file on your computer, complete the following steps:

1. Click Publish Movie on the toolbar. This starts the Publish Movie Wizard.

2. On the "Where do you want to publish your movie?" page, click "This computer" and then click Next.

3. On the "Name the movie you are publishing" page, type a name for the movie file. A default name is set for you based on the name of your project.

4. Using the "Publish to" list, select Videos to publish the movie to your personal *Videos* folder, or Public Videos to publish the movie to the shared *Public Videos* folder. Alternatively, click Browse to display the Browse for Folder dialog box and select a different folder.

5. Click Next. On the "Choose the settings for your movie" page, shown in Figure 10-45, choose "More settings" and then choose the desired movie setting. Note the estimated space required and ensure that you have enough free space for this setting.

 When choosing a format, keep in mind the quality and resolution of the original media items. Windows Movie Maker will let you create a full-length video in DV-AVI for a whopping 60 GB of space, but if your original media isn't high-quality, you'll be wasting a lot of disk space.

6. Click Publish to publish the movie to the previously selected folder. As shown in Figure 10-46, you can track the progress of the publish process by minutes remaining and percent complete. The bit rate of the movie setting you choose will largely determine how long it takes to publish the movie.

7. When Windows Movie Maker finishes publishing the movie, click Next and then click Finish.

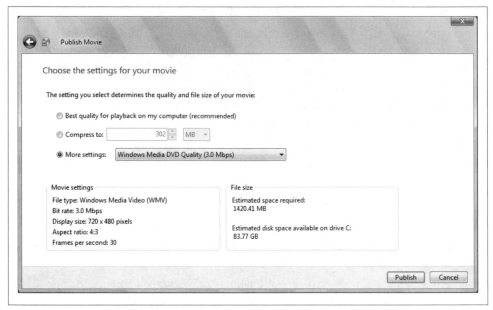

Figure 10-45. Choosing the movie settings

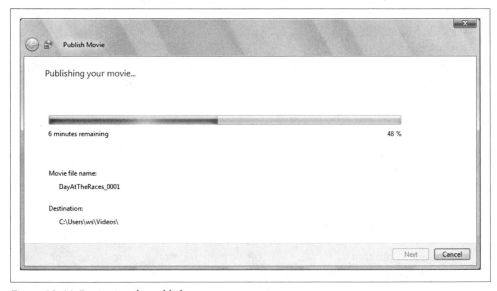

Figure 10-46. Reviewing the publish progress

To create a finished DVD with your movie, complete the following steps:

1. Click Publish Movie on the toolbar. This starts the Publish Movie Wizard.
2. On the "Where do you want to publish your movie" page, click DVD and then click Next.
3. Windows 7 will save and close your project and then open Windows DVD Maker. At the warning prompt, click OK to continue.
4. In Windows DVD Maker, you can produce the finished DVD as discussed previously.

Opening and Producing Saved Projects

You can open saved projects using the Search box on the Start menu. Click Start and then type mswmm into the Search box to see a list of all movie project files. Double-click the .mswmm project file you want to open. Windows 7 will then start Windows Movie Maker and open the selected project file for editing.

Alternatively, in Windows Movie Maker, you can open saved projects by completing the following steps:

1. Click File and then click Open Project file. This displays the Open Project dialog box.
2. In the Open Project dialog box, the last folder location you used for saving project files is opened by default. If this isn't the folder you want to use, browse to the folder containing the saved project file.
3. Click the project file and click Open. Windows Movie Maker will then read the project file and begin adding the items it references.
4. When Windows Movie Maker finishes adding items, review the movie storyboard and timeline.
5. After you make any necessary changes, click Publish Movie to start the Publish Movie Wizard and produce your movie.

Windows Movie Maker tracks the location of resources you use in your projects. If you move resources to a new location, you'll see grayed-out frames in your project. You'll need to double-click each grayed-out frame in turn to locate each missing resource. Each time when you are prompted to confirm that you want to locate the missing resource, select Yes and then use the "Browse for..." dialog box to locate the resource.

Creating Movies with Windows Live Movie Maker

Windows Live Movie Maker is one of several free programs available as part of the Windows Live Essentials program from Microsoft. You can get Windows Live Movie Maker and other programs by visiting *http://www.windowslive.com/desktop*.

Getting Started with Windows Live Movie Maker

When you are working with Windows Live Photo Gallery, you can select the initial pictures and videos you want to work with, click Make and then click "Make a Movie" to open Windows Live Movie Maker with these items selected. Otherwise, you can start Windows Live Movie Maker by clicking Start→All Programs→Windows Live→Windows Live Movie Maker.

As Table 10-4 shows, Windows Live Movie Maker works with a wide variety of image, sound, and video formats. This list is different from the formats supported by Windows DVD Maker. The key change is that Windows Live Movie Maker supports AIFF and AU sound formats, and Windows DVD Maker does not.

 Windows Live Movie Maker can open Windows Movie Maker project files with the file extension *.mswmm*. When you open a Movie Maker project file, it is imported and converted to the Windows Live Movie Maker format. If you later save the project, it will be saved with the file extension *.wlmp*.

Table 10-4. File formats supported by Windows Live Movie Maker

File format/type	File extensions
Bitmap image	.bmp
DIB image	.dib
GIF image	.gif
Icon image	.ico, .icon
JPEG image	.jpg, .jpe, .jpeg, .jfif
PNG image	.png
TIFF image	.tif, .tiff
Word Perfect image	.wdp
Windows Meta File	.wmf, .emf
Other image types	.rle, .exif
Sound formats	
MP3 audio	.mp3
WAV audio	.wav
Windows Media Audio	.wma
Video formats	
AVCHD video	.m2t, .m2ts, .mts
AVI video	.avi
DVD video	.mpa, .m1v, .m2ts, .mp2v, .mpv2
MPEG 1 and MPEG 2 video	.mpe, .mpeg, .mpg, .ts, .tts

File format/type	File extensions
MPEG-4 video	*.m4v, .mp4, .mp4v*
MOD and other formats	*.mod, .vob*
Audio/Video format	
3GPP2 Audio/Video	*.3g2, .3gp, .3gp2, .3gpp*
Windows Media Audio/Video Professional	*.asf, .wm, .wmv*
Recorded TV format	
Microsoft Digital Video Recorder	*.dvr-ms, .wtv*

Windows Live Movie Maker works with files that are already in the proper formats and doesn't include features for converting formats. When you start working with Windows Live Movie Maker, shown in Figure 10-47, you'll see that it has these key features:

A menu ribbon
> Has Home, Animations, Visual Effects panes with options for the common tasks that you may need to perform when making a movie as well as View, Edit and Options panes for preview, editing and configuring additional settings. These panes are accessed by selecting the related tab. The menu button to the right of the Home tab is referred to as the Movie Maker button.

A Preview pane
> Allows you to preview the video.

A work area
> Allows you to manage the media items you've added to the video.

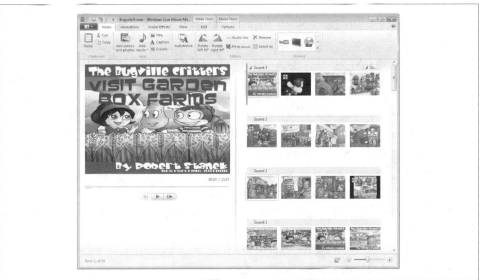

Figure 10-47. Getting started with Windows Live Movie Maker

Using the options provided in the main window, you create movies by following a series of prescribed steps. The basic steps are as follows:

1. Create your live storyboard.
2. Edit the live storyboard.
3. Add effects and transitions.
4. Add narration, music, and other audio.
5. Add titles, credits, and captions.
6. Preview and save your video project.
7. Publish your movie.

I discuss tasks related to each step in the sections that follow.

Creating and Editing Your Live Storyboard

In Windows Live Movie Maker, each video you are producing is created as a video project with a live storyboard. The live storyboard provides a representation of each media item you've added to the video in the order the items are played. In this way, the live storyboard not only serves as an outline for the presentation, but it also lets you visualize the project in a way you otherwise would not be able to. At a glance, you can see the work from start to finish, and this is extremely important in the way you conceptualize the project.

As you add media items to your video, you build the live storyboard and set the play order for each item you are including. To your live storyboard, you can add text, effects, and transitions. Unlike Windows DVD Maker, Windows Live Movie Maker doesn't put pictures into a separate folder. Instead, all media items are added to the same storyboard.

As with Windows DVD Maker, you can select all the pictures and videos you want to use in Windows Live Photo Gallery first, and then add the selected items automatically to Windows Live Movie Maker. After you use the same tricks discussed in "Creating Video DVDs with Windows DVD Maker" on page 380, click Make and then click "Make a Movie" to open Windows Live Movie Maker with these media items.

In Windows Live Movie Maker, you can select the items to add to your video by completing the following steps:

1. Click Home and then click Add Videos and Photos.
2. As shown in Figure 10-48, use the Add Videos and Photos dialog box to browse to a folder containing pictures or videos you want to add.
3. Select the items to add using one of the following techniques:
   - Select an individual item by clicking it.

Figure 10-48. Adding videos and pictures

- Select a series of items by clicking the first item, pressing and holding the Shift key, clicking the last item, and then releasing Shift.

- Select multiple items individually by clicking the first item, pressing and holding the Ctrl key, clicking each additional item in turn, and then releasing Ctrl.

4. The items you selected are added to the storyboard. The first item in the first row will be displayed first, the second item in the first row will be displayed second, and so on.

As you add media items to the storyboard, Windows Live Movie Maker lists the runtime of the video as the second time entry in the preview area. This runtime may change if you modify the transitions and effects applied.

After you add items, you can fine-tune the play order. To change the play order of an item or a group of items, select the item or items and then drag left, right, up or down until you reach the desired position. To remove an item, right-click it and then select Remove. Removing an item removes it from the storyboard but does not delete it from your computer.

00:18 / 12:10

Figure 10-49. Using the Preview controls to manage playback

While you are optimizing the play order, you may want to preview the video. As Figure 10-49 shows, the Preview pane provides the following button controls:

Play/Pause
> If you click the Play button, the video plays from the current position in the storyboard. Clicking the Play button again pauses playback.

Previous Frame
> Rewinds to the previous frame of the video.

Next Frame
> Advances to the next frame of the video.

Timeline
> Tracks the video timeline and the current frame position within the video. If you click and drag the Current Frame button on the end of the timeline slider, you can fast-forward or rewind through a video. If you click a specific part of the timeline, you can go to that time in the video.

By default, each picture in the slideshow is displayed for 3 seconds, and transitions last for a portion of the display time. You can change the display time for a selected picture

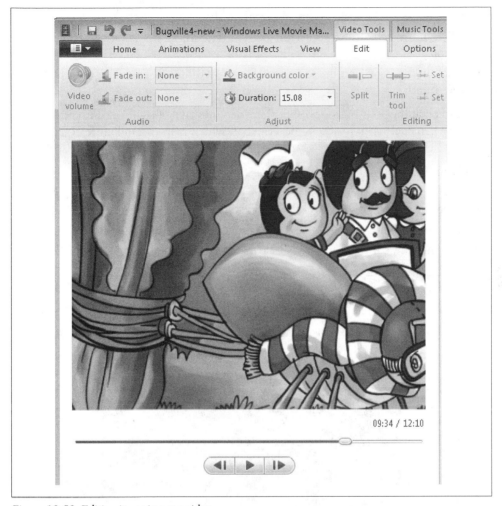

Figure 10-50. Editing items in your video

or pictures by clicking Edit on the toolbar to display the Edit bar and then entering a new display time in the Duration text box (see Figure 10-50).

When deciding the length of time to display pictures, keep in mind the prospective audience and the tempo of your soundtrack. If the music in your soundtrack has a relatively fast beat, you may want to use a shorter display duration. If the music in your soundtrack has a slower beat, you might want to use a longer display duration. In most cases, you'll want pictures to be displayed for between 3 and 10 seconds.

Anytime you are working with a video clip, you have several editing options. To view these options, click Edit on the toolbar to display the Edit bar. On the Video panel of the Edit bar, you have sound and video editing options. To control the sound in the video, you can:

- Click Video Volume and then change the volume or mute the sound of the video.
- Click in the Fade In list to use the Slow, Medium, or Fast fade in options for the sound.
- Click in the Fade Out list to use the Slow, Medium, or Fast fade out options for the sound.

You can click the Split button to split the video into two clips at the current position. You also can click Trim to access the Trim bar, which is shown in Figure 10-51. While working with the Trim bar, you can:

- Trim the beginning of the video clip by clicking and dragging the Trim Beginning slider
- Trim the ending of the video clip by clicking and dragging the Trim Ending slider
- Save the trimmed values and exit the Trim bar by clicking Save Trim
- Exit the trim bar without saving by clicking Cancel

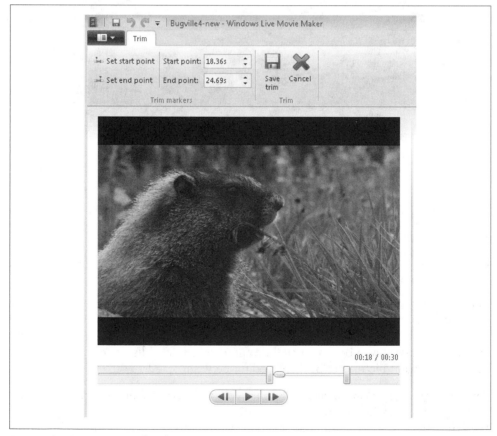

Figure 10-51. Trimming video clips

While you are fixing your storyboard, you can use the Undo button (Ctrl-Z) to undo any changes you don't like, or the Redo button (Ctrl-Y) to redo changes you previously undid.

Creating a Live AutoMovie

After you finish creating and editing your storyboard, you are ready to move on to the next phase of video production, which involves adding effects, transitions, titles, credits, and a soundtrack. Though you can perform each of these tasks manually, you can also have Windows Live Movie Maker perform them for you automatically using the AutoMovie feature. Not only is this a great timesaver, but it also allows you to see firsthand how various approaches to video production work.

To create an AutoMovie, complete the following steps:

1. In Windows Live Movie Maker, click the AutoMovie button on the Home pane.

2. If you are prompted to confirm, select the "Don't show this message again" checkbox and then click OK.

3. As you haven't added any sound to the video yet, you'll be able to add music now. When prompted, click Yes and then use the dialog box provided to select a song to add to the movie.

4. Windows Live Movie Maker will then attempt to fit the video to the song you've selected. If this process fails, you'll see a warning prompt. Click OK. Later, you can choose a longer song, add more songs, or remove some photos or videos from the movie to make the soundtrack fit.

5. Windows Live Movie Maker will then create the AutoMovie by inserting a title frame at the start of the movie, setting each picture or video to use a cross-fade transition with automatic effects, and then adding a credits frame to the end of the movie.

6. As shown in Figure 10-52, if you click the title frame on the storyboard and then click in the Preview pane, you'll be able to edit the movie title and frame formatting. By default, the title frame doesn't use a transition or effects. You can add a text effect by clicking any of the available effects on the Format pane.

7. If you click the credits frame on the storyboard and then drag the Timeline slider to the right, you'll see the end credits. Click in the Preview pane and then click the credits to edit them.

8. Click the Save Project button (or press Ctrl-S) to have Windows Live Movie Maker create the movie for you. If you don't like the results, you can always fine-tune the movie before finalizing it.

Figure 10-52. Setting the movie title

Adding Animations and Visual Effects to Your Live Video

Your videos can have animations that are used when moving between media items. Each item can have one transition, one pan and zoom effect, or both a transition and a pan and zoom effect. For example, you can transition by cross-fading and then pan right.

Your videos also can have visual effects. Visual effects act as filters and include a black-and-white filter as well as black-and-white filters with various color tones.

You work with transitions and pan and zoom effects on the Animations pane. You work with visual effects on the Visual Effects pane. Any transition or effect that you can apply to a single item can be added to multiple items simultaneously as well. Just select all of the items that should have be modified before applying the transition or effect.

An item with a transition has transition marker, as shown in Figure 10-53.

Figure 10-53. An item with a transition

An item with an effect has an effects icon as shown in Figure 10-54.

Figure 10-54. An item with an effect

An item with both a transition and a pan and zoom effect has an effects icon as shown in Figure 10-55.

Figure 10-55. An item with a transition and an effect

You can add transitions and pan and zoom effects to media items by completing the following steps:

1. In Windows Live Movie Maker, click Animations on the toolbar to display the available transitions and pan and zoom effects, as shown in Figure 10-56.
2. Select the item or items to which you want to apply a particular transition or effect.
3. Click a transition to apply it to the selected item or items. So you can see how a transition works, the Preview pane shows how the transition is applied. To remove a transition, use the up button to scroll all the way up through the list and then select the No Transition option.

There are about 70 transitions and not all of them can be viewed at the same time in the Transitions pane. Use the up and down buttons provided on the right side of the Transitions pane to navigate through the list of available transitions. Alternatively, click the More button in the lower-right corner of the pane to expand the Transitions pane for easy navigation.

4. Click an effect to apply it to the selected item or items. The Preview pane shows how the effect is applied. To remove an effect, use the up button to scroll all the way up through the list and then select the No Effect option.

There are about 20 effects and not all of them can be viewed at the same time in the Pan and Zoom pane. Use the up and down buttons provided on the right side of the Pan and Zoom pane to navigate through the list of available effects. Alternatively, click the More button in the lower-right corner of the pane to expand the Pan and Zoom pane for easy navigation.

Figure 10-56. Selecting transitions and effects

5. Transitions and effects have separate duration values. To set the transition duration, click the transition and then choose or enter the desired duration. To set the
pan and zoom effect duration, click the effect and then choose or enter the desired
duration. The default duration of a transition or effect is one second. The combined
duration for transitions and effects cannot exceed the display duration of the item.

You can add visual effects to media items by completing the following steps:

1. In Windows Live Movie Maker, click Visual Effects on the toolbar and then select
the item or items to which you want to apply a particular visual effect.

2. Click a visual effect to apply it to the selected item or items. So you can see how a
transition works, the Preview pane shows how the transition is applied. There are
about 20 visual effects and not all of them can be viewed at the same time in the
Effects pane. Use the up and down buttons provided on the right side of the Effects
pane to navigate through the list of available transitions. To remove a transition,
use the up button to scroll up through the list and then select the No Effect option.

3. Use the Brightness option to adjust the brightness of an item. Click the Brightness
button and then slide the slider to the left to darken or slide to the right to brighten.

Adding a Soundtrack to Your Live Video

You can associate a multiple audio files with your live video. The audio files then become the sound track for the video. After adding a soundtrack, you can adjust the

duration of your movie to match the soundtrack. You also can set the mix volume for included videos and the soundtrack. To manage a video's soundtrack, complete the following steps:

1. In Windows Live Movie Maker, use the Timeline slider or click an item to set the starting point for the audio you want to add.

2. Click Home on the toolbar and then click "Add music at current point."

3. Use the Add Music dialog box to select the audio file that you want to use and then click Open.

4. To automatically fit the movie to the soundtrack, click Fit to Music. Clicking Fit adjusts the length of time that pictures are displayed. By default, pictures are displayed for 3 seconds.

5. By default, the audio levels are set to mix the audio from video clips and the audio/music you've added at equal levels of volume. You can control whether the audio from video clips or the audio/music you've added should have precedence by clicking Audio Mix. Move the Volume Mixer slider to the left to increase the playback volume of videos relative to the volume of the soundtrack. Move the Volume Mixer slider to the right to increase the playback volume for the soundtrack relative to the volume of videos.

 To play your audio/music without hearing the audio from video clips, move the slider all the way to the right. To mix the audio from the video clips back in, move the slider to the left. The more you move the slider to the left, the more prevalent the audio from the video will be.

Adding Text Overlays to Your Live Video

Each item in your video can have a text overlay. The text overlay is display for as long as the item is displayed. You can use text overlays to add titles, credits and other text to your video.

You can add a title frame to the beginning of your video by completing these steps:

1. In Windows Live Movie Maker, click Home on the toolbar and then click Title.

2. Enter your title text. The default font is 36-point Arial Black.

3. If you want to change the font used for the title, click the Font list and select the font you want to use. You can change the font size, or add bold or italic. To change the font color, click the Font Color button (it shows the letter A) and then choose a color in the Color dialog box.

4. By default, the text is opaque. To set the transparency level, click the Transparency button and then use the slider provided to set the desired transparency level.

5. By default, the background is black. To set a different background color, click the Background Color button and then select a desired color.

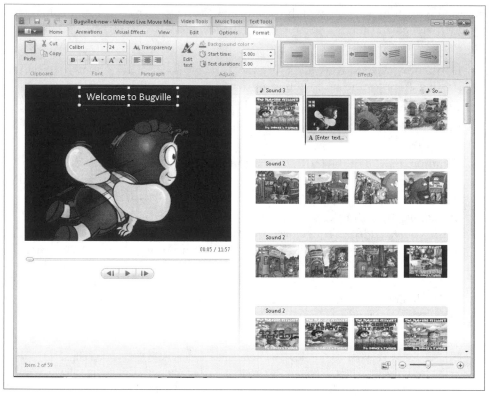

Figure 10-57. Adding text overlays to a frame

You can add a credits frame to the end of your video by completing these steps:

1. In Windows Live Movie Maker, click Home on the toolbar and then click Credits.

2. Enter your credit. The default font is 20-point Arial.

3. Edit the text and the frame background as you would with a title frame.

You can add text overlays to your video by completing these steps:

1. In Windows Live Movie Maker, select the item to which you want to add a text overlay.

2. Click Home on the toolbar and then click Caption.

3. As shown in Figure 10-57, a text box is added to the selected item and the Format pane is displayed. Enter your caption. The default font is 24-point Calibri. Format the text as appropriate using the options provided.

4. Use the Start Time box to specify at what time in the movie the caption should be displayed.

5. Use the Text Duration box to specify the length of time the text should be displayed.

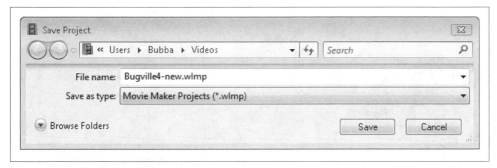

Figure 10-58. Saving your live video project

With any type of overlay text, you can:

- View the finished frame with the overlay by deselecting the text box (do this by clicking a different part of the frame).

- Edit the text by clicking the text box in the Preview pane.

- Move the text box by clicking and dragging it to a desired location.

- Click a text effect to apply it to the text. The Preview pane shows how the effect is applied. To remove an effect, use the up button to scroll all the way up through the list and then select the None option.

- Delete the text by selecting the border of the text box and pressing the Delete key.

Previewing and Finishing Your Live Video Project

Once you've fine-tuned your live video, you'll want to preview it to ensure that the movie is exactly as you want it to be. You can preview the movie at full-screen size by clicking the Play button. When you are ready to continue, you can save your video as a Windows Live Movie Maker Project. Project files are saved with the file extension *.wlmp*. Although Windows Live Movie Maker Project files can be up to multiple megabytes in size, they are still considerably smaller than your final movie file.

You can save as a project file by completing the following steps:

1. Click Movie Maker button and then select Save Project As.

2. In the Save Project dialog box, shown in Figure 10-58, select a save location.

3. Type a descriptive name for your video and then click Save.

After you save your project, you can publish your movie. Publishing your movie creates the finished video file. In most cases, you'll want to publish the movie to your computer or to a DVD. If you publish the movie to your computer, you'll have the encoding options shown in Table 10-5. Plug-ins are available for uploading your videos to Facebook, YouTube, and other online services.

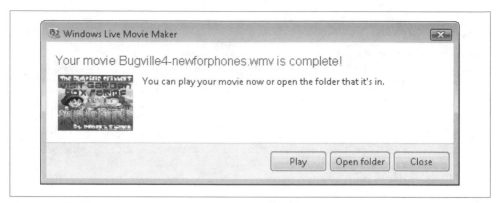

Figure 10-59. Finishing your movie

Table 10-5. Movie encoding settings for Windows Live Movie Maker

File type	File extension	Aspect ratio	Bit rate	Display size	Frames per second
High Definition (1080p)	.wmv	16:9	7.98 Mbps	1,920 × 1,080	30
High Definition (720p)	.wmv	16:9	6.03 Mbps	1,280 × 720	30
Widescreen (480p)	.wmv	16:9	2.99 Mbps	720 × 480	30
Standard Definition	.wmv	4:3	2.99 Mbps	640 × 480	30
Portable Device or Mobile Phone	.wmv	4:3	1.69 Mbps	320 × 240	15
E-mail or Instant Messaging	.wmv	4:3	291.02 Kbps	320 × 240	15

To publish your movie to a video file on your computer, complete the following steps:

1. Click the Movie Maker button and then select Save Movie.

2. Click the desired output option, such as Widescreen (480p) or For E-mail or Instant Messaging.

3. In the Save Movie dialog box, the last folder location you used for saving project files is opened by default. If this isn't the folder you want to use, browse to the folder you want to use.

4. Type a descriptive name for your video and then click Save.

5. You can track the progress of the publish process by percent complete. The bit rate of the movie setting you choose will largely determine how long it takes to publish the movie.

6. When Windows Live Movie Maker finishes publishing the movie, click Play to view the movie or Open Folder to open the file location, as shown in Figure 10-59.

Opening and Producing Saved Projects

You can open saved projects using the Search box on the Start menu. Click Start and then type `movie` into the Search box to see a list of all movies and related movie project files. Double-click the *.wlmp* project file you want to open. Windows 7 will then start Windows Live Movie Maker and open the selected project file for editing.

Alternatively, in Windows Live Movie Maker, you can open saved projects by completing the following steps:

1. Click the Movie Maker button and then click Open Project. This displays the Open Project dialog box.

2. In the Open Project dialog box, the last folder location you used for saving project files is opened by default. If this isn't the folder you want to use, browse to the folder containing the saved project file.

3. Click the project file and click Open. Windows Live Movie Maker will then read the project file and open it.

4. When Windows Live Movie Maker finishes opening, review the movie.

5. After you make any necessary changes, click Save Movie on the Movie Maker menu and then click an output option to produce your movie.

Windows Live Movie Maker tracks the location of resources you use in your projects. If you move resources to a new location, you'll see grayed-out frames in your project. You'll need to double-click each grayed-out frame in turn to locate each missing resource. Each time when you are prompted, select Find and then use the "Browse for ..." dialog box to locate the resource.

CHAPTER 11

Securing and Sharing Your Data

As discussed in earlier chapters, User Account Control (UAC) is a core part of Windows 7's security architecture, and it is meant to help protect your computer from malicious software and network-based attacks. In upcoming chapters, you'll learn about built-in security programs, such as Windows Defender and Windows Firewall, which are also designed to protect your computer from malicious software and network-based attacks. Though these security features work wonderfully and do their job if configured properly, they don't protect you from insiders whose computers are connected to the same local network as your computer, or from those who have a user account on your computer.

Without some additional protections for your files and data, your roommate, co-worker, teenager, or anyone else with local access to your computer will be able to read your email messages and go through your files and records. Just think what might happen if one of these people finds that picture of you—you know the one, the one you thought you deleted but didn't—and then prints or sends it out to a few dozen of your closest friends. This is where file access and sharing permissions come into the picture.

File access permissions control who can access your files and other data. *Sharing permissions* control who can access files and other data that you want to share selectively. If your computer doesn't have properly configured file access and sharing permissions, you don't have any private files or data. You might as well print out the photos, letters, or whatever other private files are on your computer and hand out copies to everyone at the office or at home. Because you don't want to do that and because you *do* want to keep your private files private, you should take the time to properly configure file access and sharing permissions. Best of all, thanks to a feature called *inheritance*, which ensures that any permissions you apply to the root folder of a disk drive or any other folder are also applied to the new files created in that folder, you will rarely have to change permissions once you configure them appropriately.

Securing Your Files

Disk drives and devices with removable storage are formatted with a *filesystem*. The filesystem allows you to create and manage files. The format of the disk that you are working with determines the file security options that are available. You can format disks by using either File Allocation Table (FAT) or NT File System (NTFS). As discussed in the following sections, FAT and NTFS are a bit different in the way they work.

FAT Versus NTFS

Both FAT and NTFS come in several different variations, and in some cases, the type of device you are working with determines which variation is used. With FAT, the number of bits used with the allocation table determines the variant you are working with and the maximum volume size. You'll find that USB flash devices and MP3 players with 4 GB or less of storage are usually formatted with the 16-bit version of FAT. FAT16, also known simply as FAT, defines its file allocation tables using 16 bits. FAT16 is used because it is the most efficient version of FAT for volume sizes of up to 4 GB.

If you use devices with removable storage that have storage larger than 4 GB, such as a removable hard disk, the device will in most cases use the 32-bit version of FAT, known as FAT32. FAT32 defines its file allocation tables using 32 bits, which allows you to have volumes larger than 32 GB. Devices with removable storage use FAT because it has no security controls, allowing you to access your data on multiple computers simply by connecting your device to those computers.

On the other hand, NTFS allows you to control access to files and folders by assigning permissions. At home, your computer will typically have file access permissions only for accounts configured on the local computer. At the office, your computer will typically have file access permissions for accounts configured on the local computer as well as accounts configured for your network. Although NTFS supports just about any volume size you'll want to work with, you can't necessarily move devices formatted with NTFS from one computer to another and gain access to all the data on these devices. You may not be able to do this because NTFS access permissions are set using accounts that are specific to a single computer, to a network, or to both.

File Attributes

All files and folders, whether on FAT- or NTFS-formatted disks, can be marked with *attributes* that give you limited control over how a file or folder is used. The file attributes you can use are:

Read-only
　　Specifies that the file or folder is read-only and cannot be modified.

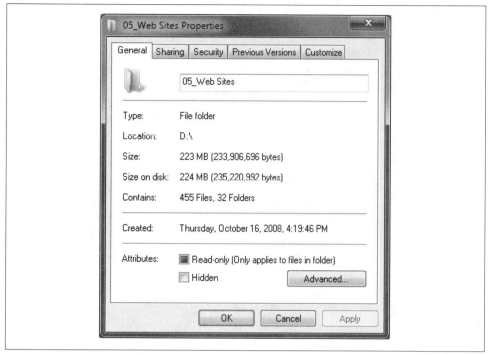

Figure 11-1. Viewing and setting file attributes

Hidden

Specifies that the file or folder is hidden and can be viewed only if the folder option "Show hidden files, folders, and drives" is enabled.

System

Identifies a system file or folder that can be viewed only if the folder option "Hide protected operating system files" is disabled.

You can view or change the Read-Only and Hidden attributes on a file or folder by completing the following steps:

1. In Windows Explorer, right-click the file or folder and select Properties to display its Properties dialog box.

2. On the General tab, shown in Figure 11-1, select the Read-only checkbox to make a file or folder read-only. Clear the Read-only checkbox to allow a file or folder to be read and modified.

3. To hide a file or folder so that it can be viewed only if the folder option "Show hidden files, folders, and drives" is enabled, select the Hidden checkbox. Otherwise, clear this checkbox to allow a file or folder to be viewed normally.

4. Click OK to save your changes.

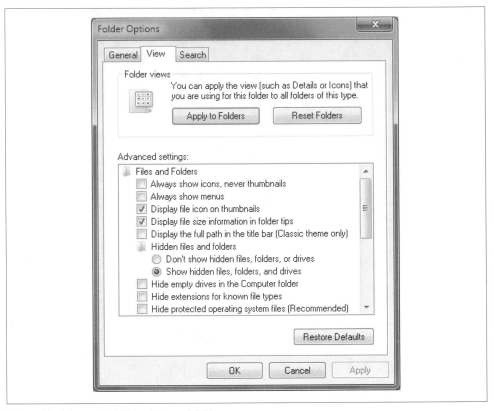

Figure 11-2. Showing hidden files and folders

Generally, Windows 7 manages the System attribute. Windows 7 marks files and folders that you shouldn't modify as system files. You can view files and folders marked with the hidden and system attributes by completing the following steps (see also "Setting Folder Options" on page 203 in Chapter 6):

1. In Windows Explorer, click Organize on the toolbar and then select Folder and Search Options.

2. On the View tab, shown in Figure 11-2, select "Show hidden files and folders" to show hidden files and folders.

3. To show system files and folders, clear the "Hide protected operating system files" checkbox.

4. Click OK to save your settings.

Although these attributes can be set on files and folders, anyone with access to a disk or device can override or change these settings. This means that without additional permission controls, these attributes provide no safeguards for file access or deletion that someone can't override easily.

NTFS Permissions

Access flags are your only choice for controlling how files or folders are used with FAT, but NTFS allows you to control the way files are used with both access flags and NTFS permissions. NTFS permissions provide granular control over the way files and folders are used. When you strip away all the needless stuff you really shouldn't worry about, NTFS permissions boil down to these five things:

Basic permissions
> Top-level permissions that you can assign to user and group accounts

Special permissions
> Low-level permissions that you can assign to user and group accounts

Ownership permissions
> Permissions that identify a file or folder's highest permission holder

Inherited permissions
> Permissions that are inherited from the folder in which a file or folder is stored

Effective permissions
> Permissions in effect for a particular user or group based on the combination of all permissions assigned to that user or group

You assign basic permissions and other permissions to the various user and group accounts available on your computer or on your network. Accounts on your computer include those accounts created by the operating system as well as accounts you've created. Local accounts on your computer are named using the following syntax:

    ComputerName\AccountName

This means that if your computer is named DadsComputer and your user account is Dad, you'll see the account referenced as DadsComputer\Dad.

Network accounts are named using the following syntax:

    DomainName\AccountName

This means that if your workplace domain is TheOffice and your user account is WilliamS, you'll see the account referenced as TheOffice\WilliamS.

If you want to manage permissions for multiple users, you will typically do this using group accounts. Your computer has several standard group accounts, including Administrators and Users. Any user that is a member of your computer's Administrators group has administrator access permissions on your computer. Any user that is a member of your computer's Users group has user access permissions on your computer. On a domain, your network has Administrators and Users groups that apply to the entire network as well.

Controlling Access to Your Data

When your disk drive or storage device is formatted using NTFS, you can use NTFS permissions to control access to your data. As mentioned earlier, NTFS permissions can be broken down into five broad categories: basic permissions, special permissions, ownership permissions, inherited permissions, and effective permissions. The sections that follow discuss how to use each type of permission.

Basic Permissions

With NTFS, permissions are stored in the filesystem as part of the access control list (ACL) assigned to a file or a folder. As described in Table 11-1, files and folders have a slightly different set of basic permissions.

 When working with permissions, keep in mind that some permissions are inherited based on the permissions of a parent folder. Inherited permissions are applied automatically, and you cannot edit inherited permissions without first overriding them. If you try to access a folder on your local computer and do not have appropriate permissions to do so, Windows will prompt you to provide administrator permissions (by default). Once you enter the administrator permissions, you'll be able to access the local folder as an administrator.

Table 11-1. Basic permissions for files and folders

Permission	How it's used	Used with
Full Control	Grants full control over the selected file or folder. Permits reading, writing, changing, and deleting files and subfolders. Also permits changing permissions, deleting files in the folder regardless of their permissions, and taking ownership of a folder or a file. Selecting this permission selects all the other permissions as well.	Files and folders
Modify	Permits reading, writing, changing, and deleting a file or folder. With folders, permits creating files and subfolders, but does not allow taking ownership of a file or folder. Selecting this permission selects all the permissions below it.	Files and folders
Read & Execute	Permits executing files. With folders, permits viewing and listing files and subfolders as well as executing files. If applied to a folder, this permission is inherited by all files and subfolders within the folder. Selecting this permission selects the List Folder Contents and Read permissions as well.	Files and folders
List Folder Contents	Permits viewing and listing files and subfolders as well as executing files. Inherited only by subfolders and not by files within the folder or its subfolders.	Folders only
Read	Permits viewing and listing the contents of a file or folder. Permits viewing file attributes, reading permissions, and synchronizing files. Read is the only permission needed to run scripts. Read access is required to access a shortcut and its target.	Files and folders

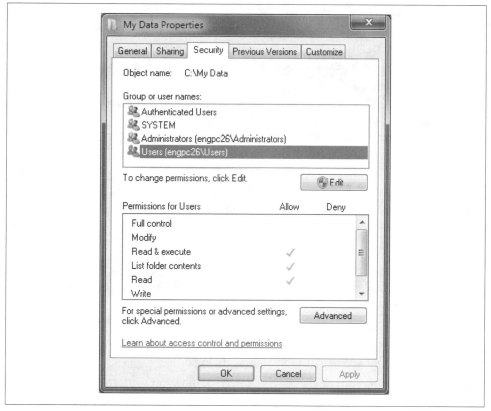

Figure 11-3. Working with basic permissions

Permission	How it's used	Used with
Write	Permits creating new files in folders and writing data to existing files. Permits viewing file attributes, reading permissions, and synchronizing files. Doesn't prevent deleting a folder or file's contents.	Files and folders

Viewing and modifying existing basic permissions

You can view or modify a file or folder's existing basic permissions by completing the following steps:

1. In Windows Explorer, right-click the file or folder you want to work with and then select Properties.

2. In the Properties dialog box, select the Security tab. As shown in Figure 11-3, the "Group or user names" list shows all users and groups with basic permissions for the selected file or folder. If you select a user or a group in this list, the assigned permissions are displayed in the "Permissions for Users" or "Permissions for Groups" list.

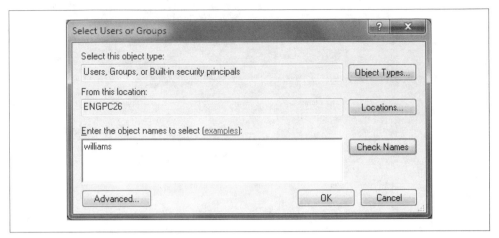

Figure 11-4. Select Users or Groups dialog box

 If permissions are shaded (unavailable), it means they have been inherited from a parent folder. I cover inheritance in detail in the section "Inherited Permissions" on page 459 later in this chapter.

3. Before you can change or remove permissions, you must click Edit. This opens an editable view of the Security tab in a new dialog box.

4. Click the existing user or group whose permissions you want to modify.

5. To modify existing permissions, use the Allow and Deny columns in the "Permissions for Users" list. Select checkboxes in the Allow column to add permissions, and clear checkboxes to remove permissions.

6. To prevent a user or a group from using a permission, select the appropriate checkbox in the Deny column. Denied permissions have precedence over other permissions.

7. Click OK to save your changes.

Adding new basic permissions

You can add new basic permissions to a file or folder by completing the following steps:

1. In Windows Explorer, right-click the file or folder you want to work with and then select Properties.

2. In the Properties dialog box, select the Security tab. The "Group or user names" list shows all users and groups with basic permissions for the selected file or folder.

3. If a user or group whose permissions you want to assign isn't already listed, click Edit. This opens an editable view of the Security tab in a new dialog box.

4. Click Add to display the Select Users or Groups dialog box, shown in Figure 11-4.

5. Type the name of a user or a group account. Click Check Names and then do one of the following:

   - If a single match is found for each entry, the dialog box is automatically updated as appropriate and the entry is underlined.
   - If multiple matches are found, you'll see an additional dialog box that allows you to select the name or names you want to use, and then click OK.
   - If no matches are found, you've probably entered an incorrect name. Modify the name in the Name Not Found dialog box and then click Check Names again.

6. Configure permissions for each user and group you added by selecting an account name and then allowing or denying access permissions as appropriate.

7. Click OK to save your settings.

Removing basic permissions

You can remove a user or group's basic permissions by following these steps:

1. In Windows Explorer, right-click the file or folder you want to work with and then select Properties.
2. In the Properties dialog box, select the Security tab. The "Group or user names" list shows all users and groups with basic permissions for the selected file or folder.
3. Click Edit to open an editable view of the Security tab in a new dialog box.
4. Click the existing user or group whose permissions you want to remove, and then click Remove.
5. Click OK to save your changes.

Special Permissions

Each basic permission is actually a set of *special permissions*. Because of this, whenever you allow or deny a basic permission, Windows 7 works behind the scenes to manage the related special permissions for you. Table 11-2 lists the special permissions related to each basic permission.

Table 11-2. Basic permissions and the related special permissions

Basic permission	Related special permissions
Read	List Folder/Read Data
	Read Attributes
	Read Extended Attributes
	Read Permissions
	Synchronize
Read & Execute or List Folder Contents	All special permissions for Read listed previously
	Traverse Folder/Execute File

Basic permission	Related special permissions
Write	Create Files/Write Data
	Create Folders/Append Data
	Write Attributes
	Write Extended Attributes
	Read Permissions
	Synchronize
Modify	All special permissions for Read listed previously
	All special permissions for Write listed previously
	Delete
Full Control	All special permissions listed previously
	Delete Subfolders and Files
	Change Permissions
	Take Ownership

Viewing and modifying existing special permissions

You can view and set special permissions for a file or a folder by completing the following steps:

1. In Windows Explorer, right-click the file or folder you want to work with and then select Properties.

2. In the Properties dialog box, select the Security tab and then click Advanced. In the "Advanced Security Settings for" dialog box, the permissions are presented much as they are on the Security tab. The key difference is that you now have additional advanced options.

3. On the Permissions tab, click Change Permissions. This opens an editable view of the Permissions tab in a new dialog box, as shown in Figure 11-5.

4. Click the existing user or group whose permissions you want to modify, and then click Edit. This displays an editable "Permission Entry for" dialog box (see Figure 11-6). If any permissions are shaded (unavailable), they are being inherited from a parent folder. You can override the inherited permission, if necessary, by selecting the opposite permission, such as Deny rather than Allow.

5. To modify existing permissions, use the Allow and Deny columns in the Permissions For list. Select checkboxes in the Allow column to add permissions, and clear checkboxes to remove permissions.

6. To prevent a user or a group from using a permission, select the appropriate checkbox in the Deny column. Denied permissions have precedence over other permissions.

7. Click OK to save your changes.

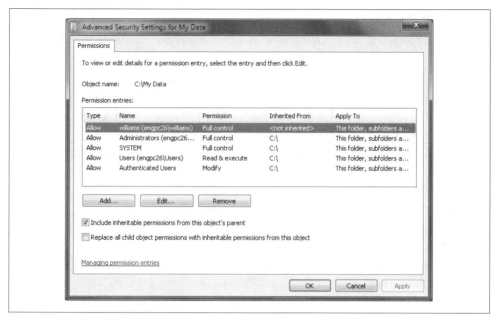

Figure 11-5. Working with advanced permissions

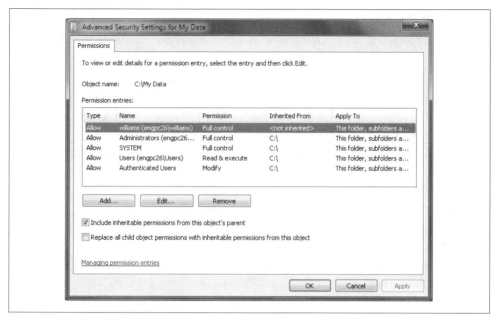

Figure 11-6. Setting individual advanced permissions

Adding new special permissions

You can add new special permissions to a file or folder by completing the following steps:

1. In Windows Explorer, right-click the file or folder you want to work with and then select Properties.

2. In the Properties dialog box, select the Security tab and then click Advanced. This opens the "Advanced Security Settings for" dialog box.

3. On the Permissions tab, click Change Permissions. This opens an editable view of the Permissions tab in a new dialog box.

4. If a user or group whose permissions you want to assign isn't already listed, click Add to display the Select User or Group dialog box.

5. Type the name of a user or a group account. Click Check Names and then do one of the following:

   • If a single match is found for each entry, the dialog box is automatically updated as appropriate and the entry is underlined.

   • If multiple matches are found, you'll see an additional dialog box that allows you to select the name you want to use, and then click OK.

   • If no matches are found, you've probably entered an incorrect name. Modify the name in the Name Not Found dialog box and then click Check Names again.

6. In the "Permissions Entry for" dialog box, configure permissions for the user or group you added by allowing or denying access permissions as appropriate.

7. Click OK to save your settings.

Removing new special permissions

You can add new special permissions to a file or folder by following these steps:

1. In Windows Explorer, right-click the file or folder you want to work with and then select Properties.

2. In the Properties dialog box, select the Security tab and then click Advanced. This opens the "Advanced Security Settings for" dialog box.

3. On the Permissions tab, click Change Permissions. This opens an editable view of the Permissions tab in a new dialog box.

4. Click the existing user or group whose permissions you want to remove, and then click Remove.

5. Click OK to save your changes.

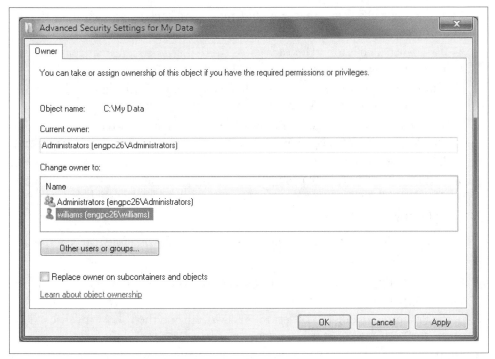

Figure 11-7. Assigning ownership permission

Ownership Permissions

The owner of a file or a folder is the highest permission holder. Regardless of whether the permissions on the file or folder allow the owner to open the file or folder, the owner can always reset the permissions via the file or folder's Properties dialog box. The default owner of a file or a folder is the person who created the resource.

You can assign or take ownership if you have the required permissions or privileges. Individuals with the required permissions include the owner and anyone with an administrator account.

If you are an administrator or the current owner of a file, you can assign ownership of a file or a folder to another user or group by completing these steps:

1. In Windows Explorer, right-click the file or folder you want to work with and then select Properties.
2. In the Properties dialog box, select the Security tab and then click Advanced. This opens the "Advanced Security Settings for" dialog box.
3. On the Owner tab, click Edit. This opens an editable view of the Owner tab in a new dialog box (see Figure 11-7).
4. Click "Other users or groups" to display the Select User or Group dialog box.

5. Type the name of a user or a group account. Click Check Names and then do one of the following:

   - If a single match is found for each entry, the dialog box is automatically updated as appropriate and the entry is underlined.

   - If multiple matches are found, you'll see an additional dialog box that allows you to select the name you want to use, and then click OK.

   - If no matches are found, you've probably entered an incorrect name. Modify the name in the Name Not Found dialog box and then click Check Names again.

6. In the "Change owner to" listbox, select the new owner. If you're taking ownership of a folder, you can take ownership of all subfolders and files within the folder by selecting the "Replace owner on subcontainers and objects" checkbox.

7. Click OK twice to save your settings.

If you are an administrator, you can take ownership of a file or a folder by completing the following steps:

1. In Windows Explorer, right-click the file or folder you want to work with and then select Properties.

2. In the Properties dialog box, select the Security tab and then click Advanced. This opens the "Advanced Security Settings for" dialog box.

3. On the Owner tab, click Edit. This opens an editable view of the Owner tab in a new dialog box.

4. In the "Change owner to" listbox, select the new owner. If you're taking ownership of a folder, you can take ownership of all subfolders and files within the folder by selecting the "Replace owner on subcontainers and objects" checkbox.

5. Click OK twice to save your settings.

 If you encounter a file or folder that doesn't allow you to take ownership, the `takeown` command-line utility can often get the job done. To use it, open an elevated, administrator Command Prompt by clicking Start→All Programs→Accessories, then right-clicking on Command Prompt and selecting Run as Administrator. Next, use the `cd` command to change to the directory that contains the file or folder, and enter:

```
takeown /f filename
```

where *filename* is the name of the file you want to take ownership of. This will assign ownership to the currently logged-on user. `takeown` has a number of other options. Enter `takeown /?` to list them.

Inherited Permissions

By default, all files and folders contained in a folder inherit the permissions assigned during installation or assigned by you when you modify folder permissions. For a disk or other storage device, the top-level folder for inherited permissions is the root folder. For example, the top-level folder for the C: drive is the C:\ folder. Any permissions assigned to this folder are inherited by all other folders on the C: drive automatically. The same is true when you assign permissions to folders at any other level of the folder hierarchy. For example, if you change the permissions for the C:\Data folder, all files and folders contained in the C:\Data folder inherit these permissions by default.

When you are working with permissions, you can easily determine whether a permission is inherited. Inherited permissions are shaded (unavailable) and directly assigned permissions are not shaded. If you don't want a file or a folder to have the same permissions as a parent folder, you have several choices. You can:

- Access the parent folder and configure the permissions you want all included files and folders to have.

- Try to override an inherited permission by selecting the opposite permission. In most cases, Deny overrides Allow.

- Stop inheriting permissions from the parent folder and then copy or remove existing permissions as appropriate.

If you want a file or a folder to stop inheriting permissions from a parent folder, follow these steps:

1. In Windows Explorer, right click the file or folder you want to work with and then select Properties.

2. In the Properties dialog box, select the Security tab and then click Advanced. This opens the "Advanced Security Settings for" dialog box.

3. On the Permissions tab, click Change Permissions. This opens an editable view of the Permissions tab in a new dialog box.

4. Clear the "Include inheritable permissions from this object's parent" checkbox.

5. In the Windows Security dialog box, shown in Figure 11-8, click Add to convert and add the permissions that were applied previously through inheritance, or click Remove to remove the inherited permissions and apply only the permissions that you explicitly set on the folder or file.

6. After you modify or remove additional permissions as necessary, click OK to save your settings.

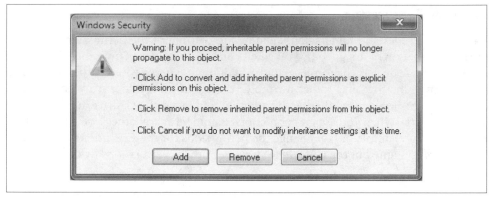

Figure 11-8. Copying or removing permissions

Effective Permissions

Because anyone with a user account can belong to multiple groups and those groups can all have different permissions with regard to a file or folder, it is sometimes difficult to figure out exactly what permission you or someone else has with regard to a file or folder. To remove the guesswork involved, Windows 7 lets you view the exact set of effective permissions for a particular user or group by completing just a few steps.

If you want to view effective permissions, follow these steps:

1. In Windows Explorer, right-click the file or folder you want to work with and then select Properties.

2. In the Properties dialog box, select the Security tab and then click Advanced. This opens the "Advanced Security Settings for" dialog box.

3. On the Effective Permissions tab, click Select to display the Select User or Group dialog box.

4. Type the name of a user or a group account. Click Check Names and then do one of the following:

   • If a single match is found for each entry, the dialog box is automatically updated as appropriate and the entry is underlined.

   • If multiple matches are found, you'll see an additional dialog box that allows you to select the name you want to use, and then click OK.

   • If no matches are found, you've probably entered an incorrect name. Modify the name in the Name Not Found dialog box and then click Check Names again.

The complete set of effective permissions for the selected user or group is listed as shown in Figure 11-9.

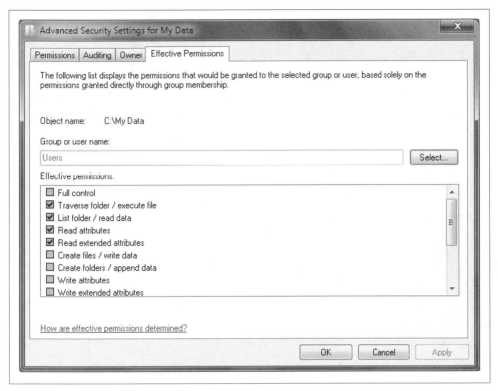

The following list displays the permissions that would be granted to the selected group or user, based solely on the permissions granted directly through group membership.

Object name: C:\My Data

Group or user name:

Users

Select...

Effective permissions:

- ☐ Full control
- ☑ Traverse folder / execute file
- ☑ List folder / read data
- ☑ Read attributes
- ☑ Read extended attributes
- ☐ Create files / write data
- ☐ Create folders / append data
- ☐ Write attributes
- ☐ Write extended attributes

How are effective permissions determined?

OK   Cancel   Apply

Figure 11-9. Viewing effective permissions

Sharing Your Data

You'll often find that you want to share your documents, pictures, videos, and other types of files with someone else. One of the most basic ways to share your files is to send a file to someone by attaching it to an email message. Most instant messaging programs will allow you to share files with other people while you are chatting with them as well. Other ways to share files include copying the files to a data disk or a device with removable storage, such as a USB flash device. Windows 7 offers other ways to share your data beyond these basic techniques, and these built-in sharing features are the subject of this section.

Enabling Sharing

Whether your computer is part of a domain, workgroup, or homegroup, Windows 7 supports two file-sharing models: standard folder sharing and public folder sharing. With standard folder sharing, you can share files from any folder on your computer. Because you don't need to move files from their current location, standard folder sharing is also referred to as *in-place folder sharing*.

You can enable standard folder sharing only on disks formatted with NTFS. Two sets of permissions determine precisely who has access to shared files: NTFS permissions and share permissions. Together, these permissions enable you to control who has access to shared files and the level of access assigned. You do not need to move the files you are sharing.

With public folder sharing, you share files from a computer's *Public* folder simply by copying or moving files to the *Public* folder. Public files are available to anyone who logs on to your computer locally regardless of whether he or she has a standard user account or an administrator user account on the computer. You can also grant network access to the *Public* folder. If you do this, however, there are no access restrictions. The *Public* folder and its contents are open to everyone who can access your computer over the local network.

Computers running Windows 7 can use both sharing models at the same time, and you also have several new sharing options. A key part of this is a home networking feature called the *homegroup*. Within homegroups, you can share your libraries automatically.

When you set up a computer running Windows 7 and are connected to a home network, the Setup program creates a homegroup automatically if one doesn't already exist on your home network. Setup won't create a homegroup if it detects an existing homegroup or if your computer is connected to a domain. Don't worry: you can create a homegroup or join your computer to an existing homegroup at any time. To do so, however, the computer's network location must be set to Home.

You can change the computer's network location and configure basic homegroup options by completing the following steps:

1. Click Start→Control Panel→Network and Internet →Network And Sharing Center.
2. The Network and Sharing Center appears, showing the current network type (see Figure 11-10).
3. If the current network type is Work or Public and you are actually connected to a home network, click the "Work network" or "Public network" link.
4. When prompted to select a location for the network, click "Home network."
5. Windows will then start the Create a Homegroup or Join a Homegroup Wizard. (If you were a member of a homegroup in the past, Windows will rejoin that homegroup.)
6. When you are creating a homegroup, you'll be able to specify the libraries to share, as shown in Figure 11-11. After you specify the libraries to share, click Next. Windows will then generate a password for the homegroup. If you want to join other computers to the homegroup, enter this password when prompted. Click Finish.
7. When you are joining an existing homegroup, you'll need to specify the homegroup password. When you click Next, your computer will join the homegroup and you'll be able to specify the libraries you want to share with other computers. Click Finish.

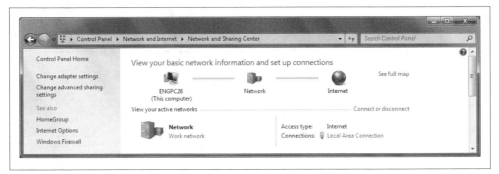

Figure 11-10. Changing the network location

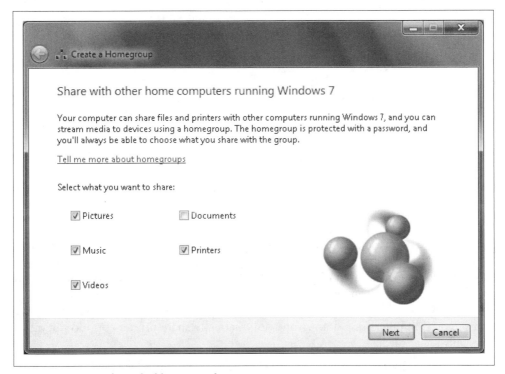

Figure 11-11. Specifying the libraries to share

 Computers running the Starter or Home Basic edition of Windows 7 can join a homegroup but cannot be used to create one. For more information on homegroups and networking, see Chapter 14.

When your computer is part of a homegroup, one of the easiest ways to share folders is simply to include a folder in a shared library (right-click the folder, select Include In Library and then select the appropriate library, such as Documents). In a homegroup,

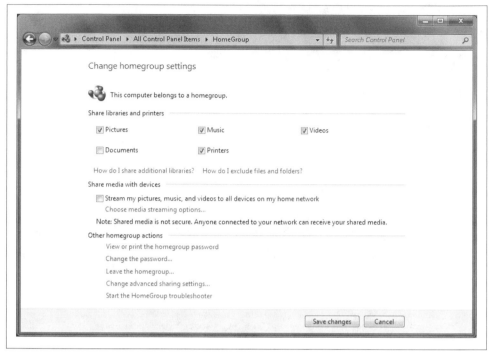

Figure 11-12. Configuring homegroup sharing options

you also have the option to share a folder directly with anyone in the homegroup as read-only or read-write. In a workgroup or domain, you have the option of sharing with specific people.

Another type of sharing is printer sharing. Windows 7 allows you to share printers attached to your computer. Windows 7 also allows you to share media in your Windows Media Player library. When you share your media, you can play media from another computer or from an Xbox 360 or other networked digital media player, and let others who can log on to your computer over the network play media from your computer. Computers in a homegroup automatically share printers but do not automatically share media.

When your computer is member of a homegroup, keep in mind that what is and isn't shared to members of the homegroup is controlled using homegroup settings. However, the overall control for whether sharing is permitted or not is still controlled using the advanced sharing settings.

You can manage the homegroup sharing settings by completing the following steps:

1. Click Start→Control Panel→Network and Internet →Homegroup.
2. On the "Change homegroup settings" page, shown in Figure 11-12, share libraries, printers, and media as appropriate and then click "Save changes."

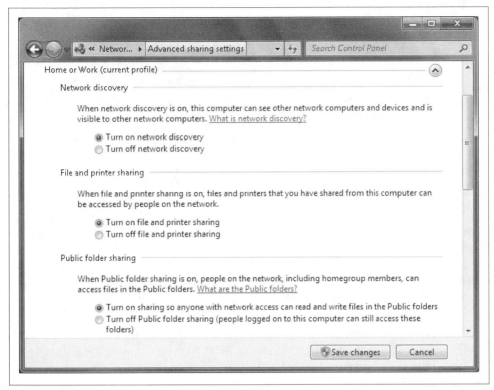

Figure 11-13. Viewing the sharing configuration

When you use your computer in a homegroup, password-protected sharing is enabled automatically and any user that wants access to shared data must either be logged on to a computer that is a member of the homegroup or have a user account and password on your computer. You can enable password-protected sharing in workgroup and domain configurations as well. When you do, only users who have an account and password on your computer can access shared data.

You can manage the various file-sharing features by completing the following steps:

1. Click Start→Control Panel→Network and Internet →Network and Sharing Center.

2. In the Network and Sharing Center, click "Change advanced sharing settings" in the left pane.

3. Windows creates a separate network profile for each network you use. Use the expand button to display the profile you want to work with, as shown in Figure 11-13.

4. Network discovery affects whether a computer can find other computers and devices on the network and whether other computers on the network can find this computer. To enable network discovery, select "Turn on network discovery." To disable network discovery, select "Turn off network discovery."

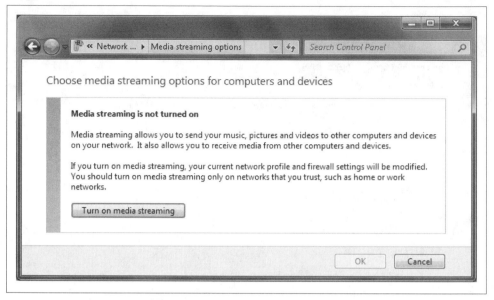

Figure 11-14. Turning on media streaming

5. File and printer sharing controls whether a computer can share files and printers. To enable file sharing, select "Turn on file and printer sharing." To disable file sharing, select "Turn off file and printer sharing."

6. Public folder sharing options control Public folder sharing on your computer. To enable public folder sharing, select "Turn on sharing." To disable public folder sharing, select "Turn off public folder sharing."

7. Media streaming allows you to share your Windows Media Player library. You can configure media streaming as follows:

   • If media streaming is turned off and you want to enable it, click Choose Media Streaming Options, click Turn On Media Streaming and then click OK (see Figure 11-14). By default, Windows streams your Music, Pictures, Recorded TV, and Video libraries to all devices on the local network and to media programs on your computer and to remote connections to your computer.

   • To specify the media that is streamed, click Choose Media Streaming Options and then click Choose Default Settings. Under Choose Parental Ratings, select Only and then select or clear checkboxes for media types as appropriate. Under Star Ratings, select Only and then specify the star rating or set or clear the "Include unrated files" checkbox.

   • To turn off media streaming, click Choose Media Streaming Options and then click Block All.

8. Windows uses encryption to securely transfer your shared data. By default, the encryption level is set to 128-bit encryption. However, before you enable 128-bit encryption, you'll want to ensure all computers and devices you are sharing with support this level of encryption.

The procedure you use to determine the level of encryption supported depends on the type of device. Generally, all computers running Windows 7 will support 128-bit encryption.

9. Password-protected sharing allows you to restrict access so that only people with a user account and password on your computer can access shared files, shared printers, and the *Public* folder. To enable password-protected sharing, select "Turn on password protected sharing." To disable public folder sharing, select "Turn off password protected sharing."

10. In a homegroup, Windows manages connections to other homegroup computers automatically. Generally, this is the preferred configuration. If you want to revert to the standard workgroup behavior and require users to have accounts on each computer, select "Use user accounts and passwords to connect to other computers."

11. Click "Save changes" to save your settings.

In a homegroup, you should not turn off password-protected sharing. Computers in a homegroup use the homegroup password for password-protected sharing. If you turn off password-protected sharing, anyone on the network can access your data.

For *Public* folder sharing, printer sharing, and media sharing, turning on sharing is all you need to do. For homegroup sharing, joining a homegroup is all you need to do. For folder sharing, however, you have more work to do. You must specify files and folders to share, and configure sharing permissions.

Configuring Standard Folder Sharing

With standard folder sharing, two levels of permissions are used: share permissions and NTFS permissions. Share permissions define the maximum level of access, and no one can ever have more permissions than those granted by the share. NTFS permissions set on files and folders further restrict the permitted actions. Table 11-3 lists the share permissions you can assign.

Table 11-3. Share permissions

Permission	How it's used
Owner	Grants full access to the shared file or folder. People with this permission can read files, change files, change file and folder permissions, and take ownership of files and folders.
Read/Write	Grants permission to read files, create files and subfolders, modify files, change attributes on files and subfolders, and delete files and subfolders.
Read	Grants permission to view file and subfolder names, read files and file attributes, access the subfolders of the share, and run program files.

As with NTFS permissions, you can assign share permissions to both users and groups. If you've granted share permissions to a group and a user is a member of that group, the user also has those permissions. If a user is a member of multiple groups, the user's effective share permissions are the highest level assigned. For example, if someone is a member of both Group A, to which you've assigned Reader permission, and Group B, to which you've assigned Owner permission, this person's effective permissions are those of Owner.

You can override this behavior by specifically denying an access permission. Denying permission takes precedence and overrides permissions that you've granted to groups. If you don't want a user or a group to have a permission, configure the share permissions so that the user or the group is denied that permission. For example, if you don't want the user to have Owner permission, deny this permission to the user's account.

When you create the first standard folder share on a computer, Windows creates the File and Printer Sharing exception in Windows Firewall to allow other computers on the network to access the share. This inbound exception is configured for Server Message Block (SMB).

Windows Explorer supports basic sharing and advanced sharing. With basic sharing, you can share any folder except for the root folder of a drive. With advanced sharing, you can share the root folder of a drive and any other folder. Keep the following in mind:

- When you create a share outside of your profile, users access the share by using the UNC path to the share. For example, if you share the *C:\My Data* folder as *Data* on EngPC26, other people can access the folder using the UNC path *EngPC26\Data*.

- When you share a folder within your profile, other people access the share by using a path that is relative to the *Users* folder on your computer. This occurs because Windows configures sharing in relation to where the folder is located in the *Users* folder. For example, if my login name is WilliamS and I share my *Documents* folder on EngPC18, the UNC path to the share is *EngPC18\Users\WilliamS\Documents*.

To use basic sharing, right-click the folder you want to share in Windows Explorer, click Share With and then do one of the following:

- Select Nobody to turn off sharing.
- Select Homegroup (Read) to create a read-only shared folder for computers in the homegroup.
- Select Homegroup (Read/Write) to create a read-write shared folder for computers in the homegroup.
- Select Specific People to explicitly specify who should be able to access the shared folder.

When you select Specific People, Windows Explorer opens the File Sharing Wizard, shown in Figure 11-15.

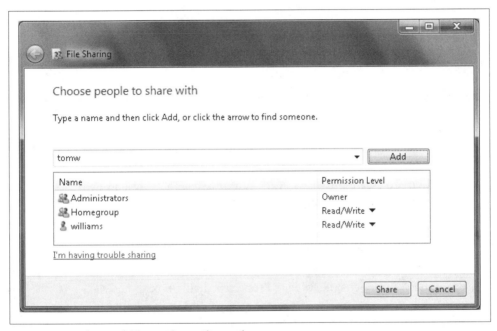

Figure 11-15. Sharing folders with specific people.

Use the wizard to specify the users and groups that have access to the share by completing the following steps.

1. Type a name, and then Click Add, or click the selection arrow to find someone. In homegroups, you'll be able to select Homegroup to share the folder within the homegroup. In workgroups, computers will always show only local accounts and groups. In domains, you'll see local users and groups and also be able to find users in domains.

2. When you click Add, the selected users and groups are added to the Name list. You can then configure permissions for each user and group by clicking an account name to display the Permission Level options and then choosing the appropriate

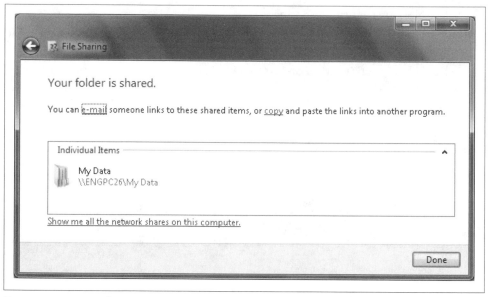

Figure 11-16. Write down or copy the share name

permission level. The options for permission levels are Read, Read/Write, and Remove. You can't assign ownership when working with file shares.

3. Click Share to create the share. After Windows creates the share, write down the share name or click the "copy" link to copy the link so you can paste into another program (see Figure 11-16). Click Done.

You can use advanced sharing by following these steps:

1. In Windows Explorer, right-click the folder you want to share and then select Properties. This opens the folder's Properties dialog box.

2. On the Sharing tab, click Advanced Sharing. In the Advanced Sharing dialog box, shown in Figure 11-17, select "Share this folder."

3. Windows sets the share name to the folder name by default. You can change the name if you want to.

4. Click Permissions. Use the "Permissions For..." dialog box to configure access permissions for the share. The options for permission levels are Full Control (which is the equivalent of Owner), Change (which is the equivalent of Read/Write) and Read. Click OK.

5. Click Caching. Use the Offline Settings dialog box to specify whether and how data is cached for offline use. Click OK.

6. On the Sharing tab, you'll see the network path to the share. Write down the share path. Click Close.

Figure 11-17. Configuring advanced file sharing

To stop sharing a folder, right-click a folder that is shared, point to Share With and then select Nobody.

Accessing Shared Data

Once you share your data, other people can connect to it as a network resource or map to it by using a driver letter on their computer. Once a network drive is mapped, other people can access it just as they would a local drive on their computer.

You can map a network drive to a shared file or folder by following these steps:

1. Click Start and then click Computer. In Windows Explorer, select Map Network Drive from the menu bar. This displays the Map Network Drive dialog box, shown in Figure 11-18.
2. Use the Drive field to select a free drive letter to use.
3. Click the Browse button to the right of the Folder field. In the Browse for Folder dialog box, expand the Network folders until you can select the name of the computer with which you want to work.
4. You'll see a list of shared folders. Select the shared folder you want to work with and click OK.
5. Select "Reconnect at logon" if you want Windows 7 to connect to the shared folder automatically at the start of each session.

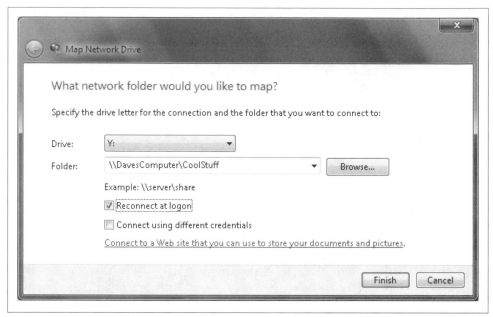

Figure 11-18. Mapping a network drive

6. If your current logon doesn't have appropriate access permissions for the share, click the "Connect using different credentials" checkbox.

7. Click Finish. If you specified that you wanted to connect with different credentials enter the username and password of the account with which you want to connect to the shared folder. Select "Remember my credentials" to have Windows remember the credentials so that you don't need to provide them each time you connect. Click OK.

You can stop mapping a network drive to a shared file or folder by completing the following steps:

1. Click Start and then click Computer.

2. In Windows Explorer, under Network Location, right-click the network drive icon and choose Disconnect.

Accessing Shared Folders Offline

An offline folder is a shared folder designated for use offline. Offline folders provide an easy way for you to use files on shared folders regardless of where you are. You use offline folders as follows:

1. When you are using a laptop computer to access a shared folder over the network, you might want to make the shared folder available for offline use.

2. You then designate the files that your computer should store so that you can use them while disconnected from the network.

3. When you later connect to the network, your computer automatically synchronizes any changes you make back to the shared folder.

 As with just about every feature discussed in this book, it is important to remember that your office administrators can enable and disable offline folders. If they have disabled this or another feature, they probably did so for a good reason. Offline folders are sometimes disabled to prevent problems with multiple users changing the same documents, or to protect potentially sensitive documents.

You can configure a shared folder so that it is available for offline use by completing the following steps:

1. In Windows Explorer, right-click the folder you want to use offline and then select Properties.

2. In the Properties dialog box, select the Sharing tab. The details on this tab indicate whether the folder is shared already. The folder must be shared to configure it for offline use.

3. Click Advanced Sharing.

4. In the Advanced Sharing dialog box, click Caching.

5. In the Offline Settings dialog box, shown in Figure 11-19, select one of the following options:

   Only the files and programs that users specify are available offline
   With this option, only files you specifically designated will be available for offline use.

   All files and programs that users open from the shared folder are automatically available offline
   With this option, all files in the selected folder will be available for offline use. Note that the Optimize for Performance option is only used with Windows XP and earlier versions of Windows.

6. Click OK three times.

You designate a network file or folder as available offline by right-clicking it and selecting Always Available Offline. Once you've ensured that a folder is available for offline use, you can specify the files and folders to use offline.

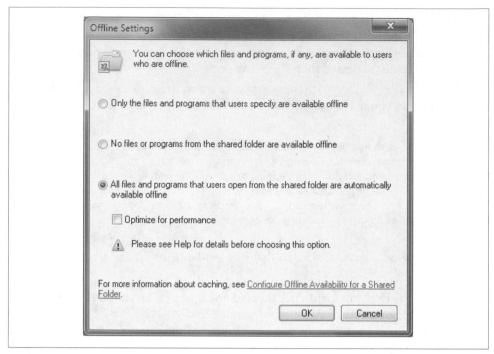

Figure 11-19. Configuring offline file settings

To include an offline folder in a library, complete the following steps:

1. Click Start and then click Computer. This opens the Computer console.
2. Under Network Location, right-click the shared location, select Include In Library and then select the appropriate library, such as Documents.

Working Offline and Syncing

Whenever your computer is not connected to the local area network (LAN), you are considered to be working offline. When you are working offline, you can access only network folders that are cached on your computer for offline use. When you reconnect to the network, Windows 7 automatically will synchronize any changes you've made to the files while offline.

Windows 7 includes many enhancements for offline files, including change-only syncing and unavailable file and folder ghosting. Windows 7 uses change-only syncing to provide fast synchronization at the file block level. Thus, rather than syncing all file blocks in a file, Windows 7 syncs only the changed blocks in a file. Windows 7 creates ghosted entries of other files and folders to preserve the online context whenever you make only part of a folder available offline. When you are not connected to a remote location, you'll see ghost entries for online items as well as normal entries for offline items.

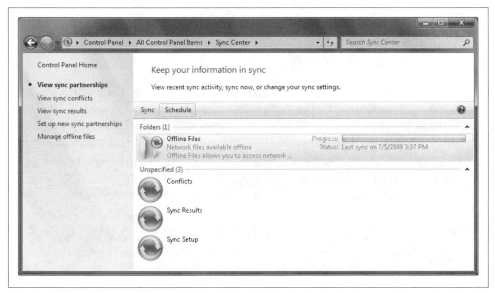

Figure 11-20. Checking the sync status

Sometimes there may be conflicts between changes you've made to files and changes other people have made to files. You can manage conflicts and the synchronization process in the Sync Center, shown in Figure 11-20.

In the Sync Center, you'll see a sync partnership for every shared folder that has locally cached contents. Work with the Sync Center as follows:

1. Click Start→All Programs→Accessories and then click Sync Center.
2. In the Sync Center, currently defined sync partnerships are listed according to name, status, progress, conflict count, error count, and category.
3. To work with offline files, double-click the Offline Files entry. You can now manage syncing of offline files using the following techniques:

    • To manually sync all offline files and folders, click Sync All. If you've selected a sync partnership, you'll need to deselect it by Control-clicking it or clicking in an unused area of the list.

    • To manually sync a specific network share, click the sync partnership that you want to work with and then click Sync.

    • To check for errors, click "View sync results" under Tasks. You can use the sync details to determine when syncing was started, stopped, or completed, and to determine whether there are problems with the synchronization configuration.

Synchronization conflicts can occur if you make changes to a file offline that is updated online by someone else. You can view and resolve synchronization conflicts by following these steps:

1. In the Sync Center, click "View sync conflicts" under Tasks.
2. Any existing conflicts are listed in the main pane. Double-click a conflict you want to resolve.
3. You can now:
   - Click the version you want to keep. To keep the local version and overwrite the network version, click the version listed as On This Computer. To keep the network version and overwrite the local version, click the version listed as being on the shared network location.
   - Click Keep Both Versions to write the local version to the shared network location with a new filename. The new filename will be the same as the old filename, but with a numeric suffix, indicating the version increment.

 Devices you've used with Windows Media Player can have sync partnerships with your computer as well. You manage those sync partnerships in Windows Media Player as discussed in Chapter 8.

In Windows 7, offline files are synchronized automatically. When you connect to a network with a latency of more than 80 milliseconds, Windows 7 uses background synchronization rather than foreground synchronization. You can control when synchronization occurs in Sync Center. In Sync Center, click Offline Files and then click Schedule. Select the folders to sync according to a schedule and then click Next. You'll then be able to configure syncing at a scheduled time or when an event occurs. For example, you can synchronize folders everyday at 3:00 p.m. or every time you log on to your computer.

CHAPTER 12

Setting Up Printers, Scanners, and Fax Machines

Not unlike many offices, scattered about my office is a jumbled assortment of printers, scanners, and fax machines. The good news is that getting these devices—some of them more than a few years old—to work with Windows 7 was much easier than with any previous version of Windows. Still, I did encounter some problems and most of these related to software installation disks that weren't designed for Windows 7. Because of problems such as these, you might find that getting your printers, scanners, and fax machines to work with Windows 7 is a frustrating experience, and this is why in this chapter I'll give you quick and easy workarounds for problems you may encounter, and more. In addition, I have to let Windows 7 off the hook on this one. The underlying problems I encountered weren't Windows 7's fault. The problems were the fault of setup programs and drivers that weren't designed for Windows 7—not unlike many of the setup programs and drivers you'll probably use with your printers, scanners, and fax machines as well.

Installing Printers, Scanners, and Fax Machines

To Windows 7, printers, scanners, and fax machines are all pretty much the same thing. Windows 7 prints to and accepts input from any of these devices in similar ways. What sets these devices apart, however, is the way they are connected.

Printers, scanners, and fax machines can be either physically attached or network-attached. A physically attached device is connected directly to your computer with a USB cable. A network-attached device is connected directly to your network via Ethernet, Bluetooth, or Wi-Fi, and is accessed remotely rather than directly.

If your computer has a built-in fax modem, it will appear in the Windows Fax and Scan utility (see "Working with Scanners and Fax Machines" on page 504, later in this chapter).

Many networked scanners can be used over the Web without needing an install. If you know the IP address or hostname of your scanner, open Internet Explorer and navigate to http://SCANNER, replacing SCANNER with the host name or IP address of the scanner. If you see an informational web page, look around for an option called Scan or Webscan. This will let you access most of the scanner's functions over the Web without needing to install a driver.

Both physically attached and network-attached devices can be shared as well. The computer sharing these devices for other computers on the network is referred to as a *print server*, regardless of whether the computer is actually running a server version of Windows. The print server also handles sending the formatted document and receiving an incoming document. For ease of reference, I'll refer to both processes as *spooling*. A key advantage of using a computer as a print server is that your printers, scanners, and fax machines will have a central queue that you can manage.

At home or at the office, you don't have to share printers, scanners, or fax machines from your computer, or any computer, for that matter. Instead, you can have everyone connect directly to a network-attached device. When you do this, the network device is handled much like a local device attached directly to a computer. However, everyone who uses a network-attached device will then have separate queues, which can make tracking down problems extremely difficult.

Installing Physically Attached Printers, Scanners, and Fax Machines

Physically attached printers, scanners, and fax machines are connected directly to your computer through a USB cable. Although Windows 7 will automatically install most devices that are Plug and Play–compatible automatically, printers, scanners and fax machines are exceptions in some cases. Why? Windows 7 won't automatically install drivers that aren't designed for and known to be fully compatible with the operating system. Additionally, Windows 7 won't automatically install non–Plug and Play devices. Unfortunately, many older printers, scanners, and fax machines fall into one of these two categories and it'll take a bit more work to install and use them with Windows 7.

Some very old printers may connect directly via serial or parallel cables. Windows 7 continues to support these devices and you'll need to install them using the manual installation technique.

Most printers come with management software and device drivers on a CD. To avoid problems, my advice is this: unless you are installing a network-attached printer and are an administrator, you probably do not need to install and use the management software. The reason for this is that Windows 7 includes device and printer management features and these can be used accessed by clicking Start→Devices and Printers and then double-clicking the printer you want to manage.

With respect to device drivers shipped by the manufacturer, my advice is this: if the device software wasn't designed for Windows Vista or later, don't use it. Instead, rely on Windows 7's automatic or manual installation process to install the printer, scanner, or fax device. If during a manual installation your device is not listed, check Windows Update for driver software first and then check the manufacturer's website.

You can install most physically attached printers, scanners, and fax machines by completing the following steps:

1. Turn on the printer, scanner, or fax device.
2. Connect the device to your computer using the appropriate USB cable.
3. Let Windows 7 automatically detect and install the device. Your computer will search its driver cache and may search the Windows Update site.

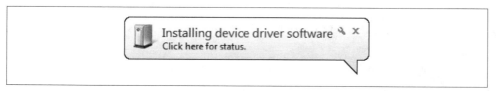

Figure 12-1. Windows 7 detects the printer, scanner, or fax device

Windows 7 should automatically detect the printer, scanner or fax device as shown in Figure 12-1, and then automatically install a built-in driver to support it. As shown in Figure 12-2, the Driver Software Installation component handles the installation task. The printer, scanner, or fax device should then run immediately without any problems.

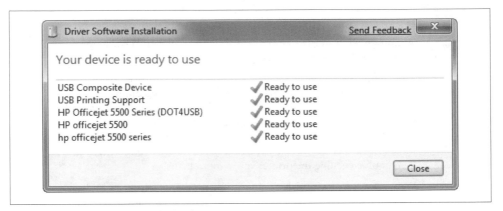

Figure 12-2. Windows 7 installs the device

You can confirm that the printer, scanner, or fax device is available by clicking Start→Devices and Printers. As shown in Figure 12-3, the printer, scanner, or fax device should be listed as an available device. Double-click the printer, scanner, or fax device to check its status. The device status should be "Ready," as shown in Figure 12-4.

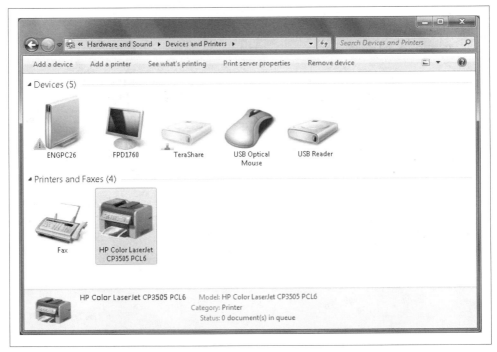

Figure 12-3. Confirming that the device is installed

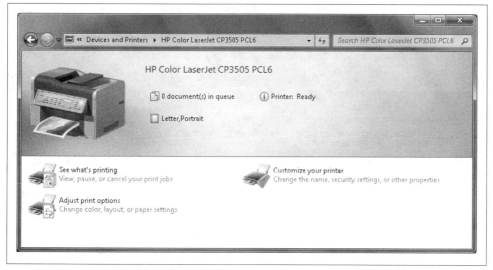

Figure 12-4. Confirming that the device is available and ready for use

Automatic installation is great when it works, but it doesn't work 100 percent of the time. Windows 7 might also automatically detect the printer, scanner, or fax device, but the Driver Software Installation component may run into problems installing the device. If this happens, you'll see errors similar to those shown in Figure 12-5. For example, the HP printer that installed automatically on 32-bit Windows 7 would not install automatically on 64-bit Windows 7. Why? At the time, the 64-bit printer driver was not designed for and known to be fully compatible with the operating system.

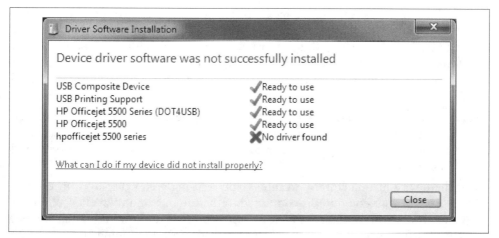

Figure 12-5. Windows 7 is unable to install the device

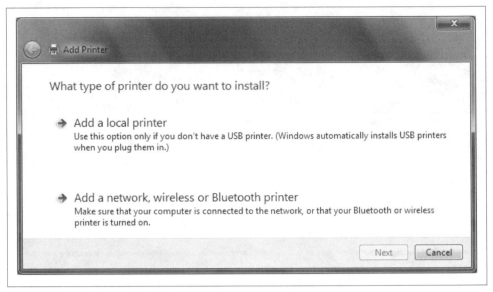

Figure 12-6. Installing a printer manually

Installing a printer or fax machine manually

If automatic installation fails, you can install the printer or fax machine manually by completing the following steps:

1. With the printer, scanner, or fax device powered on and connected to your computer using the appropriate cable, Start→Devices and Printers.

2. In Devices and Printers, click "Add a printer."

3. In the Add Printer Wizard, shown in Figure 12-6, click "Add a local printer."

4. On the "Choose a printer port page," ensure that "Use an existing port" is selected, choose the printer port to use, and then click Next. If you are trying to manually install a USB printer that did not install automatically, choose USB001 (Virtual Printer Port for USB), as shown in Figure 12-7. Otherwise, choose the COM port (for serial printers) or LPT port (for parallel printers) that your printer is connected to.

5. As shown in Figure 12-8, you must now specify the device manufacturer and model. This allows Windows 7 to assign a driver to the device. If the device manufacturer and model you are using are displayed, choose a manufacturer and a model, and then skip steps 6–9.

6. If the device manufacturer and model you're using aren't displayed in the list, ensure that your computer is connected to the Internet and then click Windows Update. Windows will then update the list of printers to show additional models. This feature is part of Windows 7's automatic driver provisioning and it can take several minutes to retrieve the updated list.

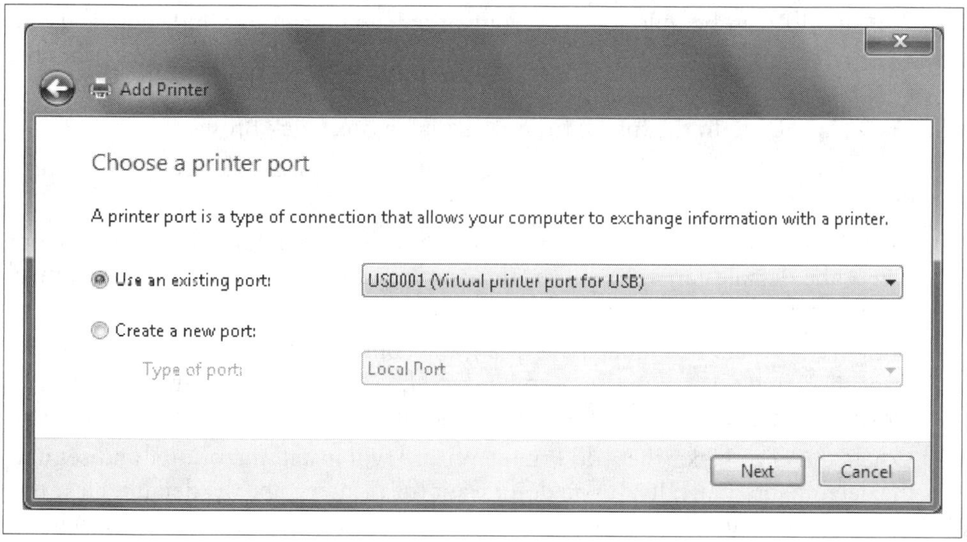

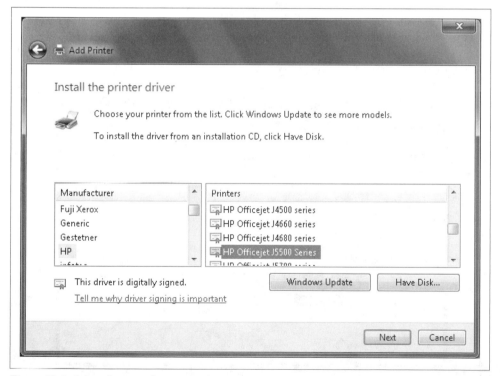

Figure 12-7. Select the port to use

Figure 12-8. Select the manufacturer and printer type

7. You should then be able to select your printer manufacturer and model. If you aren't, download the driver from the manufacturer's website and then extract the driver files.

8. Click Have Disk. In the Install from Disk dialog box, click Browse.

9. In the Locate File dialog box, locate the *.inf* driver file for the device and then click Open.

10. Click Next. On the "Type a printer name" page, type a name for the device or accept the default name. You'll see this name on the Printers page in the Control Panel. Click Next, and the printer driver will be installed.

11. The printer or fax machine is automatically configured for sharing. If you don't want the printer or fax machine to be shared, select "Do not share this printer." Otherwise, you can set the share name and location, and add an optional comment.

12. When you click Next, the Add Printer Wizard will install the printer and set it as the default automatically. If you don't want the printer to be the default, clear the "Set as the default printer" checkbox (you will see this checkbox only if you had a default printer before you installed this one).

13. To print a test page, click Print a Test Page. The wizard will then print a test page. Click Close.

14. Click Finish. Click Start→Devices And Printers. The Devices and Printers page in the Control Panel will have an additional icon with the name set the way you specified (see Figure 12-9). You can change the printer or fax properties and check printer or fax status at any time.

Figure 12-9. Confirming that the device was installed

Installing a scanner manually

You can install a scanner manually by completing the following steps:

1. In Windows Explorer, access *C:\Program Files\Windows Photo Viewer*, where C: is your system drive, and then double-click *ImagingDevices.exe*.

2. In the Scanners and Cameras window, click Add Device. This starts the Scanner and Camera Installation Wizard.

3. Click Next.

4. You must now specify the device manufacturer and model. This allows Windows 7 to assign a driver to the device. If the device manufacturer and model you are using are displayed, choose a manufacturer and a model, and then skip steps 5–7.

5. If the device manufacturer and model you're using aren't displayed in the list, download the driver from the manufacturer's website and then extract the driver files.

6. Click Have Disk. In the Install from Disk dialog box, click Browse.

7. In the Locate File dialog box, locate the *.inf* driver file for the device and then click Open.

8. Click Next. On the "What is the name of your device?" page, type a name for the scanner or accept the default name. You'll see this name in the Scanners and Cameras window.

9. Click Next and then click Finish.

10. The Scanners and Cameras window will have an additional icon with the name set the way you specified. You can change the scanner properties and check scanner status at any time.

Installing Wireless and Bluetooth Printers

Windows 7 fully supports wireless and Bluetooth. Often, wireless and Bluetooth printers will include installation software that you may be able to use to install and begin using the device. Before you use the installation software, however, you should ensure it is compatible with Windows 7. If it isn't, you may want to check the device manufacturer's website for updated software.

Some wireless and Bluetooth printers connect directly to a computer. Others connect to a computer via a network. You can connect a wireless or Bluetooth printer directly to a computer by completing the following steps:

1. Typically, wireless and Bluetooth devices require that you connect a receiver to the computer. You'll need to plug the receiver into a USB slot on the computer.

2. Position the computer and receiver so that the receiver is within range of the printer to which you want to connect.

3. Configure the printer as necessary and ensure that it is powered on.

4. Click Start→Devices and Printers. In Devices and Printers, click "Add printer."

5. In the Add Printer Wizard, shown in Figure 12-10, click "Add a network, wireless or Bluetooth Printer."

6. As shown in Figure 12-11, your computer will then search for available printers. If the printer you want to use is shown in the list of available printers, select the printer, and then click Next.

 If your computer can't find the wireless printer, make sure that the printer is powered on and that the wireless/Bluetooth transmitter is switched on. If you suspect the printer is out of range, try moving it closer to the computer. Make sure the printer is positioned away from air conditioning units, microwave ovens, etc. Then click Search Again to have your computer search again for the printer. If this resolves the problem, select the printer and then click Next to continue this procedure. Otherwise, click "The printer that I want isn't listed," and then click Next.

On the "Find a printer by name or TCP/IP address" page, select "Add a printer using a TCP/IP address or hostname," and then click Next. On the "Type a printer hostname or IP address" page, use the "Device type" list to select the type of device. If you don't know the type of device, choose Autodetect. In the "Hostname or IP address" text box, type the hostname or Internet Protocol (IP) address of the device. If you are unsure, use the device's control menu to print a configuration page. The port name is set for you based on the hostname or IP address entry. The port name doesn't matter as long as it's unique for your computer.

When you click Next, the wizard attempts to contact the device. If the wizard is unable to detect the print device, make sure that the print device is turned on and connected to the network. Also, ensure that you typed the correct IP address or printer name in the previous page. If you entered incorrect information, click the Back arrow and then retype this information. Complete the installation by setting the printer name and sharing options as discussed in steps 7–11.

7. On the "Type a printer name" page, type a name for the device or accept the default name. You'll see this name on the Printers page in the Control Panel. Click Next.

8. The printer is automatically configured for sharing. If you don't want the printer to be shared, select "Do not share this printer." Otherwise, you can set the share name and location, and add an optional comment.

9. When you click Next, the Add Printer Wizard will install the printer and set it as the default automatically. If you don't want the printer to be the default, clear the "Set as the default printer" checkbox (you will see this checkbox only if you had a default printer before you installed this one).

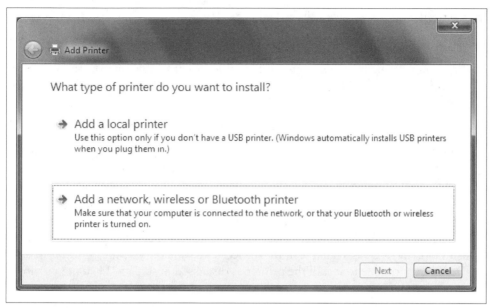

Figure 12-10. Add a network, wireless, or Bluetooth printer

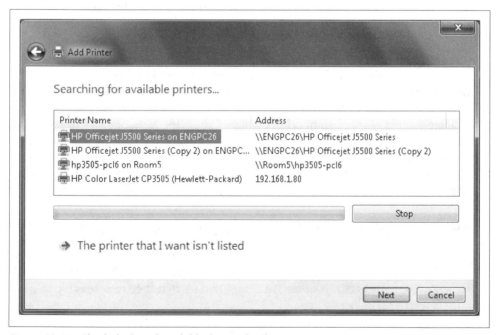

Figure 12-11. Check the list of available devices for the printer

10. To print a test page, click Print a Test Page. The wizard will then print a test page. Click Close.

11. Click Finish. Click Start→Devices and Printers. The Devices and Printers page in the Control Panel will have an additional icon with the name set the way you specified. You can change the printer properties and check printer status at any time.

To connect a wireless printer to a computer via a network, do the following:

1. Power on the printer. Configure its initial settings as appropriate for the network. For example, you may need to configure TCP/IP settings to use Dynamic Host Configuration Protocol (DHCP) or you may need to use a static IP address.

2. Wait 30–60 seconds for the device to be detected. The device should be detected and installed automatically. If the device isn't detected and installed, click Start and then click Devices and Printers. In Devices and Printers, ensure that the device isn't already listed as available. If the device isn't available yet, click "Add printer." You'll then be able to install the printer as discussed in steps 5–11 of the previous procedure.

3. If you have trouble connecting to the printer, make sure that a firewall isn't blocking connectivity to the printer. You may need to open a firewall port to allow access between the computer and the device. Also double-check the printer's TCP/IP configuration. If your network consists of multiple subnets connected together, try to connect the device to the same network subnet.

4. Keep in mind that Network Discovery settings control whether your computer can find other computers and devices on the network and whether other computers on the network can find your computer. By default, Network Discovery is not enabled (but you may have enabled this feature already by creating a homegroup, sharing folders, or performing other tasks). To enable Network Discovery, click Start→Control Panel→Network and Internet→Network and Sharing Center. In the left pane, click "Change advanced sharing settings." Access the appropriate network profile, such as Home or Work. Under Network Discovery, click "Turn on network discovery," and then click Save Changes.

Installing Network-Attached Printers, Scanners, and Fax Machines

A network-attached printer, scanner, or fax machine is a device that's attached directly to the network using a wireless connection or a network cable. Network-attached printers, scanners, and fax machines are configured so that they're accessible to network users as shared devices.

If you configure the printer and enable sharing, the computer on which you configure the print device becomes an additional print server for it. When you install this printer on another computer, you might see two listings: one for the device itself, and another for the shared printer on the computer that is sharing it. Unless you want your computer to act as a print server, you might want to select "Do not share this printer" in step 5.

You can install a network-attached printer or fax machine by completing these steps:

1. Click Start→Devices and Printers. In Devices and Printers, click "Add printer." This starts the Add Printer Wizard.

2. In the Add Printer Wizard, click "Add a network, wireless or Bluetooth printer." The Add Printer Wizard will then begin searching for available devices.

3. If the wizard finds the device you want to use, click it in the list of devices found. Click Next.

If your computer can't find the network printer, make sure that the printer is powered on and that a firewall isn't blocking connectivity to the printer. You may need to open a firewall port to allow access between the computer and the printer. If your network consists of multiple subnets connected together, try to connect the printer to the same network subnet. Also, make sure the printer is configured to broadcast its presence on the network. Although most network printers automatically do this, this isn't always the case. Finally, make sure that the printer has an IP address and proper network settings. With DHCP, network routers assign IP addresses automatically as printers connect to the network. After you've double-checked everything, click Search Again to have your computer search again for the printer. If this resolves the problem, select the printer and then click Next to continue this procedure. Otherwise, skip the remaining steps and follow the next procedure to install the printer manually.

4. On the "Type a printer name" page, type a name for the device or accept the default name. You'll see this name on the Printers page in the Control Panel. Click Next.

5. The printer is automatically configured for sharing. If you don't want the printer to be shared, select "Do not share this printer." Otherwise, you can set the share name and location and add an optional comment.

6. When you click Next, the Add Printer Wizard will install the printer and set it as the default automatically. If you don't want the printer to be the default, clear the "Set as the default printer" checkbox (you will see this checkbox only if you had a default printer before you installed this one).

7. To print a test page, click "Print a test page." The wizard will then print a test page. Click Close.

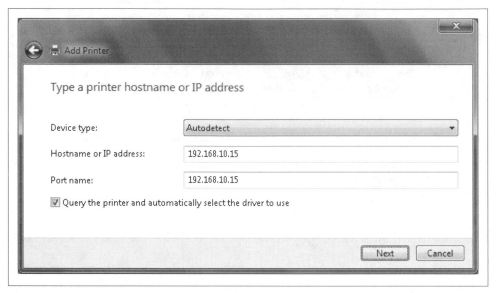

Figure 12-12. Setting the printer options

8. Click Finish. Click Start→Devices and Printers. The Devices and Printers page in the Control Panel will have an additional icon with the name set the way you specified. You can change the printer properties and check printer status at any time.

If the Add Printer Wizard doesn't find the network printer you want to use, complete the installation by following these steps:

1. On the "Searching for available printers" page, click "The printer that I want isn't listed" and then click Next.

2. On the "Find a printer by name or TCP/IP address" page, select "Add a printer using a TCP/IP address or hostname," and then click Next.

3. On the "Type a printer hostname or IP address" page, shown in Figure 12-12, use the "Device type" list to select the type of device. If you don't know the type of device, choose Autodetect.

4. In the "Hostname or IP address" text box, type the hostname or Internet Protocol (IP) address of the device. If you are unsure, use the device's control menu to print a configuration page.

5. The port name is set for you based on the hostname or IP address entry. The port name doesn't matter as long as it's unique for your computer.

6. When you click Next, the wizard attempts to contact the device and automatically determine the protocol details as well as the adapter type. If the wizard is unable to detect the print device, make sure that the print device is turned on and connected to the network. Also, ensure that you typed the correct IP address or printer

name in the previous page. If you entered incorrect information, click the Back arrow and then retype this information.

7. Complete the installation by setting the printer name and sharing options as discussed in the previous procedure.

Xerox makes a network-attached scanner called the Xerox WorkCentre Pro Scanner. This device and other similar devices install in the same way as a directly attached scanner. When you complete the installation, the scanner should be configured automatically. If it isn't, follow these steps to set the IP address for the scanner:

1. In Windows Explorer, access *C:\Program Files\Windows Photo Viewer*, where C: is your system drive, and then double-click *ImagingDevices.exe*.

2. In the Scanners and Cameras window, click the scanner and then click Properties.

3. On the Device Settings tab, type the hostname or IP address of the scanner and then click OK.

Sharing Printers, Scanners, and Fax Machines

After you install printers, scanners, and fax machines, you can use the devices with your computer. When you are printing, scanning, or faxing, all you need to do is select the device in your application. If you want other people on your network to be able to use printers, scanners, and fax machines you've installed, you can do that, too.

Sharing Printers and Fax Machines

After you install a physically attached or network-attached printer or fax machine, you can allow anyone else on your network to connect to it by sharing it. Friends and coworkers on your network can then connect to the shared printer or fax machine.

You can share a printer or fax machine by following these steps:

1. Ensure that printer sharing is enabled on your computer. To do this, click Start→ Control Panel→Network and Internet→Network and Sharing Center. In the left pane, click Change Advanced Sharing Settings. Access the appropriate network profile, such as Home or Work. Under File and Printer, "Turn on file and printer sharing" should be selected. If this option isn't selected, select it and then click Save Changes.

2. Click Start→Devices and Printers. In Devices and Printers, right-click the printer you want to configure and then select Printer Properties (not Properties).

3. On the Sharing tab, you'll see any current sharing options. If there are no current sharing options, all sharing options are dimmed, as shown in Figure 12-13.

Some types of fax machines cannot be shared. If this is the case with your fax machine, this will be stated on the Sharing tab.

4. To change the sharing options, select the "Share this printer" checkbox, Windows 7 fills in a share name for you. You can change the default name as necessary.

5. By default, print jobs are generated on the computer of the person printing a document. This is usually the desired setting. If you want to generate the print file on your computer, clear the "Render print jobs on client computers" checkbox.

6. Click Additional Drivers. In the Additional Drivers dialog box, select the types of processors other people on the network are using to ensure that your computer provides the appropriate drivers during setup. If you are using an X86-based computer, you'll likely need to enable printers for X64-based computers. Similarly, if you are using an X64-based computer, you'll likely need to enable printers for X86-based computers (see Figure 12-14).

7. Click OK.

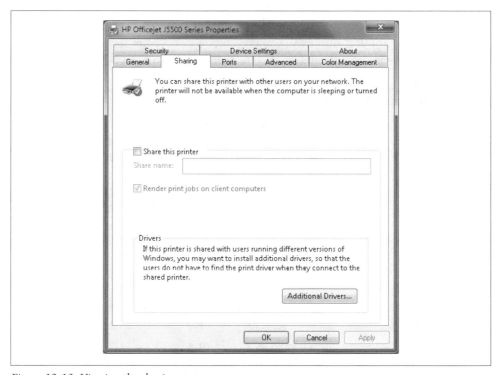

Figure 12-13. Viewing the sharing status

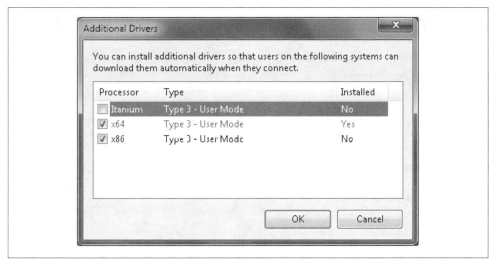

Figure 12-14. Enabling drivers for other processor architectures

Connecting to Shared Printers and Fax Machines

When you are sharing printers and fax machines, you need to keep in mind that other people on your network might not be running Windows 7. Don't worry, though: connecting to a shared printer with Windows 2000 or later is easy. Why? Because computers running Windows 2000 or later can install the printer drivers automatically once a printer is shared. The trick, of course, is to ensure that your computer provides the necessary drivers when someone tries to connect to your printer or fax machine. When you were sharing your printer or fax machine, you selected drivers for other computers as part of the sharing configuration. If you need to, you can add drivers for other types of computers by completing the following steps:

1. Click Start→Devices and Printers. In Devices and Printers, right-click the printer you want to configure and then select Printer Properties (not Properties).

2. On the Sharing tab, click Additional Drivers.

3. In the Additional Drivers dialog box, select the types of processors other people on the network are using to ensure that your computer provides the appropriate drivers during setup.

4. Click OK.

Once you've shared the printer and ensured that the drivers are available, anyone running Windows 2000 or Windows XP can connect to and use the printer by following these steps:

1. In Windows Explorer, click the Folders button on the toolbar to display the Folders pane.

Figure 12-15. Selecting the printer to use

2. Expand My Computer, expand the Control Panel, and then select Printers and Faxes.

3. In the Folders pane, expand My Network Places and then navigate My Network Places to the computer sharing the printer.

4. When you select the Printers and Faxes node on this computer, you'll see the shared printers and fax machines (see Figure 12-15).

5. Click the printer or fax machine and drag it to My Computer→Control Panel→Printers and Faxes.

Anyone running Windows Vista or later can connect to and use the printer by following these steps:

1. Click Start→Devices and Printers.
2. Open a second window by clicking Start and then clicking Network.
3. In the Network window, double-click the computer sharing the printer.
4. In the Network window, click the printer or fax machine and drag it to the Devices and Printers window.

Sharing and Connecting to Scanners

Physically attached and network-attached scanners cannot be shared in the same way as printers and fax machines can. Physically attached scanners must be connected directly to the computer of the person who wants to use the scanner. Although network-attached scanners are technically shared, they don't have sharing settings you need to configure through your computer. You connect to and use a network-attached scanner by performing an install, as discussed previously.

Configuring Printer, Scanner, and Fax Machine Properties

Like any other device, printers, scanners, and fax machines have properties that you can configure. This section looks at the properties you'll work with most.

Changing Ports for Printers, Scanners, and Fax Machines

If a setup program works correctly but configures the device incorrectly, the likely problem is the associated port. Each printer, scanner, and fax machine you use with your computer is configured to work with a specific port. USB printers, fax machines, and scanners use virtual USB ports. Parallel and serial printers use LPT and COM ports. Network-attached printers use standard Transmission Control Protocol/Internet Protocol (TCP/IP) ports. A problem you may encounter is the case of a printer being configured to print using the FILE port instead of the correct port. Because the FILE port prints documents to a raw printer file, your computer won't spool to the device.

You can view and set the ports for a printer or fax machine by following these steps:

1. Click Start→Devices and Printers. In Devices and Printers, right-click the printer you want to configure and then select Printer Properties (not Properties).
2. In the Properties dialog box, select the Ports tab, as shown in Figure 12-16.
3. In the Port column, clear the checkbox for the incorrect port and then select the checkbox for the correct port.
4. Click OK.

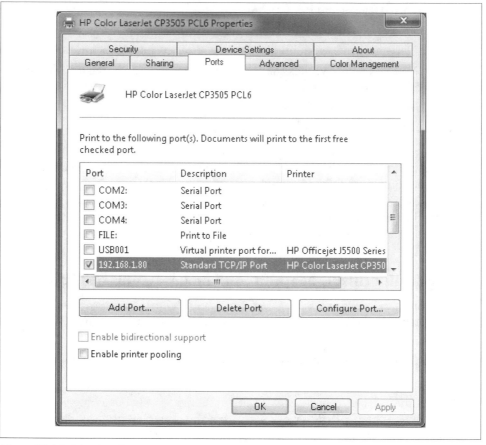

Figure 12-16. Selecting the correct printer port

If you are experiencing problems with a TCP/IP port, ensure that the IP address associated with the port is correct. The IP address typically is listed as part of the name of the port. If the IP address isn't correct and no port is available for the correct IP address, follow these steps to resolve the problem:

1. On the Ports tab, click Add Port.

2. In the Printer Ports dialog box, click Standard TCP/IP Port and then click New Port.

3. In the Add Standard TCP/IP Printer Port Wizard, click Next.

4. As shown in Figure 12-17, type the IP address of the printer or fax machine and then click Next.

5. When you click Next, the wizard attempts to contact the device and automatically determine the protocol details as well as the adapter type. If the wizard is unable to detect the print device, make sure that the print device is turned on and is connected to the network. Also ensure that you typed the correct IP address or printer

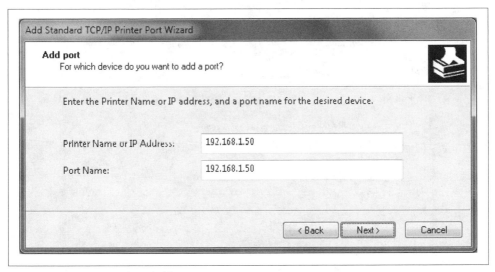

Figure 12-17. Entering the IP address

name in the previous page. If you entered the incorrect information, click the Back button and then retype this information.

6. Before you click Finish, note the protocol and adapter type details. This information must be correct for your computer to work with the printer. Click Finish and then click Close.

7. If the protocol and adapter type were incorrect, click the port in the Properties dialog box and then click Configure Port. Use the options in the Configure Standard TCP/IP Port Monitor dialog box to specify the correct information and then click OK twice. (See Figure 12-18 for an example.)

To resolve a problem with a network-attached scanner, follow these steps:

1. In Windows Explorer, access *C:\Program Files\Windows Photo Viewer*, where *C:* is your system drive, and then double-click *ImagingDevices.exe*.

2. In the Scanners and Cameras window, click the scanner and then click Properties.

3. On the Device Settings tab, the current hostname or IP address is listed. If this information isn't correct, enter the correct hostname or IP address of the scanner, and then click OK.

Changing Printer, Scanner, and Fax Machine Drivers

You can manage drivers for printers, scanners, and fax machines just like you can any other drivers. To change the drivers for a printer or fax machine, follow these steps:

1. Click Start ›Devices and Printers. In Devices and Printers, right-click the printer you want to configure and then select Printer Properties (not Properties).

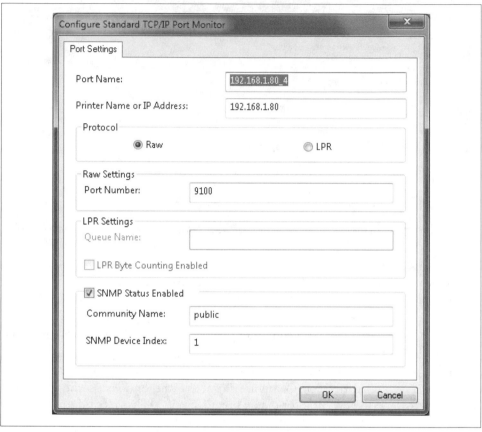

Figure 12-18. Correcting the protocol and adapter details

2. On the Advanced tab, click New Driver.

3. Use the Add Printer Driver Wizard to select and install the new driver.

To change the drivers for a scanner, follow these steps:

1. In Windows Explorer, access *C:\Program Files\Windows Photo Viewer*, where *C:* is your system drive, and then double-click *ImagingDevices.exe*.

2. In the Scanners and Cameras window, click the scanner and then click Properties.

3. On the Device Settings tab, click New Driver.

Setting Printer Scheduling, Prioritization, and Other Options

The Advanced tab of the Printer properties dialog box provides most of the options you'll want to configure. You can use these options to configure your printer by completing the following steps:

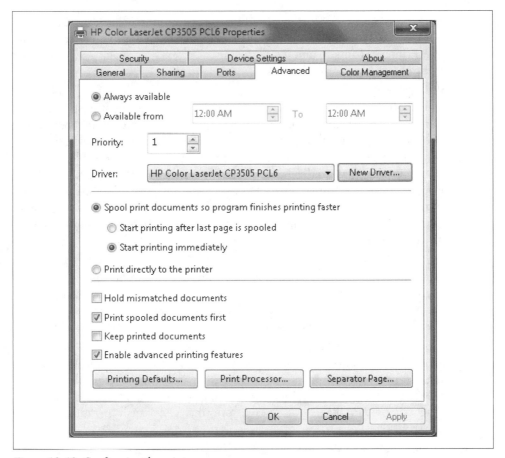

Figure 12-19. Configuring the printer as necessary

1. Click Start→Devices and Printers. In Devices and Printers, right-click the printer you want to configure and then select Printer Properties (not Properties).

2. In the Properties dialog box, select the Advanced tab, as shown in Figure 12-19.

3. Use the following options to optimize the printer configuration:

   Always available and Available from

   > Printers are either always available or available only during the hours specified. Select "Always available" to make the printer available at all times or select "Available from" to set specific hours of operation. Print jobs sent outside the designated hours are held in the printer's queue until the scheduled use time.

   Priority

   > Print jobs always print in order of priority. Jobs with higher priority print before jobs with lower priority. Use the Priority box to set the default priority.

Driver

Shows the current driver being used for the printer. If you click the Driver list, you'll see a list of all printer drivers being used on your computer. See "Changing Printer, Scanner, and Fax Machine Drivers" on page 497 for more information.

Spooling options

The spooling options control whether and how a document is spooled to a hard disk before being sent to the printer. Spooling a document before printing allows applications to finish printing faster. To enable spooling, select "Spool print documents so program finishes printing faster." To disable spooling, select "Print directly to the printer." With spooling, select "Start printing after last page is spooled" if you want to ensure that the entire document makes it into the print queue before printing. Otherwise, select "Start printing immediately" if you want printing to begin immediately when the print device isn't already in use.

Hold mismatched documents

A mismatch can occur if a document tries to use a form or type of paper not currently available in a printer tray. Typically, printers will stop all printing and wait for the mismatch to be resolved. If you want the printer to hold mismatched documents rather than try to prevent them, select this option.

Print spooled documents first

Select this option to allow the printer to print jobs that have completed spooling before jobs in the process of spooling, regardless of whether the spooling jobs have higher priority. This helps to maximize printer efficiency by ensuring that documents that have started printing can finish printing without interruption.

Keep printed documents

Select this option to keep a copy of documents in the printer queue on the print server. If you're printing files that can't easily be recreated, you might want to use this option so that you can easily reprint a document without having to recreate it.

Enable advanced printing features

Select this option to allow the use of advanced printing options, if available, such as "Page order" and "Pages per sheet." If you encounter compatibility problems when using advanced options, you can disable the advanced printing features by clearing this checkbox.

Printing Defaults

Clicking this button displays the Printing Defaults dialog box, which you can use to specify defaults for paper sources, document sizes, color matching, print resolution, and more.

Print Processor

> Clicking this button displays the Print Processor dialog box, which you can use to set the print processor and default data type for a printer. The print processor is the software component that tells your computer how to render the raw printer data. About the only time you may need to configure print processor options is when you are working with an older Unix printer.

Separator Page

> At the office, separator pages may be a requirement. To select a separator page to print before each document, click the Separator Page button. In the Separator Page dialog box, click Browse, scroll down, and then click *Sysprint.sep* if you have a PostScript printer or *Pcl.sep* if you have a PCL printer. Click Open and then click OK.

Managing Print, Fax, and Scan Jobs

Documents you print can be either spooled or sent directly to the printer. When you use spooling with printing rather than direct-to-printer printing, documents that are waiting to print or are in the process of printing are stored on the print server as a print job. If you encounter problems while printing, you may want to check the status of print jobs and pause or cancel a print job as necessary. Because fax machines and scanners typically can be used to both send and receive documents, they typically have incoming jobs and outgoing jobs that you can manage.

Working with Print Jobs

You manage the print jobs associated with a printer using the print management window. If the printer is configured on your computer, you can access the print management window by completing the following steps:

1. Click Start→Devices and Printers.
2. In Devices and Printers, right-click the printer you want to work with and then select "See what's printing."

If the printer isn't configured on your computer, you can manage the printer remotely by completing these steps:

1. Click Start and then click Network.
2. Double-click the computer sharing the printer.
3. Double-click the printer.

You can now manage print jobs for the selected printer using the print management window shown in Figure 12-20. The print management window provides details about documents being printed or waiting to print on the selected printer. These details include:

Document Name

> Shows the name of the application that printed the document, and the document name.

Status

> The status of the print job. Document status entries you'll see include Printing and Error–Printing.

Owner

> The person who printed the document.

Pages

> The number of pages in the document.

Size

> The document size in kilobytes or megabytes.

Submitted

> The time and date the print job was submitted.

Port

> The port used for printing.

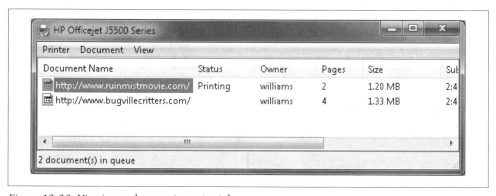

Figure 12-20. Viewing and managing print jobs

You can set the status of individual documents using the Document menu in the print management window. To cancel printing or change the status of a document, follow these steps:

1. Select the document in the print management window.

2. On the Document menu, use one of the following options to change the status of the print job:

   Cancel

   > Cancels printing of the document and removes the print job.

   Pause

   > Puts the document on hold and lets other documents print.

Resume

Resumes printing of a paused document. Printing resumes from where it left off.

Restart

Starts printing the document again from the beginning.

Sometimes when you cancel a print job that's currently printing, the printer might continue to print part of the document or all of it. This can occur because most printers cache documents in an internal buffer and may print the contents of this cache before checking for updates.

Working with Printers

The title bar in the print management window provides details on the status of the printer itself. If printing is paused or the printer is offline, you'll see related status details on the title bar, as shown in Figure 12-21.

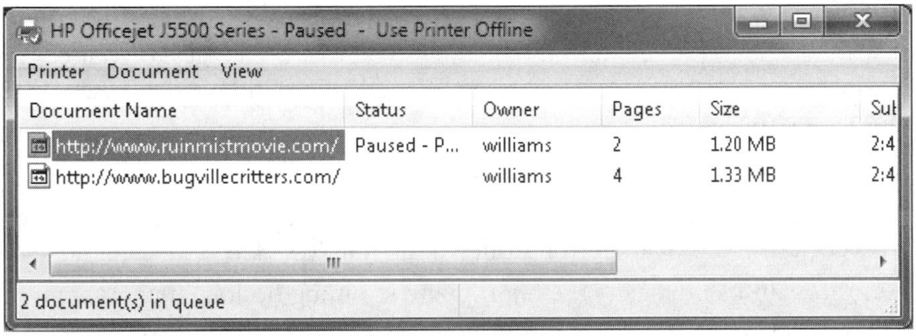

Document Name	Status	Owner	Pages	Size	Sul
http://www.ruinmistmovie.com/	Paused - P...	williams	2	1.20 MB	2:4
http://www.bugvillecritters.com/		williams	4	1.33 MB	2:4

HP Officejet J5500 Series - Paused - Use Printer Offline

Printer   Document   View

2 document(s) in queue

Figure 12-21. Checking the status of the printer as well as print jobs

Before you try to repair or resolve a problem with a printer shared with multiple people, you may want to pause printing. Using the print management window, you do this by selecting the Pause Printing option from the Printer menu. A checkmark indicates that the option is selected. When you pause printing, the printer completes the current job and then puts all other print jobs on hold. When printing is paused, the printer accepts but does not print new print jobs. To resume printing, select the Pause Printing option a second time. This should remove the checkmark next to the option.

When you have problems with a printer, you may find that many of the print jobs currently waiting to print are simply reprints of the same document or of documents that are no longer needed. In this case, you can use the print management window to empty the print queue and delete all its contents. To do this, select the "Cancel all documents" option from the Printer menu.

In addition to pausing a printer, you can also designate a printer as being offline. Using the print management window, you specify that a printer is offline by selecting the "Use printer offline" option from the Printer menu. A check mark indicates that the option is selected. When the printer is offline, the printer does not accept new print jobs but will print existing jobs waiting to print as long as printing is not paused. To designate that a printer is back online, select the "Use printer offline" option a second time. This should remove the checkmark next to the option.

 If a printer is designated as being both offline and paused, you must clear both to restore normal printing operations.

Working with Scanners and Fax Machines

Unlike printers, scanners and fax machines use helper applications when receiving and sending documents. The default helper application is Windows Fax and Scan.

Scanning images

Most scanners have a menu option that allows you to scan images to your computer, to a memory card, or to an email message. With this in mind, you can scan an image by completing the following steps:

1. Put the image you want to scan on the scanner bed.
2. Click the Scan button on the scanner. This should display a Scan menu. You can also click the New Scan button from within Windows Fax and Scan.
3. On the Scan menu, select the appropriate scanning option, such as Scan to PC, and then press the OK or Start button. If you are scanning from Windows Fax and Scan, select the appropriate options and click the Preview button to preview and select the scanning area, then click Scan to create the final scan.

Managing scanned documents

You can access a scanner management window for your scanner by completing these steps:

1. Click Start→Devices and Printers. In Devices And Printers, double-click the scanner you want to work with. This opens Windows Fax and Scan.
2. To view scans sent to the computer, click Scan in the Navigation pane. As shown in Figure 12-22, scans are listed by date, filename, file type, size, and source.
3. You can preview a scan by selecting it in the Documents list.
4. Use the following options on the toolbar to manage the scan:

Delete
>Deletes the scan from the computer

Forward as Fax
>Forwards the scan as a fax file

Forward as E-mail
>Forwards the scan as an attachment to an email message

Save as
>Saves the scan to a file on your computer

Print
>Prints the scanned document to a printer

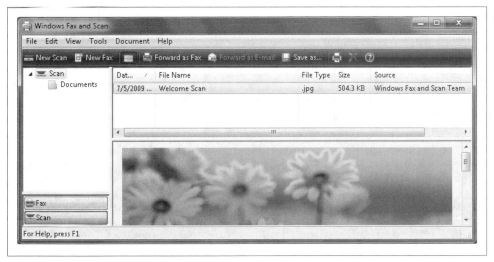

Figure 12-22. Viewing scans sent to the computer

Managing faxed documents

You can access a fax management window for your fax machine by completing these steps:

1. Click Start→Devices and Printers. In Devices and Printers, double-click the scanner you want to work with. This opens Windows Fax and Scan.

2. To view faxes sent or received by the computer, click Fax in the Navigation pane, as shown in Figure 12-23.

3. In the Navigation pane, select one of the following to view related options:

   Incoming
   >Shows incoming faxes that are in the process of being received

Inbox
> Shows incoming faxes that have been received and are waiting for your attention

Drafts
> Shows drafts of faxes that have not been sent

Outbox
> Shows outgoing faxes that are in the process of being sent

Sent Items
> Shows outgoing faxes that have been sent

4. Use the following options on the toolbar to manage faxes:

Delete (shown as an X)
> Deletes the fax from the computer

Forward as Fax (shown as a Fax machine with an arrow)
> Forwards the fax to another fax machine

Forward as E-Mail
> Forwards the fax as an attachment to an email message

Print (shown as a printer)
> Prints the faxed document to a printer

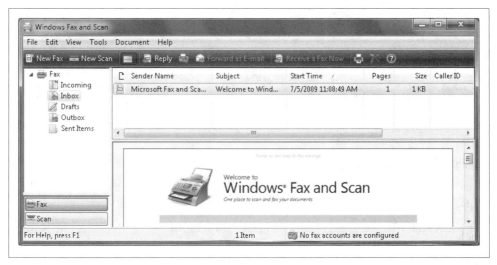

Figure 12-23. Viewing incoming and outgoing scans

You can save a fax as a TIFF image file on your computer by following these steps:

1. In Windows Fax and Scan, select the fax you want to save.
2. Click "Save as" on the File menu.
3. In the "Save as" dialog box, select a save location, type a name for the file, and then click Save.

Receiving faxes

Most fax machines will receive faxes automatically if they are connected to a telephone line. If your computer has a fax card or your fax machine can send you faxes directly, the fax should be received automatically into the Inbox of Windows Fax and Scan. In some cases, you may need to tell your computer to receive the fax. In Windows Fax and Scan, you can answer an incoming phone call and receive a fax by clicking the Receive a Fax Now button on the toolbar.

CHAPTER 13

Making the Most of Windows' Accessories

If you haven't already noticed, let me be the first to tell you that Windows 7 has more accessories than you'll probably ever use. Hidden among all those accessories are some true gems, including the Snipping Tool, a handy utility that you can use to capture screens and windows; Sticky Notes, a scratch pad for creating memos; and Windows Speech Recognition, a program you can use to dictate documents and control programs using your voice and a microphone. You'll find plenty of extras for both laptops and Tablet PCs, too, including the Mobility Center, Pen Flicks, Input Panel, and Windows Journal. You'll also find accessories for making your computer more accessible to the handicapped, including the Ease of Access Center, Magnifier, Narrator, and On-Screen Keyboard.

Capturing Screens and Windows with the Snipping Tool

One of my favorite accessories is the Snipping Tool, which is included with all editions of Windows 7 except Starter. The Snipping Tool captures any screen elements that you select, including text and images. A captured element is referred to as a snip, and you can insert snips easily into documents and email messages.

Creating Snips

You can open the Snipping Tool by clicking Start→All Programs→Accessories→selecting Snipping Tool. The Snipping Tool starts in New Snip mode, which is the mode for capturing snips. The Snipping Tool has four capture modes:

Free-form Snip
> In this mode, you outline the area that you want to snip by drawing freehand around it. You capture a snip in this mode by clicking and then dragging to outline the area you want to capture.

Rectangular Snip
> In this mode, you outline the area that you want to snip by drawing a rectangle around it. You capture a snip in this mode by clicking and then dragging around the area that you want to capture.

Window Snip
> In this mode, you capture an entire window as a snip. You capture a snip in this mode by moving the mouse pointer over the window that you want to capture, and then clicking.

Full-screen Snip
> In this mode, you capture the full screen as a snip. When you select this mode, the full screen is captured automatically.

Figure 13-1 shows the Snipping Tool in New Snip mode. From left to right, the buttons on the toolbar are used as follows:

New
> Starts a new capture using the default mode or the last capture mode you used.

Capture Options
> A downward-pointing triangle to the right of the New button that sets the capture mode.

Cancel
> Cancels the current capture.

Options
> Sets capture options.

Figure 13-1. Using the Snipping Tool to capture windows and screens

You can capture a snip by following these steps:

1. Click Start, click All Programs→Accessories→Snipping Tool. The Snipping Tool is displayed in the foreground, and the rest of the screen is lightened automatically to make it easier to distinguish the Snipping Tool interface elements from the background elements you are capturing.

2. Click the Capture Options button and select the capture mode you want to use.

3. Capture your snip. As Figure 13-2 shows, you capture a rectangular snip by clicking and then dragging around the area that you want to capture.

Figure 13-2. Selecting your snip area by clicking and dragging to highlight the area to copy

4. When you release the mouse button, the Snipping Tool captures the snip and shows the editing view. You can then use the editing view to edit the snip, as discussed in the next section.

Editing and Saving Your Snips

After you've captured a snip, the Snipping Tool window changes to Edit Mode. In this mode, you can mark up a snip by using the pen, highlighter, or eraser tool. By default, snips you capture of the desktop are formatted using the Portable Network Graphics (PNG) format and snips you capture within a web browser are formatted using the single-file HTML (MHT) format. The MHT format is used for browser snips because the web page URL is included below the snip by default. You also can save snips as JPEG or GIF image files so that the entire snip is handled as a single picture.

Figure 13-3 shows the Snipping Tool in Edit Mode. From left to right, the buttons on the toolbar are used as follows:

New Snip
> Switches to New Snip Mode and discards the current snip. If you click New Snip before saving a snip, the current snip is lost.

Save As

Allows you to save the current snip as a single-file HTML document or as a JPEG, PNG, or GIF image.

Copy

Copies the current version of the snip to the Windows clipboard. You can then paste it into documents or email messages using Ctrl-V.

Send Snip

Allows you to send the snip to someone in an email message. Click the Send Snip Options button to see additional send options, such as "Send to e-mail recipient (as attachment)."

Pen

Selects the pen so that you can use it to add notes to the snip. Obviously, this feature works best when you have a pen input device. If you click the Pen Options button, you can set the pen color. The default pen color is blue. To change the ink thickness, change the pen tip type. To select a custom color, click the Customize option.

Highlighter

Selects the highlighter so that you can use it to highlight areas of the snip.

Eraser

Allows you to erase pen ink and highlights by clicking on them.

After you edit your snip, you can copy it to the clipboard by clicking Copy and then paste it into a document or email message by accessing the document or message and then pressing Ctrl-V. To save your snip to a file, click Save As. In the Save As dialog box, type a filename for the snip, use the "Save as type" list to select the file type, such as JPEG or PNG, and then click Save.

Setting Snipping Options

By default, any snips you capture are copied to the Windows clipboard as well as to the Snipping Tool. This allows you to paste snips into programs that support images simply by pressing Ctrl-V. Other default options are used to prompt you to save snips before exiting, show a screen overlay when the Snipping Tool is active, and to include web page URLs when you capture snips from web pages.

Any snips you capture can have a thick red selection line around them. The selection line is meant to help you distinguish snips from other content if you later add the snips to other documents. You can change the color of the line, start or stop using the selection line by following these steps:

1. In the Snipping Tool, click Tools and then click Options. This opens the Snipping Tool Options dialog box, shown in Figure 13-4.

2. To set the ink color for the selection line, click the "Ink color" list and then choose the color to use.

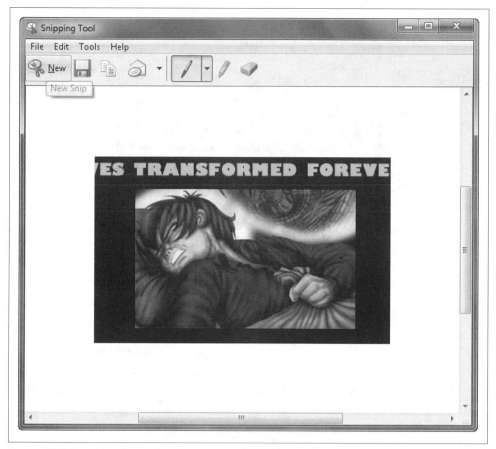

Figure 13-3. Editing your snip

3. To start or stop using the selection line, select or clear the "Show selection ink after snips are captured" checkbox as appropriate.

4. Click OK.

Creating Sticky Notes

Sticky Notes provides a scratch pad for creating memos. Because any sticky notes you create remain on the desktop until you delete them, you don't have to worry about losing notes when you log off or shut down your computer. Sticky Notes is not included in Starter editions of Windows 7.

You can start Sticky Notes by clicking Start→All Programs→Accessories, and then selecting Sticky Notes. As shown in Figure 13-5, Sticky Notes gives you a scratch pad on which you can write notes using the keyboard (or a stylus on a tablet PC). You can

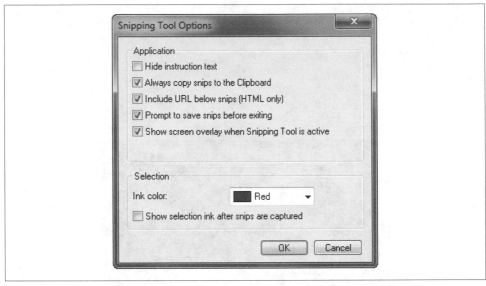

Figure 13-4. Setting snipping options

create a new note by clicking the New Note (+) button or pressing Ctrl-N. To modify a note, click the sticky note to select it and then enter the changes.

As you add notes, the number of sticky notes on your desktop grows. You can copy the contents of a note and insert it into a word processing document by following these steps:

1. Click the sticky note to select.
2. Press Ctrl-A and then press Ctrl-C to select and then copy all the text in the note.
3. In your word processing document, press Ctrl-V to insert the note.

If you no longer want a sticky note, click the note and then click the Delete button (the red X) on the toolbar. Confirm the action by clicking Yes.

Getting Your Computer to Listen

If you hear someone talking to his computer, odds are he's not going crazy—he's using Windows 7's built-in speech recognition software to take his computing experience to the next level. Speech recognition software allows you to dictate documents and email messages. It also allows you to browse the Web and navigate program menus using voice controls. Not only does this allow you to create documents quickly and perform common tasks, but it can also reduce the risk of repetitive stress injuries.

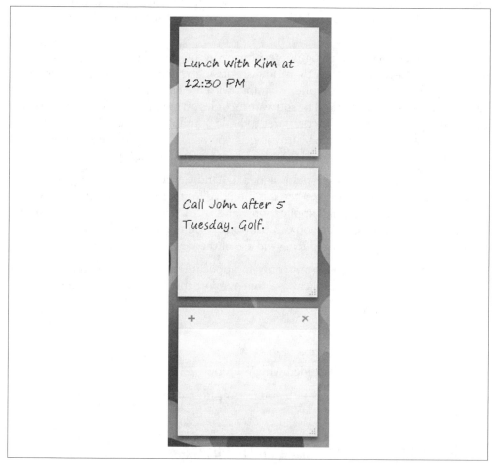

Figure 13-5. Creating written memos

Getting Started with Speech Recognition

You can access Windows 7's speech recognition software by clicking Start→All Programs→Accessories→Ease of Access→Windows Speech Recognition. However, before you do this, you should take a moment to learn more about this powerful feature.

Speech recognition allows you to control your computer by speaking into a microphone. When you talk, the software uses context-sensitive controls to determine whether to convert your words to text, as with dictation, or to navigate program menus, as with control commands. Generally, when you use speech recognition, Windows 7 enters your dictation text into the current active document and your control commands are used to navigate the current active program's menus.

Speech recognition works best when you use a quality microphone, such as a USB headset microphone or an array microphone. The environment in which you use the microphone should be relatively quiet. If it isn't, you may find that background noise is interpreted as spoken speech. A microphone with noise cancellation technology may resolve this problem.

Having started with speech recognition software in the early days of Dragon Dictate, I found the built-in software easy to use and surprisingly reliable. The software provides enhanced user interfaces that offer a simple yet efficient way to dictate text, make changes, and correct mistakes. The software includes an interactive tutorial that teaches you while you are training the computer to understand your voice. The software also improves in accuracy over time by learning as you use it, and by prompting for clarification when you give a command that can be interpreted in multiple ways.

Windows Speech Recognition isn't designed to handle every type of writing or to work with every type of application. Rather, it is intended for those who frequently use word-processing applications, email applications, and web browsers. By using speech recognition with these programs, you can use your voice to enter text and perform commands, thereby significantly reducing the use of the keyboard and mouse.

Speech recognition dictation works only in applications that support the Microsoft Text Services Framework. Applications that support this framework include:

- Microsoft Office Word
- Microsoft Office Outlook
- Microsoft Internet Explorer
- Nearly all applications included with Windows 7

Speech recognition won't work with applications that don't support the Text Services Framework.

Configuring Speech Recognition for First Use

Before you can use Windows Speech Recognition, you must ensure that your computer has a sound card and that the sound card is properly configured. If your computer does not have a built-in microphone (most portables do), you must then connect a microphone to the computer's microphone jack.

Once you've connected your microphone, ensure that the microphone is enabled and adjust the microphone volume to a proper level before you configure Windows Speech Recognition for first use. Although Windows Speech Recognition will help you set the audio input levels as part of the microphone setup process, the related wizard will not enable your microphone if it is muted and it will not boost the decibel levels of the microphone, which may be required to achieve proper input levels. To ensure that the microphone is ready to be used, follow these steps:

1. Click Start, and then click Control Panel.
2. In the Control Panel, click Hardware and Sound→Sound.

3. In the Sound dialog box, go to the Recording tab and double-click on the microphone you wish to use.

4. On the Levels tab, the Microphone button is used to mute or unmute the microphone. If the microphone is muted, click the button to unmute it, as shown in Figure 13-6.

5. Optionally, use the Microphone slider to set base the input level for the microphone. During the microphone setup process, Windows Speech Recognition will adjust the input levels for you.

6. Use the Microphone Boost slider if you need to boost the input levels for your microphone.

7. Click OK.

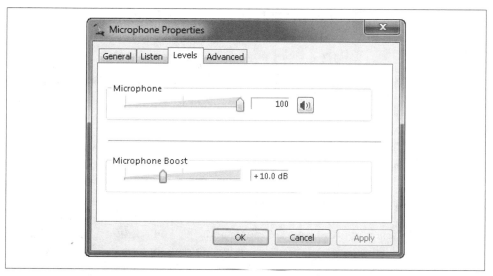

Figure 13-6. Setting the audio input levels for your microphone

To set up the speech software for first use, complete the following steps:

1. Click Start, click All Programs→Accessories.

2. Click Ease of Access→Speech Recognition. This starts the Set up Speech Recognition Wizard.

3. On the Welcome to Speech Recognition page, read the introductory text and then click Next.

4. On the "What type of microphone is Microphone" page, shown in Figure 13-7, select the type of microphone you are using. If you are using a portable PC with a built-in microphone, select Other as the microphone type.

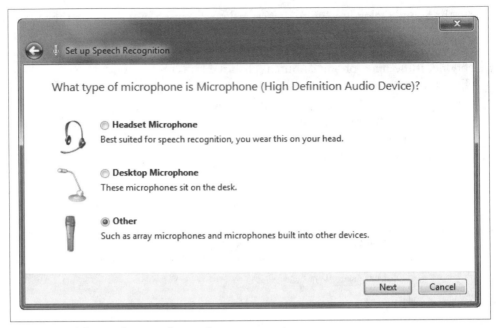

Figure 13-7. Selecting the type of microphone you are using

5. On the "Set up your microphone" page, follow the instructions for setting up and positioning your microphone. Different directions are provided for each type of microphone. Click Next.

6. On the "Adjust the volume of Microphone" page, shown in Figure 13-8, read the sample text aloud into your microphone. Ensure that you are positioned where you will be when you use your computer and that you speak in a natural voice. Your voice will be used to automatically adjust the microphone volume if the levels are too low or too high.

7. Click Next twice. On the "Improve speech recognition accuracy" page, specify whether the speech recognition software should scan your documents and email messages to learn the words and phrases you use. If you want to enable this feature, click "Enable document review." Otherwise, click "Disable document review" to turn off this feature. Click Next.

8. On the "Choose an activation mode" page, specify how the speech recognition software is activated after you say "stop listening." To activate the software by clicking the Microphone button or by pressing the Ctrl-Windows keys, select "Use manual activation mode." To activate the software by saying "start listening," select "Use voice activation mode."

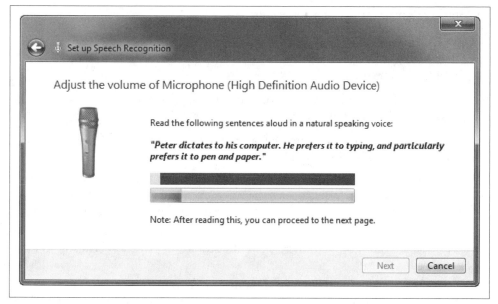

Figure 13-8. Reading the sample to check the input levels

The Microphone button is displayed on the Speech Recognition toolbar. By default, this toolbar is docked at the top of the screen. You can undock the toolbar by clicking and dragging it to a new location. If you click the toolbar's Minimize button, the toolbar is minimized to the Notification area of the taskbar.

You can rerun microphone setup by right-clicking on the speech recognition toolbar and selecting Configuration→"Set up my microphone."

9. On the "Print the speech reference card" page, click "View reference sheet." In Windows Help and Support, click Print to print out the reference sheet.

10. Click Next. By default, the speech recognition software will run each time you start your computer. If you'd rather start the software yourself, clear the "Run Speech Recognition at Startup" checkbox.

11. Click Next and then click Start Tutorial. Follow the prompts and work your way through the tutorial. While you are learning about speech recognition, Windows Speech Recognition will also train the computer to recognize your voice. The tutorial requires a minimum resolution of 1,024 × 768.

Using Speech Recognition for Dictation

The most common way you'll use speech recognition is for dictating documents. You dictate documents by following these general steps:

1. Start your word-processing application.
2. Create a new document or open an existing document.
3. Dictate the document.
4. Save the document.

In Microsoft Office Word or WordPad, you can use speech recognition to perform these tasks by following these steps:

1. If speech recognition is not running, start it. Click Start→All Programs→Accessories→Ease of Access→Speech Recognition.
2. The way the software starts depends on the activation mode you selected. With automatic activation, you can start the software by saying "start listening." With manual activation, you can start the software by clicking the Microphone button or by pressing the Ctrl-Windows keys.
3. Say "open Word" to open Microsoft Office Word or "open WordPad" to open WordPad.
4. Start dictating. Use the spoken-word commands for punctuation marks and special characters as necessary. For example, to insert a comma, you say "comma." To end a sentence with a period, you say "period."
5. To correct mistakes, say "correct" and the word that the computer typed by mistake. Select the correct word from the list offered, or say the correct word again. For example, if the computer misrecognized days as daze, say "correct daze," and then select the right word from the list or say the word "days" again.
6. The way you save the document depends on the program you are using:
   • To save the document using Office Word 2003 or WordPad, say "file," say "save as," and then say the name of the document, such as "My Shopping List." Finish by saying "save."
   • To save the document using Office Word 2007 or later, say "Office button," say "save as," and then say the name of the document, such as "My Shopping List." Finish by saying "save."

Using Laptop and Tablet PC Extras

All laptop computers include the Mobility Center for optimizing laptop settings. When you are working with laptops, you may also need to connect to a network projector, and there's an option for this, too. When you are working with Tablet PCs, you'll find even more accessories, including tools for configuring Tablet PC pens, Input Panel for entering text using a pen, and Windows Journal for creating journal entries using a pen.

Tablet PC extras are provided as Windows features that you can turn on and off. Click Start→Control Panel→Programs→"Turn on or off Windows features." This displays the Windows Features dialog box. Select or clear Tablet PC Optional Components as appropriate, and then click OK.

Navigating the Windows Mobility Center

The Windows Mobility Center provides a central console for accessing the most commonly used mobile PC settings. On a laptop or Tablet PC, you can access the Mobility Center by right-clicking the Power icon in the taskbar's notification area and then selecting Windows Mobility Center. However, if you've disabled the display of the Power icon, you won't be able to access it on the taskbar. Instead, click Start→Control Panel→Hardware and Sound→Mobility Center.

As Figure 13-9 shows, each configurable mobile PC setting is managed through a separate *control tile*. Generally, control tiles allow you to make direct adjustments to your mobile PC settings by using available options such as a toggle button to turn presentation settings on and off, or a slider to adjust the brightness of the screen.

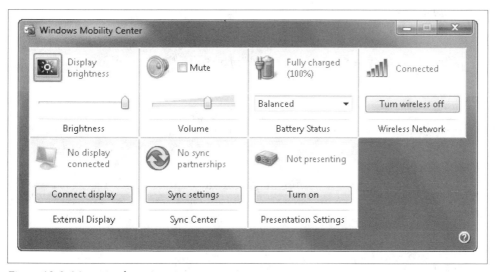

Figure 13-9. Managing laptop settings

The control tiles available depend on the type of mobile PC and the mobile PC manufacturer. Typically, laptops have seven standard control tiles and Tablet PCs have either seven or eight standard control tiles. The most common control tiles are:

Brightness

Displays the current brightness setting. If brightness is configurable on your computer, you can use the slider provided to adjust the brightness of the display. Click the Display icon to edit the settings of the currently selected power plan.

Volume

Displays the current volume setting. If volume is configurable on your computer, you can use the slider provided to adjust the volume. Click the Speaker icon to access the Sound dialog box.

Battery Status

Displays the status of the computer's battery. You can use the selection list provided to change quickly from one power plan to another. If you've created custom power plans, these are available as well. Click the Battery icon to access the Power Options page in the Control Panel.

Wireless Network

Displays the status of your wireless network connection. Click "Turn wireless on" to enable your wireless connection for use. Click "Turn wireless off" to disable wireless networking. Click the Wireless Networking icon to display the Network Connections dialog box.

External Display

Provides options for connecting a secondary display to give a presentation. If a secondary display is available and you've connected the cables, you can click "Connect display" to connect to the display. Click the Display icon to access the Screen Resolution page in the Control Panel.

Sync Center

Displays the status of file synchronization. Click Sync to start a new sync using Sync Center. Click the "Sync settings" button or the Sync icon to access Sync Center.

Presentation Settings

Displays whether you are in presentation mode. In presentation mode, the display and hard disk do not go into sleep mode due to inactivity. Click "Turn on" to enter presentation mode. Click the Projector icon to access the Presentation Settings dialog box.

Tablet Display

Displays the current display orientation. Click "Change orientation" to change from landscape to portrait display or vice versa. (Tablet PC only)

If your mobile PC includes other control tiles, these were probably provided by the PC manufacturer. You can learn more about these control tiles from the documentation that came with your mobile PC, or by visiting the manufacturer's website.

Connecting to Projectors

Before you use your laptop or Tablet PC for presentations, you may want to configure the default presentation settings (Figure 13-10). To do this, follow these steps:

1. In Windows Mobility Center, click the Presentation icon.
2. In the Presentation Settings dialog box, select "Turn off the screen saver" to disable the computer's screen saver when you are giving a presentation.
3. To override the output volume when you are giving a presentation, select "Set the volume to" and then use the related slider to set the desired volume level.
4. To show an alternative desktop background, select "Show this background" and then select a background image to use. Images from your Pictures library are listed and available for selection by default. Choose None to display a black background. Click Browse to select a different background.
5. Click OK to save your settings.

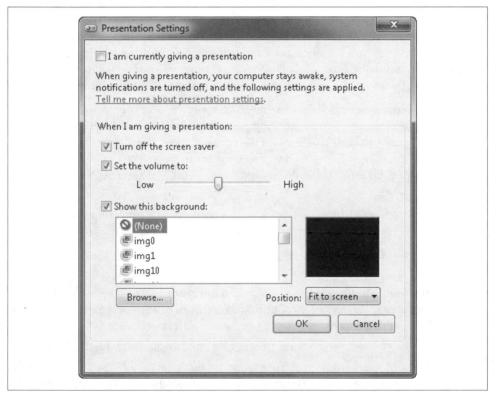

Figure 13-10. Configuring presentation settings

Basic projectors connect to computers via a cable. To use this type of projector, you must connect the projector cable to your laptop or Tablet PC. Once you've connected the cable, you can connect your computer to the projector by completing the following steps:

1. To use the presentation settings you specified previously, access Windows Mobility Center and then click Turn On in the Presentation Settings control.

2. Click Start→All Programs→Accessories→Connect to a Projector. You can also use the keyboard shortcut Windows-P.

3. Select one of the following output options for the display:
   - Select Duplicate to duplicate the computer's display to the projector.
   - Select Extend to extend the computer's display to the projector.
   - Select "Projector only" to show the computer's display on the projector only.

4. Your computer's display is configured per your selection. Typically, Windows will resize the computer screen automatically, using a resolution that is appropriate for use with projectors.

5. When you are done with your presentation, click Start→All Programs→Accessories→Connect to a Projector or press Windows-P. In the Connect to a Projector dialog box, select Disconnect Projector. Your computer will disconnect from the projector and also will stop using the presentation settings.

At the office, you may find that your meeting rooms and conference centers have networked projectors set up for use during presentations. To use this type of projector, you must connect your laptop or Tablet PC to the LAN and then connect to the project over the network. In most cases, connecting your computer to the network is as simple as plugging in an Ethernet cable or ensuring that you are using the correct wireless network connection.

Once you are connected to the network in the conference or meeting room you are using, you can connect to the networked projector by completing the following steps:

1. Click Start→All Programs→Accessories→Connect to a Network Projector.

2. The first time you use a network projector with your laptop, you'll see a warning prompt about Windows Firewall, as shown in Figure 13-11. To use the projector, you must allow Windows 7 to communicate through Windows Firewall, so click "Allow the network projector to communicate with my computer."

3. Specify how you want to connect to the projector, as shown in Figure 13-12.

4. If you want to select from projectors found on the local network, click "Search for a projector." The wizard searches for projectors on the network and returns its results along with a list of any projectors you've used recently. Click the projector you want to use, provide the access password for the projector if necessary, and then click Connect.

5. If you know the network address of the projector, click "Enter the projector network address." On the "Enter the network address of a projector" page, shown in Figure 13-13, type the network address of the projector, such as *http://intranet.the-office.local/projectors/projector4*. Enter any required access password, and then click Connect.

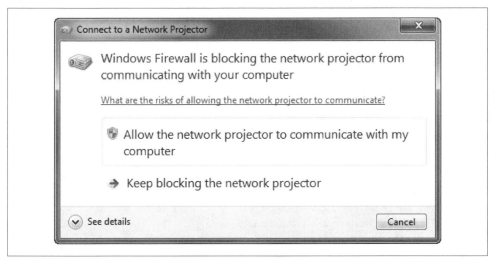

Figure 13-11. Allowing your computer to communicate with the projector

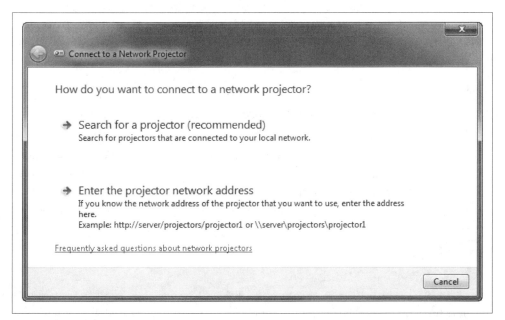

Figure 13-12. Selecting a connection option

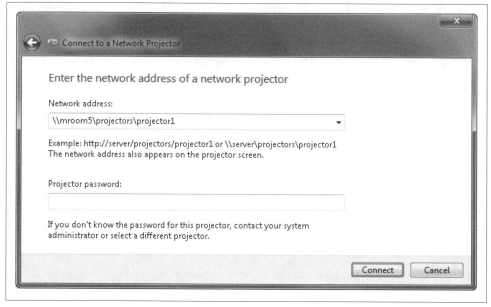

Figure 13-13. Entering the projector address and password

Using Your Tablet PC Pen

Tablet PCs use pens as input devices. You can use pens for writing as well as for interacting with items on the screen by tapping and flicking. To ensure that your Tablet PC recognizes your tapping and flicking actions, you should take a few minutes to configure the related options.

Tapping your pen

Pen taps allow you to perform actions equivalent to using a mouse. You can perform the following actions:

- Double-tapping the pen on the screen is equivalent to a double-click mouse action.
- Pressing and holding the pen to the screen is equivalent to a right-click mouse action, or pressing the pen button to perform a right-click.
- On some Tablet PC pens, you can grip the top of the pen to erase ink from the screen.

You can set pen tap options by following these steps:

1. Click Start→Control Panel.
2. In the Control Panel, click Hardware and Sound, scroll down, and then click Pen and Input Devices. This displays the Pen and Input Devices dialog box with the Pen Options tab selected.

3. To configure double-tapping, click "Double-tap" in the "Pen action" section and then click Settings. You can then adjust how quickly you can tap the screen and the distance the pointer can move between tapping. Use the test area provided to test your settings. Fine-tune your settings as necessary and then click OK.

4. To configure pressing and holding, click "Press and hold" in the "Pen action" section and then click Settings. You can then change the amount of time you must press and hold the pen to the screen to perform the equivalent of a right-click, and the amount of time to perform the right-click action. Use the test area provided to test your settings. Fine-tune your settings as necessary and then click OK.

5. To open Input Panel automatically when you move the pen quickly from side to side while it is positioned slightly above the screen, click Start Tablet PC Input Panel in the "Pen action" section and then click Settings. Select the "Enable start input panel gesture" checkbox. Use the slider to specify the relative distance you must move the pen from side to side, and then click OK.

6. To allow clicking the pen button to be used as a right-click equivalent, select the "Use the pen button as a right-click equivalent" checkbox.

7. To allow erasing ink by gripping the top of the pen (if supported) select the "Use the top of the pen to erase ink" checkbox.

8. Click OK to save the settings.

Each tapping action of the pen is accompanied by some type of visual feedback. To view or change visual feedback options, follow these steps:

1. Click Start→Control Panel→Hardware and Sound, scroll down, and then click Pen and Input Devices.

2. In the Pen and Input Devices dialog box, click the Pointer Options tab.

3. A different type of visual feedback is provided for each pen tap action. If you don't want to see visual feedback for a tap action, clear the related checkbox.

4. If you don't want pen cursors to be shown instead of mouse cursors when you use the pen, clear the "Show pen cursors instead of mouse cursors when I use my pen" checkbox.

5. Click OK to save the settings.

Flicking your pen

Pen flicks allow you to perform navigation and editing actions by flicking the pen in a specific direction. Only navigational flicks are enabled by default.

The navigational flicks are as follows:

- Flick left to go back—equivalent to clicking the Back button in Windows Explorer or Internet Explorer.

- Flick right to go forward—equivalent to clicking the Forward button in Windows Explorer or Internet Explorer.

- Flick up to drag up—equivalent to dragging a selected item up or to using a scroll-bar to scroll up the page in an extended document or the browser window.
- Flick down to drag down—equivalent to dragging a selected item down or to using a scrollbar to scroll down the page in an extended document or the browse window.

The editing flicks you can enable are as follows:

- Flick up and to the right to copy a selected item to the clipboard.
- Flick down and to the right to paste a previously selected item into a document or email message.
- Flick up and to the left to delete a selected item.
- Flick down and to the left to undo a previous action.

You can set pen flick options by following these steps:

1. Click Start→Control Panel→Hardware and Sound, scroll down, and then click Pen and Input Devices.
2. In the Pen and Input Devices dialog box, select the Flicks tab.
3. To enable flicks, select the "Use flicks to perform common actions quickly and easily" checkbox. Clear this checkbox to disable flicks.
4. When flicks are enabled, use the options provided to enable only navigational flicks or both navigational and editing flicks.
5. If you've enabled both navigational and editing flicks, you can click Customize to define alternative actions for each possible pen flick. Any alternative actions override the default actions.
6. Use the Sensitivity slider to adjust how easily pen flicks are recognized. In most cases, you'll want the sensitivity to be midway between Relaxed and Precise. However, if you are having issues with accidental flicks, you may want to use a more precise setting.
7. Click OK to save the settings.

Writing with your Tablet PC pen

When you are using a Tablet PC, you can enter text using the Tablet PC pen and a utility program called Input Panel. Input Panel converts to typed text any handwriting you enter using the pen, and it supports AutoComplete, Back-of-Pen Erase, and scratch-out gestures.

On a Tablet PC, the Input Panel icon is displayed next to text entry areas in programs that accept handwriting input from a Tablet PC pen. With Microsoft Office Word, Windows Mail, and other Windows programs, this allows you to display Input Panel by tapping the icon. You can then use the pen to write and insert the converted text by clicking the Insert button. In Input Panel, the Insert button is displayed below and to the right of your converted text. You can also start Input Panel by selecting Start→All Programs→Accessories→Tablet PC, and then selecting Tablet PC Input Panel.

Input Panel has changed in several ways since it was introduced with Microsoft Windows XP Tablet PC Edition. When you run Input Panel, it appears as a tab on the left side of the screen. To open Input Panel, move the mouse pointer over the tab and then click to slide Input Panel out from the edge of the screen. Clicking the Close button hides Input Panel.

By default, Input Panel floats in a separate window. You can move Input Panel by dragging it to a desired position or by docking it at the top or bottom of the screen. If you then hide Input Panel, it will slide out from the same location the next time you open it. The Input Panel tab on the side of your screen remains available even if the program you are using is running in full-screen mode.

Input Panel has two input modes:

Writing Pad Mode

Use this mode, shown in Figure 13-14, when you want to write continuously with the pen as though you are writing on a lined sheet of paper. Each word you write is converted to text separately and then displayed. If you click the word, you can correct letter case, change punctuation around the word, modify the letters, or delete letters. The buttons on the right provide quick access to common functions. Click Num to display the number pad, which contains the digits 0 through 9 and arithmetic symbols. Click Sym to display the symbols pad, which contains options for the most commonly used characters. Click Web to display the web pad, which contains character shortcut options for entering URLs.

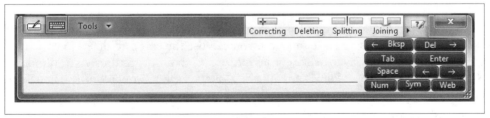

Figure 13-14. The writing pad

On-Screen Keyboard Mode

Use this mode, shown in Figure 13-15, to display an onscreen keyboard that allows you to use pen taps to select characters, press function keys, or click a special-purpose key, such as Home, Page Up, or Insert. To use the function keys, you must first tap the Fn key. Also, note that the Ctrl, Windows, and Alt keys are provided, allowing you to enter keystroke combinations, such as Ctrl-Alt-Delete, by tapping each required key. Between the right Alt key and the right Ctrl key, you'll find a properties button. Clicking this button is the equivalent of right-clicking and selecting Properties in the active window.

Figure 13-15. The onscreen keyboard

With Input Panel, AutoComplete works much like AutoComplete in other Microsoft programs. As you enter text, AutoComplete lists possible matches based on items that you've entered before. If an item in the list matches the text that you want to enter, simply tap the suggestion to enter it in the text entry area.

You can enable and disable AutoComplete and other Input Panel options by following these steps:

1. In Input Panel, click Tools, and then click Options. This opens the Options dialog box shown in Figure 13-16.

2. On the Text Completion tab, select or clear the "Suggest matches in Input Panel when possible..." checkbox as appropriate.

3. Optionally, select or clear the "Show text prediction alternates..." checkbox as appropriate.

4. Click OK.

Back-of-Pen Erase allows Input Panel to support Tablet PC pens that have erasers. If the Tablet PC pen has an erase function, you can use the eraser to delete entries from Input Panel. Another way to delete entries is to use scratch-out gestures. As in Windows XP, the Windows 7 Input Panel supports the Z-shaped scratch-out gesture. If you draw a Z over an entry or a series of entries, the entry or entries are deleted.

Windows 7 supports these scratch-out gestures as well:

Strikethrough scratch-out
    Delete entries by drawing a horizontal line across an entry or a series of entries. You can draw the horizontal line from right to left or left to right.

Angled scratch-out
    Delete entries by drawing a line at an angle across an entry or a series of entries. You can draw the line at an angle from the upper right to the lower left or from the upper left to the lower right.

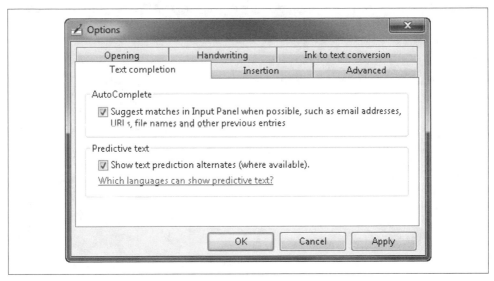

Figure 13-16. Configuring Input Panel options

Vertical scratch-out

Delete entries by drawing an M or a W from right to left over an entry or a series of entries. The M or W should be larger than the entries you are deleting.

Circular scratch-out

Delete entries by drawing a circle over an entry or a series of entries. You can draw the circle around or within the entries.

Creating a Windows Journal

Another Tablet PC extra is Windows Journal. Windows Journal gives you a virtual journal that you can use with the Tablet PC pen in much the same way you would use a stationery pad and an ink pen. You may prefer Windows Journal to Sticky Notes when you are writing longer notes and memos with the Tablet PC pen.

You can open Windows Journal by clicking Start→All Programs→Accessories→Tablet PC, and then selecting Windows Journal. The first time you start Windows Journal you'll be prompted to install the Journal Note Writer print driver. When prompted, click Install to allow Windows 7 to install the driver. When Windows 7 finishes installing the driver, click Close. By installing the driver, you ensure that you can navigate, print, annotate, and share your journal.

As shown in Figure 13-17, the Windows Journal main window looks like a notepad with lined paper, and you can use the Tablet PC pen to write your notes directly on the paper. Using Windows Journal is similar to using Sticky Notes. Your journal can have a stack of pages just like a real journal. When a journal has multiple pages, you can

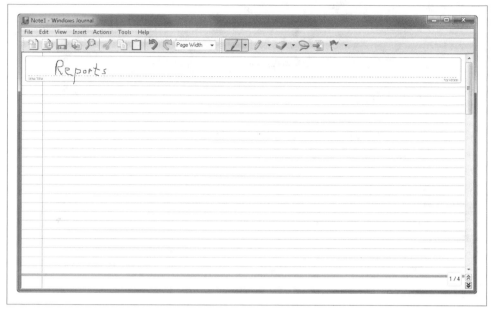

Figure 13-17. Creating a journal to take notes

navigate pages by clicking and dragging the scroll bar down and up. Beneath the scroll bar are several buttons:

Previous

   Displays the previous page. You can also display the previous page by pressing Page Up on the keyboard. If you're on the first page of the journal, this button is dimmed.

Next

   Displays the next page. You can also display the next page by pressing Page Down on the keyboard. If you're on the last page of the journal, this button is replaced by the New Page button.

New Page

   Creates a new page. This button works only if you're on the last page of the journal and you've written on the page.

Using the pen, you can convert handwriting to text, edit converted text, and copy converted text to the clipboard. This allows you to use handwriting entered into Windows Journal as text in other programs. To copy handwriting as text and edit it, follow these steps:

1. Click the Selection Tool button on the toolbar or choose Selection Tool on the Edit menu.

2. Press and hold the pen to the screen.

3. Drag the pen around the handwriting you want to select.

4. Right-click the selection and then choose Copy as Text. Windows Journal converts the handwriting to text automatically and then displays the Copy as Text dialog box, as shown in Figure 13-18.

5. In the Copy as Text dialog box, optionally tap any word or character that you want to correct and then choose a replacement from the Alternative list as necessary.

6. Click Copy to copy the text to the clipboard.

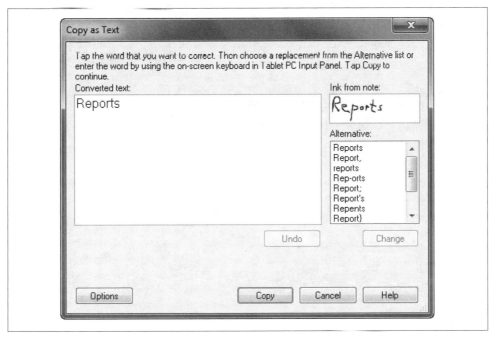

Figure 13-18. Copying handwriting as text

When working with Windows Journal, you might also want to insert a page before the current page. To insert a page before the current page, click New Page on the Insert menu. The Insert menu also has options for inserting text boxes, flags, and pictures. You use a text box to insert typed text. You use a flag to mark a part of the journal with a flag icon. To insert a picture, follow these steps:

1. In Windows Journal, click Insert and then click Picture.

2. In the Insert Picture dialog box, select the picture to insert and then click Insert. Pictures can be in JPEG, GIF, PNG, WMF, EMF, or BMP format.

3. The selected picture is inserted into the journal and selected so that you can click it and drag it within the journal.

4. After you drag the picture to the desired location, you can drop the picture in that location by clicking another part of the journal.

5. If you later want to move the picture, choose the Selection Tool option on the Edit menu and then click the picture to select it. You can then drag and drop the picture in a new location.

Windows Journal uses a college-ruled notepad as the default stationery style. You can change to other stationery as well. To do this, follow these steps:

1. In Windows Journal, click Options on the Tools menu.

2. On the Stationery panel, make sure that the Stationery option is selected, and then click Default Page Setup.

3. In the Default Page Setup dialog box, click the Style tab, as shown in Figure 13-19.

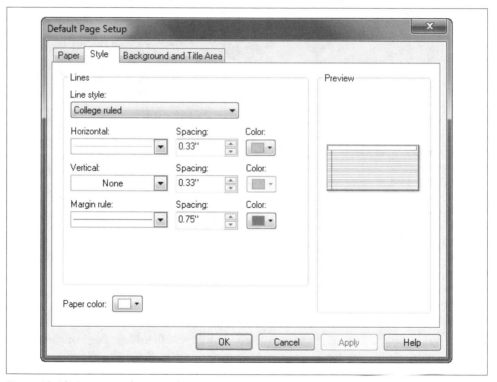

Figure 13-19. Setting up the journal pages

4. Use the "Line style" list to choose the style to use. Options include Standard ruled, Narrow ruled, College ruled, Wide ruled, Large grid, Small grid, and Blank.

5. Use the Horizontal list to select the style for horizontal lines on the paper and the related Color list to select a line color.

6. Use the Vertical list to select the style for vertical lines on the paper and the related Color list to select a line color.

7. Use the "Margin rule" list to select the style for margin rule lines on the paper and the related Color list to select a line color.

8. Use the "Paper color" list to select a background color for the paper.

9. Click OK twice.

 This change affects new notes you create with File→New Note. To change the settings for your current journal note, go to File→Page Setup and make these changes there instead.

Making Your Computer More Accessible

Windows 7's accessibility tools are designed mainly to help users who have some form of visual or motor impairment. And users without such impairments can sometimes benefit from using them as well.

Using the Ease of Access Center

In Windows 7, all accessibility tools are accessible from the Ease of Access page in the Control Panel. To display this page, as shown in Figure 13-20, click Start, click Control Panel, click Ease of Access, and then click Ease of Access Center. You can also use the keyboard shortcut Windows-U. The Ease of Access page has three main areas:

Quick access to common tools
Use these options to turn common accessibility features on and off. These features include High Contrast, Narrator, Magnifier, and On-Screen Keyboard utilities. By default, Windows 7 uses the Narrator feature to read these options aloud and automatically highlights each option in turn. When an option is highlighted, you can press the Space bar to select it.

Get recommendations...
When you click the "Get recommendations..." link, Windows 7 starts a Recommendation Wizard that is similar to, but more intuitive than, the Accessibility Wizard in Windows XP. The five questions in this Recommendation Wizard are designed to help Windows 7 determine and suggest the best accessibility options for you to use.

Explore all settings
If you don't want to use the Recommendation Wizard, you can use the additional options provided to find related settings that might improve accessibility. You can optimize the computer for the blind, optimize the visual display to make it easier to see, set up alternative input devices, adjust settings for the mouse and keyboard, use text or visual alternatives to sounds, and adjust settings for easier reading and typing.

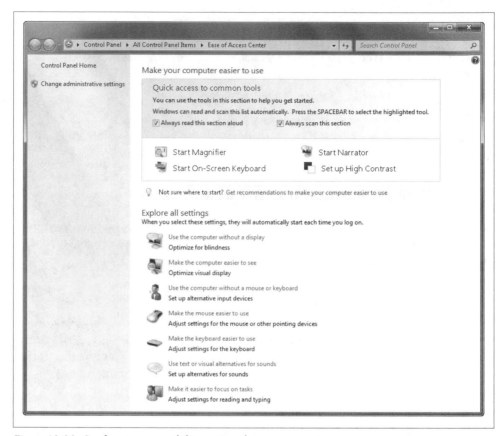

Figure 13-20. Configuring accessibility options for your computer

Using the Magnifier

The Magnifier enlarges part of the screen in a separate window to make it easier for those with limited vision to work with a computer. On an Aero-capable system, Magnifier functions in full-screen mode by default, with a limited viewport on the full screen. Move the cursor around to see other areas of your screen. On a non-Aero system, the Magnifier window is docked at the top of the screen and displays the area around the cursor, the text you are editing, or the focus of the keyboard. You can resize the Magnifier window by moving the mouse pointer over the edge of the window and then dragging the window border. If you move the mouse pointer over the Magnifier window, you can click and drag the window to make it float.

You can turn on and use the Magnifier by completing these steps:

1. Click Start→Control Panel→Ease of Access→Ease of Access Center. (You can also press Windows-U to quickly open the Ease of Access Center.)

2. Click Start Magnifier. As you move the mouse pointer to a desired area of the screen, the current position is shown magnified.

To exit the Magnifier and prevent it from starting automatically, follow these steps:

1. Click the Magnifier taskbar button. This displays a Properties dialog box.
2. Click the Magnifier window and then press Alt-X.

While the Magnifier is running, you can increase magnification by pressing the Windows key and the equals sign (=) key, or decrease magnification by pressing the Windows key and the minus sign (–) key. You can set Magnifier options by completing the following steps:

1. Click the Magnifier taskbar button. This displays a Properties dialog box.
2. Press the + or – button to set the magnification level of the Magnifier window. The default magnification is 200 percent, or twice normal, and you can select a value as high as 1600 percent.
3. To reverse the colors on the screen, click the gear icon and select the "Turn on color inversion" checkbox.
4. By default, the Magnifier is docked at the top of the screen. Click the Views menu to switch between Full Screen, Lens, or Docked mode. Full Screen and Lens requires an Aero-capable computer and Windows 7 edition.
5. When you have finished configuring your settings, click the Magnifier taskbar button again to close the Properties dialog box. Your preferences are remembered each time you start and use the Magnifier.

Using the On-Screen Keyboard

The On-Screen Keyboard is designed to make it easier to use a mouse or an alternative input device for typing. Similar to Input Panel, characters typed on the On-Screen Keyboard are inserted into the current application.

You can turn on the On-Screen Keyboard by completing these steps:

1. Click Start→Control Panel→Ease of Access→Ease of Access Center. (You can also press Windows-U to quickly open the Ease of Access Center.)
2. Click Start On-Screen Keyboard.

To exit the On-Screen Keyboard and prevent it from starting automatically, click File and then click Exit.

When the keyboard is on, as shown in Figure 13-21, use the mouse, pen, or other input device to select characters, press function keys, or click a special-purpose key, such as Home, Page Up, or Insert.

Figure 13-21. Using the On-Screen Keyboard to input text, and pressing keys using a mouse, joystick, or Tablet PC pen

Ctrl, Windows, and Alt keys are provided, allowing you to enter keystroke combinations, such as Ctrl-Alt-Delete, by clicking each required key. Between the right Windows logo key and the right Ctrl key, you'll find a Properties button. Clicking this button is the equivalent of right-clicking and selecting Properties in the active window.

By default, the keyboard is configured to type characters when you click the keys. You can also configure the keyboard to use hovering to select characters or to accept input from a joystick. With hovering, you move the pointer over a character for a specified period, such as 1 second, to select that character. With a joystick, you move the joystick and then click the joystick button when over a character to select that character.

You can configure the way characters are selected by completing the following steps:

1. In the On-Screen Keyboard, click the Options button.
2. In the Options box, shown in Figure 13-22, choose an appropriate typing mode.
3. To click to select a key, choose "Click on keys."
4. To hover to select a key, choose "Hover over keys" and then set the minimum hover time, such as 1.00 seconds.
5. To use a joystick or space bar to select a key, choose "Scan through keys" and then set the interval at which Windows 7 scans for button presses on the joystick or space bar, such as 0.50 seconds.
6. Click OK to save your settings. Your preferences are remembered each time you start and use the On-Screen Keyboard.

Using Narrator

Narrator is a text-to-speech program that reads aloud what is displayed on the screen as you navigate the keyboard. You can use the program to read aloud users' keystrokes, system messages, menu commands, and dialog box options.

You can turn on Narrator by completing these steps:

1. Click Start→Control Panel→Ease of Access→Ease of Access Center. (You can also press Windows-U to quickly open the Ease of Access Center.)
2. Click Start Narrator.

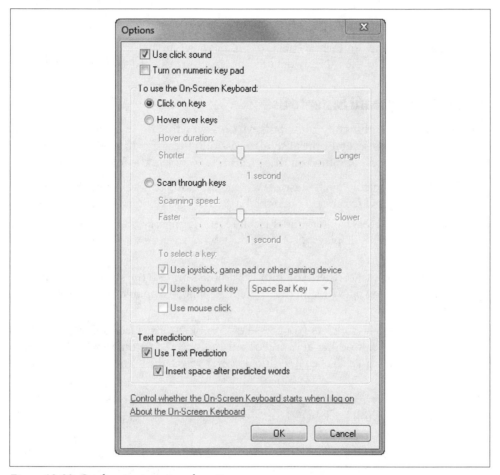

Figure 13-22. Configuring typing mode options

To exit Narrator and prevent it from starting automatically, click File and then click Exit.

Narrator's default voice is Microsoft Anna. You can configure Narrator using the following techniques:

- By clicking the Voice Settings button in the Microsoft Narrator window, you can modify the speed, volume, and pitch of the default voice.

- By default, Narrator echoes user keystrokes and announces system messages. You can also configure it to announce scroll notifications and automatically monitor screen elements. You can use the Preferences menu options to toggle these options on and off.

- By selecting Preferences and then clicking "Background message settings," you can configure whether and when background messages are discarded if they have not been presented to the user. By default, messages are discarded after 30 seconds.

Making the Keyboard Easier to Use

For those who have difficulty pressing keys on keyboards or reading onscreen text, Windows 7 includes several other useful accessibility features to make the keyboard easier to use. To access and turn on these features, complete the following steps:

1. Click Start→Control Panel→Ease of Access→Ease of Access Center. (You can also press Windows-U to quickly open the Ease of Access Center.)

2. In the Ease of Access Center, under Explore All Settings, click "Make the keyboard easier to use." This displays the "Make the keyboard easier to use" page, shown in Figure 13-23.

3. The Mouse Keys feature lets you move the mouse around the screen using the left, right, up, and down arrows on the numeric keypad. To enable Mouse Keys, select the "Turn on Mouse Keys" checkbox.

4. The Sticky Keys feature lets you press key combinations, such as Ctrl-Alt-Delete, one key at a time. Modifier keys are locked and selected automatically if you press them twice in a row. To enable Sticky Keys, select the "Turn on Sticky Keys" checkbox.

5. The Toggle Keys feature plays a warning tone whenever you press the Caps Lock, Num Lock, or Scroll Lock key. To enable Toggle Keys, select the "Turn on Toggle Keys" checkbox.

6. The Filter Keys feature lets you automatically filter unintentional keystrokes. When this feature is enabled, you must press and hold a key for a specific length of time before it is accepted or repeated. To turn on Filter Keys, select the "Turn on Filter Keys" checkbox.

7. Click Save to save and apply your settings.

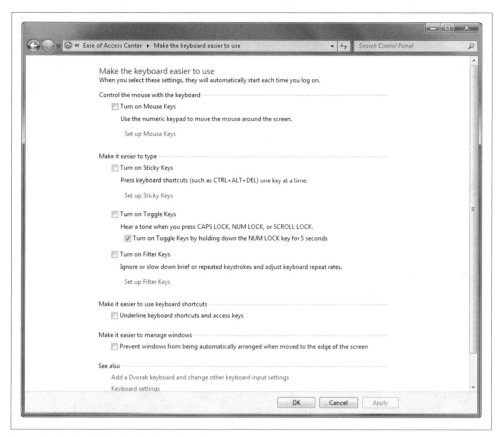

Figure 13-23. Making the keyboard easier to use

PART III

Connecting and Networking

CHAPTER 14

Setting Up Your Network

One of the best features of today's computers is their capability to connect to and communicate with one another over networks. Whether you are working at home, at the office, or away from home, you might want to set up a network, too. Setting up a network allows you to connect your computer to other computers so that you can easily share files, media, and devices. You might also want to set up a network to connect your computer to your Xbox, TiVo, and other devices, such as a network printer.

For Windows 7, Microsoft has introduced new networking tools that replace the tools used in earlier releases of Windows. Although there are many changes, the earlier functionality has remained, and new features have been added. Before diving into the specifics of the new networking features, I'll discuss the essentials of setting up a home or small-business network for use with wired and wireless networks. If you run into problems setting up your networking, see the troubleshooting tips at the end of this chapter.

Understanding Home and Small-Business Networks

With a small investment in time and resources, you can set up a home or small-business network to connect multiple computers and devices together to share files, media, and resources. Unlike a network at a larger organization that uses Active Directory domains, your network will use peer-to-peer networking, with each computer configured as part of the same workgroup or separate workgroups. In a workgroup configuration, member computers can connect to and communicate with one another and with other devices on the network. When you want to access resources on remote computers over the network, you'll need to have a logon account on that computer or other appropriate logon credentials. If other people want to connect to your computer, they'll need a logon account on your computer or other appropriate logon credentials as well.

Requirements for Building a Small Network

Every computer you want to connect to your network requires a *network interface card (NIC)*, also called a *network adapter*. Most computer and motherboard manufacturers include a network adapter on the board, which means that you can probably connect to a network easily, whether you are using a portable computer or a desktop PC, including one you built yourself. You can purchase additional network adapters at any office supply store or computer hardware supplier. Ethernet is the single most common wired network standard in the world, and on desktop machines, integrated network adapters usually fall into this category. All-in-one PCs and portable computers such as notebooks usually include both Ethernet and Wi-Fi adapters. Additional network standards exist, and they work very well with Windows 7, but Ethernet and Wi-Fi have the most use. This chapter discusses Wi-Fi and Ethernet only as network media for shared network resources. Aside from installation and setup differences, Wi-Fi and Ethernet are interchangeable from the perspective of any networked application you use, such as a web browser or email client.

 Although it is possible to skip the network cabling and use only Wi-Fi for your network, this is only recommended for very small networks. Wi-Fi networks, even the fastest ones available, share a limited amount of bandwidth between all devices. As a result, transferring a large file or streaming high-definition video between computers can degrade performance for every user of the network.

It is best to use wired Ethernet for servers, media center devices, desktop computers, and even notebook computers (at least while you're using them at a desk). Wi-Fi is best reserved for notebook computers and handheld devices that need to roam around your home or office.

Networking machines together requires several different items to allow the functionality you desire. Table 14-1 lists the different requirements and functionality of the components available.

Table 14-1. Small-network functionality requirements

Hardware	Internal network	Internet connectivity	Internal network with Internet	Internal network with secure Internet
Network cables or Wi-Fi	X	X	X	X
Network cards	X	X	X	X
Cable/DSL modem		X	X	X
Ethernet and/or Wi-Fi router	X		X	X
Firewall				X

As the table shows, you can set up an isolated internal network using network cables (or wireless), network cards, and a router. I recommend a router rather than a hub or switch to allow you to connect your network to the Internet later, without having to purchase a separate router. As an example, the D-Link Ethernet Broadband router has four Ethernet ports for connecting your computers and network devices, and an additional port for connecting to the Internet. The LinkSys Wireless G Broadband router has four Ethernet ports for connecting your computers and network devices, wireless connection capability, and an additional port for connecting to the Internet.

You can create a simple network to connect one computer to the Internet using a network card, two network cables, and a cable/DSL modem. Typically, your ISP will supply the necessary cable/DSL modem.

By merging the components required for an internal network with those that are required for connecting to the Internet, you could create an internal network with Internet connectivity. This type of network would allow multiple computers to share resources and to connect to the Internet through your ISP's cable/DSL modem. Although most ISPs will allow you to connect multiple computers to the Internet through their cable/DSL service, some won't, and you might need to purchase a service upgrade to allow this type of connectivity.

For secure connectivity to the Internet, you'll need a firewall. Though Windows 7 includes Windows Firewall, this software firewall protects only your computer. It doesn't protect the other computers or devices on your network. Both of the broadband routers mentioned previously include a hardware firewall, which will fully protect your network.

On a home or small-business network, you shouldn't stop using Windows Firewall just because your network has a firewall. In most cases, your computer still needs the protection Windows Firewall offers.

You can expand your home or small-business network beyond the ports on your Ethernet router by connecting network hubs or switches to the router instead of individual computers or devices. Hubs and switches work in a similar manner, allowing computers or devices to connect to a network. Each allows a central point of connectivity, but hubs and switches work in different ways.

Hubs send all packets transmitted on the network to each host, making connectivity very simple. The downside of hubs falls directly on their inability to send packets to only a single host, which forces each host connected to the hub to share bandwidth. This drastically decreases the amount of available bandwidth to transmit data. If you have a 100 Mbps hub with 10 hosts using the network at once, each host has approximately 10 Mbps of network bandwidth available to transmit data. The transmission of data happens only in a half-duplex manner, greatly reducing network throughput. The upside of a hub lies in its capability to transmit data to all ports at the same time.

When you have network difficulties and you want to mirror the data on the network for monitoring purposes, hubs offer this functionality by default.

Switches differ from hubs with their inherent capability to transmit data from a single host to another single host, without sending the packets to all the hosts on the switch. This functionality allows for greater data throughput. If you have a 100 Mbps switch, each host on the switch may transfer data at 100 Mbps. A switch stores a routing table to keep track of the hosts connected. The routing table holds the machine (MAC) address of the network adapter for each computer or device, and the switch uses this table to determine to which host to send the data.

Installing Network Adapters in Your Computers

Installing network adapters in your computers requires you to open the case of the computer and install a card. If you do not feel comfortable completing this task, contact a computer repair or service company to install the network card. If installing cards is an "old hat" routine for you, then power down, unplug the computer, open the case, find the first available slot in your machine, insert the card with the gold leads down into the slot, and press firmly to insert the card. Once you have completed this task, screw in the top of the card to connect it to your chassis. This alleviates "wiggle" in the card, which could create shorts or cause intermittent connectivity problems.

On the other hand, if you are using an integrated network card in your machine that has not been enabled, reboot the system into the BIOS. Most OEMs (Original Equipment Manufacturers, the companies that make computers) configure their computers to use the Delete key. Press the Delete key every second or so after you reboot to enter the main BIOS section. Usually, you can find the network card settings under Integrated Devices. Once you have found the network card settings in your BIOS, select the desired device and enable it. If you need two network cards and the board has two network cards, enable each one. Very rarely will you need this type of configuration on a standard home system. Once you have enabled the device(s) on your system, save the changes in the BIOS, and reboot the system into the operating system.

After installing or enabling the network card physically or logically, allow the system to boot into the operating system. When you have completed this task, click the Start button, right-click the Computer option, and select Manage. This opens the Computer Management window, which allows you greater flexibility in managing the different aspects of your system. Once Computer Management starts, click the Device Manager node in the left pane. In the main pane, expand the Network Adapters node by clicking on the wedge-shaped icon to view the network adapters installed in your machine. Right-click on the adapter you previously installed or enabled, and select Properties. On the Driver tab, verify the Driver Provider details. As necessary, install the device driver as discussed in Chapter 5.

If you do not see a network adapter listed in the Device Manager screen under Network Adapters, you should verify that the device does not show up under Other Devices as a network controller. If this happens, don't worry. Simply install the device driver as discussed in Chapter 5.

Installing Ethernet Routers, Hubs, and Switches

Installing an Ethernet router, hub, or switch requires you to remove the device from the packaging and plug it into a power source using the power cable provided by the manufacturer. After you plug in the device, you should see it begin to flash green- and amber-colored lights. The network device will accept connections and begin transmitting data when the initialization process completes. You can tell that the initialization process has completed when most of the lights on the unit settle down and quit flashing.

After the initialization process completes, you need to connect the network cables to the Ethernet router to provide connectivity to the computers and devices that you want to network together. To establish an Internet connection, connect a network cable between your cable/DSL modem and the Ethernet router's Internet port. Cable modems should automatically assign an IP address to your router for external connectivity to the Internet. DSL modems usually require a client username and password. You should have received this information when you signed up for Internet connectivity, or you can contact support and receive this information from your ISP.

When you have added the first connection to the Ethernet router, you must then connect the cables to the network cards on your computers and devices. When you have completed this task, you should see a green LED light up on each network card and possibly see the amber activity light. If you see both of these signs, you have successfully completed the physical connectivity portion of the networking process. If you do not see both of these lights, it does not mean you have failed, as there may be no data transmission on the line while you are connecting the cables.

If you want to connect more computers or devices than the ports on the Ethernet router allow, you'll need a hub or switch. With a hub or switch, you connect a network cable between the hub/switch and the Ethernet router. Then, instead of connecting the cables for computers or devices directly to the Ethernet router, you connect the cables to the hub or switch.

To finalize the router setup, you need to configure the network services available on your router. Using the DHCP, you can assign IP addresses to the computers and devices connected to your router.

With the help of your router's user manual, log on to the router and select the screen to configure DHCP. Usually, this requires opening your web browser and typing the address of the router's configuration page, which is either *http://192.168.0.1* or *http://192.168.1.1*. Then when prompted, enter the default username and password for the router. Typically, the username is *admin* and the password is either blank or one of the following words: *admin* or *password*. If these don't work, refer to the documentation for the router.

You need to assign a network IP range for use on your network. If you have only a small group of users, use the 192.168.0.1 range for use on your network, or a similar network ID. Most routers have the functionality turned on automatically. You may also need to input the DNS addresses of your ISP or the MAC address of a network card.

To complete connectivity to the network, you must configure the network cards on your computers and devices. See the section "Configuring IPv4, IPv6, and Other Protocols" on page 567 for details.

Setting Up a Wireless Router or Access Point

The basic setup of a wireless router or access point is similar to the basic setup of an Ethernet router. After you to remove the device from the packaging and plug it into a power source using the power cable provided by the manufacturer, you will need to logon to the router and configure it.

Most wireless routers and account points purchased after November 2009 will be compatible with Windows 7 and support Windows Connect Now (WCN). You can set up a wireless router or wireless access point that supports WCN by completing these steps:

1. Set up and plug in the router to a power source.
2. Click the Network icon in the system tray, click the default network of the router, which is identified by the manufacture name, and then follow the prompts to set up the router.
3. During the setup process, you may need to connect one end of an Ethernet cable to the Internet port on your router and the other end into modem or other device supplied by your Internet provider. This will allow the device to connect to the Internet. If you don't connect the router to the Internet during setup, you'll need to do so afterward.
4. Your computer will be connected to the router's network automatically. To connect other computers, click the Network icon in the system tray, click the network of the router. If the router supports WCN or WPS and has an activate/connect button, you can push the button on the router and then wait for the router to automatically set up the connection to the new computer. If the router doesn't have an activate/connect button, you are prompted for a security key, enter it and then click OK.

If the wireless router or access point doesn't support WCN, you can set it up by completing these steps:

1. Set up and plug in the wireless router or access point.

2. Open your web browser and type the address of the router's configuration page, which is either *http://192.168.0.1* or *http://192.168.1.1*.

3. When prompted, enter the default username and password for the router. Typically, the username is *admin* and the password is either blank or one of the following words: *admin* or *password*. If these don't work, refer to the documentation for the router.

4. In your browser, you should have an option to run the router's setup utility. If there isn't a setup utility, specify a name for the router's network, select the encryption level and choose a security key for accessing the router. Be sure to change the administrator password so that the router is protected from other people.

5. Once you've set up the router, you can connect to it by clicking the Network icon in the system tray, and clicking the network of the router. Enter the security key when prompted and then click OK.

Mapping Your Networking Infrastructure

Windows 7 provides a whole new way to navigate and manage the networking features of your computer. For mapping your networking infrastructure, Windows 7 provides the Network and Sharing Center, Network Map, and Network Connections. You can access and work with these utilities as discussed in the following sections.

Using the Network and Sharing Center

The Network and Sharing Center is a central console for managing your networking experience. You can access the Network and Sharing Center by following these steps:

1. Click Start, and then click Control Panel.

2. In the Control Panel, click Network and Internet→Network and Sharing Center.

Once you've accessed the Network and Sharing Center, shown in Figure 14-1, you can use it to manage your general network settings and network status. When you are connected to a network, the Network and Sharing Center provides an overview of your networking configuration. The main areas in the Network and Sharing Center are:

Network overview
> Provides a visual overview of your network infrastructure, including whether you are connected to a network and whether you can access the Internet from that network. If your computer has multiple active network connections, the network overview states that you are connected to multiple networks. Clicking "See full

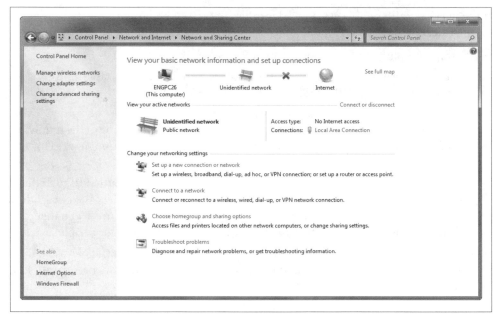

Figure 14-1. Viewing your network and sharing configuration

map" opens the Network Map window. See "Viewing the Network Map" on page 557, later in this chapter, for more information.

Network details

Provides details about the network(s) to which the computer is connected and the types of access for those networks. A connection to a LAN is shown as "Local only" or "No Internet access." A connection to a LAN that in turn connects to the Internet is shown as Local and Internet. Clicking the connection name (next to "Connections:") allows you to manage the related network connection. See "Viewing and Managing Your Network Connections" on page 559, later in this chapter, for more information.

In the Network and Sharing Center, you'll see several links at the bottom of the main pane. Clicking "Set up a new connection or network" allows you to manage the different types of network connections available to you. As shown in Figure 14-2, you may connect to the Internet, set up a wireless router or access point, manually connect to a wireless network, connect to a workplace, or set up a dial-up connection. Not visible in the figure are choices for setting up a wireless ad hoc (computer-to-computer) network and connecting to a Bluetooth personal area network (PAN). Options include:

Set up a new network

If you need to set up a wireless router or access point on your network, select this option from the list and click Next. The wizard allows you to configure a wireless router or access point, set up the properties for file and printer sharing, save the

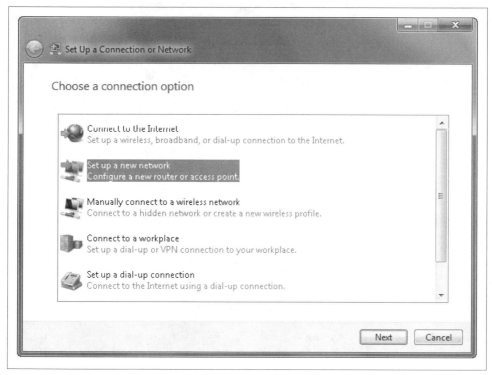

Figure 14-2. Setting up a new network

network configuration for future use, and make the network a private network. If you have all of the required information to set up your wireless network, click the Next button and follow the steps provided by the wizard.

Connect to a network

Clicking this option allows you to connect to an available network using the window shown in Figure 14-3. This includes wired connections to known networks discovered, as well as wireless connections Windows 7 discovered during the browsing process while opening the window. If you see the desired network you want to connect to, click Connect, and Windows 7 will automatically try to connect you to the network. You can also disconnect from a network by clicking the network and then clicking Disconnect.

Choose homegroup and sharing options

Clicking this option allows you to configure homegroup settings. As Figure 14-4 shows, you can share libraries and printers with other computers in the homegroup; stream media to devices; and view, print or change the homegroup password. You also can leave a homegroup. For more information on homegroups, see "Sharing Your Data" on page 461 in Chapter 11.

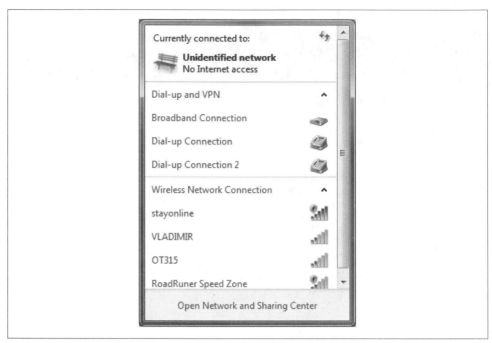

Figure 14-3. Connecting to a network or disconnecting from a network

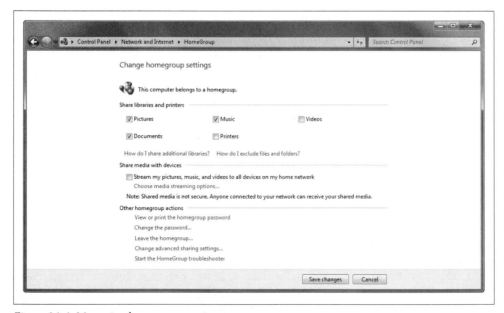

Figure 14-4. Managing homegroup settings

You can configure homegroup settings only when you are connected to the homegroup. If you are not connected to a home network, you won't able to change homegroup settings.

Troubleshoot problems

Clicking this option provides access to the built-in network and printing troubleshooters. The network troubleshooters allow you to have Windows 7 automatically try to detect problems with your networking configuration. As Figure 14-5 shows, each troubleshooter is related to a specific type of problem, such as Internet connections or Homegroups. To start a troubleshooter, simply click its listing. Network Diagnostics can help to identify different problems related to an inability to connect to the Internet, connect to network resources, or find resources on the network. Although these tools help to identify network problems, they are not a substitute for the tools available to find and diagnose low-level problems, such as the Event Viewer and command-line tools like `ping` and `tracert`. The troubleshooters will enable and disable your network adapter, check for a new IP address from the DHCP server, and check for connectivity. If you have recently set up a network connection and you find that it does not work, the troubleshooters will help to identify these simple problems.

The network and printing troubleshooters are designed for resolving specific types of problems. They work well when you think you know the source of a problem. For example, if you suspect that your computer has a problem with the network adapter configuration, you can use the Network Adapter troubleshooter to try to diagnose and resolve the problem.

In the Network and Sharing Center, the Network Overview shows warning icons. Similar warning icons are displayed on the Network Map as well. Clicking one of these warnings icons starts Windows Network Diagnostics, which runs a high-level network diagnostics that makes use of the appropriate network troubleshooters automatically.

In the left pane of the Network and Sharing Center screen, you'll find options to manage wireless networks, change adapter settings, and change advanced sharing settings:

Manage wireless networks

This option allows you to see wireless connections already configured or available for your use, as shown in Figure 14-6. You may also:

- Add a wireless connection by selecting the Add button. When you select this option, you are presented with a window asking you for specific information about how you want to add a network. You can add a network that is in range of the computer, manually create a network profile, or create an ad hoc

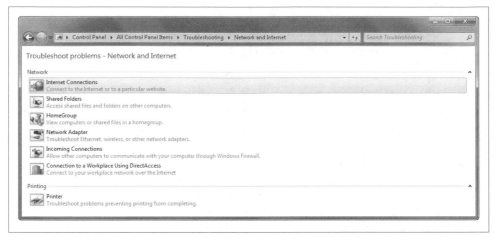

Figure 14-5. Use troubleshooters to diagnose and resolve problems

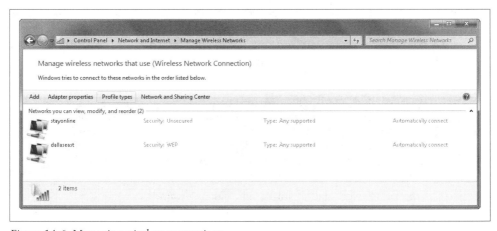

Figure 14-6. Managing wireless connections

(computer-to-computer) network. If you have already enabled a wireless connection, select the first option, which allows you to connect to the wireless network and saves a configuration profile for future use. If you would like to create a new wireless profile, you need to know the network name, security type and security key, if enabled. This option also creates a configuration profile for the wireless network for future use. The last option allows you to create an ad hoc network connection. An ad hoc network is a temporary network for the transmission of files among machines not connected via a wireless access point. This option works well if you need to transfer data with someone else and you both have a wireless card in your computer.

- View the properties of a selected wireless adapter by clicking the "Adapter properties" button. You will see a window that allows you to manipulate the different protocols associated with the wireless adapter, including TCP/IP properties, file and printer sharing, and the Microsoft network client protocol. These settings reside on the Networking tab; the Sharing tab allows you to configure Internet Connection Sharing (ICS) for this adapter. Selecting the Configure button on the Networking tab allows you to view and manage additional features of your wireless adapter.

- Choose the type of profile to assign to new wireless networks by clicking the Profile types button. The default setting in Windows 7 is "Use all-user profiles only." This setting allows connections to wireless networks from your computer to be accessed only by those with user accounts on the computer. Selecting the "Use all-user and per-user profiles" allows users to create connections accessible only to them, which can cause a loss of network connectivity if you log off or switch users on the local system. Microsoft recommends that you use the "Use all-user profiles only" option, which allows greater flexibility and lessens the chance of lost network connectivity.

Change adapter settings

This allows you to view and change the properties of your computer's network adapters. As shown in Figure 14-7, this includes standard network adapters, wireless adapters, Microsoft VPN connections, and any other software or hardware adapter allowing you network connectivity.

Change advanced sharing settings

This shows the status of different aspects of network discovery and sharing. As shown in Figure 14-8, Windows creates a separate profile for each type of network you use. You can choose specific options for each profile. Clicking the Expand button for a profile allows you to manage the aspects of that profile. Clicking the Shrink button minimizes the management section for a profile. Network discovery must be on to discover information about your network. When you are connected to a home, work, or domain network, network discovery is turned on automatically to allow you to discover computers and devices. When you are connected to a public network, network discovery is turned off to prevent other people from discovering and then trying to access your computer. To enable network discovery if it isn't already enabled, click "Turn on Network Discovery" and then click Save Changes.

Viewing the Network Map

When network discovery is enabled, you can use the Network Map to display an expanded view of your network. As Figure 14-9 shows, the expanded Network Map view includes your computer, the computers near your computer, and the devices near your computer. You can access the Network Map by following these steps:

1. Click Start, and then click Control Panel.

2. In the Control Panel, click Network and Internet→Network and Sharing Center.

3. In the Network and Sharing Center, under Network Map, click "See full map."

4. If your computer has more than one network connection, use the "Network map of" list to select the network connection for which the map should be created.

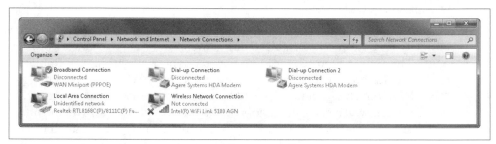

Figure 14-7. Managing network connections

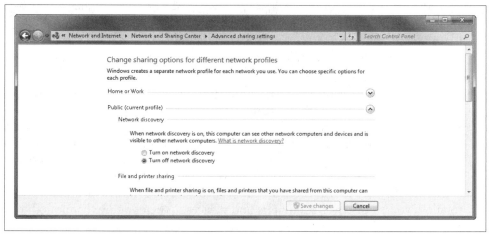

Figure 14-8. Changing advanced sharing settings

On the Network Map, you'll see solid lines connecting the selected network connection to your network devices. You may also see dashed lines to other devices for alternative connections. If there's a problem with a particular segment of your connection, you'll see a yellow warning symbol or a red X on the connecting line. Clicking either warning icon starts Windows Network diagnostics, which runs a high-level network diagnostic check that makes use of the appropriate network troubleshooters automatically.

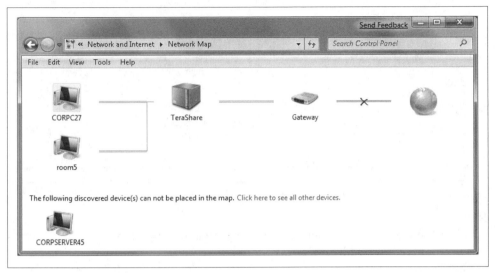

Figure 14-9. Viewing a Network Map

Viewing and Managing Your Network Connections

Network connections contain the configuration properties that allow your computer to connect to a network. Windows 7 automatically creates a local area connection for each network adapter you've configured. As you configure dial-up, broadband, or wireless, Windows 7 will create related connections as well.

 Windows will usually configure connections for devices that it supports out-of-the-box, including wireless and Ethernet connections.

You can quickly obtain a list of network connections for your computer by completing the following steps:

1. Click Start, and then click Control Panel.
2. In the Control Panel, click Network and Internet and then click Network and Sharing Center.
3. In the Network and Sharing Center, click "Change adapter settings." This opens the Network Connections window, shown in Figure 14-10.

The Network Connections window has several different views. You can access these views by clicking the Views button and then selecting the desired view. The view you'll use most often is the Details view. This view shows you:

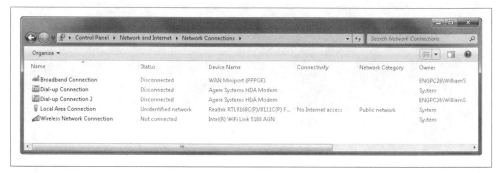

Figure 14-10. Viewing network connections

Name
> The name of your computer's connections, organized by connection type, such as LAN or High-Speed Internet

Status
> The name of the network to which a connection is connected, or another status, such as "Unavailable–device missing," "Not connected," "Disconnected," or "Network cable unplugged"

Device Name
> The manufacturer and type of network adapter

Connectivity
> The type of connectivity for active connections, such as "No Internet access" or "Internet Access"

Network Category
> The network category, which can be Private, Public, or Domain

Owner
> The owner of the connection, such as the System account

Type
> The type of connection, such as Dial-up

Phone # or Host Address
> The phone number associated with a dial-up connection, or the host address associated with a remote access connection

When you select a connection in the Network Connection window, the toolbar options allow you to work with the connection in several different ways. The option buttons are used as follows:

Diagnose This Connection
> Opens Network Diagnostics for troubleshooting the connection

View Status of This Connection
>Displays the connection's Status dialog box, which you can use to get details about and manage the TCP/IP configuration

Change Settings of This Connection
>Displays the connection's Properties dialog box, which you can use to manage the TCP/IP configuration

Disable This Network Device
>Allows you to disable the network device so that your computer doesn't try to use it

Rename This Connection
>Allows you to change the name of a selected connection by clicking this button, typing the new name for the connection, and then pressing Enter

Start/Connect To
>Allows you to start or connect to the selected connection

Networking with TCP/IP

Although Windows 7 has the capability of using several networking protocols, the primary protocols used are TCP and IP. Windows 7 uses the TCP/IP protocol for networking among peer-to-peer networks, domain-controlled networks, and the Internet. TCP/IP is a vital protocol set for using your operating system fully.

Windows 7 contains a new TCP/IP stack, referred to as a dual stack, that works with IP version 4 (IPv4) and IP version 6 (IPv6). IPv4 uses a limited 32-bit address space, defined by four octets and a subnet mask composed of four octets. IPv6 uses a 128-bit addressing scheme, allowing for the needed IP growth of the Internet.

Understanding IPv4

IP addresses used with IPv4 can be divided into two parts: the network ID and the host ID. The network ID identifies the network on which a computer or device is located and the host ID identifies the computer or device.

An example of an IPv4 address is 192.168.1.1, which shows the four distinct sets of numbers divided by a period, or dot. Each section separated by a dot is referred to as an *octet*, which correlates to an eight-bit number in binary form.

The second set of numbers associated with an IPv4 address is the subnet mask. The subnet mask identifies which parts of the IP address belong to the network ID and which parts belong to the host ID.

Subnet masks use four distinct octets separated by a period, or dot, just like the IP address. Subnet masking correlates to the network ID and the actual host ID of the computer by giving binary values of either a 1, for a bit that belongs to the network ID, or 0, for a bit that belongs to the host ID. An example of a subnet mask is 255.0.0.0, which is read in binary as 11111111.00000000.00000000.00000000. Thus, the first 8 bits of the IP address belong to the network ID and the final 24 bits belong to the host ID.

When you use standard subnet masks, you are said to be using a *classful network*. Classful networks are defined in three different classes: Class A, Class B, and Class C. Table 14-2 shows examples of the different classful networks. Table 14-3 shows network ID examples, and Table 14-4 gives some examples of subnet forms translated into binary to help you understand the differences in their formats and to differentiate the network ID portion of the subnet from the host ID portion of the subnet.

Table 14-2. IPv4 subnet example

Subnet class	Example	Maximum nodes
Class A	255.0.0.0	16,777,214
Class B	255.255.0.0	65,534
Class C	255.255.255.0	254

Table 14-3. IPv4 network example

Network ID	Subnet mask	Host IP range	Broadcast address
10.0.0.0	255.0.0.0	10.0.0.1–10.255.255.254	10.255.255.255
169.254.0.0	255.255.0.0	169.254.0.1–169.254.255.254	169.254.255.255
192.168.1.0	255.255.255.0	192.168.1.1–192.168.1.254	192.168.1.255

Table 14-4. IPv4 subnet to binary form example

Decimal subnet form	Binary subnet form
255.0.0.0	11111111.00000000.00000000.00000000
255.255.0.0	11111111.11111111.00000000.00000000
255.255.255.0	11111111.11111111.11111111.00000000

For every network, two host addresses are reserved: the network address and the broadcast address. The network address is used to identify the unique network. The broadcast address is used to broadcast a message to all hosts on a network. On a classful network, address 0 is reserved to indicate the network number, and address 255 is reserved for the broadcast address.

Class A networks use the first octet in the range of 1–126. The remaining three octets define unique host IDs. Each Class A network may contain up to 16,777,214 nodes.

Class B networks use the first two octets in the range of 128–191. The remaining two octets define the unique host IDs. Each Class B network may contain up to 65,534 nodes.

Class C networks use the first three octets in the range of 192–223. The remaining octet is for unique host IDs. Each Class C network may contain up to 254 hosts.

 Out of these IP address ranges, you may note that some ranges are missing. The 127 network is reserved for local loopback. Your computer typically uses the address 127.0.0.1 to send messages to itself. The network addresses from 224 to 239 are used for multicast IPv4 addresses.

When you are working with IPv4, data is sent in discrete packets of information with a header and a payload. IPv4 headers are variable in size, between 20 and 60 bytes, in 4-byte increments. Each bit range is broken into different sections, which correspond to the range of a related field in a packet. Bit ranges consist of 0–3, 4–7, 8–15, 16–18, and 19–31. These correspond to the values 0, 32, 64, 96, 128, 160, and 160/192+ for data. See Table 14-5 for examples of the ranges and their use. The IP payload is of variable size as well, ranging from 8 bytes to 65,515 bytes (with sizing primarily depending on network protocols and other options). Although most people will never use this information on a regular basis, it is very useful for understanding how to troubleshoot network problems.

Table 14-5. IPv4 packet information

+	Bits 0–3	4–7	8–15	16–18	19–31
0	Version	Header length	Type of service	Total length	
32	Identification			Flags	Fragment offset
64	Time to Live (TTL)		Protocol	Header checksum	
96	Source address information				
128	Destination address information				
160	Optional information				
160/192+	Data transmitted				

Using Private IPv4 Addresses and Networking Protocols

Some IP addresses designated for Class A, B, and C networks are defined as public and others are defined as private. Public IP addresses are assigned by ISPs. ISPs obtain their IP addresses from a regional Internet registry. When you connect directly to the Internet through dial-up or by connecting an ISP's cable/DSL modem directly to your computer, your computer uses a public IP address assigned by your ISP. Not every computer that connects to the Internet needs its own IP address, however. If it did, the IPv4 addressing scheme would have run out of new addresses a long time ago. This is where private IP addresses come into the picture.

When you set up a network, you assign the computers on the network private IP addresses. Private IP addresses are defined as follows:

- Class A private IP addresses include the addresses from 10.0.0.0 through 10.255.255.255.
- Class B private IP addresses include the addresses from 172.16.0.0 through 172.31.255.255.
- Class C private IP addresses include the addresses from 192.168.0.0 through 192.168.255.255.

Because private IP addresses are not routable to the Internet, your network can use the same private IP addresses that other people are using with their networks. When a computer is connected to a network that in turn connects to an ISP, your broadband router is the device that is assigned a public IP address. Your broadband router uses some tricks to allow computers with private addresses to access the Internet, despite the fact that private addresses are not routable to the Internet. Generally speaking, the router's public IP address is the address by which all the computers on your network will be identified when they are accessing resources on the Internet.

On a network, private IP addresses are assigned in one of three ways:

Static IP address
 A fixed IP address that you manually assign to a computer or device.

Dynamic IP address
 An IP address automatically assigned to a computer or device by DHCP.

Automatic private IP address
 An IP address automatically assigned to a computer by the operating system when a DHCP server cannot be contacted. Sometimes referred to as *link-local* addresses.

On a home or small-office network, you can use the DHCP service capability of your Ethernet router to assign IP addresses. Refer to the user manual of your router to find the correct procedure to configure the DHCP service to assign IP addresses automatically to computers and devices connecting to your network. Once you've configured the DHCP service, you may need to configure the network adapters of computers and devices to use DHCP, although it is typically the default IP addressing scheme.

Understanding IPv6

Although IPv4 allows for more than four billion networked computers and devices, the world is running out of available IPv4 addresses. Rather than allow there to be a shortage of available addresses, organizations have worked together to create several solutions to the problem. One of these solutions is IPv6. Unlike IPv4, which uses 32-bit addresses, IPv6 uses 128-bit addresses, which offer literally enough IP addresses so that there are thousands of IP addresses for each square yard of the Earth's surface. Or put another way, there are about 340,282,367,000,000,000,000,000,000,000,000,000,000 available addresses—give or take a few hundred million quadrillion.

To make it easier to track all those IP addresses, IPv6 uses hexadecimal numbers rather than decimal numbers to define the address space. This means that instead of allowing only the numbers 0 through 9 for each position in the IP address, IPv6 allows the values 0 through 9 and A through F, with A representing 10, B representing 11, and so on, up to F representing 15. Thus, the values 0 through 15 can be represented using the values 0 through F.

IPv6's 128-bit addresses are divided into eight 16-bit blocks delimited by colons. With standard IPv6 addresses, the first 64 bits represent the network ID and the last 64 bits represent the network interface being used. Since many IPv6 address blocks are set to 0, a contiguous set of 0 blocks can be expressed as ::, a notation referred to as the *double-colon notation*. Table 14-6 shows an example of an IPv6 IP address and an abbreviated IP address.

Table 14-6. IPv6 address example

IPv6 address	Abbreviated IPv6 address
FE80:0:0:033C:FB:B335:FE4F: 752B	FE80::033C:FB:B335:FE4F:752B

Just as there are different types of IPv4 addresses, there are different types of IPv6 addresses. As Table 14-7 shows, the type of an IPv6 address is identified by the high-order bits of the address. The IPv6 address 0:0:0:0:0:0:0:1 is used for local loopback. IPv6 addresses beginning with FF00 are used for multicast transmissions. IPv6 addresses beginning with FE80 are used for link-local unicast transmissions. Link-local unicast IPv6 addresses are the equivalent of IPv4 automatic private addresses. IPv6 addresses beginning with FEC0 are used for site-local unicast transmissions. Site-local unicast IPv6 addresses are the equivalent of IPv4 private addresses. Global unicast IPv6 addresses are the equivalent of IPv4 public addresses because they are globally reachable on the Internet and must be assigned by an IP address authority.

Table 14-7. IPv6 subnet prefix example

IPv6 subnet prefix length	Associated network addresses
2001:1234:5678::/48	2001:1234:5678:: through address 2001:1234:5678::FFFF:FFFF:FFFF:FFFF

IPv6 doesn't use subnet masks to identify which bits belong to the network ID and which bits belong to the host ID. Instead, each IPv6 address is assigned a subnet prefix length that specifies how the bits in the network ID are used. The subnet prefix length is represented in decimal form. For example, if 48 bits in the network ID are used, the subnet prefix length is written as /48. Table 14-8 shows an example of the subnet prefix length and the associated network range.

Table 14-8. IPv6 address types

Address type	Binary prefix	IPv6 notation
Unspecified	000000	::/128
Loopback	000001	::1/128
Multicast	11111111	FF00::/8
Link-Local unicast	1111111010	FE80::/10
Global unicast	All other addresses	

IPv6 allows for a greater than 64 KB payload in an IPv4 packet, which designers refer to as a *jumbogram*. These jumbograms greatly increase the throughput of high-performance networks. IPv4 does not support this type of transmission, and it has a 64 KB payload limit.

IPv6 packets are composed of two parts: a header and a payload section. The first 40 octets of an IPv6 packet contain the header, composed of the source and destination addresses, including an IPv4 version where necessary, traffic class section, flow label (for packet priority information), payload length, next header addressing section, and hop limit. The payload section consists of the actual data sent during transmission. The payload section can contain either 64 KB of information, like the IPv4 standard, or a jumbogram for true IPv6 "high-throughput" networking architectures. Table 14-9 shows an example of an IPv6 packet.

Table 14-9. IPv6 packet example

+	Bits 0–3	4–7	8–11	12–15	16–19	20–23	24–27	28
0	Version	Traffic class		Flow Label				
32	Payload Length				Next Header		Hop Limit	
64	Source address information							
192	Destination address information							

IPv6 developers also implemented IP Security (IPSec) into the protocol. IPSec lies within the IP network layer, and encrypts and authenticates as an integrated part of the protocol by default. This eliminates additional overhead in encoding and decoding packets using IPSec functionality.

Configuring IPv4, IPv6, and Other Protocols

Each network adapter configured on your computer has a separate IP addressing configuration, which you can manage through the associated network connection. The network connection for the first network adapter on the computer is named Local Area Connection; the second network adapter is named Local Area Connection 2, and so on. Connections for wireless, dial-up, or broadband have either default names or the names you assigned when you created the connection.

During installation of the operating system, the Setup program automatically installed the necessary networking components for your computer if a network adapter was detected. In addition to TCP/IPv4 and TCP/IPv6, Windows 7 uses the following networking components:

Client for Microsoft Networks
Allows you to connect to Microsoft-based networking services. If you are connecting to a Windows domain, you are required to use this protocol.

QoS Packet Scheduler
Offers the capability to define which protocols and applications have precedence in a situation where multiple applications or protocols request access to the same network resources. This protocol gives you the ability to raise or lower the priority of the requests made. Basically, the Quality of Service (QoS) Packet Scheduler works as a traffic cop by allowing you to control the rate of flow and prioritization of services available.

File and Printer Sharing for Microsoft Networks
Allows other computers to connect to and access resources on your computer when using Microsoft networking protocols. This feature also allows you to access resources on remote machines connected to your network and on the Internet.

Link-Layer Topology Discovery Mapper I/O Driver
Allows your computer to discover and locate other computers and devices on the network. Also used to determine the available network bandwidth.

Link-Layer Topology Discovery Responder
Allows your computer to be discovered and located by other computers and devices on the network.

Although you will probably use only IPv4 on your home or small-office network, you should understand how IPv6 works and be able to configure the protocol. You can manually assign IPv4 and IPv6 addresses using static IP addresses, or automatically assign them using dynamic IP addresses. You configure the IPv4 and IPv6 protocols in exactly the same way, with the following exceptions:

- IPv4 uses subnet masks, and IPv6 uses subnet prefix lengths.
- IPv4 uses both DNS and WINS for locating computers and devices on the network, and IPv6 uses only DNS.

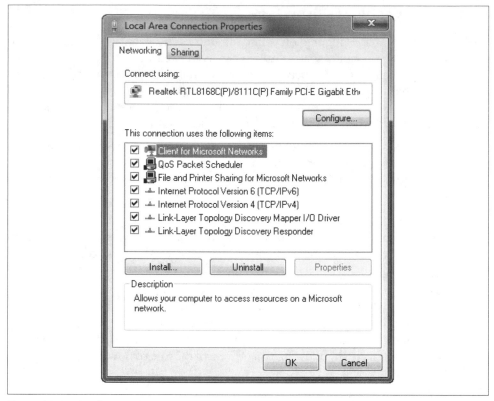

Figure 14-11. Configuring connection properties

- IPv4 allows for automatic private IP addressing if a DHCP server cannot be located, and IPv6 simply assigns the computer a link-local unicast (private) IP address based on the MAC address of the network adapter.

On a per-network-connection basis, you can configure the networking protocols used by completing the following steps:

1. Click Start, and then click Control Panel.
2. In the Control Panel, click Network and Internet→Network and Sharing Center.
3. In the Network and Sharing Center, click "Change adapter settings." This opens the Network Connections window.
4. Right-click the network connection you want to configure and then select Properties. This displays a Properties dialog box, as shown in Figure 14-11.
5. On the Networking tab, you can use the checkboxes provided to manipulate the different protocols associated with the network adapter. You can turn the different protocols on and off by clicking the checkbox associated with each protocol:

- If you are using file and printer sharing on your network, you must enable both Client for Microsoft Networks, and File and Printer Sharing for Microsoft Networks.

- The QoS protocol offers greater flexibility in the flow of data by prioritizing the different requests made by the client.

- If you are using the IPv6 protocol for connectivity, you also must use the QoS Packet Scheduler, which Windows selects by default. If you are not using this protocol, you should disable it by unchecking the box associated with this protocol.

- If you are using the IPv4 protocol for connectivity, you must leave the Internet Protocol version 4 (TCP/IPv4) box checked.

- If you are using the IPv6 protocol for connectivity, you must leave the Internet Protocol version 6 (TCP/IPv6) box checked.

- If you want to be able to use the network connection to discover and locate other computers and devices, you must leave the Link-Layer Topology Discovery Mapper I/O Driver box checked.

- If you want other people to be able to discover your computer through the network connection, you must leave the Link-Layer Topology Discovery Responder box checked.

> Although the discovery protocols add some overhead to your computer, they offer some real value to the capabilities of networking in Windows 7. Most of the time, you should leave these protocols enabled, unless you are leery of security issues associated with other people discovering your computer. If you are concerned about the security aspects, verify that you have Windows Firewall enabled on your computer and make sure the hardware firewall on your Ethernet router is properly configured. Although firewalls will not eliminate all problems associated with security, they will drastically decrease the potential to have data stolen.

6. To configure IPv4 or IPv6, double-click Internet Protocol version 4 (TCP/IPv4) or Internet Protocol version 6 (TCP/IPv6) as appropriate. As Figure 14-12 shows, the options available are nearly identical whether you are working with IPv4 or IPv6. Repeat this as necessary to configure both IPv4 and IPv6.

7. The General tab allows you to select either "Obtain an IP address automatically" or "Use the following IP address." If you have enabled DHCP on a network device such as a router, you should choose the first option. This allows DHCP to configure the options of the protocol for IP addressing and the default gateway for accessing the network. You should also choose "Obtain DNS server addresses automatically" to ensure that your computer gets the correct DNS servers for name lookups.

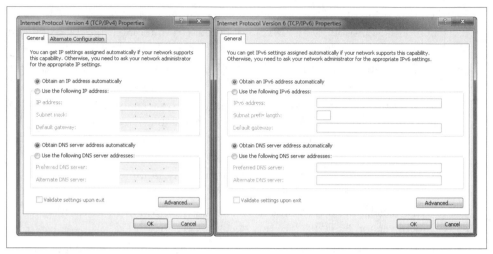

Figure 14-12. Configuring IPv4 and IPv6

Windows 7 defaults to the automatic configuration, as you'll typically have a device providing your IP addressing dynamically.

8. To configure the network adapter to use a manually assigned IP address, do the following:

 a. Select the "Use the following IP address" option. For IPv4 addressing, enter the IP address you want to associate with the network adapter in the "IP address" text box and then enter the subnet mask in the "Subnet mask" text box. For IPv6 addressing, enter the IP address in the IP address text box and then enter the subnet prefix in the "Subnet prefix length" text box.

 b. Select the "Use the following DNS server addresses" options. Enter the DNS server address of either your local DNS server or your ISP into the "Preferred DNS server" text box. If you have additional DNS server information to provide, enter the address into the "Alternate DNS server" text box.

9. Click OK to save your settings.

 If you are manually configuring your IP address, you must have an IP address, subnet mask or subnet prefix, and IP addresses for DNS servers. If you have a computer that connects to a network router that in turn connects to your ISP's cable/DSL modem, you should configure private IP addresses for your internal network. When enabling network connectivity without a hardware firewall, you should verify that Windows Firewall is on. You should also carefully consider whether you need file and printer sharing. Enabling file and printer sharing without a firewall may make your computer accessible to other people.

Regardless of how you connect to a network, you are required to add your computer to a homegroup, a workgroup, also know as a peer-to-peer network, or a domain. Homegroups, described in Chapter 11, are small groups of computers with very permissive sharing. Workgroups are small groups of computers with individual user rights assigned by the computer. Domains are groups of computers with a centralized authentication mechanism. Each works to its own benefit and small networks seldom use domains, unless you are willing to put the capital out to purchase a server operating system. To add your computer to an existing workgroup or connect to a domain, use the techniques discussed in the section "Configuring the Computer Name and Membership" on page 772 in Chapter 20.

Advanced Networking Concepts

Windows 7 includes support for advanced network features, which include IPSec and VPN. These protocols have existed for some time, but they are more readily available and usable in Windows 7 than they were in earlier releases of Windows. I'll also take a brief look at the Open Systems Interconnection (OSI) model.

Introducing VPN

If you are a traveler and you work in a corporate environment, you have probably used a VPN connection to connect to your corporate network on the road, in order to check your email, or possibly to update sales orders and the like. VPN makes connecting to remote networks secure and easy.

VPN allows remote users to connect to a network confidentially over a public network. VPN uses standard protocols (TCP/IP, SSL) to traverse the public network, making it very easy to use. VPN consists of two types: Secure VPN and Trusted VPN. Each type uses different processes to gain connectivity to a remote network.

Secure VPN uses cryptographic tunneling protocols to gain private access to the remote network. Secure VPN can use IPSec to encrypt the data traversing the VPN connection. Secure VPN also supports SSL to encrypt the data, essentially creating a web proxy, not really a VPN connection. Point-to-Point Tunneling Protocol (PPTP), the original VPN protocol, has aged and does not secure data as well as Layer 2 Tunneling Protocol (L2TP). In addition, Layer 2 Tunneling Protocol version 3 (L2TPv3) also works in Windows 7.

Trusted VPN does not use a cryptographic set to allow tunneling. Instead, it uses the provider's network to encrypt data. Usually, Multi-Protocol Label Switching (MPLS) makes up the trusted VPN tunnel, but this type of VPN also supports use of the Layer 2 Forwarding (L2F) protocol.

Most networks supporting VPN give you access to a VPN client, which you install. If you use Routing and Remote Access Service (RRAS) on your network, you can use the

Connect to a Workplace option in the "Set up a new connection or network" window. You have the choice of dialing directly to your workplace or using your Internet connection. Dialing directly requires a phone line and does not use the Internet. Of course, the other choice requires you to have a connection to the Internet. Click your desired option and enter the name of the server, or IP address. Give the destination a meaningful name; select the security properties, which consist of Smart Cards, Sharing, and Just Set Up; and then click the Next button. Enter your username, password, and optional domain information and then click the Create button. To connect, click the Connect Now button and you should connect to the VPN server.

Introducing IPSec

IPSec offers the ability to encrypt network transmissions at the adapter level. IPSec varies from Secure Sockets Layer (SSL) in terms of the OSI layer it encrypts. SSL typically encrypts at the application/protocol layer (OSI layer 7), and IPSec encrypts data at the transport layer (OSI layers 4–7). Because SSL works only at the application protocol layer, if you transmit data over any other port or use any application other than the one bound to the SSL protocol, that data is not encrypted (for example, when you use an HTTPS URL to connect to your bank's website, only that web session is protected by SSL). IPSec, however, encrypts all of the data transmitted from the network adapter at the transport layer.

IPSec includes two encryption mechanisms: *transport* and *tunneling*. Most implementations use the tunneling version, which encapsulates the entire packet. This feature allows for routable information to other hosts to be unencrypted while the internal header and the rest of the data stay encrypted. This makes it possible to use Network Address Translation (NAT), which lets you use a single device to allow traffic into and out of the network using private IP addressing—something your broadband router does for you automatically.

The transport mechanism usually consists of one-to-one communication among computers on the same network. Transport encrypts the data, not the header, and creates a hash of the packet. Using the transport method does not allow you to use NAT, thereby making external communications difficult. The reason lies in the method: transport creates a hash of the packet; when it hashes the packet, it rewrites part of the header, making the header value mismatch the rest of the packet, thereby rendering the packet invalid.

You may ask yourself, "How does it encrypt the data?" That is a very good question. First, the adapters create a trusted relationship by importing a digital certificate into each network adapter. When the adapter connects to the network, possibly via a VPN tunneling server or Active Directory domain controller, it verifies the digital certificate, trades private and public keys that are associated with the certificate, and verifies the MAC address of the network adapter. The adapter creates a hash value for each packet transmitted to the adapter, including a timestamp, alleviating replay attacks against the adapter.

Understanding the OSI Model

The Open Systems Interconnection (OSI) model defines the ways protocols operate by breaking the different aspects of protocols into layers. The OSI model uses seven layers with different purposes to define how protocols function. Each layer may use the functionality of the first layer below it and export functionality to the next layer above it. See Table 14-10 for a detailed listing of the OSI model's layers.

Table 14-10. OSI layer reference

Layer level	Layer name
Layer 1	Physical
Layer 2	Data Link
Layer 3	Network
Layer 4	Transport
Layer 5	Session
Layer 6	Presentation
Layer 7	Application

OSI layer 1 covers all of the physical connectivity specifications of devices. This includes any electrical voltage, pin-outs, connectors, cables, and hubs. Layer 1 defines all network adapters, network devices that do not work in layer 2, and host bus adapters used in storage area networks (SANs). The main purpose of layer 1 includes establishing a connection or disconnection from a network medium. Layer 1 also covers modulation and flow control over the network medium.

OSI layer 2 controls the means of controlling data transfer among network entities. Layer 2 also handles the control mechanism of data transferred among network entities. Bridges and switches both work within layer 2. Although there are layer 3 switches, they work on layer 2 without the use of a router.

OSI layer 3 controls the functional means of transferring data among network entities. Layer 3 handles the variable length sequences to and from destinations among networks. It also handles QoS for the transport layer. Routing also occurs at layer 3 (in fact, routing is the most common use of layer 3).

OSI layer 4 controls the transfer of data among users, and provides reliable data transfer to the layers above itself. Layer 4 controls flow as well as errors. This layer controls the retransmit of packets lost in transport among users. TCP uses this layer as the control portion of the protocol. Layer 4 also converts data into the User Datagram Protocol (UDP) and Stream Control Transmission Protocol (SCTP) formats.

OSI layer 5 controls the networked communications between computers. This includes managing and terminating connections among machines. Layer 5 controls duplex modes on network traffic, which includes full- and half-duplex operations. TCP uses layer 5 to control the flow of data and to terminate connections.

OSI layer 6 provides a standard interface to transform data into the correct format for the application layer. Standard uses of layer 6 include data encryption, compression, and specific types of encoding, including MIME encoding. Layer 6 also allows for the transformation into and out of the XML format.

OSI layer 7 controls the means a user needs to access network resources through an application. Programs that use layer 7 include SMTP, HTTP, FTP, Telnet, IPSec, IM, and other applications.

Each layer of the OSI model handles different portions of the networking process and helps to define the process of finding errors, or just understanding how the complex process of networking actually works. Armed with the information from the OSI model, we can begin to truly understand, create, and even fix networks as well as the protocols used to transmit data across networks.

Troubleshooting Common Problems on Small Networks

As with any type of technology, sometimes things just don't work out the way you want them to. This truth brings us to the troubleshooting portion of this chapter. Learning about the different tools available to help identify and solve problems with networking is paramount to successfully sharing resources locally or across the globe.

The first step to learning about troubleshooting falls into the theoretical arena with the OSI model. See Table 14-10 for a list of the OSI model layers and their names. The OSI model helps us break networks into different layers in terms of how they correspond to the different applications and protocols we use to transmit data. Each protocol works in different ways, and the OSI model helps us understand how they function and what they do.

Using the Network Diagnostics and Repair Option

Windows 7 offers the ability to self-diagnose network connectivity problems using Windows Network Diagnostics. This feature can help to identify problems with network adapters and TCP/IP issues. If you do not have a cable properly connecting the adapter to the network, it will also notify you of this problem. The wizard goes through a simple set of tests to determine the problem, alleviating the need to complete these tasks manually. However, if the wizard cannot fix the problem, you must determine the problem yourself, as discussed in the other troubleshooting sections of this chapter.

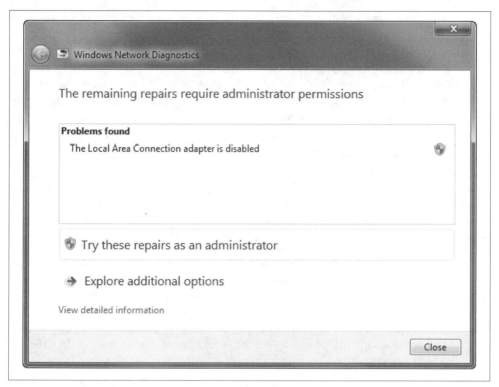

Figure 14-13. Diagnosing your networking problem

You can diagnose and repair network problems by completing these steps:

1. Click Start, and then click Control Panel.
2. In the Control Panel, click Network and Internet→Network and Sharing Center.
3. In the Network and Sharing Center, click "Change adapter settings." This opens the Network Connections window.
4. Right-click the network connection you want to troubleshoot and then select Diagnose.
5. When Windows Network Diagnostics finishes testing your network configuration, you'll see a list of possible solutions, as shown in Figure 14-13. Follow the instructions provided to try to correct the problem, or click a solution to have Windows Network Diagnostics perform a troubleshooting task for you.

Checking Physical Connectivity

Using the functionality of the OSI model, you can identify where protocols function to aid in troubleshooting network problems. If you are unable to connect to a network, you should begin at the layer 1 level. This layer tells you to look specifically at the physical connectivity of your computer to the network. Identifying whether your cabling works correctly should be the first step of network troubleshooting. You can usually verify that you have connectivity by making sure that the link light is lit on the network adapter. Usually if your link light is lit and the activity light is showing activity by flashing, you can assume the computer has connectivity. With wireless routers, you can go a step further by logging in to the router and confirming whether the device shows up as being currently connected.

If you complete the troubleshooting steps in the section but you still have issues connecting to the network properly, replace the network cable or check the wireless configuration settings. If you have doubts as to whether you have connectivity with Ethernet, take a few minutes to replace the network cable, as it is easy and inexpensive to replace this piece of equipment. Telltale signs that you need to replace your cable include no link light when connected to a powered-on network device, and the fact that you can either only send or only receive data.

If you have verified that you have connectivity, you must determine whether the network adapter exists within Device Manager on your computer. If your computer sees the network adapter, verify that you have the latest driver installed. Sometimes you can have problems with network functionality due to an old device driver associated with the network adapter. This scenario can happen after a software update to the operating system and when a third-party application makes changes to a shared control file, or to a file the driver relies upon for quality communications.

If you still cannot connect to the network, check your TCP/IP configuration settings, as discussed previously in the section "Configuring IPv4, IPv6, and Other Protocols" on page 567 of this chapter. You can also use the techniques discussed in the upcoming sections "Using the Command Line to Diagnose Network Problems" on page 577 and "Fixing Network Problems" on page 580 to help you with troubleshooting configuration issues. If none of these efforts resolves the problem, try replacing the network adapter with a second network adapter. This should verify connectivity problems or resolve the issue. If the problem follows the adapter, you can assume the adapter has a problem. If you still cannot connect to the network with a new adapter, verify that the slot in the motherboard works correctly. If your network adapters are integrated into the motherboard, you can still add a different physical network adapter into a slot on the motherboard. You may then want to disable the integrated adapters in firmware to avoid IRQ conflicts on your computer.

To check the functionality of the slot in the motherboard, install the network adapter into a different slot on the motherboard. If you still cannot connect to the network or see an adapter, you should update firmware on your motherboard or contact the manufacturer's technical support to either identify the problem with the board or get a replacement board, assuming you have warranty support on the board in question. Once you have the replacement board, you can connect the network adapter to verify connectivity.

Using the Command Line to Diagnose Network Problems

Microsoft offers many different tools to help diagnose network problems. The best tools for testing your network are those available at the command line. For troubleshooting, be sure to start the command line with elevated privileges by completing the following steps:

1. Click Start, click All Programs, and then click Accessories.
2. Right-click Command Prompt and then select "Run as administrator."
3. This opens an administrator command prompt that you can use to perform any necessary troubleshooting procedures.

To begin troubleshooting, you should first determine the IP configuration for all network adapters on your computer. To accomplish this task, type `IPconfig /all` at the command prompt you opened previously. You will see the output of the TCP/IP stack as well as some physical details concerning the characteristics of your local machine, similar to Example 14-1, which gives you a great view of the properties controlling access to your network and its resources. You can see immediately the name of the host, type of connection, routing capability, DNS name, MAC address, IP address, DHCP server IP address, subnet, default gateway, and IP address for each adapter connected to the computer.

Example 14-1. IPConfig /all output

```
C:\>IPconfig /all
Windows IP Configuration
    Host Name . . . . . . . . . . . . : RC1-5600
    Primary Dns Suffix  . . . . . . . :
    Node Type . . . . . . . . . . . . : Hybrid
    IP Routing Enabled. . . . . . . . : No
    WINS Proxy Enabled. . . . . . . . : No
    DNS Suffix Search List. . . . . . : globalsuite.net

Wireless LAN adapter Wireless Network Connection:
    Media State . . . . . . . . . . . : Media disconnected
    Connection-specific DNS Suffix  . : ok.cox.net
    Description . . . . . . . . . . . : Broadcom 802.11g Network Adapter
    Physical Address. . . . . . . . . : 00-14-A5-A0-15-F1
    DHCP Enabled. . . . . . . . . . . : Yes
    Autoconfiguration Enabled . . . . : Yes

Ethernet adapter Local Area Connection:
    Connection-specific DNS Suffix  . : globalsuite.net
    Description . . . . . . . . . . . : Realtek RTL8139/810x Fast Ethernet NIC
    Physical Address. . . . . . . . . : 00-16-36-46-FF-15
    DHCP Enabled. . . . . . . . . . . : Yes
    Autoconfiguration Enabled . . . . : Yes
    Link-local IPv6 Address . . . . . : fe80::2da2:3d:9f2e:297c%10(Preferred)
    IPv4 Address. . . . . . . . . . . : 158.18.184.133(Preferred)
    Subnet Mask . . . . . . . . . . . : 255.255.0.0
    Lease Obtained. . . . . . . . . . : Tuesday, October 12, 2009 2:02:32 PM
```

```
Lease Expires . . . . . . . . . . : Wednesday, October 13, 2009 2:35:32 PM
Default Gateway . . . . . . . . . : 158.18.0.1
DHCP Server . . . . . . . . . . . : 158.18.0.1
DHCPv6 IAID . . . . . . . . . . . : 234886710
DNS Servers . . . . . . . . . . . : 4.2.2.1
NetBIOS over Tcpip. . . . . . . . : Enabled
```

The first setting you need to verify is the IP address of the computer. If you are using DHCP on a network device, make sure you see DHCP Enabled. . . . . : Yes in the output of the IPCONFIG /ALL command. If you see this setting, verify that you have received an IP address. If you do not have an IP address, check whether you can see an address for the DHCP server. When identifying the IP address, if you see either 0.0.0.0 or 169.265.X.X as an IP address, you did not connect to the DHCP server. You can try to reapply for an IP address by typing the IPconfig /renew command at the command line. If this fails to give you an IP address, try inputting a static IP address within the subnet of the DHCP server to see if you can gain access to the network (you'll need to visit the adapter's configuration as described in "Configuring IPv4, IPv6, and Other Protocols" on page 567, earlier in this chapter). If you can, make sure the DHCP server is running correctly. Alternatively, simply unplug and then plug in the device to force it to reset itself.

Windows offers a host of commands for testing your network, but by far the king of all commands is ping. Pinging allows you to direct specific-size packets at a computer to verify connectivity. Ping actually echoes back with information on the connectivity to another computer. If you wanted to verify your ability to send packets, you should first ping your computer on the local loopback address, 127.0.0.1. The loopback address provides a simple mechanism for testing the Windows network stack.

Next, proceed to verify that name resolution is working correctly. You can accomplish this task by pinging the name of a computer on the Internet, such as a website. If you are unable to ping the computers on the Internet, check the TCP/IP settings of the network adapter to verify that you have enabled the TCP/IP protocol. See Example 14-2 for examples of how to ping different network hosts by name or IP address.

Example 14-2. Ping command

```
C:\>ping 127.0.0.1

Pinging 127.0.0.1 with 32 bytes of data:

Reply from 127.0.0.1: bytes=32 time<1ms TTL=128
Reply from 127.0.0.1: bytes=32 time<1ms TTL=128
Reply from 127.0.0.1: bytes=32 time<1ms TTL=128
Reply from 127.0.0.1: bytes=32 time<1ms TTL=128

Ping statistics for 127.0.0.1:
    Packets: Sent = 4, Received = 4, Lost = 0 (0% loss),
Approximate round trip times in milliseconds:
    Minimum = 0ms, Maximum = 0ms, Average = 0ms
```

```
C:\>ping google.com

Pinging google.com [72.14.207.99] with 32 bytes of data:

Reply from 72.14.207.99: bytes=32 time=52ms TTL=235
Reply from 72.14.207.99: bytes=32 time=75ms TTL=235
Reply from 72.14.207.99: bytes=32 time=51ms TTL=235
Reply from 72.14.207.99: bytes=32 time=52ms TTL=235

Ping statistics for 72.14.207.99:
    Packets: Sent = 4, Received = 4, Lost = 0 (0% loss),
Approximate round trip times in milliseconds:
    Minimum = 51ms, Maximum = 75ms, Average = 57ms
```

If you cannot receive packets by pinging another computer, you should proceed to ping the IP address of your default gateway. You can find the IP address of your default gateway in the output of the IPconfig /all command.

If you are unable to ping your default gateway, either contact your network administrator or check the gateway. In most instances, your gateway consists of a broadband router or similar device, and you should check the device for proper functionality. You can identify errors with packets on the device by looking for status lights identifying packet collisions or another error. Try resetting the device by unplugging it, waiting a few seconds, and powering it on again. Alternatively, if the device has a Reset button, you can press this button as well. If this process does not work, you may need to update firmware on or replace the network device. If your default gateway consists of a cable modem or DSL router, contact your service provider for steps to alleviate your problem.

If you can ping your default gateway but are unable to connect to the Internet and you are using a network router or other personally managed network device for a gateway, check the cable going to your outside provider. You should also try to ping outside your internal network to test for outside connectivity. If you can successfully ping an external IP address your gateway should be in good shape. If you can ping by IP address externally but not to a name, such as Google.com, you need to verify that you have input the IP address of your DNS server properly in the TCP/IP configuration. With DHCP, the network device usually provides the DNS server address, so you would need to check the configuration of the device. If you verify these settings but still cannot connect to the Internet, use the NSLookup command to check for DNS resolution. See Example 14-3 for an example of how to use the NSLookup command.

Example 14-3. NSLookup output

```
C:\>nslookup
Default Server: ns1.securestream.net
Address:  69.150.220.8

> securestream.net
Server:  ns1.securestream.net
Address:  69.150.220.8
```

```
Name:     securestream.net
Address:  69.150.220.9
```

To verify DNS resolution for connectivity to the Internet or possibly your Active Directory domain, type `NSLookup` at the command line. You should receive a `>` prompt. Type the name of the domain to which you want to connect and press the Enter key. If you receive output showing the IP addresses of the domain, your resolution works correctly. If you receive output that says something like "Non-Existent" domain, you should try another DNS server for output or contact your ISP to find out why its DNS server fails queries.

If you can query the DNS name correctly but are still having problems with Internet connectivity, use the `tracetrt` command to check the routing device hops between yourself and the desired location. At the command line, you can accomplish this task by typing:

```
tracert <Destination IP or Name>
```

You will see a maximum of 30 hops to the destination, including an IP address, and possibly the name of the device. If you see timeouts or other error messages for addresses outside your network, there are problems outside of your control. You should contact your service provider to determine whether it is aware of these problems and is working to correct them.

Fixing Network Problems

TCP/IP networking has many different facets, and additional protocols that ride on top of it. Although it is the single most prolific technology in use today, there are inherent problems with some implementations. Use Table 14-11 to help diagnose common problems with network connectivity or protocol issues.

Table 14-11. Troubleshooting matrix

Problem	Resolution
No IP Address	Check DHCP scope on the router or server.
	Input a static IP address.
Cannot Ping Machine	Ping `<Host Name>`.
	Ping `<Default Gateway>`.
Cannot Ping 127.0.0.1	Verify that the TCP/IP protocols are enabled on the adapter.
	Verify that the adapter is enabled in Device Manager.
Cannot Ping Default Gateway	Verify that the gateway has network connectivity.
	Check the cables connecting your computer to the network device.
	Reset the network device by powering it off and then powering it on.
	Contact your ISP.

Problem	Resolution
	Replace the network device.
Cannot Reach Internet	Check gateway connectivity using TRACERT <IP Destination>.
	Verify DNS resolution using NSLookup.
	Input DNS server addresses as part of the network device DHCP configuration.
	Input DNS server addresses in the TCP/IP properties of the network adapter.
No Network Connectivity	For Ethernet, check the cable connecting the network adapter to the network.
	For wireless, reorient antenna, relocate router, or try a different channel.
	Check Link/Activity status on the adapter.
	Update the network adapter driver.
	Flash firmware on motherboard (integrated adapters only).
	Move the network adapter to a different slot on the motherboard.
	Replace the network adapter.
Only Send or Receive Packets	For Ethernet, reseat the network cable or replace the network cable. For wireless, reorient antennae, relocate router, or try a different channel.

CHAPTER 15

Protecting Your Computer with Windows Defender and Windows Firewall

Hackers and malicious individuals enjoy nothing more than creating nasty programs that destroy your data or cause your computer to crash. Your computer is at risk every time you connect to the Internet, browse the Web, or work with files from another computer. To protect your computer and your data, you need to secure your computer with protection software.

Microsoft has taken a firm stance with security in Windows 7. It has added many new security features in this release, alleviating some of the most common security threats used against Windows users. This chapter discusses the nature of many common security threats, and the applications Microsoft offers to eliminate them. I will discuss malware, viruses, spyware, and the tools available to eliminate these threats from your Windows 7 installation. I will also discuss Windows Defender and the Windows Firewall.

Please take the time to read this chapter and understand how to use the products Windows 7 offers to help you retain the data on your computer, reduce security problems, and eliminate programs that may try to leech computer resources or exploit your personal data. Malware, viruses, and spyware are serious problems, and protecting against them is vital to the use of a computer housing any type of confidential or private information.

Navigating the Computer Security Maze

It seems like every time Microsoft or other software providers find a better way to protect your computer, hackers and malicious individuals find new ways to exploit computer vulnerabilities. In this section, we'll introduce the various techniques being used to attack computers and discuss the software programs used to prevent these types of attacks.

Introducing Malware

Many people spend a lot of time on the Internet browsing websites, downloading data, and never thinking of the potential problems of malicious software (malware) creeping onto their computers. Some such software simply reports your surfing habits, and other software tries to take control of your computer. Malware consists of programs that are suspicious in nature and have the malicious intent of infiltrating your computer without your consent. The industry also defines malware as software with a legitimate purpose that contains harmful bugs that ravage a computer.

Before the proliferation of broadband Internet connections, most malware was kept in check by the limited bandwidth of dial-up Internet connections. When you dialed into your service provider, you didn't really have the bandwidth to allow your computer to be compromised without your knowledge and most computers were not left online all the time for people to try to connect to and harm. However, because broadband connections are fast and always on, many people today simply leave their computers connected to the Internet all the time. This works against the computer owner, especially if she connects directly to a cable or DSL modem. With a direct connection to the Internet, you have left your computer open to numerous attacks. This is where malware comes into play. Malicious individuals have the opportunity to fingerprint your computer in an attempt to find vulnerabilities, and eventually your computer succumbs to an attack, which allows someone to load software on your computer without your consent.

 When you are troubleshooting a problem with your ISP, you may be asked to disconnect your computer temporarily from your router and connect directly to the cable or DSL modem. Before you do this, you should be sure that you have the latest updates to Windows and that your antivirus and antimalware software is up to date. Many of the attackers are actually automated scripts that sweep large chunks of IP addresses at a time, so it is only a matter of time before your computer is probed by one of these scripts.

At the time of this writing, the SANS Internet Storm Center reported that an unpatched Windows system would be likely to survive for no more than 70 minutes upon being connected to the Internet without protection. For more information and precautions you can take, see *http://isc.sans.org/survivaltime.html*.

Another way for malicious software to get onto your computer is via your own use of the Internet. You may recall a time when you visited a website and were faced with numerous pop-ups asking you to vote for a website or install specific add-ons in order to see the content of a website. More than likely, you either purposefully clicked, allowing the malicious program to load, or you were misled into clicking the wrong button and the software loaded by itself. Many of these websites load harmful software to take advantage of your computer without your consent. Some even load dialers onto your computer to use your modem to make phone calls that are then charged to you.

Other malicious programs get loaded onto a computer without the owner knowing they are there because they are able to mask their running processes. The industry calls this particularly heinous type of software a *rootkit*. Rootkits conceal their running processes and files, and sometimes they even morph process names and files to conceal their true nature. Most of the time rootkits disguise themselves as drivers, parts of the operating system, or kernel modules.

Kernel-level rootkits replace portions of code programmed into the computer kernel. The modified code added by the rootkit usually hides an additional program, allowing remote users to use the infected computer. Usually kernel-level rootkits replace a computer driver, device driver, or additional module to accomplish their goal. If the rootkit has bugs in the code, it may compromise the integrity of the computer from a stability standpoint, in addition to introducing the security implications of infection. These types of rootkits are extremely difficult to identify and clean, which makes them extremely dangerous.

Other common types of rootkits include library-level kits and application-level rootkits. A library-level kit will replace a computer call with modified code to mask the information about the hijacked module. Application-level rootkits replace common applications with modified code or a Trojan. These applications mimic the behavior of the previous application and mask their modification of the computer. Sometimes application-level rootkits replace patches loaded onto a computer for security purposes.

Virtualized rootkits modify the boot sequence of a computer to load their content instead of the intended operating system. Once they have introduced their payload, they load the operating system as a virtual computer, which enables them to gain control of all calls to the hardware by the guest operating system. Although no virtualized rootkits exist in the wild, they do exist in controlled environments. For example, Microsoft and the University of Michigan jointly developed a virtual rootkit, which they termed Virtual Machine Based Rootkit, or VMBR.

Rootkits also serve as a tool to abuse an infected computer using a program called a *backdoor*. Backdoors also fall into the category of malware. Backdoors are programs that allow attackers to use a computer for their personal use or profit. Backdoors allow the attacker to manipulate the compromised computer to perform single or even strategic attacks against other people's computers. In addition to allowing remote connectivity to the computer, backdoors may also allow an attacker to run software at an elevated level usually reserved for administrators of the compromised computer.

Additional malware programs include key loggers and denial-of-service attack tools. Key loggers usually log or directly send keystrokes from the compromised computer to another user on a remote computer. Denial-of-service attack tools are loaded by an attacker or rootkit and allow the compromised computer to be used against web servers, denying users the ability to connect to the web server.

Denial-of-service tools accomplish their task by overloading the server with requests until the computer under attack runs out of available resources to honor the overwhelming number of requests for a particular resource. Although a standard denial-of-service attack uses a single computer to try to accomplish this goal, a distributed denial-of-service attack uses any number of compromised computers, making it even more difficult to stop the attack by blocking requests from a single IP address.

Whatever the flavor of malware, most of it provides no value to the computer on which it exists. Malware has many impractical purposes, including malicious use of the infected computer. It may also allow the use of personal information housed on the infected computer for profiteering, or identity theft. Malware makes up a very large portion of the problems inherent to the Internet in its current state, and it poses a great threat to private information housed on private networks. The worst part of malware seems to be computer users' lack of knowledge of how to remove and prevent these types of programs from infecting their computers. This includes home users and corporate IT professionals alike. Malware may arguably be the worst threat against computers to date.

Understanding Antimalware Programs

Recently more companies have realized the potential harm of malware programs, and they have tried to take steps to begin removing malware from their environments. With the onset of the Sarbanes-Oxley and HIPAA acts, compliance is on the rise and many people have started to realize how vulnerable their private data has become to outside entities. Armed with this knowledge, security practices have become increasingly important for many organizations, and everyone feels the pain as we struggle to maintain a balance between user-friendly computing and secure computing. To combat the problem with malware, many vendors now offer tools that will remove even the toughest malware out there. The industry refers to these programs as *antimalware tools*.

Antimalware tools scan and remove malware from infected computers. If you type "antimalware" in a search engine, you will discover some of the more than 6 million web pages on the topic. The reason for this relates directly to the inexhaustible amount of malware floating around on the Internet. As discussed previously, most users have become aware of the problem with this type of software only in the last few years. Some people were aware of the problem early and tried to explain to others how difficult it may become, especially in the corporate world, but mostly it was ignored. Now antimalware has taken the lead in the battle for securing your data.

Antimalware programs work similarly to antivirus scanners—identifying malicious programs on the suspect computer, whether in RAM, on the hard drive, or on network shares connected to the computer. Once the antimalware program has identified the threat, it will either alert the user for further instructions on how to handle the problem, or it will delete the program and eliminate any registry entries associated with the rogue program.

As with antivirus engines, multiple malware scanners are your best bet for eliminating malware programs from suspect computers. You can find these types of programs online, and using them will eliminate the vast majority of malware on an infected computer. For the purposes of malware removal, Windows 7 offers Windows Defender, arguably the largest and most powerful antimalware engine available.

Antimalware programs can identify and remove many of the unwanted programs on your computer, including unwanted browser help objects, startup programs, registry settings, toolbar buttons, Winsock hijackers, Internet Explorer plug-ins, ActiveX controls, DNS hacks, and anonymous proxy rerouters. Each type of unwanted program relates to methods that malware writers employ to get their malicious code onto your computer. Some of the methods employ deceptive tactics to make you believe you are loading a beneficial program onto your computer while manipulating data on your computer so that it can be accessed on remote servers. These programs leave you vulnerable to the less than savory strategy of the malware writer.

Currently many antivirus companies are beginning to enter the world of malware removal by either using third-party applications or purchasing the engines of antimalware programs and integrating them into their own products for malware identification and removal. Although malware may seem similar to a virus, it is indeed a separate category of malicious code. Viruses replicate themselves from computer to computer; malware is a silent threat that users usually unknowingly install.

Also, note that you may have to hand-edit the registry to remove some types of malware. If you require this type of intervention, take great care when editing your computer's registry. Editing the registry can render a computer unusable and require the intervention of a recovery service or large amounts of time to correct. If you are not comfortable editing the registry, consult a computer service or repair shop to remove these types of malicious programs. Most computer service companies can remove these programs within a short period and require only a small fee to clean your computer. This can help immensely when the programs are embedded into the computer or have metamorphic qualities.

Understanding Computer Viruses

The industry defines a computer *virus* as a program that spreads by inserting itself into executable code, documents, or programs, and then self-replicates to other documents, users, or computers when the compromised file is shared. We refer to a computer with a virus as *infected*, and we try to inoculate the computer against future infections. Viruses are usually malicious and sometimes harbor backdoors or Trojans.

Viruses were extremely prevalent in the earlier days of personal computing and they had a devastating effect on computers. Viruses come in all shapes and sizes, as well as varying strengths of maliciousness. Some of the methods viruses used to execute included time bombs that would go off at a predetermined time, and logic bombs that a user triggered by completing some predefined action on the computer.

Another very nasty virus included the stealth boot virus, which attacked the boot sector of the host computer or floppy disk. This virus would not allow the computer to boot, and it required considerable work to remove. This type of virus was more common due to the lack of networks available. Most files were moved from computer to computer via floppy disks. Once the infected floppy was inserted into the receiving computer, the virus code executed, infecting the new computer.

Viruses are terrible in the sense that they can replicate themselves at an inexhaustible rate. Luckily, because more people use virus protection, they are not as widespread as before. However, now that we have the ability to transmit data at gigabit speeds and process data in the gigahertz range, viruses pose an even greater threat than previously known. This brings us to the subject of worms.

Computer worms have taken on the traditional bogeyman role of the computer virus, though viruses continue to present a real threat. A *worm* is defined as a piece of software using a computer network to copy itself and generate new hosts by compromising security flaws in applications or the host operating system. Once a worm makes it onto a network, it begins to scan for other computers with a similar or identical flaw used to infect the first host. The more hosts the worm can find to replicate itself, the greater the impact it has on the host computer and network. Some worms have generated so much traffic that they have literally brought the Internet to its knees.

The first worm was created at the Xerox PARC laboratory in Palo Alto, California. One of the computer scientists at the lab created a worm to use on the different host computers in the facility to process data for a centralized program. This was in the early days of the PC. Before this, all users connected to a CPU. To garner the processing power of the individual PCs in the facility as a single unit, the scientist broke his data into chunks for each PC to process. Once the PCs finished their work, they transmitted the results back to the controlling node. At one point, the worm began using more and more resources of the host's computers, until it failed to give the user computer availability. This required the creator to find a way to disarm the worm, which in turn gave the user use of the infected computer and the network it flooded with traffic. Although this worm had no malicious intent against the host computer, some of the more recent incarnations of this type of program have caused considerable damage to entire networks. Some worms have rendered entire networks unusable for days, weeks, and even months, due to their inherent capability to replicate themselves.

The most recent embodiment in the computer virus family comes in the form of email viruses. Recent years have given us some particularly nasty specimens, including (but not limited to) the ILOVEYOU, MELISSA, and, of course, Mydoom viruses. Each of these email viruses had a devastating effect on computers, causing many providers to turn off their email computers to prevent the virus from taking over and spreading.

Most email viruses use the address book of the user executing an email program to spread themselves to other users, who in turn execute the program, allowing their address books to be manipulated by the virus and spread even farther.

Almost all viruses execute with the use of another program, replicate themselves, and continue their path of destruction. Some replace executable files on the computer they infect, which the operating system executes, releasing the virus to spread to other computers. All types of computers are susceptible to viruses. Additionally, all operating systems have vulnerabilities allowing the execution of virus-ridden code, so no one vendor offers a completely safe product.

Although some viruses try to inundate a network to eliminate its use, others are malicious and want to destroy data on a computer. Viruses can be embedded in all types of files, including video, audio, document, and image files. Some of the newer viruses are embedded into JPEG images for execution. This is especially dangerous because the browser has the intrinsic capability to execute and display images. Browsers make up the largest group of applications in use on computers today. With this fact evident, the propagation of viruses could become even greater in the future than in the past.

As with malware, viruses that take the place of programs used by the operating system may cause instability of the host computer. This can cause crashes, hangs, and intermittent lock-ups. Trojans fall into this category as well, but they work slightly differently than viruses. Trojans follow true to their name. Trojans are also referred to as Trojan horses, relating to the famous story told by Homer in *The Iliad* of the great battle between the Greeks and the Trojans over Princess Helen. To get a Trojan on your computer, you must invite the program onto your computer. Usually you do this by loading a utility or other program that has a purported valid use on the computer. Unbeknownst to you, the program includes a Trojan, which gives an external user the ability to use the computer remotely. The remote user can then cause great harm to the data on the computer or expose its use for personal gain.

The Trojan may lie dormant on the computer until you open the program, and then it may require the use of a specific program to open a predefined network port. Once you meet the criteria for the Trojan to work, it allows a remote user to manipulate the infected computer for his purposes. These purposes usually fall in line with malicious uses including profiteering, denial-of-service attacks, distributed denial-of-service attacks, key logging, and identity theft.

As you can see, the lines between malware and viruses are very blurry in terms of the devastation they can wreak on a computer. The difference lies in the way the program comes to reside on the infected host computer. Malware makes its way onto the computer without your knowledge and allows remote control of the computer. Malware does not necessarily replicate itself to gain the use of other computers. Viruses always replicate themselves. Sometimes viruses employ the same method of installation on the infected host computer, but they always replicate themselves to other computers. They act in very much the same way as a virus acts in the human body, which is how they received their name. The good news is that since the popularity of the Internet, many viruses have been permanently eradicated from the industry, due to the capability to transfer code to eliminate the viruses from infected computers.

Introducing Antivirus Programs

The intent of an antivirus program is to identify, inoculate, disinfect, or clean a virus or other malware program from a computer. Antivirus programs usually work in two different ways. Most scan a computer in its entirety, looking for known viruses based on their databases of virus listings, and then they delete, inoculate, remove, or quarantine the infected file. Other antivirus programs watch file behavior on the computer. If the program detects unusual behavior, it will usually capture the file, scan it, and then either ask the user for input on how to handle the issue or quarantine the file for further inspection and possible deletion.

Most current commercial antivirus programs use both of these methods to detect and eradicate viruses from infected computers. This helps eliminate the threat of infection by watching the most consistent way viruses try to infiltrate computers. The most common elements of virus removal involve repair of the file itself. This consists of the antivirus program trying to remove the offending code from the infected file. If the removal process does not work, the antivirus program usually will quarantine the file discovered and prompt you for further instructions on how to handle the problem with the infected file. When you log on to the computer after the quarantine process, you must decide whether to try to repair the file again or delete the infected file.

It should be noted that you should always attempt to use multiple antivirus programs to repair either files of a sensitive nature or those used by the operating system before deleting the files. If you have a virus in a file you want to keep, you should try to use multiple antivirus engines to repair the file. This also holds true for operating system files. Operating system files infected with viruses may render the infected computer incapable of operating correctly, sometimes to the point where the infected computer will not boot into the operating system. Infections of this type sometimes require a boot disk with an antivirus program to remove the virus from the computer.

Antivirus programs detect viruses via dictionary scans, behavior analysis, and other methods. Each detection technique follows a specific type of logic in order to find, repair, remove, or delete an infected file. Each approach is unique. Most antivirus engines employ at least two of these types of analysis in order to identify viruses. The third category is usually used only when specific types of viruses are encountered. Each approach helps us to identify the methods virus writers employ to launch their code so that we can begin the process of eradicating viruses from our environment:

Dictionary scanning
> This approach uses a database of known antivirus types. When the antivirus program scans the computer in question, it looks for specific code listed in the files it scans. If it discovers suspect code, it will try to identify the virus strain, report the

infection, and complete whatever predefined options the user has defined in case of corruption. Usually a dictionary-based antivirus program scans the files when the operating system opens the files for use. This includes files, programs, email, and other known methods of attack.

Not all virus writers allow their code to remain static. That means the code may be able to change or "morph" into something different to eliminate the effectiveness of dictionary scanning. These types of viruses fall into the *polymorphic* and *metamorphic* categories. They modify themselves to prevent detection, and even employ encryption to help hide portions of themselves from antivirus programs.

Polymorphic code changes into different forms while keeping the original algorithm intact, allowing the same action to occur when executed but letting the code slip past dictionary analysis. This helps the code hide its presence from antivirus programs trying to detect and rid infected computers of viruses. Malicious-virus programmers use this type of mechanism to keep their code "in the wild," allowing the virus to propagate freely without detection.

Metamorphic code literally reprograms itself by translating itself into a similar representation, and then back into the original form. Metamorphic code can also use different operating systems affected by the virus. That means a single virus could employ different methods of infecting Windows, Linux, and BSD in the same code. This method allows the virus to slip through detection of dictionary analysis by antivirus programs. Programmers go to great lengths to see that their viruses do maximum damage by eliminating the simplest of detection efforts by the public.

Checking for suspicious behavior

This is a different approach to virus identification. This approach does not employ dictionary databases to find and eradicate viruses. Instead, it monitors a program's behavior on the computer. When the antivirus program sees a program attempt to write data into an executable program, the antivirus program will identify the behavior, flag it as a potential problem, and ask the user what to do with the offending file.

Metamorphic viruses that reprogram themselves create brand-new types of viruses. Because the new virus does not have a signature to match in a database, the behavior analysis method allows the antivirus program to capture and begin to identify the new offending virus. However, if the user accepts the behavior of the offending virus, this allows the virus to propagate, eliminating the effectiveness of the antivirus program. This type of analysis also lends itself to lots of false positives, making it a less effective technique than other methods of virus identification and eradication.

Other approaches

Other approaches to identify, capture, and eliminate viruses include *heuristic analysis* and *sandboxes*. Each method employs different processes to identify and capture viruses in an effort to eradicate their capability to propagate. Heuristic analysis may emulate the beginning lines of code executed by a program to identify the program's behavior as self-modifying, or it may use a similar technique to discover that a program is looking for other executable files. In either case, the antivirus program may flag the file as a virus. Heuristic filters employ replicable methods to study, ascertain, or identify viruses through their perceived behavior.

Sandboxes emulate an operating system and allow code to run in a simulated environment. When the code runs, the antivirus program analyzes the emulated operating system for changes that are perceived as a virus. These types of analysis require sophisticated programs and use large amounts of computer resources to run. These features lend themselves to finding new viruses and keeping them out of the user environment, but they do not lend themselves to real-time analysis, requiring the antivirus program to run either as a managed background process or during off-peak usage times.

Each process lends itself to different types of virus identification and removal processes. Not all antivirus programs use the same methods of identification and no one antivirus program can identify and eliminate all viruses. Because of this, you may want to supplement scans of your installed virus software with online scans using a different virus engine. Take the time to research the different antivirus programs available, including free scanners online, to help identify and eliminate viral code from your computer.

Understanding Spyware

Spyware falls into a broad category of software designed to gain control of a computer without the user's consent. As the name suggests, the program loaded onto the computer spies on the user, and the industry has come to realize that spyware also allows a remote user to control how the computer operates. Sometimes spyware only offers the data housed on the computer for use in spying on a user's habits. Some companies use this data for targeted advertising or to manipulate content based on the user's browsing habits.

Spyware watches what you do on your computer and sends the data over the Internet to a collection point for future use. Sometimes these collection points are data warehouse computers that let marketing groups purchase browsing habits to begin an advertising campaign based on the way you and other people browse the Web, thereby allowing them greater financial gain. Some types of spyware will attempt to record your keystrokes in the hopes of getting personal information for monetary gain. These programs try to intercept any usernames, passwords, or credit card information you use while online, and they are the most dangerous type of spyware.

Other spyware programs monitor the use of websites on the compromised computer. They then attack you with a barrage of pop-up windows. Some simply begin popping up advertisements of competitor websites in the hopes of gaining advertising dollars through your clicking on the advertisements. Most of these types of programs fall into a category called *adware*. Not all pop-up windows are associated with programs loaded on the computer; some simply are generated by the code on a website. With this in mind, if you see pop-ups on a regular basis whenever you use your browser, you probably need to look into cleaning spyware off your computer. If you visit a website and get the same pop-up or a similar pop-up every time, it is probably due to the code on the website. For example, the Barnes & Noble website (*http://www.bn.com*) used to display a pop-up with the latest advertisement whenever you visited the home page. This type of pop-up is not the result of adware or spyware. However, if you visited the Barnes & Noble website and got pop-ups for competing or unrelated sites, this was probably the result of adware or spyware.

Most spyware capitalizes on the integration of the Internet Explorer browser into the Windows operating system. This integration allowed individuals to write code to get information from the browser and the operating system, and it allows companies to pull information from unsuspecting users when they visit a website using ActiveX controls and other applications loaded onto your computer.

An example of a program that integrates the Internet Explorer browser into the Windows operating system is the Alexa toolbar. The Alexa toolbar is an application defined as a browser helper object that includes some useful tools, such as a pop-up blocker, a search engine, and a link to Alexa.com and Amazon.com. The toolbar also reports the website usage of the local computer to a collection point at Alexa. Some dispute the Alexa toolbar spyware classification, because the user has to agree to an end-user license agreement (EULA).

One of the most prolific spyware programs was Gator. This program offered to house your personal passwords for applications and websites. Although the program held on to your personal data, it also spied on the browsing habits of users and sent the information back to Claria Corporation. Another prolific spyware program was called Bargain Buddy. Bargain Buddy loaded onto the computer in a not-so-above-the-board manner. Exact Advertising then paid the installing website money for loading the software, and the program began popping up advertisements to the user.

Some of the more recent applications of spyware include software advertised as a spyware removal tool. Though these tools advertise removal of spyware on infected computers, they actually cause damage to the computer on which they are installed. Some argue against the use of the term *spyware* for these programs because they actually require the user to install them on the computer, and some include a EULA, which flies in the initial definition of spyware.

Another prolific installation path for spyware programs includes the offer of a usable program for peer-to-peer file transfers or other uses that then piggyback the spyware onto the computer when the user installs the program. Kazaa worked in this manner by tricking the user into installing the program, and then allowing the spyware to work in the background without the user's knowledge. After its prolific use on the Internet, someone noticed the problem with the application and made it publicly known that the software was pilfering data from the computer on which it was installed. Kazaa then proceeded to create a new, "lite" version of the product without the spyware attached.

Of course, most of these programs have fallen under attack by the Recording Industry Association of America (RIAA) in the battle against music theft and user rights, and they do not have the same user base as they once did.

Not all spyware comes packaged in the cloak-and-dagger style. Another prolific spyware program, named BonziBUDDY, advertised itself as a companion for children while they surf the Web. It even claimed to allow product price comparisons for the user. What the user did not understand when he or she loaded the program was that it was spying on the usage of the computer. It goes to show that you need to take the time to research the programs asking for your approval before you install them on your computer.

You are the main line of defense against spyware and other malicious programs targeting your computer. Take the time to consider what you are installing, and block your children's ability to install programs onto computers. Some spyware applications come packed with freeware utilities or even games. This makes children a prime target for the installation of programs that may undermine the stability of the computer or that may allow someone to steal your private data.

Introducing Antispyware Programs

Antispyware falls into the same category as antimalware does. Before the proliferation of this type of code across the Internet, a distinction was made between the two types of programs. However, in recent years, these antispyware and antimalware programs have morphed into the same program. Usually you can eliminate spyware using freeware antimalware tools or antivirus scanners. Some specialty tools list themselves as spyware removal tools, but they also help eradicate malware.

It may be more accurate to call spyware *adware* or *nuisance software*. Although some of these offending programs do actually send user data across the Web, they usually do not have a malicious intent against the user. They typically use the data to advertise goods or services to the user by scanning the user's computer for patterns of behavior on browser use. Windows Defender, which is included with Windows 7, will find most types of spyware programs on your computer.

For many in the industry, spyware programs were both a wake-up call and the proverbial straw that broke the camel's back. Many companies in the security business underestimated the threat posed by spyware and were not ready to combat the unique problems it created. This left many people running McAfee, Norton, and other security products without real protection against spyware, until recently. Not only did this leave many longtime users of these security products outraged, but it also created a backlash that was heard throughout the security industry. Why did this occur? Well, most of the security products—even those sold as total security shields—protected your computer from viruses, hackers, abuse, and sometimes even spam, but they did not protect your computer from spyware. In fact, only the 2007 and later editions of the McAfee and Norton security products truly protect you from spyware as well as all the other bad things out there on the Internet.

The backlash created by consumer outrage did have some positive effects, though. As ISPs noticed that people were increasingly canceling their memberships because their computers simply could not be made safe on the Internet, many began offering free security solutions. At the time of this writing, two of the largest ISPs in the United States—Comcast and AOL—provide McAfee security products free to subscribers. Comcast subscribers get a free subscription to McAfee VirusScan, Personal Firewall Plus, Privacy Service, and SpamKiller. AOL included McAfee VirusScan and Personal Firewall Plus in the AOL Safety and Security Center, and also offers spyware protection, phishing protection, and spam protection.

You should note that not all antispyware programs work as advertised. Some of these programs disguise themselves as removal tools, but in fact they install and advertise themselves for use to remote users for malicious intent, or they install advertisement programs onto the computers themselves. Take the time to research any product before you install it on your computer. All reputable programs have websites explaining the use and purpose of their programs, and should have reviews on reputable websites and publications.

Most of the tools available require you to go online to update their databases of known spyware to aid in the removal of these programs. As with any tool you use to remove unwanted programs, take the time to either update it regularly or allow it to connect and retrieve its updates automatically. Most of these programs have a mechanism built in to allow this type of automation and allow the user to go on without the effort to check them as frequently. This does not mean you should set it and forget it. You still need to take the time to verify that they are updating correctly, because from time to time they may not work as advertised.

As with malware, you may occasionally have to hand-edit the registry to remove some types of spyware. If you require this type of intervention, please take great care when editing your computer's registry. Editing the registry can render a computer unusable and require the intervention of a recovery service or large amounts of time to correct. If you are not comfortable editing the registry, consult a computer service or repair shop to remove these types of malicious programs. Most computer service companies can remove such programs within a short period and require only a small fee to clean your computer. This can help immensely when the programs are embedded into the computer or have metamorphic qualities.

Introducing Action Center

Microsoft introduced the Security Center in Windows XP. Windows 7 replaces Security Center with Action Center, which offers greater flexibility. Here you are presented with a console to manage the most common security and maintenance tasks as well as

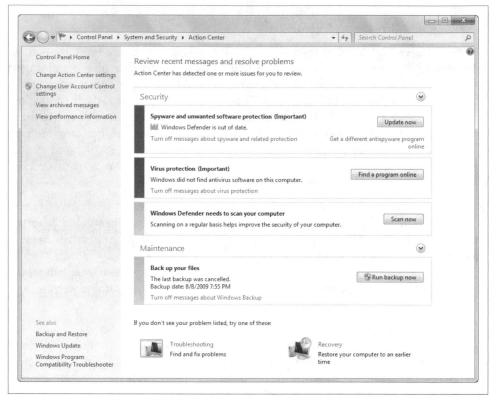

Figure 15-1. Viewing the security status of your computer

elements associated with your computer. Microsoft has made it very simple and effective to use, and continues with the standard "lighting" scheme of red, yellow, and green for ease of use. Figure 15-1 shows an example of the Action Center management window and its available features.

The Action Center offers you the ability to manage security and maintenance operations on the computer from a single interface. You can find the Action Center in the Control Panel. To open the Action Center, follow these steps:

1. Click Start and then click Control Panel.

2. In the Control Panel, click the "Review your computer's status" link under the System and Security heading.

3. On the Security panel, you'll see the status of security-related features, including you computer's default spyware and antivirus program. If you are using Windows Defender, you'll see alerts about required updates and scans as well.

4. On the Maintenance panel, you'll see the status of maintenance-related features, including your computer's backup status and update requirements. If there are maintenance tasks that need to be performed, you'll have related options.

When working in a workgroup configuration, you'll be able to use related security tools to manage the related security features. In a domain configuration, however, it's unlikely that you'll be able to change security-related settings, because they're usually managed through Group Policy.

Using the Action Center, you can easily identify common security features and the tasks associated with securing your operating system. With the Action Center, you can view the status of Windows Firewall, Windows Update, Windows Defender, Internet Options, User Account Control, and Network Access Protection. The Action Center also lists virus protection status and indicates whether you have installed an antivirus solution on the computer.

Using Windows Defender

With the advent of so much suspicious software on the Internet freely working its way onto individual computers, a solution was bound to surface. Microsoft has introduced Windows Defender to champion the removal of spyware and other unwanted software from your computer. Windows 7 uses Windows Defender by default to aid in the identification and removal of spyware and malicious programs from your computer. You may remember Microsoft AntiSpyware as a software program for removing and quarantining spyware on early releases of Windows. Microsoft has greatly enhanced this program and renamed it Windows Defender.

Working with Windows Defender

Microsoft purchased an antispyware tool originally created by GIANT Company Software, called GIANT AntiSpyware. This product originally aided in the fight against spyware on Windows 95 and Windows 98. When Microsoft purchased the product, it did not keep support for these older versions of Windows.

Microsoft announced the release of Windows Defender (then called Microsoft Anti-Spyware) at the 2005 RSA security conference. With the announcement, it stated that the product was freely available to all valid licensed users of the Windows 2000, XP, and Server 2003 products. It championed Microsoft AntiSpyware as a product to help users worldwide in the fight against spyware and malware. Windows Defender offers even greater capability than the older versions, helping to ward off infection by employing several real-time security agents monitoring well-known areas of Windows that spyware and malware change regularly.

Microsoft has also integrated support for Microsoft SpyNet into the Windows Defender product. This support allows users to report spyware and malware to Microsoft in an effort to help update a centralized database that Microsoft houses to thwart the spread of spyware and malware. Microsoft uses these reports to determine the validity of the code submitted. This helps all computer users fight the spread of malicious programs across the Internet.

Microsoft significantly redesigned its antispyware product in the release of Windows Defender. It has rewritten the core engine in C++, replacing the original GIANT engine written in Visual Basic. This change alone allows for considerably greater performance because it is now compiled code. Windows Defender also offers an easier user interface, and now runs as a service under the Windows 7 operating system, giving you greater protection because it runs all the time, not just when you log on and use your computer. To ensure that you have a valid license for the operating system, Windows Defender uses the Windows Genuine Advantage validation routine when updating content.

Windows Defender for Windows Vista was the first iteration of a code rewrite since Microsoft purchased the original GIANT product. Previous releases were rebrandings of the original GIANT product, with some added functionality. Microsoft has also introduced more points of entry into the Windows Defender program than previously available in the rebranded product releases, making it easier to find and manage the product in Windows 7.

Microsoft integrated Windows Defender into the Internet Explorer browser engine to offer protection from files downloaded during your browser session. Windows Defender scans programs in real time. This feature allows greater flexibility in the fight against malicious code on your computer. It also helps in identifying and removing accidental download of malicious code without your knowledge. Windows Defender also allows you to schedule scanning and removal of unwanted programs. This gives you the option of choosing a specific time that works better with your usage of the computer.

To keep the detection database up-to-date, you have the option of allowing Windows Defender to complete automatic updates. This lets you continue working without having to update your antispyware definitions manually. However, you should still check the program periodically to verify that it has updated itself correctly.

Configuring Windows Defender

You can start Windows Defender by clicking Start→Control Panel. In Control Panel, click Small Icons or Large Icons on the View By list and then click Windows Defender (you can return to the default Category view from the View By list as well). Figure 15-2 shows an example of the Windows Defender management window.

You can always access the Windows Defender main page by clicking the Home button on the toolbar. In the main window, you will see the status of protection against malicious and unwanted software. In the lower portion of the window, you will see the status of the product, including the last scan date, scan type, scan schedule, real-time protection status, and definitions version. Windows Defender offers you several default

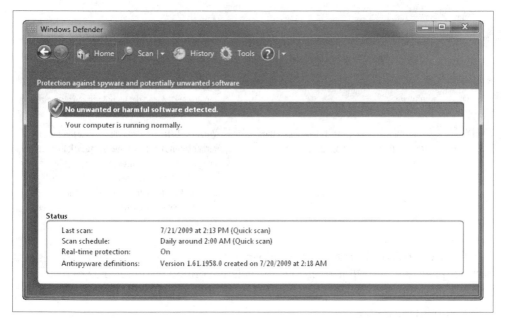

Figure 15-2. Checking the status of Windows Defender

options for how to handle potential spyware. These default options are based on definitions.

Windows Defender has five different alert levels, each associated with an action. Windows Defender follows actions dictated by alert levels. Table 15-1 provides an overview of the different alert levels, their associated descriptions, and the actions Windows Defender takes in the default configuration state.

Table 15-1. Windows Defender alert levels

Alert level	Associated with	Action taken
Severe	Widespread or exceptionally malicious programs, similar to viruses or worms, which negatively affect your privacy and the security of your computer, and can damage your computer.	Windows Defender removes this type of software immediately.
High	Programs that might collect your personal information and negatively affect your privacy or damage your computer—for example, by collecting information or changing settings, typically without your knowledge or consent.	Windows Defender removes this type of software immediately.
Medium	Programs that might affect your privacy or make changes to your computer that could negatively impact your computing experience—for example, by collecting personal information or changing settings.	Windows Defender alerts you. Review the alert details to see why the software was detected. If you do not like how the software operates or if you do not recognize and trust the publisher, consider blocking or removing the software.

Alert level	Associated with	Action taken
Low	Potentially unwanted software that might collect information about you or your computer or change how your computer works, but is operating in agreement with licensing terms displayed when you installed the software.	Windows Defender alerts you. Review the alert. This software typically is benign when it runs on your computer, unless it was installed without your knowledge. If you are not sure whether to allow the program to run, review the alert details or see if you recognize and trust the publisher of the software.
Not Yet Classified	Programs that typically are benign unless they are installed on your computer without your knowledge.	Windows Defender alerts you. Review the alert. If you recognize and trust the software, allow it to run. If you do not recognize the software or the publisher, review the alert details to decide how to take action. If you are a SpyNet community member, check the community ratings to see whether other users trust the software.

If you click the Tools button on the toolbar and then click Options on the Tools and Settings page, you'll be able to change the default configuration settings to meet your needs. The options are divided into seven broad categories:

- Automatic scanning
- Default actions
- Real-time protection options
- Excluded files and folders
- Excluded file types
- Advanced options
- Administrator options

The "Automatic scanning" settings, shown in Figure 15-3, allow you to change how the automatic scanning of your computer works. You have the following options:

- To enable or disable automatic scanning, select or clear the "Automatically scan my computer" checkbox as appropriate.
- Use the Frequency list to control the frequency at which Windows Defender scans the computer. You can choose Daily to scan daily, or you can choose to scan on a specific day of the week, such as Sunday.
- Use the "Approximate time" list to choose the approximate time at which Windows Defender will scan the computer. The actual time of the scan will depend on whether the computer is started and the current activity level. If your computer is off during a scheduled scan time, Windows Defender will try to scan your computer the next time you turn it on.
- Use the Type list to choose the type of scan you desire. You can perform a quick (partial) scan or a full computer scan.

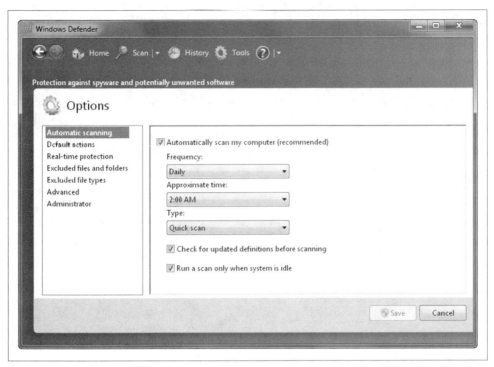

Figure 15-3. Configuring automatic scanning options

- To enable or disable automatic updating before scanning, select or clear the "Check for updated definitions before scanning" checkbox as appropriate.

The "Default actions" settings, shown in Figure 15-4, allow you to customize the default actions to take when Windows Defender detects potential spyware. The default action is based on the settings in the spyware definition file. You can configure severe-alert, high-alert, medium-alert, and low-alert items separately so that the items are allowed, removed, or quarantined. Be sure to select "Apply recommended actions" to ensure recommended actions are applied after items are detected.

The "Real-time protection" options, shown in Figure 15-5, allow you to customize the way in which real-time protection works. First, you can turn this feature either on or off. Second, you have the ability to customize the security agents that are run as part of real-time protection.

The available security agents are:

Downloaded files and attachments
Monitors files and programs that are designed to work with web browsers. Turning on this option allows you to control the behavior of these files and programs, and removes their capability to spy on you without your knowledge. This helps maintain the integrity of the computer by blocking, or alerting you, about potentially

dangerous types of downloads. This also helps maintain the integrity of the browser by blocking potentially malicious browser add-ons from installing and running. Together, these features help maintain a first line of defense against malware or malicious content coming through the browser.

Programs that run on your computer

Monitors how programs react when started and while running on the computer. This feature allows Windows Defender to watch how programs interact with the operating system. Windows Defender maintains a record of actions by programs processing on the computer and to stop a program if suspicious behavior begins. This helps prevent spyware and malware from collecting information about your computer and also eliminates unwanted background processing on the computer.

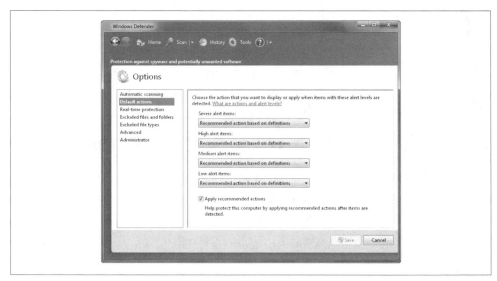

Figure 15-4. Configuring default actions

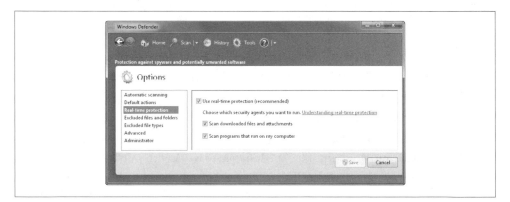

Figure 15-5. Configuring real-time protection options

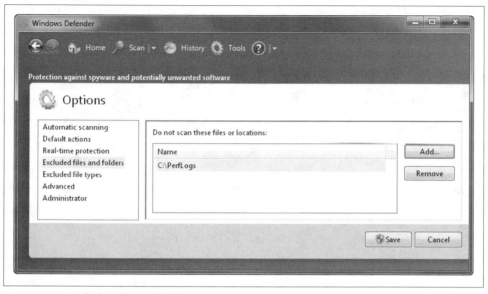

Figure 15-6. Excluding files and folders from scans

Each real-time protection option works in conjunction with the alerts defined within Windows Defender. This allows Windows Defender to operate behind the scenes to protect the computer in real time. These options happen automatically without the need for user intervention to handle mundane tasks associated with elimination of threats to the computer.

The "Excluded files and folders" option, shown in Figure 15-6, allow you to identify locations that should not be scanned. For example, if a file is being incorrectly flagged as malware, you can tell Windows Defender not to scan the file; if scans are taking too long you can speed them up by excluding folders that rarely change. To add a file or folder exclusion, follow these steps:

1. Click Start→Control Panel. In Control Panel, click Small Icons or Large Icons on the View By list and then click Windows Defender (you can return to the default Category view from the View By list as well).

2. In Windows Defender, click Tools and then click Options.

3. Under Options, click "Excluded files and folders."

4. Click Add. Use the Browse for Files or Folders dialog box to select the file or folder to exclude and then click OK.

5. Click Save to save your changes.

The "Excluded file types" option, shown in Figure 15-7, allow you to identify types of files that should not be scanned. For example, you may want to exclude certain types of picture files from scans to speed up the scanning process and you can use this option to identify the types of picture files that should not be scanned. Note that you probably

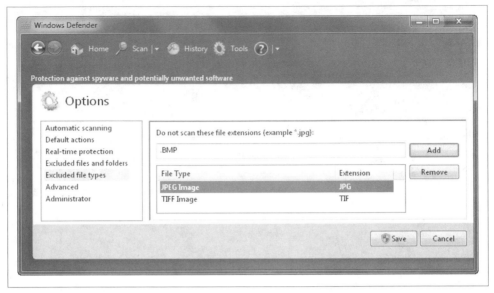

Figure 15-7. Excluding file types from scans

don't want to exclude any document and executable file types, as they are the most likely types of files to contain malware or spyware. To add a file type exclusion, follow these steps:

1. Click Start→Control Panel→Small Icons or Large Icons on the View By list→Windows Defender (you can return to the default Category view from the View By list as well).

2. In Windows Defender, click Tools→Options.

3. Under Options, click "Excluded file types."

4. Enter the file extension that you want to exclude, such as .JPG or .TIF, and then click Add.

 Here, I'm using .BMP, .JPG and .TIF as examples. I'm not advising you to exclude them. Files with seemingly innocuous extensions can contain malware.

5. Click Save to save your changes.

The "Advanced" options, shown in Figure 15-8, allow you to control the way scanning works. By default, "Scan archive files," "Use heuristics," and "Create restore point" are selected, and this is generally the configuration you'll want to use. By allowing Windows Defender to scan archived files and folders, you ensure that archived files and folders, such as those that are stored in a *.zip* file, are scanned. Because some malware programs will try to hide in archived files and folders, scanning archives is a good idea.

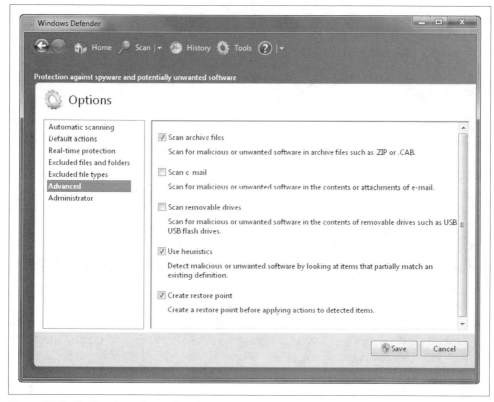

Figure 15-8. Configuring advanced options

It is also a good idea to allow Windows Defender to use heuristics to detect new types of malware and to ensure that a restore point is created before applying actions to detected items. If you also want to scan e-mail, removable drives or both, you can select the related options as well.

Using Heuristics ensures that you are notified about potentially dangerous software that hasn't yet been classified by Windows Defender. By selecting this option, you can help Windows Defender detect new types of malware and malware that is embedded in otherwise benign software.

The "Administrator" options, shown in Figure 15-9, control whether Windows Defender is enabled and whether items from all users are displayed. By default, Windows Defender is turned on and anyone who logs on locally to the computer can use it. This is the configuration you should use to ensure that your computer is protected from malware.

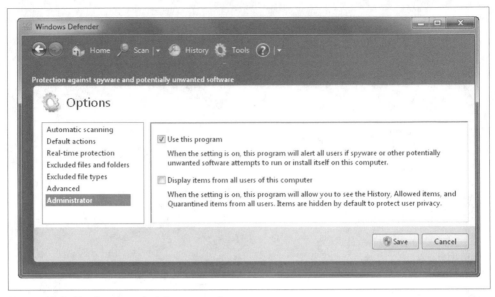

Figure 15-9. Configuring administrator options

You can also control whether Windows Defender should display items for only the currently logged-on user or all users. By default, only history, allowed items, and quarantined items for the currently logged-on user are available. This setting is designed to protect user privacy. However, you'll get a better picture of what's happening on your computer if you can see items from all users. If you have administrative permissions and want to see items for all users, select "Display items from all users of this computer." Note that Windows Defender scans all files as appropriate, regardless of whether you select or clear this option.

When you have finished changing your settings, click the Save button. This ensures that your configuration settings are saved for future use. This also keeps you from having to change the options again.

Which options you select in Windows Defender depend on how you use your computer. Take the time to consider the implications of turning these options on or off. If you want to turn off a setting that is normally turned on, realize the gap in protection you are opening on your computer, and take related action to protect your computer in another manner, if possible.

You are the first and last lines of defense against malicious programs on your computer. Pay close attention to the content you access with your browser. Also, take the time to scan your computer regularly for spyware content to help Windows Defender protect your computer. As with antivirus programs, no one antimalware program can identify and eliminate all spyware. Because of this, you may want to supplement scans made by Windows Defender with online scans using a different antimalware engine.

Scanning Your Computer for Spyware and Malware

In Windows Defender, you can run a quick scan of your computer by clicking the Scan button on the toolbar. A quick scan checks the most common areas of the computer affected by spyware, including the computer's memory and the program executable files and registry settings currently in use. Figure 15-10 shows an example of a quick scan being performed.

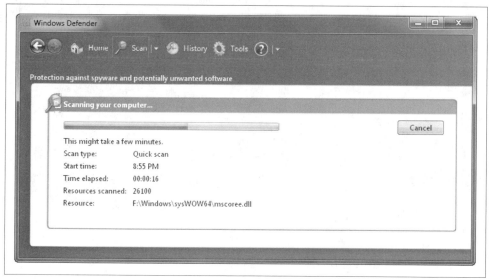

Figure 15-10. Scanning your computer for malware and spyware

Using the Scan Options button to the right of the Scan button on the toolbar, you have the option of performing a full scan or a custom scan, in addition to a quick scan. A full scan scans the entire operating system and every file on the hard drive. A custom scan allows you to define the specific areas you want to scan for spyware or malware on the computer.

Regardless of which type of scan you choose, you'll see a results window, similar to the one shown in Figure 15-11, when the scan completes. The scan statistics show you the start time of the scan, the total elapsed time of the scan, and the number of items scanned. The scan status shows the last scan date and time, scan type, scan schedule, real-time protection status, and a definition version of the product.

By default, Windows Defender is configured to perform a quick scan daily. You should manually run a full scan monthly or weekly.

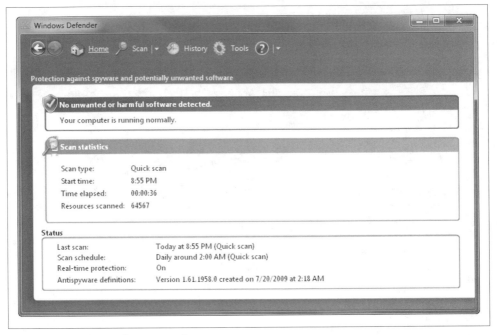

Figure 15-11. Viewing the scan results

Using Windows Defender Tools

In Windows Defender, you can access the Tools and Settings page, shown in Figure 15-12, by clicking the Tools button on the toolbar. As the previous sections discussed how to configure general and administrative options, and how to perform a scan, let's now look at the other selections available on this page.

Clicking Microsoft SpyNet lists Microsoft SpyNet features and options that allow you to join this service offered by Microsoft. Microsoft SpyNet is an online community that helps users determine how to respond to potential threats to their computers. You have three options to choose from: join with a basic membership, join with an advanced membership, or not join at all.

The default setting is a basic membership. A basic membership sends very little information to Microsoft about the software Windows Defender detects and the alert actions the computer uses. Advanced membership sends more information to Microsoft about spyware and other potentially unwanted programs encountered on the computer. Microsoft does not send any personal identification information in these updates. Of course, the "I don't want to join" option does not send any information to Microsoft, but you also do not get the benefits of using SpyNet. Make sure you click the Save button to allow Windows to update your profile for future use of Windows Defender.

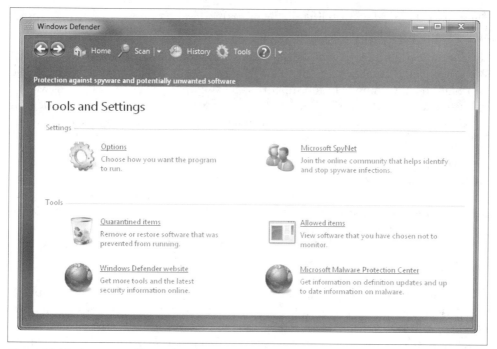

Figure 15-12. Accessing additional settings and tools

"Quarantined items" lists the different programs and files Windows Defender has identified as threats against the computer. This feature also lists the default action taken against the listed objects, and the date the computer found the potentially unwanted program. You have three options for working with quarantined items:

Remove All
> Permanently removes all quarantined items from your computer.

Remove
> Selecting a quarantined item and then clicking Remove removes the quarantined item from your computer.

Restore
> Selecting a quarantined item and then clicking Restore allows the item to run on your computer.

The top of the "Quarantined items" window lists the membership level if you have joined Microsoft SpyNet, and it allows you to change your membership level.

"Allowed items" lists the programs and files that you've allowed to run after Windows Defender alerted you about a potential threat. Each program or file is listed by name, alert level, and recommended action. If you want to remove a program or file from the "Allowed items" list, click it and then select "Remove from list." Windows Defender will then be able to monitor the program or file for potentially malicious activity.

The top of the window also lists the membership level if you have joined Microsoft SpyNet, and it allows you to change your membership level.

Selecting the link to the Windows Defender website takes you directly to the official Windows Defender area of Microsoft's website. The related pages have invaluable information concerning help and support using Windows Defender, as well as Microsoft's stance against spyware. You can find some wonderful information, in addition to an online community dedicated to helping users with problems using Windows Defender.

Also available is a link to the Malware Protection Center website. The Malware Protection Center performs malware research and response for the Windows operating system. You can learn more about the latest definitions for Windows and various other Microsoft products. There's also lots of information about malware as well as lists of protection software and resources.

Troubleshooting Windows Defender

As with all programs associated with computers, you can sometimes have problems getting Windows Defender to work. The single most common problem with Windows Defender is it not starting at all. If this happens, you must make sure that you have enabled Windows Defender to run on the computer. To check this setting, open the Action Center in the Control Panel by clicking "Review your computer's status" under System and Security. Click Security to reveal current security settings. Under Spyware and unwanted software protection, make sure that Windows Defender protection is on.

If you do not see this listing, you will see "Windows Defender is turned off" and a button labeled "Turn on now." Click the button to turn on the Windows Defender feature and allow the program to scan the computer for spyware or malware infections. You will then see an "On" entry, showing that the feature is enabled on the computer.

If you have problems turning on the Windows Defender feature, or if you receive an error stating that the Windows Defender service was unable to start, you can troubleshoot using Computer Management. To open Computer Management, click the Start button, right-click on the Computer icon, and then select Manage from the context menu provided.

Once you've opened Computer Management, click the Services and Applications node and then double-click Services. In the Services view, scroll down on the right side of the window until you see Windows Defender. Double-click the entry to view the properties of this service, as shown in Figure 15-13. If the service status is not listed as Started, click the Start button to start the service. If the Start button is dimmed, click the Stop button and then click the Start button. While you are working with the Windows Defender service, ensure that the "Startup type" is set to Automatic (Delayed Start).

If you still cannot get the service to work correctly, you can check the event logs for additional information. In Computer Management, expand the Event Viewer node by

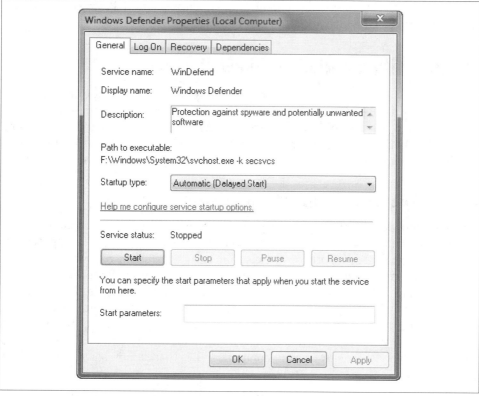

Figure 15-13. Checking the status and startup type of the service

double-clicking it, do the same with the Windows Logs node, and then select the System log. Look for stop errors for Windows Defender. If the stop error lists an unauthorized account that is preventing the service from starting, access the Logon tab of the Properties dialog box for the Windows Defender service and verify that the "Log on as" option is set to "Local system account." If it isn't, select this option and then click Start on the General tab to start the service.

If you still cannot start the service, you can visit *http://support.microsoft.com* and enter the information from the Event Viewer as your search parameters to help you determine the source of the problem. Try using the Event ID number or error text as the search text. Usually you can find information on Microsoft's support pages to help identify existing problems and resolutions for errors on your computer. Other available options include checking for updates to Windows Defender on Microsoft's website, or even reinstalling Windows Defender using the download link listed at the site. Although these may not be the most appealing options, they do work from time to time.

If you continue to have problems getting Windows Defender to work correctly, you may need to run an antivirus program on the computer to determine if a computer file was corrupted, or you may need to contact a computer service company. Calling in a professional support representative is the most expensive option. Professional support would also be the last-ditch effort to fix the problem.

Working with the Windows Firewall

With Windows 7, Microsoft offers you the ability to manage Windows Firewall in several different ways. You can manage the basic functionality of the firewall using the Windows Firewall in Control Panel, and the advanced functionality of the firewall using the Windows Firewall with Advanced Security console. This section looks at the basic Windows Firewall. You'll learn more about the advanced firewall in the next section.

Windows Firewall Features and Improvements

When Windows Firewall was first introduced, it enabled built-in exceptions for file sharing and similar protocols that allowed some ports to be open on the computer, but it disallowed most other ports on the computer. In subsequent revisions, Microsoft added the ability to manage the firewall using Group Policy, enabling administrators to manage the feature throughout an enterprise. Later, Microsoft implemented the same changes into Windows Server 2003, which brought the same improvements to the server operating system. Unfortunately, in order to correct some of the problems associated with Windows Firewall, you often had to disable the product completely to make things work efficiently on your computer—and that definitely was not good for computer security.

The current version of Windows Firewall includes IPv6 support, outbound packet filtering, and a host of other features (see Table 15-2). Together, these features offer great improvements over the Windows Firewall that was first introduced with Windows XP. These features also help alleviate the need to turn off Windows Firewall, as you had to do with early offerings of the product.

Table 15-2. Windows Firewall features

Feature	Description
IPv6 connection filtering	Allows filtering of connections using the IPv6 protocol
Outbound packet filtering	Allows control of outbound ports
Advanced packet filtering	Allows filtering rules specified by source and destination IP addressing, or complete port ranges
IPSec integration	Manages connections through the use of IP Security (IPSec) and a certificate
Encryption requirement	Manages connections through the ability to require encryption
Separate firewall policies for domains, private, and public network enrollment	Manages rule enforcement based on the network enrollment of the computer
Management Console (MMC)	MMC snap-in, called Windows Firewall with Advanced Security

IPv6 connection filtering enables you to use the IPv6 protocol in a secure fashion. This ability did not exist under Windows XP. Because of this feature, your IPv6 connections will be as secure as your IPv4 connections.

Firewall rules for inbound packet filtering make up the majority of configuration efforts on firewalls. These rules determine how network traffic flows through the computer. You manage the flow of inbound and outbound traffic through these rules. The firewall inspects the packets as the computer receives them, and then determines based on the configured rules—how the computer will handle a particular packet. If Windows Firewall determines that the packet should be accepted, it passes the packet along internally to the computer. If the packet does not meet the requirements of the rule set, it discards the packet.

Outbound packet filtering enables you to manage outbound connections from your computer. This option did not exist as part of the Windows Firewall in early versions. Outbound packet filtering lets you keep spyware or malware from uploading personal data that's been collected. To use this type of functionality in Windows XP, you had to purchase a third-party application. Microsoft now offers this ability as part of the operating system. When the computer encounters a packet requesting outbound access, Windows Firewall inspects the packet to determine its purpose, verifies the packet against the firewall rules, and then either allows the packet to be delivered or discards it completely.

Advanced packet filtering allows you to create rules associated with multiple IP addresses. This feature gives you greater flexibility in managing connections using a source or destination IP address. You even can manage a range of IP addresses for connectivity to the computer. With Windows XP, you could filter with only a single IP address, never a range of IP addresses. This is a marked improvement over early versions of the product.

IPSec integration allows you to manage connections using encryption. With IPSec integration, you can require that a connection have the proper certificate in order to connect to the computer. This allows for incredibly strong security and much greater flexibility when transferring data among computers.

 IPSec requires the use of certificates to transfer data. These certificates use public and private keys to determine whether the connecting entity has authorization to transfer data. This option makes transferring data much more secure among computers than before, especially among computers connected across the Internet.

Separating policies by network enrollment enables you to manage how your computer reacts to requests in different network environments. You can associate a very hardened security policy when you are using an insecure network, a fairly open security policy when connected to your corporate network, and a moderately secure policy when connected to your home network. The beauty of this feature is that you do not have to configure the settings over and over; Windows 7 allows you to create a profile for each type of environment and forget it. You specify the type of environment when you create the network connection.

Windows Firewall with Advanced Security offers the greatest flexibility in managing the advanced security options This allows you to manage the different types of connections and rules through a single interface. And administrators can easily manage the Windows Firewall connections and associate the settings with Group Policy.

Overall, Microsoft brings a very capable firewall into Windows 7. It offers excellent security features, and truly supplements a network perimeter firewall. Although you may have more difficulty configuring some of the advanced features of Windows Firewall, you will find considerably fewer intrusions and false positives on your computer when the firewall is configured correctly.

Configuring Security for the Basic Windows Firewall

The basic Windows Firewall provides essential firewall security for your computer. You can use the basic firewall to protect your computer from many types of attacks. In Control Panel, you can configure the basic firewall by clicking System and Security and then clicking Windows Firewall.

As Figure 15-14 shows, the main page in Windows Firewall provides an overview of the firewall configuration and status. You can use this information to tell at a glance whether the firewall is on or off, whether notifications are displayed when a program is blocked, and to which type of network you are currently connected. The network type determines which firewall profile is currently being applied. There are separate profiles for:

- Home or work (private) networks
- Public networks
- Domain networks

In the left pane are links for accessing management settings, including:

- Allow a program or feature through Windows Firewall
- Change notification settings
- Turn Windows Firewall on or off
- Restore defaults
- Advanced settings

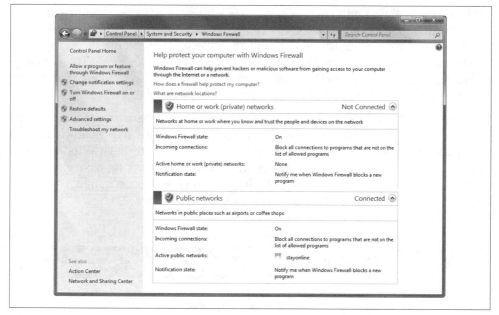

Figure 15-14. Viewing the status of Windows Firewall

Clicking either "Change notification settings" or "Turn Windows Firewall on or off" opens the Customize Settings page. You can use the options on the Customize Settings page to turn the firewall on or off (see Figure 15-15) for each profile. To turn the firewall on, click "Turn on Windows Firewall." This setting allows the firewall to block incoming connections. To turn the firewall off, click "Turn off Windows Firewall (not recommended)." This setting turns the firewall off and makes your computer vulnerable to remote attacks through network and Internet connections.

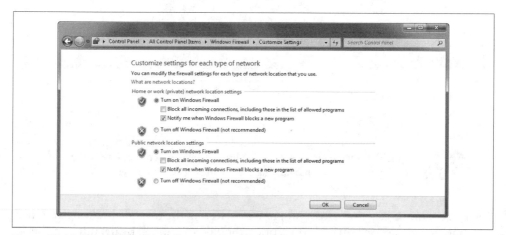

Figure 15-15. Turning the firewall on or off

When you are connecting to networks that are less secure, you may want to turn the firewall on and block all incoming connections to your computer. To do this, select the "Turn on Windows Firewall" option and the "Block all incoming connections…" checkbox. This setting ignores all settings in the firewall configuration and blocks every connection to your computer. You can turn off notifications by selecting the "Notify me when Windows Firewall blocks a new program" checkbox.

Back on the Windows Firewall main page, clicking "Allow a program or feature through Windows Firewall" opens the Allowed Programs page. This page, shown in Figure 15-16, allows you to control how programs communicate through Windows Firewall. Many Windows components commonly used for networking have exceptions listed in the Program or Port list. By default, you can view the configured exceptions but cannot make changes. To modify the settings, click Change Settings.

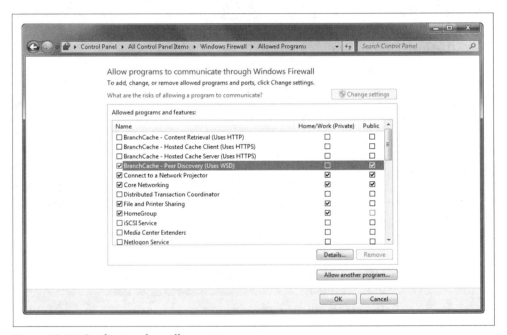

Figure 15-16. Configuring firewall exceptions

 Keep in mind that changing or disabling the default configuration of Windows Firewall may leave your computer in a vulnerable state. Take considerable care when changing these configuration settings.

You can enable an exception for a program by selecting the related checkbox and then selecting the profiles on which the exception should be enabled. By default, the checkbox for the active profile is selected.

To disable an exception for a profile, clear the related profile checkbox. To disable an exception entirely, clear the program checkbox or clear all the related profile checkboxes.

To learn more about an exception for a Windows component, select the exception by clicking it and then click Details.

Using the "Allow another program" button, you can add new programs to the exception list, giving you greater control over your computer's security parameters. You can permanently remove any exception you add by clicking the exception and then clicking Remove.

Clicking "Restore defaults" and then clicking the Restore Defaults button allows you to remove all Windows Firewall settings that you can have configured for all network profiles. Although this might cause some programs to stop working, it resets the Windows Firewall to its original post-installation configuration.

Troubleshooting the Basic Windows Firewall

Like Window Defender, Windows Firewall runs as a service on your computer. Because of this, you can use procedures similar to those discussed in the section "Troubleshooting Windows Defender" on page 610, earlier in this chapter, to troubleshoot Windows Firewall. If you begin to experience problems connecting to your network or you cannot connect to a specific computer or resource on the network, you may be experiencing problems associated with Windows Firewall. Other telltale signs of firewall problems include other computers failing to connect to your computer or the inability to `ping`, `tracert`, or access network resources even though you have an IP address.

As with Windows Defender, start your troubleshooting by making sure that Windows Firewall is on. If the firewall is on and you are blocking all incoming connections, you might want to clear this setting for your troubleshooting. Next, you should verify that the Windows Firewall service is running through the Services node in Computer Management. Verify that the service status is listed as Started, and make sure the "Startup type" is set to Automatic. If the service is not listed as Started, click the Start button to start the service. Also, verify the logon credentials using the Log On tab associated with the service's Properties dialog box. You should see "Local service" as the selected account.

If the firewall still isn't working properly, you need to verify the network location. When you click the Windows Firewall option in Control Panel, the main firewall window shows the connected networks. If you are on a private or domain network, other computers should be able to connect to you by default. If you are on a public network, most types of connections to your computer are disabled. If the wrong location type is listed, you can change the location type in the Network and Sharing Center by clicking the network type link, selecting the desired location type, and then clicking Close. Don't change the location type without first considering the possible ramifications of doing so. If you are on a public network such as a wireless hotspot in a cafe or airport, and you specify that you are on a private network, you will open your computer to attack.

If the firewall still isn't working properly, check the exceptions that are listed on the Allowed Programs page. In most configurations, a home or work (private network) should have the following exceptions enabled:

- Core Networking
- File and Printer Sharing
- HomeGroup
- Network Discovery
- Remote Assistance

You might also have exceptions for:

- Connect to a Network Projector
- Windows Live Call
- Windows Live Messenger
- Windows Live Sync
- Windows Media Player
- Windows Media Player Network Sharing Service

If you believe the appropriate exceptions are enabled and you still have problems, you can click the Restore Defaults button on the main firewall page and then click the Restore Defaults button to go back to the original postinstallation Windows Firewall settings and remove any changes you have made to these settings since installing the operating system. Keep in mind that this will also disable any custom exceptions you have created, possibly causing certain programs to function incorrectly. This is especially true for networked games, so you will need to reenable your custom settings after verifying that your network connections work correctly after resetting the default configuration. If you continue to have problems with connections, refer to the section "Troubleshooting Advanced Firewall Problems" on page 627, later in this chapter, for more information.

Configuring Advanced Firewall Security

In addition to the basic Windows Firewall, Windows 7 includes Windows Firewall with Advanced Security. At home, you probably won't work much with this feature. At the office, however, especially if you work in a medium or large organization, you may find it critical to know how the advanced firewall works.

Windows Firewall with Advanced Security allows you to open a custom management console for use in managing advanced firewall features. As Figure 15-17 shows, this

Figure 15-17. Configuring advanced firewall settings using Windows Firewall with Advanced Security

console gives you direct control over inbound, outbound, and connection security rules for the firewall's domain profile, private profile, and public profile. One way to open the firewall console is to click the "Advanced settings" link in the main page for the basic firewall. Another way to open Windows Firewall with Advanced Security is to follow these steps:

1. Click Start and then click Control Panel.
2. In the Control Panel, click System and Security and then click Administrative Tools.
3. In Administrative Tools, double-click Windows Firewall with Advanced Security.

Windows Firewall with Advanced Security gives you a host of additional features and management options over the basic Windows Firewall. You have object classes on the left side of the window, and their associated properties on the right side of the window. This follows the classic design of Microsoft products, making management very intuitive. To configure specific settings, simply click the desired object from the left and manage it from the right. You also can right-click a selected object to get context menus with more options. Table 15-3 lists the objects and their associated properties from the Windows Firewall with Advanced Security management console.

Table 15-3. Windows Firewall with Advanced Security features

Feature	Associated properties
Windows Firewall with Advanced Security	Provides an overview of the firewall profiles associated with the local computer as well as Getting Started options.
Inbound Rules	Provides an at-a-glance listing of the inbound packet filtering rules. Lists the associated inbound rules created on the computer according to the rule name, associated program group, profile, enabled status, action, and more.
Outbound Rules	Provides an at-a-glance listing of the outbound packet filtering rules. Lists the associated outbound rules created on the computer according to the rule name, associated program group, profile, enabled status, action, and more.
Connection Security Rules	Provides an at-a-glance listing of the IPSec rules. Lists the associated connection rules created on the computer according to the rule name, enabled status, endpoints, authentication mode, authentication method, and associated program group.
Monitoring	Provides a detailed summary of the firewall's domain profile, private profile, and public profile according to the firewall state, general settings, and logging settings.
Monitoring→Firewall	Lists the standard inbound and outbound connection settings and their associated status, giving you one place to look for monitoring the currently active inbound and outbound rules.
Monitoring→Connection Security Rules	Lists the status of connection security rules.
Monitoring→Security Associations	Lists the security associations for Main Mode and Quick Mode, as well as their status.

Windows Firewall with Advanced Security maintains a separate firewall profile for each type of network to which you can connect. For each profile, you can manage settings for the firewall state, inbound connections, outbound connections, notification, unicast response, and logging. As Table 15-4 shows, the default configuration for each setting is the same for each profile.

It's important to note that the standard network profile types differ slightly in the advanced firewall. The advanced firewall has domain, private and public network profiles. The private profile is the same as the home or work (private) profile in the basic firewall.

Table 15-4. Default configuration for Windows Firewall with Advanced Security

Setting	Domain profile	Private profile	Public profile
Firewall State	On	On	On
Inbound Connections	Block	Block	Block
Outbound Connections	Allow	Allow	Allow
Notification	Yes	Yes	Yes
Unicast Response	Yes	Yes	Yes
Log Dropped Packets	No	No	No
Log Successful Connections	No	No	No

You can configure the settings for the domain, public, and private profiles by completing these steps:

1. In Windows Firewall with Advanced Security, select the Windows Firewall with Advanced Security node.

2. In the main pane, click the Windows Firewall Properties link. You'll find this link in the Overview section below the profile status listings. This opens the management dialog box, shown in Figure 15-18.

3. Select the tab for the profile type you want to manage.

4. Use the "Firewall state" list to turn the firewall on or off for the selected profile.

5. Use the "Inbound connections" list to allow or block inbound connections when using this profile. You can also specify that you want to override the profile settings and block all connections when using this profile.

6. Use the "Outbound connections" list to allow or block outbound connections when using this profile.

7. Under Settings, you may also elect to customize the specific settings of a profile by selecting the Customize button. Settings customization allows you to turn notifications on or off, and to allow or disallow unicast responses to multicast or broadcast traffic.

8. Under Logging, you may also elect to customize the logging options of a profile by selecting the Customize button. Logging customization allows you to enable or disable logging of dropped packets and successful connections. When you use logging, you can also set the location and size of the firewall log.

9. Click OK to save your settings.

Figure 15-18. Managing the settings for each firewall profile

You can configure the default IPSec settings by completing these steps:

1. In Windows Firewall with Advanced Security, select the Windows Firewall with Advanced Security node.

2. In the main pane, click the Windows Firewall Properties link. You'll find this link in the Overview section below the profile status listings. This opens the management dialog box.

3. On the IPSec tab, click the Customize button. This displays the Customize IPSec Settings dialog box, shown in Figure 15-19.

4. In the Customize IPSec Settings dialog box, you can specify key exchange settings, including the security methods applied. These include SHA1 AES-128 and SHA1 3DES by default, with Kerberos V5 for authentication.

5. If you want to add a method for key exchange, do the following:

    a. Click the Advanced option under "Key exchange" and then click the related Customize button.

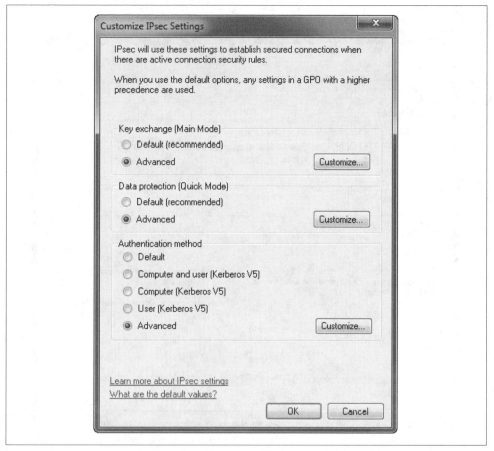

Figure 15-19. Customizing IPSec

   b. In the Customize Advanced Key Exchange Settings dialog box, shown in Figure 15-20, click Add.

   c. Select the integrity algorithm and the related encryption algorithm to use. Your options for encryption algorithms are AES-CBC-256, AES-CBC-192, AES-CBC-128, 3DES, and DES. Your options for integrity algorithms are SHA1, MD5, SHA-256, and SHA-384.

   d. Use the "Key exchange algorithm" option to select the desired key exchange algorithm and then click OK. The default algorithm is Diffie-Hellman Group 2. Your other options are to select Elliptic Curve Diffie-Hellman P-384, Elliptic Curve Diffie-Hellman P-256, Diffie-Hellman Group 14, and Diffie-Hellman Group 1.

   e. In the "Security methods" list, use the options provided to set the relative priority of each configured algorithm. As the security method listed first is tried

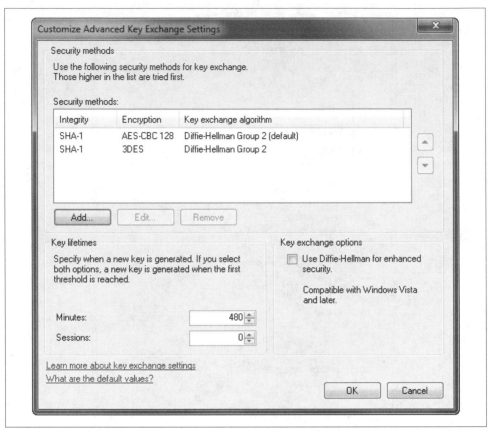

Figure 15-20. Customizing advanced key exchange settings

first, you'll usually want the strongest supported encryption method to be listed first. Click OK.

6. If you want to require encryption for all connection security rules or add data integrity and encryption algorithms, return to the Customize IPsec Settings dialog if necessary and do the following:

   a. Click the Advanced option under "Data protection" and then click the related Customize button.

   b. In the Customize Data Protection Settings dialog box, shown in Figure 15-21, select the "Require encryption . . ." checkbox if you want to require encryption for all connection security rules.

   c. By default, IPSec uses ESP with SHA1 and AH with SHA1 for data integrity. You can also use ESP and AH with MD5, AES-GMAC 128, AES-GMAC 192, and AES-GMAC 256. To do this, click Add under "Data integrity," select the

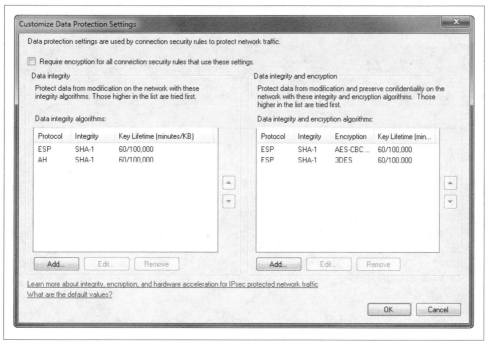

Figure 15-21. Customizing data protection settings

desired security protocol and the desired integrity algorithm, and then click OK.

d. By default, IPSec uses ESP with SHA1 integrity and AES-CBC-128 encryption as well as ESP with SHA1 integrity and 3DES encryption. You can add support for the AH security protocol, various encryption algorithms, and various integrity checking algorithms if desired. To do this, click Add under "Data integrity and encryption," select the desired security protocol, the desired encryption algorithm, and the desired integrity algorithm, and then click OK.

e. In both the Data Integrity Algorithms and the Data Integrity and Encryption Algorithms lists, use the options provided to set the relative priority of each configured algorithm. As the security method listed first is tried first, you'll usually want the strongest supported encryption method to be listed first. Click OK.

7. If you want to configure the authentication mechanism to use, return to the Customize IPsec Settings dialog if necessary and do the following:

a. Click the Advanced option under Authentication Method and then click the related Customize button.

b. In the Customize Authentication Methods dialog box, shown in Figure 15-22, Kerberos V5 is listed as the first authentication method. You can

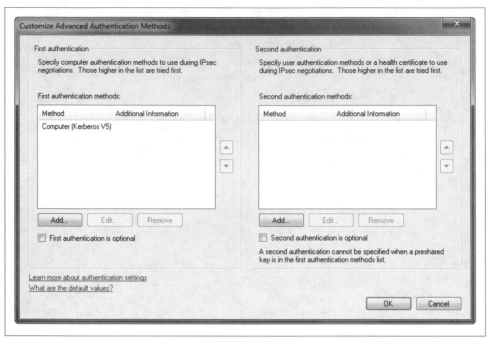

Figure 15-22. Customizing authentication methods

also use NTLMv2, computer certificates, and preshared keys for authentication.

c. To add an authentication method for use in authenticating your computer, click Add under "First authentication methods," select the desired authentication method, provide additional information as necessary, and then click OK.

d. To add an authentication method for use in authenticating your user account, click Add under "Second authentication methods," select the desired authentication method, provide additional information as necessary, and then click OK.

e. In the Methods lists, use the options provided to set the relative priority of each configured authentication method. As the method listed first is tried first, you'll usually want the strongest supported authentication method to be listed first. Click OK.

8. Be sure to click OK to save your changes, or click Cancel to avoid changing these options if you are unsure of the implications.

To create inbound or outbound rules, right-click the Inbound Rule or Outbound Rule node as appropriate and then select New Rule from the context menu provided. You have the option of choosing a program, port, predefined selection, or custom rule. You must then determine the action taken by the rule, the profile with which to associate the rule, and the name you want to give the rule. Managing existing rules only requires you to double-click the rule to view the properties and manage the settings associated with the rule.

Numerous feature sets are available for each rule, allowing you to configure the associated users or computers, protocols and ports, scope of the rule, standard enablement, and allow or block action. You may select which program or service to associate with a rule. You also can change the profile associations, interface types, and edge traversal with the advanced feature options. Edge traversal allows traffic to and from the Internet to bypass specified devices, including NAT routers, as may be necessary when using IPSec in a rule.

Windows Firewall with Advanced Security also offers you the ability to filter rules by profiles or state. You can manage the stopping, starting, and disablement of rules using the options on the Action menu. You can import and export rules by selecting the desired operation from the Action menu. This makes managing multiple computers a snap. You can create the rules you desire for all your computers on a single computer, export those settings, and then use them in Group Policy to manage your entire network.

Troubleshooting Advanced Firewall Problems

Troubleshooting advanced firewall configurations can become very complicated in a hurry. This is true especially if you have created customized authentication methods, applied certificate-based communications, or edited the standardized listings available within the management console. You must be methodical and patient when pursuing these problems in some cases. Don't become discouraged, because you can always fall back to the postinstallation configuration by restoring the default settings.

When you are experiencing problems with advanced firewall configurations, the first thing to set is the logging feature for each profile associated with Windows Firewall. Although you must enable logging separately for each profile, the firewall records all logged activities—dropped packets, successful connections, or both—in a central log-file. The default location for the firewall log is *%SystemRoot%\System32\logfiles\firewall\pfirewall.log*. This log can help you diagnose problems, and offers some insight into additional issues associated with the advanced firewall features.

If you are having problems with inbound or outbound connections, refer to the profile settings for the active profile. When you select the Monitoring node in Windows Firewall with Advanced Security, the active profile is listed as such. Check the status of your current profile. If the firewall is on and you are blocking all incoming connections, select Block instead of Block All Connections. If the firewall is on and you are blocking outgoing connections, select Allow instead of Block.

If you have created IPSec policies for specific connection types or you require IPSec for communications, verify that you have the correct certificate installed or make sure the certificate has not expired or become untrusted. You will also want to verify that the remote computer has the same authentication methods set to allow proper authentication among them. You may also want to enable IPSec exemptions to allow ICMP traffic to flow regularly with IPSec. This can save a lot of time when determining specific network issues without IPSec blocking echo requests.

If a specific program does not work, make sure that you have not created a customized rule that denies the desired behavior. Look in the inbound and outbound rules to make sure the settings are correct for the port, protocol, and IP address requirements as well as associated computers or users. Make sure you have enabled or disabled the rule, depending on your specific situation. You should also try to determine the correct ports and protocols in use for the program to operate correctly. Once you have the correct information, ensure that you have either created the custom rule for inbound and outbound traffic, or changed the predefined listing to work correctly according to your information.

Sometimes it helps to restart the Windows Firewall service to make sure something has not ended up in an unusable state due to configuration changes. Also, confirm that the desired functionality works with the firewall disabled. This can help to determine whether you have a separate issue besides the firewall configuration.

You may also want to check Event View in Computer Management to determine whether errors are being logged for Windows Firewall. If you find a stop error, use the specified information to look up errors with Microsoft's Support site to determine how to fix your specific problem.

When all else fails, you may consider restoring the default settings. To do so, follow these steps:

1. In Windows Firewall with Advanced Security, select the Windows Firewall with Advanced Security node.

2. On the Action menu, select Restore Default Policy.

3. When prompted to confirm the action, click Yes to change Windows Firewall back to the default settings when first installed. Keep in mind that this will also disable any custom exceptions you have created, possibly causing certain programs to function incorrectly. This is especially true for networked games, so you will need to reenable your custom settings after verifying that your network connections work correctly once you've reset the default configuration.

When all else fails, you can either consult with a professional computer repair service, contact your network administrator, consult with the Microsoft online forum for specific answers to detailed questions, or use any errors you find in the Event Viewer to determine whether someone else has this problem by searching for it online. Microsoft offers an automated network troubleshooting link in the main page of the basic firewall. Clicking this link displays a list of network and Internet troubleshooters. Use the Incoming Connections troubleshooter to help you diagnose and resolve configuration problems with the Windows Firewall.

CHAPTER 16

Using Windows Live for Email, Calendars, and Contacts

Many programs are available that are designed to help you communicate with other people and share information, but few are as important to your everyday life as email. For many people, sending email is the most important thing they do on a computer. As the popularity and importance of email have grown over the years, some serious risks have emerged. Enter Windows Live Mail. Windows Live Mail includes features that help you reduce the risks, while enjoying the many benefits of email.

Although you may spend a lot of time using Windows Live Mail for messaging, don't overlook the benefits of Windows Live Contacts and Windows Live Calendar. To help you keep track of all the people and events in your life, Windows Live Mail includes Windows Live Contacts and Windows Live Calendar. Using Windows Live Contacts, you can create a virtual address book with the names, email addresses, and other contact information for friends, coworkers, business connections, and more. When you have meetings, commitments, appointments or tasks to track, Windows Live Calendar is there to help you.

Getting Started with Windows Live

Windows Live is a free, web-based service offered by Microsoft. You can sign up for the service at *http://home.live.com*. As part of the sign-up process, you'll need to create a Windows Live ID and an email account with Windows Live Hotmail. The ID gets you into all the Windows Live services and your email account.

 You can use Windows Live ID just for signing in to the service. You do not need to use the Windows Live Hotmail account with Windows Live Mail, Contacts, or Calendars. If you have a Windows Live ID, you will be able to synchronize your contacts and calendars with Windows Live and access other email accounts.

When you sign in to the service, you'll see your home page (see Figure 16-1). From the home page, you'll be able to:

- View and edit your Windows Live profile
- Get the free desktop programs
- View your Windows Live contacts and add people to your network
- Access email in your Windows Live Hotmail account
- View and edit your online photo albums
- View and edit your Windows Live calendars
- Plan Windows Live Events and send invitations to guests

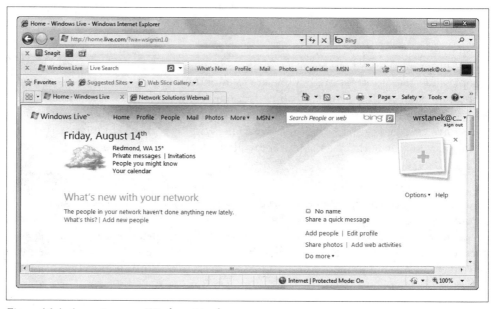

Figure 16-1. Accessing your Windows Live home page

Other programs and services related to Windows Live are also available. These include:

Windows Live SkyDrive

A free web-based service that allows you to store documents and other types of files online. When you access your SkyDrive, you'll have default folders for documents, favorites, and photos. By default, the *Documents* and *Favorites* folders are secure and accessible only by you, the *Shared Favorites* folder is accessible by anyone in your network, and the *Public* folder is accessible by everyone. You can create additional folders and set permissions on these folders to share with everyone, your network, select people, or just you. At the time of this writing, you could store up to 25 GB of data for free.

Windows Live Groups

A free web-based service that allows you to create discussion groups for connecting with others and collaborating online. Membership in the group can be open to allow anyone to join or by invitation only. The group will appear in Windows Live Messenger and will have a discussions area, a shared calendar, a photos folder, and a SkyDrive.

Windows Live Spaces

A free home page that you can use to share photos, create a blog, add lists and more. When you create a live space, you can choose a web address for it and then add items to it. As your Windows Live profile is also accessible from your Windows Live space, you'll want to edit your profile and configure permissions to specify who can access various parts of your profile. By default, your Windows Live space is shared with the public, meaning everyone can access it. To change the permissions, click the Profile link at the top of your Windows Live Home page, click Permissions, choose Space, and then clear the Everyone (public) checkbox. You can then share with your network of contacts or specify individual contacts. Be sure to save your changes.

Windows Live Mobile

A free web-based service that allows you to access your Windows Live account from your mobile phone. If your phone has a web browser, you can access your account by visiting *http://mobile.live.com*. You also can register your phone for Short Messaging Service (SMS). You can then send text messages to Windows Live and receive a text message with the result. For example, send the text message "today" to Windows Live to get your calendar events for today or send the text message "tomorrow" to Windows Live to get your calendar events for tomorrow.

Don't confuse Windows Live with Office Live. Office Live is another free, web-based service offered by Microsoft. When you sign up for the service at *http://www.officelive .com*, you create an Office Live Workspace. In your workspace, you can store Office documents (as well as other types of files) online, collaborate with others on a single Office document, and view Office documents right in your web browser. No program downloads are required.

Using Windows Live Mail

Windows Live Mail is a combined email, calendar, and contacts program that replaces three products that were available previously with Windows Vista: Windows Mail, Windows Calendar, and Windows Contacts. If you haven't purchased Microsoft Office Outlook, you can use Windows Live Mail to send and receive email. For connecting to email servers and receiving email, Windows Live Mail supports Post Office Protocol 3 (POP3) and Internet Message Access Protocol 4 (IMAP4). For sending email, Windows Live Mail supports Simple Mail Transfer Protocol (SMTP). Windows Live Mail also supports Hyper Text Transfer Protocol (HTTP) for use with Web-based email services, such as Windows Live Hotmail.

Getting to Know Windows Live Mail

Windows Live Mail is one of several free desktop programs available as part of the Windows Live Essentials. You do not need to sign up for Windows Live to use these programs, but most of them include enhanced functionality available to Windows Live users (such as uploading photos and synchronizing contacts online).

To install Windows Live Essentials, click Start→All Programs→Accessories→Getting Started. Use the option titled Go Online to get Windows Live Essentials to download and run the Windows Live Setup program. When Setup starts, select the programs you want to install and then click Install. That's it! Once you install the Windows Live programs, they are available by clicking Start→All Programs→Windows Live and then selecting the program that you want to run.

You start Windows Live Mail by clicking Start→All Programs→Windows Live→Windows Live Mail. As Figure 16-2 shows, Windows Live Mail has an interface similar to earlier versions of Outlook Express. From the deceptively similar interface, you might think that Windows Live Mail is essentially Outlook Express with a face-lift. The truth is, however, that Windows Live Mail is dramatically different.

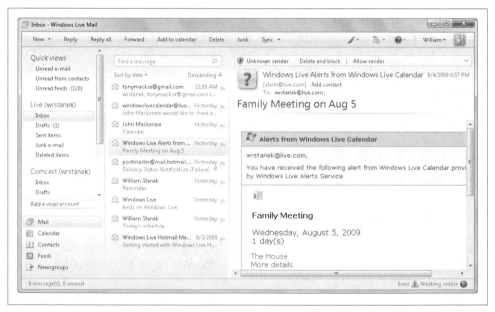

Figure 16-2. Creating and managing your email

You can configure Windows Live Mail to send and receive email for multiple accounts. When you do, you'll have a separate inbox and working areas for each account.

If you browse your personal folders, you'll find the folders Windows Live Mail uses under *%LocalAppData%\Microsoft\Windows Live Mail*. In the main folder, Windows Live Mail stores messaging data in the Message Store database and you'll have one top-level folder for each mailbox you've configured as well as additional folders for your calendar data, your outbox, and more.

 AppData and all the folders and files it contains are stored on your computer as hidden folders and files. See the section "File Attributes" on page 446 of Chapter 11 for details on displaying hidden files.

In the mailbox folders, Windows Live Mail stores email messages as separate Email Message (*.eml*) files. The *.eml* file format is a raw email message file format that includes the routing information for the message. These folders also include the following subfolders:

Inbox
Stores individual *.eml* files for email you've received from other people

Sent Items
Stores individual *.eml* files for email you've sent to other people

Deleted Items
Stores your deleted email messages as individual *.eml* files until you empty the *Deleted Items* folder

Drafts
Stores individual *.eml* files for messages you've drafted but have not sent

Junk Email
Stores junk email you've received as individual *.eml* files

The Message Store database (*Mail.MSMessageStore*) tracks the folder location and the email items within individual folders. Windows Live Mail uses the database to help manage your email.

Because of how the database and *.eml* files work, at a very basic level Windows Live Mail is really just an organizer and viewer for your email. Whether you are working with the Search Results window or the individual Windows Live Mail folder, you can:

- Open an email by double-clicking it.
- Forward an email to someone else by right-clicking it and selecting Forward.
- Reply to an email by right-clicking it and selecting Reply to Sender or Reply All as appropriate.

In the left pane of Windows Live Mail, you'll find a familiar folder structure, starting with a Quick Views node for quickly accessing unread email from any email account. Under the node for each configured mailbox, you'll have subnodes for Inbox, Sent

Items, Deleted Items, Drafts, and Junk Email. There's also an Outbox, which stores outgoing messages for all mailboxes (the messages will appear in the appropriate Sent Items folder once they have been sent).

In Windows Live Mail, you can search your email by selecting the starting folder and typing your search text into the Search box provided. If you select the top-level folder for a particular account, you can search all of the email folders associated with that account at once.

Even more exciting is that you can search your email and read email returned in search results without ever having to open Windows Live Mail. You can do so by following these steps:

1. Click Start and then click your logon name to access your personal folder in Windows Explorer.

2. In Windows Explorer, type `kind:=email` in the Search box and then type the text you want to search for within your email. In the search results, you'll see a list of emails that match your search text by the sender's email address and message subject.

3. When you click an email that you want to view, you'll see the complete text of the email in the Preview pane.

 If the Preview pane is not displayed, click the Show Preview pane toolbar button. As discussed in Chapter 6, the Windows Search service automatically indexes email folders used with Office Outlook and Windows Live Mail. This means you also can use this technique with Office Outlook.

Windows Live Mail periodically synchronizes your messaging, calendar, and contacts data between the program running on your computer and the online service. Keep the following in mind:

• With Windows Live Hotmail or any IMAP account, synchronization ensures your Inbox, Drafts, Sent Items, Junk E-Mail, and Deleted Items folders have the same contents whether you are using the desktop program or logged in to the online service. With POP3 mail servers, synchronization retrieves email from the inbox and by default leaves the email on the server. By leaving the mail on the POP3 server, you can check mail on one computer and still download it to your home or office computer later. However, this also means that you need to delete and file mail in more than one place. With Windows Live Hotmail and IMAP, you'll see the same folder view no matter which computer or device you're using to read email.

• With Windows Live Contacts, synchronization ensures your basic contact data is the same whether you are using the desktop program or logged in to the online service. Basic contact data includes your personal profile, personal contacts you've created and contact categories you've defined, but does not include people networks available when you are accessing the online service.

- With Windows Live Calendar, synchronization ensures your basic calendar data is the same whether you are using the desktop program or logged in to the online service. Basic calendar data includes personal calendars you've created and events you've added to personal calendars as well as group calendars for Windows Live Groups you've created or joined and shared calendars to which you've subscribed online, but does not include the calendar agenda items or calendar to-do lists that are available when you are accessing the online service.

The Windows Live Mail team has also devised a much easier way for you to back up your email. The previous Outlook Express clients did not make it very easy to back up and restore your email repository. With Windows Live Mail, backing up and restoring your email is easy. You really need to back up only one folder, and that's the *%Local-AppData%\Microsoft\Windows Live Mail* folder.

Setting Up Windows Live Mail and Configuring Email Accounts

When you first start using Windows Live Mail, the Add An Email Account Wizard will guide you through the process of configuring your first email account. Using this wizard, you can set up your default email account by completing the following steps:

1. Type the email address and password for the account you are configuring (see Figure 16 3). To successfully send and receive email, you must use the email address the email server expects—either the email address you've been assigned or the one you selected to use when initially setting up your email account.

2. In the Display Name text box, enter the display name for the email account and then click Next. The display name is the name that will appear in the From field when you send email to other people.

3. If you are configuring email for Hotmail, Yahoo, or another online service, Windows Live Mail will automatically configure itself for the service and then attempt to connect to the service to download your mailbox and related folders. In some cases, you may be required to change settings in order to use Windows Live Mail with the service. If Windows Live Mail successfully connects to the service, you're done and don't need to follow the remaining steps. If Windows Live Mail can't connect to the service, ensure you've entered the correct email address and password, or perform a required procedure, such as upgrading to Yahoo Plus or enabling IMAP with Google Gmail.

4. If you're configuring a connect to mail servers in your organization or other mail servers Windows Live Mail doesn't recognize, you'll need to manually configure mail. As shown in Figure 16-4, select the incoming email server type from one of POP3, IMAP4, or HTTP.

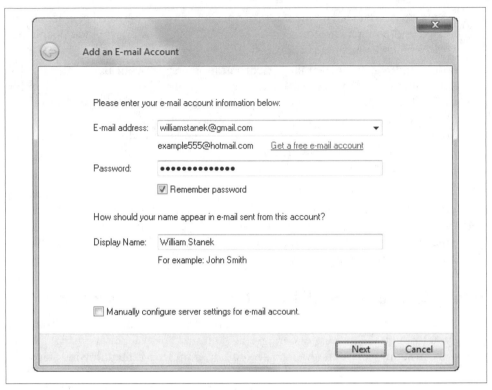

Figure 16-3. Setting the email address, password, and display name for your account

5. If you selected HTTP, you must enter the fully qualified domain name for the incoming mail server.

6. If you selected POP3 or IMAP4, you must do the following:

   • In the "Incoming server" text box, type the fully qualified domain name of the incoming email server, such as *mail.microsoft.com*. The incoming email server is the POP3 or IMAP4 server from which you receive email.

   • In the "Outgoing server" text box, type the fully qualified domain name of the outgoing email server, such as *smtp.microsoft.com*. The outgoing email server is the SMTP server to which you submit email that you want to send to other people. Just about every email server in the world uses SMTP for submitting messages.

   • Select a logon authentication mechanism. If you are unsure, select Clear Text Authentication. If the incoming, outgoing or both servers requires a secure connection, select the related checkbox to enable SSL.

   • Confirm that the port information is correct. Windows Live Mail sets the port for the incoming and outgoing servers based on the options you select. With POP3 for the incoming server, the default unsecure port is 110 and the default

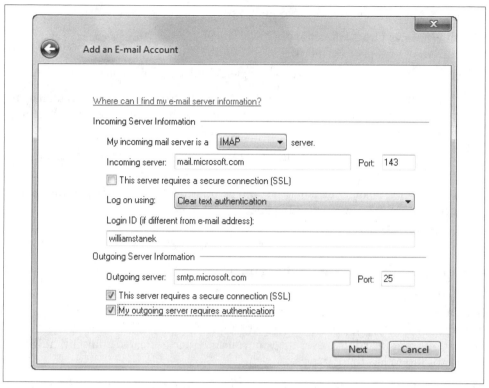

Figure 16-4. Setting the email address for your account

secure port is 995. With IMAP4 for the incoming server, the default unsecure port is 143 and the default secure port is 993. With SMTP for the outgoing server, the default port is 25 (whether you are using a secure or unsecure connection). If you get connection errors using port 25, try 587.

- If the mail server requires a user name and password when a user sends email in addition to when a user retrieves email, select the "My outgoing server requires authentication" checkbox.

 Most email servers require a user name and password for both sending and receiving mail. If a password isn't required for sending mail, the mail server may be vulnerable to exploitation.

7. Confirm that the login id is correct. The login id is usually the same as the email user name. For some email servers, however, you might need to enter the name of the domain in the form *domain\email_alias*, such as northamerica\williams (note the backslash). In some cases, you might need to type this information in the form *domain/email_alias*, such as northamerica/Williams (note the forward slash).

8. Click Next, and then click Finish to complete the configuration.

You can set up additional email accounts by following these steps:

1. In Windows Live Mail, click the "Add email account" link that appears at the bottom of your list of mailboxes.

2. Follow the previous procedure to complete the account configuration.

Once you configure your email accounts, you'll be able to send and receive email using the configured accounts. As necessary, you can modify the settings of an email account by following these steps:

1. In Windows Live Mail, right-click the top-level node for your account, and then click Properties.

2. As necessary, change the email account settings, including the user information, server information, and type of connection.

3. Click OK to save your settings.

Creating, Sending, and Receiving Email

In Windows Live Mail, you can create and send an email simply by clicking the New button on the toolbar, entering the necessary email addresses in the To field, typing a message subject, typing your message text, and clicking Send. That's it; it's that easy. When you want full control over the way your message is created and sent, however, you'll want to follow these steps:

1. To create an email message, click the New button on the toolbar. Alternatively, you can click the New options button to the right of the New button and select E-Mail Message or press Ctrl-N.

2. The From field of your message is set to your default email address and your email will be routed through the outgoing email server associated with this account. If you've configured multiple email accounts, the From field becomes a selection list from which you can select the email address and email server to use (see Figure 16-5).

3. In the To field, and optionally the Cc or Bcc fields (click the link labeled Show Cc & Bcc), enter the email addresses for the people to whom you are sending the message. If you've created contacts or contact groups, these are available as well by clicking the Address Book button to the left of the To, Cc, or Bcc field. Alternatively, you can enter part of a name or email address and then click the name in the match list to fill in the contact information automatically.

4. In the Subject field, type the message subject.

5. Click in the message body and then use the Font and Font Size lists to set the desired font. After you type the text of your message, click the Check Spelling button on the toolbar to check the spelling.

6. To attach a file to the message, click the Attach button on the toolbar. Use the Open dialog box to locate the file to attach, and then click Open.

7. Click Send to send your email.

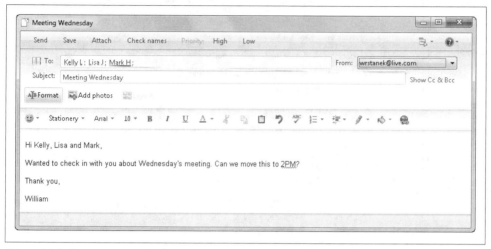

Figure 16-5. Creating your email message

When you click Send, Windows Live Mail will always try to send your email immediately. It won't necessarily check for new email as quickly as you might like, however. By default, Windows Live Mail will:

- Send and receive messages when you start the program.
- Send messages when you click Send after drafting an email message.
- Check for new messages every 30 minutes and play a sound when they arrive.

You can change the way Windows Live Mail sends and receives messages by following these steps:

1. In Windows Live Mail, click the Menus button on the toolbar, and then click Options.

2. On the General tab, shown in Figure 16-6, you can control the way Windows Live Mail sends and receives email using the following options:

   Play sound when new messages arrive
   Clear this checkbox if you don't want Windows Live Mail to play a sound when new email arrives. Otherwise, select this checkbox and Windows Live Mail will alert you when new email arrives by playing a sound.

   Send and receive messages at startup
   Clear this checkbox if you don't want Windows Live Mail to send and receive messages at startup. Otherwise, select this option to allow Windows Live Mail to check for new email and send email in your Outbox at startup.

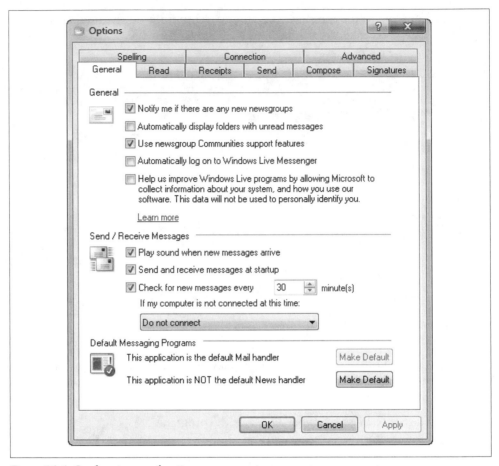

Figure 16-6. Configuring email options

> *Check for new messages every*
> > Clear this checkbox if you don't want Windows Live Mail to check for new messages automatically. Otherwise, select this checkbox and enter the desired interval to allow Windows Live Mail to check for new email sent to your configured email accounts.

3. Click OK to save your settings.

You can manually send and receive messages for all configured accounts by clicking the Sync Options button on the toolbar to the right of the Sync button and then clicking "All email accounts," or by pressing F5. To send and receive email for a specific account only, click the Sync Options button to the right of the Send/Receive button and then select the account to use.

Clicking Sync or clicking the Sync Options button and then selecting Everything (Ctrl-F5) synchronizes all email, calendar, and contact data with the Windows Live service.

Protecting Yourself from Junk Email

Unwanted junk email (spam) is annoying and disruptive, forcing us to wade through huge amounts of useless or offensive messages just to find the ones we need. To help reduce this problem, Windows Live Mail includes a built-in filter that automatically screens email to identify and separate the junk email from legitimate email. Unlike other filters that require you to "train" the filter to identify junk email correctly, Windows Live Mail automatically identifies many types of junk email from the first use, often without the need for feedback from you. It does this by shifting the required "training" to the Microsoft servers and using a version of filtering called *Bayesian spam filtering*.

Bayesian spam filtering is the process of using Bayesian statistical methods to classify documents into categories. Particular words have particular probabilities of occurring in spam email and in legitimate email. For instance, most email users will frequently encounter the word *Viagra* in spam email but will seldom see it in other email. Typically, the filter doesn't know these probabilities in advance and must first be trained so that it can build them up. To train the filter, you generally must indicate manually whether a new email is spam. For all words in each email you've identified as junk, the filter adjusts the probabilities that each word will appear in spam or legitimate email in its database. For instance, Bayesian spam filters typically will have learned a very high spam probability for the words *Viagra* and *refinance*, but a very low spam probability for words seen only in legitimate email, such as the names of friends and family members.

Fortunately, you do not have to have a degree in mathematics or programming skills to use this feature or to change the filtering to be more effective. Windows Live Mail comes ready with an initial database that you can use to distinguish between spam and legitimate email. You can choose to adjust the sensitivity of the filter to block more email or to block less email, depending on your needs. You can also specifically designate senders as either safe or blocked.

By default, Windows Live Mail moves any email identified as junk to the Junk E-mail folder. This ensures that you don't have to wade through junk email but can review the messages before deleting them as necessary. Checking your Junk E-mail folder periodically for regular email that has been incorrectly filtered is important to optimize junk email filtering. If an email is marked as junk but isn't junk, right-click it, point to Junk E-mail, and then select Mark As Not Junk.

You can set the filter level for junk email as well as safe senders and blocked senders by following these steps:

1. In Windows Live Mail, click the Menus button on the toolbar, and then click Safety Options.

2. In the Safety Options dialog box, shown in Figure 16-7, you can set the filter level for junk email on the Options tab. Choose one of the following filter levels:

No Automatic Filtering
Turns off automatic filtering. Only email addresses on your Blocked Senders list are filtered.

Low
Ensures that only email with the highest probability of being junk is filtered.

High
Uses rigid screening to detect the highest number of junk email possible, but may also incorrectly flag regular email as junk.

Safe List Only
Filters all email except for recipients specifically designed as Safe Senders.

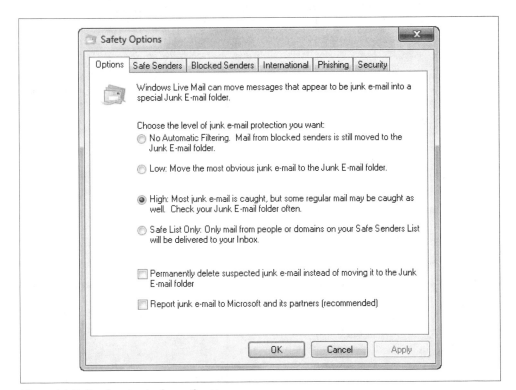

Figure 16-7. Configuring junk email options

3. You can permanently delete suspected junk email rather than moving it to the Junk E-mail folder by selecting the "Permanently delete suspected junk e-mail instead of moving it to the Junk E-mail folder" checkbox. If you do this, keep in mind that legitimate email could also be deleted automatically.

4. Messages from email addresses designated as safe senders will never be treated as junk email. Use the following options on the Safe Senders tab to manage your Safe Senders list:

   Add
   > Allows you to add a safe sender. Click Add, type the email address or Internet domain to add to the Safe Senders list, and then click OK.

   Edit
   > Allows you to edit an existing safe sender entry. Click the entry you want to edit and then click Edit. As necessary, edit the email address or Internet domain and then click OK.

   Remove
   > Allows you to remove a safe sender entry. Click the entry you want to remove and then click Remove.

5. Messages from email addresses designated as blocked senders are always treated as junk email. Use the following options on the Blocked Senders tab to manage your Blocked Senders list:

   Add
   > Allows you to add a blocked sender. Click Add, type the email address or Internet domain to add to the Blocked Senders list, and then click OK.

   Edit
   > Allows you to edit an existing blocked sender entry. Click the entry you want to edit and then click Edit. As necessary, edit the email address or Internet domain and then click OK.

   Remove
   > Allows you to remove a blocked sender entry. Click the entry you want to remove and then click Remove.

6. Click OK to save your settings.

Protecting Yourself from Phishing Links

Phishing is a type of fraud designed to steal your identity. In phishing scams, scam artists try to get you to disclose valuable personal data such as credit card numbers, passwords, account data, or other information. They usually do this by convincing you to provide the information under false pretenses. Phishing emails claim to be from a trusted party, such as a financial institution or online service, but they aren't. By including links to fraudulent websites, these email messages can trick you into providing your personal information to sites you wouldn't normally use. Windows Live Mail has a phishing filter that analyzes email to help detect these fraudulent links and help protect you from these online scams. Although links in suspected phishing emails are blocked automatically, phishing emails are not moved automatically to the Junk E-mail folder.

You can configure phishing filtering by completing the following steps:

1. In Windows Live Mail, click the Menus button on the toolbar, and then click Safety Options.

2. In the Safety Options dialog box, select the Phishing tab, as shown in Figure 16-8.

3. To block links in phishing emails so that they cannot be clicked, select the "Protect my Inbox from messages with potential Phishing links" checkbox.

4. To move suspected phishing emails to the Junk E-mail folder, select the "Move phishing E-mail to the Junk e-mail folder" checkbox.

5. Click OK to save your settings.

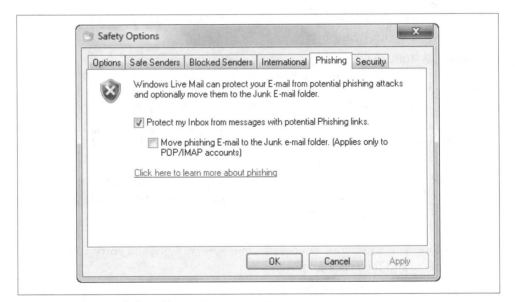

Figure 16-8. Setting phishing filter options

Changing Windows Live Mail Security Settings

By default, to protect you from viruses, Windows Live Mail treats all email as though it is from a restricted site. As discussed in the section "Restricting Permissions Using Security Zones" on page 265 of Chapter 7, this setting ensures that Windows Live Mail uses the maximum safeguards and disables all types of potentially unsafe content. To prevent certain types of phishing and marketing scams as well as nefarious programs, Windows Live Mail also blocks images and other types of external content in HTML email automatically. In most cases, this is the best configuration to safeguard your computer and your data. With these settings, very few viruses can slip through. Plus, if you are sure an email is from a safe sender, you can right-click an image or other type of blocked external content in a message and then select Download to display the blocked contents.

You can use the Security tab in the Windows Live Mail Options dialog box to change settings for virus protection and secure email. To access and configure the Security tab options, follow these steps:

1. In Windows Live Mail, click the Menus button on the toolbar, and then click Options.

2. In the Options dialog box, click the Security tab, as shown in Figure 16-9.

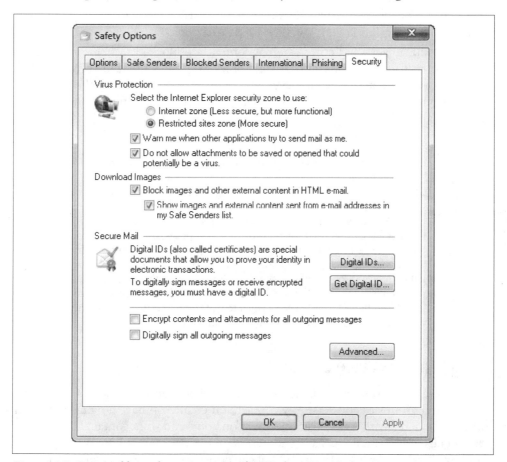

Figure 16-9. Setting additional security options for Windows Live Mail

3. For virus protection, select either the less secure Internet zone or the highly secure Restricted sites zone as the Internet Explorer security zone to use.

4. By default, Windows Live Mail warns you whenever another program tries to send email as you. This option is designed to protect other people from a virus that has infected your computer and is trying to spread itself through email. Clear the "Warn me when other applications try to send mail as me" option if you don't want to be warned when other applications try to send email as you. Otherwise, leave this option selected to help protect other people from viruses that spread themselves through email.

5. By default, any suspect attachments in messages are blocked so that they can't be saved or opened. Clear the "Do not allow attachments to be saved or opened that could potentially be a virus" checkbox if you want to allow all attachments to be saved and opened. Otherwise, leave this option selected to help protect your computer and your data.

6. By default, images and other external content are blocked to help protect your computer. Clear the "Block images and other external content in HTML e-mail" checkbox if you always want images and other external content to be displayed. Otherwise, leave this option selected to help protect your computer and your data.

7. Click OK to save your settings.

 Secure Mail is the last set of security options on the Security tab. To use Secure Mail as it is offered here, you will have to acquire a digital certificate that you will need to import and configure. The digital certificate has settings that determine how you can use it. Some certificates are used just for SSL encryption, others for IPSec or network encryption, and some can be used for both of these purposes, and more. If you already have a digital certificate that is enabled for email encryption and/or digital signing, you can choose whether you want all emails to be encrypted and/or digitally signed automatically using the "Encrypt" and "Digitally sign" checkboxes. If you don't already have a digital certificate, Windows Live Mail gives you a few places you can enroll for one. Just click the Get Digital ID button and follow the prompts.

Using Windows Live Contacts

You can use Windows Live Contacts to create a virtual address book of individual contacts and groups of contacts. Any contact you create can have a name and email address associated with it as well as full details on home and work contact information. You can also add instant messaging addresses, notes, and digital IDs. When you use Windows Live Contacts to create contract categories, you can send email to everyone in the contact category simply by specifying the name of the contact category in your email message.

Don't confuse Windows Live Contacts with Windows Contacts. Windows Live Contacts is part of the Windows Live service and its desktop version is accessed through Windows Live Mail. Windows Contacts is the contact program introduced with Windows Vista. Windows Contacts is a special view for Windows Explorer that is available when you access the Contacts folder within your personal profile. Windows Contacts stores individual contacts and groups of contacts as separate files. Contact files for individuals are saved as *.contact* files. Contact files for groups are saved as *.group* files. In your profile, you'll find these files in the *Contacts* folder. You can use Windows Contacts to create contacts and contact groups for your use and reference. These contacts will be separate from your Windows Live Contacts.

Getting to Know Windows Live Contacts

Windows Live Contacts is integrated into Windows Live Mail. You can start Windows Live Contacts from within Windows Live Mail by clicking the Contacts button in the left pane. From within Windows Live Contacts, shown in Figure 16-10, you can organize your contacts, add new contacts and contact categories, import contacts (from CSV, VCF, WAB, and more formats), and export contacts (to CSV and VCF). You display and configure individual contacts using a dialog box that is actually quite similar to the old Windows Address Book Contacts Properties dialog box. The big change is that you have view selection buttons in a left pane instead of tabs for accessing various categories of information related to the selected contact.

Figure 16-10. Creating and managing your contacts

Windows Live Contacts is designed to replace other storage mechanisms for personal contacts, including Windows Contacts. You can use Windows Live Contacts to keep track of people and organizations by creating contacts for them. Each contact contains the information for one person or organization. When you need to look up a friend's email address or phone number, you can open Windows Live Contacts and find it there. When you want to take notes about a contact, you can store the notes along with the contact.

Windows Live Contacts also functions as the address book for Windows Live Mail. When you create an email message in Windows Live Mail, you select recipients from your contacts list. Even if you don't use Windows Live Mail as your email program, you can still use Windows Live Contacts to store information about people and organizations. Use Windows Live Contacts to keep track of all the people and organizations with which you communicate.

Any Windows Live Contacts you create, modify, or delete in the related desktop program are automatically created, modified, or deleted in your contacts in the Windows Live service and vice versa. For this to work, you must sign in by clicking the Sign In link in the upper right of the Windows Live Mail main window.

Synchronization occurs when Windows Live Mail checks for new messages, which occurs every 30 minutes by default. You can change the synchronization options by following these steps:

1. In Windows Live Mail, click the Menus button on the toolbar, and then click Options.

2. On the General tab, ensure the "Check for new messages every" checkbox is selected and then specify the desired interval.

3. Click OK to save your settings.

 When you are working with the Mail view in Windows Live Mail, you can manually synchronize all email, calendar, and contact data with the Windows Live Service by clicking the Sync button or by clicking the Sync Options button and then selecting Everything (Ctrl-F5).

What's in a Live Contact?

You can store as much or as little information as you like about each contact. Windows Live Mail offers you the ability to store email addresses, phone numbers, addresses, family information, website addresses, and notes, all associated with your contact.

You can store personal, work and other email addresses for a contact, and set a single email address as the primary address for your contact. The primary email address is the one Windows Live Mail uses when you want to send someone an email quickly, without selecting from the different email addresses stored for the contact you selected.

You can store separate home and work contact numbers for phone, fax, and cell/pager. Windows Live Mail also offers you the ability to store personal and family information about your contact. The categories include a contact's nickname, significant other, birthday, and anniversary information. This can help you considerably if you try to keep track of your contact's personal information for sending cards or gifts, or for other personal reasons. You also have the ability to keep notes associated with a contact, making it easy to find specific information you have noted about a particular contact.

Creating Live Contacts for Individuals

Windows Live Contacts allows you to create contacts in one of two ways. You can use the Quick Add function to quickly enter basic information about a personal contact or you can use the standard add function to create a contact with detailed information. Any Windows Live Contacts you create in the related desktop program are automatically copied to your contacts in the Windows Live service and vice versa.

To quickly add a new personal contact, follow these steps:

1. In Windows Live Mail, click Contacts in the left pane. This opens Windows Live Contacts.

2. Click New on the toolbar or press Ctrl-Shift-N. This opens the Add a Contact dialog box like the one shown in Figure 16-11.

Figure 16-11. Creating a new contact

3. The Quick Add view is selected by default. Enter the contact's first and last name. This sets the name under which the contact will be filed and the display name that will be used in Windows Live Mail.

4. Type an email address and home phone number for the contact.

5. Optionally, enter a company name.

6. Click Add Contact to create the contact.

To create a new contact with detailed information, follow these steps:

1. In Windows Live Mail, click Contacts in the left pane. This opens Windows Live Contacts.

2. Click New on the toolbar or press Ctrl-Shift-N. This opens the Add a Contact dialog box.

3. On the Contact page, type the name information for the contact by doing the following:

   - Enter the contact's first and last name. This sets the name under which the contact will be filed and the display name that will be used in Windows Live Mail.

   - Optionally, enter a middle name or middle initial for the contact.

   - Optionally, enter a nickname for the contact. If you specify a nickname, this is the name under which the contact will be filed and the display name that will be used in Windows Live Mail.

4. Enter an email address or addresses for the contact in the fields provided. The personal email address you add is set automatically as the preferred email address. The preferred email address is the default for Windows Live Mail. If you add multiple email addresses to a contact, you can use the Primary E-Mail Address list to set the preferred email address.

5. On the Personal page, use the options provided to enter the home contact information, including the street address, city, state, and postal code, as well as phone and fax. You can also enter the contact's personal website address.

6. On the Work page, use the options provided to enter the work contact information, including the street address, city, state, and postal code, as well as work phone, other phone and pager numbers. You can also enter the contact's business website address.

7. On the IM page, enter the contact's Windows Live Messenger address or other instant messaging address.

8. On the Notes page, enter any additional notes about the contact.

9. Click Add Contact to create the contact.

Importing and Exporting Contacts

You can import contacts from the address books of other programs, including Office Outlook and Windows Contacts. As contacts you import are not deleted from their original location, you are still able to use contacts in the original program.

To import contacts from Office Outlook, follow these steps:

1. In Windows Live Contacts, click the Menus button or press Alt-M.
2. Click Import and then click Microsoft Office Outlook Address Book.
3. Windows Live Contacts will begin importing the contacts from Microsoft Office. When it finishes, click OK.

To import contacts from Windows Contacts, follow these steps:

1. In Windows Live Contacts, click the Menus button or press Alt-M.
2. Click Import and then click Address Book For Current Windows Users.
3. Windows Live Contacts will begin importing the contacts from Windows Contacts. When it finishes, click OK.

You can export contacts from the address book in Windows Live Contacts so that you can use the contacts in other programs. At the time of this writing, two export formats were supported: vCards in .VCF format and .CSV (lists of comma-separated values) format. Contacts you export are not deleted from Windows Live Contacts.

To export contacts from Windows Live Contacts, follow these steps:

1. In Windows Live Contacts, click the Menus button or press Alt-M.
2. Click Export and then click the desired export format.
3. Use the Browse For Folder dialog box to select a save location for the .VCF or .CSV file.
4. A .VCF or .CSV file is created in the location you select.
5. Import this file into another program, such as Office Outlook.

Creating Contact Categories

In addition to creating contacts for individuals, you can create Contact Categories, which combine multiple individual contacts into a single group. Creating a contact category enables you to send email to many people at once. If you send an email message to a contact category, it will be sent to everyone you added to the category. In this way, sending email to a contact category can be a lot easier than adding names one at a time to an email message, especially if you often send messages to the same group of people.

You can create a contact category by following these steps:

1. In Windows Live Mail, click Contacts in the left pane. This opens Windows Live Contacts.

2. In the left pane, click the "Create a new category" link that appears under the list of predefined categories such as All Contacts, Buddies, and Coworkers.

3. In the Create a New Category dialog box, shown in Figure 16-12, enter a category name, such as Bridge Club or Golf Team.

4. Click the contacts you want to add to the category. As you click contact names, the contact's display name is entered into a semicolon-separated list. Alternatively, you can enter the email address of a contact directly in the list. Just make sure each entry is separated with a semicolon.

5. Click Save. If you entered email addresses directly and one or more of the email addresses is not already associated with a contact, a new contact is created automatically. You'll likely want to edit the contact information to make it more complete. To do this, simply double-click the contact entry, enter the desired information and then click Save.

Figure 16-12. Creating a contact category

As with email addresses, you can enter contact category names in the To, Cc, or Bcc fields in an email message. Contact categories are used internally by Windows Live Mail. When you send a message to a category, Windows Live Mail will list each individual email address.

Using Windows Live Calendar

Windows Live Calendar lets you schedule events in one or more calendars, send information about these events to contacts, and share your calendar with others—all from one easy-to-use application. Microsoft designed Windows Live Calendar to be used with Windows Live Mail and Windows Live Contacts, allowing you to share and coordinate calendar information with family and friends.

Getting to Know Windows Live Calendar

One of Windows Live Calendar's most useful features is the ability to create multiple calendars for different people or different purposes. Because calendars and their respective events are color-coded, you can quickly and easily differentiate between one person's appointments and commitments and another's. Windows Live Calendar also makes it easy for you to access any available calendars and for you to allow others to access your calendars. If you want to access someone else's calendar, you can ask that person to publish the calendar so that you can subscribe to it. If you want others to be able to access your calendar, you can publish your calendar as a shared calendar.

You can start Windows Live Calendar from within Windows Live Mail by clicking the Calendar button in the left pane. As Figure 16-13 shows, Windows Live Calendar has a navigation pane and a work pane. On the left, the Navigation pane shows the current month and the available calendars. The main window in the center displays the current view of the active calendar.

You can use the toolbar to navigate the calendar, change views, and perform essential tasks. From left to right, the buttons on the toolbar are:

New
    Creates a new event in the selected calendar.

Send in e-mail
    Sends a select event to one or more contacts as an email message.

Delete
    Deletes a selected event.

View
    Provides options that set the calendar to the Day, Week, or Month view.

Print
    Prints the Day, Week, or Month view of the dates you select as the start and end dates under Print Range.

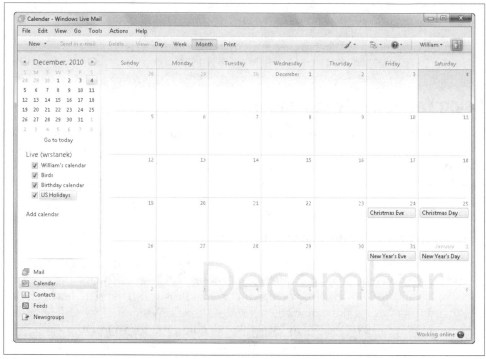

Figure 16-13. Setting up your calendar

When you are working with the Date section of the Navigation pane, you can use the Month view of the calendar to select individual dates to view in the main window. Using the Previous Month and Next Month buttons on the calendar, you can navigate to previous and next months. Other techniques to navigate the calendar are as follows:

• While viewing a particular month, you can navigate to previous or next months by clicking the month and year entry to display the 12 months of the year. You can then select any month to view by clicking it.

• While viewing the 12 months of the year, you can change the year by clicking the Previous Year or Next Year button.

• At any time, you can click the "Go to today" link to go back to the current date.

In Windows Live Calendar, the Day, Work Week, Week, and Month views in the main window show appointments and meetings associated with all the calendars you've created or to which you've subscribed. When you are working with the Calendars section of the Navigation pane, you can select the calendar you want to work with to make it the active calendar for when you are scheduling events or setting calendar properties.

Any calendar events you create, modify or delete in the related desktop program are automatically created, modified, or deleted in your contacts in the Windows Live service and vice versa. Synchronization occurs when Windows Live Mail checks for new messages, which occurs every 30 minutes by default. When you are working with the Mail view in Windows Live Mail, you can manually synchronize all email, calendar and contact data with the Windows Live Service by clicking the Sync button or by clicking the Sync Options button and then selecting Everything (Ctrl-F5).

You can change the synchronization options by following these steps:

1. In Windows Live Mail, click the Menus button on the toolbar, and then click Options.
2. On the General tab, ensure the "Check for new messages every" checkbox is selected and then specify the desired interval.
3. Click OK to save your settings.

Creating and Using Calendars

The true power of Windows Live Calendar is its capacity for creating and managing multiple calendars. If you would like to have separate calendars for work and play, or perhaps you would like to manage the calendars for each of your family members and see them all together at a glance to avoid conflicts, you can do this by creating multiple calendars. Because each calendar has a separate color code, it is easy to tell which appointments, meetings, and commitments are related to which calendar.

To create a new calendar, all you need to do is click the "Add calendar" link or click the Options button to the right of the New button on the toolbar and then select Calendar. Alternatively, you can press Ctrl-Shift-D to create a new calendar. In the Add a Calendar dialog box, shown in Figure 16-14, you can then set the name of the new calendar and select a color for the calendar's events. You can also enter a description of the calendar and optionally make the calendar your primary calendar.

When you create events, Windows Live Calendar adds them to the active calendar by default. Calendars have two key properties that you can manage: a title and an associated color. You can edit calendar details by clicking the calendar name and then selecting Properties.

When selecting a color to associate with a calendar's events, use a unique color for each calendar so that it is easy to distinguish the owner or purpose in the master calendar. For example, you might want to use red, blue, green, yellow, and orange as the colors for five different calendars.

By default, items for all calendars are shown on the master calendar. To hide a calendar's items, clear the related checkbox. If you later want to display the calendar's items and tasks, select the related checkbox. You also can hide the calendar's items and hide the calendar's entry by clicking the calendar and selecting the "Hide this calendar from list" option. To restore hidden calendars, click any available calendar and then select the "Add hidden calendars to list" option.

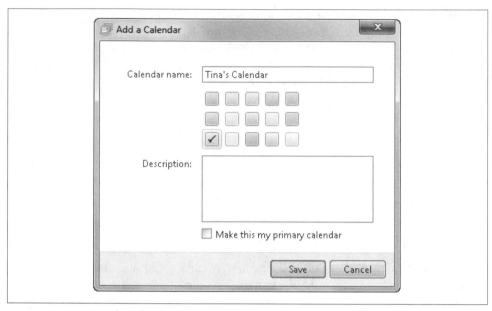

Figure 16-14. Setting the calendar name and color

If you no longer need a calendar, you can permanently delete the calendar and all related events. To delete the calendar, click it, and then select Delete from the menu that pops up. When prompted to confirm that you want to delete the calendar, click Delete again.

Sharing Your Calendars with Others

Windows Live Mail synchronizes your calendar data between the desktop program and the online service. If you create or join Windows Live Groups, the group calendar will be added to the desktop program. You also can subscribe to other people's calendars. If you do, these shared calendars will be added as well. To subscribe to or share calendars, you must be logged in to Windows Live and accessing the service through your web browser.

You can publish any calendars you've created, so that other users can access and subscribe to them. To publish a calendar for sharing, follow these steps:

1. After accessing your calendars online in the Windows Live service (*http://calendar .live.com*), click the Share option and then select the calendar to share.

2. Select "Share this calendar" and then select the appropriate sharing options (see Figure 16-15). Keep the following in mind:

   • If you choose to share your calendar with your friends and family, click Add People and then select the people to share with. Afterward, use the list provided to choose how much these people can see and do and then click Add. Only the people you selected can subscribe to your calendar.

- If you want to send friends a view-only link of your calendar, click "Get your calendar links" if the links do not appear and then click the appropriate link or links. Each link you click will display a URL that you must copy and paste into an email so that people can see your calendar. No one can subscribe to a view-only calendar.

- If you choose to make your calendar public for all the world to see, set the permission level and time zone and then click "Get your calendar links" if the links do not appear. Each link you click will display a URL that you must copy and paste into an email so that people can access your public calendar. Anyone can view or subscribe to a public calendar.

3. Click Save to save your sharing options. Confirm that you want to do this when prompted. If you are sharing your calendar with friends and family, an invitation with the calendar URL is sent to each person.

4. As shown in Figure 16-16, the email message sent to your friends and family allows the person to accept or decline the invitation. If the person accepts the invitation and is using Windows Live Mail or is signed into to the Windows Live service, they'll be automatically subscribed to the calendar. The invitation also contains accept and decline links that can be copied and pasted into a browser.

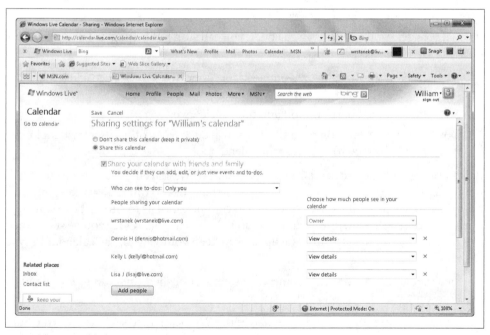

Figure 16-15. Publishing your calendar

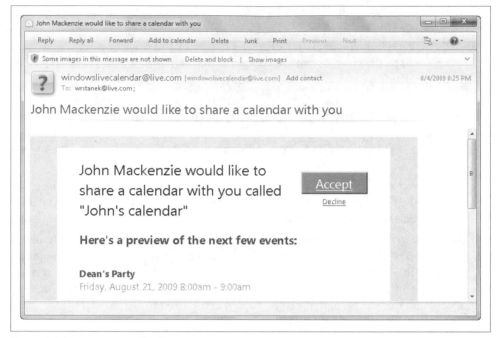

Figure 16-16. Viewing a calendar invitation

If you no longer want to publish a calendar, you can stop publishing it. To do so, follow these steps:

1. After accessing your calendars online in the Windows Live service, click the Share option and then select the calendar to stop sharing.

2. Select the "Don't share" option and then click Save.

3. You'll see a confirmation prompt. When you click Save, other users will no longer be able to subscribe to or access the calendar.

Being able to publish a calendar is pretty cool, but we haven't even begun to touch upon the new features that Windows Live Calendar has to offer. Now, keeping with our scenario, we just published a calendar, so your next task is to subscribe to someone else's calendar so that it will appear in Windows Live Calendar. Once you've subscribed to a calendar, you can get automatic updates to keep your view of the calendar in sync with the published view.

To subscribe to a calendar that someone else has published (including *.ics* calendars used on some websites), follow these steps:

1. After accessing your calendars online in the Windows Live service, click the Subscribe option.

2. As shown in Figure 16-17, you can subscribe to a public calendar or a private calendar shared to you. To do this, select the "Subscribe to a public calendar"

Figure 16-17. Subscribing to a calendar

option and then type the URL path to the calendar to which you want to subscribe. This can be any iCalendar-formatted (*.ics*) and published calendar.

 As calendar URL paths can be quite long and complex, you'll usually want to copy and paste the path. This will help ensure you enter the correct path.

3. Type the display name you want to use for the calendar to which you are subscribing. This doesn't have to be the same as the name used by the person who shared the calendar.

4. Click "Subscribe to calendar" to complete the procedure. If you entered the calendar URL incorrectly, you'll see an error and will need to retype the URL. To reduce the possibility of making a mistake, copy and paste the URL path.

Once you've subscribed to a calendar, Windows Live Mail will retrieve and display updates as they become available and when synchronization occurs. If you don't want to see the events for a subscribed calendar, clear the checkbox for the calendar. When you are working with Windows Live Calendar (and not the online service in your browser), you can unsubscribe from a calendar by clicking the calendar and selecting Delete. When prompted to confirm, click Delete.

Synchronizing Google Calendar with Windows Live Calendar

You can subscribe to your Yahoo! and Google calendars, too. For Google, the steps you use should be similar to the following:

1. In Internet Explorer, browse to the Google calendar to which you want to subscribe, and log on.

2. On the left-hand side of the page, under My Calendars, click Settings.

3. Under Sharing, click on "Share this calendar." Similar to Windows Live Calendar, you have the option to make the calendar public or share the calendar with specific people. If you make the calendar public, everyone in the world will be able to see it and you'll need to copy and paste the calendar URL into an email. If you share the calendar with specific people, you can set a permission level to control how much these people can see and do.

4. After you select the sharing options for this calendar, click Save. If you are sharing your calendar with specific people, you have the option of sending an email invitation to each person. You probably don't want to do this as the invitation requires registering for a Google account and then accessing the calendar via Google.

5. On the left-hand side of the page, under My Calendars, click the options button and then click Calendar Settings. This displays the Calendar Details page.

6. Scroll down. You'll see a Calendar Address and a Private Address section.

   • With a public calendar, you'll have several different calendar formats for the calendar address. You should be interested in only iCal for now. Right-click on iCal under "Calendar Address," and then click "Copy shortcut." This is the shortcut you use to synchronize your Google Calendar with Windows Live Calendar (or another iCalendar-enabled calendar).

   • With a private calendar (one shared with friends), you'll have several different calendar formats for the private address. You should be interested in only iCal for now. Right-click on iCal under "Private Address," and then click "Copy shortcut." This is the shortcut you use to synchronize your Google Calendar with Windows Live Calendar (or another iCalendar-enabled calendar).

7. After accessing your calendars online in the Windows Live service, click the Subscribe option.

8. You can now subscribe to the public calendar or the private calendar shared to you. To do this, select the "Subscribe to a public calendar" option and then type the URL path to the calendar to which you want to subscribe.

 As calendar URL and file paths can be quite long and complex, you'll usually want to copy and paste the path. This will help ensure you enter the correct path.

---

9. Type the display name you want to use for the calendar to which you are subscribing. This doesn't have to be the same as the name used when publishing the calendar.

10. Click "Subscribe to calendar" to complete the procedure. If you entered the calendar URL incorrectly, you'll see an error and will need to retype the URL. To reduce the possibility of making a mistake, copy and paste the URL path.

Because web interfaces tend to change more frequently than program interfaces, I won't repeat the example for Yahoo!. However, you'll use a similar procedure to share your Yahoo! calendar so that you can subscribe to it in Windows Live Calendar.

Scheduling Appointments and Meetings

Windows Live Calendar can help you track appointments, meetings, and other commitments for yourself and any calendars to which you've subscribed. All these events can have a subject and location associated with them. On the master calendar, the subject is shown first, followed by the location in parentheses. When you create an event, you can specify start and end times or you can specify that an event lasts all day. Windows Live Calendar also allows you to specify whether events are recurring and to add reminders to events so that you are notified a specified amount of time prior to an event.

 Windows Live Calendar doesn't try to distinguish between meetings, appointments, or other types of commitments and simply refers to them all as events. This is the same approach used by most calendaring and scheduling programs. This is because with appointments, meetings, and other types of commitments, you must be somewhere at a particular time to meet someone or do something, and programmatically it doesn't make sense to create separate sets of features that do essentially the same thing.

You can create an event by following these steps:

1. In Windows Live Calendar, click New or press Ctrl-Shift-E. This opens the New Event dialog box, shown in Figure 16-18.

2. In the Subject text box, type a subject for the event.

3. In the Location text box, type the location for the event.

4. Use the Start and End options to set the start and end times for the event. Or for an all-day event, select the "All day" checkbox.

5. If the event is not for your default, primary calendar, click in the Select a Calendar list and select the calendar where the event should be created. You can create events only on calendars to which you have read/write access.

Figure 16-18. Creating your appointment

6. Click in the "Select Availability" list and choose whether the event should be shown as busy, free, tentative or away.

7. If the event should repeat, use the Recurrence list to select the interval at which the event repeats, such as Weekly, Monthly, or Yearly. If you want to use a recurrence schedule other than the default, select the Custom option. You can then set the appointment to repeat every *n*th day, week, month, or year.

8. To have Windows Live Mail remind you prior to the appointment, use the Reminder list options to set the amount of time prior to the appointment to display a reminder. For example, if you select 1 hour, Windows Live Mail will remind you 1 hour before the appointment.

9. Click Save & Close to create the event.

If you want to remove an event from a unsubscribed calendar, you can do so by right-clicking the event and selecting Delete. You cannot delete events from subscribed calendars. If you no longer want to see events from a subscribed calendar, clear the related checkbox under Calendars or delete the subscribed calendar.

When you try to delete a recurring event, you'll be given the opportunity to delete the series, delete the selected occurrence, or cancel the deletion. The related dialog box is shown in Figure 16-19.

Viewing Agendas and Creating To-Do Lists

When you are logged in to the Windows Live service, you have several extra features for your calendars. One of the calendar extras is an agenda, which is displayed when you select the Agenda tab. As Figure 16-20 shows, an agenda is a handy list of upcoming events from all your personal and subscribed calendars.

Another handy calendar extra is the to-do list, which is displayed when you select the "To-do list" tab. The Windows Live service can help you manage to-do lists for your

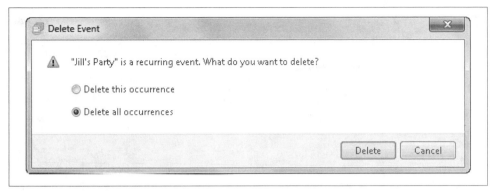

Figure 16-19. Deleting a recurring event

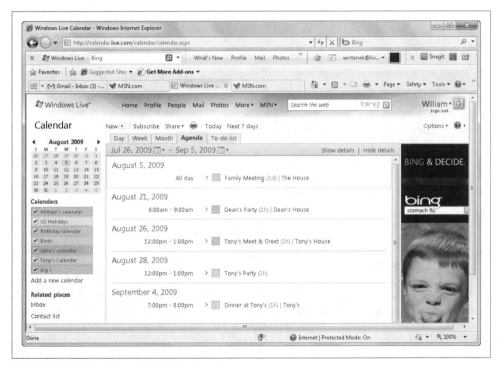

Figure 16-20. Viewing your agenda

personal and group calendars. As Figure 16-21 shows, the to-do list shows upcoming tasks that need to be completed by their title, due date, and status.

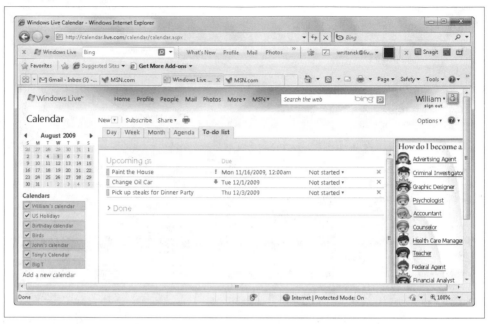

Figure 16-21. Creating to-do lists

In the to-do list, upcoming tasks are listed under the Upcoming heading and completed tasks are listed under the Done heading. Tasks have three basic states:

Not started
A task that has not yet been started

In progress
A task that you are working on but has not yet been completed

Done
A completed task

When you create a task, you can specify a priority to indicate the task's relative importance. You can set start and due dates. You can also add reminders so that you are notified a specified amount of time prior to a task's expected due date.

 Each task is color-coded to the calendar to which it relates and can also have a priority indicator to the left due date. High-priority tasks are shown with an exclamation point. Low-priority tasks are shown with a down arrow. Normal priority tasks don't have a priority indicator.

You can create a task by following these steps:

1. When you are working with calendars while signed in to the Windows Live service, select the "To-do list" tab.
2. Click the New link on the toolbar. This displays the "Add a to-do" dialog box, shown in Figure 16-22.
3. In the What text box, type a title for the task.
4. If the task is not for your default, primary calendar, click in the Calendar list and select the calendar with which the task should be associated.
5. If desired, use the Priority list to set the task's relative priority as High, Normal, or Low.
6. Use the "Due date" options to specify the date when the task must be completed. Optionally, you can specify a time the task is due.
7. To set the task status, set a reminder or add a description, click the "Add more details" link. You'll then be able to use the Status list to set the task's status, the Send Reminder list to specify when a reminder should be sent before the due date, and add a description of the tasks.
8. Click Save to add the task to your to-do list.

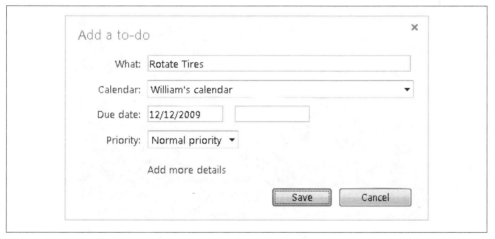

Figure 16-22. Configuring your task

Any uncompleted tasks created on your personal calendar or other calendars are displayed under the Upcoming heading. You can change a task's status by clicking the current status and selecting a different status. When you mark a task as done, it is displayed under the Done heading. However, by default, completed tasks are hidden and you must click the Done heading to retrieve the list of completed tasks.

When you complete tasks, you may want to delete them. You can delete a task by clicking the related Delete button. You can delete all completed tasks by clicking the "Delete all" link and then clicking OK when prompted to confirm.

CHAPTER 17

Mastering Dial-Up, Broadband, and On-the-Go Networking

As our need for information increases, our use of networks and communications has become increasingly important. Windows 7 allows greater flexibility and options for managing network infrastructure, and gives more flexible options to access networks than were previously available. This flexibility enhances support for standard networking and wireless technologies, and fully supports the next generation of networks.

Many of us spend time on the road trying to make connections to the corporate network, or even to our home network, to get information or files we need while away. While some of us are not as well connected as the quintessential road warrior, many of us require Virtual Private Network (VPN) connections, Wi-Fi hotspot connectivity, or dial-up connections to get our email or download something from a file server located remotely. This chapter discusses the different aspects of mobile computing with Windows 7.

Configuring Dial-Up, Broadband, Wireless, and VPN

Do you remember the last time you were sitting in a hotel room trying to make a remote connection to your corporate or home network? Windows 7 has eased the pain of making remote connections to your network by offering much greater flexibility in the ability to network. Windows 7 also offers many updated security measures to protect your data when connecting to remote networks or when gaining access to your critical data on an unsecured network.

Windows 7 allows you to make VPN connections, dial-up connections, wireless connections, and broadband connections. When working with the network features of your computer, you need to start with the Network and Sharing Center. You can easily access the Network and Sharing Center by following these steps:

1. Click Start→Control Panel.
2. In the Control Panel, click Network and Internet→Network and Sharing Center. This opens the Network and Sharing Center, shown in Figure 17-1.

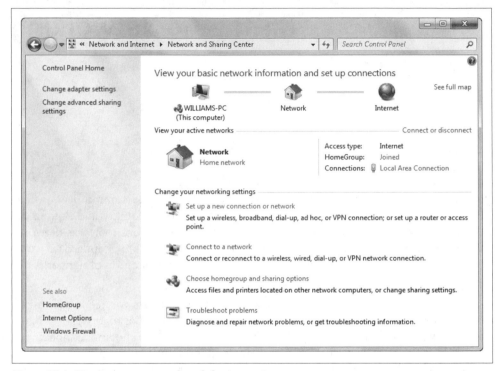

Figure 17-1. Viewing your network and sharing settings

After you have opened the Network and Sharing Center, you can use the console to manage your network settings, view your network status, and get an overview of your networking configuration. The left pane of the console offers you different tasks to choose from when managing your network features.

Your choices are:

- Manage wireless networks

 The wireless networks option is only available if your computer has a configured wireless adapter. See "Wireless Networking" on page 692, later in this chapter, for more information.

- Change adapter settings
- Change advanced sharing settings

- HomeGroup
- Internet Options
- Windows Firewall

The Network and Sharing Center houses the main features for managing your computer's networking capabilities. When you need to create, connect, or manage your network, this console offers you the ability to handle all of the management aspects available in Windows 7.

You can set the properties of your current network by following these steps:

1. Click Start→Control Panel.
2. In the Control Panel, click Network and Internet→Network and Sharing Center.
3. If you have a valid connection to a network, click the icon for the network (it will appear under the header "View your active networks").
4. Use the options in the Set Network Properties dialog box to set the network name and network icon. Click OK.

Windows automatically applies the default network settings based on the network location type. The three network location types are:

Home Network
> A network for computers that are configured as members of a homegroup and are not connected directly to the public Internet.

Work Network
> A network for computers that are connected to the corporate domain to which they are joined or are being used in a workgroup.

Public Network
> A network in a public place, such as a coffee shop or airport, rather than for an internal network.

In the Network and Sharing Center, the current network location type is displayed below the network name. You can set the network location type by clicking the current location type and then selecting a location type for the network.

> Your computer saves settings separately for each network location type. This allows you to specify different networking and sharing settings for each network location. The first time you connect your computer to a network, you'll see a dialog box that allows you to specify whether you are at home, at work, or in a public location. If Windows 7 is unable to determine the network location, it uses the public network location type. If you join a computer to a domain, the network to which the computer is connected changes to a work network.

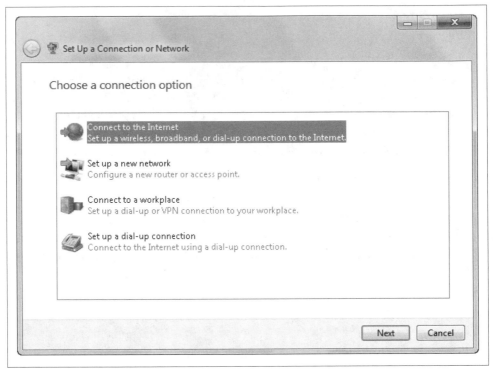

Figure 17-2. Setting up a network connection

In the Network and Sharing Center, you can create network connections by clicking "Set up a new connection or network" link. This opens the Set Up a Connection or Network Wizard, shown in Figure 17-2. You can use this wizard to create connections to the Internet and set up wireless networks and access points, ad hoc wireless networks, dial-up connections, and VPN connections to your workplace. Chapter 14 explains how to use this wizard to connect to a wired network.

Creating Dial-Up Connections

In the Network and Sharing Center, you can set up a dial-up connection by following these steps:

1. Click "Set up a new connection or network." This opens the Set Up a Connection or Network Wizard.

2. In the wizard, click "Set up a dial-up connection," and click the Next button.

3. The Create a Dial-up Connection window appears and asks for specific information to configure your dial-up connection. See Figure 17-3 for an example.

4. In the "Dial-up phone number" text box, type the telephone number provided by your ISP or network administrator.

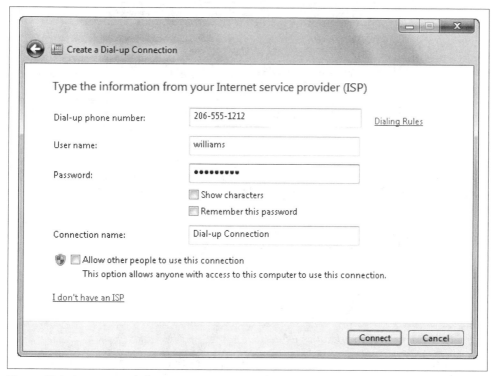

Figure 17-3. Setting up a dial-up connection

5. In the "User name" text box, type the username provided by your ISP or network administrator.

6. In the Password text box, type the password provided by your ISP or network administrator.

7. As necessary, select the "Show characters" checkbox when you are typing your password to view your entry. This will help eliminate any typing mistakes. Also, uncheck this selection after you confirm the correct spelling of your password to eliminate the possibility of anyone else seeing your password later.

8. Select the "Remember this password" checkbox to save your password for future connections. If you do not check this box, you will have to enter your password every time you use your dial-up connection.

9. In the "Connection name" text box, type a descriptive name for the connection. The default name is Dial-up Connection.

10. Select the "Allow other people to use this connection" checkbox if you want to allow anyone with access to your computer to use this connection.

11. If you haven't previously set up a dialing location, click the Dialing Rules link. The wizard will prompt you to provide the specific location information for your

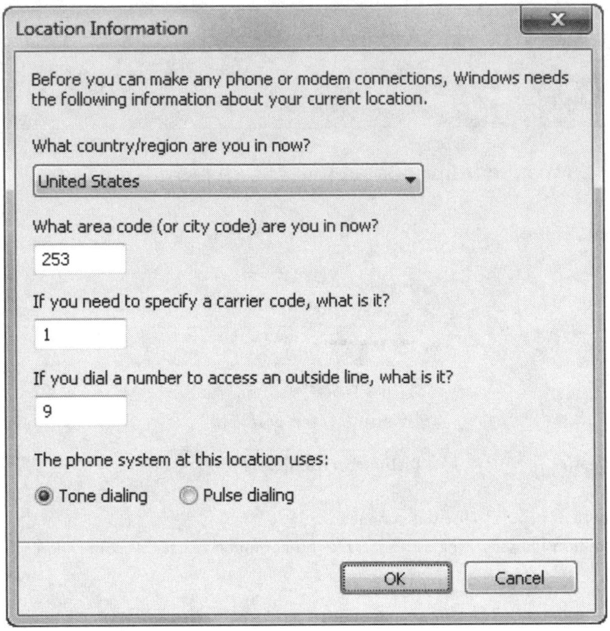

Figure 17-4. Configuring your location information

connection, as seen in Figure 17-4. When prompted, enter your country/region, area code, carrier code, and dial-out number as necessary. Click "Tone dialing" or "Pulse dialing" to identify your phone type. Windows 7 saves this information into a dialing rule location named My Location for future use. See the next section for more information on Dialing Rules configuration.

12. Click Connect to create the connection. If you don't want to connect via dial-up now, click Skip to bypass the connection activation and then click Close.

Setting a connection to use dialing rules

Dialing Rules, as seen in Figure 17-5, offers you the ability to control how your dial-up connections function in defined locations. These rules apply to outgoing phone calls from your modem. When you specify the phone number to dial, the dialing location determines whether the area code applies to the current call, and whether a calling card applies. To configure Dialing Rules, you must open the Phone and Modem Options dialog box.

To open the Phone and Modem Options dialog box, use the following steps:

1. Click Start→Control Panel.
2. In Control Panel, click Large Icons or Small Icons in the View By list. When you're done, you may want to set it back to Category view.

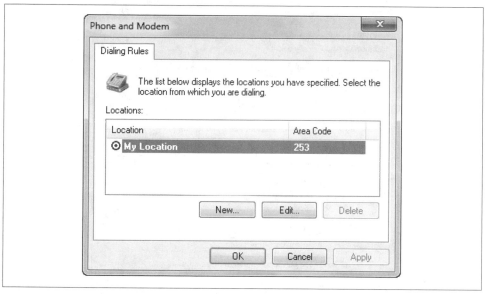

Figure 17-5. Configuring phone and modem options

   3. Click Phone and Modem.

If you have never opened the Phone and Modem Options dialog box, you will have to provide the default location information for your connections. When prompted, enter your area code, country/region, carrier code, and dial-out number, if you have one. Click "Tone dialing" or "Pulse dialing" to identify your phone type.

To configure Dialing Rules for your connection, use the following steps:

   1. In the Phone and Modem Options dialog box, the Dialing Rules tab is selected by default.

   2. Click My Location to highlight the selection, and then click Edit.

   3. The Edit Location dialog box appears and gives you three tabs to customize your rules. These tabs are listed as General, Area Code Rules, and Calling Card.

The General tab contains the basic information about your dialing rule. You have six areas to enter information that aids and defines aspects of your rule. See Table 17-1 for a detailed list of the areas covered.

Table 17-1. General information for dialing rules

Options	Description
Location Name	The name you have given your location. The default name is My Location.
Country/Region	The country or region you live in. The default is based on the information provided during setup and stored in your system.
Area Code	This field holds the area code in which you currently reside.

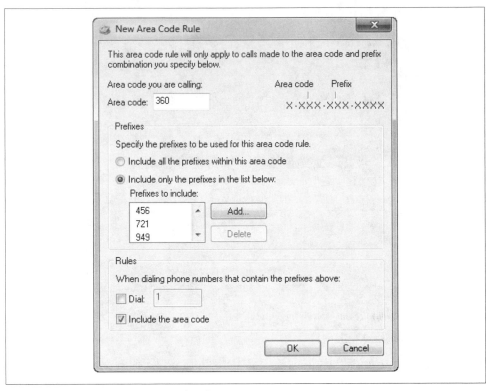

Figure 17-6. Creating a new area code rule

Options	Description
Dialing Rules	This heading allows you to change multiple details. You can quickly change settings for the number you use to dial a local outside call, the number you dial for a long-distance call, the carrier code used to make a long-distance call, and the carrier code to make international calls.
Disable Call Waiting	Check this option and enter the specific sequence to disable your call-waiting feature. Your options are *70, 1170, and 70#. You can also enter your own sequence.
Tone/Pulse Dialing	Select the appropriate radio button for either tone or pulse dialing.

The Area Code Rules tab provides options for creating and managing area code rules. These rules determine how phone numbers are dialed from your current area code to different area codes. These settings also determine how numbers are dialed within your current area code. To create a new area code rule, follow these steps:

1. Click New. This displays the New Area Code Rule dialog box shown in Figure 17-6.

2. In the "Area code" text box, type the area code to which you want the rule to apply.

3. Use the Prefixes options to set the desired prefixes to use in the current area code rule. You can specify to use all of the prefixes or you can enter specific prefixes:

- To use all prefixes, select the "Include all the prefixes within this area code" option.
- To specify prefixes to use with this rule, select the "Include only the prefixes in the list below" option and then click Add. In the Add Prefix dialog box, enter one or more prefixes separated by commas or spaces, and then click OK.

4. When dialing phone numbers that contain the prefixes you've selected, you have the option to set the number to dial, as in dialing a 1 to call a long-distance number. Select the Dial checkbox and then enter the number to dial.

5. To include the area code when dialing the call, select the "Include the area code" checkbox.

When gaining access to the Internet, you may want to use a calling card for long-distance expenses. Windows 7 supports the use of calling cards within the dialing rules associated with your dial-up connection. The Calling Card tab, as shown in Figure 17-7, allows you to enter information about a predefined calling card you use. Windows 7 supplies a prepopulated list of common calling cards. If you cannot find your calling card company, you can create a new entry for it.

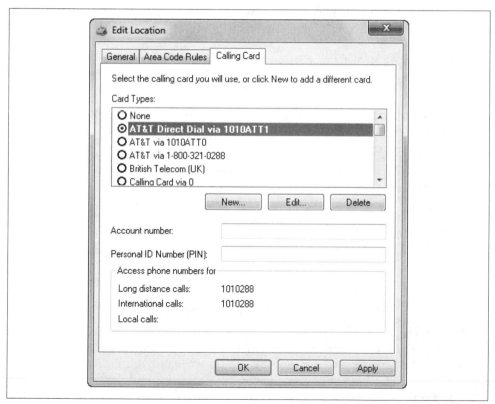

Figure 17-7. Selecting a calling card to use

To create a new calling card entry, click New, and the New Calling Card window appears. There are four tabs with which to define your new calling card. The four tabs are listed in Table 17-2.

Table 17-2. Calling card information for dialing rules

Tab	Related options
General	This tab allows you to name your new calling card settings, letting you assign an easy-to-remember name. In the "Account number" box, type your calling card account number. In the "Personal Identification Number (PIN)" box, type your PIN.
Long Distance	This tab provides the options required to dial a long-distance call, and allows you to specify the steps required to make a connection using the card. Enter the number required for long-distance calls into the "Access phone number for long distance calls" field. Use the buttons provided to sequence the steps required to dial a call. Use the Move Up, Move Down, and Delete buttons for your sequencing needs.
International	This tab provides the options required to dial an international call, and allows you to specify the steps to make a successful connection using the calling card. Enter the number required for the call into the "Access phone number for international calls" field provided. Use the buttons provided to sequence the steps required to dial a call. Use the Move Up, Move Down, and Delete buttons for your sequencing needs.
Local	This tab provides the options required to dial a local call. Enter the number to dial for a local call into the "Access phone number for local calls" field. Use the buttons provided to sequence the different aspects for a successful call. Use the Move Up, Move Down, and Delete buttons to move your sequence into the desired arrangement.

Configuring dial-up connection properties

When connecting using a dial-up connection, you may need to configure additional options for your connection. Windows 7 enables you to change the properties of your dial-up connection to alter your phone numbers, manage redial attempts, and manage your personal security settings. You can also configure the network protocol options and network sharing options.

To change the properties of your network connection, you need to open the Network Connections window and the Dial-up Connection Properties dialog box by following these steps:

1. Click Start→Control Panel.
2. In the Control Panel, click Network and Internet→Network and Sharing Center.
3. In the Network and Sharing Center, click "Change adapter settings" in the left pane.
4. Right-click the entry for your dial-up connection and then select Properties.

The Dial-up Properties window gives you five tabs of features to configure. The different tabs are labeled General, Options, Security, Networking, and Sharing. Each tab enables you to manage the different features available for use with your modem and dial-up connections. Table 17-3 shows the different tabs available and the features you can manage through the Dial-up Properties window.

Table 17-3. Dial-up connection properties feature settings

Tab	Related options
General	Modem device configuration
	Phone number to dial
	Alternative phone numbers to dial
	Associate dialing rules with this dial-up connection
Options	Dialing options
	Redialing options
	PPP settings
Security	Data encryption
	Authentication
	Interactive logon and scripting options
Networking	Internet Protocol version 6 (TCP/IPv6)
	Internet Protocol version 4 (TCP/IPv4)
	File and Printer Sharing for Microsoft Networks
	Client for Microsoft Networks
Sharing	Internet Connection Sharing

The General tab of the Dial-up Properties dialog box allows you to manage the device configuration of your modem by clicking the Configure button. See Figure 17-8 for an example. The Modem Configuration dialog box that appears allows you to change the maximum transfer speed of your modem and the hardware features available for your modem. Using the "Hardware features" options, you can turn a feature on or off by checking the associated checkbox for each feature listed:

- Enable hardware flow control
- Enable modem error control
- Enable modem compression
- Enable modem speaker

From the General tab, you can also edit the phone number to dial for calls. Editing the "Phone number" field allows you to change the stored phone number to dial. If you have multiple numbers to choose from through your service provider or VPN provider, you can add these phone numbers using the Alternates button. Clicking the Alternates button provides you with the ability to add new numbers, change their dialing priority, and use error checking to go to the next number in the list.

The Options tab allows you to configure the dialing options available for your dial-up connection. You can have Windows 7 display progress while connecting by checking

Figure 17-8. Optimizing the modem configuration

the box next to this feature. You can have Windows prompt for a name and password, certificate, and so on, by checking the box for this feature. You can also turn on the "Include Windows logon domain" feature by checking its associated checkbox, and the "Prompt for phone number" feature, which opens a dialog box for you to fill in the appropriate phone number to dial. See Figure 17-9 for an example of the Options tab.

Figure 17-9. Configuring additional modem options

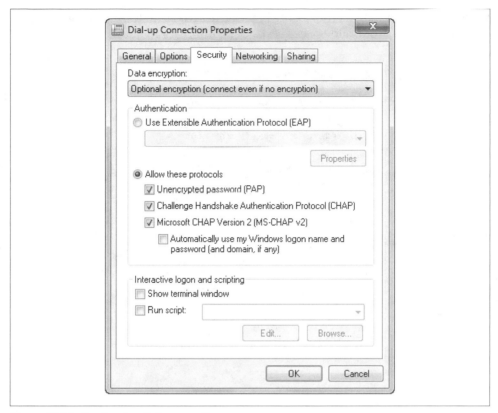

Figure 17-10. Configuring dial-up security

The Options tab also allows you to configure the options used to redial a connection. Use the "Redial attempts" text box to set the number of attempts Windows 7 makes to dial a connection. You can also use the "Time between redial attempts" listbox to change the behavior Windows 7 uses between call attempts. Setting the "Idle time before hanging up" feature allows you to turn off a connection automatically when you are no longer using the connection for active data transfers on the network. This feature can save you money if you are using a calling card or if long-distance charges apply to your dial-up connection.

As Figure 17-10 shows, default settings on the Security tab allow you to validate your identity with secured and unsecured password use. With a secured password, you can specify whether you want to use your Windows logon name and password automatically and whether data encryption is required.

If the default settings don't meet your needs, you can configure data encryption and authentication. With data encryption, you can require encryption or specify that maximum encryption must be used. With authentication, you can choose to use the

Extensible Authentication Protocol (EAP) in one of several modes, including Protected EAP, Secured Password, and Smart Card. See Figure 17-11 for an example.

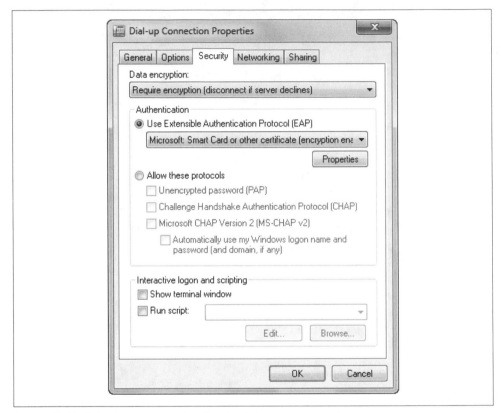

Figure 17-11. Using encryption and authentication

As shown in Figure 17-12, the Networking tab gives you the ability to configure the protocols associated with your dial-up connection. You can enable or disable a protocol by checking its associated checkbox. To configure the individual protocol properties, you may either double-click the desired protocol or highlight the protocol and choose the Properties button to open the dialog box associated with its properties. By default, dial-up connections have file and printer sharing as well as Client for Microsoft Networks disabled. If you are connecting directly to your workplace using dial-up, you'll need to enable Client for Microsoft Networks to connect to servers and printers on the work network (File and Printer Sharing will allow people to connect to resources on your computer).

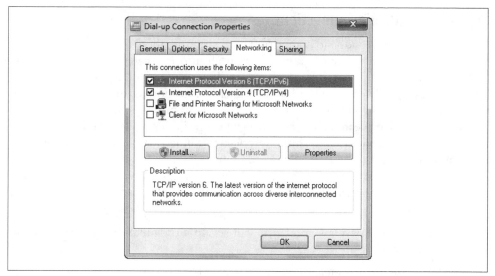

Figure 17-12. Configuring the networking protocols to use with the dial-up connection

The Sharing tab allows you to configure the Internet Connection Sharing feature of Windows 7, as seen in Figure 17-13. To enable this feature, check the associated box. This will allow other users to connect to the connection you define from the drop-down menu. You have the option to associate any network connection defined to your system with this feature.

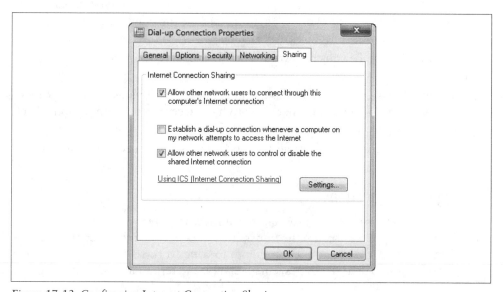

Figure 17-13. Configuring Internet Connection Sharing as necessary

Creating Broadband Connections

Most people have a broadband connection to the Internet these days. Broadband connections are defined by their bandwidth and fall into five categories: cable, ADSL, SDSL, fiber to the premises, and broadband wireless. Any of these types of connections provides high-speed access to the Internet. Each connection requires service from an ISP. If the ISP allows you to connect without having to provide a username and password, such as with cable modem service, you typically don't need to establish a separate broadband connection. Instead, you simply need to connect your computer to the cable modem provided by the cable provider (see Chapter 14 for more details). On the other hand, if your broadband provider requires you to use a username and password it has assigned, you'll need to create a broadband connection that sets the username and password for you.

In the Network and Sharing Center, you can set up a broadband connection by following these steps:

1. Click "Set up a new connection or network." This opens the Set Up a Connection or Network Wizard.

2. In the wizard, click Connect to the Internet, and click the Next button.

3. If your computer has existing connections that could be used to connect to the Internet, you'll see a list of the existing connections. Select "No, create a new connection" and then click Next.

4. The wizard gives you three selections from which to choose. The choices are Wireless, Broadband (PPPoE), and Dial-up. Click Broadband (PPPoE).

5. On the "Type the information . . ." page, shown in Figure 17-14, type the username and password provided by your ISP in the text boxes provided. As necessary, select the "Show characters" checkbox to see your password and verify the correct syntax.

6. Select the "Remember this password" checkbox to save your password for future use.

7. Windows 7 also enables you to share your connection with anyone with access to your computer. If you want other users to have access to this connection, check "Allow other people to use this connection."

8. Click Connect to create the connection and establish a connection to the ISP.

Creating VPN Connections

Many organizations use VPN connections to gain access to their networks. These connections use encryption to secure the transmitted data between the user and the network. They also provide remote connectivity to a network so that you can access network resources, such as file shares, email servers, and terminal service connections.

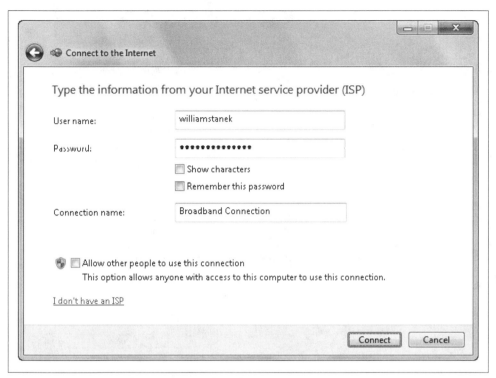

Figure 17-14. Providing the necessary credentials

Most organizations use Internet connections to allow VPN client connections to their network. If you do not have the correct information to connect to the VPN service, contact your network administrator for specific information on how to connect to the network. Some organizations use specific VPN client applications, which require the installation of a separate VPN client application. To determine whether the default VPN client included in Windows 7 will work with your VPN connection, contact your network administrator. If your organization is running Microsoft's Routing and Remote Access Service (RRAS), the VPN client in Windows 7 will work by default.

In the Network and Sharing Center, you can set up a VPN connection by following these steps:

1. Click "Set up a new connection or network." This opens the Set Up a Connection or Network Wizard.

2. In the wizard, click "Connect to a workplace," and click the Next button.

3. If your computer has existing dial-up connections that could be used to connect to your workplace, you'll see a list of the existing connections. Unless your system administrator has specifically directed you to use one of these connections, select "No, create a new connection" and then click Next.

4. On the "How do you want to connect?" page, you have two choices:

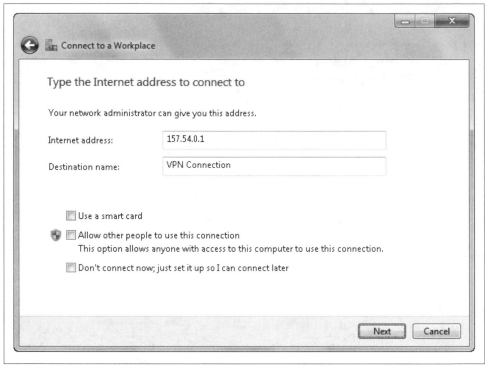

Figure 17-15. Configuring the connection address and options

Use my Internet connection

This feature connects you to a workplace using a VPN connection through the Internet. It requires a username and password for connecting to your VPN server.

Dial directly

This feature connects you to a workplace using a VPN connection with a modem by directly dialing a phone number to your workplace without going through the Internet.

To use an existing Internet connection for a VPN connection, follow these steps:

1. Click "Use my Internet connection (VPN)" to use an Internet connection for a VPN connection.

2. If you aren't currently connected to the Internet, you'll see the "Before you connect" page. On this page, choose the connection that you want to use to connect to the Internet, and then click Next.

3. On the "Type the Internet address to connect to" page, shown in Figure 17-15, type the IP address provided by your network administrator. This is the IP address of your organization's remote access server.

4. In the "Destination name" text box, type a name for the connection. The default name is VPN Connection.

5. Check "Use a smart card" if you have a smart card for use in authenticating you to your VPN connection.

6. Check "Allow other people to use this connection" if you want anyone with access to your computer to be able to use this VPN connection.

7. Check "Don't connect now; just set it up so I can connect later" if you want to create the VPN connection, but not actually connect to it.

8. Click Next. On the "Type your user name and password" page, the wizard prompts you to enter your username and password. In the "User name" text box, enter the domain username for your workplace. In the Password text box, enter the password for your domain user account. As necessary, click "Show characters" to view your password. This helps you identify the correct syntax and find typos.

9. Click "Remember this password" to save your password for future use.

10. As necessary, enter the name of the domain at your workplace into the Domain text box. This setting is optional, but it remembers your domain so that you do not have to type it in each time you use the connection.

11. After entering the correct data into the fields provided by the wizard, click the Connect button to create the connection and connect. If you chose "Don't connect now; just set it up so I can connect later" in the earlier step, click Create to create the connection without actually connecting and then click Close.

To use a dial-up connection for a VPN connection, follow these steps:

1. Click "Dial directly" to use your modem to make the VPN connection.

2. On the "Type the telephone number" page, enter the phone number provided by your network administrator.

3. Complete steps 4–10 of the previous procedure. After providing the necessary information, click Create to create the dial-up VPN connection. If you chose "Don't connect now; just set it up so I can connect later" in the earlier step, click Create to create the connection without actually connecting and then click Close.

Configuring Proxy Settings

Many organizations today use proxies to protect their users from intrusion and to use smaller amounts of publicly routed IP addresses. A *proxy* is a server that sits between you and the Internet. It receives all client requests to the Internet, fulfills the request itself, and then sends the information to the client. When creating network connections, you may need to configure a proxy in order to gain access to the Internet or other external servers.

Windows 7 offers support for adding proxies inside Internet Explorer's settings. You can configure the proxy server and port to support the different protocols you use for accessing services that require a proxy within your organization.

 If you use a different web browser, such as Mozilla Firefox, that browser may have its own proxy settings that you must configure using its settings or options dialog. Some browsers, such as Google Chrome, use the system-wide proxy settings that you learn to configure in this section.

You can enable or disable proxy settings on a per-connection basis as well as for the LAN. You should enable proxy settings only when using a proxy is required. If you enable proxy settings and a proxy is not required, you won't be able to use the related connection to access the Internet or resources on your network. This happens because your computer will look for a proxy that isn't there. Malware programs sometimes target your proxy settings, and you may have to enable or disable these settings as a result.

You can configure a proxy for a LAN connection by completing these steps:

1. Click Start, and then click Control Panel.
2. Click Network and Internet, and then click Internet Options.
3. In the Internet Options dialog box, click the Connections tab.
4. Click the LAN Settings button.
5. To enable the use of a proxy server, check the box for "Use a proxy server for your LAN (These settings will not apply to dial-up or VPN connections)," as shown in Figure 17-16.
6. Enter the IP address of the proxy in the Address text box.
7. Enter the port number of the proxy in the Port text box.
8. If you want to bypass the proxy server for local IP addresses, select the "Bypass proxy server for local addresses" checkbox.
9. Click OK to complete the proxy configuration process.

You can configure a proxy for a dial-up or VPN connection by completing these steps:

1. Click Start→Control Panel. Click Network and Internet→Internet Options→ Connections tab.
2. Under Dial-up and Virtual Private Network Settings, click the connection you want to work with and then click Settings.
3. In the Connection Settings dialog box, enable the use of a proxy server by checking the box for "Use a proxy server for this connection (These settings will not apply to other connections)."

Figure 17-16. Configuring LAN proxy settings as necessary

4. Enter the IP address of the proxy in the Address text box.

5. Enter the port number of the proxy in the Port text box.

6. Click OK to complete the proxy configuration process.

Whenever you change network connection settings, you should verify that you can establish a connection and access resources. If you are having difficulty connecting to the Internet after changing your connection settings, check your proxy settings in Internet Options to enable or disable your proxy configuration as appropriate for each connection.

Enabling and Disabling Windows Firewall

Windows Firewall helps prevent hackers and malicious programs from gaining access to your computer. The firewall blocks access to your computer through network or Internet connections. The firewall can also block packets being sent by your computer, helping to protect others from malicious content on your computer, such as a virus or worm. The firewall is essential to help protect your computer and your data, and you will want to leave it enabled.

If you use Windows Firewall, make sure you do not run other software firewalls on your computer, as it takes considerable effort to troubleshoot networking issues when you have multiple firewalls enabled on your computer. If you are using an Ethernet or Wi-Fi router, you should enable the firewall on the router as well, as this will also help block attacks against your network. Although no firewall has the capability to stop all

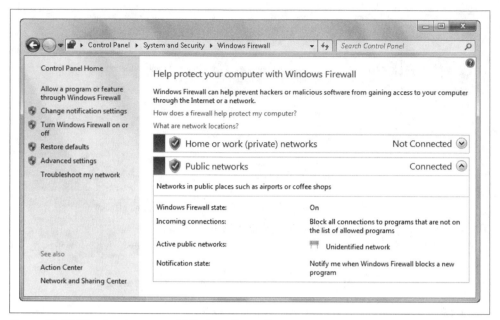

Figure 17-17. Viewing the status of Windows Firewall

harmful attacks against your computer, it is well worth the time to configure Windows Firewall and any firewall that may be available on your router.

Windows 7 offers you the ability to configure the options of the Windows Firewall feature by giving you an easy-to-use interface. For more information on the Windows Firewall, see Chapter 15. The Windows Firewall is enabled by default for all connections and can be enabled or disabled for each type of network to which a user connects. You can determine the status of Windows Firewall for each network location type by following these steps:

1. Click Start→Control Panel→System and Security heading→Windows Firewall.

2. As shown in Figure 17-17, you'll see a summary of the firewall status and configuration. To change the basic firewall settings, click "Change notification settings."

3. As Figure 17-18 shows, Windows Firewall settings for each network type to which a user can connect are listed in the Customize Settings page. Select Turn on Windows Firewall or Turn off Windows Firewall for each network type as appropriate. Note that turning the firewall off makes your computer vulnerable to remote attacks through network and Internet connections.

4. When you are connecting to networks that are less secure, you may want to block all incoming connections to your computer. To do this, select the "Block all incoming connections" checkbox. This setting ignores all settings in the firewall configuration and blocks every connection to your computer.

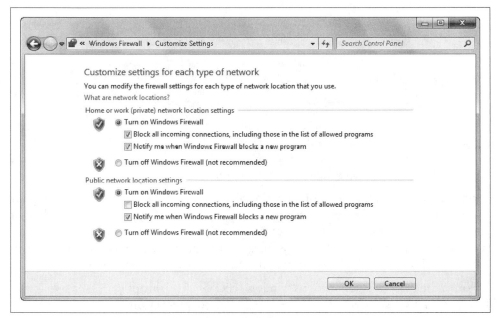

Figure 17-18. Changing basic settings in the Windows Firewall

5. By default you are notified when Windows Firewall blocks a new program. If you don't want to be notified, clear the "Notify me when Windows Firewall blocks a new program" checkbox.

6. Once you have completed making changes to the firewall settings, complete the steps by clicking OK, and Windows 7 applies your changes to the system. If you are a member of a domain and you cannot change some of your firewall configuration options, your network administrator may be controlling the settings through Group Policy. You also need the correct credentials to change your firewall settings. If you do not have local administrative rights, some features of Windows Firewall are unavailable for your configuration.

Establishing Network Connections

Network connections are the actual settings that allow you to connect to a network. They require several configurations in order to work. First, you must have a hardware device offering you connectivity to the network. You also need a profile associated with the network connection, and you must configure the network protocols to use on the related network adapter. Each setting is required for any connection to work properly.

You must have a connection defined in order to establish a connection to a network. To verify that you have a connection defined, you can use the Network Connections window (from Network and Sharing Center, click Change Adapter Settings), as shown in Figure 17-19. The Network Connections window holds all of the network

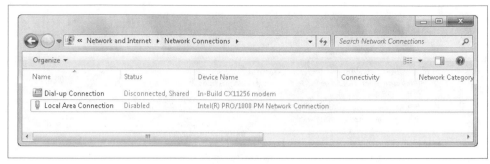

Figure 17-19. Viewing and establishing network connections

connections defined for your computer. When you install network hardware in your computer, Windows 7 creates a connection in the Network Connections window. If you install an Ethernet card, Windows 7 creates a Local Area Connection in the Network Connections window. If you install a wireless network adapter, Windows 7 creates a Wireless Network Connection in the Network Connections window.

To open the Network Connections window, click Start→Control Panel→Network and Internet→Network and Sharing Center→"Change adapter settings" in the left pane.

In the Network Connections window, you will see the status of each connection. If a connection is active, you will see a connectivity entry that shows whether the connection has access to the Internet. Once you've verified that you have network connection entries but do no have an active connection, you will want to connect to a network or the Internet using dial-up, broadband, or VPN.

To activate a connection that is not connected, right-click the connection and then select Connect. Confirm or provide the required username and password and then click Dial or Connect as appropriate. If your connection fails, Windows 7 displays an error dialog box. With dial-up and broadband, you are able to redial/retry to try to make the connection again using the same settings.

 Some connections, such as wireless broadband adapters that use cellular networks, should be started and stopped using the utility supplied by your cellular provider.

To enable a disabled connection, right-click the connection and select Enable.

Wireless Networking

If you travel frequently, chances are you are quite familiar with the existence of wireless networks. Most hotels, coffee shops, airports, and libraries offer Wi-Fi or 802.11 networks. Many cities are beginning to offer Wi-Fi connections also, offering low-cost Internet access to residents. Eventually wireless networks may become so prevalent that we'll be able to connect to the Internet from just about anywhere. With this in mind, Windows 7 makes creating and connecting to wireless networks very easy. With Windows 7, Microsoft has taken the time to revamp the wireless networking interface, making it considerably easy to create and connect to wireless networks.

The beauty of wireless networking correlates directly to the word *wireless*. Wireless networks allow you the freedom to move about, whether in your home or on the road, which can make your life considerably easier when you need to connect to a network. With wireless networking, you gain the complete functionality of a standard network without the need for any cables to connect the computers or devices. This eases the requirements and restrictions of regular networks, but it adds some complexity and additional pitfalls to the networking process.

Wireless Network Technologies

The most common wireless network technologies fall under the Institute of Electrical and Electronics Engineers (IEEE) 802.11 specification. Although other wireless technologies exist, they are not as prevalent as 802.11 (Wi-Fi) networks. Wi-Fi networks transmit radio waves between devices to allow network communications. Wi-Fi uses the 2.4 GHz and 5 GHz spectrums. There are three major standards within the Wi-Fi designation. See Table 17-4 for a listing of the major standards and their specifications.

Table 17-4. Common wireless networking technologies

Version	Transmission frequency	Transmission rate
802.11a	5 GHz	Up to 54 Mbps
802.11b	2.4 GHz	Up to 11 Mbps
802.11g	2.4 GHz	Up to 54 Mbps
802.11n	2.4 GHz, 5 GHz, or both	Up to 540 Mbps

The 802.11b specification was the first Wi-Fi technology introduced to the market. It uses the 2.4 GHz spectrum to transmit data at 11 Mbps. The 802.11b specification uses Complimentary Code Keying (CCK) coding to transmit data. While 802.11b has enjoyed the most widespread use, the lowering costs of faster technologies are rapidly replacing it with newer technologies.

The 802.11a specification transmits in the 5 GHz spectrum at a transmission rate of 54 Mbps. This specification uses Orthogonal Frequency-Division Multiplexing (OFDM) to transmit data, which is considerably better than the CCK coding standard. Additionally, 802.11a has more usable channels than 802.11b. This, plus the fact that the 5 GHz spectrum typically has less interference than 2.4 GHz, gives 802.11a a considerably faster transmission rate.

The 802.11g specification transmits in the 2.4 GHz spectrum at a transmission rate of 54 Mbps. This specification also uses OFDM to transmit data, and it enjoys the most widespread use of the newer technologies.

The 802.11n specification transmits in the 2.4 GHz, 5 GHz, or both spectrums. 802.11n offers up to 540 Mbps while using Multiple-Input-Multiple-Output (MIMO) technology. Essentially this means that the client computer and the wireless access point will use multiple receivers and multiple transmitters to achieve improved performance. Although multiple data streams can help your computer achieve higher throughput, many standard 802.11n devices combine strong, weak, and reflected signals into one data stream to maximize the range.

These technologies fall under the Wi-Fi designation, since devices that use the 802.11 family of standards are typically certified for interoperability by the Wi-Fi Alliance. Windows 7 supports each of these wireless technologies and the devices used to make connections to these types of networks.

New networking standards are also in the marketplace today. It bears noting that early adoption of new technologies does not always favor the consumer, because some products in the market may support early adoption of a standard that is not yet finalized. Therefore, if you purchase products too early, you may have to purchase additional hardware to support the additional features defined in the final version of the standard. Though this is not always true, be wary of purchasing the latest and greatest wireless products. Take some time to research the technology before buying equipment on impulse.

Not all 802.11 specifications are about transmission speed and rate, however. The 802.11i specification offers enhanced security. The 802.11h specification offers frequency and power control management. The 802.11e specification offers quality of service enhancements.

 The 802.1x specification is not part of the 802.11 family of protocols. It works with wireless and wired network protocols and provides a framework for authenticating users and controlling their access to a protected network.

Another emerging wireless technology is Worldwide Interoperability for Microwave Access (WiMax). WiMax is not really a technology, but a stamp of approval for use with the 802.16 specification in broadband wireless deployments in metropolitan areas. WiMax-certified equipment usually uses the 2.5 GHz spectrum, but the 3.5 GHz, 2.3 GHz, and 5 GHz spectrums are available in some regions. Currently, a movement exists to use the 700 MHz spectrum for future WiMax deployments.

Wireless Network Devices

Wireless devices come in different shapes and sizes. A wireless device is the network adapter used to make the connection to wireless networks. A wireless network adapter is the actual hardware device you install into a slot or port in your computer. You must have a wireless network adapter to create a wireless network connection, which in turn allows you to connect to a wireless network.

Most new portable computers offer integrated wireless networking adapters. Older cards are available for older laptops that go into the PC Card or PCMCIA slot, but these are increasingly less common to find. PCI cards exist for the desktop and workstation. USB adapters are now more prevalent in the market, and they will work in all computers with a USB slot (although computers without USB 2.0 slots may experience performance or compatibility problems).

You can find wireless network adapters at just about any store that carries electronics. Most office supply, electronics, and retail stores offer you the ability to purchase wireless adapters for your computer. Make sure that you purchase the correct card for the type of wireless technology you are using. If you are in doubt, you might want to buy an 802.11g adapter, since it can use both 802.11g and 802.11b technologies to communicate. Although likely more expensive, an 802.11n adapter can use 802.11a, 802.11b, and 802.11g, as well as 802.11n.

The device to which your wireless adapter connects is a wireless router or a wireless access point. At the office or out on the town, you may be able to use someone else's wireless router or wireless access point to access the Internet. At home, however, you must purchase the necessary wireless router or a wireless access point. Several manufacturers produce wired/wireless router combinations. A wired/wireless router, such as the Linksys Wireless N Broadband router, has ports for network cables that use wired communications as well as receivers for receiving wireless communications.

Installing and Configuring a Wireless Adapter

You must have a wireless adapter or chip in your computer in order to create a wireless connection. You can see the devices installed in your computer using Device Manager. Device Manager allows you to manage the different devices in your system from a single console. You have the ability to enable or disable devices, update or roll back the device drivers, and uninstall devices.

You can open the Computer Management console to use Device Manager by following these steps:

1. Click Start, right-click Computer, and then select Manage.
2. In the Computer Management console, click Device Manager in the left pane.
3. Your computer's wired and wireless adapters should be listed under the Network Adapters node. Expand this node by double-clicking it.

If you have a PCI card to install, install it as discussed in Chapter 5. If you have a PC Card, ExpressCard, or a USB adapter, slide the card into the appropriate slot in your computer. Once you have installed the PC Card, ExpressCard, or USB adapter into your computer, Windows 7 should automatically see the device and install a driver for the adapter or ask you to install a driver for the adapter. See Chapter 5 for details on installing the device driver.

If you are using an integrated wireless network card in your computer and this card is not enabled in firmware, reboot the computer into the firmware. (Most OEM manufacturers use the Delete key, but some use F2 or Esc. Press the Delete, F2, or Esc key every second or so after the reboot to enter the main firmware screen.) Usually, you can find the network card settings under Integrated Devices. Once you have found the wireless network card settings in your firmware, select and enable the device. After you have enabled the device, save the changes in the firmware and reboot your computer into the operating system.

When you have completed the setup process, you will need to open Device Manager to verify that the installation of the wireless adapter finished correctly. In Device Manager, right-click on the adapter you previously installed or enabled and select Properties from the context menu. On the Driver tab, verify that the details for the Driver Provider listing are correct. If you see Microsoft listed as the driver vendor, you should go to your network adapter manufacturer's website and download the latest driver for your network card. This allows you to use the entire functionality of the card. Microsoft drivers usually allow you only the lowest common features of the card.

If you do not see a network adapter listed in the Device Manager screen under Network Adapters, you should verify that the device does not show up under Other Devices as a network controller. If this happens, you should go to your network adapter manufacturer's website and download the latest driver for your network card. If you continue to have problems installing the network card, refer to the networking troubleshooting section in Chapter 14.

Connecting to and Managing Wireless Connections

Windows 7 greatly simplifies the process of connecting to wireless networks by auto-negotiating the required settings, making it really easy to connect your computer to any available wireless network. To connect to a wireless network, click the Network icon in the system tray, click an available wireless network and then click Connect. If you are connecting to a secured network, type the security key when prompted and then click OK.

You will only need to enter the key once. The next time you connect, Windows will remember the key and supply it for you. If you entered the security key incorrectly, simply reenter the key when prompted and then click OK again.

If you aren't within range of a wireless connection, you can pre-create the connection to use when you are within range. For some types of secured networks, you may need to pre-create the connection by walking through the steps below but not actually connecting as this ensures the right security settings are used. You also can create connections to establish an ad hoc wireless network between your computer and other

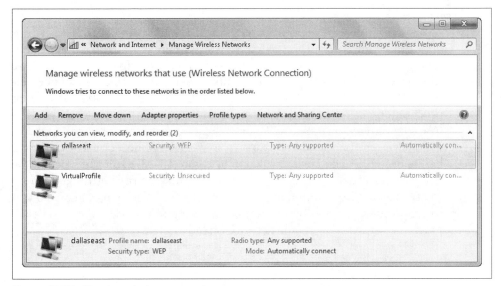

Figure 17-20. Viewing wireless connections

computers. In an ad hoc wireless network, the connections are created directly between the participating computers and no other networking equipment is needed.

You can view available wireless network connections and create new wireless network connections by following these steps:

1. Click Start→Control Panel→Network and Internet→Network and Sharing Center.

2. In the Network and Sharing Center, click "Manage wireless networks" in the left pane.

3. In the "Manage wireless networks" window, shown in Figure 17-20, you'll see a list of any currently defined wireless network connections.

4. Click Add. This starts the "Manually connect to a wireless network" Wizard, as shown in Figure 17-21.

5. Select one of the following options:

   Manually create a network profile
   Making this selection creates a new wireless network profile and saves the profile to your computer. As shown in Figure 17-22, you are prompted for the Network name, Security type, Encryption type, and Security Key/Passphrase for access to the wireless network. Select the "Start this connection automatically" checkbox if you want to connect to this network without prompting. Click "Connect even if the network is not broadcasting" if you have a wireless network that has been configured not to broadcast its SSID (this is sometimes called *stealth mode*, though it does not adequately protect you from snoopers). When you click Next, the wizard adds the network to your list and prompts you to open the connection properties dialog box to review the settings.

Create an ad hoc network

Making this selection allows you to create a computer-to-computer network with other computers using only the wireless network adapters installed in your computer. You can use these types of connections to share files or share Internet connections with other computers. Generally, devices in ad hoc networks must be within 100 feet of one another indoors and 300 feet of each other outdoors. When making the connection to the ad hoc network, you will lose connectivity to any active Wi-Fi connection that uses the same adapter as the one you use for the ad hoc connection (wired Ethernet connections should be unaffected). Click Next. As shown in Figure 17-23, enter the name of the network, select a security type, and then enter the security key or pass phrase to use. You have the option to save this network for future use, allowing you to keep your settings without prompting during future use. When you click Next, the wizard tells you the network is ready to use.

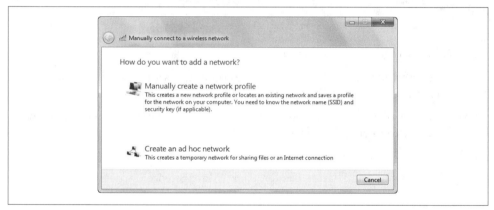

Figure 17-21. Adding a wireless connection

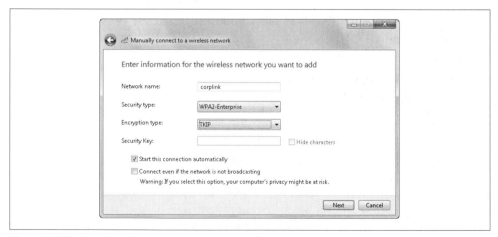

Figure 17-22. Entering the necessary connection information

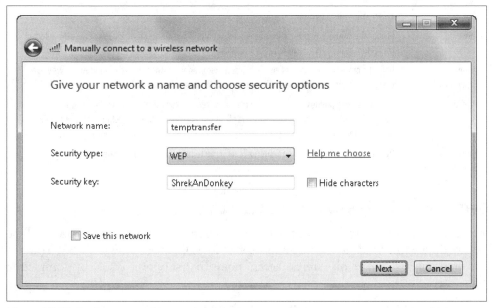

Figure 17-23. Setting up an ad hoc network

Configuring Available and Preferred Wireless Networks

You can connect to and configure wireless networks using the Network and Sharing Center. You have the option of setting the preferences of wireless networks defined to your computer and the order in which you connect to the available networks. You can even set your network connections to start automatically.

You can manage wireless network connections by following these steps:

1. Click Start→Control Panel→Network and Internet→Network and Sharing Center.
2. In the Network and Sharing Center, click "Manage wireless networks" in the left pane. This opens the "Manage wireless networks" window.

In the "Manage wireless networks" window, you will see the wireless networks defined for your computer. You also have a toolbar with different options for managing your wireless networks. Table 17-5 lists the options available for your use.

Table 17-5. Properties for managing wireless networks

Option	This feature allows you to
Add	Add wireless network connections to your computer.
Remove	Remove a selected wireless network connection from your computer.
Move Down	Change the connection preference of a wireless network to a lower state. This will allow other wireless connections to connect before this one.

Option	This feature allows you to
Move Up	Change the connection preference of a wireless network to a higher state. This will allow the selected connection to connect before other connections you've created.
Adapter Properties	Open the properties window of your wireless network adapter. The properties window allows you to change the network protocol definitions and services available.
Profile Types	Change the way profiles are handled on the computer. You can use all-user profiles, or all-user and per-user profiles. All-user profiles allow all users of the computer to use the connection. Per-user profiles apply only to the logged-on user, and may cause an interruption in connectivity when you log off or switch users.
Network and Sharing Center	Open the Network and Sharing Center, allowing you to manage more of your network settings.

Setting Up a Wireless Router or Access Point

Most wireless routers and account points you purchase after November 2009 will be compatible with Windows 7 and support Windows Connect Now (WCN). You can set up a wireless router or wireless access point that supports WCN by completing these steps:

1. Set up the router and plug it into a power source.

2. Click the Network icon in the system tray, click the default network of the router, which is identified by the manufacturer name, and then follow the prompts to set up the router.

3. During the set up process, you may need to connect one end of an Ethernet cable to the Internet port on your router and the other end into modem or other device supplied by your Internet provider. This will allow the device to connect to the Internet. If you don't connect the router to the Internet during setup, you'll need to do so afterward.

4. Your computer will be connected to the router's network automatically. To connect other computers, the Network icon in the system tray, click the network of the router. If the router supports WCN or WPS and has an activate/connect button, you can push the button on the router and then wait for the router to automatically set up the connection to the new computer. If the router doesn't have an activate/connect button, you are prompted for a security key; enter it and then click OK.

If the wireless router or access point doesn't support WCN, you can set it up by completing these steps:

1. Set up and plug in the wireless router or access point.

2. Connect one end of a network cable to your computer's wired network adapter and then connect the other end of the cable to the wireless router. On the router, use a port that isn't labeled "Internet," "WAN," or "WLAN."

3. Open your web browser and type the address of the router's configuration page, which is usually *http://192.168.0.1* or *http://192.168.1.1*. Consult your router's documentation to be sure.

4. When prompted, enter the default username and password for the router. Typically, the username is *admin* and the password is either blank or one of the following words: *admin* or *password*. If these don't work, refer to the documentation for the router.

5. In your browser, you should have an option to run the router's setup utility. If there isn't a setup utility, specify a name for the router's network, select the encryption level and choose a security key for accessing the router. Be sure to change the administrator password so that other people on your network can't modify the router's configuration.

6. Once you've set up the router, you can connect to it by clicking the Network icon in the system tray, then clicking the network of the router. Enter the security key when prompted and then click OK.

PART IV

Managing and Supporting Windows 7

CHAPTER 18

Managing User Accounts
and Parental Controls

In Windows 7, you use user accounts to manage access to your computer and parental controls to manage the types of content users can access while logged on. User accounts and parental controls are the two main areas of the operating system where you're likely to have entirely different sets of features and functions at home and at the office. At home, you'll use local accounts on your computer and you'll have full access to parental controls. While you are logged on to your computer with a local account, local computer security is applied to your account through Local Group Policy and through other local computer security components.

On the other hand, at the office, your computer will typically be a member of a domain and you'll typically use domain accounts to log on to computers and the network. While you are logged on to the network with a domain account, domain security is applied to your account through Active Directory Group Policy and through other domain security components. Although you can log on to a domain computer using a local account, some of the domain security changes will still affect what you can do and how you can work with user accounts.

 If you work in an office that does not use domains or does not centralize its management using group policy, your office computer will behave much like a home computer in these respects.

When working with domain computers, one of the biggest changes you'll notice is that there are no parental controls, and this remains true whether you log on with a local account or a domain account. Another big change is in the available options for managing local computer accounts. Local computer account options for domain computers are completely different from the options for managing local computer accounts on nondomain computers.

Managing Access to Your Computer

Windows 7 provides user accounts and group accounts. User accounts are designed for individuals. Group accounts, usually referred to as *groups*, have users as members and are used to manage the file access permissions and privileges of multiple users. Although you can log on to a user account, you can't log on to a group account.

On a domain, your IT administrators will create and manage the user account you need to log on to the network. You can use the techniques discussed in the section "Logging On, Switching, Locking, Logging Off, and Shutting Down" on page 21 of Chapter 1 to log on to the network and access your account. If you have a problem with your account, you can ask your IT administrators to help you resolve it.

At home (or in a small organization that doesn't use domains), you have complete control over your computer. During installation, you created the user account that you need to log on to your computer. When you are logged on with an administrator account rather than a standard user account, you can create other accounts to allow other people to log on to your computer. You can also manage user account settings as necessary.

Though the user and group names are what Windows 7 displays to you, these names aren't the actual identifiers Windows 7 uses. Behind the scenes, when you create a user or group account, Windows 7 assigns each user or group a unique security identifier (SID). The SID consists of a computer or domain security ID prefix combined with a unique relative ID for the user or group. The SID allows Windows 7 to track an account independently from its display name. Windows 7 does this to enable you to easily change account names, and delete accounts without worrying that someone might gain access to resources simply by creating an account with the same name as one you've deleted.

Thus, when you change a username or group name, you tell Windows 7 to map a particular SID to a new display name. When you delete a user or group, you tell Windows 7 that a particular SID is no longer valid. If you later were to create an account with the same username or group name, the new account would not have the same privileges and permissions as the previous one. This occurs because the new account will have a new SID.

When you install Windows 7, the operating system installs several types of default accounts. The default user accounts are Administrator and Guest. The default system accounts include LocalSystem, LocalService, and NetworkService. You use these accounts as follows:

Administrator
A standard account that provides complete access to your computer. To protect your computer, the Administrator account should have a secure password.

Guest

A standard account that provides limited privileges on your computer. Because this account can potentially put your computer at risk, the Guest account is disabled by default.

LocalSystem

A system account for running system processes and handling system tasks. The operating system manages this account.

LocalService

A system account for running services with fewer privileges and logon rights than the LocalSystem account. The operating system manages this account.

NetworkService

A system account for running services that need network access privileges. The operating system manages this account.

In most cases, you don't need to modify these or other default accounts. Although you can configure Administrator and Guest so that you can use them for logon, in most cases you should use a user account with administrator privileges instead. An administrator user account is one of two types of user accounts you can create. You can also create standard user accounts. When a user needs the highest level of permissions possible, create that account as an administrator user account. Otherwise, create the account as a standard user account.

Managing Your User Account

Your user account has many properties associated with it. These properties include a password, picture, account name, and account type designation. Unless your computer is on a domain, you can manage the properties associated with your user account by following the techniques discussed in this section. Most account management tasks require you to have an administrator account or the username and password of an administrator account.

 If your computer is part of a domain, you won't be able to use these techniques to manage your account, even if you log on to your computer using a local account. As discussed previously, when your computer is a member of a domain, different security components and features are in effect.

Changing Your Account Name

Because your computer tracks your account with an SID, you can safely change your account name at any time without worrying that this will cause problems with your access permissions or privileges. If you want to change your account name, follow these steps:

1. Click Start→Control Panel→User Accounts and Family Safety→User Accounts.
2. Select "Change your account name."
3. On the Change Your Name page, shown in Figure 18-1, type the new name for your account and then click Change Name.

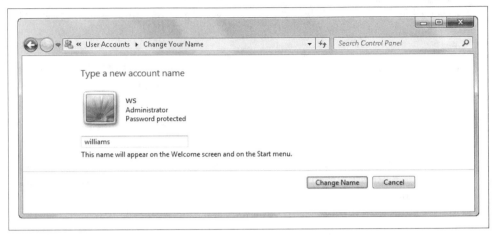

Figure 18-1. Changing your account name

Changing Your Account Picture

Your account picture is displayed on the logon screen and on the Start menu. If you want to change your account picture, follow these steps:

1. Click Start→Control Panel→User Accounts and Family Safety→User Accounts.
2. Select "Change your picture."
3. On the Change Your Picture page, shown in Figure 18-2, click the picture you want to use, or click the "Browse for more pictures" link to select any BMP, GIF, JPEG, PNG, DIB, or RLE picture to use.
4. Click Change Picture.

When you use a picture other than a default picture provided by Microsoft, Windows 7 automatically optimizes the picture and saves the optimized copy as part of your personal Contact entry in Windows Contacts. Although it may seem strange to save the picture as part of your personal *.contact* file, doing so is a quick and easy shortcut for the operating system. Most pictures are optimized to a file size of 50 KB or less—even high-resolution pictures.

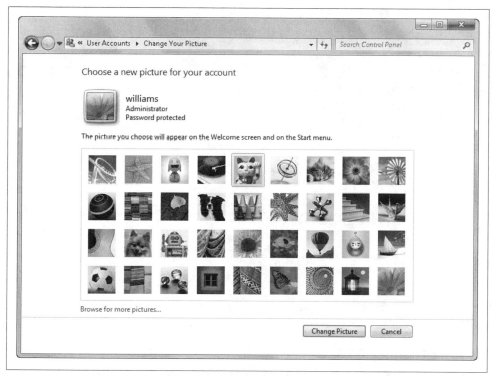

Figure 18-2. Changing your account picture

Changing Your Account Type

You can configure your user account as a standard user account or as an administrator user account. If you are logged on with a standard user account, you can change the account type to Administrator. If you are logged on with an administrator account, you can change the account type to Standard User.

 Your computer must have at least one administrator account. If your account is the only administrator account, you won't be able to change the account type to Standard User.

You can change the account type by following these steps:

1. Click Start→Control Panel→User Accounts and Family Safety→User Accounts.
2. Select "Change your account type."
3. On the "Select your new account type" page, shown in Figure 18-3, set the account type as either Standard user or Administrator.
4. Click Change Account Type.

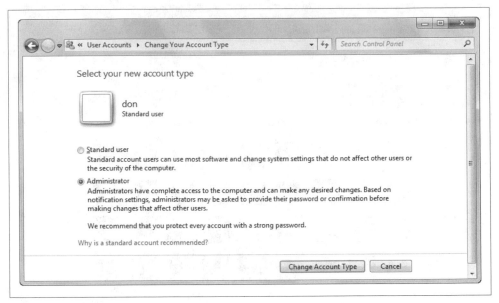

Figure 18-3. Changing your account type

Creating Your Password

To protect your computer, your user account should have a strong password. You can create a password for your account by completing the following steps:

1. Click Start→Control Panel→User Accounts and Family Safety→User Accounts.

2. Select "Create a password for your account."

3. On the "Create a password for your account" page, shown in Figure 18-4, type a password and then confirm it.

4. Afterward, type a unique password hint. The password hint is a word or phrase that can help you remember the password if you forget it. This hint is visible to anyone who uses your computer, so be careful what you use.

5. Click "Create password."

Changing Your Password

You should periodically change your password to help protect your computer. You can change the password on your account by completing the following steps:

1. Click Start→Control Panel→User Accounts and Family Safety→User Accounts.

2. Select "Change your password."

3. On the "Change your password" page, shown in Figure 18-5, type your current password in the first text box.

Figure 18-4. Creating your account password

4. Type your new password in the second text box.

5. Confirm your new password by retyping it in the third text box.

6. Afterward, type a unique password hint. The password hint is a word or phrase that can help you remember the password if you forget it. Because this hint is visible to anyone who uses your computer, you'll want to be careful what you use as the hint.

7. Click "Change password."

Storing Your Password for Recovery

You can store your password in a secure, encrypted file on a floppy disk or USB flash drive, and then use this file to recover your password if you forget it.

To store your password for recovery, complete these steps:

1. Press Ctrl-Alt-Delete and then click the Change a Password option.

2. Click "Create a password reset disk" to start the Forgotten Password Wizard.

3. In the Forgotten Password Wizard, read the introductory message and then click Next.

4. You can use a floppy disk, USB flash drive, or a flash memory card as your password key disk. To use a floppy disk, insert a blank, formatted disk into the A: drive and

Figure 18-5. Changing your account password

then select Floppy Disk Drive (A:) in the drive list. To use a USB flash drive, select the device you want to use on the drive list. Click Next.

 If you insert a USB flash device after clicking Next, it won't be displayed on the list automatically. Click Back and then click Next to update the list to include the device you just inserted.

5. Type your current password in the text box provided and then click Next.

6. After the wizard creates the password reset key, click Next and then click Finish.

7. Remove the disk, USB flash drive, or flash memory card and store it in a safe location. Anyone who has this disk or drive can use it to access your account.

Recovering Your Password

Windows 7 provides two ways for recovering passwords: password hints and password reset disks. You can access your password hint or recover your password by completing the following steps:

1. On the logon screen, click your username to display the Password prompt.

2. Click the button to the right of the password text box without entering a password.

3. When you click OK, the password hint for your account is displayed on the logon screen.

4. Type your password and click the logon button. If you log on successfully, skip the remaining steps. Otherwise, click OK and continue with password recovery.

5. On the logon screen, click Reset Password.

6. When the Reset Password Wizard starts, click Next.

7. Insert the disk into the *A:* drive or the USB flash key containing your password recovery file, and then click Next.

8. Type a new password in the first text box.

9. Confirm your new password by retyping it in the second text box.

10. Type a new password hint in the third text box.

11. Click Next to log on with your new password.

Managing Other People's User Accounts

You can allow other people to log on to your computer by creating a user account for them. As with your user account, you can create the account for other people as a standard user account or as an administrator user account. Both account types have passwords, pictures, account names, and account type designations associated with them. Unless your computer is part of a domain, you can manage the properties associated with other people's accounts by following the techniques discussed in this section. You must have an administrator account to manage other people's accounts, or the username and password of an administrator account.

 On a computer that's part of a domain, you won't be able to use these techniques to manage other people's accounts, even if you log on to your computer using a local account. As discussed previously, when your computer is a member of a domain, different security components and features are in effect.

Creating User Accounts for Other People

Your computer can, and probably should, have multiple user accounts configured as administrators. However, not everyone who logs on to your computer should be configured with an administrator account. Remember, anyone with administrator privileges can read any file on your computer and make changes to your computer's configuration. If you're in doubt as to whether a person needs an administrator account, create that account as a standard user account first. When he or she is trying to perform tasks that require administrator privileges and cannot, you should encourage the user to ask you for help. You can then type in your username and password to allow him or her to perform the task, or explain to the user why he or she shouldn't be trying to perform this type of task on your computer.

Before other people can log on to your computer, you'll need to create a user account for them. You can create a local user account on a computer by following these steps:

1. Click Start→Control Panel→User Accounts and Family Safety→Add or Remove Users Accounts.

2. On the "Choose the account you would like to change" page, you'll see a list of existing accounts on the computer. If an account has a password, it is listed as being password-protected. If an account is disabled, it is listed as being off.

3. Click "Create a new account." This displays the Create New Account page shown in Figure 18-6.

4. Type the name of the local account. This name is displayed on the Welcome screen and Start menu.

5. Set the type of account as either Standard user or Administrator.

6. Click Create Account.

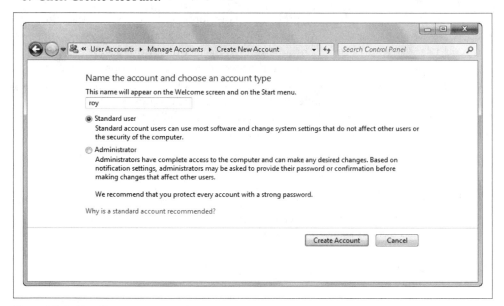

Figure 18-6. Creating a new account

Windows 7 will create a user profile and personal desktop for this user the first time he or she logs on to your computer.

Changing User Account Names for Other People

Your computer tracks account names with SIDs. This allows you to safely change account names at any time without worrying that this will cause problems with access permissions or privileges. If you want to change someone else's account name, follow these steps:

1. Click Start→Control Panel→User Accounts and Family Safety→Add or Remove Users Accounts.

2. On the "Choose the account you would like to change" page, you'll see a list of existing accounts on the computer. Click the account you want to work with.

3. On the "Make changes to..." page, click "Change the account name."

4. On the "Type a new account name for...account" page, shown in Figure 18-7, type the new name for the account and then click Change Name.

Figure 18-7. Changing the account name

Changing the Account Picture for Other People

Every user account can have a unique picture associated with it. This picture is displayed on the logon screen and on the Start menu. If you want to change the picture associated with another person's account, follow these steps:

1. Click Start→Control Panel→User Accounts and Family Safety→Add or Remove Users Accounts.

2. On the "Choose the account you would like to change" page, you'll see a list of existing accounts on the computer. Click the account you want to work with.

3. On the "Make changes to..." page, click "Change the picture."

4. On the "Choose a new picture for...account" page, shown in Figure 18-8, click the picture you want to use, or click the "Browse for more pictures" link to select any BMP, GIF, JPEG, PNG, DIB, or RLE picture to use.

5. Click Change Picture.

If the user for whom you are setting the picture hasn't logged on to the computer yet, the picture data is saved temporarily in your profile. When the user logs on, Windows 7 will create the user's profile and copy the picture you've assigned into this profile. Most pictures are optimized to a file size of 50 KB or less—even high-resolution pictures.

Figure 18-8. Changing the account picture

Changing the Account Type for Other People

You can create user accounts as standard user or administrator accounts. You can change the account type at any time by following these steps:

1. Click Start→Control Panel→User Accounts and Family Safety→Add or Remove Users Accounts.

2. On the "Choose the account you would like to change" page, you'll see a list of existing accounts on the computer. Click the account you want to work with.

3. On the "Make changes to..." page, click "Change the account type."

4. On the "Choose a new account type for..." page, shown in Figure 18-9, set the account type as either Standard user or Administrator.

5. Click Change Account Type.

Figure 18-9. Changing the account type

Creating a Password for Other People's Accounts

To protect your computer, every user account should have a strong password. You can create a password for someone else's account by completing the following steps:

1. Click Start→Control Panel→User Accounts and Family Safety→Add or Remove Users Accounts.

2. On the "Choose the account you would like to change" page, you'll see a list of existing accounts on the computer. Click the account you want to work with.

3. On the "Make changes to..." page, click "Create a password."

4. On the "Create a password for...account" page, shown in Figure 18-10, type a password for the account and then confirm the password by retyping it in the second text box.

5. Afterward, type a unique password hint. The password hint is a word or phrase that can help this person remember the password if he or she forgets it. Because this hint is visible to anyone who uses the computer, you'll want to be careful what you use as the hint.

6. Click "Create password."

Create a password for an account only if this person doesn't have encrypted files, personal certificates, or stored passwords for websites. If the user does have these items and you create a password, he or she will lose all the associated data. To keep this from happening, simply ask the user to log on and create his or her own password. Alternatively, you can log on as this person and create the password for the account. Follow the instructions discussed in the section "Creating Your Password" on page 710.

Figure 18-10. Creating the account password

Changing the Password on Other People's Accounts

Everyone who logs on to your computer should periodically change his password to help protect your computer. The best way to change passwords is to have the person log on and change the password himself. This way, he won't lose any encrypted files, personal certificates, or stored passwords for websites. Alternatively, you can log on as this person and change his password for him by following the instructions discussed in the section "Changing Your Password" on page 710.

If a user loses his password and you have no password recovery file, you can change the password on that person's account by completing the following steps:

1. Click Start→Control Panel→User Accounts and Family Safety→Add or Remove Users Accounts.

2. On the "Choose the account you would like to change" page, you'll see a list of existing accounts on the computer. Click the account you want to work with.

3. On the "Make changes to..." page, click "Change the password."

4. On the "Change...password" page, shown in Figure 18-11, type the new password for this user's account in the first text box.

5. Confirm the new password by retyping it in the second text box.

6. Afterward, type a unique password hint and then click "Change password."

 Change a password for an account only if this person doesn't have encrypted files, personal certificates, or stored passwords for websites. If the user does have these items and you create a password, he or she will lose all the associated data. To keep this from happening, simply ask the user to log on and create his or her own password.

Figure 18-11. Changing the account password

Storing Another Person's Password for Recovery

To ensure that another person can recover his or her password if he or she forgets it, you can store the password in a secure, encrypted file on a floppy disk or USB flash drive, and then use this file to recover his or her password if it's forgotten. To store another person's password for recovery, have the person log on to the computer. Follow the steps discussed in the section "Storing Your Password for Recovery" on page 711.

In step 5, be sure to have the other person type his or her password and not your current password.

Recovering Another Person's Password

To help another person remember or recover his or her password, complete the following steps:

1. On the logon screen, click this person's username to display the Password prompt.
2. Click the button to the right of the password text box without entering a password.
3. When you click OK, the password hint for the account is displayed on the logon screen.
4. Have the other person type the password if he or she remembers it, and click the logon button. If the user logs on successfully, skip the remaining steps. Otherwise, click OK and continue with password recovery.
5. On the logon screen, click Reset Password.
6. When the Reset Password Wizard starts, click Next.
7. Insert the disk into the A: drive or the USB flash drive containing the other person's password recovery file, and then click Next.
8. Have the other person type a new password in the first text box.
9. Have the user confirm his or her new password by retyping it in the second text box.
10. Have him or her type a new password hint in the third text box.
11. Have him or her click Next to log on with the new password.

Enabling Local User Accounts

User accounts on your computer can become disabled for several reasons. If a user forgets a password and tries to guess it, he or she might exceed the security settings for bad logon attempts. Another person with an administrator account could have disabled the account as well. When an account is disabled or locked out, you can enable it by following these steps:

1. Click Start→Control Panel→System and Security→Administrative Tools.
2. Double-click Computer Management.
3. In Computer Management, double-click Local Users and Groups under System Tools and then select the Users node.
4. Right-click the account name and then select Properties. This displays a Properties dialog box for the account, as shown in Figure 18-12.
5. Clear the "Account is disabled" checkbox if selected.
6. Clear the "Account is locked out" checkbox if selected.
7. Click OK.

Figure 18-12. Enabling the account for logon

Controlling the Way Account Passwords Are Used

User accounts can have three flags that control the way passwords are used with the account. You can specify that a particular person:

- Must change his password the next time he or she logs on.
- Cannot change his or her password.
- Has a password that never expires.

To manage these settings for passwords for a user account, follow these steps:

1. Click Start→Control Panel→System and Security→Administrative Tools.
2. Double-click Computer Management.
3. In Computer Management, double-click Local Users and Groups under System Tools and then select the Users node.
4. Right-click the account name and then select Properties. This displays a Properties dialog box for the account, as shown previously in Figure 18-12.
5. If you want this person to have to change his password the next time he or she logs on, select the "User must change password at next logon" checkbox.
6. If you don't want this person to be able to change his or her password, select the "User cannot change password" checkbox.

7. If you don't want this person's password to expire, select the "Password never expires" checkbox.

8. Click OK.

Deleting Local User Accounts

Every account has a user profile and personal folders associated with it. The user profile stores the desktop configuration and preferences as well as other settings and data. When an account is no longer needed and you are sure the user has no settings or personal data that is needed, you can delete the account.

To a delete a person's account, follow these steps:

1. Click Start→Control Panel→User Accounts and Family Safety→Add or Remove Users Accounts.

2. On the "Choose the account you would like to change" page, you'll see a list of existing accounts on the computer. Click the account you want to delete.

3. On the "Make changes to... " page, click "Delete the account."

4. On the "Do you want to keep...files?" page, shown in Figure 18-13, you have two options. You can:

   • Click Keep Files to create a folder on your desktop containing a copy of the user's personal data, and then delete the account.

   • Click Delete Files to delete all personal settings and personal data for this account, and then delete the account.

 Regardless of which option you choose, the user's email, preferences, and other settings are deleted with the account.

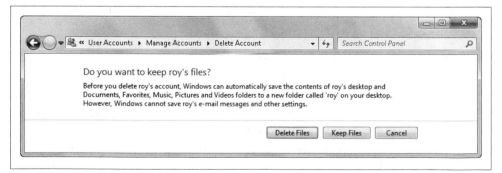

Figure 18-13. Deleting the user account

Managing Access Permissions with Group Accounts

On a computer that's not connected to a domain (most home and many small office computers), the best and easiest way to share files with other people who log on to your computer is to simply copy or move files you want to share to the *Public* folder or a related subfolder. If you use this technique, you don't have to worry about file access permissions or privileges, because Windows 7 sets the access permissions for you. As discussed in Chapter 11, if you configure password-protected sharing, you can be sure that only people with accounts on your computer can access your shared data.

For folders other than your personal folders, the personal folders of other people, or *Public* folders, you can set access permissions to control who has access. As also discussed in Chapter 11, you can assign access permissions to individual users or groups.

Every Windows 7 computer has the same set of default groups, which includes groups for performing administrative and maintenance tasks. If you're using an administrator account, your account is a member of the Administrators group. If you're using a standard user account, your account is a member of the Users group. For most at-home uses of Windows 7, these are the only groups you'll ever need to use.

Although all Windows 7 computers have the same set of default groups, each computer sees its groups as being different from the local groups on any other computer. This occurs because computers track groups with unique SIDs rather than display names. At the office, your network will have its own unique groups, which are also different from your computer's groups.

Creating Local Groups

If you find that you need additional groups beyond the Administrators and Users groups, you can create local groups on your computer. You create local groups by completing the following steps:

1. Click Start→Control Panel→System and Security→Administrative Tools.
2. Double-click Computer Management.
3. In Computer Management, double-click Local Users and Groups under System Tools.
4. Select the Groups node to display a list of the current groups on your computer, as shown in Figure 18-14.

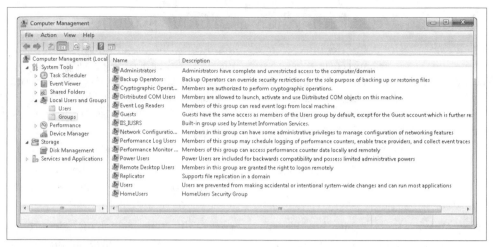

Figure 18-14. Viewing the groups on your computer

5. Right-click Groups and then select New Group. This opens the New Group dialog box, shown in Figure 18-15.

Figure 18-15. Creating a group and adding members

6. Type a name and description for the group.
7. Click the Add button.
8. In the Select Users dialog box, shown in Figure 18-16, type the name of a user you want to add to the group. This must be the username rather than the full name of the account.

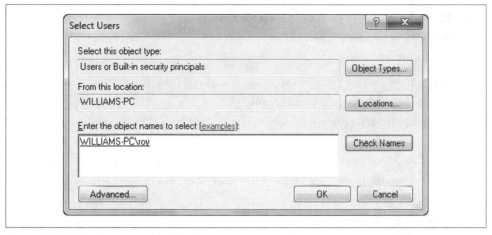

Figure 18-16. Selecting users to add to the group

9. Click Check Names and then do one of the following:

   • If a single match is found for each entry, the dialog box is automatically updated as appropriate and the entry is underlined.

   • If multiple matches are found, you'll see an additional dialog box that allows you to select the name or names you want to use, and then click OK.

   • If no matches are found, you've probably entered an incorrect name. Modify the name in the Name Not Found dialog box and then click Check Names again.

 You must enter the username rather than the full name of the account. If you changed the username by following the directions in the sections "Changing Your Account Name" on page 707 or "Changing User Account Names for Other People" on page 714, earlier in this chapter, you actually changed the full name associated with the account rather than the username. To view the usernames associated with accounts on your computer, open Computer Management. Double-click Local Users and Groups under System Tools. Select the Users node and then double-click the user account.

10. Repeat step 11 as necessary. When you are finished selecting names, click OK to close the Select Users dialog box.

11. The New Group dialog box is updated to reflect your selections. If you made a mistake, select a name and remove it by clicking Remove.

12. Click Create when you're finished adding or removing group members.

Adding and Removing Local Group Members

You add and remove local group members using Local Users and Groups. Complete the following steps:

1. Click Start→Control Panel→System and Security→Administrative Tools.
2. Double-click Computer Management.
3. In Computer Management, double-click Local Users and Groups under System Tools.
4. Select the Groups node to display a list of the current groups on your computer.
5. Double-click the group with which you want to work.
6. Use the Add button to add user accounts to the group via the Select Users dialog box, as discussed previously.
7. Use the Remove button to remove user accounts from the group. Select the user account you want to remove from the group and then click Remove.
8. Click OK when you are finished.

Renaming Local User Accounts and Groups

Because your computer tracks users and groups with SIDs, you can safely change account names at any time without worrying that this will cause problems with access permissions or privileges. Although you can rename any user and group accounts you've created, you shouldn't rename the default user and group accounts without considering the impact these changes may have on other users. For example, if you change the name of the Administrators group to HeadHonchos, you may be the only person who knows that this group was originally the Administrators group. If a year or so from now you forget that you renamed Administrators, you may think this group has mysteriously disappeared from your computer.

To rename a user or group account, complete the following steps:

1. Open Computer Management.
2. In Local Users and Groups, select the Users or Groups folder as appropriate.
3. Right-click the group or account name and then select Rename.
4. Type the new account name and then click a different entry.

Deleting Groups

Deleting a group permanently removes it. Once you delete a group, you can't simply create another group with the same name to get the same permissions because the SID for the new group won't match the SID for the old group. Deleting built-in accounts can have far-reaching effects on your computer, so don't do it.

To delete a group, complete the following steps:

1. Open Computer Management.
2. In Local Users and Groups, select the Users or Groups folder as appropriate.
3. Right-click the group and then select Delete.
4. When prompted to confirm, click Yes.

Keeping Your Family Safe While Using Your Computer

As a parent, teacher, or librarian, you'll want to use parental controls to help keep young people safe when they are on the Internet and to prevent them from accessing types of content they shouldn't be accessing. Parental controls enable you to manage three broad categories of Windows settings:

Time restrictions
> Control the times when a user can use the computer by blocking or allowing specific hours of the day.

Game restrictions
> Control whether a user can play games and the types of games this person can play.

Application restrictions
> Control the types of applications a user can run while using the computer.

When parental controls are turned on, you can also collect information about computer usage, and select a game rating system.

Turning On Parental Controls

You can set parental controls for standard user accounts on the local computer only. You cannot set parental controls for administrators, and you cannot set parental controls for computers configured to use domain user accounts (typically used in large organizations or companies). Any user designated as an administrator on the local computer can configure parental controls and view activity reports for users subject to parental controls.

You can turn on parental controls by completing the following steps:

1. Click Start→Control Panel→User Accounts and Family Safety→Parental Controls.
2. On the "Choose a user and set up Parental Controls" page, shown in Figure 18-17, you'll see a list of all users on the computer and a summary of their current account configuration. Any account that has parental controls turned on is listed as such.
3. All Administrator accounts on your computer should have a password to prevent your kids or other people with standard user accounts from bypassing or turning off parental controls. If there are Administrator accounts on your computer that

have no password, you'll see a warning on the "Choose a user and set up Parental Controls" page.

4. To clear the password warning, if displayed, click the warning text to display the Ensure Administrator Passwords page shown in Figure 18-18. On this page, the "Force all administrator accounts to set a password at logon" checkbox is selected by default. To force all users with an administrator account to set a password the next time they log on, accept this setting and click OK.

5. Click the account for which you want to turn on parental controls.

6. On the "Set up how...will use the computer" page, shown in Figure 18-19, click "On, enforce current settings" under Parental Controls to turn on parental controls.

7. Click OK to apply these settings and then configure the Windows settings to control, as discussed in the sections that follow. Be sure to select a game rating system as appropriate.

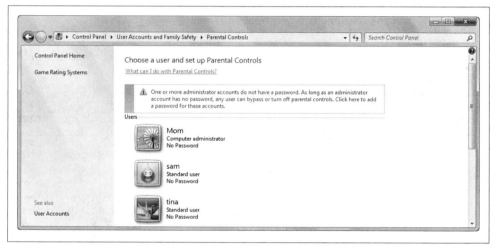

Figure 18-17. Setting up parental controls

Figure 18-18. Ensuring that administrators have passwords

Figure 18-19. Configuring parental controls

Selecting a Game Rating System

Game rating systems, such as those used by the Entertainment Software Ratings Board (ESRB), are meant to help protect young people from specific types of mature content in computer games and on the Internet. You can learn more about the available rating systems and select a default rating system to use by completing these steps:

1. Click Start→Control Panel→User Accounts and Family Safety→Parental Controls.

2. In the left panel of the main Parental Controls page, click "Game Rating Systems."

3. On the "Game Rating Systems" page, shown in Figure 18-20, you can review the game rating systems available. The default rating system used depends on the country or region settings for your computer.

4. If you want to change the default rating system, click the rating system you want to use. Beneath each option, you'll find a link to the home page for the game rating organization. If you have questions about a rating system, click this link to open the home page in Internet Explorer. You can then read about the organization and the related rating system.

5. Click OK to apply your changes and go back to the Parental Controls page in the Control Panel.

Configuring Time Restrictions

Time restrictions control the times when a user can use the computer by blocking or allowing specific hours of the day. If you've turned on parental controls, allow hours

Figure 18-20. Choosing a game rating system

are permitted by default. You can configure time restrictions by completing the following steps:

1. Click Start→Control Panel→User Accounts and Family Safety→Parental Controls.

2. Click the account you want to restrict.

3. On the "Set up how...will use the computer" page, click "Time limits" under Windows Settings.

4. On the "Control when...will use the computer" page, shown in Figure 18-21, you can specify what times you allow and what times you block.

5. Click and drag over allowed hours to change them to blocked hours.

6. Click and drag over blocked hours to change them to allowed hours.

7. Click OK to save your settings.

Configuring Game Restrictions

Game restrictions control whether a user can play games and the types of games that this person can play. If you've turned on parental controls, users are allowed to play games and no types of games are blocked by default. You can configure game restrictions by completing these steps:

1. Click Start→Control Panel→User Accounts and Family Safety→Parental Controls.

2. Click the account you want to restrict.

3. On the "Set up how...will use the computer" page, click Games under Windows Settings.

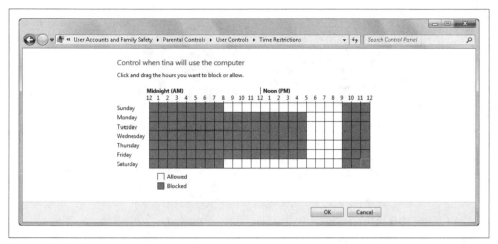

Figure 18-21. Configuring time restrictions

4. On the "Control which types of games...can play" page, shown in Figure 18-22, "Can...play games?" is set to Yes by default and the user is allowed to play games. To block game playing, click No under "Can...play games?"→OK, and skip the remaining steps.

5. To block or allow games by rating and content type, click "Set game ratings," choosing which game ratings are OK for the user to play, and then click OK.

6. To block or allow games installed on the computer by name, click "Block or Allow specific games," choose allowed or blocked games, and then click OK.

7. Click OK to save your settings.

Configuring Application Restrictions

Application restrictions control the types of applications a user can run while using the computer. If you've turned on parental controls, users are allowed to run any programs installed on the computer by default, and no programs are restricted. You can configure application restrictions by completing these steps:

1. Click Start→Control Panel→User Accounts and Family Safety→Parental Controls.

2. Click the account you want to restrict.

3. On the "Set up how...will use the computer" page, click "Allow and Block specific programs" under Windows Settings.

4. On the "Which programs can...use?" page, the "Use all programs" option is selected by default. To restrict program use so that only programs specifically allowed can be run, select the "...can only use the programs I allow" option. You'll then see a list of every program installed on the computer, as shown in Figure 18-23.

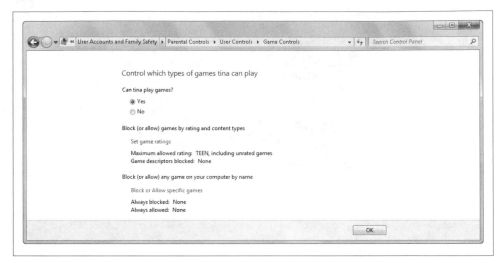

Figure 18-22. Configuring game restrictions

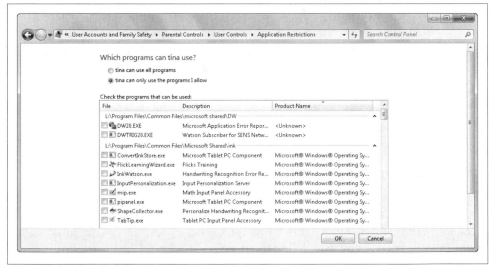

Figure 18-23. Configuring application restrictions

5. You can now control the allowed programs. Select the checkbox for a program you want the user to run. Clear the checkbox for a program you don't want the user to run. Alternatively, click Check All to select all programs and then selectively clear the programs the user shouldn't be able to run.

6. Click OK to save the settings. Whenever you install new programs on the computer that you want the user to be able to run, you'll need to repeat this procedure to allow running the program and its related executable files.

Configuring Additional Controls

In addition to the basic controls, you can install additional controls that restrict the websites a user can access, control who your child can talk to, and generate activity reports. These additional controls are available from some service providers. If you download Windows Live Essentials (*http://download.live.com*), one of the available programs is Windows Live Family Safety.

After you download and install Windows Live Family Safety, you can run the program (Start→All Programs→Windows Live→Windows Live Family Safety) to specify the Windows Live ID and password of the parent who will be the primary Family Safety administrator. You can then access the Family Safety area of the Windows Live website, shown in Figure 18-24, to configure web filtering, choose permitted contacts, and view activity reports about where your child went on the Web.

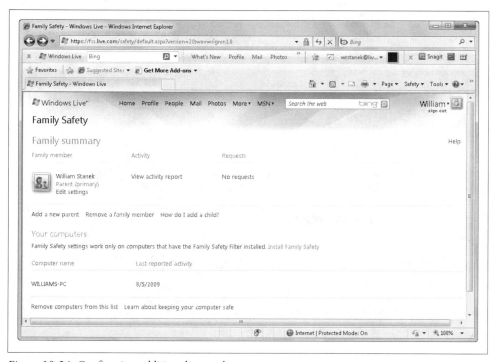

Figure 18-24. Configuring additional controls

Once you enable Windows Live Family Safety, everyone using your computer must start Windows Live Family Safety and log into Windows Live. From then on, the websites that a person can visit are controlled by the child safety settings you've established. You also can set up the computer to log in automatically for a child.

To stop using Windows Live Family Safety, you must uninstall the Family Safety filter on your computer. To do this, complete the following steps:

1. Sign in to Windows Live Family Safety and access the Family Safety area of the Windows Live website.

2. Under Your Computers, click the "Remove computers from this list" link.

3. On the Remove Computers page, shown in Figure 18-25, select the computer or computer to remove from filtering and then click Save.

4. When prompted to confirm, click Remove.

Figure 18-25. Removing a computer from filtering

CHAPTER 19

Managing Disks and Drives

The disks and drives configured within or attached to your computer provide storage for the operating system and your personal files. You use internal storage devices and external storage devices in different ways. You use internal storage devices for the operating system and your primary storage. You use external storage devices for your secondary storage only.

Disks and drives are one area of computer configuration that you won't work with often. Primarily, this is because disks and drives are something you need to prepare only one time, and once you've prepared a disk, you perform maintenance tasks on it rather than configuration tasks. Preparing a disk for use involves three main tasks:

- Partitioning the disk with volumes
- Formatting the disk volume
- Mounting the disk volume

You can partition a disk into one or more volumes. You then format the volumes with an appropriate filesystem. Finally, you mount the volume to a drive letter or file path. When you format volumes with the NT File System (NTFS), you can use compression to reduce the disk space used, or encryption to add an extra layer of protection to your data.

Configuring Disks and Drives

Like filesystems, disks have a particular formatting that determines how you can use the disk. Windows 7 allows you to configure disks to be either the basic disk type or the dynamic disk type. Basic disks are the traditional disk type Windows has used since it was first introduced. Dynamic disks are a newer disk type that was introduced with Windows 2000.

The differences between the two disk types largely concern what you can do with the disks. Consider the following:

- With basic disks, Windows 7 supports both primary and extended partitions. A primary partition is used to start the operating system. You access a primary partition directly by its drive designator. You cannot subdivide a primary partition. In contrast, an extended partition is designed to be subdivided. After you create an extended partition, you must divide it into one or more logical drives. You can then access the logical drives independently of each other.

- With dynamic disks, Windows 7 uses volumes instead of partitions. The most basic type of volume is a simple volume. A simple volume is a volume on a single disk that can be used to start the operating system and for general data storage.

In a significant change over previous releases of Windows, Windows 7 allows you to span and stripe drives using the basic disk type as well as the dynamic disk type. Previously, you could only perform these tasks using dynamic disks. A spanned drive is a drive with partitions or volumes that extend across several disks. A striped drive uses allocated disk space from partitions or volumes on multiple disks and stripes the data as it is written to give you faster read/write access.

Dynamic disks do continue to have several advantages over basic disks, including improved error detection and error handling. Also, you can mirror only dynamic drives. A mirrored drive is a drive that combines a volume on two different drives to create a single fault-tolerant volume.

Although dynamic disks have advantages over basic disks, when you want to boot your computer to a non-Windows operating system, such as Linux, or a pre-Windows 2000 operating system, you'll usually want to have a basic disk. Further, you cannot create dynamic disks on any removable-media drives. You can convert external disks attached via FireWire or USB to dynamic disks in some cases, but typically you won't want to use dynamic disks with external disks.

Using Disk Management

Your primary tool for working with your computer's disks is Disk Management. You will use Disk Management to partition disks, format disk volumes with filesystems, and mount disk volumes. You can also use Disk Management to convert a disk from the basic disk type to the dynamic disk type and vice versa. However, while you can convert from a basic disk type to the dynamic disk type without losing data, you must remove disk volumes on a dynamic disk before you can convert the disk to the basic disk type.

Using an Administrator account, you can start and work with Disk Management by completing the following steps:

1. Right-click Computer on the Start menu.

---

2. On the shortcut menu, choose Manage to start Computer Management.

3. In the left pane of the Computer Management window, select Disk Management under Storage.

As Figure 19-1 shows, Disk Management provides an overview of the storage devices configure within or attached to your computer. By default, Disk Management's main windows show the Volume list view in the upper panel and the Graphical view in the lower panel. The third view available but not displayed is the Disk List view.

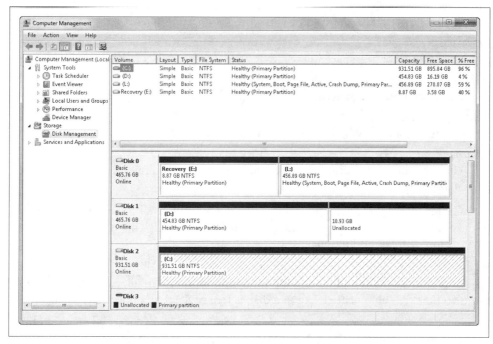

Figure 19-1. Managing your computer's disks

You can set the view for the top or bottom pane using options from the View menu. To change the top view, select View, choose Top, and then select the view you want to use. To change the bottom view, select View, choose Bottom, and then select the view you want to use.

Volume list view provides a detailed summary of internal drives and external devices with removable storage. Devices with removable media, such as CD-ROM and DVD-ROM drives, are listed only if you've inserted a CD or DVD. The volume details provide the following information:

Volume
    The drive letter or the volume name and drive letter, such as C: or Primary (C:)

Layout
    The layout type of the volume, such as simple

Type
> The drive type, such as basic or dynamic

File System
> The filesystem type, such as FAT or NTFS

Status
> The status of the volume, as well as any relevant volume designations, such as Healthy (Active, Primary Partition)

Capacity
> The amount of data the volume can store

Free Space
> The amount of free space in megabytes (MB) or gigabytes (GB)

% Free
> The amount of free space as a percentage of total volume capacity

Fault Tolerance
> An indicator as to whether the volume uses fault tolerant features

Overhead
> The total additional disk space required because of the fault tolerant feature used (if applicable)

The Graphical view provides a graphical overview of internal drives, external drives with removable storage, and devices with removable media. This is the view you use to partition, format, and mount disks.

In the Graphical view, you can see the individual areas of allocated and unallocated space on internal disks and disks with removable storage. An allocated area of a disk has a volume. An unallocated area of a disk is free space that's not being used.

As Figure 19-2 shows, the summary information regarding disks and devices with removable storage includes the disk number, drive type, disk capacity, and overall status. For each volume allocated on a disk, you'll see the volume name, drive letter, volume capacity, filesystem type, and status as well.

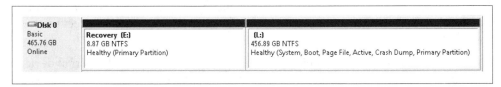

Figure 19-2. Viewing disk and volume details

Although Disk Management can show only two view panes at a time, you can display the Disk List view in either the upper or the lower pane of the main window. As Figure 19-3 shows, the Disk List view provides summary information about physical drives. This information includes:

Disk

The disk designator and number, such as Disk 0 or CD-ROM 1.

Type

The drive or media type, such as basic, dynamic, removable, CD, or DVD. Also displays the drive letter if one is assigned.

Capacity

The amount of data the drive, device, or media can store.

Unallocated Space

The amount of space that hasn't been allocated (if any).

Status

The drive or device status, such as online, online (errors), no media, or offline.

Device Type

The device interface type, such as Integrated Drive Electronics (IDE), Small Computer System Interface (SCSI), USB, or FireWire (1394).

Partition Style

The partition style of the disk or device. Windows 7 supports both Master Boot Record (MBR) and GUID Partition Table (GPT) partition styles. For the most part, the partition style used is determined by your computer's processor architecture and the type of device.

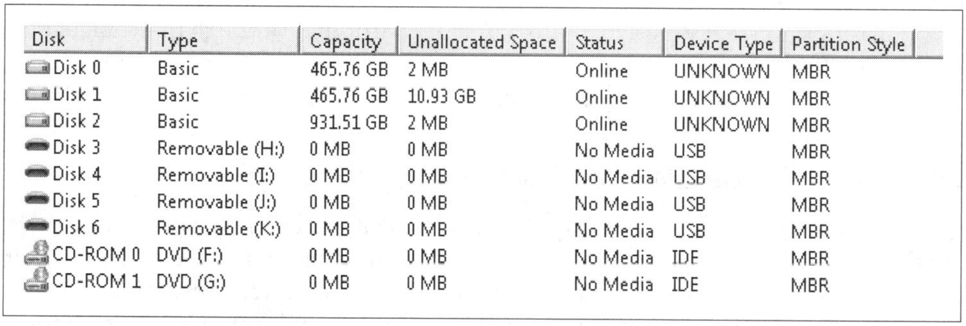

Disk	Type	Capacity	Unallocated Space	Status	Device Type	Partition Style
Disk 0	Basic	465.76 GB	2 MB	Online	UNKNOWN	MBR
Disk 1	Basic	465.76 GB	10.93 GB	Online	UNKNOWN	MBR
Disk 2	Basic	931.51 GB	2 MB	Online	UNKNOWN	MBR
Disk 3	Removable (H:)	0 MB	0 MB	No Media	USB	MBR
Disk 4	Removable (I:)	0 MB	0 MB	No Media	USB	MBR
Disk 5	Removable (J:)	0 MB	0 MB	No Media	USB	MBR
Disk 6	Removable (K:)	0 MB	0 MB	No Media	USB	MBR
CD-ROM 0	DVD (F:)	0 MB	0 MB	No Media	IDE	MBR
CD-ROM 1	DVD (G:)	0 MB	0 MB	No Media	IDE	MBR

Figure 19-3. Viewing a list of disks

When you are working with basic or dynamic disks, you should note the special designations assigned to drive sections. Drive sections can have one or more of the following designations:

Active

The drive section used for system cache and startup. Some devices with removable storage may be listed as having the active partition, such as when you use ReadyBoost.

System
> The drive section containing the boot manager files needed to load the operating system. A drive section with this designation can't be part of a striped or spanned volume.

Boot
> The drive section containing the operating system and its related files.

Page File
> A drive section containing a paging file used by the operating system.

Crash Dump
> The drive section to which the computer attempts to write dump files in the event of a system crash.

Your computer has one active, one system, one boot, and one crash dump drive section. The page file designation is the only drive designation you might see on multiple drive sections.

Depending on the disk type and status, you might also see the following designations:

At Risk
> A drive section with this designation is at risk of failing, and probably also has an error status, such as Online (Errors). See the section "Troubleshooting Disk Problems" on page 757, later in this chapter, for details on how to resolve the problem.

Primary Partition
> A drive section that is designated as a primary partition. Although this designation is usually displayed only for fixed disks, you may see this designation on devices with removable storage and on devices with removable media.

Installing and Initializing New Disks

With the dramatic increase in the quality and capacity of external disk drives, there aren't many good reasons to bother going inside your computer to install an internal disk anymore. In fact, if you follow the tips and advice in Chapter 5 regarding USB and FireWire devices, you can have an external hard disk up and running in five minutes or less.

With that said, if you want to install a disk inside your computer, you'll also find tips and advice for doing so in Chapter 5. When you are finished installing the disk inside your computer and you turn your computer on, you need to log on and start Disk Management. If the new disks have already been initialized with disk signatures by the manufacturer, they should be brought online automatically if you select Rescan Disks from the Action menu. If you are working with new disks that have not been initialized with disk signatures by the manufacturer, Disk Management will display the Initialize Disk dialog box as soon it detects the new disk.

In this case, you can initialize the disk by completing these steps:

1. In the Select Disks list, the disk or disks you added can be selected for initialization automatically. Select the disk or disks you want to initialize. Click Next.

2. By default, the disk partition style is set to MBR (Master Boot Record) if the total disk size is less than 2 TB. If you want to use the GPT (GUID Partition Table) style, select the related option.

3. Click OK. The disk or disks are initialized with the basic disk type. If you want to convert the new disk or other disks from the basic disk type to the dynamic disk type, you'll need to do this manually, as discussed in the next section.

Converting a Basic Disk to a Dynamic Disk

Windows 7 allows you to convert a basic disk to a dynamic disk. Moving from a basic disk to a dynamic disk is considered an upgrade. When you upgrade to a dynamic disk, partitions become volumes of the appropriate type.

To upgrade successfully to a dynamic disk, keep the following caveats in mind:

- There must be at least 1 MB of free space at the end of the disk. Disk Management reserves this free space automatically, but other disk management tools might not.

- Devices with removable media or removable storage can't be converted. In most cases, these devices can be configured only as basic drives with primary partitions.

- Disks with the system, boot, or both partitions can't be converted if they are part of a spanned or striped volume. You'll need to stop the spanning or striping of system or boot partitions before you perform the conversion.

- Dynamic disks are not supported on portable computers.

You can convert a basic disk to a dynamic disk by completing the following steps:

1. In Disk Management, right-click the disk designator for the basic disk that you want to convert in the Graphical view and then select Convert to Dynamic Disk.

2. In the Convert to Dynamic Disk dialog box, the disk you selected is listed, as shown in Figure 19-4.

3. If the disk you are converting has no formatted volumes, the disk is automatically selected for conversion and clicking OK converts the disk. You do not need to follow the remaining steps.

4. If the disk you are converting has formatted volumes, you may need to select the disk and then click OK. Continue with the remaining steps to complete the conversion.

5. As shown in Figure 19-5, the Disks to Convert dialog box shows the disk you're converting so that you can confirm the conversion. The value in the Will Convert column should be Yes as long as the disk meets the conversion criteria.

6. Click the disk and then click Details to see the volumes on the selected disk. When you are ready to continue, click OK to close the Convert Details dialog box.

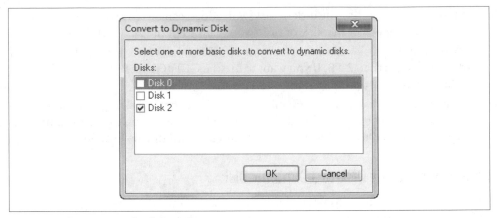

Figure 19-4. Converting the disk

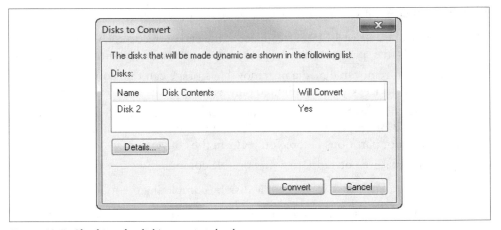

Figure 19-5. Checking the disk's associated volumes

7. Click Convert. Disk Management warns you that once you convert the disk, you won't be able to boot other operating systems from volumes on the selected disk. Click Yes to continue.

8. If disks are mounted and active, Disk Management warns you that it needs to dismount the disk to convert its volumes. Click Yes to continue.

9. If a selected drive contains the boot partition, the system partition, or a partition in use, Disk Management will need to restart the computer and you will see another prompt.

Converting a Dynamic Disk to a Basic Disk

Downgrading to the basic disk type from the dynamic disk type is not so easy. Before you convert a dynamic disk to a basic disk, you must delete all the volumes on the disk.

This results in the loss of all data in those volumes if you do not back up or move the data to another disk beforehand.

You can convert a dynamic disk to a basic disk by completing the following steps:

1. In Windows Explorer, copy or move all data on all the disk's volumes to another disk. Confirm that all data has been copied or moved before continuing.

2. In Disk Management, delete all volumes on the dynamic disk by right-clicking and selecting Delete Volume. Because this destroys all the data on the volumes, Disk Management displays a warning prompt (see Figure 19-6). If you are sure you want to delete the volume, click Yes.

3. When you delete the last volume, Windows changes the dynamic disk to a basic disk, and you can then partition and format the disk for use.

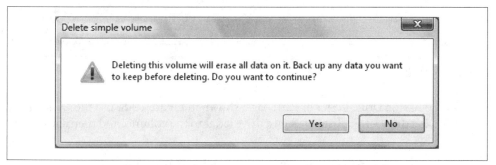

Figure 19-6. Confirming that you want to delete the volume

Preparing Disks for Use

Disk Management uses the same set of dialog boxes and wizards whether you are partitioning basic disks or dynamic disks. By default, the first three volumes on a basic drive are created automatically as primary partitions. If you try to create a fourth volume on a basic drive, the remaining free space on the drive is converted automatically to an extended partition with a logical drive that is the same size as the extended partition. Any subsequent volumes are created in the extended partitions as logical drives automatically.

In Disk Management, you create partitions, logical drives, and simple volumes on an internal or external hard disk drive by completing the following steps:

1. In Disk Management's Graphical view, right-click an unallocated or free area and then choose New Simple Volume.

2. In the New Simple Volume Wizard, click Next.

3. On the Specify Volume Size page, shown in Figure 19-7, size the volume within the maximum and minimum size limits. If you want the volume to use all the space

available, set the volume size equal to the value shown for the maximum disk space in MB. Click Next.

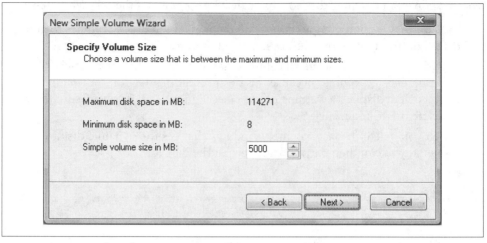

Figure 19-7. Setting the volume size

4. On the Assign Drive Letter or Path page, shown in Figure 19-8, use the "Assign the following drive letter" list to assign a drive letter to the volume, and then click Next.

 On most systems, the drive letter B and drive letters E through Z are available, with drive letter A reserved for a floppy disk, C assigned to the primary disk, and D assigned to the CD/DVD drive. If your computer has a secondary hard disk, a secondary CD/DVD drive, or both, you may find that drive letter E or the drive letters E and F are already assigned as well.

5. On the Format Partition page, shown in Figure 19-9, use the "File system" list to set the filesystem type. The options you have depend on the size of the volume and type of device, and they include FAT, FAT32, and NTFS. NTFS is selected by default in most cases. If you create a filesystem as FAT or FAT32, you can later convert it to NTFS. However, you can't convert NTFS partitions to FAT or FAT32.

6. The "Allocation unit size" list sets the cluster size for the filesystem. A cluster is a logical grouping of file sectors. In most cases, you'll want the "Allocation unit size" list to be set to Default. This allows Windows 7 to optimize the cluster size based on the volume size.

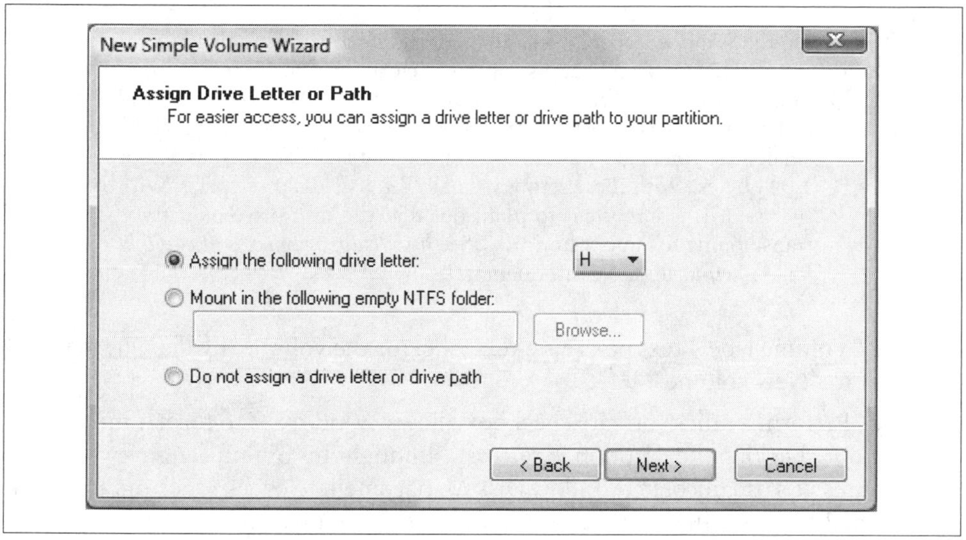

Figure 19-8. Assigning a drive letter

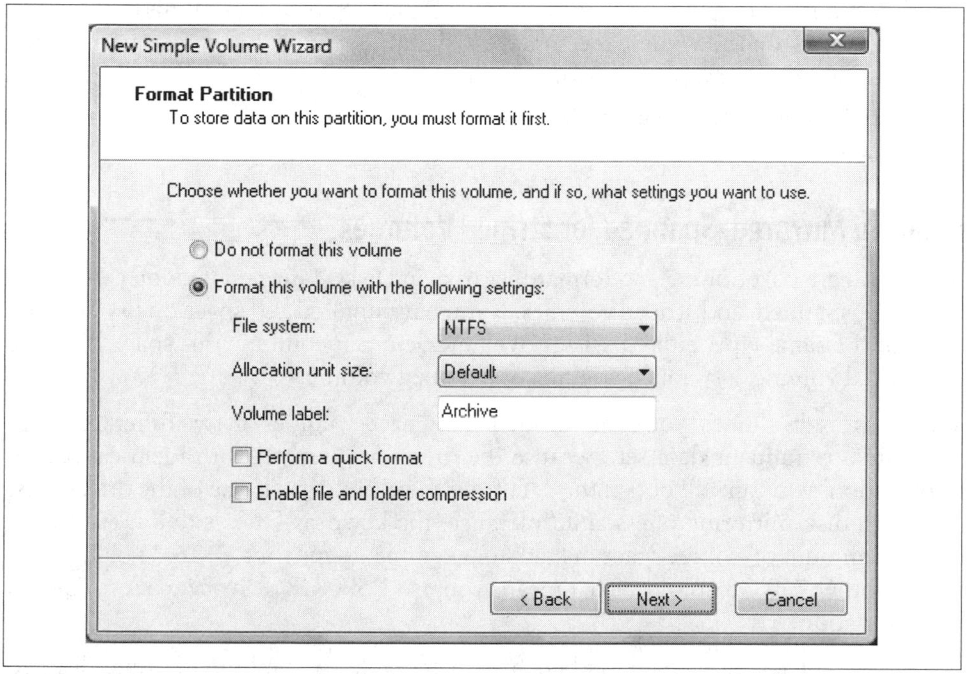

Figure 19-9. Setting the formatting options

On the Windows operating system, most disk drives use a fixed sector size of 512 bytes, and because of this, a cluster is typically made up of multiple sectors. For example, if the cluster size is 4,096 bytes, there will be four 512-byte file sectors per cluster. If you create large quantities of small files, you might want to use a smaller cluster size, such as 512 or 1,024 bytes. With these settings, small files use less disk space. With that said, it is important to point out that the disk drive industry is transitioning to large-sector disks. See *http://support.microsoft.com/kb/923332/en-us* for more information.

7. The "Volume label" text box sets a text label for the volume. By default, the label is set to "New volume."

8. The "Perform a quick format" checkbox allows Windows 7 to format the volume without checking the partition for errors. Although this option can save you a few minutes, it's usually better to allow Disk Management to check for errors and mark any bad sectors it finds on the disk so that they aren't used.

9. The "Enable file and folder compression" checkbox turns on compression for the disk. Built-in compression is available only for NTFS. If you select this option, files and folders on the volume are compressed automatically. See the section "Compressing Drives" on page 760 for more information.

10. Click Next and then click Finish. Disk Management will create and format the new volume.

Creating Mirrored, Spanned, or Striped Volumes

When you are partitioning and formatting disks in Disk Management, you can create mirrored, spanned, and striped volumes. If you have unallocated space on two or more disks of the same type, either basic or dynamic, you can combine this space to create a mirrored volume, a spanned volume, or a striped volume.

With mirrored volumes, you combine identically sized volumes on two different drives to create a redundant data set. Because the drives are written with identical sets of information, you can still obtain the data from the other drive if one of the drives fails. Although disk mirroring offers fault tolerance, the key drawback is that it effectively cuts the amount of storage space in half. For example, to mirror a 750 GB volume, you need another 750 GB volume. That means you use 1,500 GB of space to store 750 GB of information.

With spanned volumes, the only benefit is being able to combine multiple disks to create a single volume. Files are written to the entire spanned volume randomly and there are no read/write benefits. There is a huge downside, however. If any disk in a spanned volume fails, the entire volume fails as well, and all data will be lost.

Although you can only create mirrored volumes on dynamic disks, Windows 7 will allow you to initiate mirroring on basic disks. Here's how this works: if your computer has free space on multiple disks, you'll be able to right-click an unallocated area and then choose New Mirrored Volume. When you complete the creation process and click Finish, you'll see a warning prompt telling you that the operation you selected will convert the selected basic disks to dynamic disks. You are also asked whether you are sure you want to continue. If you click Yes, Disk Management will convert the disks and then mirror the volumes. If you click No, you'll cancel the conversion process and the mirrored volume will not be created.

With striped volumes, you also can combine multiple disks to create a single volume. You get faster read/write access to data because data is read from and written to multiple disks. For example, with a three-disk striped volume, data from a file will be written to Disk 1, then to Disk 2, and then to Disk 3 in 64 KB blocks. However, like a spanned volume, a striped volume has no fault tolerance. If any disk in a striped volume fails, the entire volume will fail as well, and all data will be lost. Additionally, although you can extend simple and spanned volumes to increase their volume size, you cannot extend striped volumes.

In Disk Management, you create mirrored, spanned, or striped volumes by completing the following steps:

1. In Disk Management's Graphical view, right-click an unallocated area and then choose New Mirrored Volume, New Spanned Volume, or New Striped Volume as appropriate. When the wizard starts, click Next.

2. On the Select Disks page, shown in Figure 19-10, available disks are shown in the Available listbox. Select a disk in this listbox and then click Add to add the disk to the Selected listbox. If you make a mistake, you can remove disks from the Selected listbox by selecting the disk and then clicking Remove.

3. The "Maximum available space" text box shows you the largest area of free space that can be used on a selected disk; the "Total volume size" text box shows you the total disk space currently allocated to the volume.

4. Specify the space that you want to use on each disk by selecting each disk in the Selected listbox and then using the "Select the amount of space in MB" listbox to specify the amount of space to use on the selected disk. Although spanned volumes can use all available space on any selected disk, mirrored, and striped volumes must use an equal amount of space on each disk. Click Next.

5. Follow steps 4–10 in the preceding section, "Preparing Disks for Use" on page 743.

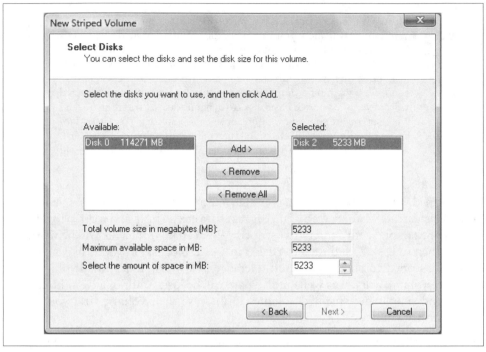

Figure 19-10. Selecting the disks to span or stripe

Adding a Mirror to an Existing Volume

You can use an existing volume to create a mirrored set. To do this, the volume you want to mirror must be a basic partition or simple volume, and you must have an area of unallocated space on a second drive of equal or larger size than the existing volume.

In Disk Management, you can mirror an existing volume by following these steps:

1. Right-click the basic partition or simple volume you want to mirror, and then click Add Mirror. This displays the Add Mirror dialog box, shown in Figure 19-11.

2. In the Disks list, select a location for the mirror, and then click Add Mirror. Keep in mind that only disks that have an area of unallocated space that is equal or larger in size are listed.

3. If you are trying to mirror a partition on a basic disk, you'll see the warning prompt shown in Figure 19-12. This indicates that the disk will be converted to a dynamic disk.

4. Windows 7 begins the mirror creation process. In Disk Management, you'll see a status of Resynching on both volumes. The disk on which the mirrored volume is being created has a warning icon. Once mirroring is complete the mirrored volume

Figure 19-11. Select a location for the mirror

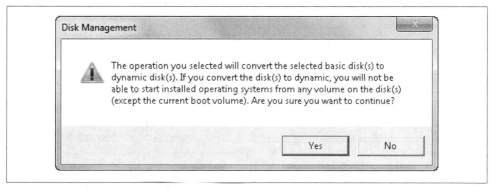

Figure 19-12. Mirroring a partition requires upgrading to a dynamic disk

should have a Healthy status. This is the status of a redundant volume that is performing correctly.

Shrinking or Extending Volumes

In Disk Management, you can change the size of partitions, simple volumes, and spanned volumes. When you reduce the size of a volume, you shrink the volume to free up available space. When you increase the size of a volume, you extend the volume into unallocated space. For spanned volumes on dynamic disks, the extended space can come from any available dynamic disk, not only those on which the volume was originally created. This enables you to combine areas of free space on multiple dynamic disks and use those areas to increase the size of an existing volume.

You can shrink and extend volumes only if they are formatted and the filesystem uses NTFS. You can't shrink or extend striped or mirrored volumes.

You can shrink a volume by completing the following steps:

1. In Disk Management's Graphical view, right-click the volume that you want to shrink and then select Shrink Volume. After checking the disk to determine how much space can be removed, Disk Management displays the Shrink dialog box shown in Figure 19-13.

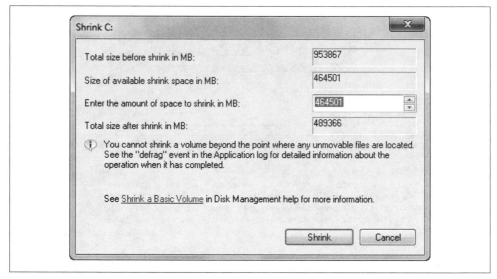

Figure 19-13. Shrinking the volume

2. The Shrink dialog box provides the following information:

Total size before shrink in MB
Shows the current capacity of the volume in MB. This is the formatted size of the volume.

Size of available shrink space in MB
Shows the maximum amount by which you can shrink the volume. This doesn't represent the total amount of free space on the volume. Instead, it represents the maximum amount of space that can be removed safely.

Enter the amount of space to shrink in MB
Shows the total amount of space that will be removed from the volume. The initial value defaults to the maximum amount of space that you can remove from the volume.

Total size after shrink in MB
Shows what the total capacity of the volume in MB will be after the shrink. This is the new formatted size of the volume.

3. Enter the amount of space to shrink the volume and then click Shrink to shrink the volume.

You can extend a volume by completing the following steps:

1. In Disk Management's Graphical view, right-click the volume that you want to extend and then select Extend Volume.

2. When the Extend Volume Wizard opens, read the introductory message and then click Next.

3. On the Select Disks page, shown in Figure 19-14, the disk you right-clicked is listed in the Selected list with all of its remaining unallocated space selected for use in extending the volume.

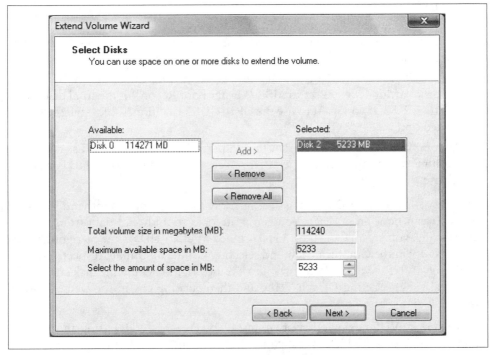

Figure 19-14. Extending the volume

4. In the Available list, you'll see available space on other dynamic disks. If you add one or more of these additional disks to the Selected list, you'll be able to use the free space on these disks as well. However, doing so will create a spanned volume with no fault tolerance.

5. Click Next and then click Finish. Disk Management will extend the volume.

Creating and Attaching Virtual Hard Disks

Windows 7 also allows you to create and attach virtual hard disks (VHDs). You can create a virtual hard disk by completing the following steps:

1. In Disk Management, select the Create VHD option on the Action menu.

2. In the "Create and Attach Virtual Hard Disk" dialog box, click Browse. Use the Browse Virtual Disk Files dialog box to select the location where you want to create the *.vhd* file for the virtual hard disk, and then click Save.

3. In the "Virtual hard disk size" list, enter the size of the disk in MB, GB, or TB.

4. Specify whether the size of the VHD dynamically expands to its fixed maximum size as data is saved to it or uses a fixed amount of space regardless of the amount of data stored on it.

5. Click OK to create the VHD.

6. The VHD is attached automatically and added as a new disk in Disk Manager. To initialize the disk for use, right-click the disk entry in the Graphical view and then select Initialize Disk.

7. In the Initialize Disk dialog box, the disk is selected for initialization. By default, the disk partition style is set to MBR (Master Boot Record) if the total disk size is less than 2 TB. If you want to use the GPT (GUID Partition Table) style, select the related option. Click OK.

8. After initializing the disk, right-click the unpartitioned space on the disk and create a volume of the appropriate type. After you create the volume, the VHD is available for use.

You can work with a VHD in much the same way as you work with other disks. Your computer can boot off a VHD. You can write data to and read data from a VHD. Additionally, you are able to take a VHD offline or put a VHD online by right-clicking the disk entry in the Graphical view and selecting Offline or Online, respectively. You can detach a VHD if you no longer want to use it by right-clicking the disk entry in the Graphical view, selecting Detach VHD, and then clicking OK in the Detach Virtual Hard Disk dialog box.

You can create VHDs using other programs. If you created a VHD using another program or have a detached VHD that you want to attach, you can do so by completing the following steps:

1. In Disk Management, select the Attach VHD option on the Action menu.

2. In the Attach Virtual Hard Disk dialog box, click Browse. Use the Browse Virtual Disk Files dialog box to select the location where you want to create the *.vhd* file for the virtual hard disk, and then click Open.

3. If you want to attach the VHD in read-only mode, select Read-only.

4. Click OK to attach the VHD.

Formatting Volumes

Formatting a volume creates a filesystem that you can use to store your data. If you format an existing volume that you've already used, you will permanently delete any existing data. You can format a volume by following these steps:

1. In Disk Management's Graphical view, right-click the volume that you want to format and then select Format. This displays the Format dialog box shown in Figure 19-15.

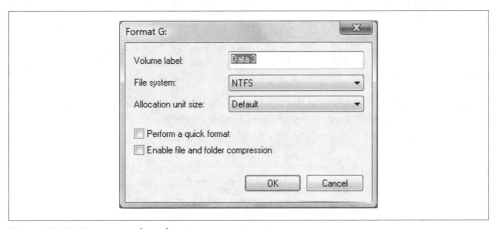

Figure 19-15. Formatting the volume

2. In the "Volume label" text box, type a text label for the volume.

3. Use the "File system" list to set the filesystem type. The options you have depend on the size of the volume and type of device, but they include FAT, FAT32, and NTFS.

4. The "Allocation unit size" list sets the cluster size for the filesystem. A cluster is a logical grouping of file sectors. In most cases, you'll want the "Allocation unit size" list to be set to Default. This allows Windows 7 to optimize the cluster size based on the volume size.

5. The "Perform a quick format" checkbox allows Windows 7 to format the volume without checking the partition for errors. Although this option can save you a few minutes, it's usually better to allow Disk Management to check for errors and mark any bad sectors it finds on the disk so that they aren't used.

6. The "Enable file and folder compression" checkbox turns on compression for the disk. Built-in compression is available only for NTFS. If you select this option, files

and folders on the volume are compressed automatically. See the section "Compressing Drives" on page 760 for more information.

7. Click OK to continue. Because formatting a volume destroys any existing data, Disk Management displays a warning. Click OK to start formatting the volume or Cancel to cancel.

Changing Drive Letters

Assigning a drive letter to a volume is the fastest and easiest way to access and work with a volume. On most systems, the drive letter B and drive letters E through Z are available, with drive letter A reserved for a floppy disk, C assigned to the primary disk, and D assigned to the CD/DVD drive. If your computer has a secondary hard disk, a secondary CD/DVD drive, or both, you may find that drive letter E or the drive letters E and F are already assigned as well.

To prevent potential startup problems, you should rarely if ever change the drive letter for the system and boot volumes. However, you can change the drive letters for other volumes at any time. To change a drive letter, follow these steps:

1. In Disk Management's Graphical view, right-click the volume that you want to work with and then select Change Drive Letter and Path. This displays the "Change Drive Letter and Paths for" dialog box shown in Figure 19-16.

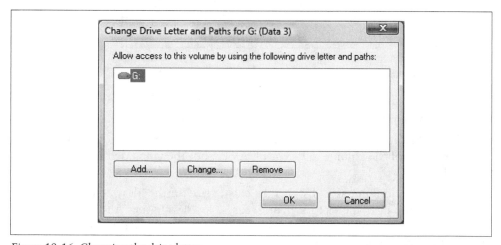

Figure 19-16. Changing the drive letter

2. To change the drive letter, select the current drive letter and then click Change. In the Change Drive Letter or Path dialog box, choose a different letter to assign to the drive. Only those drive letters that aren't currently assigned will be available.

Although volumes can have multiple drive letters or be mounted to file paths instead of drive letters, I recommend that you avoid these options. You'll prevent possible confusion and it always will be clear how your drives are accessed.

3. Click OK to save your settings, then click Yes when you are warned about the effects that changing a drive letter may have on installed applications.

Changing Volume Labels

The *volume label* is a text descriptor for a volume that is displayed when the volume is accessed in Windows Explorer and other Windows programs. If your computer has multiple volumes, giving each volume a descriptive label will help you easily navigate between volumes. For example, you might have a volume named Documents and a volume named Archive.

To change or set a volume label, follow these steps:

1. In Disk Management's Graphical view, right-click the volume that you want to work with and then select Properties.
2. On the General tab of the Properties dialog box, use the Label field to type a new label for the volume.
3. Click OK.

Converting a Volume to NTFS

Windows 7 provides the Convert utility for converting FAT or FAT32 volumes to NTFS. Convert is a command-line utility that requires administrator privileges to run. When you convert a volume, Convert preserves the file and folder structure and no data is lost.

Windows 7 does not provide a utility for converting NTFS to FAT or FAT32. The only way to go from NTFS to FAT or FAT32 is to delete the volume and then recreate the volume with FAT or FAT32 as the filesystem format.

You can convert any volume to NTFS, including the active, boot, and system volumes. If you try to convert the boot or system volume, Windows 7 displays a prompt asking whether you want to schedule the volume to be converted the next time you start your computer. If you choose Yes, you can restart the system to begin the conversion process. In most cases, it will take several restarts to convert the boot or system volume. Don't interrupt the conversion process and don't attempt to shut down your computer during the conversion process.

Convert needs a block of free space that's approximately equal to 25 percent of the total space used on the drive. For example, if the drive stores 5 GB of data, Convert needs about 500 MB of free space. If there isn't enough free space, Convert will not convert the volume and will instead tell you that you need to free up disk space.

You can convert a volume by following these steps:

1. Click Start→All Programs→Accessories.
2. Right-click Command Prompt and then select Run As Administrator.
3. At the command prompt, use the following syntax to convert the volume:

       convert *volume* /FS:NTFS

   where *volume* is the drive letter followed by a colon (:). For example, if you wanted to convert the H volume to NTFS, you would use the following command:

       convert H: /FS:NTFS

4. Type the volume name when prompted. This confirms that you are converting the correct volume.

Deleting Volumes

Occasionally, you may need to delete volumes that you no longer need. You might also need to delete a volume if you want to extend or reconfigure another volume on the same disk drive. Because deleting a volume erases all data on the volume, you will want to copy or move all data on the volume and then verify the copy or move prior to deleting the volume.

You can't delete the system or boot volume. However, Windows 7 will let you delete an active volume if it isn't also designated as boot, system, or both. Always check to ensure that the volume that you are deleting doesn't contain important data or files.

You can delete a volume by following these steps:

1. In Disk Management's Graphical view, right-click the volume that you want to delete and then select Delete Volume.
2. When prompted to confirm that you want to delete the volume, click Yes.

Maintaining and Recovering Volumes

As part of routine preventive maintenance for your disks, you should periodically check disks for errors, defragment volumes, and clean up unnecessary temporary files. Windows 7 provides separate utilities for each of these tasks; they are discussed in Chapter 20.

Troubleshooting Disk Problems

When you experience problems with a disk, you can use Disk Management to help you troubleshoot. In most cases, partitions and simple volumes are easier to troubleshoot and recover than mirrored, spanned, and striped volumes. With partitions and simple volumes, only one disk is involved. If a disk with a partition or simple volume has problems, you might see the Failed, Online (Errors), or Unreadable status. This occurs because after a certain number of errors, Windows flags the disk, and although this is likely a sign of a serious problem, you can attempt to use the disk by right-clicking the volume and selecting Reactivate Disk. If this doesn't work, click Rescan Disks on the Action menu. If a disk is listed as Failed or Unreadable and won't return to a Healthy status, you should replace the volume. If a disk is listed as Online (Errors) and won't return to an Online status without errors, you should check the disk for errors, as discussed in Chapter 20. Keep in mind that a disk with recurring errors is likely on the way out and will likely stop working eventually.

Sometimes you might need to reboot your computer to get a disk back online. The Online (Errors) status can also be an indicator of a failing disk, so if you see this status several times on the same disk, check for problems with the drive, its controller, and its cables.

 In a desktop or server computer, a bad power supply could also be the source of the problem, so make sure that the components in your computer (drives, video cards, CPU, etc.) do not draw more power than your power supply can handle. Excessive heat and inadequate space for ventilation can cause a power supply to operate below its rated wattage. You may need to upgrade to a more capable power supply.

With disks that have mirrored, striped, and spanned volumes, the drive status might show as Failed, Online (Errors), or Unreadable. In many cases, you can resolve these problems using the same techniques as with simple volumes. Right-click the volume and select Reactivate Disk. If this doesn't work, click Rescan Disks on the Action menu. You might also see the Missing or Offline status if drives have been disconnected or powered off. In this case, you can try to reactivate or rescan, but this probably won't work. To resolve the problem, you may need to check the disk to ensure that it is connected and that its power supply is connected. If you can't fix the problem, you'll need to replace the disk. Shut down your computer before you try to examine your computer's hardware.

Breaking or Removing Mirroring

You may want to break a mirrored set or remove mirroring. Breaking a mirrored set and removing a mirror are two very different operations. When you break a mirrored set, you stop mirroring and break the mirrored set into two independent volumes—both of which contain all the original data. When you remove a mirror, you stop mirroring and remove all data from one on the volumes so that you can use it for other purposes.

You also may need to break a mirrored set to repair a mirrored set. For example, if one of the mirrored drives in a set fails, disk operations can continue. However, at some point you'll need to fix the mirror, and to do this you must break the mirror and then reestablish it.

In Disk Management, you can break a mirrored set by following these steps:

1. Although breaking a mirror doesn't delete the data in the set, you should always back up your data before you break the mirror. This ensures that if you have problems, you can recover your data.

2. Right-click one of the volumes in the mirrored set, and then click Break Mirrored Volume.

3. Confirm that you want to break the mirror by clicking Yes. If the volume is in use, you'll see another warning dialog box. Click Yes to confirm that it's OK to continue.

4. Windows breaks the mirror, creating two independent volumes.

In Disk Management, you can remove one of the volumes from a mirrored set. When you do this, all data on the mirror you remove is deleted, and the space it used is marked as Unallocated. To remove a mirror, follow these steps:

1. In Disk Management, right-click one of the volumes in the mirrored set, and then click Remove Mirror. This displays the Remove Mirror dialog box.

2. In the Remove Mirror dialog box, select the disk from which to remove the mirror.

3. Confirm the action when prompted. All data on the removed mirror is deleted.

Resynchronizing and Repairing a Mirrored Set

As part of the mirroring process, Windows is constantly synchronizing the data on mirrored drives. When problems arise, however, data on mirrored drives can become out of sync. For example, if one of the drives goes offline, data is written only to the drive that's online.

You need to get both drives in the mirrored set online. Because a disk in the set has failed, the mirrored set's status should read Failed Redundancy. You can use various techniques to resynchronize and repair mirrored sets. The corrective action you take depends on the failed volume's status:

- When a drive has a status of Missing or Offline, ensure that the drive has power and is connected properly. Then start Disk Management, right-click the failed volume, and then click Reactivate Volume. The drive status should change to

Regenerating and then to Healthy. If the volume doesn't return to the Healthy status, right-click the volume, and then click Resynchronize Mirror.

- When a drive has a status of Online (Errors), right-click the failed volume, and then click Reactivate Volume. The drive status should change to Regenerating and then to Healthy. If the volume doesn't return to the Healthy status, right-click the volume, and then click Resynchronize Mirror.

- When one of the drives shows a status of Unreadable, you might need to rescan the drives on the system by selecting Rescan Disks from Disk Management's Action menu. If the drive status doesn't change, you might need to reboot the computer.

If you've tried the previously listed techniques to repair the mirrored set and one of the drives still won't come back online, right-click the failed volume, and then click Remove Mirror. Next, right-click the remaining volume in the original mirror, and then click Add Mirror. You now need to mirror the volume on an unallocated area of a different drive. If you don't have unallocated space on another drive, you need to create space by deleting other volumes or replacing the failed drive. Note that you must rebuild the set using disks with the same partition style—either MBR or GPT.

Repairing a Mirrored System or Boot Volume

When you're mirroring the system or boot volume, or both, and the primary mirror drive has failed, the drive failure might prevent your system from booting. Don't worry: Windows 7 should have added an entry to the system's boot manager that allows you to boot to the secondary mirror. Resolving a primary mirror failure is much easier with this entry in the boot manager file than without it, because you can easily boot to the secondary mirror and then repair the problem. If you mirror the boot volume and a secondary mirror entry is not created for you, you can modify the boot entries in the boot manager to create one using the BCD Editor (*Bcdedit.exe*). For more information on the BCD Editor, see Chapter 23.

If the primary mirror fails and your computer has a secondary boot entry, restart your computer and select the Boot Mirror–Secondary Plex option for the operating system you want to start. Your computer should start up normally. After you successfully boot the computer to the secondary drive, you can rebuild the mirror with these steps:

1. Break the mirror set, and then re-create the mirror on the drive you replaced, which is usually Drive 0. Right-click the remaining volume that was part of the original mirror, and then click Add Mirror. This displays the Add Mirror dialog box.

2. In the Disks listbox, select a location for the mirror, and then click Add Mirror. Windows 7 begins the mirror creation process. In Disk Management, you'll see a status of Resynching on both volumes. The disk on which the mirrored volume is being created has a warning icon.

3. If you want the primary mirror to be on the drive you added or replaced, use Disk Management to break the mirror again. Make sure that the primary drive in the

original mirror set has the drive letter that was previously assigned to the complete mirror. If it doesn't, assign the appropriate drive letter.

4. Right-click the original system volume, and then click Add Mirror to recreate the mirror.

5. Check the boot configuration and ensure that the original system volume is used during startup. You may need to modify the boot configuration to ensure this.

Using Compression and Encryption

When you format volumes with NTFS, you can use compression to reduce the disk space used or encryption to add an extra layer of protection to your data. Because these two options are mutually exclusive, a file or folder can be either compressed or encrypted, not both. Although you can compress or encrypt entire drives, you can also compress or encrypt individual files and folders. Windows 7 Home Premium and Starter do not support NTFS encryption.

In Windows Explorer, compressed or encrypted NTFS files and folders are shown in color by default. Compressed files and folders are shown in blue. Encrypted files and folders are shown in green.

Compressing Drives

When you format a volume with NTFS, Windows 7 allows you to turn on compression for the entire disk. With compression enabled, any files created on or moved to the disk are compressed automatically. When you open files or access folders, Windows 7 expands the files or folders for viewing as well. This behind-the-scenes compression and expansion makes NTFS compression completely transparent, but it does use some of your computer's processing power. With that said, there's an enormous benefit: you can store much more information on a compressed drive.

You cannot compress encrypted data. If you try to do so, Windows 7 automatically decrypts the data and then compresses it. Likewise, if you try to encrypt compressed data, Windows 7 expands the data and then encrypts it.

Compressing a drive

You can compress a drive and all its data by completing these steps:

1. In Windows Explorer or Disk Management, right-click the drive that you want to compress and then select Properties.

2. On the General tab, select "Compress drive to save disk space" and then click OK.

3. In the Confirm Attribute Changes dialog box, shown in Figure 19-17, specify whether you want to compress only the top-level folder of the drive or the entire drive:

- To compress only the drive's top-level folder, select "Apply changes to drive X:\ only."
- To compress the drive's top-level folder, subfolders, and files, select "Apply changes to drive X:\, subfolders and files."

4. Click OK.

Any files or folders you create on a compressed drive are compressed automatically.

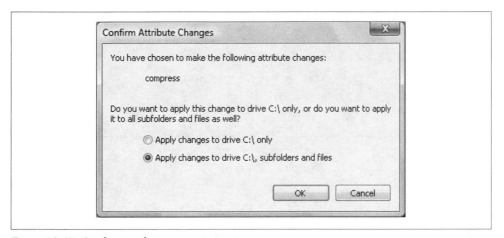

Figure 19-17. Confirming the compression options

Expanding a drive to remove compression

If you later decide that you no longer want to compress a drive, you can remove compression from the drive. However, before you do this, you should ensure that the drive has adequate free space to accommodate the expanded files. Typically, you'll need at least 50 percent more free space on the disk to expand its contents successfully. If a compressed disk currently uses 40 GB of space, this means you'd probably need about 20 GB of free space to expand the disk successfully.

You can expand a disk by completing these steps:

1. In Windows Explorer or Disk Management, right-click the drive that contains the disk that you want to expand and then select Properties.

2. On the General tab, clear the "Compress drive to save disk space" checkbox and then click OK twice.

3. In the Confirm Attribute Changes dialog box, shown in Figure 19-18, specify whether you want to expand only the top-level folder of the drive or the entire drive:

- To expand only the drive's top-level folder, select "Apply changes to drive X:\ only."
- To expand the drive's top-level folder, subfolders, and files, select "Apply changes to drive X:\, subfolders and files."

4. Click OK.

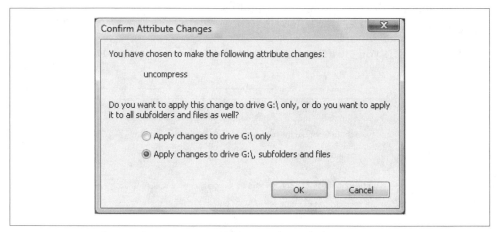

Figure 19-18. Confirming the uncompress options

Compressing Files and Folders

In addition to compressing an entire drive, Windows 7 allows you to compress files and folders selectively. When you compress a folder, you can elect to compress only the folder and the files it contains, or the folder, its subfolders, and all related files.

Compressing a file or folder

Any files or folders you create in a compressed folder are compressed automatically. When you move an uncompressed file or folder to a compressed drive or folder, the file or folder is compressed automatically when you are moving between drives. However, if you move an uncompressed file or folder to a compressed folder on the same NTFS drive, the file or folder isn't compressed automatically and you will need to compress the file or folder manually.

You can compress a file or folder by completing these steps:

1. In Windows Explorer, right-click the file or folder that you want to compress and then select Properties.
2. On the General tab of the Properties dialog box, click Advanced.
3. In the Advanced Attributes dialog box, shown in Figure 19-19, select the "Compress contents to save disk space" checkbox and then click OK.

4. For an individual file, Windows 7 marks the file as compressed and then compresses it. For a folder, Windows 7 marks the folder as compressed. If a folder contains files or subfolders, Windows 7 displays the Confirm Attribute Changes dialog box, shown in Figure 19-20:

- To compress only the folder, select "Apply changes to this folder only" and then click OK. Newly created files in this folder will be compressed.

- To compress the folder, subfolders, and all related files, select "Apply changes to this folder, subfolders and files" and then click OK. All existing files and newly created files in this folder will be compressed.

Figure 19-19. Compressing the disk

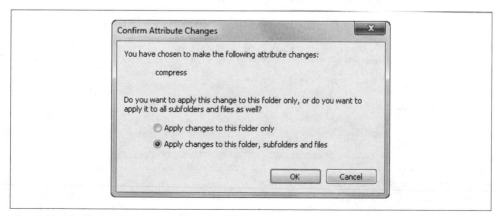

Figure 19-20. Choosing the compression options

Expanding a file or folder to remove compression

If you later decide that you no longer want to compress a folder or file, you can remove compression. Before you do this, you should ensure that the drive has adequate free space to accommodate the expanded files. Typically, you'll need at least 50 percent more free space on the disk to expand its contents successfully. If a compressed folder currently uses 2 GB of space, this means you'd probably need about 1 GB of free space to expand the folder successfully.

You can expand a file or folder by completing these steps:

1. In Windows Explorer, right-click the file or folder that you want to expand and then select Properties.

2. On the General tab of the related property dialog box, click Advanced.

3. In the Advanced Attributes dialog box, clear the "Compress contents to save disk space" checkbox and click OK twice.

4. For a file, Windows 7 removes compression and expands the file. For a folder, Windows 7 turns off compression for that folder. If the folder contains subfolders or files, Windows 7 displays the Confirm Attribute Changes dialog box, shown in Figure 19-21:

   - To expand only the folder, select "Apply changes to this folder only" and then click OK. Newly created files in this folder will not be compressed.

   - To expand the folder, subfolders, and all related files, select "Apply changes to this folder, subfolders and files" and then click OK. All existing files and newly created files in this folder will be uncompressed, and newly created files will not be compressed.

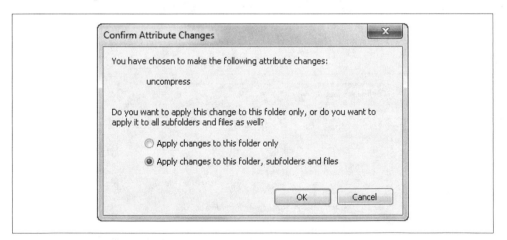

Figure 19-21. Choosing the uncompress options

Encrypting Files and Folders

You can use encryption to protect your files and folders so that only you can access them regardless of the NTFS permissions assigned to those files or folders. The first time you encrypt a file or folder, Windows 7 creates a personal certificate containing your encryption key. A personal certificate is similar to other types of certificates used by computers in that it contains both private key and public key encryption data. The certificate is extremely important. If it is damaged or removed from your computer, you won't be able to access your encrypted data.

Unlike NTFS compression, you can't encrypt entire drives. You can't encrypt compressed files, system files, or read-only files, either. If you try to encrypt compressed files, they are automatically uncompressed and then encrypted. If you try to encrypt system files, you'll get an error message.

The Windows 7 component that handles encryption is called the Encrypting File System (EFS). EFS encrypts files and folders using an encryption key that is automatically generated and unique for each person that uses encryption on your computer. When you encrypt a file or folder, the associated data is converted to an encrypted format so that only you can access the file or folder.

By default, you are the only person who can access your encrypted files and folders. However, as you might expect there are some caveats. If your computer has any assigned *recovery agents*, those recovery agents have the authority to decrypt any encrypted files and folders on your computer. You can think of a recovery agent as having a master key. Additionally, you can grant another user the right to access your encrypted files and folders. When you do this, this person's encryption key is added to the file or folder's encryption data, allowing the person to access the file or folder just like you can.

Encrypting a file or folder

You can encrypt a file or folder by completing these steps:

1. In Windows Explorer, right-click the file or folder that you want to encrypt and then select Properties.
2. On the General tab of the related property dialog box, click Advanced.
3. In the Advanced Attributes dialog box, select the "Encrypt contents to secure data" checkbox and then click OK.
4. For an individual file, Windows 7 marks the file as encrypted and then encrypts it. If the file is in a folder that is not encrypted, Windows 7 displays the Confirm Attribute Changes dialog box:
   - To encrypt the file and its parent folder, select "Encrypt the file and its parent folder" and then click OK.
   - To encrypt the file only, select "Encrypt the file only" and then click OK.

5. For a folder, Windows 7 marks the folder as encrypted. If the folder contains sub-folders or files, Windows 7 displays the Confirm Attribute Changes dialog box:

- To encrypt only the folder, select "Apply changes to this folder only" and then click OK. Newly created files in this folder will be encrypted.
- To encrypt the folder, subfolders, and all related files, select "Apply changes to this folder, subfolders and files" and then click OK. Newly created files in this folder will be encrypted, along with existing folders and files.

Before other people can access your encrypted data, you must decrypt the file or you must grant special access permission. Once you encrypt a file or folder, you can work with it just like any other file or folder. You can copy, move, and rename an encrypted file or folder just like any other files or folders. However, if you move an encrypted file to a disk or device formatted using FAT, the file is decrypted automatically.

Removing encryption from files and folders

If you later decide that you no longer want to encrypt a folder or file, you can remove encryption by completing the following steps:

1. In Windows Explorer, right-click the file or folder you want to decrypt and then select Properties.
2. On the General tab of the related property dialog box, click Advanced.
3. In the Advanced Attributes dialog box, clear the "Encrypt contents to secure data" checkbox and then click OK twice.
4. For a file, Windows 7 decrypts the file and restores it to its original format. For a folder, Windows 7 turns off encryption for that folder. If the folder contains sub-folders or files, Windows 7 displays the Confirm Attribute Changes dialog box:

- To decrypt only the folder, select "Apply changes to this folder only" and then click OK. Newly created files in this folder will not be encrypted.
- To decrypt the folder, subfolders, and all related files, select "Apply changes to this folder, subfolders and files" and then click OK. All existing files and newly created files in this folder will be unencrypted, and newly created files will not be encrypted.

Sharing encrypted files

If you want other people to be able to access an encrypted file, you must either remove encryption or grant the person special access to the file. When you grant a person special access to the file, this person's encryption key is added to the file encryption data, allowing the person to access the file just like you can.

The person to whom you are granting access must have an encryption key on your computer. The easiest way to get an encryption key is to have the person log on and

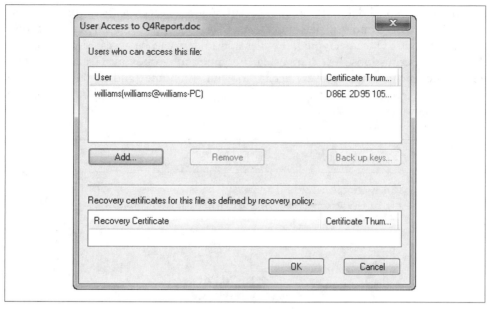

Figure 19-22. Viewing users who can access the encrypted file

then encrypt a file. Because Windows 7 generates an encryption key automatically the first time a person encrypts a file, this person will then have an encryption key.

You can grant access to an encrypted file by completing the following procedure:

1. In Windows Explorer, right-click the file for which you are granting access and then select Properties.
2. On the General tab of the file's property dialog box, click Advanced. The Advanced Attributes dialog box appears.
3. Click Details. In the User Access dialog box, shown in Figure 19-22, users who have access to the encrypted file are listed by name.
4. To allow another user access to the file, click Add.
5. In the Encrypting File System dialog box, shown in Figure 19-23, you'll see a list of every user who has an encryption key on your computer.
6. Select the user's name in the list provided and then click OK three times.

Backing up your encryption keys

As discussed previously, the first time you encrypt a file or folder, Windows 7 creates an encryption key for you. This key is critically important because if it becomes damaged or is removed, you won't be able to access your encrypted files or folders ever again. Several safeguards are put in place to prevent catastrophic data loss. The first is a feature called the *recovery agent*. A recovery agent is a person who is issued a master key for all encrypted data on a computer. Although recovery agents cannot use their master keys to open and read files and folders, they can use their master keys to decrypt files and folders. Once decrypted, the files and folders can be accessed according to their NTFS permissions. If you are using encryption at work, your IT administrators will create and manage recovery agents for you. At home (and at the office as a supplement to recovery agents), you can back up your encryption key to a USB flash drive or memory card.

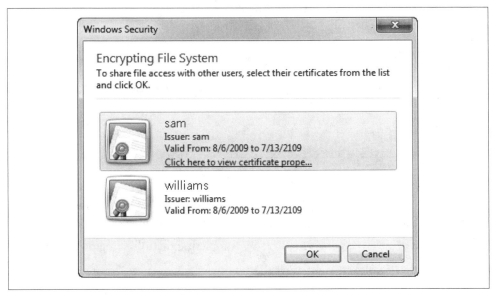

Figure 19-23. Sharing file access with another person

The first time you create an encryption key, Windows 7 will display a notification icon in the System Tray telling you to back up your encryption key. If you click this icon and then click "Back up now," you'll start the Certificate Export Wizard. You can use this wizard to back up your encryption key by completing the following steps:

1. In the Certificate Export Wizard, shown in Figure 19-24, read the introductory message and then click Next twice.

2. To help safeguard your encryption key, you must protect it with a password. This password should not be the same one you use to log on to your computer, but it should be one you can easily remember. On the Password page, type a password and then confirm it by typing it again. Click Next.

3. As necessary, connect a USB flash device or memory card to your computer.

4. On the File to Export page, click Browse.

5. Use the Save As dialog box to select the USB flash device or memory card as the save location.

6. Type a name for the encryption key file and then click Save.

7. Click Next and then click Finish. If the export was successful, you'll see a dialog box confirming this. Click OK.

Figure 19-24. Backing up your encryption key by exporting it

If your encryption key is damaged or you need to recover encrypted files moved to a new computer, you can do so by completing the following steps:

1. Connect the USB flash device or memory card containing the encryption key file.

2. Click Start. On the Start menu, type MMC in the search box and then press Enter.

3. In the Console window, click Add/Remove Snap-in on the File menu. In Add or Remove Snap-ins, select Certificates under Available Snap-ins and then click Add. When prompted, click OK to accept the default value of "My user account" and add the Certificates snap-in to the console.

4. In the left pane, double-click Certificates→Current User, right-click Personal, point to All Tasks, and then select Import. This starts the Certificate Import Wizard. Click Next.

5. On the File to Import page, shown in Figure 19-25, click Browse. Use the Open dialog box to select the location where you previously saved the key file.

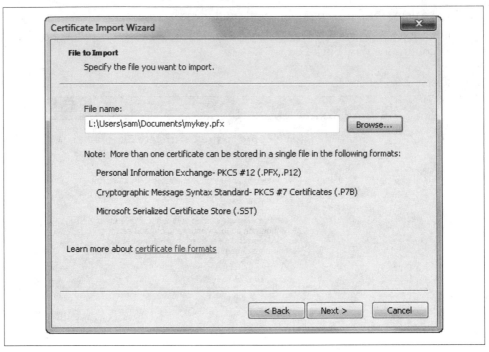

Figure 19-25. Selecting the encryption file to import

6. Your key file is saved as a Personal Information Exchange file. You won't see this file type until you use the "File type" list to the right of the "File name" text box to select Personal Information Exchange as the file type.

7. Click your key file and then click Open.

8. Click Next. Type the password you assigned to the key file.

9. Click Next twice and then click Finish.

You can now decrypt any files that were encrypted using this encryption key.

CHAPTER 20

Handling Routine Maintenance and Troubleshooting

Often, when people ask me to help them solve computer problems, I ask them when they last performed preventive maintenance on their computers. The most common responses I receive are a blank stare and a sheepish grin—as if it had never occurred to them that a computer was something they had to maintain, or as if they're embarrassed to admit they don't do anything to maintain their computers. The problem is that a computer—just like a home or a car—needs to be maintained. Although most people wouldn't neglect their homes or cars, a surprisingly high number of people neglect their computers. They think of a computer as something they turn on and off, like a car stereo. They forget about the computer's dozens of interconnected components, such as the hard disk they're filling up with data, the programs they're installing and uninstalling, and all the other processes that must work together to make their computer operate normally. They don't realize that a poorly maintained computer is a computer that doesn't run as efficiently as it should, or that the problems they're experiencing with long startup times, slow responsiveness, and delays when performing tasks have everything to do with the fact that they're not maintaining their computer.

Sometimes, though, it's not a matter of neglecting your computer, but of knowing where to start. Most people who have told me they don't maintain their computers have also told me they just don't know where to start or what to do. Your new car comes with an owner's manual and on page 62 or thereabouts it says to change the oil every 5,000 miles, rotate the tires every 10,000 miles, get this maintenance done at 30,000 miles, and get that maintenance done at 60,000 miles. Your computer, on the other hand, doesn't come with an owner's manual that spells out the specific maintenance tasks you should perform—but maybe it should. Maybe if a computer came with a maintenance checklist, we'd all have far fewer problems with our computers. Until that happens, though, you can use this chapter and the next chapter as your guide to practically everything you need to know to perform routine and not-so-routine maintenance on your computer.

Maintaining Your System Configuration

As part of routine maintenance, you should periodically review your computer's core configuration. You control many of your computer's core configuration properties through the System Properties dialog box. You use the System Properties dialog box to manage settings for your computer's network identity, environment variables, user profiles, and much more. The System Properties dialog box has five tabs:

- Computer Name
- Hardware
- Advanced
- System Protection
- Remote

The sections that follow discuss how to use the related options to configure the computer name (including domain, workgroup, and homegroup membership), view hardware settings, set advanced options, and manage remote access. Chapter 21 covers how to configure system protection options.

Configuring the Computer Name and Membership

Whenever you access resources on another computer, you do so using the computer's name. Generally, when computers are in the same domain, homegroup, or workgroup, you'll have an easier time accessing and working with them. When your computer is a member of a domain, it uses a different naming scheme than when it is a member of a homegroup or workgroup. At the office, the full computer name is essentially the Fully Qualified Domain Name (FQDN) of the computer, which identifies the computer's name as well as its place on the network. At home, your computer has a computer name and a homegroup or workgroup associated with it.

As Figure 20-1 shows, you can determine the domain or workgroup membership for your computer on the Computer Name tab in the System Properties dialog box. If you have appropriate permissions, you can also use this tab to modify the computer's name and its domain or workgroup membership.

You can access the Computer Name tab in the System Properties dialog box by completing these steps:

1. Click Start→System and Security→System.
2. In the System Console, click "Change settings" under "Computer name, domain, and workgroup settings." Alternatively, click Advanced System Settings in the left pane.
3. Click the Computer Name tab, if the tab isn't already selected.

Figure 20-1. Viewing the computer name

You can use the options on the Computer Name tab to join a computer to a domain or to change a computer's name. To join a computer to a domain, follow these steps:

1. On the Computer Name tab of the System Properties dialog box, click Network ID to start the Join a Domain or Workgroup Wizard.

2. Click Next three times to accept the default options.

3. As shown in Figure 20-2, enter the name of your domain user account, the password for this account, and the name of the domain. You will use this account to connect to the domain.

4. When you click Next, the wizard will search for a computer account in your user account domain. If the wizard can't find a computer account, you'll need to specify the computer name and computer domain to use, and then click Next.

5. As necessary, type the domain username, password, and domain of an account with permission to join the computer to the previously specified domain, and then click OK.

6. If you receive an error stating that the computer could not be joined to the domain because your computer couldn't resolve the DNS name of the domain controller, click OK and then do the following:

   • Click Start→Control Panel→Network and Internet→Network and Sharing Center.

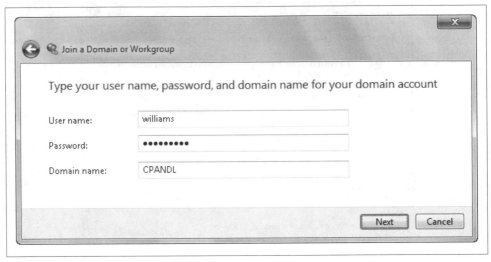

Figure 20-2. Providing your credentials for connecting to the domain

- In Network and Sharing Center, click Change Adapter Settings in the left pane. Right-click the active connection and then select Properties.
- In the Properties dialog box, click Internet Protocol version 4 (TCP/IPv4) and then click Properties.
- In the Internet Protocol version 4 (TCP/IPv4) Properties dialog box, confirm that the IP address settings are correct for the domain you are trying to join. You may need to temporarily use a static IP address that is on the same network as the domain.
- Confirm that the DNS server addresses are set correctly. You likely will need to specify the IP address of a preferred DNS server in the domain you are trying to join.
- Click OK and then click Close. If you made changes to the IP configuration and your domain uses DHCP, you'll likely need to configure the TCP/IPv4 settings to use dynamic addressing and obtain the DNS server addresses automatically after you successfully join the domain.
- In the Domain User Name and Password dialog box, click OK to try to join the domain again. If you've configured the settings correctly, your computer should be able to join the domain.

7. On the "Do You Want to Enable a Domain User Account on This Computer?" page, specify whether you want to add a domain user account to your computer. Typically, you'll want to add the account listed to your computer, so accept the default selection and then click Next. On the next page, choose an account type. Typically, you'll want to choose Administrator or another account that grants the appropriate access level, such as Backup Operator. Click Next.

8. Click Finish. Click OK in the System Properties dialog box. You'll see a prompt stating that you need to restart the computer. Click Restart Now to restart the computer.

You can move a computer from a domain to a workgroup by following these steps:

1. On the Computer Name tab of the System Properties dialog box, click Change. This displays the Computer Name/Domain Changes dialog box, shown in Figure 20-3.

Figure 20-3. Changing the membership of the computer

2. If you want to change the computer name, type the new name for the computer in the Computer Name text box.

3. Select the Workgroup option and then type the name of the workgroup to join.

4. Click OK. Read the warning prompt and then click OK again.

5. When prompted that your computer has joined the previously specified workgroup, click OK.

6. You'll see a prompt stating that you need to restart the computer. Click OK.

7. Click Close and then click Restart Now to restart the computer.

You can change the computer name by following these steps:

1. On the Computer Name tab of the System Properties dialog box, click Change. This displays the Computer Name/Domain Changes dialog box.

2. Type the new name for the computer in the Computer Name text box.

3. You'll see a prompt stating that you need to restart the computer. Click OK.

4. Click Close and then click Restart Now to restart the computer.

Creating or Joining a Homegroup

Whenever your computer is in a workgroup, you have the option of creating or joining a homegroup. To do this, follow these steps:

1. Click Start→Control Panel→Network and Internet→Network and Sharing Center.

2. Under the "View your active networks" heading, click the link that shows the type of network to which you are connected, such as "Work network."

3. In the Set Network Location dialog box, click Home Network.

4. If no homegroup exists on your network, Windows prompt you to select the sharing settings for a new homegroup. As shown in Figure 20-4, select what you want to share and then click Next. Write down the homegroup password and then click Finish.

5. If a homegroup exists on your network, you are notified that a homegroup was detected. As shown in Figure 20-5, select what you want to share in this homegroup and then click Next. When prompted, enter the homegroup password and then click Next.

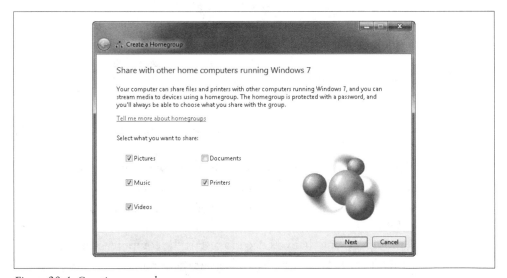

Figure 20-4. Creating a new homegroup

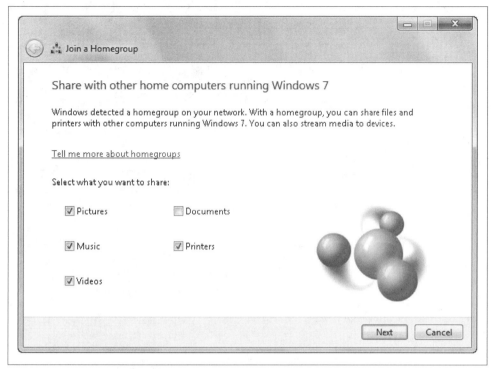

Figure 20-5. Joining an existing homegroup

Once you've created and/or joined a homegroup, you can manage the homegroup settings and homegroup sharing options on the HomeGroup page in the Control Panel (see Figure 20-6). To access this page, click Start→Control Panel→Network and Internet→HomeGroup.

Viewing Hardware Settings

You can use the Hardware tab in the System Properties dialog box to access Device Manager and Windows Update (see Figure 20-7). You can access the Hardware tab in the System Properties dialog box by following these steps:

1. Click Start→Control Panel→System and Security→System.
2. In the System console, click "Change settings" under "Computer name, domain, and workgroup settings." Or click Advanced System Settings in the left pane.
3. Click the Hardware tab.

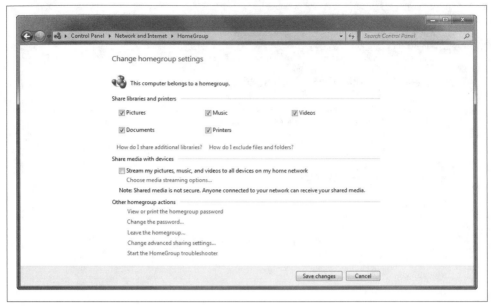

Figure 20-6. Configuring your homegroup settings

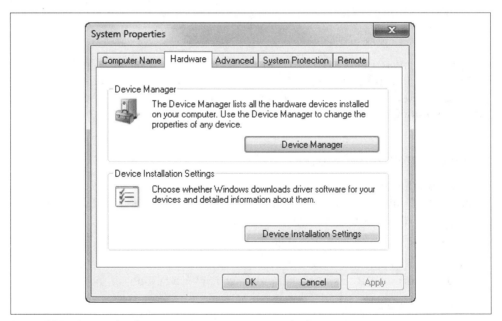

Figure 20-7. Viewing hardware settings

I discuss Device Manager and Device Installation Settings options in Chapter 5. See the sections "Learning About Your Computer's Hardware Devices" on page 151 and "How

Does the Operating System Obtain Driver Updates?" on page 149 for more information.

Configuring User Profiles, Environment Variables, and Startup and Recovery

You can use the Advanced tab in the System Properties dialog box to configure application performance, virtual memory usage, user profiles, environment variables, and startup and recovery. I cover configuring application performance and virtual memory in the section "Optimizing Performance" on page 98. This section looks at options related to user profiles, environment variables, and startup and recovery.

User profiles

When you create a user account on a computer, your computer creates a user profile for that account the first time the user logs on. A user profile contains the global settings and configuration options that are unique to a particular user account. Whenever you make changes to your desktop or other settings that affect only you rather than everyone who logs on to your computer, the changes are saved in your user profile. This is also where your computer stores all your personal files. Any documents, music, or other files you've put into your personal folders are actually stored within your profile.

I could easily spend 50 pages extolling the details of profiles, but what you really need to know is this:

- On a computer connected to a domain, your IT administrators will largely control the ways you can use your profile. If your IT administrators create a special type of profile, called a *roaming profile*, for your account, you can use the same profile on every computer you use, and this would ensure that you always have a consistent user environment. When you have a roaming profile, your profile is stored on a Windows server and a cached copy is stored on your computer.

- At home or in an organization that does not use domains, you are in complete control of your profile. Your profile contains your desktop settings and user-specific configuration settings. Your profile contains all the files and folders listed when you click Start and then click your username on the Start menu. Because your account settings and your personal data are stored in your profile, any problems with your profile could prevent you from logging on and could result in catastrophic data loss.

You can view the profiles on your computer by following these steps:

1. Click Start→Control Panel→System and Security→System.

2. In the System console, click "Change settings" under "Computer name, domain, and workgroup settings." Alternatively, click Advanced System Settings in the left pane.

3. On the Advanced tab, click Settings under User Profiles.

4. In the User Profiles dialog box, shown in Figure 20-8, you'll see a list of profiles stored on your computer according to the associated account name, size, type, status, and date last modified.

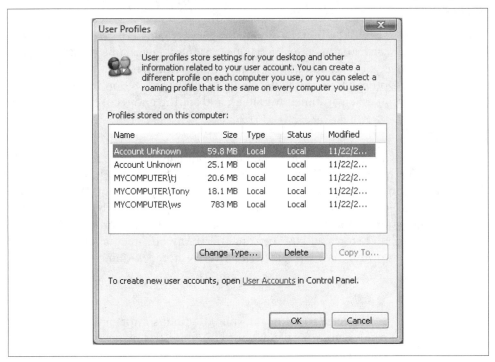

Figure 20-8. Viewing user profiles

As you can see from the list of profiles, profiles can grow quite large. On this computer, my profile is 783 MB in size. On my primary computer, my profile is a whopping 5.2 GB in size. That's a lot of data for the computer to drag around. In the profile list shown in Figure 20-8, you should also note that several names are listed as "Account Unknown." These entries aren't for corrupt profiles or necessarily for profiles that should be deleted. Rather, these entries are typically for profiles created when a computer was a member of a domain, and since the computer was removed from the domain, it no longer recognizes the related accounts to which the profiles belong.

In the User Profiles dialog box, you can:

Change the type of profile

> On a domain, your IT administrators may use the Change Type option to change your profile from the default profile type—local profile—to a roaming profile or vice versa. Other settings you must configure in your user properties to ensure that you get the correct environment when you log on.

Create a copy of a profile

Use the Copy To option to create a copy of a profile and all its related data. As you cannot copy a profile that is active, you'll likely only be able to create a copy of the default profile.

Delete a profile

Use the Delete option to delete a profile that is no longer needed. You cannot delete a profile that currently is logged on. If you delete a profile from an account that is still being used, the computer will create a new profile the next time the other person logs on.

Because so much of your important personal data is stored in your user profile, you might want to create a backup copy of your profile. As long as you aren't logged on to an account using a profile, you can copy a profile to a folder by completing these steps:

1. In Windows Explorer, create a new folder for storing the profile data.

2. In the User Profiles dialog box, click the profile you want to copy and then click Copy To.

3. In the Copy To dialog box, shown in Figure 20-9, click Browse, locate the folder you created for storing the profile data, and then click OK.

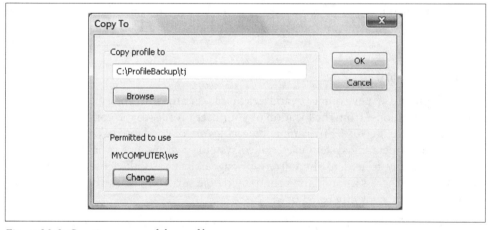

Figure 20-9. Creating a copy of the profile

4. Under "Permitted to use," click Change. Use the Select User or Group dialog box to specify the user or group who should be granted the Full Control permission for the profile data and then click OK. No other user or group will be granted access to the profile data.

5. In the Copy To dialog box, click OK.

6. In the Confirm Copy dialog box, click Yes to confirm that you want to delete the contents of the new folder you created and store the profile in this location.

7. You'll now have a complete backup copy of the profile.

To ensure that a corrupt profile can't prevent you from logging on, you should create at least one additional administrator account on your computer. If you find that you can't log on to your primary account due to a profile or other problem, you can log on to the backup administrator account to try to resolve the problem. When you are logged on to the backup administrator account, you can try to use System Restore, as discussed in Chapter 21, to restore your computer to a previous point in time. Although the restore may cause you to lose your most recent setting changes, you won't lose all the data in your user profile. If you find that you aren't able to restore your computer with a working profile for your primary account, you can try to restore your computer from backup, also discussed in Chapter 21. Alternatively, you can do the following to restore logon:

1. Log on to your computer with the backup administrator account.
2. Create a copy of your profile in a working folder, or create copies of your profile folders in Windows Explorer.
3. Delete your profile. When you delete your profile, all your personal data will be permanently lost if you haven't backed it up or copied it.
4. Log off the backup administrator account.
5. Log on to your primary account. When you log on, Windows 7 will create a new profile for you. You can then copy your personal data back into your personal folders.

Environment variables

Your computer uses environment variables to track many different aspects of the computer configuration—from the location of your user profile, to the computer name, to the processor architecture. Environment variables are divided into two general classes: those that the operating system uses, called system environment variables; and those that are specially related to the currently logged on user, called user environment variables. If you access a command prompt and type set, you'll see all the environment variables that are currently being used.

In the System Properties dialog box, you can view and configure environment variables by completing these steps:

1. Click Start→Control Panel→System and Security→System.
2. In the System console, click "Change settings" under "Computer name, domain, and workgroup settings." Alternatively, click Advanced System Settings in the left pane.
3. On the Advanced tab, click Environment Variables. This displays the Environment Variables dialog box shown in Figure 20-10.
4. You can now configure environment variables using the following techniques:

- To create an environment variable, click New under "User variables" or under "System variables," whichever is appropriate. In the New Variable dialog box, type the variable name and value in the fields provided and then click OK.

- To edit an existing environment variable, select the variable in the "User variables" or "System variables" listbox. Click Edit under "User variables" or under "System variables," whichever is appropriate. In the Edit Variable dialog box, type a new value in the Variable Value field and then click OK.

- To delete an environment variable, select it and click Delete.

Figure 20-10. Configuring your computer's environment variables

When you create or edit system environment variables, the changes affect the entire system when you restart the computer. When you create or edit user environment variables, the changes take effect the next time you log on.

 Programs that you run from the Start menu or Run dialog will pick up the new environment variables when you quit and restart them. So if you are setting an environment variable for use in the Command Prompt, you need only close it and reopen it for the new environment variable to take effect.

Startup and recovery

Startup and recovery options control the way Windows 7 starts and handles failures. You can view and configure startup and recovery options by completing these steps:

1. Click Start→Control Panel→System and Security→System.
2. In the System console, click "Change settings" under "Computer name, domain, and workgroup settings." Alternatively, click Advanced System Settings in the left pane.
3. On the Advanced tab, click Settings under Startup and Recovery. This displays the Startup and Recovery dialog box shown in Figure 20-11.

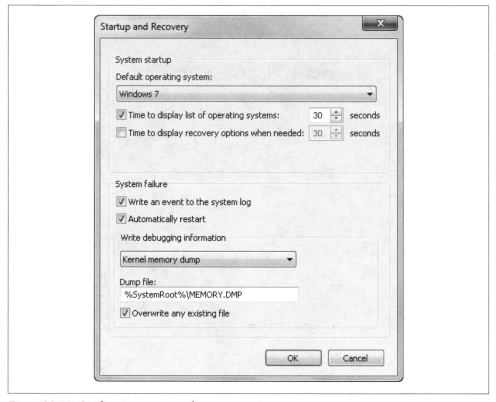

Figure 20-11. Configuring startup and recovery options

4. If your computer has multiple bootable operating systems, you can set the default operating system by selecting one of the operating systems on the "Default operating system" list. These options change the configuration settings that Windows Boot Manager uses.
5. At startup of a computer with multiple bootable operating systems, Windows 7 displays the startup configuration menu for 30 seconds by default. To boot

immediately to the default operating system, clear the "Time to display list of operating systems" checkbox. To display the available options for a specific amount of time, select the "Time to display list of operating systems" checkbox and then set the desired time delay in seconds.

6. When the system is in a recovery mode and is booting, a list of recovery options might be displayed. To boot immediately using the default recovery option, clear the "Time to display recovery options when needed" checkbox. To display the available options for a specific amount of time, select the "Time to display recovery options when needed" checkbox and then set a time delay in seconds.

7. System Failure options control what happens when the system encounters a fatal system error (also known as a STOP error). The available options for the System Failure area are used as follows:

Write an event to the system log
   Logs the error in the system log, which allows you to review the error later using the Event Viewer.

Automatically restart
   Check this option to have the system attempt to reboot when a fatal system error occurs.

Write debugging information
   Choose the type of debugging information to write to a dump file if a fatal error occurs. You can then use the dump file to diagnose system failures.

Dump file
   Sets the location for the dump file. The default dump locations are *%SystemRoot%\Minidump* for small memory dumps and *%SystemRoot%\MEMORY.DMP* for all other memory dumps.

Overwrite any existing file
   Ensures that any existing dump files are overwritten if a new STOP error occurs.

8. Click OK to save your settings.

Configuring Remote Access

The Remote tab in the System Properties dialog box controls Remote Assistance invitations and Remote Desktop connections. With Remote Assistance, you can send invitations to support technicians, enabling them to service your computer remotely. With Remote Desktop, you can connect remotely to another person's computer and access its resources.

Remote Assistance

When you have a problem with your computer, you can use Remote Assistance to ask an expert for help. At the office, this is an easy way to allow a support technician either to guide you through a configuration task or to solve a problem for you. At home, if you have a home network, you can use this feature to ask a trusted person to do the same. You should rarely, if ever, however, ask others to help you when they are connecting over the Internet.

Remote Assistance is enabled by default. You can configure Remote Assistance by following these steps:

1. Select Control Panel→System and Security→System.

2. On the System page, click Remote Settings in the left pane. This opens the System Properties dialog box to the Remote tab, as shown in Figure 20-12.

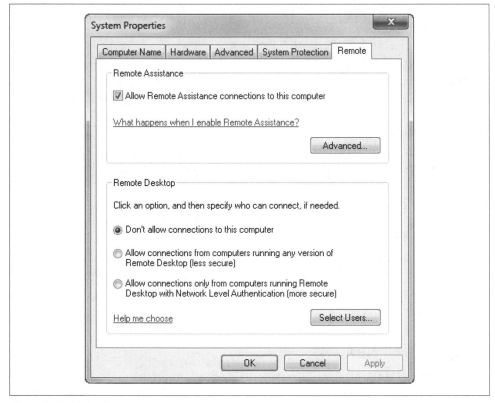

Figure 20-12. Viewing remote access options

3. To disable Remote Assistance, clear the "Allow Remote Assistance connections to this computer" checkbox, and then click OK. Skip the remaining steps.

4. To enable Remote Assistance, check the "Allow Remote Assistance connections to this computer" checkbox.

5. Click Advanced. This displays the Remote Assistance Settings dialog box shown in Figure 20-13.

6. To allow assistants to view and control the computer, select the "Allow this computer to be controlled remotely" checkbox. To provide view-only access to the computer, clear this checkbox.

7. By default, Remote Assistance invitations are valid for six hours and then expire. The helper must initiate a Remote Assistance session within this time limit. As necessary, use the Invitations options to set a different time limit.

8. Because Windows 7 offers improved security and enhanced management, you might want to create invitations that only computers running Windows Vista or later can answer. If so, select the related checkbox.

9. Click OK to save your settings. See Chapter 21 for details on getting help.

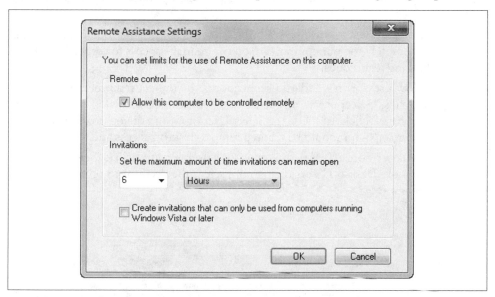

Figure 20-13. Configuring Remote Assistance options

Remote Desktop access

Remote Desktop is a feature you can use to connect to your home computer when you are at work or to your work computer when you are at home. Unlike Remote Assistance, this feature is not designed to allow someone to use a computer locally while the computer is being access remotely. If someone is currently logged on to the desktop locally and then you try to log on remotely, the local desktop locks automatically and the remote user can then access all of the currently running applications just as if he or she were sitting at the keyboard. If no one is logged on locally and you try to log on remotely, Windows creates a new user session and you are then able to work with the computer remotely just as if you were sitting at the keyboard.

Remote Desktop is not enabled by default. You can configure Remote Desktop access by completing these steps:

1. Select Control Panel→System and Security→System.

2. On the System page, click Remote Settings in the left pane. This opens the System Properties dialog box to the Remote tab.

3. To disable Remote Desktop, select "Don't allow connections to this computer" and then click OK. Skip the remaining steps.

4. To enable Remote Desktop, you can select "Allow connections from computers running any version of Remote Desktop" to allow connections from any version of Windows, or you can select "Allow connections only from computers running Remote Desktop with network level authentication" to allow connections only from Windows Vista or later computers (and computers with secure network authentication).

5. By default, only users who have administrator accounts on your computer can connect remotely to your computer. You can manage access for other users using the following techniques:

   • To allow users with standard user accounts to connect remotely to your computer, click "Select users." In the Remote Desktop Users dialog box, shown in Figure 20-14, click Add. Use the Select User or Group dialog box to specify the user or group who should be granted remote desktop access and then click OK.

   • To revoke remote access permissions for a user account, click "Select users." In the Remote Desktop Users dialog box, select the account to remove and then click Remove.

6. Click OK to save your settings.

Figure 20-14. Configuring Remote Desktop users

General Maintenance Tools

Windows 7 provides a wide range of tools to help you maintain your computer. They include the following:

Automatic Updates
> Allows you to keep your computer up-to-date with the latest hot fixes and security updates

Disk Cleanup
> Allows you to check disk drives for files that aren't needed

Check Disk
> Allows you to check disks for errors in the filesystem and on the disk volume itself

Disk Defragmenter (Dfrg.msc)
> Allows you to optimize disk performance by reducing fragmentation of files

The following sections discuss how you can use each tool to perform preventive maintenance and routine checkups on your computer.

Updating Your Computer

Ensuring that your computer is up to date with the most recent hot fixes, security updates, and service packs is the most important preventive maintenance task you can perform. The great news is that you can completely automate the update process so that as updates become available, you can have your computer automatically download and install them.

The feature in Windows 7 that handles updates is called Windows Update. Windows Update is an enhanced version of the standard automatic update feature included in earlier releases of Windows. With Windows Update, you can be sure that all operating system components and related programs that ship with the operating system are updated automatically. If you installed the Windows Live desktop programs, these can be updated automatically as well.

You can even take this process a step further by having your computer download and install updates for related Microsoft products, including Microsoft Office, via an extension component called Microsoft Update. Microsoft Update extends Windows Update to provide a total update shield for your computer and key Microsoft products.

Installing Microsoft Update

When you install some Microsoft products, Microsoft Update is downloaded and installed automatically. For example, if you downloaded and installed the Windows Live desktop programs, Microsoft Update is installed automatically as part of the setup process.

You can determine whether your computer is using Microsoft Update by following these steps:

1. Click Start→All Programs→Windows Update. This displays the Windows Update page in the Control Panel.
2. If your computer is configured to use Microsoft Update, you'll see the following message in the lower portion of the page:

   `You receive updates: For Windows and other products from Microsoft Update.`

You can install Microsoft Update by completing these steps:

1. Click Start→All Programs→Windows Update. This displays the Windows Update page in the Control Panel.
2. Click the "Get updates for more products" link. This opens the Windows Update page at the Microsoft web site in Internet Explorer.
3. After you read about Microsoft Update, scroll down, select "I accept the Terms of Use," and then click Install.

 When you are using Microsoft Office, related Office applications, Visual Studio, and some other Microsoft products, you'll want to use Microsoft Update to ensure that your computer downloads and installs updates for these programs according to your Automatic Updates settings. This will help ensure security patches, updates, and service packs for these applications are installed as they are released.

Configuring Automatic Updates

You can configure Automatic Updates by completing these steps:

1. Click Start→All Programs→Windows Update. This displays the Windows Update page in the Control Panel.
2. In the left panel, click "Change settings." This displays the "Change settings" page, shown in Figure 20-15.
3. You can now specify whether and how updates should occur. To download and install updates automatically, select "Install updates automatically" and then set the interval for installing updates. By default, your computer periodically checks for and downloads updates when you are connected to the Internet. However, updates are installed only on the specific days and times you set. If you shut down your computer after updates have been downloaded, the updates are installed automatically before the computer shuts down, unless you elect to shut down without installing updates.
4. To ensure that recommended updates for device drivers included with the operating system and other optional updates are downloaded when they are available, select the "Give me recommended updates the same way I receive important

updates" checkbox. Recommended updates are not installed automatically. Instead, you are notified when recommended updates become available.

5. To ensure that you receive updates for other Microsoft products and periodically check for new optional software from Microsoft, select the "Give me updates for Microsoft products and check for new optional Microsoft software when I update Windows" checkbox.

6. To receive detailed notifications about optional software from Microsoft, select the "Show me detailed notifications…" checkbox.

7. Click OK to save your settings.

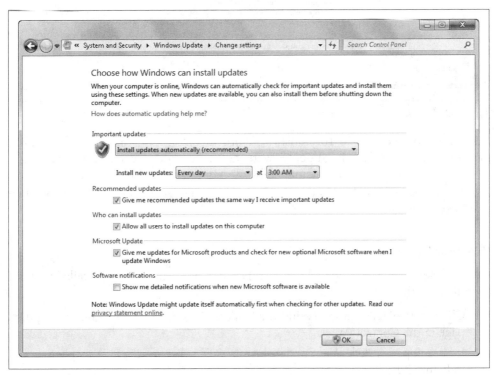

Figure 20-15. Configuring your Automatic Updates settings

Checking for updates

You can check for and install updates manually at any time by following these steps:

1. Click Start→All Programs→Windows Update. This displays the Windows Update page in the Control Panel.

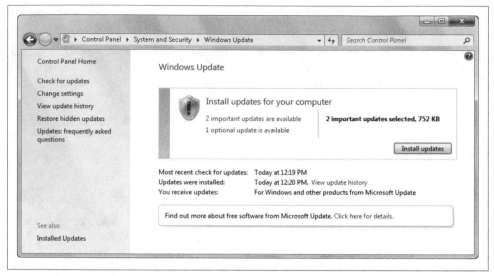

Figure 20-16. Checking for updates

2. As shown in Figure 20-16, statistics are provided regarding the most recent check for updates, the last time updates were installed, and the current update configuration. If you want to check manually for updates, click "Check for updates."

3. If updates are available, they are downloaded. To install downloaded updates, click "Install updates."

Viewing update history

You can view a detailed update history and a list of both successful and failed updates by following these steps:

1. Click Start→All Programs→Windows Update. This displays the Windows Update page in the Control Panel.

2. In the left panel, click "View update history." This displays the History page shown in Figure 20-17.

3. On the History page, updates listed with a Successful status were downloaded and installed. Updates listed with an Unsuccessful status were downloaded but failed to install.

4. To remove an update while accessing the History page, click Installed Updates. Then on the Installed Updates page, right-click the update that you do not want and select Uninstall.

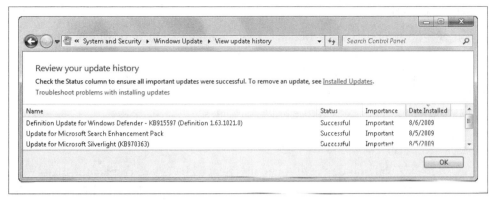

Figure 20-17. Viewing the update history

Removing updates and resolving update problems

Occasionally your computer may experience problems due to installing updates. Although this happens rarely, it does happen. You can remove updates if you need to by following these steps:

1. Click Start→All Programs→Windows Update. This displays the Windows Update page in the Control Panel.

2. In the left panel, click "View update history" and then click Installed Updates.

3. Select the update you want to modify or remove and then click Change or Uninstall as appropriate.

A problem I've experienced several times with Automatic Updates occurs due to a conflict between McAfee Security Center and Automatic Updates. As this is an equal opportunity conflict, I've also seen it occur due to a conflict between Norton Security and Automatic Updates. Normally, when you shut down your computer and there are updates to install, these updates are installed automatically. The problem I've experienced is that the update process gets locked when I shut down my computer, and there are multiple updates that affect components protected by McAfee or Norton as part of their antivirus or antimalware protection.

To shut down my computer, I had to press and hold the power button—something you should never do when updates are being installed. When I later started my computer, the computer froze as soon as either McAfee or Norton started, and I was at a complete standstill. If you experience this problem, too—and you might—you'll need to boot your computer to Safe Mode, as discussed in Chapter 21, and restore your computer to a previous point in time using System Restore, which is also discussed in Chapter 21.

Restoring declined updates

If you decline an update that you later want to install, you can restore the update so that you can install it by completing these steps:

1. Click Start→All Programs→Windows Update. This displays the Windows Update page in the Control Panel.
2. In the left pane, click "Restore hidden updates."
3. On the Restore Hidden Updates page, select an update you want to install and then click Restore.
4. Windows 7 will unhide the declined update. Click Back to display the main Windows Update page, and then click "Install updates" to install the previously declined update.

Cleaning Up Your Disk Drives

Over time, the many types of temporary files created when you browse the Internet, install programs, or update your computer can eat up the free space on your computer's disks. As your computer's primary disk fills to 85 percent or more of its total capacity, you may start to notice that it's not as responsive as it used to be. Your computer may slow down as its primary disk fills to capacity, because it depends on this free space to write the page file and other temporary files it needs to use. To help prevent performance problems due to your primary disk being too full, you should periodically clean up your computer's disks using Disk Cleanup. Table 20-1 provides a summary of the types of temporary files Disk Cleanup can help you track down and remove.

Table 20-1. Temporary files that you can clean up

Type of temporary file	Description
Downloaded program files	Contains programs downloaded for use by your browser, such as ActiveX controls and Java applets. These files are temporary, and you can delete them.
Microsoft Office temporary files	Contains logfiles that Office created as well as other temporary files that Office uses. These files are temporary, and you can delete them.
Offline files	Contains local copies of network files that you've designated for offline use. These files are stored to enable offline access, and you can delete them.
Offline web pages	Contains web pages that have been stored locally for viewing offline.
Recycle Bin	Contains files that have been deleted from the computer but not yet purged. Emptying the Recycle Bin permanently removes the files.
Previous Windows Installations	Previous Windows installations are saved under *Windows.old*. After you've saved any necessary data from previous Windows installations, including user data, you can use remove the related files and free up space.
Setup logfiles	Contains logfiles that Windows created during setup. If your computer is fully installed and you have no problems with the installation, you can delete the setup logfiles.

Type of temporary file	Description
System error memory dump files	Contains dump files Windows created because of a STOP error. If you've resolved the problem that caused the STOP error or do not plan to send the dump file to Microsoft or another support technician, you can delete the dump files.
System queued Windows error reporting files	Windows Error Reporting creates several types of temporary files that are used for error reporting and solution checking. Once you've resolved any problems or if there are no current problems, you can delete these temporary files.
Temporary files	Contains information stored in the Temp folder. These files are primarily temporary data or work files for applications.
Temporary Internet files	Contains web pages stored to support browser caching of pages. These files are temporary, and you can delete them.
Temporary offline files	Contains temporary data and work files for recently used network files. These files are stored to enable working, and you can delete them.
Thumbnails	Contains thumbnails of pictures, videos, and documents Windows 7 has created. When you access a folder the first time, Windows 7 creates thumbnails of pictures, videos, and documents. These thumbnails are saved so that they can be quickly displayed the next time you access a folder. If you delete thumbnails, they are re-created the next time you access a folder.

You can clean up temporary files by completing the following steps:

1. Click Start→All Programs→Accessories→System Tools→Disk Cleanup.
2. In the Disk Cleanup: Drive Selection dialog box, shown in Figure 20-18, select the disk that you want to clean up and then click OK.

 For best results on a computer with multiple drives, perform this procedure twice. The first time, select the primary system disk as the drive you want to clean up. The second time, select the primary disk that you use for saving documents and related files as the drive you want to clean up.

3. Disk Cleanup then examines the selected drive, looking for temporary files that can be deleted and files that are candidates for compression. The more files on the drive, the longer the search process takes.
4. When Disk Cleanup finishes, you'll see a list of files that can be deleted. To add system files to the clean up list click the "Clean up system files" button, select the primary system drive and then click OK. The primary system disk is the disk with the Windows logo.
5. You'll see a list of both user and system files that can be deleted, similar to the list shown in Figure 20-19. Only a few types of temporary files are selected by default. Because of this, you'll want to carefully review the other types of temporary files that you can delete. As shown in the example, only 8.02 MB of data was selected

for deletion by default, but I was able to increase this to 46.4 GB by selecting other types of unnecessary files.

6. After you select additional checkboxes as necessary, click OK. When prompted to confirm the action, click Yes.

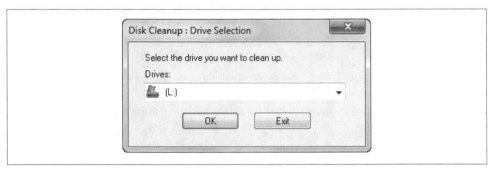

Figure 20-18. Selecting the drive to clean up

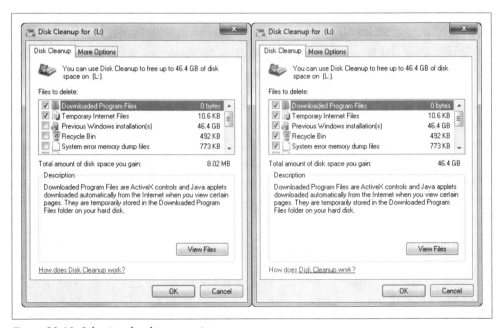

Figure 20-19. Selecting the cleanup options

When Disk Cleanup finishes, I recommend that you restart your computer and consider the two additional options it provides:

Program Clean Up
Helps you free up space by removing programs that you do not use

System Restore and Shadow Copy Clean Up
Helps you free up space by removing all but the most recent restore point and shadow copy

I recommend backing up and restarting your computer before using these cleanup options to ensure that your computer is in a bootable state, that no updates need to be applied, and that no current errors need to be resolved. You can use Disk Cleanup to help you clean up programs, as well as system restore and shadow copies, by completing these steps:

1. Click Start, type `cleanmgr` in the Search box, and then press Enter.
2. In the Disk Cleanup Options dialog box, select a disk to clean up and then click OK.
3. Click the "Clean up system files" button, select the primary system drive and then click OK.
4. In the Disk Cleanup dialog box, select the More Options tab, as shown in Figure 20-20.
5. To remove all system restore and shadow copies except for the current restore point, click "Clean up" under System Restore and Shadow Copies. When prompted to confirm that you want to delete this data, click Delete.
6. To find programs to clean up, click "Clean up" under Programs and Features. On the Programs and Features page in the Control Panel, select a program that you want to remove and then click Uninstall.

Checking Your Disks for Errors

Your primary disk is one of the most-used pieces of hardware on your computer. Your computer is constantly reading and writing data. If it experiences the slightest hiccup, the wrong data can be written to parts of the disk. If a particular sector or cluster on a disk is damaged or otherwise cannot be written to, your computer will experience problems whenever it tries to read or write data to this sector or cluster. Though Windows 7 and hardware controllers on the disk drives themselves both do a good job of correcting problems, neither one can correct all disk problems. To keep your computer's disks running optimally, you need to check your computer's disks periodically for errors and correct any errors found.

You can check disk drives for errors and correct any errors found by following these steps:

1. Click Start→Computer. Under Hard Disk Drives, right-click the drive you want to check and then select Properties.

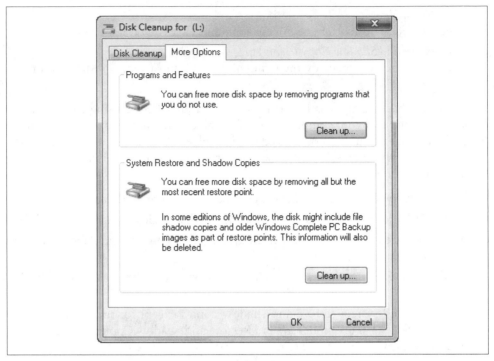

Figure 20-20. Cleaning up programs and other files as necessary

2. On the Tools tab, click Check Now. This displays the Check Disk dialog box, shown in Figure 20-21.

Figure 20-21. Checking your disk for errors

3. To check for errors and attempt to resolve them, select either or both of the following options, and then click Start:

   Automatically fix file system errors
   > When this is selected, Windows 7 fixes any filesystem errors it finds.

   Scan for and attempt recovery of bad sectors
   > When this is selected, Windows 7 checks for bad sectors and attempts to recover readable information from them.

4. With the primary disk or other disks that are in use, Check Disk displays a prompt that asks whether you want to schedule the disk to be checked the next time you restart the system. Click Yes to schedule this check.

5. When Check Disk finishes analyzing and repairing the disk, click OK.

Optimizing Disk Performance

Another problem that causes disk drives to perform poorly is fragmentation. Fragmentation occurs when a file can't be written to a single contiguous area on the disk, and the operating system often must write a single file to several smaller areas on the disk. Having to seek different parts of the disk slows down not only the write process, but also the read process. Because fragmentation is the number-one cause of disk performance problems (second only to disks being packed with too much information), Windows 7 uses Disk Defragmenter to defragment disks automatically.

Windows 7 runs Disk Defragmenter automatically at 1:00 a.m. every Wednesday by default. As long as the computer is on at the scheduled runtime, automatic defragmentation will occur. You can cancel automatic defragmentation or modify the defragmentation schedule by following these steps:

1. Click Start and then click Computer. Under Hard Disk Drives, right-click a drive and then select Properties.

2. On the Tools tab, click Defragment Now. This displays the Disk Defragmenter dialog box, shown in Figure 20-22.

3. Click Configure schedule and the Modify Schedule dialog box, shown in Figure 20-23, appears.

4. To cancel automated defragmentation, clear "Run on a schedule" and click OK, and then click Close.

5. To modify the defragmentation schedule, ensure that "Run on a schedule" is selected and then choose the desired settings. For example, you might want to schedule automatic defragmentation to occur every Thursday at 9:00 a.m. during your weekly staff meeting. Click OK, and then click Close.

6. Click OK.

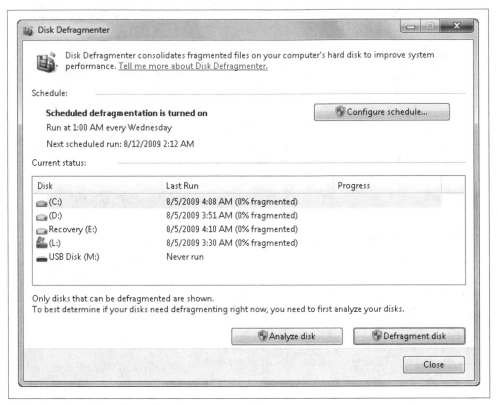

Figure 20-22. Viewing the Disk Defragmenter configuration

 Windows 7 will defragment your disks only if the computer is on, meaning that the computer isn't sleeping or powered off. To ensure that your computer's disks are defragmented periodically, you'll want to use a time when you know you'll be in the office or at home on the computer. Because of performance improvements to Windows 7, you might not even notice defragmentation is running. Why? Well, unlike Windows XP and other earlier releases of Windows, Windows 7 gives whatever programs you are running priority over background housekeeping tasks such as disk defragmentation.

When you access Disk Defragmenter, the last runtime and next runtime are listed. If your computer hasn't been automatically defragmented in several weeks or months, you can defragment a disk manually by completing the following steps:

1. Click Start→Computer. Under Hard Disk Drives, right-click a drive and then select Properties.

2. On the Tools tab, click Defragment Now.

3. In the Disk Defragmenter dialog box, click "Defragment disk."

4. Defragmentation can take several hours. You can select a disk that's being defragmented, then click "Stop operation" at any time to stop defragmentation.

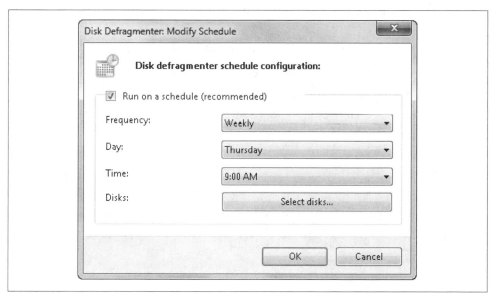

Figure 20-23. Modifying the run schedule

Scheduling Maintenance Tasks

You can automate any routine task that you perform. To do this, you can use the Task Scheduler service to schedule the task to run automatically. Not only can you schedule tasks to run once or periodically, but you can also schedule them to run when the computer starts, when you log on, or when a specific event occurs.

Getting Started with Task Scheduling

You use the Task Scheduler to view and work with scheduled tasks. To access the Task Scheduler, click Start→Control Panel→System and Security→Administrative Tools→Schedule Tasks.

As Figure 20-24 shows, scheduled tasks are stored in the Task Scheduler Library. Task Scheduler displays tasks created by you or other users when you select the Task Scheduler Library node in the left pane. Unlike earlier versions of Windows, Windows 7 makes extensive use of scheduled tasks. In the Task Scheduler Library, you'll find system tasks under *Microsoft\Windows* and *Microsoft\Windows Defender*. Tasks under *Microsoft\Windows* handle many of the background housekeeping tasks on your computer. Tasks under *Microsoft\Windows Defender* are used to automate malware scans.

To ensure that you don't accidentally delete or modify system tasks, most system tasks are locked so that you cannot edit them. Some system tasks are also hidden. In Task Scheduler, you can view hidden tasks by selecting Show Hidden Tasks on the View menu.

Tasks can have many properties associated with them, including:

- Triggers that specify the circumstances under which a task begins and ends
- Actions that define the action a task performs when it is started
- Conditions that qualify the conditions under which a task is started or stopped
- Settings that affect the behavior of the task

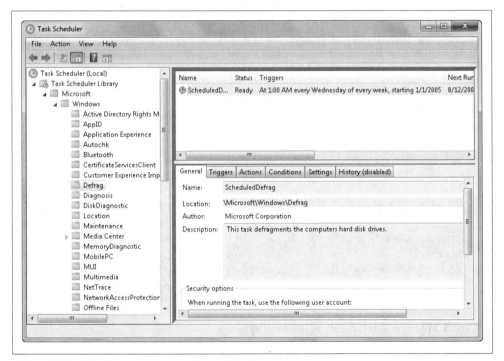

Figure 20-24. Viewing your computer's scheduled tasks

Based on these properties, you can use Task Manager to create two types of tasks: basic tasks and advanced tasks. Basic tasks have only triggers and actions, and are meant to help you quickly schedule a common task. Advanced tasks have triggers, actions, conditions, and settings, and are meant to be used by advanced users or administrators.

Creating Basic Tasks

You can create a basic task by completing these steps:

1. Click Start→Control Panel→System and Security→Administrative Tools→Schedule Tasks.

2. Click the Action menu and then select Create Basic Task. This starts the Create Basic Task Wizard.

3. On the Create a Basic Task page, type a name and description of the task. Click Next.

4. On the Task Trigger page, select a run schedule for the task. You can schedule tasks to run periodically (daily, weekly, or monthly), or when a specific event occurs, such as when the computer starts or when the task's user logs on. Click Next. The next page you see depends on when the task is scheduled to run.

5. If you've selected a daily running task, the Daily page appears, as shown in Figure 20-25. Configure the task using these fields and then click Next:

    Start
    > Use the Start options to set a start date and time.

    Recur every
    > Allows you to run the task every day, every other day, or every *n*th day, beginning with the start date you set. For example, if you want the task to run every other day, you'd set the "Recur every X days" text box to 2 days.

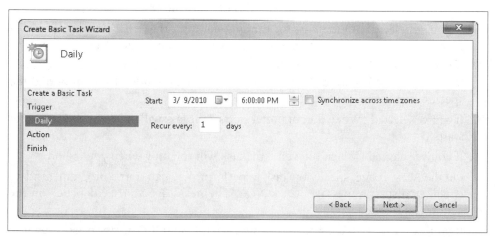

Figure 20-25. Configuring a daily scheduled task

6. If you've selected a weekly running task, the Weekly page appears, as shown in Figure 20-26. Configure the task using these fields and then click Next:

Start
> Use the Start options to set a start date and time.

Recur every
> Allows you to run the task every week, every other week, or every *n*th week.

Days of the week
> Sets the day(s) of the week when the task runs, such as on Tuesday or on Tuesday and Friday.

7. If you've selected a monthly running task, the Monthly page appears, as shown in Figure 20-27. Configure the task using these fields and then click Next:

Start
> Use the Start options to set a start date and time.

Months
> Use this selection list to choose which months the task runs. You can select all months or months individually.

Days
> Sets the day(s) of the month the task runs. For example, if you select 2 and 8, the task runs on the second and eighth days of the month.

On
> Sets the task to run on the *n*th occurrence of a day in a month, such as the second Monday or the third Tuesday of every month.

8. If you've selected "One time" for running the task, the "One time" page is displayed. Use the Start options to set a start date and time. Click Next.

9. If you've selected "When a specific event is logged," the "When a specific event is logged" page is displayed. You'll need to select the event log to monitor and the specific event source, event ID, or both. Click Next.

10. If you've selected "When the computer starts," the task will run when the computer starts.

11. If you've selected "When I log on," the task will run only when you log on.

12. On the Action page, specify the task to perform. You can start a program, send an email, or display a message. Click Next. The next page you see depends on the action you selected.

13. If you've selected Start a Program, you'll see the Start a Program page, shown in Figure 20-28. Click Browse to display the Open dialog box and then select the program or script to run. You'll find system utilities, such as Disk Cleanup (*cleanmgr.exe*), in the *%SystemDrive%\Windows\System32* folder. Click Next.

14. If you've selected Send an E-mail, you'll see the Send an E-mail page. You can then configure the automated email to send by completing the From, To, Subject, and Text fields of the email message. In the "SMTP server" text box, enter the FQDN

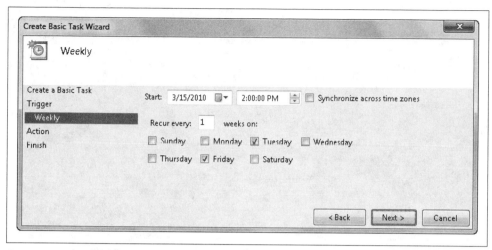

Figure 20-26. Configuring a weekly scheduled task

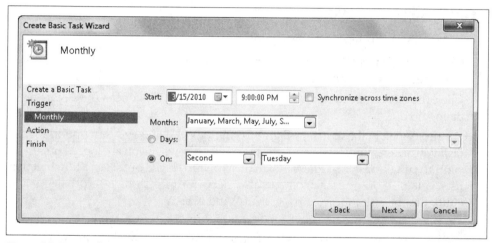

Figure 20-27. Configuring a monthly scheduled task

(Fully Qualified Domain Name) of the mail server through which you will send your message. Click Next.

15. If you've selected Display a Message, you'll see the Display a Message page. You can then configure the message to display on the desktop when the task is started. Enter the title and text of your message in the text boxes provided. Click Next.

16. On the Summary page, review the task details and then click Finish. By default, basic tasks you create run under your account and will run only when you are logged on.

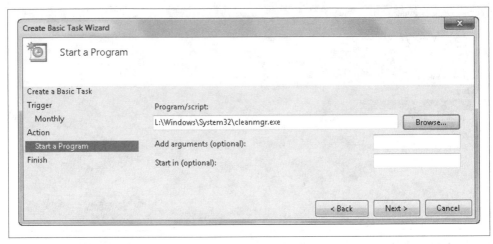

Figure 20-28. Selecting the program to start

Creating Advanced Tasks

You can create an advanced task by completing these steps:

1. Click Start→Control Panel→System and Security and then click the Schedule Tasks link under Administrative Tools.

2. Click the Action menu and then select Create Task. This opens the Create Task dialog box.

3. On the General tab, shown in Figure 20-29, type a name and description for the task you are creating. By default, the task runs only when you are logged on. If you want to run the task regardless of whether you are logged on, select "Run whether user is logged on or not." You can also elect to run with highest privileges and configure the task for earlier releases of Windows.

4. On the Triggers tab, create and manage triggers using the options provided. Using triggers, you can schedule tasks to run periodically (daily, weekly, or monthly), or when a specific event occurs, such as when the computer starts or when the task's user logs on. To create a trigger, click New, use the options provided to configure the trigger, and then click OK.

5. On the Actions tab, create and manage actions using the options provided. You can start a program, send an email, or display a message. To create an action, click New, use the options provided to configure the action, and then click OK.

6. On the Conditions tab, specify any limiting conditions for starting or stopping the task.

7. On the Settings tab, choose any additional optional settings for the task.

8. Click OK to create the task.

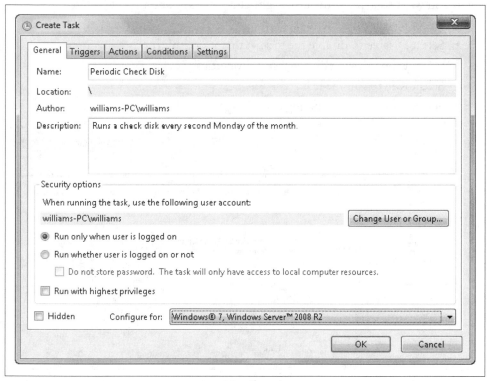

Figure 20-29. Configuring the settings for the task

Managing and Troubleshooting Tasks

You can access the current tasks configured on your computer through the Task Scheduler. You can view and manage scheduled tasks that you or other people created by completing the following steps:

1. Click Start→Control Panel→System and Security→Administrative Tools→Schedule Tasks.

2. In the left pane, select the Task Schedule Library node to display tasks created by you or other people.

3. Select a task to view its properties using the tabs provided (see Figure 20-30). Note the task status, last runtime, and last run result. If a task has a status of Queued, it is waiting to run at a scheduled time. If a task has a status of Ready, it is ready to run on its next runtime. If a task should be running automatically but has a Last Run Time of Never, you'll need to check the task's properties to determine why it isn't running. If the Last Run Result is an error, you'll need to resolve the referenced problem so that the task can run normally.

4. If you want to manage the task, right-click the task and then:
   - Select Delete to delete the task.
   - Select Disable to disable the task so that it doesn't run.
   - Select Properties to edit the task's properties.
   - Select Run to run the task.
   - Select End to stop a running task.

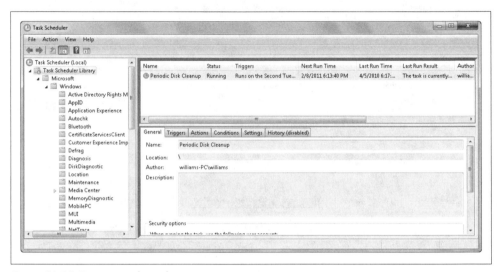

Figure 20-30. Reviewing the task status

You can view all running tasks by selecting Display All Running Tasks on the Action menu. When checking for problems with tasks, keep in mind that a task that is listed as Running might not in fact be running, but instead might be a hung process. You can check for hung processes using Last Run Time, which tells you when the task was started. If a task has been running for more than 24 hours, there is usually a problem. To stop the task, right-click it in the Task Scheduler and then select End. When prompted to confirm, click Yes.

CHAPTER 21

Getting Help and Handling Advanced Support Issues

Computers have dozens—and in some cases, hundreds—of different devices, services, and applications configured on them. Keeping all these components working properly is a big job that Windows 7 handles aptly with your help. Still, it's a fact of life that stuff happens: computers crash, services and applications stop working, and devices fail. Fortunately, Windows 7 includes many features to help ensure that your computer keeps running optimally and to help you resolve any problems you may encounter. In addition to the traditional tools available in Windows XP and earlier releases of Windows, you'll find a comprehensive diagnostics framework that can detect problems as they occur, new tools for helping you recover your computer and data, and more.

Although the built-in diagnostics features attempt to provide solutions to common problems, not all problems can be diagnosed automatically, and you'll often need to work to resolve problems on your own. This is why Windows 7 includes a variety of troubleshooting tools as well as tools for backing up and restoring your computer. When disaster strikes, it's too late to configure these tools, so make sure that your computer's backup and restore features are configured properly as part of your periodic preventive maintenance.

Detecting and Resolving Computer Problems

Windows 7 includes an extensive diagnostics and problem resolution architecture. Although Windows XP and earlier versions of Windows include some help and diagnostics features, those features are, for the most part, not self-correcting or self-diagnosing. Windows 7, on the other hand, can detect many types of hardware, memory, and performance issues and can either resolve them automatically or help users through the process of resolving them. When the automated features are unable to resolve problems for you, you may have to do more extensive troubleshooting by using the event logs and checking the status of essential services.

Throughout this book, you'll find troubleshooting tips and techniques for specific components, features, and applications as well. Don't overlook these additional resources in your troubleshooting. If you have problems that you can't resolve yourself and you are able to load the operating system, you can also use Remote Assistance to get help from other people, regardless of where they may be located. See the section "Getting Help and Giving Others Assistance" on page 845 details.

Solving the Tough Problems Automatically (and Sometimes with a Little Help)

Windows 7's built-in diagnostics framework is designed to monitor the operating system and your computer's hardware components. The diagnostics framework has many components, including:

- Application compatibility alerts to warn you about possibly incompatible programs
- Disk fault monitoring to alert you about a disk that is failing and may need to be replaced
- Corrupt file monitoring to detect and recover corrupted system and application files
- Memory leak detection to detect memory allocation and heap problems caused by programs or components, and to automatically free memory
- Boot performance monitoring to detect and alert you about conditions that affect startup
- Standby/resume performance monitoring to detect and alert you about conditions that affect standby/resume
- Shutdown performance monitoring to detect and alert you about conditions that affect shutdown
- System performance monitoring to detect and alert you about conditions that affect system responsiveness
- Virtual memory monitoring to detect and alert you about low memory conditions that affect system performance

All these diagnostics components work together to help ensure that your computer runs as smoothly and efficiently as possible. The alerts and notifications these components generate are displayed on the screen in dialog boxes and are recorded in the event logs. Although the alerts and notifications vary depending on the type of performance problem, most alerts provide you with a diagnosis and a possible resolution. For example, if your computer is running low on available virtual memory, you'll see the "Close programs to prevent information loss" dialog box. This dialog box will alert you about the low memory condition and provide options for closing the biggest resource hogs to free up memory.

With disk faults, hardware diagnostics alerts you about a disk that is failing and helps guide you through the process of backing up your computer. Performance problems addressed by built-in diagnostics include slow application startup, slow boot, slow standby/resume, and slow shutdown. If a computer is experiencing degraded performance, performance diagnostics can detect the problem and provide possible solutions for resolving it.

Some of the more serious problems you may be alerted to are memory leaks and failing memory modules. Memory leaks are caused by applications or system components that don't free up memory they've previously allocated, and this can cause your computer to run out of available memory. Failing memory can also be exceptionally difficult to troubleshoot. To detect system crashes possibly caused by failing memory, memory diagnostics works with the Microsoft Online Crash Analysis tool. If your computer crashes due to failing memory and memory diagnostics detects this, you are prompted to schedule a memory test the next time the computer is restarted. If you suspect that your computer has a memory problem, you can run Windows Memory Diagnostics manually as well by completing these steps:

1. Click Start→All Programs→Accessories.
2. Right-click Command Prompt and then select Run As Administrator.
3. At the command prompt, type `mdsched.exe`.
4. Choose whether to restart the computer and run the tool immediately or schedule the tool to run at the next restart.
5. Windows Memory Diagnostics runs automatically after the computer restarts and performs a standard memory test automatically. If you want to perform fewer or more tests, press F1, use the Up and Down arrow keys to set the Test Mix as Basic, Standard, or Extended, and then press F10 to apply the desired settings and resume testing.
6. When testing is completed, the computer restarts automatically. You'll see the test results when you log on.

Windows 7 uses the Startup Repair Tool to resolve problems that prevent your computer from starting. This tool is installed during the initial setup of the operating system and started automatically when your computer fails to boot. When started, the tool attempts to determine the cause of the startup failure by analyzing startup logs and error reports and then tries to fix any identified problems automatically. If the Startup Repair Tool is unable to resolve the problem, it restores the system to the last known working state and then provides diagnostic information and support options for further troubleshooting.

As compared to Windows XP and earlier releases, Windows 7:

- Prevents many common causes of hangs and crashes by using more reliable and better performing device drivers. Improved input/output (I/O) cancellation for device drivers ensures that there are fewer blocking disk I/O operations and that Windows 7 can recover gracefully from any blocking calls that do occur.

- Reduces downtime and restarts required for application installations and updates by marking in-use files for update and then automatically replacing the files the next time the application is started. In some cases, Windows 7 can save the application's data, close the application, update the in-use files, and then restart the application.

- Improves the overall system performance and responsiveness by using memory more efficiently. Windows 7 provides ordered execution for groups of threads, and provides new process scheduling mechanisms. By optimizing memory and process usage, Windows 7 ensures that background processes have less impact on system performance.

- Provides improved guidance on the causes of unresponsive conditions. Windows 7 makes it easier to identify and resolve problems by including additional error reporting details in the event logs.

- Attempts to resolve the issue of unresponsive applications by using Restart Manager. Restart Manager can shut down and restart unresponsive applications automatically. This means you might not have to intervene to try to resolve issues with frozen applications.

Windows 7 also tracks failed installation and unresponsive conditions of applications and drivers through the Action Center console. Should an installation fail or an application become unresponsive, the built-in diagnostics adds an alert to Action Center. You can see alerts when you click the Action Center icon in the system tray. If you click an alert message, Windows 7 opens the message details in Action Center, which either provides a ready solution or enables you to check for solutions to the problem. You can view a list of current problems at any time by following these steps:

1. Click the Action Center icon in the system tray and then click the Open Action Center link. If the Action Center icon is not visible, click Start→Control Panel→System and Security→Action Center.

2. In Action Center, expand the Security and Maintenance panels to see security and maintenance issues, respectively.

3. Click the button provided for the issue to get more information and in many cases a link to a solution.

If your computer has a problem that is not automatically detected, you can try to use one of the built-in troubleshooters to resolve the problem. When you are working with the main page in Action Center, clicking the "Troubleshooting" link opens the Troubleshooting window. As Figure 21-1 shows, Windows 7 includes multiple

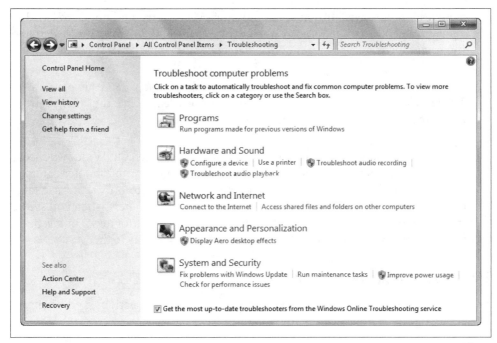

Figure 21-1. Accessing the built-in troubleshooters

troubleshooters. These troubleshooters are designed to help you quickly resolve common problems. The available troubleshooters include:

- The Programs Troubleshooter, for resolving compatibility issues with applications designed for earlier versions of Windows.

- The Hardware and Sound Troubleshooter, for resolving issues with hardware devices, audio recording, and audio playback.

- The Network and Internet Troubleshooter, for resolving issues with connecting to networks and accessing shared folders on other computers.

- The Appearance and Personalization Troubleshooter, for resolving issues with the display appearance and personalization settings. To quickly resolve display issues with Aero, click Display Aero Desktop Effects.

- System and Security Troubleshooter for resolving issues with Windows Update, power usage, and performance. Click Run Maintenance Tasks to clean up unused files and shortcuts and perform other routine maintenance tasks.

In the left pane of the Troubleshooting page you'll find several important links, including:

View All

Lists all available troubleshooters alphabetically by name, description, location, category, and publisher. When a troubleshooter is listed as being Local, the troubleshooter is available on your computer. When a troubleshooter is listed as being Online, the troubleshooter is available online and will be downloaded and run each time you use it.

View History

Provides a history of which troubleshooters you've run and when you've run them. To view troubleshooters run with administrator privileges, click the "Include troubleshooters that were run as an administrator" link.

Change Settings

Allows you to manage how troubleshooters are used. By default, Windows checks for routine maintenance issues and remotes you when a troubleshooter can help fix a problem. Windows also allows you and other users to browse for available troubleshooters online and begins troubleshooting immediately when you start a troubleshooter. If you don't allow Windows to check online for new troubleshooters, your computer won't install updates for troubleshooters, either.

Tracking Errors in the Event Logs

Windows 7 stores errors generated by processes, services, applications, and hardware devices in logfiles. Two general types of logfiles are used:

Windows logs

Logs that the operating system uses to record general system events related to applications, security, setup, and system components

Applications and services logs

Logs that specific applications or services use to record application-specific or service-specific events

You can access event logs using the Event Viewer node in Computer Management. To open Computer Management, click the Start button, right-click on the Computer icon, and then select Manage from the context menu provided.

You can access the event logs by completing the following steps:

1. Open Computer Management. You are connected to the local computer by default. If you want to view logs on a remote computer, right-click the Computer Management entry in the console tree (left pane) and then select Connect to Another Computer. Then, in the Select Computer dialog box, enter the name of the computer that you want to access and click OK.

2. Expand the Event Viewer node and then expand the Windows Logs node, the Applications and Services Logs node, or both to view the available logs.

3. Select the log that you want to view.

As shown in Figure 21-2, Windows 7 records entries in log files according to the activity date, time, and warning level. The various warning levels you'll see are as follows:

Information
    An informational event, which is generally related to a successful action

Audit Success
    An event related to the successful execution of an action

Audit Failure
    An event related to the failed execution of an action

Warning
    A warning about a component, service, or application that can be useful in resolving current problems or preventing future problems

Error
    A noncritical error that you should examine

Critical
    An error for which there is no recovery

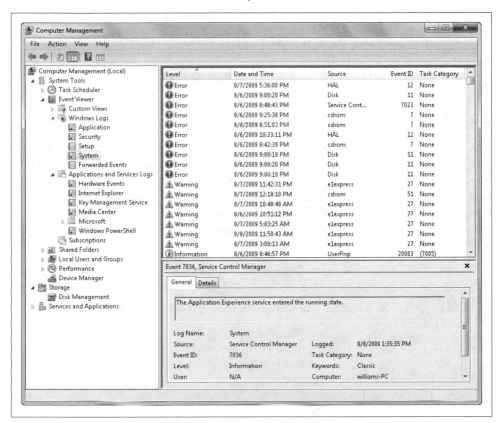

Figure 21-2. Tracking and reviewing errors and warnings in the event logs

In addition to the date, time, and warning level, the summary and detailed event entries provide the following information:

Source
> The application, service, or component that logged the event

Event ID
> An identifier for the specific event

Task Category
> The category of the event, which is sometimes used to further describe the related action

User
> The user account or system process that was logged on when the event occurred or that caused the event to occur

Computer
> The name of the computer where the event occurred

Details
> A text description of the event followed by any related data or error output

You can examine events by double-clicking the entry to view the detailed event description. Use the information provided to help you resolve problems. To learn more about the error or warning, click the link provided in the error description or search the Microsoft Knowledge Base for the event ID or part of the event description.

Resolving Problems with System Services

Just about every advanced facet of the operating system runs as a system service. If an essential service stops, the related functionality will not be available and your computer won't work as expected. When you are troubleshooting problems, you'll want to ensure that essential services are running as expected early in your troubleshooting process. To manage system services, you'll use the Services entry in the Computer Management console. Start Computer Management and access the Services entry by completing the following steps:

1. Click the Start button, right-click on the Computer icon, and then select Manage from the context menu provided.

2. In Computer Management, double-click the Services and Applications node and then select Services.

3. As Figure 21-3 shows, you'll now see the available services. Services are listed by:

   Name
   > The name of the service.

   Description
   > A short description of the service and its purpose.

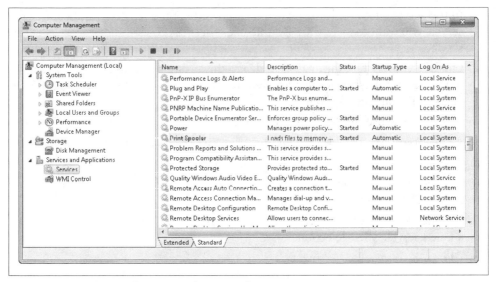

Figure 21-3. Tracking and reviewing the status of services

Status
> The status of the service. If the entry is blank, the service is stopped.

Startup Type
> The startup setting for the service.

Log On As
> The account the service logs on as. The default in most cases is the local system account.

Once you've accessed the Service node in Computer Management, you can work with services by completing the following steps:

1. In the Services view, scroll down on the right side of the window until you see the service you want to work with. Double-click the entry to view the properties of this service (see Figure 21-4).

2. If the service startup type is listed as Automatic and the service status is not listed as Started, click the Start button to start the service.

3. If the Start button is dimmed, click the Stop button and then click the Start button.

4. If a service that should have a startup type of Automatic has a different configuration, set the startup type as Automatic.

5. Click OK.

As part of the comprehensive overhaul of the Windows operating system, essential services in Windows 7 are set to restart automatically if they fail. You can review and configure the restart settings for a service by following these steps:

1. In the Services view, scroll down on the right side of the window until you see the service you want to work with. Double-click the entry to view the properties of this service.

2. On the Recovery tab, the first, second, and third restart actions are listed as shown in Figure 21-5. Restart actions you'll see include Take No Action, Restart the Service, and Restart the Computer.

3. As necessary, use the "First failure" list to set the first failure option.

4. As necessary, use the "Second failure" list to set the second failure option.

5. As necessary, use the "Subsequent failures" list to set the third failure option.

6. Use the "Reset fail count after" text box to set the expiration period for the failure count. The default value is 1 day.

7. Use the "Restart service after" text box to set how long Windows 7 waits to restart a failed service after detection.

8. Click OK to save your settings.

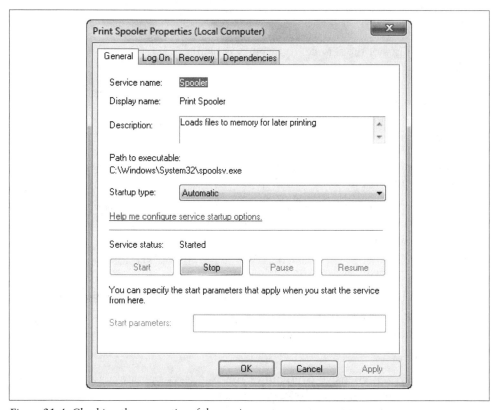

Figure 21-4. Checking the properties of the service

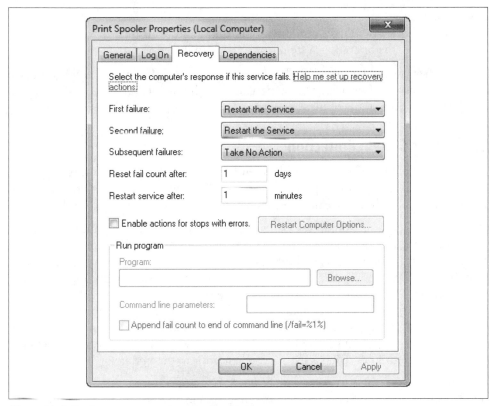

Figure 21-5. Setting recovery options for the service

Creating Backups and Preparing for Problems

Windows 7 includes a number of backup features that can help safeguard your computer against disaster. The ones you'll want to use are as follows:

System Protection
Used to back up the configuration and settings of your computer for easy restoration without having to reinstall the operating system

Previous Versions
Used to back up previous versions of files and folders so that you can easily recover your data

Automated Backup
Used to back up your personal data and optionally your system drives automatically so that you can recover it easily

System Image Backup
> Used to back up your system drives and optionally your data drives so that you can recover the operating system from a backup image

None of these features is meant to be used in lieu of the other; you should configure and use all four backup features. As part of periodic maintenance, you should also regularly check the status of these features.

Configuring System Protection

You use System Protection to fix problems and undo changes to Windows. With System Protection enabled, your computer makes periodic snapshots of the system configuration. These snapshots are called *restore points*.

Restore points include Windows settings, device settings, and program settings. Restore points are intended to be used to recover your computer to the state it was in prior to performing a task that changed the configuration of the operating system, devices, or programs. If your computer has problems starting or isn't working properly because of a configuration change, you can use a restore point to restore the computer to the point at which the snapshot was made. For example, suppose your computer is working fine until you install a security patch or a service pack. Although you uninstall the update, your computer still doesn't work correctly, so you decide to use System Restore to restore the computer using a snapshot taken prior to the update.

System Protection can provide several different types of restore points. One type, System Checkpoint, is scheduled by the operating system and occurs at regular intervals. Another type of snapshot, Installation Restore Point, is created automatically based on events that the operating system triggers when you install applications. Other snapshots, known as Manual Restore Points, are ones you create manually. You should create a Manual Restore Point prior to performing any operation that might cause problems on your computer.

You can restore your computer when it is running in normal mode or safe mode. In normal mode, a restore point is created prior to restoration of the computer. But in safe mode, a restore point is not created, because changes you make in safe mode aren't tracked and you can't undo them using restore points. However, you can use safe mode to restore any previously created restore point.

You control how System Protection works using the System Protection tab of the System Properties dialog box. System Protection saves system checkpoint information for all monitored drives and requires at least 300 MB of disk space on the System volume to save restore points. System Protection reserves additional space for restore points as necessary—up to 100 percent of the total disk capacity—but this additional space is always available for user and application storage. If System Protection needs to create a restore point and has no more allocated space, the operating system overwrites previously created restore points.

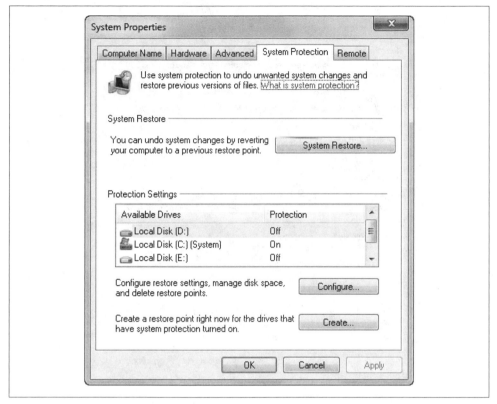

Figure 21-6. Checking the System Protection configuration

You can manage System Protection monitoring of your computer by completing these steps:

1. Click→Control Panel→System and Security→System→System Protection in the left pane.

2. System Protection is enabled on the System disk by default (see Figure 21-6). You should enable System Protection on all disks that store system, program, and personal files.

3. To configure System Protection for a volume, select the volume in the Protection Settings list, and then click Configure. This displays the "System Protection for" dialog box, shown in Figure 21-7.

4. If you are configuring System Protection for the System volume or a volume on which you've installed programs, choose the "Restore system settings and previous versions of files" option to keep copies of system settings and previous versions of files. This option ensures that you can restore the computer and programs and also recover previous versions of important data files.

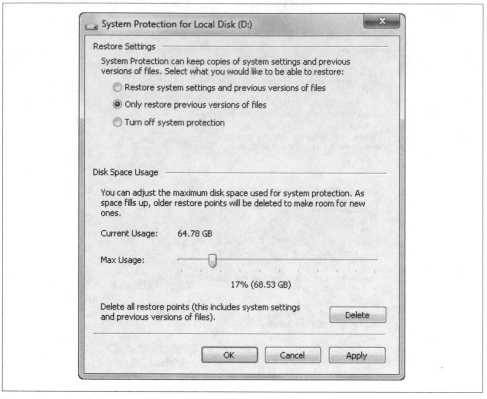

Figure 21-7. Configuring System Protection

5. If you are configuring System Protection for a data volume choose the "Only restore previous versions of files" option to keep previous versions of files but not keep copies of system settings. This option ensures you can recover previous versions of important data files but doesn't try to track system settings (which data volumes don't have).

6. If you don't want the volume to use System Protection, choose the "Turn off system protection" option. This option turns off System Protection but is not recommended because you will not be able to restore the computer or recover previous versions of files.

7. If you've enabled System Protection, you can use the Disk Space Usage slider to adjust the maximum disk space that System Protection can use. When the maximum size is reached, System Protection deletes older restore points to make room for new ones.

8. When you are finished making configuration changes, click OK to the return to the System Properties dialog box. Repeat steps 5–9 to configure other volumes.

You can create a manual restore point for all drives that have system protection turned on by following these steps:

1. Click Start→Control Panel→System and Security→System→System Protection in the left pane→Create.

2. Enter a description for the restore point and then click Create.

3. When your computer finishes creating the restore point, click OK.

Configuring Previous Versions

Using System Restore to restore files and settings does not affect personal data. You can recover your computer to a restore point without affecting your application data, cached files, or documents. System Restore doesn't write any information to any of your personal document folders, either. However, as a new feature in Windows 7, restore points include previous versions of your data. Because of this, you should enable System Protection for all disks on your computer that store system and program data as well as disks that store personal data. If you've configured System Protection only for the System disk, you should update the configuration to include any disks that store personal data as well. See the section "Restoring Previous Versions of Files" on page 834 for more information on previous versions.

Scheduling and Managing Automated Backups

Windows 7 is capable of automatically backing up your personal data and optionally your computer's system data. You use personal data backups to create periodic backups of pictures, music, videos, email, documents, and other types of important files. You use system image backups to create periodic backups of the files needed to recover the operating system and the programs you've installed. You can write your automated backups to internal or external disks, CD/DVD drives, and network locations.

When you are working with automated backups, keep the following in mind:

- The computer must be turned on at the scheduled runtime for automated backups to work. By default, scheduled backups are created every Sunday at 7:00 p.m.

- Although you cannot save backups to the system disk, the boot disk, or tape, you can now save backups to USB flash drives, CD/DVD drives, external FireWire or USB drives, and network locations, as long as they are formatted with NTFS.

- When you use CD/DVD drives, make sure that you remove the CD or DVD from the previous backup and insert a new CD or DVD prior to the scheduled backup. For best results, keep in mind the size of the data you are backing up and use the appropriate media. Most CDs can store up to 700 MB of data, and most single-sided single-layered DVDs can store 4.7 GB of data. If the backup doesn't fit on one disk, you'll need to be available to insert disks when prompted to do so.

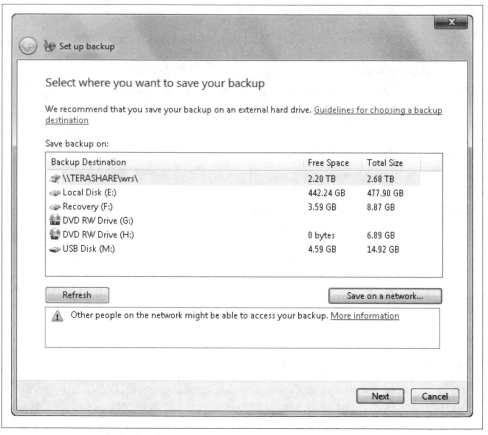

Figure 21-8. Setting the backup location

- You might need a system repair disc to restore a system image. Additionally, only one system image per computer can be stored in a particular backup location. Therefore, if you wanted to keep multiple system image backups, you'd need to select different backup locations for each.

If you haven't previously configured automated backups, you can do so by following these steps:

1. In the Control Panel, under the System and Security heading, click the "Back up your computer" link. This opens the Backup and Restore page in the Control Panel.

2. On the Backup and Restore page, click "Set up backup."

3. On the "Select where you want to save your backup" page, shown in Figure 21-8, use the options provided to specify a backup location on a local disk, a CD/DVD drive, or USB flash drive and then click Next.

Alternatively, to back up to a network location, click Save On a Network. On the "Select a network location" page, type the UNC path to the network share or click Browse to use the Browse for Folder dialog box to select a network share. Enter the network credentials required to access this location in the Username and Password text boxes and then click OK. The wizard will then validate the network location and ensure the credentials you've specified are correct. If you entered invalid credentials, you'll need to reenter the credentials and then click OK again. When you are ready to continue, click Next.

4. On the "What do you want to back up?" page, select Let Windows Choose if you want to backup all personal data in user profile folders and libraries and also create a system image or select Let Me Choose if you want to select personal and system data to backup. Click Next.

5. If you select Let Windows Choose, data files that are saved in local library files, on the desktop and in default Windows folders for all users are backed up. Library files on a different computer, on the same drive as the one being used for the backup, or on a non-NTFS drive are not included in the backup. Default Windows folders that are backed up include AppData, Contacts, Desktop, Downloads, Favorites, Links, Saved Games and Searches. System images include all your programs, any files used by the operating system, all drivers and registry settings.

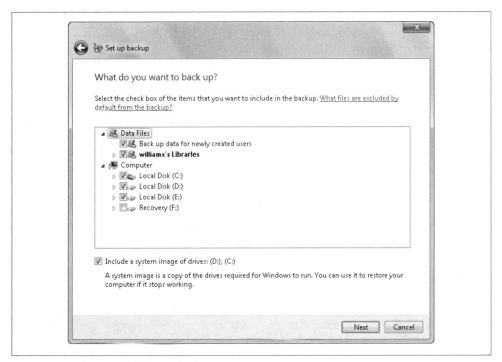

Figure 21-9. Choosing the data to back up

6. If you selected Let Me Choose, use the options provided to select personal data to back up (see Figure 21-9). You can expand the Data Files and Computer nodes and subnodes to select specific folders and libraries. After making your selections and clearing unwanted options, click Next. Note the following:

- Files in known system folders as well as files for installed programs will not be backed up even if you select the folder they are stored in.

- Typically, the "Include a system image of drives" checkbox is selected by default to ensure that system image backups are created (which is what you'll usually want to do). If selected, the system image will include all your programs, any files used by the operating system, all drivers, and registry settings.

7. On the "Review your backup settings" page, shown in Figure 21-10, review what will be included in your automated backups as well as any warnings being displayed. Click the Back button if you want to change the backup settings.

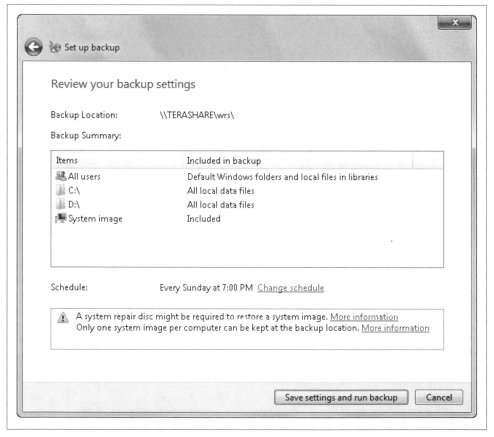

Figure 21-10. Reviewing the backup settings

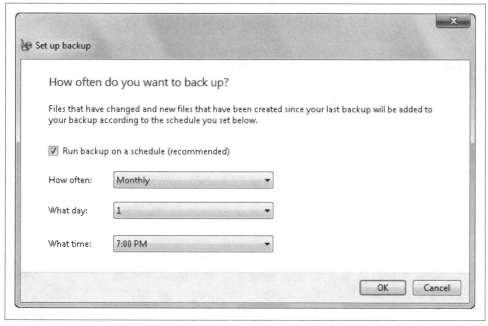

Figure 21-11. Setting how often backups should be created

8. Click Change Schedule. On the "How often do you want to create a backup?" page, shown in Figure 21-11, use the options provided to set the desired backup schedule. The "How often" selection list lets you choose Daily, Weekly, or Monthly as the run schedule. If you choose a weekly or monthly run schedule, you'll need to set the day of the week or day of the month using the "What day" selection list. Finally, the "What time" selection list lets you set the time of the day when automated backup should occur. Be sure to pick a time when your computer will typically be on, and a time that the backup process will cause the least disruption to your work.

9. If you are creating the initial backup, click "Save settings and run backup" to save your settings and then have Windows create the initial backup. If you've already created the initial backup for the computer, you'll have the "Save settings and exit" option instead.

10. As shown in Figure 21-12, you can track the backup progress on the Backup and Restore page. You'll also see any errors that are generated as a result of this backup or future backups. If an error occurs, you'll have troubleshooting options. For example, if the backup fails because there is not enough free space, you'll see a related error and will be able to click the Troubleshoot button to display trouble-shooting options, which should include an option to try to run the backup again and an option to change the backup settings.

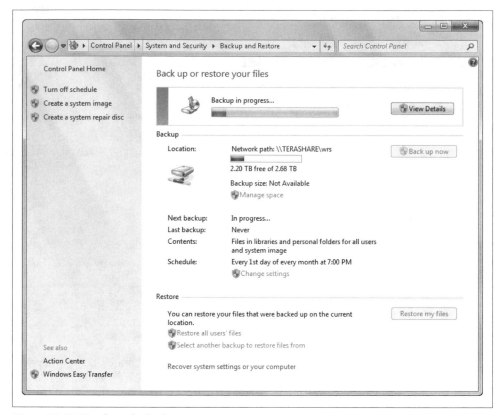

Figure 21-12. Tracking the backup progress

 Insufficient storage space is one of the most common errors you'll see. You'll see this error if the backup device you've selected doesn't have enough free space to either start or complete the backup. For example, although the backup program will let you use a device with removable storage as a backup location, the device might not have enough free space to start or complete the backup.

To modify the backup schedule or configuration, follow these steps:

1. In Control Panel, under the System and Security heading, click the "Back up your computer" link.

2. On the Backup and Restore page, click "Change settings" and then complete steps 3–9 of the previous procedure.

Once you've configured automated backups, you can run a backup manually to add new or updated files to your backup. To do this, complete the following steps:

1. In Control Panel, under the System and Security heading, click the "Back up your computer" link.
2. On the Backup and Restore page, click "Back up now."

To manually create a system image backup, follow these steps:

1. In Control Panel, under the System and Security heading, click the "Back up your computer" link.
2. On the Backup and Restore page, click "Create a system image" in the left pane.
3. On the "Where do you want to save the backup?" page, use the options provided to specify a backup location. Click Next.
4. On the "Which drives do you want to include in the backup?" page, the computer's system drive is selected by default. You cannot change this selection, but you can add other drives to the backup image by selecting the related checkboxes. Click Next to continue.
5. Click Start Backup to start the backup.

You can turn automated backups on and off by following these steps:

1. In Control Panel, under the System and Security heading, click the "Back up your computer" link.
2. If automated backups are on and you want to turn them off, click the "Turn off schedule" in the left pane. To protect your personal data, you'll need to create backups manually or reenable automated backups.
3. If automated backups are off and you want to turn them on, click the "Turn on schedule" option next to the Schedule entry. The settings you configured previously are used for automated backups.

When you are using automated backups, you can always view the status of the last backup by clicking the "Manage space" option on the Backup and Restore page. Clicking "Manage space" opens the "Manage Windows Backup disk space" dialog box, shown in Figure 21-13. This dialog box allows you to do the following:

- View the space usage summary for the backup location, including used, available and total disk space
- Browse the backup location by clicking the Browse link
- Manage data files by clicking View Backups and then selecting backup sets to delete
- Change settings for system image backup to save space

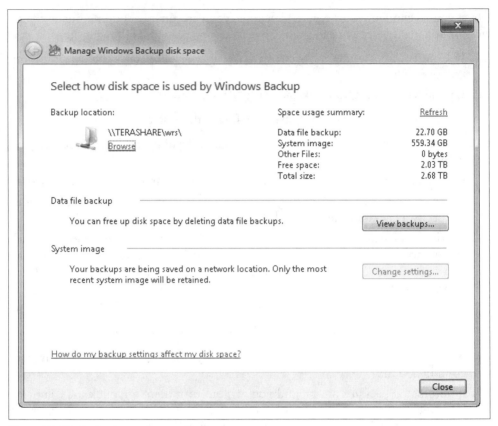

Figure 21-13. Reviewing and managing backups

Recovering After a Crash or Other Problem

Windows 7 includes a number of features to help you recover your computer and your data in case disaster strikes. The recovery features to use are as follows:

Restore points
Use restore points to fix problems and undo changes to the operating system, programs, and devices.

Previous versions
Use previous versions of files to help you recover files that were accidentally deleted or incorrectly edited.

File recovery from backup
Use file recovery from backup to recover files when previous versions aren't available.

Force restart or shutdown
> Use this technique to recover after your computer hangs so that you can restart or shut down.

Failed resume recovery
> Use this technique to recover after a failed resume.

Startup repair
> Use this technique to repair system files so that you can start the operating system.

System image recovery
> Use this technique to recover Windows and install programs in the event that restore points and startup repair do not resolve your problem.

System repair disc
> Use this technique to recover your computer if the Windows Recovery Environment partition has been corrupted or you cannot otherwise access the repair tools.

Operating system reinstall
> Use this technique to reinstall the operating system in the event that no other recovery technique works.

Table 21-1 provides an overview of problems you may have that force you to use recovery techniques, and the techniques you should use to resolve the problem.

Table 21-1. Recovery techniques

Issue	Recovery technique
Need to recover pictures, music, video, email, documents, and other types of important personal files	1. Use Previous Versions. 2. Use File Recovery from Backup.
Need to resolve resume, restart, or shutdown issues	1. Use Force Restart or Shutdown, or use Failed Resume Recovery.
Need to resolve startup problem due to corrupt system files	1. Use Startup Repair. 2. Use system image recovery. 3. Use operating system reinstall.
Need to recover by undoing changes to the operating system, programs, and devices	1. Use Restore Points. 2. Use system image recovery. 3. Use operating system reinstall.
Need to recover but the recovery tools are not available	1. Use System Repair disc.

Recovering Using Restore Points

You use restore points to fix problems and undo changes to the operating system, programs, and devices. When selecting a restore point, keep in mind that any programs that were added to your computer since the restore point was made will be deleted and any programs that were removed since the restore point was made will be restored.

If the restore point doesn't resolve your problem, you can undo it (in most cases) or choose another restore point. However, if you started the computer in Safe Mode or are using the Recovery Environment, the System Restore cannot be undone.

If you cannot start your computer, you can try to access System Restore in the Windows Recovery Environment (Windows RE). For more information, see "Repairing a Computer to Enable Startup" on page 840, later in this chapter.

 Although using a restore point does not affect personal data, user accounts and passwords on the computer can be affected. If you or any other user on your computer changed passwords recently, you may want to create a Password Reset disk before trying to restore the computer.

If you can start your computer and log on, you can try to recover the computer using a restore point by following these steps:

1. Click Start→Control Panel→System and Security.
2. Click the "Restore your computer to an earlier time" link under the Action Center heading.
3. Click Open System Restore. This starts the System Restore Wizard. Click Next.
4. System Restore recommends one or more recent restore points, as shown in Figure 21-14. Restore points are listed by date, time, description, and type. To get more information and access additional options, do the following:

   • To see additional restore points that are available, click Show More Restore Points.

   • To determine what programs the restore will affect, click the restore point and then click Scan For Affected Programs.

 Typically, it will take System Restore several minutes to scan the restore point and determine the affected programs. You'll then see two separate lists. The first list shows you programs and drivers that will be deleted if you apply the restore point. The second list shows you programs and drivers that might be restored if you apply the restore point.

5. Click the restore point you want to use. Restore points you've created have the type *Manual*. Restore points created by Windows 7 have the type *System*.
6. Click Next and then click Finish. When prompted, click Yes to confirm that you want to restore the computer's system files and settings using the selected restore point. Do not interrupt the restore process once it has started.

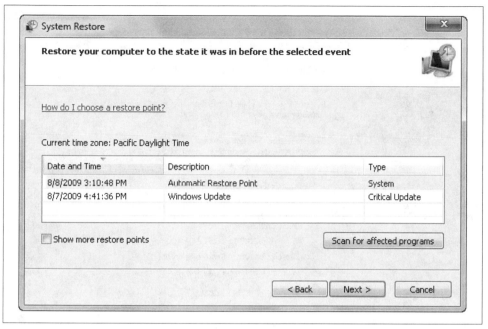

<figure>

Date and Time	Description	Type
8/8/2009 3:10:48 PM	Automatic Restore Point	System
8/7/2009 4:41:36 PM	Windows Update	Critical Update

</figure>

Figure 21-14. Choosing a restore point

7. System Restore will then prepare to restore your computer. During the restoration, System Restore restarts your computer. During startup, System Restore uses the settings from restore points you've selected.

8. After your computer restarts and you log in, a System Restore dialog box is displayed. Read the message provided and then click Close.

If Windows 7 isn't working properly after the restore operation, you can apply a different restore point or try to reverse the restore operation by following these steps:

1. Click Start→Control Panel→System and Security.

2. Click the "Restore your computer to an earlier time" link under the Action Center heading.

3. Click Open System Restore. On the "Restore system files and settings" page, shown in Figure 21-15, do one of the following:

   • Select "Undo System Restore," click Next and then follow the prompts to recover the system to its previous state.

   • Select "Choose a different restore point," click Next and then follow the prompts to select a different restore point.

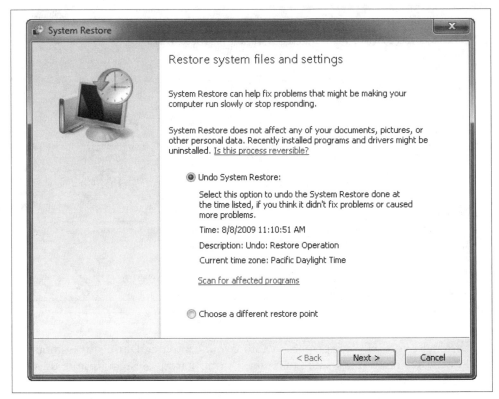

Figure 21-15. Undoing a restore point

Restoring Previous Versions of Files

Windows 7 tracks changes in files and folders using Previous Versions. When you configure System Protection for a disk, System Protection creates previous versions of files and folders automatically as part of restore points. Any personal file or folder that was modified since the last restore point is saved and made available as a previous version.

 Typically, restore points are made once a day. If you modify a file more than once in the same day, only the version of the file that was current at the time of the restore point is saved as a previous version.

Previous versions are created for pictures, music, videos, email, documents, and other types of personal files. Previous versions are not created for files and folders that the operating system uses.

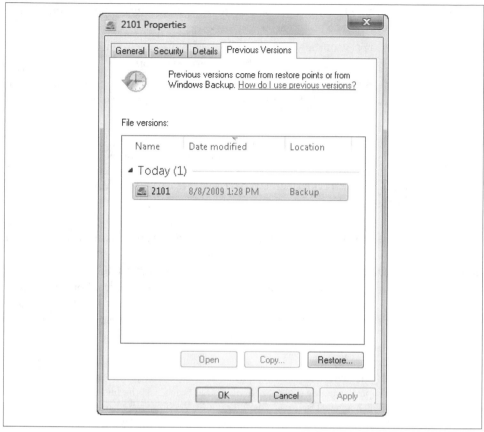

Figure 21-16. Checking for previous versions

You can use previous versions of files to restore files that were inadvertently changed, deleted, or damaged. Although System Protection creates previous versions daily for all drives being monitored by System Protection, only those versions of files that are actually different from the current version are stored as previous versions. You can enable or disable previous versions by enabling or disabling System Protection on a particular drive.

Accessing previous versions of files and folders is a snap. To view previous versions of a file or folder, right-click the file or folder and then select "Restore previous versions." This opens the file or folder's Properties dialog box to the Previous Versions tab, as shown in Figure 21-16. Your computer will then search the available restore points and applicable backups for previous versions of the selected folder or file. When previous versions are available, the Previous Versions tab lists the previous versions of a file by name, date, and location and previous versions of folders by name and date. Select the previous version you want to work with and then click:

- Open to open the selected previous version. By opening the file you can ensure it's the version you want to restore.

- Copy to create a copy of the selected previous version. By copying the file, you can keep the current version and the selected previous version.

- Restore to revert the file or folder to the selected previous version. By restoring the file or folder, you overwrite the current version. The restore cannot be undone.

 Although you can restore previous versions of files from backup locations, you cannot restore previous versions of folders from backup. Additionally, only the Restore option is available with previous versions of files that are in backup locations. You cannot open or copy files created by Windows Backup.

If no previous versions are found, you'll see a message stating this. In this case, you may need to check your computer's configuration to ensure that System Protection is monitoring the related disk. Keep in mind that System Protection does not create previous versions of offline files cached on your computer or system files. For offline files, previous versions may be available on the server where the file is stored. Changes made to system files are tracked as part of restore points, and you must recover the computer to the restore point to go back to a previous state.

 If the folder in which the file was stored has been deleted, you must open the Properties dialog box for the folder that contained the file or folder that was deleted. Use this folder's Previous Versions tab to restore the folder and then access the file or folder to recover the previous version of the file you are looking for.

Recovering Files from Backup

Windows 7 allows you to recover individual files from backup locations using the Previous Versions features as discussed in the previous section. You also can recover files using Windows Backup. To recover files using Windows Backup, follow these steps:

1. In Control Panel, under the System and Security heading, click the "Back up your computer" link.

2. In Backup and Restore, click Restore My Files to restore your files or click Restore All Users' Files to restore the files of any user.

3. On the "Select the files and folders to restore" page, shown in Figure 21-17, use the following techniques to select the files and folders to restore, and then click Next:

   - To restore individual files, click the "Browse for files" button. In the "Browse the backup for files" dialog box, you'll see a list of all the folders and files in the

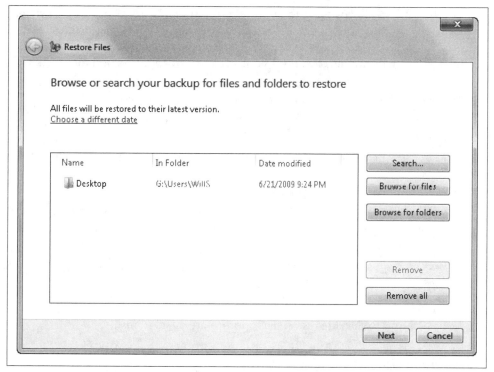

Figure 21-17. Selecting the files and folders to restore

backup. Select files to restore and then click Add Files. Repeat this process to select other individual files to restore.

- To restore folders and all their contents, click the "Browse for folders" button. In the "Browse the backup for folders" dialog box, you'll see a list of all the folders in the backup. Select a folder to restore and then click Add. Repeat this process to select other folders to restore.

- To search for a particular file or folder, click the Search button. In the "Search for files to restore" dialog box, type all or part of the filename or folder to search for, and then click Search. In the Search results, select the files or folders to restore, and then click Add. Repeat this process to search for other files and folders to restore.

 If the items you want to restore are stored in the current backup location, you can use the options in the Restore Files window to select items to restore. To restore files from a different backup, click "Choose a different date." In the Restore Files dialog box, you'll see a list of all backups by backup period. Use the Show Backups From list to select how far back the backup you want to use was made. Click the backup you want to restore files from and then click OK to return to the "Browse or Search" page.

4. On the "Where do you want to save the restored files?" page, the "In the original location" option is selected by default. You use this option to restore files to their original location. To restore files and folders to an alternative location, select "In the following location," click Browse, select a restore location, and then click OK.

5. Click Restore to restore the selected files and folders. If there is already a file or folder with the same name in the location you've selected, you can:

   • Overwrite the current version with the restored version by clicking Copy and Replace.

   • Keep the current version and discard the restored version by clicking "Don't copy."

   • Keep both versions by clicking the "Copy, but keep" option. The new filename will be the same as the old filename, but with a numeric suffix, indicating the version increment.

 If you want to use the same response for all conflicts, select the "Do this for all conflicts" checkbox before you click an option.

6. Your files and folders are restored as appropriate. Click Finish.

Resolving Restart or Shutdown Issues

The normal way to shut down or restart Windows 7 is to click Start, click the Options button to the right of the power and lock buttons, and then click Restart or Shut Down as appropriate. There are times, however, when Windows 7 won't shut down or restart normally and you must resolve the problem that is preventing the operating system from shutting down or restarting. To resolve shutdown or startup problems, follow these steps:

1. Press Ctrl-Alt-Delete to display the Windows screen and then click Start Task Manager. If your computer doesn't respond and you've waited a sufficient amount of time for it to recover by itself or complete any pending tasks, press and hold the computer's power button to force a shutdown.

2. In Task Manager, click the Application tab, as shown in Figure 21-18. Look for an application that is not responding. If all programs appear to be running normally, skip to step 5.

3. Click the application that is not responding, and then click End Task.

4. If the application fails to respond to the request, you'll see a prompt that allows you to end the application immediately or cancel the end-task request. Click End Now.

Figure 21-18. Checking for unresponsive programs

5. Try shutting down or restarting the computer. Press Ctrl-Alt-Delete, click the Shutdown button or click the Shutdown Options button (the arrow to the right of the Shutdown button), and then click Restart.

6. If the preceding steps don't work, perform a hard shutdown by pressing and holding the computer's power button or by unplugging the computer.

 If you force the computer to shut down, the Windows Error Recovery screen should be displayed automatically the next time you start the computer. You then have the option of starting the computer in one of several Safe Modes or using normal startup. After you start your computer, you may want to run Check Disk to check for errors and problems that might have been caused by the hard shutdown.

Recovering from a Failed Resume

When your computer enters sleep mode or hibernates, Windows 7 creates a snapshot of the current state of the computer. With sleep mode, this snapshot is created in memory and then read from memory when you wake the computer. With hibernate mode, this snapshot is written to disk and then read from disk when you wake the computer. Windows Resume Loader handles both the sleep and the hibernate operations.

Your computer may have a problem with resume for a variety of reasons, including errors in the snapshot, physical errors in memory, and physical disk errors. If there is a problem resuming after waking the computer, Windows Resume Loader will prompt you with a warning message similar to the following:

```
Windows Resume Loader
The last attempt to restart the system from its previous location
failed. Attempt to restart again?

Continue with system restart
Delete restoration data and proceed to system boot.

Enter=choose
```

This prompt gives you two options for resuming:

- Continue with system restart.
- Delete restoration data and proceed to system boot.

If you select "Continue with system restart," Windows Resume Loader will attempt to reload the system state again. If you select "Delete restoration data and proceed to system boot," Windows Resume Loader will delete the saved state of the computer and restart the computer. Although a full restart will typically resolve any problem, you'll lose any work you hadn't saved before the computer entered sleep or hibernate mode.

Repairing a Computer to Enable Startup

Windows 7 includes the Startup Repair tool (StR) to automatically detect corrupted system files during startup and guide you through automated or manual recovery. Once started, StR attempts to determine the cause of the startup failure by analyzing startup logs and error reports, then attempts to fix the problem automatically. If StR is unable to resolve the problem, it restores the system to the last known working state and then provides diagnostics information and support options for further troubleshooting.

When you install Windows 7, a Window Recovery Environment (Windows RE) partition is created automatically. Because of this, note the following:

- If your computer fails to shutdown properly, the Windows Error Recovery screen is shown automatically the next time you start the computer. You then have the option of starting the computer in one of several Safe Modes or using normal startup.
- If your computer fails to start, the Windows Error Recovery screen is shown automatically the next time you try to start the computer. You then have the option of running the Startup Repair tool or using normal startup.

If the Windows RE partition has been corrupted, you won't be able to access any of the repair tools. To safeguard your computer against this possibility, you can create a System Repair disc as discussed in "Safeguarding Your Computer from a Corrupted Windows RE" on page 844.

You can manually launch the Startup Repair tool by following these steps:

1. If the computer is running but has started with errors, click Start. On the Start menu, click the Shut Down options button and then click Restart.

2. During startup you can access the Windows RE, press F8 to access the Advanced Boot Options screen. If the computer has multiple operating systems, you'll see the Windows Boot Manager screen; select the operating system to work with, and then press F8.

3. On the Advanced Boot Options menu, use the arrow keys to select Repair Your Computer, and then press Enter.

4. The computer will load the Windows RE. In the System Recovery Options dialog box, select a language and keyboard layout, and then click Next.

5. To access recovery options, you need to logon using a local administrator account. Select the local administrator to log on as, type the password for this account, and then click OK.

6. In the System Recovery Options dialog box, note the location of the operating system, and then choose Startup Repair.

The Startup Repair tool checks for problems preventing your computer from starting. If problems are found, the tool tries to repair them to enable startup. The automated troubleshooting and repair process can take several minutes. During the first phase of the repair, you can click Cancel to exit.

If Startup Repair doesn't find common problems, you see the "Do you want to restore your computer using System Restore?" dialog box. Clicking Restore starts System Restore. Clicking Cancel returns to the startup repair process and the Startup Repair tool will attempt to make repairs using advanced techniques. During this advanced phase, you may not be able to click Cancel to exit the repair process.

If Startup Repair is successful, your computer will start. If Startup repair was unable to find or correct problems, you'll see a note about this and will be able to send more information about the problem to help Microsoft find solutions in the future. Select the option to send or to not send information to Microsoft. You'll then return to the Startup Repair dialog box.

To access advanced repair options, click the related link and follow the procedure discussed in the next section, "Recovering Your Computer Using Windows RE" on page 843, to continue troubleshooting. Otherwise, click Finish. You may want to disconnect any external devices that you've recently connected to your computer and then try to start your computer again. Otherwise, ask your network administrator for help or your computer manufacturer.

Corrupted system files aren't the only types of problems that can prevent proper startup of the operating system. Many other types of problems can occur, but most of these problems occur because something on the system has changed. Often you can resolve startup issues using safe mode to recover or troubleshoot system problems. When you are finished using safe mode, be sure to restart the computer using a normal startup. You will then be able to use the computer as you normally would.

You can restart a system in safe mode by completing the following steps:

1. If the computer is running but has started with errors, click Start, then click the Options button to the right of the power and lock buttons, and click Shut Down.

2. Start the computer. During startup, press F8 to access the Advanced Options screen. If the computer has multiple operating systems, you'll see the Windows Boot Manager screen; select the operating system to work with, and then press F8.

3. Use the arrow keys to select the safe mode you want to use and then press Enter. The safe mode option you use depends on the type of problem you're experiencing. In most cases, you'll want to use one of the following options:

   Safe Mode
   > Windows loads only basic files, services, and drivers during the initialization sequence. The drivers loaded include the mouse, monitor, keyboard, mass storage, and base video. No networking services or drivers are started.

   Safe Mode with Networking
   > Windows loads only basic files, services, and drivers during the initialization sequence. The drivers loaded include the mouse, monitor, keyboard, mass storage, and base video. After the initialization sequence, Windows loads the networking components.

   Safe Mode with Command Prompt
   > Windows loads basic files, services, and drivers, and then starts a command prompt instead of the Windows 7 graphical interface. No networking services or related drivers are started.

   Last Known Good Configuration
   > Windows starts the computer in Safe Mode using registry information that Windows 7 saved at the last shutdown. Only the HKEY_CURRENT_CONFIG (HKCC) hive is loaded. This registry hive stores information about the hardware configuration with which you previously and successfully started the computer.

4. If a problem doesn't reappear when you start in Safe Mode, you can eliminate the default settings and basic device drivers as possible causes. If a newly added device or updated driver is causing problems, you can use Safe Mode to remove the device or reverse the update.

5. If you are still having a problem starting the computer normally and you suspect that problems with hardware, software, or settings are to blame, remain in Safe Mode and then try using System Restore to undo previous changes.

Recovering Your Computer Using Windows RE

When you install Windows 7, a Window RE partition is created automatically for your computer. You can use Windows RE to repair the computer by following these steps:

1. During startup, press F8 to access the Advanced Boot Options screen. If the computer has multiple operating systems, you'll see the Windows Boot Manager screen; select the operating system to use and then press F8.
2. On the Advanced Boot Options menu, use the arrow keys to select Repair Your Computer, and then press Enter.
3. The computer will load the Windows RE. If the Windows RE fails to load, see the following section, "Safeguarding Your Computer from a Corrupted Windows RE" on page 844, for more recovery information.
4. In the System Recovery Options dialog box, select a language and keyboard layout, and then click Next.
5. To access recovery options, you need to log on using a local administrator account. Select the local administrator to log on as, type the password for this account, and then click OK.
6. In the System Recovery Options dialog box, note the location of the operating system, and then choose a recovery option:

   Startup Repair
   Launches the Startup Repair tool to repair problems that are preventing Windows from starting.

   System Restore
   Runs System Restore so that you can restore Windows to an earlier point in time.

   System Image Recovery
   Allows you to recover Windows using a system image created previously.

   Windows Memory Diagnostics
   Runs Windows Memory Diagnostics so that you can check for memory problems.

   Command Prompt
   Opens a command prompt so you can work with the commands and tools available in the recovery environment.

When you cannot recover Windows any other way, your final recovery option is to reinstall Windows 7. Before you do this, try to repair the computer by using Startup Repair and System Restore. If these repair techniques do not work, you should try to recover the computer using a system image.

Safeguarding Your Computer from a Corrupted Windows RE

If the Windows RE partition has been corrupted or removed, you won't be able to access any of the repair tools. To safeguard your computer against this possibility, you should create a System Repair disc. The repair disc contains a boot image that allows your computer to access a Windows Preinstallation Environment (Windows PE) that includes a Boot Manager and generalized Boot Configuration Data (BCD). The disc also includes tools for automatically fixing the boot sector on your computer's system volume.

To create a repair disc, follow these steps:

1. In Control Panel, under the System and Security heading, click the "Back up your computer" link.

2. On the Backup and Restore page in Control Panel, click "Create a system repair disc" in the left pane.

3. When prompted insert a blank CD or DVD into your computer's read-writable CD/DVD drive and then click Create Disc. If your computer has multiple read-writable CD/DVD drives, you can specify which drive to use.

4. After Backup and Restore prepares and creates the recovery disc, click Close and then click OK. Eject and label the disc "Repair Disc Windows 7 32-bit" or "Repair Disc Windows 7 64-bit" as appropriate.

The repair disc is architecture-specific but not necessarily computer-specific. Typically, you can use any 32-bit repair disc to repair any 32-bit Windows 7 installation and any 64-bit repair disc to repair any 64-bit Windows 7 Installation. So if you encounter a problem and aren't able to access the recovery tools on your computer, you can create a repair disc on another computer with the same architecture as yours and then use this disc for recovery.

To use the repair disc, insert the repair disc into your computer's primary CD/DVD drive and then boot your computer from the disc. You then be able to access the recovery environment as discussed previously under "Recovering Your Computer Using Windows RE" on page 843. If your computer doesn't allow booting from a disc, you'll need to change the boot options in firmware and then repeat this step.

Recovering Your Computer from Backup

System image backups contain all the information needed to recover the Windows operating system. This means system image backups contain your programs, any files used by the operating system, all drivers, and all registry settings. You can use a system image backup to recover the operating system and your programs to the point in time the backup was created.

You can recover the Windows operating system using a system image by following these steps.

1. If the computer is running but has started with errors, click Start. On the Start menu, click the Shut Down options button and then click Restart.

2. During startup you can access the Windows RE, press F8 to access the Advanced Boot Options screen. If the computer has multiple operating systems, you'll see the Windows Boot Manager screen, select the operating system to work with, and then press F8.

3. On the Advanced Boot Options menu, use the arrow keys to select Repair Your Computer, and then press Enter.

4. The computer will load the Windows RE. In the System Recovery Options dialog box, select a language and keyboard layout, and then click Next.

5. To access recovery options, you need to log on using a local administrator account. Select the local administrator to log on as, type the password for this account, and then click OK.

6. In the System Recovery Options dialog box, select System Image Recovery, and then click Next. Follow the prompts to recover the operating system.

Reinstalling Windows 7

When all else fails and you cannot recover Windows in any other way, you can reinstall Windows 7. This procedure follows the same steps you would follow if performing a clean install of the operating system. Reinstalling Windows 7 will result in the loss of all user settings and programs. After reinstalling the operating system, you will need to reconfigure the computer and reinstall your applications.

Getting Help and Giving Others Assistance

Windows 7 offers two similar features for getting help and remotely accessing computers: Remote Assistance and Remote Desktop. When you have a problem with your computer, you can use Remote Assistance to ask an expert for help. You can also use Remote Assistance to give others assistance. Remote Desktop is a feature you can use to connect to a computer from another location and then work with the computer as though you were sitting at the keyboard.

Getting Help from Another Person

When you want to get help from others, you must create a Remote Assistance invitation and then make this invitation available to the person from whom you want help. Although there are multiple ways to create and send invitations, the easiest and most reliable way to do this is to create an email invitation. As long as you've installed and configured an email program, such as Windows Live Mail or Office Outlook, you'll be able to send an email invitation.

You can create a Remote Assistance invitation and send it to your helper by following these steps:

1. In Control Panel, under the System And Security heading, click "Find and fix problems." In the left pane of the Troubleshooting window, click "Get help from a friend." Alternatively, click Start→All Programs→Maintenance→Windows Remote Assistance.

2. If the computer is not configured to send invitations, click Repair. After Windows Network Diagnostics analyses the problem, click "Try these repairs as an administrator" and then click "Close the troubleshooter." You will then need to repeat step 1.

3. On the "Use Remote Assistance" page, click "Invite someone to help you" and then click "Use e-mail to send an invitation."

4. On the "Choose a password" page, enter and confirm a secure password that is at least six characters long. This password is used by the person you are inviting and is valid only for this Remote Assistance session.

5. When you click Next, Windows 7 starts your default mail program and creates an email message with the invitation.

6. In the To field, type the email address of the person you are inviting and then click Send.

Once you've sent the invitation via email, the Windows Remote Assistance dialog box is displayed. This dialog box provides the following options:

Stop sharing
  Starts or stops sharing control of the computer with the helper.

Pauses
  Pauses or resumes sharing with the helper.

Chat
  Opens a chat window for sending messages between you and the helper.

Settings
  Allows you to configure the session settings.

Troubleshoot
> Allows you to troubleshoot Remote Assistance.

Help
> Allows you to open Windows Help and Support.

As long as you've allowed remote control of your computer, the helper will have a similar set of controls and will be able to access your desktop and Start menu, allowing the remote helper to fix your computer much as if he or she were sitting at the keyboard. If you haven't allowed remote control of your computer, the helper will only be able to view your desktop and guide you through chat.

 For Windows Vista and Windows 7, Remote Assistance has been enhanced in several ways. First, two people can now simultaneously connect to a computer for troubleshooting. Second, if troubleshooting requires that the computer be restarted, the Remote Assistance session is reestablished automatically after the computer reboots.

Giving Other People Assistance

Just as you can use Remote Assistance to get help, you can use Remote Assistance to help other people. Have the person send you a Remote Assistance invitation via email. When you receive the email, double-click the invitation attached to the message. You'll then see a Windows Remote Assistance dialog box with a view of the other person's computer. As long as the person has allowed remote control, the view will have a similar set of controls as previously discussed, and will provide complete access to the person's desktop and Start menu, allowing you to fix the person's problem much like you could if you were sitting at the keyboard.

If you know that a user is having problems with his or her computer, you can follow these steps to offer remote assistance rather than waiting for an invitation:

1. Click Start, type `msra`, and then press Enter.
2. In the Windows Remote Assistance wizard, click "Help someone who has invited you."
3. Click the "Advanced connection option for help desk" link.
4. Type the name or IP address of the computer you want to assist, and then click Next to connect to the computer.

Connecting to Your Computer Remotely

Sometimes you may want to be able to connect remotely to your computer. For example, if you are at home, you may want to be able to access files on your work computer. Or if you are at work, on vacation, or out wherever, you may want to be able to access files on your home computer. To access your computer remotely, you can use Remote

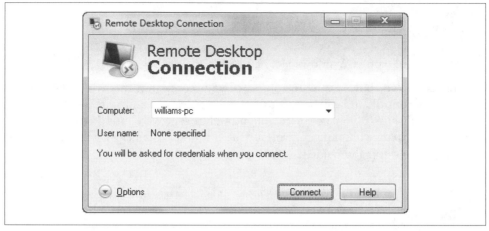

Figure 21-19. Connecting to a remote computer

Desktop, as long as you've configured port forwarding on your router for the port 3389 and opened this port on your firewall for Remote Desktop connections.

You can make a Remote Desktop connection to your computer by following these steps:

1. Click Start→All Programs→Accessories→Remote Desktop Connection. This displays the Remote Desktop Connection dialog box, shown in Figure 21-19.

2. In the Computer field, type the name of the remote computer or its IP address. For a connection over the Internet, in most cases you'll need to use the IP address (when connecting to your home computer from other places, this is the public IP address assigned by your ISP).

3. Click Connect. Your screen will go black for a moment except for a title bar at the top.

4. When you see the logon dialog box, enter the username and password of an account that is a member of the Remote Desktop Users group, and then click OK.

5. If the account is already logged on to the remote computer, the desktop on the computer will lock and you'll then see the current desktop as though you were sitting at the keyboard.

6. If someone is already logged on to the remote computer, you'll see a prompt telling you that the other person will be disconnected. Click Yes to continue. The user will then see a prompt asking if he or she wants to allow the connection. If the remote user clicks Yes, he or she will be logged off similar to what happens when you use fast user switching. The user can resume that logon session later.

When you've connected successfully, you'll see the Remote Desktop window on the selected computer, and you'll be able to work with resources on the computer. Although you are using the remote computer, the remote computer shows the welcome screen with your account listed as being logged on and locked. A person with physical access to the remote computer cannot see what you're doing at the local computer. Keep in mind that firewalls and Network Address Translation (NAT) can prevent successful remote desktop connections. Transmission Control Protocol (TCP) port 3389 must be open to any firewall between your local computer and the remote computer.

Troubleshooting Windows 7 Programs and Features

Windows 7 has so many features and components that you are bound to run into problems occasionally that I don't address in other sections of this book. When you run into these problems, please refer to this section for possible solutions for everything from installation to playback in Windows Media Player.

Resolving Problems with Programs and Features

Table 21-2 provides an extensive list of problems you may encounter while working with Windows 7. The table is organized alphabetically by program or issue, followed by details on problems you may encounter and possible resolutions to those problems. In some cases, the resolution details will also point to a specific page within the Microsoft Knowledge Base where you can look to find more information.

Table 21-2. Troubleshooting Windows 7 programs and features

Program/ Issue	Problem/Resolution
16-bit DOS-based programs	16-bit programs will not run under 64-bit Windows. On 32-bit Windows, some 16-bit DOS-based programs and the Command Prompt will not run in full-screen mode in Windows 7. This issue occurs because Windows 7 device drivers do not support running all of the DOS video modes. The device drivers are based on the Windows Display Driver Model (WDDM). To resolve this problem, you may need to install a Windows XP version of the video drivers for your video adapter.
Activation expires	You see an error stating "Your activation period has expired" or that you have a "non-genuine version of Windows 7 installed." If you have not activated Windows 7 in the time allowed or you are running a nongenuine version of Windows 7, Windows 7 will run in a reduced functionality mode. If you modify the computer hardware so that Windows 7 determines that it is running on a different computer, Windows 7 will also run in a reduced functionality mode. You'll need to activate and validate Windows 7 as necessary to resume full functionality mode.
Activation fails	Activation of Windows 7 fails over the Internet. If you connect to the Internet through a proxy server where Basic authentication is enabled, you will not be able to activate Windows 7. Change the authentication method. Alternatively, when the Windows Activation Wizard prompts you, click Use the Automated Phone System and then activate Windows 7 over the telephone.
Administrator account	The Administrator account does not appear on the Windows 7 Welcome screen. In Windows 7, the built-in Administrator account is disabled by default and you cannot use it to log on to the computer in safe mode. However, during an upgrade, if the built-in Administrator account is the only active local Administrator account, Windows 7 leaves the built-in Administrator account enabled and puts this account into Admin Approval mode.

Program/ Issue	Problem/Resolution
ATM network adapters	You receive an error message when you start Windows 7 after you install an ATM network adapter. This error occurs because Windows 7 does not support ATM.
Audio playback	You lose audio playback after you unplug a USB audio device, such as a microphone or headphones. This problem occurs because Windows Media Player does not detect that the USB audio device has been removed. To resolve this issue, stop and restart the media player or restart the computer after you unplug a USB audio device.
BitLocker Drive Encryption	You see a "BitLocker Drive Encryption key needed" error message when your computer resumes from hibernation. This occurs because the BitLocker Drive Encryption feature expects the USB key to be inserted prior to you waking the computer. As prompted, insert the USB key and then press the Esc key to reboot. To avoid this problem in the future, insert the USB key prior to waking the computer.
Burning discs	When you try to burn a disc, Windows Media Player doesn't recognize your DVD-RAM. This error occurs because you can't use Windows Media Player to burn DVD-RAM discs. You'll need to use Windows Explorer to burn DVD-RAM discs.
Computer names	After you change the name of a computer, other computers can continue to access the computer by using the previous name of the computer. This occurs because the computer name is stored in the DNS cache. At an elevated command prompt (Start→All Programs→Accessories, then right-click on Command Prompt and choose Run As Administrator), flush the DNS cache by typing `ipconfig /flushdns`.
Connecting computers	You cannot use a serial cable connection to connect a Windows XP–based computer to a Windows 7–based computer. To work around this issue, connect the computers using a network connection with Ethernet cables.
DHCP	Windows 7 cannot obtain an IP address from a router or non–Microsoft DHCP server. This can occur due to a design difference in the way DHCP is implemented. See *http://support.microsoft.com/kb/928233/en-us* for more information.
Digital still cameras	A digital still camera is not recognized. Windows 7 uses the Windows Image Acquisition (WIA) standard instead of the Windows Portable Devices (WPD) standard to import pictures and videos. To resolve this problem, configure the camera to use the Picture Transfer Protocol (PTP) standard instead of the WIA standard. See the owner's manual for the camera to configure the camera to use the PTP standard.
Digital video cameras	When you are changing modes, Windows Live Movie Maker may incorrectly detect the mode of a digital video camera. This can occur if you quickly switch between the Camera, Off, VCR, and Memory modes. To avoid this problem, pause momentarily after switching from one mode to another and before switching to another mode.
Disk drives with large sectors	Windows 7 supports large-sector hard disk drives. Newer hard disk drives may contain physical sector sizes that are larger than the traditional 512 bytes per sector. If the drive uses an emulation mode to support these large-sector sizes, your applications should continue to work without problems. If the drive doesn't use an emulation mode, some of your applications may not work. See *http://support.microsoft.com/kb/923332/en-us* for more information.
EAP-MD5	Extensible Authentication Protocol-Message Digest 5 (EAP-MD5) doesn't work. In Windows 7, EAP-MD5 has been deprecated and is not enabled. You can reenable support for EAP-MD5. See *http://support.microsoft.com/kb/922574/en-us* for more information.
Favorites in Internet Explorer	In Internet Explorer, Windows 7 does not let you type a favorite name that is longer than 227 characters. Make sure that the name of the new favorite is no longer than 227 characters.

Program/ Issue	Problem/Resolution
Fingerprint readers	You cannot use a fingerprint reader or another biometric device to log on after you upgrade to Windows 7. Windows 7 does not support the Graphical Identification and Authentication (GINA) components that the device requires. Install drivers for the device that are compatible with Windows 7.
FireWire devices	In Windows Explorer or other interfaces, you cannot see a specific FireWire (IEEE 1394a) device that you've connected to the computer. To resolve this issue, see *http://support.microsoft.com/kb/927827/en-us* for more information.
GINA/biometrics	Custom GINA modules do not work after you upgrade your computer to Windows 7. This occurs because GINA functionality that existed in earlier versions of Windows is replaced by a credential provider model in Windows 7. See *http://support.microsoft.com/kb/925520/en-us* for more information.
Help (*.hlp*) files	Windows 7 won't display Help (*.hlp*) files. The Windows Help program (*WinHlp32.exe*) is not included in Windows 7. Windows Help is no longer supported. See *http://support.microsoft.com/kb/917607/en-us* for more information.
Hosts and Lmhosts	You cannot modify the *Hosts* or *Lmhosts* file in Windows 7. This occurs because the program you are using must be in elevated mode to save the edited files. Before opening the *Hosts* or *Lmhosts* file, right-click the program shortcut and then select "Run as administrator."
Installation	Installation media is not recognized when you try to install Windows 7. If the media is damaged, you'll need to obtain replacement media. Otherwise, make sure that the CD or DVD drive is configured as a startup device in firmware and that you are inserting the media into the appropriate CD or DVD drive.
Installation	During installation, you are unable to select the hard disk you want to use. This issue can occur if the hard disk partition contains an invalid byte offset value. To resolve this issue, you'll need to follow the procedure discussed in the section "Removing Disk Partitions During Installation" on page 854, later in this chapter.
Installation	During installation of Windows 7, you see an "Error: uncaught exception" message. This error can occur if there are problems with the selected disk partitions. To resolve this problem, you'll need to remove the partitions, as discussed previously.
Installation	During installation of Windows 7, you cannot select or format a hard disk partition. If the partition is formatted with FAT32 or has other incompatible settings, this may be causing the problem. To work around this issue, you may want to boot to the current operating system, convert the partition to NTFS, and then restart the installation. As this could also be due to a problem with the drivers for the hard disk, you may need to boot to the current operating system, update the disk drivers, and then restart the installation.
Installation	During installation, you see a "This computer's hardware may not support booting to this disk" message. This can occur if the disk has not been initialized for use or if the BIOS of the computer does not support starting the operating system from the selected disk. To resolve this problem, create one or more partitions on all the hard disks that are not initialized and then restart the installation.
Language/ Keyboard	Only one keyboard layout is available during installation. If your keyboard language and the language edition of Windows 7 you are installing are different, you may see unexpected characters as you type. Select the correct keyboard language to avoid this.
Language/ Keyboard	Some user interface items are not displayed in the correct language after you change the display language. This occurs because Windows 7 cannot update language settings for currently running processes. To resolve this problem, restart your computer.
Language/ Keyboard	You see an incorrect display language when you use elevated permissions to open a dialog box. This can occur because Windows 7 uses the preferred user interface language of the administrator whose credentials you provide. This language may differ from your preferred user interface language.

Program/Issue	Problem/Resolution
Live File System	The available space on a Live File System disc is less than the capacity of the disc. This issue occurs because the Live File System reserves a small amount of disc space to accommodate link-loss area. In contrast, the Universal Disc Format (UDF) filesystem reserves at least 10 percent of the reported capacity of the disc for sparing. See *http://support.microsoft.com/kb/928353/en-us* for more information.
Mf.sys devices	You cannot install a device that requires the *Mf.sys* device driver in Windows 7. The *Mf.sys* device driver is not installed in Windows 7 by default. See *http://support.microsoft.com/kb/926171/en-us* for more information.
Network Map	In Windows 7, Network Map does not display computers that are running Windows XP. This occurs because the Link-Layer Topology Discovery (LLTD) Responder component is not installed on most Windows XP–based computers. You can download and install this component on your Windows XP computers from the Microsoft website. See *http://support.microsoft.com/kb/922120/en-us* for more information.
Networking programs	Third-party networking programs that use NDIS drivers no longer function after you upgrade to Windows 7. To resolve this issue, you must reinstall the networking program. This will ensure that the third-party NDIS driver is installed and configured correctly.
Playing DVDs	A DVD+RW or DVD-RW video disc that was formatted on a Windows 7–based computer is not recognized by a DVD player that supports DVD+RW or DVD-RW video discs. This problem can occur if Windows 7 uses a version of the UDF that the DVD player does not support. See Chapter 9 for details on UDF versions.
Playing DVDs	A video DVD does not appear in the correct aspect ratio in Windows Media Player on a Tablet PC. This problem may occur when you view the DVD in portrait mode. To resolve the problem, set the display to landscape mode.
RAW image files	You cannot view RAW image files after you copy them from a camera to your computer. This issue occurs if you do not have a RAW image codec for your camera model installed in Windows 7. To resolve this issue, install a Windows 7–compatible RAW image codec that either supports the camera model or is from the camera manufacturer.
Recording DVDs	You cannot record more data to a recordable DVD after you format and then eject the disc. This issue occurs because Windows 7 automatically closes a disc when you eject it. Closing a disc lets you use it in another computer or device. If you don't want Windows 7 to automatically close sessions, see the section "Changing Disc Close on Eject Settings" on page 854, later in this chapter, for a workaround.
Slide show playback	On a Tablet PC, the screen goes black when you switch the screen orientation during slideshow playback. To resolve this problem, exit the slideshow before you change the screen orientation, and then restart the slideshow. Or press the Esc key to restore the original screen orientation.
Sound Recorder	You do not hear any sound when you play back a recording that was recorded with the Sound Recorder. This can occur because the default volume of microphones is 0 dB. To resolve this problem, adjust the volume for the microphone, as discussed in Chapter 5.
Speech Recognition	Speech Recognition does not appear to be using the correct language. Speech Recognition is only available in U.S. English, U.K. English, French, German, Spanish, Japanese, and Chinese versions of Windows 7. Because of the way in which Speech Recognition is integrated into the operating system, the feature cannot be removed from versions of Windows 7 for which Speech Recognition is unavailable.
Speech Recognition commands	You cannot use Speech Recognition in Windows 7 to select commands on floating toolbars in Microsoft Office. With Speech Recognition, you can select commands on docked toolbars in Microsoft Office. Dock the toolbars to resolve the problem.
USB audio devices	You are unable to hear the audio from a newly connected USB audio device in Windows Media Player. To resolve this issue, restart Windows Media Player.

Program/ Issue	Problem/Resolution
USB drives	A USB drive does not appear in the Windows Connect Now window. This behavior occurs if the USB drive uses the NTFS filesystem format and you do not have permission to write to the root directory of the drive. To avoid this problem, use a device that uses the FAT filesystem format. Alternatively, you may need to take ownership of the drive and its files as discussed in "Ownership Permissions" on page 457 in Chapter 11.
USB storage devices	A connected USB storage device does not appear when you click the Safely Remove Hardware icon in the notification area in Windows 7. This problem can occur if the USB device has an embedded USB hub. In this case, you may be able to manage the device in the Computer console or you may need to shut down the computer before removing the device.
User Account Control	You encounter an unexpected error or behavior when you try to perform a task that requires elevated privileges. This issue can occur if UAC is turned off. To resolve this issue, turn UAC on, as discussed in Chapter 3.
Windows Complete PC Restore	You receive a version error message when you use the Windows Complete PC Restore program to restore a computer. If you try to restore a computer using a 64-bit version of Windows 7 using a 32-bit installation disc, you will see an error stating "This version of System Recovery Options is not compatible with the version of Windows you are trying to repair. Try using a recovery disc that is compatible with this version of Windows." To resolve this issue, start recovery using a 64-bit installation disc.
Windows Explorer menu bar	When you view files and folders by using Windows Explorer, the Windows Explorer menu bar is not displayed. To display the menu bar, press the Alt key. Press the Alt key again to hide the menu bar.
Windows Media Player	You see an "Invalid File Format" error message when you play a file in Windows Media Player. This can occur if you are trying to play a file type that Windows Media Player doesn't support. It can also occur if the file is damaged. See Chapter 8 for more information on Windows Media Player's supported file formats. If the file is in a supported format and is not damaged, you may need to reinstall Windows Media Player and then reinstall or upgrade to the latest version of Microsoft DirectX. See *http://support.microsoft.com/kb/924073/en-us* for more information.
Windows startup	In a dual-boot configuration, Windows XP does not start if you subsequently format or delete the partition on which Windows 7 is installed. This occurs because Windows 7 uses a different startup method than Windows XP does. To resolve this problem, you'll need to repair your Windows XP installation by starting an installation and selecting the Repair option. See *http://support.microsoft.com/kb/922809/en-us* for more information.
Windows 7 startup	Windows 7 won't start after you install an earlier version of the Windows operating system in a dual boot configuration. See the next section, "Restoring the Windows 7 Boot Sector" on page 853, for more information.
Wireless adapters	When running on battery, you experience connectivity or performance issues when you connect to a wireless access point. This can occur if the wireless access point doesn't support the 802.11 power save protocol. To resolve this issue, connect the computer to a power source or change the power saving options for the wireless adapter to use the Maximum Performance power saving mode (see "Network Adapters" on page 157 in Chapter 5).

Restoring the Windows 7 Boot Sector

Windows 7 won't start after you install Windows XP or an earlier version of the Windows operating system in a dual-boot configuration. This occurs because Windows 7 uses a different startup method than Windows XP and earlier versions of Windows do.

You must restore the Windows 7 boot sector and allow dual boot by following these steps:

1. Click Start, click Accessories, right-click the command prompt, and then click Run As Administrator.

2. Restore the Windows 7 boot code by typing the following command at a command prompt: `DriveLetter:\boot\Bootsect.exe -NT60 All`, where `DriveLetter` is the actual letter of the drive on which Windows 7 is installed.

3. Allow booting of the earlier operating system by typing the following commands at a command prompt, where `DriveLetter` is the actual letter of the drive on which Windows 7 is installed:

```
DriveLetter:\Windows\system32\Bcdedit -create {ntldr} -d "Description for earlier
    Windows version."
DriveLetter:\Windows\system32\Bcdedit -set {ntldr} device partition=DriveLetter:
DriveLetter:\Windows\system32\Bcdedit -set {ntldr} path \ntldr
DriveLetter:\Windows\system32\Bcdedit -displayorder {ntldr} -addlast
```

4. Restart the computer.

Changing Disc Close on Eject Settings

In Windows 7, closing a disc session lets you use it in another computer or device. If you don't want Windows 7 to automatically close sessions, follow these steps:

1. Click Start and then click Computer.

2. Right-click the writable DVD drive, and then click Properties.

3. In the Properties dialog box, click the Recording tab, and then click Global Settings.

4. Clear the "Automatically close the current UDF session when" options and then click OK twice.

Removing Disk Partitions During Installation

During installation, you may be unable to select the hard disk you want to use. This issue can occur if the hard disk partition contains an invalid byte offset value. To resolve this issue, you'll need to remove the partitions on the hard disk (which destroys all associated data) and then create the necessary partition using the advanced options in the Setup program. During installation on the "Where do you want to install Windows?" page, you can remove unrecognized hard disk partitions by following these steps:

1. Press Shift-F10 to start a command prompt.

2. At the command prompt, type `diskpart`.

3. To view a list of disks on the computer, type `list disk`.

4. Select a disk by typing select disk *DiskNumber* where *DiskNumber* is the number of the disk you want to work with.

5. To permanently remove the partitions on the selected disk, type clean.

6. When the cleaning process finishes, type exit to exit the DiskPart tool.

7. Type exit to exit the command prompt.

8. Restart the computer, and then start the Windows 7 installation.

PART V

Advanced Tips and Techniques

CHAPTER 22

Installing and Running Windows 7

Windows 7 is the latest version of the Windows operating system for personal computers. Unlike earlier releases of Windows, Windows 7 is hardware-independent and ships on media as a modular disk image.

Thanks to Windows 7's new hardware-independent architecture, all editions of Windows 7 support both 32-bit and 64-bit hardware. This means that every product edition can be used with computers that have either 32-bit or 64-bit architecture. Microsoft provides separate installation media for 32-bit computers and 64-bit computers.

Thanks to Windows 7's modular disk image, all editions of Windows 7 ship on the same media. This means that you can use any Windows 7 media disk to install any Windows 7 edition. The product key you provide during installation is what determines the edition and the features of Windows 7 that are installed.

Comparing Windows 7 Features and Versions

Windows 7 is available in six main editions:

Windows 7 Starter
   A budget edition of Windows 7 for casual users and low-powered devices such as netbook computers

Windows 7 Home Basic
   A budget edition of Windows 7 for emerging markets

Windows 7 Home Premium
   An enhanced edition of Windows 7 with premium entertainment features

Windows 7 Professional
   A basic edition of Windows 7 for use in small businesses and networks that use Windows domains

Windows 7 Enterprise
   An enhanced edition of Windows 7 for use in Windows domains with extended management features

Windows 7 Ultimate

An enhanced edition of Windows 7 with all the available home user and professional user features

Only the Professional, Enterprise, and Ultimate editions have the components needed to join a Windows domain. Table 22-1 provides an overview of the differences among these editions. Supported features are marked with a "×." Standard features that all Windows 7 editions support are not listed. Note also that Microsoft may change the included features and I'll try to update the list as appropriate at *http://www.williamsta nek.com/windows7/*.

Table 22-1. Differences among Windows 7 editions

Windows 7 feature	Windows 7 edition				
	Home Basic	Home Premium	Professional	Enterprise	Ultimate
All worldwide user interface languages				X	X
Backup of user files to network device			X	X	X
BitLocker Drive Encryption				×	×
Centralized power management through Group Policy			X	X	X
Client-side caching			X	X	X
Control over installation of device drivers			X	X	X
Desktop deployment tools for managed networks			X	X	X
Encrypting File System (EFS)			X	X	X
File and printer sharing connections	10	20	20	20	20
Folder redirection			X	X	X
Group Policy support			X	X	X
Integrated smart card management			X	X	X
Internet Information Server			X	X	X
Join a Windows domain			X	X	X
Maximum RAM on 32-bit systems	4 GB	4 GB	4 GB	4 GB	4 GB
Maximum RAM on 64-bit systems	8 GB	16 GB	192 GB	192 GB	192 GB
Multiple user interface languages				X	X
Network Access Protection Client Agent			X	X	X
Network projection		X	X	X	X
Offline file and folder support			X	X	X
PC-to-PC sync		X	X	X	X

Windows 7 feature	Windows 7 edition				
	Home Basic	Home Premium	Professional	Enterprise	Ultimate
Pluggable logon authentication architecture			X	X	X
Policy-based quality of service for networking			X	X	X
Premier Support			X	X	
Presentation settings		X	X	X	X
Remote desktop	Client only	Client only	Client and host	Client and host	Client and host
Rights Management Services Client			X	X	X
Roaming user profiles			X	X	X
Scheduled backup of user files		X	X	X	X
Small-business resources			X		X
Software Assurance			X	X	X
Subsystem for Unix-based applications				X	X
System image-based backup and recovery			X	X	X
Themed slide shows		X			X
Two-processor support		X	X	X	X
Virtual Machine Licenses			4	4	
Windows Virtual PC and Windows XP Mode			X	X	X
Volume Licensing			X	X	
Windows Aero		X	X	X	X
Windows Anytime Upgrade	X	X	X		
Windows DVD Maker		X	X	X	X
Windows Fax and Scan			X	X	X
Windows Media Center		X	X	X	X
Windows Mobility Center	Partial	Partial	X	X	X
Windows Shadow Copy			X	X	X
Windows Tablet PC support		X	X	X	X
Wireless network provisioning			X	X	X
Xbox 360		X	X	X	X

Installing Windows 7

You can install Windows 7 on new hardware or as an upgrade. When you install Windows 7 on a computer with Windows Vista, you can perform either a clean installation or an upgrade. Upgrade copies are available for Windows XP, but you can't perform an in-place upgrade. When you are upgrading from Windows XP, you'll need to use Windows Easy Transfer to transfer your files and settings and then run Windows Setup. Windows Setup will then perform a clean installation of the operating system. Afterward, you'll need to reinstall your applications.

With a clean installation, the Windows 7 Setup program completely replaces the original operating system on the computer, and all user or application settings are lost. With an upgrade, the Windows 7 Setup program performs a clean installation of the operating system followed by a migration of user settings, documents, and applications from the earlier version of Windows.

Before you install Windows 7, you should make sure that your computer meets the minimum requirements of the edition that you plan to use. Microsoft provides both minimum requirements and recommended requirements. If your computer doesn't meet the minimum requirements, you will not be able to install Windows 7. If your computer doesn't meet the recommended requirements, you will experience performance issues.

Windows 7 requires a 1 GHz or faster 32-bit (x86) or 64-bit (x64) processor, at least 1 GB RAM (32-bit) or 2 GB RAM (64-bit), and a DirectX 9 graphics processor with a WDDM 1.0 or higher driver. Although the Home Premium, Professional, Enterprise, and Ultimate editions provide two-processor support, Home Basic and Starter do not.

 Don't confuse multiprocessor support with multicore support. All editions of Windows 7 support a single processor with multiple cores. On the editions that support two processors, a computer also can have two discrete-socketed processors and those processors can have multiple cores.

Microsoft recommends that a computer have available disk space of at least 16 GB (32-bit) or 20 GB (64-bit). Additional features, such as System Restore points that include previous versions of files and folders that have been modified, can increase the size of the installation over time. You'll also want at least 15 percent of your disk to be free space at all times.

You can run Windows 7 on any computer that meets or exceeds these requirements. If you run into problems during installation, see the section "Troubleshooting Windows 7 Programs and Features" on page 849 for possible solutions. During installation on the "Where do you want to install Windows?" page, you can display a command prompt by pressing Shift-F10.

Performing a Clean Installation

To perform a clean installation of Windows 7, complete the following steps:

1. Start the Setup program using one of the following techniques:

    - For a new installation, turn on the computer and insert the Windows 7 distribution media into the computer's CD-ROM or DVD-ROM drive. Press a key to start Setup from your media when prompted. When prompted, choose your country or region, time and currency format, and keyboard layout. Click Next.

    - For a clean installation over an existing installation, start the computer and log on using an account with administrator privileges. Insert the Windows 7 distribution media into the computer's CD-ROM or DVD-ROM drive. Setup should start automatically. If it doesn't, use Windows Explorer to access the distribution media and then double-click *Setup.exe*.

2. Start the installation by clicking Install Now. If you are starting the installation from an existing operating system and are connected to a network or the Internet, choose whether to get updates during the installation. Click either "Go online to get the latest updates for installation" or "Do not get the latest updates for installation."

3. Read the license terms. Click "I accept the license terms" and then click Next.

4. Since you are performing a new installation or clean installation over an existing installation, select "Custom (advanced)" as the installation type.

5. Choose the disk drive on which you want to install the operating system and then click Next.

6. If the disk you've selected contains a previous Windows installation, Setup provides a prompt stating that existing user and application settings will be moved to a folder named *Windows.old* and that you must copy these settings to the new installation to use them. Click OK.

7. Setup starts the installation of the operating system. During this procedure, Setup copies the full disk image of Windows 7 to the location you've selected and then expands it. Afterward, Setup installs features based on the computer's configuration and detected hardware. This process requires several automatic restarts. When Setup finishes the installation, the operating system will be loaded and you can complete the installation.

8. You must next create a local machine account that will be created as a computer administrator account. Enter a username.

9. Type a computer name. Click Next.

10. Type and then confirm a password. Enter a password hint. Click Next.

11. If prompted for a product key, enter the product key and then click Next.

12. Select a Windows Update option for the computer. Usually, you'll want to use the recommended settings to allow Windows 7 to automatically install all available

updates and security tools as they become available. Choose "Ask me later" only if you want to disable Windows Update.

13. Setup displays the date and time settings, and then makes changes as necessary. Click Next.

14. If a network card was detected during setup, networking components were installed automatically. Because of this, you'll need to configure detected networking components:

- If your computer has a built-in wireless adapter and it was properly configured during installation, you'll have the opportunity to select and connect to a wireless network.

- If network connections are detected, you can configure each detected network connection. Depending on the type of location and connection, click Home for a home network, Work for a network in a workplace, or Public Location for a public network. Windows 7 will then configure networking as appropriate for this location.

- If there are multiple networks, you'll see a prompt for each network. You can configure each detected network in a different way.

- When you select Home as the connection type, you have additional options. If your home network doesn't have a homegroup, you'll be able to set up a new homegroup. If your home network already has a homegroup, you'll be able to join the homegroup and set sharing options.

15. After setting up your networking, Windows 7 will prepare your desktop.

Performing an Upgrade Installation

Although Windows 7 provides an upgrade option during installation, an upgrade with Windows 7 isn't what you think it is. With an upgrade, the Windows 7 Setup program performs a clean installation of the operating system followed by a migration of user settings, documents, and applications from the earlier version of Windows.

During the migration portion of the upgrade, Setup moves folders and files for the previous installation to a folder named *Windows.old*. As a result, the previous installation will no longer run. Settings are migrated because Windows 7 doesn't store user and application information in the same way as earlier versions of Windows do. See Chapter 1 for more information on where Windows 7 stores user data.

 After you ensure you've recovered any data that you might need, you can delete the *Windows.old* folder. As discussed in "Cleaning Up Your Disk Drives" on page 794 in Chapter 20, Disk Cleanup will also remove this folder for you.

To perform an upgrade installation of Windows 7, complete the following steps:

1. Start the computer and log on using an account with administrator privileges. Insert the Windows 7 distribution media into the computer's CD-ROM or DVD-ROM drive. Setup should start automatically. If Setup doesn't start automatically, use Windows Explorer to access the distribution media and then double-click *Setup.exe*.

2. Start the installation by clicking Install Now.

3. Choose whether to get updates during the installation. Click either "Go online to get the latest updates for installation" or "Do not get the latest updates for installation."

4. Read the license terms. Click "I accept the license terms" and then click Next.

5. Because you are performing a clean installation over an existing installation, select the installation type as Upgrade.

6. Setup will start the installation. During this process, Setup copies the full disk image of Windows 7 to the disk you've selected and then expands it. Afterward, Setup installs features based on the computer's configuration and detected hardware. When Setup finishes the installation, the operating system will be loaded and you can complete the installation.

7. If prompted for a product key, enter the product key and then click Next.

8. Select a Windows Update option for the computer. Typically, you'll want to use the recommended settings to allow Windows 7 to automatically install all available updates and security tools as they become available. If you choose "Ask me later," Windows Update will be disabled.

9. Review the date and time settings, and then make changes as necessary. Click Next.

10. If a network card was detected during setup, networking components were installed automatically. Because of this, you'll need to configure detected networking components:

    - If your computer has a built-in wireless adapter and it was properly configured during installation, you'll have the opportunity to select and connect to a wireless network.

    - If network connections are detected, you can configure each detected network connection. Depending on the type of location and connection, click Home for a home network, Work for a network in a workplace, or Public Location for a public network. Windows 7 will then configure networking as appropriate for this location.

    - If there are multiple networks, you'll see a prompt for each network. You can configure each detected network in a different way.

- When you select home as the connection type, you have additional options. If your home network doesn't have a homegroup, you'll be able to set up a new homegroup. If your home network already has a homegroup, you'll be able to join the homegroup and set sharing options.

11. After setting up your networking, Windows 7 will prepare your desktop.

Upgrading Your Windows 7 Edition

You can easily upgrade Windows 7 editions from one edition to another. Table 22-2 provides an overview of the upgrade paths you can use to upgrade from basic editions to the enhanced editions.

Table 22-2. Upgrade options for Windows 7 editions

Windows 7 Edition	Upgrades to
Windows 7 Starter	Windows 7 Home Premium, Windows 7 Ultimate
Windows 7 Home Premium	Windows 7 Ultimate
Windows 7 Business	Windows 7 Enterprise, Windows 7 Ultimate
Windows 7 Enterprise	Windows 7 Ultimate

You can upgrade the edition installed on a computer by clicking Start→Control Panel→System and Security→System. On the System page, click "Get more features with a new edition of Windows 7." Once you've determined that an edition upgrade is possible, you can begin your upgrade.

You can perform an edition upgrade using the built-in Windows Anytime Upgrade feature. To start an upgrade using the built-in Windows Anytime Upgrade feature, click Start and then click Control Panel. In the Control Panel, click System and Maintenance and then click Windows Anytime Upgrade. To complete the upgrade, you'll access the Microsoft website, where you can purchase the upgrade and find instructions for upgrading. You'll need the Windows 7 distribution media. The distribution media contains the components for all Windows 7 versions, and it is the product key you provide to unlock and install the features for a specific version.

Once you've completed the upgrade, your computer will be running the new edition and will have all the features of this edition.

CHAPTER 23

Exploring the Windows Boot Environment

Unlike earlier releases of Windows, Windows 7 uses a pre–operating system boot environment. At the core of this boot environment is the Boot Configuration Data (BCD) data store, which contains boot configuration parameters and controls how the operating system is started. The preboot environment provides a fundamental change in the way computers running Windows 7 are started. If you understand how this preboot environment works, you'll be better prepared to work with and troubleshoot Windows 7 installations. Be sure to read this chapter before you install an earlier version of Windows on a computer running Windows 7.

Introducing the Windows 7 Boot Environment

Windows computers can use several different processor architectures, several different types of firmware, and several different disk partitioning styles. Generally, computers with 32-bit x86-based processors use the Master Boot Record (MBR) disk partitioning style and BIOS. Computers with Itanium-based IA64 processors use the GUID Partition Table (GPT) disk partitioning style and Extensible Firmware Interface (EFI). Computers with 64-bit x64-based processors use the MBR disk partitioning style and Unified Extensible Firmware Interface (UEFI) which is wrapped around either BIOS or EFI.

Every computer has *firmware*. Firmware is implemented in motherboard chipsets. Just as Windows has an interface, so does firmware. The interface between the platform firmware and the operating system that handles the startup process. The way a firmware interface works and the tasks it performs depend on the type of firmware interface. Windows computers can use different types of firmware. Generally, computers with 32-bit x86-based processors use BIOS. Computers with Itanium-based IA64 processors use EFI. Computers with 64-bit x64-based processors use UEFI, which is wrapped around either BIOS or EFI. For the purposes of this discussion, a computer that uses

UEFI wrapped around BIOS is BIOS-based and a computer that uses UEFI wrapped around EFI is EFI-based.

If you are familiar with the way Windows XP and earlier versions of Windows start, you know these versions of Windows uses *Boot.ini* to initialize the startup environment and *Ntldr* to load the operating system. Windows Vista and Windows 7 don't use these boot facilities. Instead, startup is controlled using the parameters in the BCD data store:

- Entries in the BCD data store identify the boot manager to use during startup and the specific boot applications available.
- Windows Boot Manager controls the boot experience and enables you to choose which boot application is run.
- Boot applications load a specific operating system or operating system version. For example, a Windows Boot Loader application loads Windows 7.

Because BCD abstracts the underlying firmware, you can boot BIOS-based and EFI-based computers in much the same way—just as you can computers based on other firmware models. The BCD store is contained in a file called the *BCD registry*. On BIOS-based operating systems, the BCD registry file is stored in the *\Boot\Bcd* file of the hidden System Reserved partition that Windows 7 creates. This partition is visible in the Disk Management MMC Snap-In, but it is not assigned a drive letter by default. On EFI-based operating systems, the BCD registry file is stored on the EFI system partition.

The BCD store contains multiple entries. On a BIOS-based computer, you'll have one Windows Boot Manager entry. There is only one boot manager, so there is only one boot manager entry. You'll also have Windows Boot Loader application entries, with one entry for each instance of Windows Vista, Windows 7 or a later version of Windows installed on the computer.

On a computer with Windows XP or earlier operating systems installed in addition to Windows Vista, Windows 7 or later, you'll have one legacy operating system entry. The legacy entry is not for a boot application. This entry is used to initiate *Ntldr* and *Boot.ini* so that you can boot into a pre–Windows Vista operating system. If the computer has more than one pre–Windows Vista operating system, you'll be able to select the operating system to start after selecting the legacy operating system entry.

Working with Boot Configuration Data

Several tools are available to work with and manage the BCD, including the following:

- Startup and Recovery
- System Configuration utility
- BCD Editor

The following sections discuss how these tools are used.

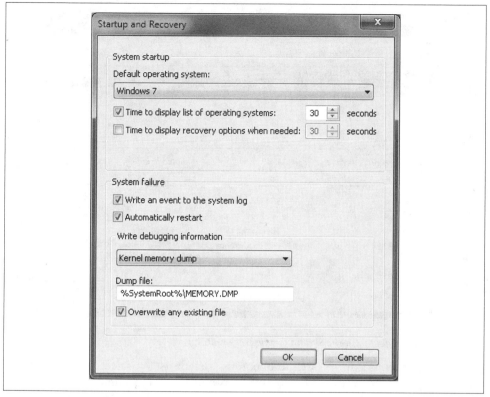

Figure 23-1. Setting Startup and Recovery options

Using the Startup and Recovery Dialog Box

The Startup and Recovery dialog box enables you to select the default operating system to start if you have multiple operating systems installed on your computer. You can also specify timeout values for operating system selection lists and recovery options.

You can access the Startup and Recovery dialog box by following these steps:

1. Click Start→Control Panel. In the Control Panel, click System and Security and then click System.

2. In the System utility, click "Advanced system settings" in the left pane.

3. On the Advanced tab of the System properties dialog box, click Settings under Startup and Recovery. This displays the Startup and Recovery dialog box, as shown in Figure 23-1.

4. Use the "Default operating system" drop-down list to specify the default operating system.

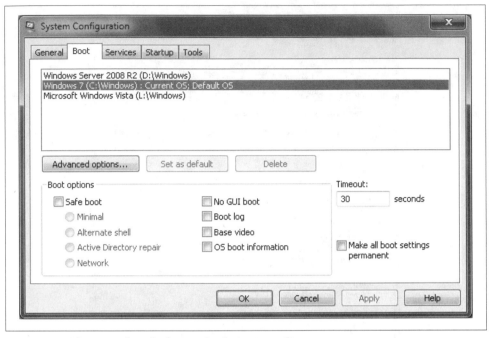

Figure 23-2. The Boot tab in the System Configuration utility

5. Set the timeout interval for the operating system list by selecting the "Time to display list of operating systems" checkbox and specifying a timeout in seconds in the field provided.

6. Set the timeout interval for the recovery options list by selecting the "Time to display recovery options when needed" checkbox and specifying a timeout in seconds in the field provided.

7. Click OK.

Using the System Configuration Utility

Using the System Configuration utility (*Msconfig.exe*), you can set the default operating system and control the way your computer starts. For example, you can configure the computer to start in Safe Mode or force the computer to use standard VGA display settings.

The basic steps for starting and using the System Configuration utility are as follows:

1. Click Start, type `msconfig.exe` in the Search box and press Enter.

2. Select the Boot tab, as shown in Figure 23-2.

3. To set the default operating system, click the operating system you want to use and then click "Set as default."

4. To start the operating system in Safe Mode for troubleshooting, select the "Safe boot" checkbox and then set other troubleshooting options as appropriate.

5. Click OK to apply your changes.

If you are using the System Configuration utility for troubleshooting, you must later remove your selective startup options. After you restart the computer and resolve any problems, access the System Configuration utility again, select Normal Startup on the General tab, and then click OK.

Using the BCD Editor

The BCD Editor (*BCDEdit.exe*) is the only tool that gives you direct access to view and manage the BCD data store. You can use *BCDEdit* to view the entries in the BCD store by following these steps:

1. Click Start, click All Programs, and then click Accessories.

2. Right-click Command Prompt and then select Run As Administrator.

3. Type **bcdedit** at the command prompt.

Example 23-1 shows an example of the output from *BCDEdit*. As the listing shows, the BCD store for this computer has three entries: one for the Windows Boot Manager, one for the Windows Legacy OS Loader, and one for the Windows Boot Loader.

Example 23-1. Examining the contents of the BCD data store

```
--------------------
Windows Boot Manager
--------------------
identifier              {9dea862c-5cdd-4e70-acc1-f32b344d4795}
device                  partition=C:
description             Windows Boot Manager
locale                  en-US
inherit                 {7ea2e1ac-2e61-4728-aaa3-896d9d0a9f0e}
default                 {1cafd2e9-e035-11dd-bbf6-bdebeb67615f}
resumeobject            {1cafd2e8-e035-11dd-bbf6-bdebeb67615f}
displayorder            {1cafd2ed-e035-11dd-bbf6-bdebeb67615f}
                        {1cafd2e9-e035-11dd-bbf6-bdebeb67615f}
                        {360a7720-e6ef-11dc-89b8-84b5c301f2c8}
toolsdisplayorder       {b2721d73-1db4-4c62-bf78-c548a880142d}
timeout                 30

Windows Legacy OS Loader
------------------------
Identifier:             {ntldr}
Type:                   10300006
Device:                 partition=C:
Path:                   \ntldr
Description:            Earlier Version of Windows
Boot debugger:          No

Windows Boot Loader
```

```
--------------------
identifier              {1cafd2e9-e035-11dd-bbf6-bdebeb67615f}
device                  partition=C:
path                    \Windows\system32\winload.exe
description             Windows 7
locale                  en-US
inherit                 {6efb52bf-1766-41db-a6b3-0ee5eff72bd7}
recoverysequence        {1cafd2f0-e035-11dd-bbf6-bdebeb67615f}
recoveryenabled         Yes
osdevice                partition=C:
systemroot              \Windows
resumeobject            {1cafd2e8-e035-11dd-bbf6-bdebeb67615f}
nx                      OptIn
```

The Windows Boot Loader entry has parameters that track the status of the no execute (NX) policy, integrity checking, kernel debugger mode, and Emergency Management Services (EMS). Although the Windows Boot Manager, Windows Legacy OS Loader, and Windows Boot Loader are the primary types of entries that control startup, the BCD also stores information about preoperating system boot environment utilities and settings. To view the BCD entries for utilities and settings, use the following command line:

```
bcdedit /enum all /v
```

This command line enumerates all BCD entries, regardless of their current state, and lists them in Verbose Mode. Example 23-2 shows the verbose entries. It is important to note that Verbose Mode provides the actual value of the GUIDs needed to manipulate entries in the BCD data store.

Example 23-2. Viewing extended BCD entries

```
Windows Boot Manager
--------------------
identifier              {9dea862c-5cdd-4e70-acc1-f32b344d4795}
device                  partition=C:
description             Windows Boot Manager
locale                  en-US
inherit                 {7ea2e1ac-2e61-4728-aaa3-896d9d0a9f0e}
default                 {1cafd2e9-e035-11dd-bbf6-bdebeb67615f}
resumeobject            {1cafd2e8-e035-11dd-bbf6-bdebeb67615f}
displayorder            {1cafd2ed-e035-11dd-bbf6-bdebeb67615f}
                        {1cafd2e9-e035-11dd-bbf6-bdebeb67615f}
                        {360a7720-e6ef-11dc-89b8-84b5c301f2c8}
toolsdisplayorder       {b2721d73-1db4-4c62-bf78-c548a880142d}
timeout                 30

Windows Boot Loader
--------------------
identifier              {1cafd2e9-e035-11dd-bbf6-bdebeb67615f}
device                  partition=C:
path                    \Windows\system32\winload.exe
description             Windows 7
locale                  en-US
inherit                 {6efb52bf-1766-41db-a6b3-0ee5eff72bd7}
```

```
recoverysequence        {1cafd2f0-e035-11dd-bbf6-bdebeb67615f}
recoveryenabled         Yes
osdevice                partition=C:
systemroot              \Windows
resumeobject            {1cafd2e8-e035-11dd-bbf6-bdebeb67615f}
nx                      OptIn

Windows Boot Loader
-------------------
identifier              {1cafd2e0-e035-11dd-bbf6-bdebeb67615f}
device                  ramdisk=[C:]\Recovery\1cafd2e0-e035-11dd bbf6 bdebeb6761
5f\Winre.wim,{1cafd2e1-e035-11dd-bbf6-bdebeb67615f}
path                    \windows\system32\winload.exe
description             Windows Recovery Environment
inherit                 {6efb52bf-1766-41db-a6b3-0ee5eff72bd7}
osdevice                ramdisk=[C:]\Recovery\1cafd2e0-e035-11dd-bbf6-bdebeb6761
5f\Winre.wim,{1cafd2e1-e035-11dd-bbf6-bdebeb67615f}
systemroot              \windows
nx                      OptIn
winpe                   Yes

Resume from Hibernate
---------------------
identifier              {1cafd2e8-e035-11dd-bbf6-bdebeb67615f}
device                  partition=C:
path                    \Windows\system32\winresume.exe
description             Windows Resume Application
locale                  en-US
inherit                 {1afa9c49-16ab-4a5c-901b-212802da9460}
filedevice              partition=C:
filepath                \hiberfil.sys
debugoptionenabled      No

Windows Memory Tester
---------------------
identifier              {b2721d73-1db4-4c62-bf78-c548a880142d}
device                  partition=C:
path                    \boot\memtest.exe
description             Windows Memory Diagnostic
locale                  en-US
inherit                 {7ea2e1ac-2e61-4728-aaa3-896d9d0a9f0e}
badmemoryaccess         Yes

Windows Legacy OS Loader
------------------------
identifier              {466f5a88-0af2-4f76-9038-095b170dc21c}
device                  unknown
path                    \ntldr
description             Earlier Version of Windows
custom:45000001         1
custom:47000005         301989892

EMS Settings
------------
identifier              {0ce4991b-e6b3-4b16-b23c-5e0d9250e5d9}
```

```
bootems                 Yes

Debugger Settings
-----------------
identifier              {4636856e-540f-4170-a130-a84776f4c654}
debugtype               Serial
debugport               1
baudrate                115200

RAM Defects
-----------
identifier              {5189b25c-5558-4bf2-bca4-289b11bd29e2}

Global Settings
---------------
identifier              {7ea2e1ac-2e61-4728-aaa3-896d9d0a9f0e}
inherit                 {4636856e-540f-4170-a130-a84776f4c654}
                        {0ce4991b-e6b3-4b16-b23c-5e0d9250e5d9}
                        {5189b25c-5558-4bf2-bca4-289b11bd29e2}

Boot Loader Settings
--------------------
identifier              {6efb52bf-1766-41db-a6b3-0ee5eff72bd7}
inherit                 {7ea2e1ac-2e61-4728-aaa3-896d9d0a9f0e}
                        {7ff607e0-4395-11db-b0de-0800200c9a66}

Hypervisor Settings
-------------------
identifier              {7ff607e0-4395-11db-b0de-0800200c9a66}
hypervisordebugtype     Serial
hypervisordebugport     1
hypervisorbaudrate      115200

Resume Loader Settings
----------------------
identifier              {1afa9c49-16ab-4a5c-901b-212802da9460}
inherit                 {7ea2e1ac-2e61-4728-aaa3-896d9d0a9f0e}

Device options
--------------
identifier              {1cafd2dd-e035-11dd-bbf6-bdebeb67615f}
description             Ramdisk Options
ramdisksdidevice        partition=C:
ramdisksdipath          \Recovery\1cafd2dc-e035-11dd-bbf6-bdebeb67615f\boot.sdi

Device options
--------------
identifier              {1cafd2e1-e035-11dd-bbf6-bdebeb67615f}
description             Ramdisk Options
ramdisksdidevice        partition=C:
ramdisksdipath          \Recovery\1cafd2e0-e035-11dd-bbf6-bdebeb67615f\boot.sdi
```

As you can see from the listing, there are a number of additional entries. Each entry has a specific purpose, and lists values that you can set, including the following:

Recovery Environment

In the Windows Boot Loader entries, you'll find entries that have a description of "Windows Recovery Environment." The Windows Recovery Environment is a custom preinstallation environment that includes components for recovery and startup troubleshooting. To enable rapid recovery, the Windows Recovery Environment (Windows RE) is installed with Windows 7 automatically. Normally, Windows RE is installed on a hard disk partition other than the one containing the Windows installation. This ensures that Windows RE is separate from the operating system.

Resume from Hibernate

The Resume from Hibernate entry shows the current configuration for the resume feature in Windows 7. The preoperating system boot utility that controls resume is *Winresume.exe*, which in this example is stored in the *C:\Windows\system32* folder. The hibernation data, as specified in the filepath parameter, is stored in the *Hiberfil.sys* file in the root folder on the filedevice (c: in this example). Because the resume feature works differently if the computer has Physical Address Extension (PAE) and debugging enabled, these options are tracked by the PAE and Debugoptionenabled parameters.

Windows Memory Tester

The Windows Memory Tester entry shows the current configuration for the Windows Memory Diagnostics utility. The preoperating system boot utility that controls memory diagnostics is *Memtest.exe*, which in this example is stored in the *\boot* folder of the hidden System Reserved partition. Because the memory diagnostics tool is designed to detect bad memory by default, the badmemoryaccess parameter is set to yes by default.

EMS Settings

The EMS Settings entry shows the configuration used when booting with Emergency Management Services. Individual Windows Boot Loader entries control whether EMS is enabled.

Debugger Settings

The Debugger Settings entry shows the configuration used when booting with the debugger turned on. Individual Windows Boot Loader entries control whether the debugger is enabled. When debug booting is turned on, Debugtype sets the type of debugger as SERIAL, 1394, or USB. With SERIAL debugging, Debugport specifies the serial port being used as the debugger port and Baudrate specifies the baud rate to be used for debugging. With 1394 debugging, you can use Channel to set the debugging channel. With USB debugging, you can use Targetname to set the USB target name to be used for debugging.

Managing the BCD Data Store

You can use the BCD Editor to add, modify, and delete entries in the BCD data store. Although I discuss related tasks in the sections that follow, only experienced users should attempt to modify the BCD data store. If you make a mistake, your computer may end up in a nonbootable state.

Changing the Default Operating System

To change the default operating system entry, you can use the /Default parameter for *BCDEdit*. The syntax for this parameter is:

```
Bcdedit /default bootldrid
```

where *bootldrid* is the GUID of the boot loader to use. You can boot to a particular installation of Windows 7 or a later Windows operating system by specifying the identifier for the related boot loader. When you view verbose details for the BCD data store, the identifiers for a particular Windows Boot Loader are listed with its entry, such as:

```
Windows Boot Loader
-------------------
identifier              {1cafd2e9-e035-11dd-bbf6-bdebeb67615f}
device                  partition=C:
path                    \Windows\system32\winload.exe
description             Windows 7
locale                  en-US
inherit                 {6efb52bf-1766-41db-a6b3-0ee5eff72bd7}
recoverysequence        {1cafd2f0-e035-11dd-bbf6-bdebeb67615f}
recoveryenabled         Yes
osdevice                partition=C:
systemroot              \Windows
resumeobject            {1cafd2e8-e035-11dd-bbf6-bdebeb67615f}
nx                      OptIn
quietboot               No
debug                   No
ems                     No
```

The Windows Boot Manager entries also list each Windows Vista or later operating system by its identifier in the displayorder field:

```
Windows Boot Manager
-------------------
identifier              {9dea862c-5cdd-4e70-acc1-f32b344d4795}
device                  partition=L:
description             Windows Boot Manager
locale                  en-US
inherit                 {7ea2e1ac-2e61-4728-aaa3-896d9d0a9f0e}
default                 {1cafd2e9-e035-11dd-bbf6-bdebeb67615f}
resumeobject            {1cafd2e8-e035-11dd-bbf6-bdebeb67615f}
displayorder            {1cafd2ed-e035-11dd-bbf6-bdebeb67615f}
                        {1cafd2e9-e035-11dd-bbf6-bdebeb67615f}
                        {360a7720-e6ef-11dc-89b8-84b5c301f2c8}
```

```
toolsdisplayorder        {b2721d73-1db4-4c62-bf78-c548a880142d}
timeout                  30
```

You could set one of the related operating systems as the default for the computer, as shown in this example:

```
bcdedit /default {1cafd2e9-e035-11dd-bbf6-bdebeb67615f}
```

If you want to use a pre–Windows 7 operating system as the default, you'd use the identifier for the Windows Legacy OS Loader. The related BCD entry looks like this:

```
Windows Legacy OS Loader
------------------------
identifier               {466f5a88-0af2-4f76-9038-095b170dc21c}
device                   partition=C:
path                     \ntldr
description              Earlier Version of Windows
```

Following this, you could set *Ntldr* as the default by entering:

```
bcdedit /default {466f5a88-0af2-4f76-9038-095b170dc21c}
```

Changing the Default Timeout

You can change the timeout value associated with the default operating system using the /timeout parameter. Set the /timeout parameter to the desired wait time in seconds, such as:

```
bcdedit /timeout 30
```

If you set the timeout to zero seconds, the system will boot automatically to the default operating system.

Enabling Physical Address Expansion

PAE is a feature that allows x86-based computers to support more than 4 GB of physical memory, effectively expanding the number of addressable bits from 32 to 36. Physical memory in addresses above the first 32 bits is accessed as regular 4 KB memory pages.

 You do not need to enable PAE on a computer running a 64-bit version of Windows, as 64-bit Windows can access more than 4 GB of memory automatically.

If you want to enable PAE through the BCD, you can use the command syntax:

```
bcdedit /set bootldrid pae paeState
```

where *bootldrid* is the identifier for the operating system that should use PAE and *paeState* specifies how you want PAE to be used:

Default

If you set *paeState* to Default, the operating system will use the default configuration for PAE.

ForceEnable

If you set *paeState* to ForceEnable, the operating system will use PAE.

ForceDisable

If you set *paeState* to ForceDisable, the operating system will not use PAE.

This means you could enable PAE for the operating system identified by this boot loader identifier:

```
Windows Boot Loader
-------------------
identifier              {0c728e1b-d009-11da-b18b-9dc1d02cdda0}
```

using the following command:

```
bcdedit /set {0c728e1b-d009-11da-b18b-9dc1d02cdda0} pae forceenable
```

Changing the Operating System Display Order

You can change the display order of boot managers associated with a particular Windows 7 or later operating system using the /Displayorder parameter. Follow the parameter with the operating system identifiers in the desired display order.

Thus you could change the display order of the operating systems identified in these BCD entries:

```
Windows Boot Loader
-------------------
identifier              {0c728e1b-d009-11da-b18b-9dc1d02cdda0}

Windows Boot Loader
-------------------
identifier              {263bf496-4ab4-11db-b478-c0671802252f}
```

using the following command:

```
bcdedit /displayorder {263bf496-4ab4-11db-b478-c0671802252f}
  {0c728e1b-d009-11da-b18b-9dc1d02cdda0}
```

You can set a particular operating system as the first entry by using /addfirst with /displayorder, such as:

```
bcdedit /displayorder {263bf496-4ab4-11db-b478-c0671802252f} /addfirst
```

You can set a particular operating system as the last entry by using /addlast with /displayorder, such as:

```
bcdedit /displayorder {263bf496-4ab4-11db-b478-c0671802252f} /addlast
```

Changing the Restart Boot Sequence

If you'd like to boot to a particular operating system one time and then revert to the default boot order, you can use the `/bootsequence` parameter to do this. Follow the parameter with the operating system to which you want to boot after restarting the computer, such as:

```
bcdedit /bootsequence {0c728e1b-d009-11da-b18b-9dc1d02cdda0}
```

Now when you restart the computer, the computer will set the specified operating system as the default for that restart only. If you restart the computer again, the computer will use the default boot order.

Managing the Boot Sector for Hard Disk Partitions

The Boot Sector Configurator (*Bootsect.exe*) is a tool you can use to manage the master boot sector on computers running Windows 7. Before you try to install Windows XP or an earlier version of Windows on a computer running Windows 7, you should familiarize yourself with this tool.

Bootsect is provided as part of the Windows Automated Installation Kit (Windows AIK), which is available as a free download from the Microsoft Download website. Visit *http://download.microsoft.com* and search for "Windows AIK."

Using the Boot Sector Configurator

You use *Bootsect* to modify the master boot code for a designated hard disk partition so that either Boot Manager or *Ntldr* is used to boot the operating system. You also can use *Bootsect* to restore the boot sector on your computer if it has been corrupted or accidentally overwritten. This tool replaces *FixNTFS*.

 Windows 7 can repair most boot sector problems. For boot sector problems that Windows 7 can't fix, you can boot to the Windows Recovery Environment, access a command prompt, and then run *Bootsect*. For more information on the Windows RE, see Chapter 21.

The hard disk partition that you want to modify is identified using one of the following identifiers:

- *DriveLetter:*, where *DriveLetter* identifies the letter of the drive to modify, followed by the colon, such as `C:`. The drive letter must be for a connected, bootable volume.

- SYS specifies that you want to modify the system partition used to boot Windows 7.
- ALL specifies that you want to modify all partitions that could be used as Windows boot volumes and exclude those that cannot be used as boot volumes.

To create a boot sector for *Ntldr* and a pre–Windows 7 operating system, you use the /nt52 parameter followed by the identifier for the disk partition you want to modify, such as:

```
bootsect /nt52 SYS
```

To create a boot sector for Boot Manager and Windows 7 or later, you use the /nt60 parameter followed by the identifier for the disk partition you want to modify, such as:

```
bootsect /nt60 D:
```

Bootsect will always try to lock and dismount the partition before updating it. If *Bootsect* cannot gain exclusive access to the drive, the drive's boot sector is modified the next time the computer is started.

 You can attempt to force a partition to dismount using the /force parameter. However, this causes all open file handles to become invalid, which may cause programs to lock or fail.

Installing a Previous Version of Windows on a Computer Running Windows 7

One scenario where *Bootsect* is particularly handy is when you are installing a previous version of Windows on a computer running Windows 7. Normally, Windows 7 won't let you install and then run a previous version of Windows. You can work around this issue using *Bootsect* and *BCDedit*.

To install a previous version of Windows onto a computer running Windows 7, follow these steps:

1. Insert the media for the previous version of Windows into your CD-ROM or DVD-ROM drive.
2. Restart the computer and run Setup for the previous version of Windows. Be sure to install the previous version of Windows onto a different partition or drive than the one running Windows 7.
3. Log on to the previous version of Windows and restore the Windows 7 boot manager. You must specify the partition where Windows 7 is installed. If Windows 7 were installed on *C:*, you'd use the following command:

```
bootsect /nt60 c:
```

4. Create a BCD entry for the pre-Windows 7 operating system you just installed using *BCDedit*. *BCDedit* is located in the *\Windows\System32* directory of the Windows 7 partition. Type the following commands exactly as shown, where `Windows_Version` is the version of Windows you installed:

```
Bcdedit /create {legacy} /d "Windows_Version"
Bcdedit /set {legacy} device boot
Bcdedit /set {legacy} path \ntldr
Bcdedit /displayorder {legacy} /addlast
```

5. Restart the computer to apply the BCD changes.

CHAPTER 24

Using Group Policy with Windows 7

Whether you are working with your computer at home or at the office, your computer is affected by Group Policy. Group Policy is a collection of policy settings that simplify management of a computer's configuration. Two general types of Group Policy are available: Active Directory Group Policy and Local Group Policy. As Active Directory Group Policy applies to all computers that are part of a Windows domain, a computer being used on many business networks is affected by Active Directory Group Policy. As Local Group Policy applies to all computers regardless of their configuration, your computer—whether on a home network or a domain network—is affected by Local Group Policy.

Policy settings are important because you can use them to manage a great many operating system features. Policy settings also typically control the things you can and cannot do with your computer. For example, the default policy configuration doesn't allow a nonadministrator user to install device drivers, but if you know how to work with policies you could modify this behavior to allow certain types of devices to be installed by users with standard user accounts. Also, as a broad set of policies known as Administrative Templates is used to configure registry settings, Group Policy has become the preferred way to manage a computer's registry settings. Collectively, the Administrative Templates settings expose hundreds of registry settings, making it much easier to manipulate operating system configuration.

Windows 7 features several fundamental changes to the way Group Policy works. This chapter looks at these features and discusses how they affect the way Group Policy is used.

Exploring Group Policy in Windows 7

In Windows 7, the Group Policy architecture includes these enhancements, as discussed in the following sections:

- Group Policy Client service
- Support for Network Location Awareness
- Multiple Local Group Policy Objects (LGPOs)
- Updated management tools and policy file formats

Introducing the Group Policy Client Service

The Group Policy Client service completely isolates Group Policy notification and processing from the Windows logon process. Separating Group Policy from the Windows Logon process:

- Ensures that a single service can deliver the needed Group Policy functionality
- Enables more dynamic control over how policy settings are applied, maintained, and updated
- Reduces the resources used for background processing of policies while increasing overall performance
- Allows delivery of new Group Policy files as part of the update process and application of those updates without restart

The Group Policy Client service is a standalone service that runs under the Svchost process and no longer uses the trace logging functionality in *userenv.dll*. As a result, Group Policy event messages are now written to the system log with the event source of Microsoft-Windows-GroupPolicy, and the Group Policy Operational log replaces previous Userenv logging. The operational event log provides detailed event messages specific to Group Policy processing. When troubleshooting Group Policy issues, you'll use this log rather than *userenv.log* as you did in Windows XP and earlier versions.

Using Multiple Local Group Policy Objects

Unlike Windows XP and earlier implementations of Group Policy, Group Policy in Windows Vista and Windows 7 allows the use of multiple LGPOs on a single computer. Previously, computers had only one LGPO. Windows Vista and Windows 7 allow you to assign a different LGPO to each local user or group. This allows the application of a policy to be more flexible and support a wider array of implementation scenarios.

Multiple LGPOs are particularly useful when computers are being used in a standalone configuration rather than a domain configuration, because local administrator users no longer have to explicitly disable or remove settings that interfere with their ability to manage a computer before performing administrator tasks. Instead, an administrator user can implement one LGPO for administrators and another LGPO for nonadministrators.

Administrator and nonadministrator LGPOs are the two standard types of LGPOs available. See "Working with Multiple Local Group Policy Objects" on page 889, later in this chapter, for more information.

Enhancing Group Policy Application

Thanks to the Network Location Awareness feature in Windows Vista and Windows 7, Group Policy can respond better to changing network conditions and no longer relies on ICMP (ping) for policy application. Network Location Awareness ensures that a computer is aware of the type of network to which it is currently connected—in other words, whether the computer is on a home, public, or work network—and is responsive to changes in the system status or network configuration. This gives Group Policy access to the resource detection and event notification capabilities in the operating system, allowing Group Policy to determine when a computer is in standby mode or resuming from hibernation, as well as when a network connection has been disabled or disconnected. In cases where the network isn't available, Group Policy won't wait for the network, allowing for faster startup.

Because ICMP (ping) is no longer used for slow link detection, business networks can filter this protocol on their firewalls. Group Policy uses Network Location Awareness to determine the network bandwidth. When mobile users connect to a business network, Group Policy can detect the availability of a domain controller and initiate a background refresh of policy over the VPN connection.

Improving Group Policy Management

Windows 7 includes the Group Policy Management Console (GPMC) and Group Policy Object Editor (GPOE) for managing Group Policy. If you are an administrator, you can install the GPMC as part of the Remote Server Administration Tools for Windows 7. GPOE is included with Windows 7.

Using the GPMC, shown in Figure 24-1, you can manage Active Directory Group Policy in an enterprise environment. To edit Group Policy for your local computer or users, skip ahead to the next example. To open the GPMC, follow these steps:

1. Log on to a computer running Windows 7 with an administrative user account.
2. Click Start, type mmc into the Search box, and then press Enter.
3. In the Microsoft Management Console, click File→Add/Remove Snap-in.
4. In the Add or Remove Snap-ins dialog box, click Group Policy Management Console, click Add, and then click OK.
5. You can now navigate through the forest and domains in the organization to view individual Group Policy Objects (GPOs).

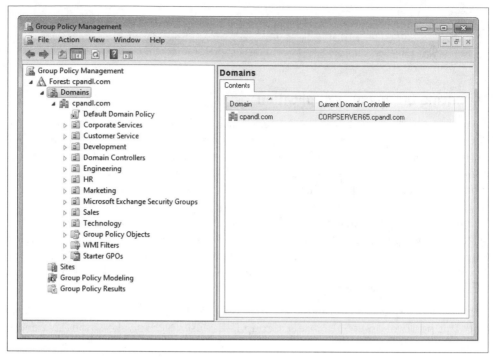

Figure 24-1. Accessing Active Directory Group Policy

6. If you expand the site, domain, or organizational unit node in which a related policy object is stored, you can right-click the policy object and then choose Edit. This opens the object for editing in the GPOE.

Using the GPOE, shown in Figure 24-2, you can manage group policy for your local computer. To open the GPOE, follow these steps:

1. Log on to a computer running Windows 7 with an administrative user account.

2. Click Start, type mmc into the Search box, and then press Enter.

3. In the Microsoft Management Console, click File→Add/Remove Snap-in.

4. In the Add or Remove Snap-ins dialog box, click Group Policy Object Editor and then click Add.

5. In the Select Group Policy Object dialog box, the default object is the Local Computer Group Policy Object. If this is the object you want to work with, click Finish. If this isn't the object you want to work with, click Browse, select the object you want to work with, and then click OK.

6. Click OK to close the Add or Remove Snap-ins dialog box.

7. You can now work with the GPO you've opened.

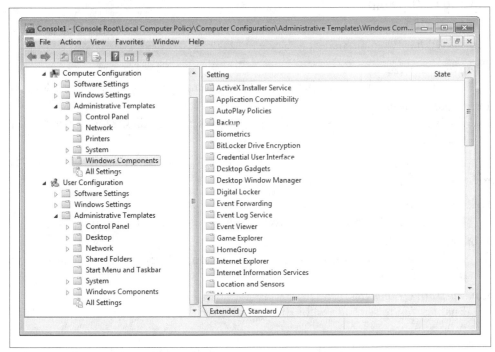

Figure 24-2. Accessing Local Group Policy

For Windows Vista and Windows 7, the GPMC and GPOE have been updated to work with XML-based Administrative Templates and use a document format referred to as ADMX. These tools can also work with the previous ADM format.

ADMX files are divided into language-neutral and language-specific file sets. The language-neutral files ensure that a GPO has the same core policies. The language-specific files allow policies to be viewed and edited in multiple languages. Because the language-neutral files store the core settings, policies can be edited in any language for which a computer is configured, thus allowing one user to view and edit policies in English and another to view and edit policies in Spanish. The mechanism that determines which language is used is the language pack installed on the computer.

In domains, ADMX files are stored in a central store—the domain-wide directory created in the System volume (Sysvol). Previously, Administrative Templates were stored with each GPO. In the new implementation, only the current state of the setting is stored in the GPO and the ADMX files are stored centrally. As a result, this reduces the amount of storage space used as the number of GPOs increases, and it reduces the amount of data being replicated throughout the enterprise. As long as you edit GPOs using Windows Vista or Windows 7, new GPOs will not contain either ADM or ADXM files inside the GPO.

Editing Group Policy

After you access a policy for editing, you can use the GPOE to work with group policies. The GPOE has two main nodes:

Computer Configuration
    Enables you to set policies that are applied to computers, regardless of who logs on

User Configuration
    Enables you to set policies that are applied to users, regardless of which computer they log on to

The Computer Configuration and User Configuration nodes have subnodes for the following:

Software Settings
    Enables you to set policies for software settings and software installation

Windows Settings
    Enables you to set policies for name resolution, scripts, printers, security, and quality of service

Administrative Templates
    Enables you to set policies for the operating system, Windows components, and programs

The policy settings you'll work with the most are those found under Administrative Templates. You can enable, disable, and configure policy settings for Administrative Templates by completing the following steps:

1. Open the policy object you want to edit. Access the GPOE for the resource you want to work with (see "Improving Group Policy Management" on page 885, earlier in this chapter, for instructions).

2. Expand Computer Configuration→Administrative Templates or User Configuration→Administrative Templates as appropriate for the type of policy you want to set.

3. After you expand the policy subfolders as appropriate, double-click a policy or right-click it and select Edit to display its Properties dialog box.

4. The Help section of the dialog shows a description of the policy, if one is available.

5. Use the following buttons to change the state of the policy:

    Not Configured
        The policy is not configured.

    Enabled
        The policy is enabled.

    Disabled
        The policy is disabled.

---

6. If you enabled the policy, set any additional parameters specified under Options and then click Apply.

7. Click OK to save your settings.

Policy changes are applied when Group Policy is refreshed. Windows automatically refreshes policy periodically. However, with some types of policies you may need to log out and then log back in, or restart the computer.

Working with Multiple Local Group Policy Objects

As discussed previously, computers running Windows 7 can have multiple LGPOs. The way you use and work with multiple LGPOs is explored in this section.

Understanding Multiple Local Group Policy Object Usage

Multiple LGPOs increase flexibility when applying policy settings and allow home and workgroup users to gain some of the benefits and controls previously available only in Windows domains. They do this by allowing a policy to be uniquely tailored to users based on the logon account and their membership in specific groups.

Windows 7 has three layers of LGPOs:

1. Local Group Policy
2. Administrators and Non-Administrators Local Group Policy
3. User-specific Local Group Policy

These layers of LGPOs are processed in order. Local Group Policy is applied first. Administrators and Non-Administrators Local Group Policy is applied second. User-specific Local Group Policy is applied third.

Local Group Policy is the only LGPO that allows both computer configuration and user configuration settings to be applied. User configuration settings applied through the LGPO apply to all users of the computer, even the built-in Administrator account. Local Group Policy works the same as it did in Windows XP.

Administrators and Non-Administrators Local Group Policy contains only user configuration settings and is applied based on whether the user account being used is a member of the local Administrators group. A user is either an administrator or a non-administrator. If the user is a member of the Administrators group, Administrators Local Group Policy is applied to the user at logon. If the user is not a member of the Administrators group, Non-Administrators Local Group Policy is applied to the user at logon.

User-specific Local Group Policy contains only user configuration settings and is applied based on whether an additional policy object has been created and applied to a user's account. In this way, you use User-specific Local Group Policy to apply policy settings to one specific user.

The available user settings are the same among all LGPOs. Because of this, it is possible that a setting in one GPO may conflict with a setting in another GPO. Windows 7 resolves conflicts in settings by overwriting any previous setting with the last read and most current setting. The final setting is the one Windows 7 uses. Because of this, the processing order is extremely important: it determines which user settings are actually applied when there are conflicting settings.

 Only the enabled or disabled state of a setting matters. If a setting is set as Not Configured, this has no effect on the state of the setting from a previous policy application.

To see how setting overwriting works, consider the following examples:

- Jim is a member of the local Administrator account and has a user-specific GPO. When Jim logs on to his computer, Local Group Policy is applied, then Administrators Local Group Policy, and then his User-specific Local Group Policy. Thus, if Local Group Policy disabled a setting, then Administrators Local Group Policy enabled a setting, and then User-specific Local Group Policy disabled the setting, the setting would be disabled.

- Tina is not a member of the local Administrator account and has a user-specific GPO. When Tina logs on to her computer, Local Group Policy is applied, then Non-Administrators Local Group Policy, and then her User-specific Local Group Policy. Thus, if a setting is disabled in Local Group Policy, then enabled in Administrators Local Group Policy, and then not configured in User-specific Local Group Policy, the setting would be enabled.

As you can see, using multiple LGPOs in a standalone configuration allows you to control precisely how policy settings are applied to users based on their logon account and group membership. In a domain configuration, however, you might not want to use multiple LGPOs because in domains, most computers and users already have multiple GPOs applied to them, and adding multiple LGPOs to this already varied mix can make it confusing to manage Group Policy.

In a domain, computers apply local policy first and then domain policy. Because domain policy is applied last, domain policy settings overwrite any conflicting settings from local policy. Further, to simplify administration, domain administrators can disable processing of LGPOs on computers running Windows 7 by enabling the "Turn off Local Group Policy objects processing" policy setting in a domain GPO. In Group Policy, this setting is located under *Computer Configuration\Administrative Templates \System\Group Policy*.

Creating Multiple Local Group Policy Objects

Using the GPOE, you can easily create and manage multiple LGPOs. By default, the only local policy object that exists on a computer is the LGPO. You can, however, create other local objects as necessary. Other objects are created when you access them in the GPOE.

Accessing the top-level LGPO

The way you create or access a particular LGPO depends on the object you want to work with. You can access the top-level LGPO by completing the following steps:

1. Log on to a computer running Windows 7 with an administrative user account.
2. Click Start, type mmc into the Search box and then press Enter.
3. In the Microsoft Management Console, click File→Add/Remove Snap-in.
4. In the Add or Remove Snap-ins dialog box, click Group Policy Object Editor and then click Add.
5. In the Select Group Policy Object dialog box, click Finish because this is the default object.
6. Click OK.

 You can use the same Microsoft Management Console to manage more than one LGPO. In the Add or Remove Snap-ins dialog box, you simply add one instance of the GPOE for each object you want to work with.

Accessing the Administrators Local Group Object or the Non-Administrators Local Group Object

You can create or access the Administrators Local Group Object or the Non-Administrators Local Group Object by completing the following steps:

1. Log on to a computer running Windows 7 with an administrative user account.
2. Click Start, type mmc into the Search box, and then press Enter.
3. In the Microsoft Management Console, click File→Add/Remove Snap-in.
4. In the Add or Remove Snap-ins dialog box, click Group Policy Object Editor and then click Add.
5. In the Select Group Policy Object dialog box, click Browse.
6. In the Browse for a Group Policy Object dialog box, click the Users tab, as shown previously in Figure 24-3. Note that the entries in the Group Policy Object Exists column specify whether a particular local policy object has already been created.
7. Select Administrators (note the "s" on the end to distinguish it from the one for the Administrator user) to create or access the Administrators Local Group Object.

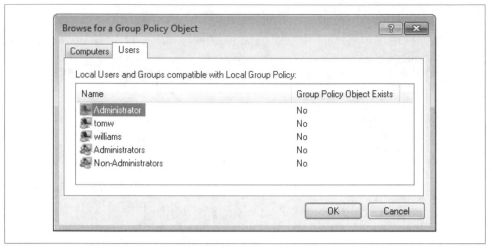

Figure 24-3. Creating or accessing the desired object

> Select Non-Administrators to create or access the Non-Administrators Local Group Object.

8. Click OK.

In the Microsoft Management Console, the policy is listed as *Local Computer\Administrators Policy* or *Local Computer\Non-Administrators Policy* (see Figure 24-4). As discussed previously, only the top-level LGPO has both computer configuration and user configuration settings. Other types of local policy objects have only user configuration settings.

Accessing a user-specific local group object

You can create or access a user-specific local group object using the procedure outlined in the preceding section. The only change is that in step 7, you select the local user whose user-specific local group object you want to create or work with. If this object doesn't already exist, it will be created. Otherwise, you'll open the existing object for review and editing.

Deleting Local Group Policy Objects

All computers have an LGPO. You cannot delete this top-level policy object. You can, however, set each policy setting to Not Configured to ensure that no related policy settings are applied.

Although you cannot delete this object, you can delete other LGPOs that you have created. When you delete an LGPO, the object and all its related settings are removed from the computer.

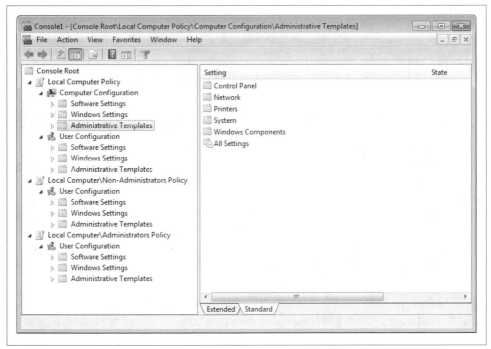

Figure 24-4. Unique labels provided for each local policy object

 An LGPO is not created until you've configured at least one of the objects underneath it. If you add the LGPO as outlined in the previous section, and then return to the Browser for a Group Policy Object, the Group Policy Object Exists column will read "No" unless you've configured one of the objects.

You can delete the Administrators Local Group Object, Non-Administrators Local Group Object, or User-specific Local Group Object by following these steps:

1. Log on to a computer running Windows 7 with an administrative user account.
2. Click Start, type mmc into the Search box, and then press Enter.
3. In the Microsoft Management Console, click File→Add/Remove Snap-in.
4. In the Add or Remove Snap-ins dialog box, click Group Policy Object Editor, and then click Add.
5. In the Select Group Policy Object dialog box, click Browse.
6. In the Browse for a Group Policy Object dialog box, click the Users tab, as shown in Figure 24-3.
7. Right-click the name of the policy you want to remove and then select Remove Group Policy Object.

8. When prompted to confirm, click Yes.

9. Click Cancel three times to exit all open dialog boxes.

10. In the Microsoft Management Console, click File→Exit. If prompted to save the console, click No.

11. Log off the computer to ensure that the policy object can be removed.

Updating Active Directory Group Policy Objects for Windows 7

On a Windows 7 computer, you'll automatically see the Windows 7 policies as well as the other policies when you work with LGPOs. The same is not true automatically, however, if you try to use the Windows 7 policies in a domain. This is because Active Directory Group Policy objects must be updated to include Windows 7 policies. A similar update is required to apply any additional policies defined in service packs or later Windows releases. Once you've performed the update and made any necessary changes, you can perform basic management, such as policy linking or blocking, using any computer. However, it is recommended that the actual policy editing be done on a computer running Windows 7 or later.

Each Active Directory Group Policy object that should include Windows 7 policies must be updated separately. Update an individual GPO by following these steps:

1. Log on to a computer running Windows 7 with an administrative user account.

2. Open Group Policy Management Console.

3. In Group Policy Management Console, expand the Forest node. This node represents the current forest to which you are connected.

4. When you expand the Forest node, you'll see Domains and Sites nodes. Expand these nodes and their subnodes to work your way to the GPO you want to work with.

5. When you find the GPO you want to work with, right-click it and then select Edit to open the GPOE.

6. In the GPOE, select the Computer Configuration node by clicking it and then select the User Configuration node by clicking it.

When you select the Computer Configuration and User Configuration nodes, the current administrative templates are read and applied to the GPO you've selected. Once Group Policy is refreshed, you can modify policy settings as necessary, and the changes will be updated as appropriate in the selected site, domain, or organizational unit. Repeat this procedure to update the GPO for other sites, domains, or organizational units.

CHAPTER 25

Mastering Windows Media Center

Microsoft introduced Windows Media Center Edition (MCE) with Windows XP, then followed through and added the functionality of MCE to later releases of Windows. In Windows 7, Windows Media Center gives you a "living room" computer that will connect to your home entertainment system and allow you to manage your media easily without the need for a keyboard, mouse, or monitor. You can connect directly to your television for a display, and you can use an optional remote control with Windows Media Center.

Windows Media Center allows you to control how you watch television by letting you record programs and schedule content, and it gives you an easy-to-use scheduling window so that you can view programming many days in advance. You can also use Windows Media Center to play your digital music, watch movies, and even burn a DVD, so you can share your content or archive it for later use. This chapter discusses the different features of Windows Media Center and gives you detailed information on how to set it up and purchase the correct hardware to make Windows Media Center come alive for your entertainment.

Understanding Windows Media Center Requirements

Only computers running Windows 7 Home Premium, Windows 7 Professional, or Windows 7 Ultimate have Windows Media Center. When considering using Windows Media Center, you should ask yourself the following questions:

- What type of entertainment equipment do I want to connect to my computer?
- What type of network bandwidth will I need for media services?
- Where do I want to locate my computer?

Each question leads to different requirements for using Windows Media Center and each feature that Windows Media Center provides requires different software and hardware.

If you want to use Windows Media Center to watch and record TV, you must have a TV tuner card. To record HD, you'll need an HD-capable TV tuner card. Also available are digital TV tuner cards that you can connect to a portable or fixed antenna to get over-the-air digital HD television for free.

Listening to music with the music library or watching a movie requires that you install a sound card. Most computers include a sound card, but some sound cards work better than others with home audio systems, particularly when you go beyond two speakers. If you want to use Windows Media Center to download album and additional online content, you need a connection to the Internet. To make it easier to navigate the TV functions and movie library features, you should purchase a programmable remote control. Table 25-1 summarizes Windows Media Center functionalities and their respective requirements for successful use.

Table 25-1. Windows Media Center functionalities and requirements

Functionality	Requirement
Watch and record TV	TV tuner card
Listen to music or watch a movie	Sound card
Download online content	Internet connection
Access via remote control	Windows Media Center IR remote control
Listen to radio stations	Radio tuner card

Selecting the Correct Hardware for Windows Media Center

As with all other operating systems, purchasing the correct hardware for use with Windows Media Center can mean the difference between using something that merely works and having a great experience while using it. Microsoft has gone to great lengths to increase the reliability of video functions within Windows 7. Drivers for the video card work differently than they did in previous operating systems. The kernel mode drivers and their functions in previous operating systems do not exist in Windows 7.

Video Cards

Windows 7 usesWindows Display Driver Model (WDDM), which offers greater flexibility than previous Windows display models. WDDM moved most of the driver components out of the kernel environment and into the user environment. This driver arrangement isolates the graphics driver from the operating system and additional applications.

You should take the time to look for the best hardware available for Windows 7. Spending the time upfront will improve your experience with Windows 7 as a whole, as well as with Windows Media Center. Currently the leading hardware manufacturers writing Windows 7 drivers and video capture drivers are ATI, Intel, and NVIDIA. Visit the manufacturers' websites and research the hardware they currently offer that works with Windows 7. Each offers tables that give you choices on price versus performance on each card they deliver for different needs. The professional-level cards will always cost considerably more than cards at the novice or enthusiast level. So, research the available hardware when you are ready to move to Windows 7. It will pay dividends in the end.

Sound Cards

Sound cards are also essential to enjoying Windows Media Center. The best advice on purchasing a sound card is similar to the advice on finding a good video card. Assess your sound needs. Do you require digital output? Are you using this professionally, or are you just an enthusiast who wants to listen to your music? If you require excellent sound, research what's available and make your decision based on how the products meet your needs. If you are planning to drive a home theater speaker system with your computer, you'll want to make sure you get a sound card (or pick a computer with a sound card) that can work with the types of speakers you want to use. Most built-in sound cards will work great with a 2.1 speaker system (stereo speakers with a sub-woofer), but more complex speaker setups may require a more advanced sound card.

Installing and Configuring Windows Media Center Using the Wizard

Windows 7 offers a Setup wizard to help you configure Windows Media Center. To set up Windows Media Center, click Start→All Programs→Windows Media Center. The Welcome screen appears, as shown in Figure 25-1. Click Continue to get started. Next, you'll see the Get Started screen, shown in Figure 25-2, which allows you to choose between Express and Custom setup.

Express setup offers the default settings most people use. If you click "Express," Windows 7 tries to automatically configure everything you need to use Windows Media Center. Therefore, if you click "Express," you are done as far as the initial configuration is concerned and you can skip the rest of this section.

Custom setup allows you to select specific applications installed on your computer, and then customize their settings for use with Windows Media Center. With the wizard, you can configure your video settings, TV signal, and other settings for optimal use. To get started, click the "Custom" option, read the introductory text, and then click Next. Setup asks you to join the Microsoft Customer Experience Improvement Project, which helps Microsoft determine how you use Windows Media Center, and periodically asks you to fill out surveys. Joining this program is optional, but it does help Microsoft improve product use and enjoyment. Once you have chosen whether to join the program and you click Next, you are asked for permission to connect to the Internet to retrieve album art information, additional music information including artist and

composer, and other assorted pieces of information about the media you have listed
for use in Windows Media Center. Click Yes and then click Next twice. The wizard
will inform you that the required part of the setup is complete.

Figure 25-1. Getting started with Windows Media Center

Figure 25-2. Selecting a setup option

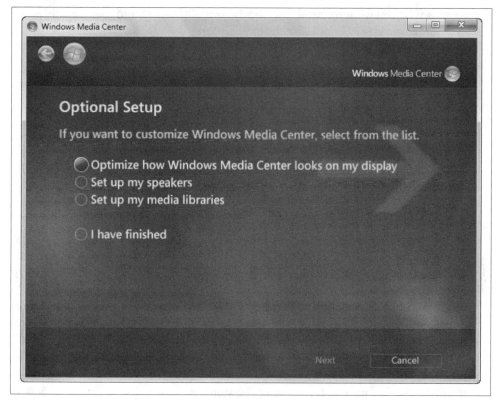

Figure 25-3. Continuing with the optional setup as necessary

At this point, you have several options from which to choose (see Figure 25-3):

Configure tuners, TV signal, and Guide

Selecting this option and clicking Next brings up the TV Setup screen, which shows you the default region used to configure your computer for local TV services, such as the United States. If the region is correct, accept the default selection of "Yes, use this region to configure TV services" and then click Next to continue. Otherwise, select "No, I want to select a different region" and then after specifying your region you'll be able to continue.

After you select the region, you'll need to enter your postal or Zip code if appropriate. This allows you to get downloadable TV Program Guide listings if they are available for your region. Click Next. When prompted, agree to the program guide terms of service and then click Next.

If you agree to the Microsoft PlayReady agreement, Windows Media Center will install a premium content protection software component called PlayReady. PlayReady allows you to watch and record premium content in Windows Media Center and also protects your premium content by only allowing authorized people to view it. If you want to install PlayReady, select "I agree" and then click Next to install the software.

Next, Windows Media Center will examine the available TV signal. If there's a problem with the signal detection, you can have Media Center try to detect the TV signal again or manually configure the TV signal. Finally, Media Center will download the TV program guide for your region, if it is available.

Optimize how Windows Media Center looks on your display
Selecting this option and clicking Next brings up the Display Configuration screen. Before you continue, make sure that you are viewing the wizard on your preferred display. If your preferred display isn't connected, connect it and then restart the setup before clicking Next. If you are prompted about watching in full-screen mode, click Yes. When prompted to confirm that you are viewing the wizard on your preferred display, click Yes and then click Next.

You have several display type choices: Monitor, Flat panel, Projector, Television, and Built-in display. Select the correct device from the list, and then click Next. Select the correct cable used to connect the device to your machine and then click Next. You have four options to choose from: Composite or S-Video; DVI, VGA, or DisplayPort; HDMI; and Component cable. Selecting the proper connection helps Windows Media Center optimize itself to your system by using the best settings for each type of cable and device connected to your system.

Once you have selected the correct cable type, you must supply information concerning the display width of your computer and then click Next. You can select from standard or widescreen format. The standard format uses a ratio of 4:3. The widescreen format uses a ratio of 16:9, which is the same format as a movie screen. These choices enable you to optimize your display settings based on the media formats and device configurations available.

After you make your choices, the wizard asks you to confirm that the current display resolution is what you want to use. If so, click Yes and then click Next. If not, click No, click Next, choose a desired display resolution and then click Next.

You now have the option of allowing the wizard to help you adjust brightness, contrast and other settings or finish the display optimization part of the setup process. If you want to adjust the display controls, select the related option, click Next and then follow the prompts to adjust various aspects of the display.

Set up your speakers
Select this option and click Next to set up your speakers for use with Windows Media Center. You must know how your speakers are connected to your computer and how many speakers are available, and then you must test your speakers.

Speaker connection types include: mini-plug (analog), dual-RCA (analog), single-RCA (analog), Toslink (digital), HDMI/DisplayPort (digital), and built-in (laptop). Once you have identified the type of speakers connected to your computer and then click Next.

Several speaker selections are available for use with Windows Media Center including: two speakers, 5.1 surround speakers, and 7.1 surround speakers. Select the correct speaker configuration and then click Next.

Select the Test button. If you heard sound from all of your speakers, click "I heard the sound from all of my speakers," click Next, and then click Finish. If you didn't hear sound from all of your speakers, click "I did not hear sound from all of my speakers," click Next, review the troubleshooting advice, and then click Finish.

Set up your media libraries

Choosing this option and then clicking Next allows you to tell Windows Media Center about folders that contain your media. Select a media library to set up, such as Pictures or Music, and then click Next. You are then able to add folders to or remove folders from the selected library.

You can add folders from your computer or another computer (if the folders are shared). After you select the folders to add to your libraries, Windows Media Center will then scan these folders for media and make the media available for use in Windows Media Center. From then on, Windows Media Center will monitor the folders you selected for new media as well, and will automatically make new media available for your use as well.

When you are working with Windows Media Center, you can add folders to or remove folders from your media libraries at any time by going to Tasks, clicking Settings and then clicking Media Libraries.

The first time you access a particular media library you also have a chance to add media to the library. If you want to add media to the library, click the "Add" option. Otherwise, click Cancel.

I am finished

Choose this option when you have finished the setup process and you're ready to begin using Windows Media Center. Click "I am finished," click Next, and then click Finish.

Navigating Windows Media Center

Once you have completed setup, you will see the main screen for Windows Media Center, as shown in Figure 25-4. The main menu works a little differently than most Windows menus. It scrolls up and down, and when you make a selection, you see the options of a related submenu on which you can scroll left to right to view and select the available options. Once you get started, the menu is rather intuitive, especially if you are using a remote control rather than a computer keyboard.

Figure 25-4. Navigating the main menu

Adding Media to Your Libraries

Before you start using Windows Media Center, you may want to ensure all your media is available. Media in your Pictures, Videos, and Music libraries are automatically available in Windows Media Center as are any media folders you've added to Windows Media Player. To add media to your library, click Tasks→Settings→Media Libraries. Select the media library to work with, such as Pictures, and then click Next. Click "Add folders to the library" and then click Next again. On the "Add Folders for" screen, specify whether the folders are on this computer, another computer or a shared folder that you want to add manually and then click Next. Continue by selecting the folder that contains the media you want to add and then clicking Next. On the Confirm Changes page, click "Yes, use these locations" and then click Finish.

When you add media to Windows Media Center and confirm the changes by clicking Finish, you are given the option of waiting while your libraries are updated or clicking OK to continue to use Windows Media Center. Rather than clicking OK, you might want to wait for your media libraries to be updated, especially if you have a very large collection of pictures and videos, because if you click OK, Windows Media Center uses a background process (rather than a foreground process) to add media. This background process is low priority and only runs when your computer isn't actively performing other tasks. If you have a very large library, it could take several hours for the background process to completely update your library. If you close Windows Media Center before the task completes, Windows Media Center will resume the update process by scanning your media folders the next time you start the program.

Working with Pictures + Videos

The Pictures + Videos menu allows you to play pictures and videos saved to folders that Windows Media Center is monitoring. On this menu, you have a Play All option for playing all available pictures and videos, as well as Picture Library and Video Library options, which let you select individual pictures and videos to view.

Both the Picture Library and the Video Library make it easy to manage your collections. You can view your content by selecting the Folders option. Play Favorites is a new option that creates a collage of all your pictures and then enters play mode where pictures are randomly displayed full size. After a while, media center will go back to collage mode and start the random selection process all over again.

Navigating your Picture Library

Using the Picture Library option, you can view pictures saved in your Pictures library, and any other folders monitored by Windows Media Center that contain pictures. As Figure 25-5 shows, the pictures options are similar to those in Windows Media Player. When you are working with pictures, you can even select "Play slide show" to play a slideshow of all your pictures or of pictures in a selected folder. To go up to the next level of the menu system from a submenu, move the pointer around the screen and then click the Back button.

You can view pictures associated with the Picture Library using the Folders view, which shows you thumbnails of the pictures available in each folder. You can also view pictures by selecting the Tags or Ratings option, which allows you to select pictures to which you have added a tag or rating for easier management. In addition, you can select pictures by the date they were taken to make it easier to manage large numbers of photos, or if you have forgotten their specific locations.

Figure 25-5. Selecting a folder and viewing your pictures

Two new options are Shared and Slide Shows. Shared is a new option that allows you to access shared pictures from other users on your computer or from other computers in your homegroup. When you select the Slide Shows option, you can create a playlist of music, pictures or both and then play this back at any time as a slideshow. To get started, select the Slide Shows option and then click Create Slide Show. On the Name Slide Show screen, shown in Figure 25-6, type a name for the slideshow, such as Family Vacation, and then click Next. Afterward, select a location to browse for media, either your Music Library or your Picture Library. I would suggest adding pictures first and then adding music.

You select pictures by navigating through the Picture folders you've added to Windows Media Center and then clicking each picture that you want to add as shown in Figure 25-7. By default, pictures in each folder are listed by name, but you can also list pictures by date or rating. To navigate from a subfolder to a top-level folder, move the mouse in the screen and then click the Back button in the upper-left corner of the screen.

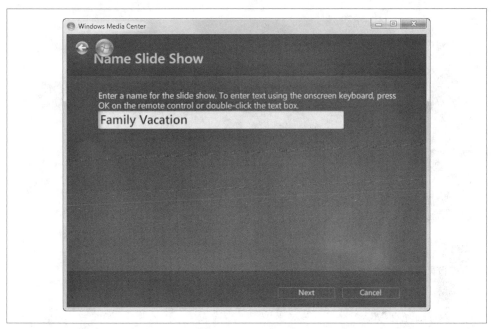

Figure 25-6. Naming your slideshow

Figure 25-7. Selecting pictures for the slideshow

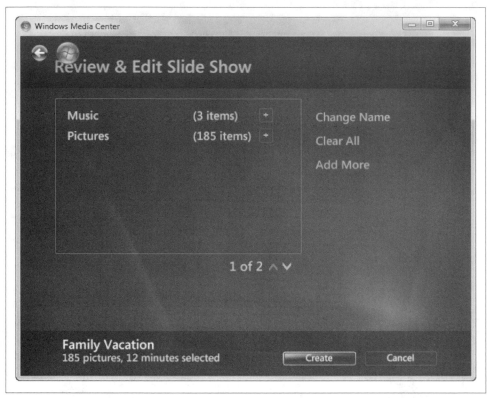

Figure 25-8. Reviewing and editing your slideshow

When you've selected the pictures you want to add to the slideshow, click Next to access the Review & Edit Slide Show screen. Click Add More to return to the Select Media screen where you can select a location to browse for media. Once you've added both pictures and music to the slideshow, the Review & Edit Slide Show screen will appear similar to the screen shown in Figure 25-8. Click Create to create the slideshow and add it to your Slide Shows list or use the other options on the screen to edit the settings.

Clicking Change Name allows you to change the name of the slide show. Clicking Add More brings you back to the Select Media screen where you can select a location to browse for media. Clicking Clear All removes all media from the slide show. To change the order of music or pictures, click the expand option (the + button) next to either Music or Pictures. Each song or picture will have up and down arrow buttons that allow you to change the order of the item as well as a delete button. Once you've made your changes, click the Back button to return to the Review & Edit Slide Show screen.

You can work with your slideshows in several different ways. Clicking a slideshow in the Slide Shows list displays summary information about the slideshow as shown in Figure 25-9. To play the slideshow, click the Play Slide Show option. The top-level

Figure 25-9. Accessing a saved slideshow

menu provides Pictures, Music, and Actions options. Selecting Pictures allows you to review the pictures in the slideshow. Selecting Music allows you to review the music in the slideshow.

Selecting the Actions option while working with a saved slideshow displays the Actions page, shown in Figure 25-10. Click the Edit Slide Show option to return to the Review & Edit Slide Show screen. Click Burn a CD/DVD to write your slideshow to a CD or DVD. Before clicking this option, you should insert a writable CD or DVD into your computer's CD/DVD burner. If you insert a CD, you can create an Audio CD that contains only the music in your slideshow or a data CD that contains your music and pictures stored as standard files. If you insert a DVD, you can create a data DVD that contains your music and pictures stored as standard files or a DVD slideshow that is written as a video DVD that you can play in any compatible DVD player. The Burn Progress dialog box tracks the progress of the CD or DVD creation process. To do other things while the disc is being burned, click OK.

When you are working with your Picture library, don't overlook the handy shortcut menus that are available when you right-click. If you right-click a picture folder in the

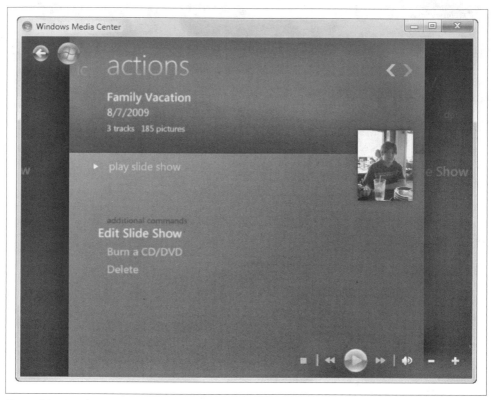

Figure 25-10. Selecting actions to perform

Folders view, or select a picture folder and then click the More Info/Options button on your remote control, your options are:

Burn a CD/DVD
 Allows you to write the pictures in the selected folder to a CD or DVD.

View Small/View Large
 Switches between the small or large view of folders.

Manage Library
 Accesses the add and remove folders options for your Pictures library directly.

Settings
 Access the Settings page directly.

If you right-click a picture, or select a picture and then click the More Info/Options button on your remote control, your options are:

Picture Details
 Displays detailed information about the picture and provides additional management commands, including View, Play Slide Show, Rotate, Print, Touch Up, Burn

a CD/DVD, and Rate. To touch up a picture, you must have modify permissions. When touching up a picture, you can correct red-eye, automatically correct contrast problems, or crop the picture. Click Preview to check your changes and then click Save to save the changes or Cancel to cancel the changes.

Delete
> Deletes the picture from your library and your computer. You are prompted to confirm that you really want to delete the picture.

Rotate
> Rotates the picture 90 degrees clockwise each time you select this option.

View Small/View Large
> Switches between the small or large view of pictures.

Manage Library
> Accesses the add and remove folders options for your Pictures library directly.

Settings
> Access the Settings page directly.

Navigating your Video Library

Using the Video Library option, you can view videos saved in your Video Library, and any other folders monitored by Windows Media Center that contain videos. As Figure 25-11 shows, the video options are similar to those for pictures but less extensive. When you are working with videos, you can select Play All to play all of your videos or all the videos in a selected folder. To go up to the next level of the menu system from a submenu, move the pointer around the screen and then click the Back button.

You can view videos associated with the Video Library using the Folders view, which shows you thumbnails of the videos available in each folder, organized by name. You can also view videos by the date they were taken, which may make it easier to manage large numbers of photos, or if you have forgotten their specific locations. Shared is a new option that allows you to access shared videos from other users on your computer or from other computers in your homegroup. If you have a folder that also contains pictures and the related folder has been added for pictures to Windows Media Center, you can click the Related Pictures option to quickly access the pictures in the folder. You can then click the Back button to return to the video view of the folder.

The Video Library also has handy shortcut menus that are available when you right-click. If you right-click a video folder in the Folders view, your options are:

Burn a CD/DVD
> Allows you to write the videos in the selected folder to a CD or DVD.

View Small/View Large
> Switches between the small or large view of folders.

Manage Library
> Accesses the add and remove folders options for your Video Library directly.

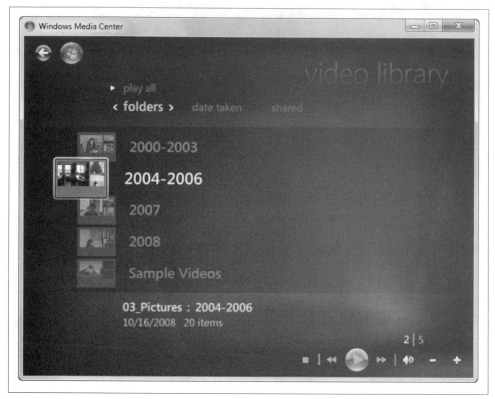

Figure 25-11. Selecting a folder and viewing your videos

Settings
    Access the Settings page directly.

If you right-click a video, or select a video and then click the More Info/Options button on your remote control, your options are:

Video Details
    Displays detailed information about the video and provides additional management commands, including Delete and Play.

Delete
    Deletes the video from your library and your computer. You are prompted to confirm that you really want to delete the video.

View Small/View Large
    Switches between the small or large view of videos.

Manage Library
    Accesses the add and remove folders options for your Video Library directly.

Settings
    Access the Settings page directly.

Working with Music

From the Music menu, you can play music saved to folders being monitored by Windows Media Center, and access Internet radio stations. You must have a sound card and speakers to play music. Additionally, you must have an Internet connection in order to use the radio management functionality. Table 25-2 lists Windows Media Center music functionality and requirements.

Table 25-2. Music and radio functionalities and requirements

Functionality	Requirement
Listen to music	Sound card and speakers
Download online updates to album information	Internet connection
Listen to Internet radio	Internet connection

On the Music menu, you have a Play Favorites option for playing all available music, as well as Music Library, Radio, and Search options. If you select the Play Favorites option, Windows Media Center will randomly select an album and song to play and then shuffle automatically between albums and songs. As shown in Figure 25-12, View Song List is the default view. Alternate views you can choose are Visualize, which works like the visualization options in Windows Media Player, and Play Pictures, which allows the Play Favorites option for pictures while Windows Media Center is randomly playing songs. Click Shuffle to turn the shuffle mode on or off. Click Repeat to turn the repeat mode on or off. Click the Back button to return to the Music menu.

Figure 25-12. Playing your favorites

If you select Music Library, you will see a list of albums and other audio files that are available. As Figure 25-13 shows, your music is organized in much the same way as it is in Windows Media Player. You can play all your music, or select albums or individual songs to play. You can also create playlists that work just like Windows Media Player playlists.

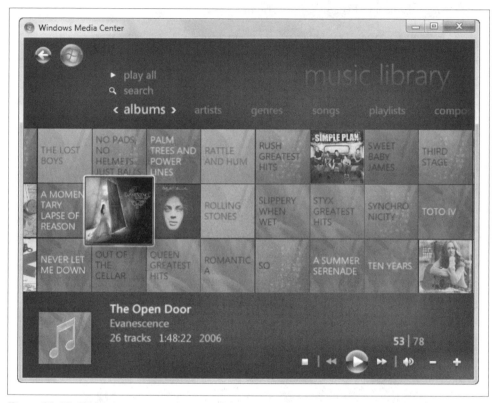

Figure 25-13. Viewing your music

 Using the Music Library option, you can access music saved in the Music folder within your profile, and any other folders monitored by Windows Media Center that contain music. From the main menu, click Tasks→Settings→Library Setup to specify additional music folders that should be monitored.

The Music Library section lets you view your music library by the following categories:

- Albums
- Artists
- Genres

- Songs
- Playlists
- Composers
- Years
- Album artist
- Shared

These categories make it very simple to find the music you want to play. You also have the option to play all of the music in your library, by selecting the Play All button.

Figure 25-14. Selecting an album within your library

When you select an album within your music library, as shown in Figure 25-14, you see detailed information about the album, including run time, song titles, song play time, and more. On the top-level Album menu, you have the following options:

Play Album
    Plays the selected album from the beginning.

Add to Now Playing
> Adds the album to the active playlist where it is queued to play after any previously queued music.

If you click Actions to access the Actions menu, you have additional options, including:

Edit Info
> Allows you to edit the album details downloaded from the Internet.

Burn
> Burns the album to an audio CD or a data CD/DVD.

Delete
> Permanently deletes the album from your computer.

 When you right-click an album, or select an album and then click the More Info/Options button on your remote control, you have a similar set of options on a shortcut menu. As with pictures and videos, you can also toggle the view between small and large icons, manage your library, or access the Settings screen.

If you select the Radio option from the Music menu, you can manage the different aspects of Internet radio, including adding new stations, managing how you sort them, and listening to the different stations you add. Clicking the Sources selection opens the Showcase menu. Selecting the Presents option takes you to a screen listing the preset options available to you. However, you must first install a radio tuner to play FM radio.

Once you install a tuner, you can select many different radio stations from any of these predefined selections. You can choose by genre or specific radio station listed. Some of the different genres available are jazz, Latin, metal, new age, oldies, pop, country, and blues. Each genre has numerous sites to choose from, and offers endless hours of music entertainment.

If you select the Search option from the Music menu, you can search your music by keyword to find a song, album, artist, and so on. Matches for text you enter are returned as you type, and you can click on a selection to view more details. To go up to the next level of the menu system from a submenu, move the pointer around the screen, and then click the Back button.

Working with Now Playing

When you are playing media, you will have the Now Playing option on the main menu for accessing media that is currently playing or is queued to play. You can think of the queue as the active playlist. When you select Now Playing, you will see the Now Playing screen, which is similar to the screen shown previously in Figure 25-12. The main options for Now Playing are as follows:

View Song List

Displays the current queue and provides options for editing and clearing the queue, saving the current queue as a playlist, shuffling the queue to create a random play order, and setting the queue to repeat automatically. The final option allows you to burn the playlist to an audio CD or a data CD/DVD. The process of burning a disc is similar to that of burning a disc in Windows Media Player.

Visualize

Displays a graphical depiction of the music being played called a visualization. Visualizations work just as they do in Windows Media Player. Use the channel +/– buttons to change the visualization.

Play Pictures

Plays a slideshow using pictures in monitored folders. When you play a slideshow, any selected and queued music will continue to play. Use the channel +/– buttons to move forward and backward through your pictures. Use the Stop button to exit the slideshow.

Shuffle

Shuffles the play order of items in the Now Playing queue.

Repeat

Sets the Now Playing queue to repeat automatically.

Buy Music

Allows you to buy music from your default online store.

Working with Movies

The Movies menu allows you to play downloaded movies saved to folders that Windows Media Center is monitoring. The top-level options are Movie Library and Play DVD. You can view your Movie library by the following categories:

- Title
- Genre
- Year
- Parental Rating
- Type
- Date Added

These categories make it very simple to find a movie you want to watch. Any movie inserted into a DVD player on your computer is available in the other category as well. When you click a movie, you access a Synopsis screen, as shown in Figure 25-15. On this screen, you can get more information about the movie and play the movie. If the movie is inserted into a DVD player, you also can eject the movie.

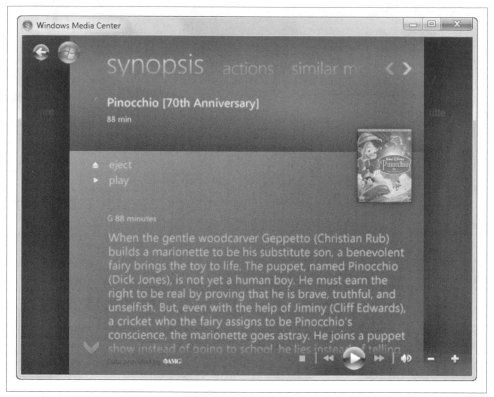

Figure 25-15. Selecting a movie

In addition to the Synopsis screen, you can access Actions, Similar Movies, Cast+Crew, and Review screens. The Actions screen allows you to edit the movie details. The Similar Movies screens displays a list of similar movies, if available. The Cast + Crew screens displays the movie credits. The Review screen displays a review of the movie, which typically is from the All Movie Guide.

If you right-click a movie, or select a movie and then click the More Info/Options button on your remote control, a shortcut menu provides the following options:

Movie Details
  Displays information about the movie.

Play
  Plays the movie. When the movie is playing, you can use the controls to manage playback. Click the Stop button to stop playing the movie and go back to the main menu.

Delete
  Permanently deletes the movie from your computer.

Burn CD/DVD
    Burns the movie to a data CD/DVD or a Video DVD.

View Small/View Large
    Switches between the small or large view of the placeholder icons for movies.

Manage Library
    Accesses the add and remove folders options for your Movie Library directly.

Settings
    Access the Settings page directly

By clicking Play DVD on the Movies menu, you can play a DVD inserted into your computer's DVD drive. If your computer has two DVD drives, you can insert a DVD into either drive. However, if DVDs are inserted into multiple drives, Windows Media Center plays the DVD in the primary DVD drive by default. The primary DVD drive is determined according to the drive letter, meaning that the DVD in drive D will play if drives D and E both have DVDs inserted into them.

Working with Recorded TV

The TV menu allows you to play recorded TV shows saved to folders that Windows Media Center is monitoring. The Recorded TV option lets you view and manage your favorite recorded TV content, as well as add TV content to your collection. You can also watch live TV from this menu. To configure these options, you must have the required hardware. You need a TV tuner card to watch live TV and a video capture card to record and manage your favorite TV shows.

Internet TV is also available. To access Internet TV, select Extras→Internet TV. At the time of this writing, Windows Media Player did not include an Internet TV tuner. However, the first time you access the Internet TV screen, you are given the opportunity to download and install an Internet TV tuner.

The Extras menu also provides access to headline news from MSNBC.com. By selecting Extras→News, you can view top stories, popular stories, stock news, economy news, and weather.

When working with Recorded TV and Live TV, you can add recorded content already scheduled and recorded for you to use. Each selection offers you the ability to view the desired content by date recorded, by title and by original air date. You may also want to view the scheduled content to be recorded by the system so that you can see what program will be recorded and the date and time of the scheduled recording for editing or configuration.

Microsoft was nice enough to include some sample recorded content for you to view. You can also add content you want to record, view scheduled recordings, and view your collection of recorded content. You can view your content by thumbnails, the date of the recording, or the title of the content.

Your recorded TV content is organized in much the same way as it is in Windows Media Player. When you select a recorded TV show by clicking it, you access a synopsis page, which is similar to the one shown for movies. You can then:

Play
>   Plays the recorded TV show. When the show is playing, you can use the controls to manage playback. Click the Stop button to stop playing the show and go back to the main menu.

Delete
>   Permanently deletes the recorded TV show from your computer.

If you click Actions to access the Actions menu, you have the additional option of burning a CD or DVD. When you right-click a recorded TV show, or select a recorded TV show and then click the More Info/Options button on your remote control, you have a similar set of options on a shortcut menu. You can also manage your Recorded TV library and access the Settings screen.

The Live TV menu allows you to view live TV. If you want to use this feature, you must have a TV tuner card installed in your machine. The submenu options available in this section include Recorded TV, Live TV, and Guide, all of which give you flexibility when managing and searching your TV content.

Once you have chosen a channel to watch, you can change channels just as though you are watching a regular television. If you have purchased an optional remote control, you can even select the Up and Down Channel options to change channels. If you select Up or Down, you will change to other channels. If you select Left or Right, you will change to other content on that channel. From here, you can also record the channel you are watching, pause live TV, rewind, or fast-forward.

With the Guide option, you can search live TV content just as though you are watching satellite dish or cable programming guides on your regular TV. The Guide refreshes periodically to update content made available to Windows Media Center. Using the Guide you can browse based on channel, categories, date, or time.

If you have purchased a remote control, finding content really does not get much easier. You can choose from the available content, record shows, or just browse the different channels available to you. The Guide content does not require any additional licensing or fee-based utilities, making recording your favorite programs easy and affordable.

If you decide not to purchase a remote control, you can still easily find, record, and browse content via the keyboard or mouse. Select the Arrow menu in the bottom-right corner to change the direction in which you want to scroll. Up and Down move you in the corresponding directions, and Left and Right do the same. You can also click the red button on the Play menu to record live TV.

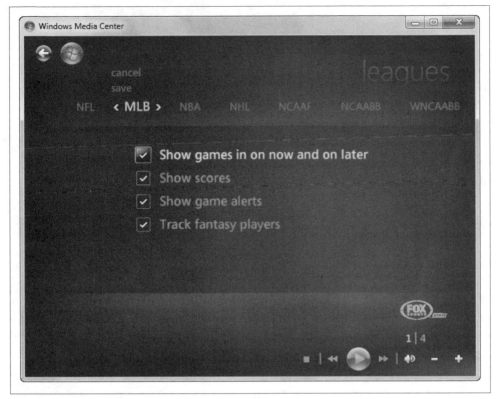

Figure 25-16. Setting up your leagues

Tracking Your Sports Players and Teams

The Sports menu provides a mini headquarters for all things related to sports. Not only can you show games on now or later on a league-by-league basis, but you can also show scores, view game statistics, get game alerts, and track players. Your options include Scores, Players, and Leagues.

The place to start is the Leagues screen. On the Leagues screen, shown in Figure 25-16, you can specify the data you want to track on a league-by-league basis. Select a league and make your selections for information to track. When you are finished modifying the settings, click Save.

 By default, Windows Media Center tracks all available information for all leagues. While the information itself doesn't take up much space on your computer, tracking the sports stats does require computer processing power and network bandwidth because the information much be downloaded from the Internet. Additionally, you won't be able to track players or configure alerts for some leagues.

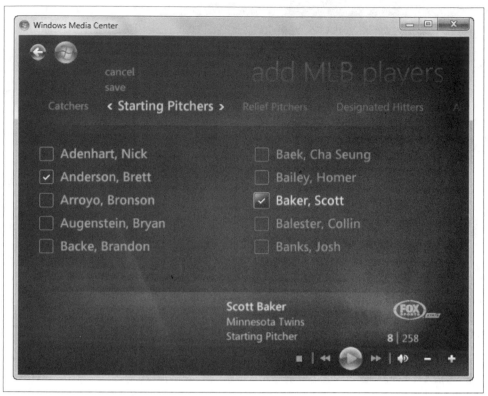

Figure 25-17. Selecting players to track

After you specify the league information to track, you may want to specify players to track. You do this on a per-league basis on the Players screen. Use the options provided to select a league, such as MLB or NHL, and then click Add Players. Windows Media Center will then load the players list for the league and organize players by position. For example, with MLB, player positions include Infielders, Outfielders, Catchers, and Starting Pitchers. If you want to track one or more starting pitchers, select Starting Pitchers and then select the starting pitchers to track, as shown in Figure 25-17.

When you are finished selecting players to track, Windows Media Center will download the stats for each player and display it as shown in Figure 25-18. The stats for these players are updated automatically from now on. If you click a player, you can see current news items on the player, vital details, and a team schedule.

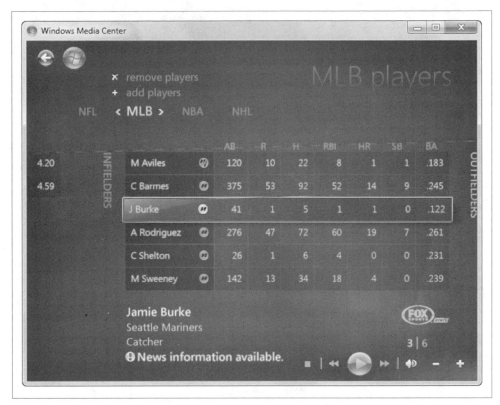

Figure 25-18. Tracking players

Working with the Extras Library

The Extras Library allows you to access your computer's program library so that you can play games on your TV rather than on your computer. When you click Extras and then click Extras Library, you will see a list of available games, as shown in Figure 25-19. Click the game you want to play, such as Chess Titans or Purble Place.

When you click Tasks→Settings→Start Menu and Extras→Extras Library Options, you'll see the Extras Library Options screen shown in Figure 25-20. From this screen, you can allow applications in the program library to control the Windows Media Center experience. By selecting the related checkbox, you allow other programs to control how Windows Media Center looks and acts. This is a default setting for Windows Media Center, and unless you have reason to change it, it is best to leave it checked.

You can also select the "Access media information" from Windows Media Center checkbox to allow other applications to retrieve and use the information that Windows Media Center collects.

Figure 25-19. Viewing your extras library

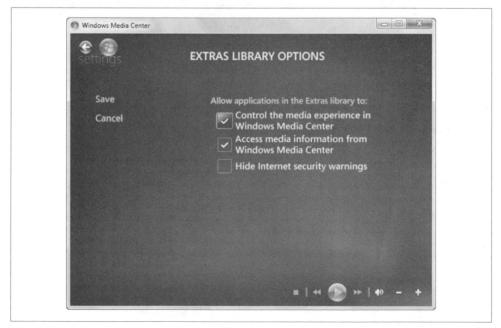

Figure 25-20. Configuring extras library options

The next selection available allows you to hide security warnings in Windows Media Center. If you do not want to see the security dialog messages concerning security issues with Windows Media Center, you can check the box next to this setting to stop them from appearing. When you are finished, click or select the Save button to save these settings in your profile.

When you click Tasks→Settings→Start Menu and Extras→Extras Library you can customize how applications interact with Windows Media Center. Choose specific applications to show or hide within Windows Media Center. Choices available include Burn CD/DVD as well as other programs. Then click or select the Save button to save these settings in your profile.

Burning Discs

Burning discs in Windows Media Center is similar to burning discs with Windows Media Player and Windows DVD Maker, but with fewer options. To burn a DVD, click Tasks and then click Burn CD/DVD. With CDs, Windows Media Center helps you burn audio and data CDs. With DVDs, it helps you burn a data DVD, Video DVD, or DVD slide show. Start by inserting the CD or DVD and then selecting the disc format, such as Video DVD, when prompted.

Next, provide a title for the disc and select a media location to browse for media:

- If you selected Audio CD as the disc format, you will be able to select albums and songs in your Music Library.
- If you selected Data CD or Data DVD as the disc format, you will be able to select from Recorded TV, Music Library, Picture Library, and Video Library options.
- If you selected Video DVD as the disc format, you will be able to select from Recorded TV and Video Library options.
- If you selected DVD Slide Show as the disc format, you will be able to select from Music Library and Picture Library options.

When creating your disc, you can mix and match different types of content from available categories by selecting a category, adding items, and then clicking Next. Afterward, on the Review & Edit List screen, click Add More, select a different category, and then add items from that category. Only categories for the selected type of disc are available, however. If you decide to go back and change the disc type, you will have to start all over again with the media item selection.

With Recorded TV, you can select the recorded TV shows to add to your disc. With Music Library, you can select albums and songs to add. With Picture Library, you can select pictures to add as a slideshow, and with Video Library, you can select videos to add. The process of burning a disc is similar to that of burning a disc in Windows Media Player.

On the Review & Edit List page, you can set the play order of media items you have selected. When you are ready to create the DVD, click Burn DVD.

Working with Tasks

The Tasks menu provides you with options to manage Windows Media Center settings and perform management tasks. Your options include:

Shutdown
> Provides options for closing Windows Media Center, logging off your computer, shutting down your computer, restarting your computer, and putting your computer in sleep mode.

Settings
> Allows you to manage Windows Media Center configuration. The main options let you configure settings for TV, Pictures, Music, DVD, and Extender. If you select Media Libraries, you can change the folders that Windows Media Center monitors for media. If you select General, you will have a completely new set of option categories. I discuss these additional options in the section that follows.

Burn CD/DVD
> Burns recorded TV, pictures, and videos to a data CD/DVD or Video DVD. See the previous section, "Burning Discs" on page 923, for more information.

Sync
> Syncs media content to a device with removable storage. This process works much like it does with Windows Media Player.

Add Extender
> Helps you set up your computer to work with a Windows Media Center extender configured on your home network. You can use extenders to allow Windows Media Center to work with other devices, such as the Xbox 360.

Media Only
> Turns the Media Only mode on and off. In Media Only mode, Windows Media Center is displayed in full screen mode and the Minimize and Close buttons are hidden.

Fine-Tuning the Settings for Windows Media Center

Selecting the Tasks list, clicking Settings, and then clicking General brings you to Windows Media Center's main configuration section (see Figure 25-21). You should take advantage of the ability to customize Windows Media Center so that you can optimize its use, as well as optimize the settings of your sound, display, and video.

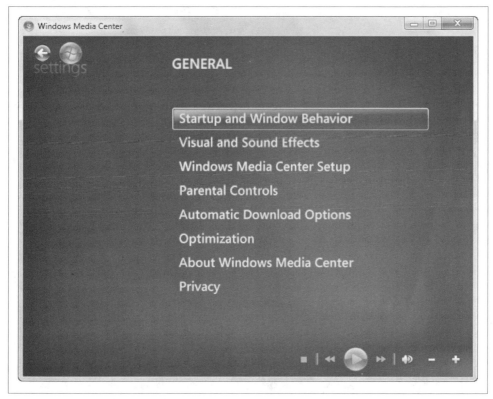

Figure 25-21. Using the General options to configure Windows Media Center

Configuring Window Behavior

When you click Tasks→Settings→General→Startup and Window Behavior, you will see the Startup and Window Behavior screen shown in Figure 25-22. From this screen, you can choose how your Windows Media Center windows behave in conjunction with other windows. You can tell Windows Media Center to always be on top of other windows on your desktop by checking the box next to this setting. You can also have Windows Media Center display a warning before displaying web pages that are not designed for Windows Media Center by checking the box next to this setting.

Selecting the checkbox next to "Start Windows Media Center when Windows starts" will allow Windows Media Center to open on the desktop display before anything else opens. This enables you to work with Windows Media Center as the main focal point of the operating system, and controlling it via a remote control allows you to use it like you would use your TV.

The last setting available, "Show taskbar notifications," allows Windows Media Center to notify you with issues or settings you need to look at in Windows Media Center. Once you have made your desired selections, click or select Save to save the settings into your profile.

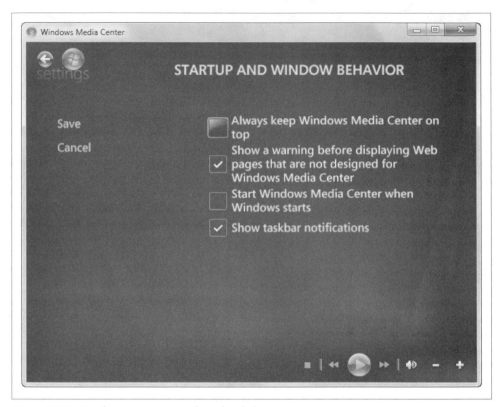

Figure 25-22. Configuring startup and window behavior

Configuring Visual and Sound Effects

When you click Tasks→Settings→General→Visual and Sound Effects, you'll see the Visual and Sound Effects screen shown in Figure 25-23. From this screen, you can control the visual and sound behavior of Windows Media Center. You can customize the behaviors of transition animations by selecting the "Use transition animations" checkbox. Checking the "Play sounds when navigating Windows Media Center" checkbox allows you to control how sound is used with Windows Media Center. If you want to hear sounds when you select menus or files, you should leave this setting checked, as it is a default setting.

Selecting the best color scheme for Windows Media Center is simple. Leave the "Windows Media Center standard" checkbox selected if you do not want to change the color scheme. If you want a higher-contrast color scheme so that you can view Windows Media Center better, select either "High contrast white" or "High contrast black" from the menu.

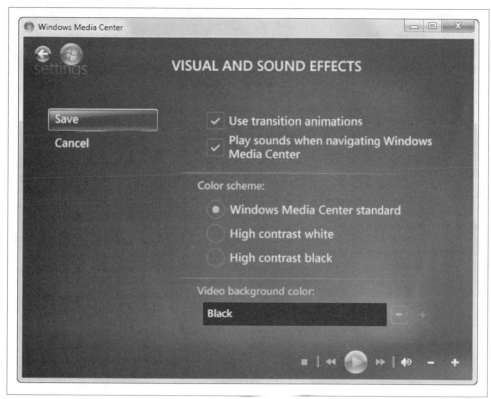

Figure 25-23. Configuring visual and sound effects

Additionally, you can change the video background color by selecting the – sign or the + sign available under "Video background color." This changes the black settings from 100 percent black to different shades of gray. This can help with specific types of eye-strain. Once you have made your desired selections, select or click the Save button to update the settings in your profile.

Configuring Parental Controls

Selecting Tasks→Settings→General→Parental Controls allows you to customize how you view specific content within Windows Media Center. These settings work similarly to adding access codes to your TV, cable, or satellite device. Once you have selected the Parental Controls option, you must enter a new four-digit access code to begin the process, and then confirm the access code to ensure that you did not mistype it. Make sure you write down and memorize this code. After completing this step, you are allowed access to the content menu, as shown in Figure 25-24.

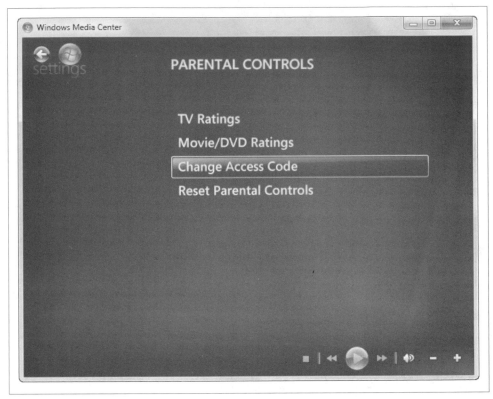

Figure 25-24. Setting parental controls to restrict usage

The content menu allows you to control specific content related to TV ratings and movie/DVD ratings, manage and reset the access code, and reset the default parental controls. For example, select TV Ratings to turn on the TV blocking attributes based on standard TV rating scales. You can select from the following choices: TV-MA, TV-14, TV-PG, TV-G, TV-Y7, TV-Y, and None. Table 25-3 provides more information concerning these settings.

Table 25-3. TV ratings

TV rating	Description
TV-MA	Mature audience only. This program selection is designed specifically to be viewed by adults and, therefore, may be unsuitable for children under 17.
TV-14	Parents strongly cautioned. This program contains some material that many parents would find unsuitable for children less than 14 years of age.
TV-PG	Parental guidance suggested. This program contains material that parents may find unsuitable for younger children.
TV-G	General audience. Most parents would find this program suitable for all ages.

TV rating	Description
TV-Y7	Directed to older children. This program selection is designed for children ages 7 and older.
TV-Y	All children. This program selection is designed to be appropriate for all children.
None	All rated programs will be blocked.

Within the selection of each setting, you can use the Advanced Options button to configure your system further. The available options are:

- Fantasy Violence
- Suggestive Dialogue
- Offensive Language
- Sexual Content
- Violence

This allows parents even greater flexibility in rating content specific to their children's needs or desires.

You can select the Movie/DVD Ratings option to control viewing of specific movie and DVD content. By turning on movie blocking, you can control movies available for viewing based on their ratings. Selections include NC-17, R, PG-13, PG, G, and None. Table 25-4 summarizes these settings and their meanings.

Table 25-4. Movie ratings

Movie rating	Description
NC-17	Not intended for anyone 17 and under.
R	Restricted. Children under 17 require an accompanying parent or adult guardian.
PG-13	Parents strongly cautioned. Some material may be inappropriate for children under 13.
PG	Parental guidance suggested. Some material may not be appropriate for children.
G	General audience. Appropriate for all ages.
None	All rated movies will be blocked.

After you have selected the settings you feel are appropriate for viewing on your system, click or select the Save button to save your settings into your profile. Failure to save the settings will leave the previous settings selected and saved to your profile.

You can change the access code for parental controls by clicking the Change Access code option, typing and confirming a new access code. You can reset the parental controls at any time and remove the access code as well as any restrictions by selecting the Reset Parental Controls option. As both options are available only when you type in the current access code, don't lose your access code.

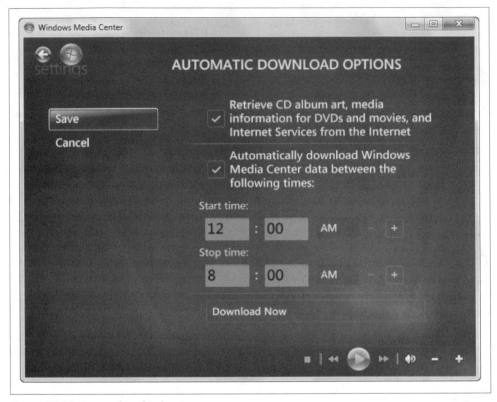

Figure 25-25. Setting download options

Configuring Automatic Download Options

Selecting Tasks→Settings→General→Automatic Download Options allows you to turn on or off the capability of Windows Media Center to connect to the Internet to retrieve information as it pertains to your CDs, DVDs, and movies. If you do not want Windows Media Center to connect to the Internet to retrieve this information, you need to un-check the box next to the "Retrieve CD album art, media information for DVDs and movies, and Internet Services from the Internet" checkbox (see Figure 25-25). To re-strict the times when Windows Media Center can download information, select the "Automatically download Windows Media Center data between the following times" checkbox and then set start and stop times.

By default, Windows Media Center will always automatically try to connect to the Internet to retrieve information, in the belief that it gives you a better user experience within Windows Media Center. Once you have made your desired selection, click or select the Save button to save these settings to your profile. If you want to use manual downloads, you must remember to access this screen periodically and then click "Download now" to retrieve media information.

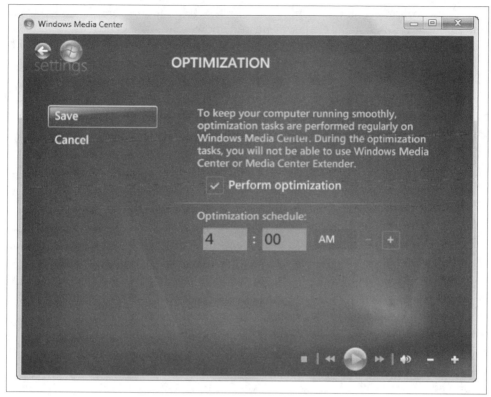

Figure 25-26. Optimizing Windows Media Center automatically

Configuring Optimization

Selecting Tasks→Settings→General→Optimization allows you to turn on and configure automatic optimization (see Figure 25-26). When optimization is enabled, your computer will periodically optimize your media to work more smoothly with Windows Media Center. Windows Media Center will perform specific optimization tasks that make it easier to use, such as reindexing your media content for faster content retrieval.

When you select the "Perform optimization" checkbox, you must choose a time for optimization to start. You can select any time during a 24-hour period, but keep in mind that during the optimization process, you will be unable to use Windows Media Center. Standard times are after 11:00 p.m., for most people, but if you require a different time, you can select it here. Once you have made the desired selection, click or select the Save button to save your configuration settings into your profile.

Using the About Windows Media Center Menu

Selecting Tasks→Settings→General→About Windows Media Center provides you with critical information concerning Windows Media Center. Within this section, you can view the software version of the application by selecting the Software Version button. The About Windows Media Center menu also allows you to view the terms of service when using the program. Finally, you can select Data Provider Credits to open a listing of the content providers for media information, allowing you to see where Windows Media Center retrieves its online content.

Viewing Privacy Information in Windows Media Center

Selecting Tasks→Settings→General→Privacy allows you to view the online Windows Media Center privacy statement, privacy settings, and customer experience settings. Clicking on the Online Windows Media Center Privacy Statement opens a window showing you the updated privacy available from Microsoft's website. To view the specific content from your browser, go to *http://go.microsoft.com/fwlink/?LinkId=8430.*

From the Privacy Settings option, you can change the Guide and Most Viewed settings available in Windows Media Center. The Guide selection allows you to turn on or off the ability for Windows Media Center to send anonymous information to Microsoft, which helps Microsoft improve the quality and accuracy of the services available within Windows Media Center. The Most Viewed selection turns on or off the favorites filter in the Windows Media Center guide. Once you have made your selections, click or select the Save button to update your local profile.

The Customer Experience Settings option lets you select whether you want to send anonymous usage and reliability information to Microsoft. When you experience an error within the program, you are asked whether to send a report to Microsoft, which helps Microsoft determine specific problems with the product and its interaction with additional programs. If you want to send this information to Microsoft, leave the checkbox selected, as it is a default setting within Windows Media Center. After you have completed your selection, click or select the Save button to save your preferences.

Using Windows Media Center Setup

If you did not use the Startup Wizard to configure your hardware and customized settings in the initial startup screen, you can select Tasks→Settings→General→Windows Media Center Setup to configure your hardware and network settings. You also can run the entire Setup Wizard again. Even if you did use the wizard to set up Windows Media Center, you can use these menu options to add new hardware or change the configuration settings.

When you select Tasks→Settings→General→Windows Media Center Setup, you will have these additional options, discussed in the following sections:

- Configuring your Internet connection
- Configuring your TV signal
- Configuring your speakers

- Configuring your TV or monitor
- Running the Windows Media Center Setup Wizard again

Configuring your Internet connection

If you have not previously configured an Internet connection for your computer, the Set Up Internet Connection option allows you to configure an Internet connection. Click Next on the first screen of the wizard. When prompted as to whether you have an always-on connection, click Yes or No as appropriate. If you are using a cable modem or DSL, select Yes and then click Next. If you are using dial-up, click No, click Next, select the dial-up connection to use with Windows Media Center, and then click Next again. If you choose a wrong selection, you can always select the Back button to change your settings.

Click the Test button to see whether you can connect to the Internet. If you can successfully connect to the Internet, you will see Connection Working listed under the test button. If you are unsuccessful, click the Back button to change your settings. If you are still having problems connecting to the Internet, refer to the section "Troubleshooting Problems with Windows Media Center" on page 936, later in this chapter.

Once you have resolved any problems and can successfully complete the connection, click the Next button to proceed to the "Setup Finished" window. Click the Finish button to complete setup of your Internet connection.

Configuring your TV signal

The Set Up TV Signal option allows you to configure your TV tuner card. Click Next on the first screen in the wizard, and then confirm your respective region. If the region selected matches your desired region, click the "Yes, use this region to configure TV services" radio button. If the settings listed do not match your region, click the "No, I want to select a different region" radio button. After making your selection, click the Next button to proceed. This section moves forward on the assumption that your region is now correct. Next, you see the Download TV Setup Options screen. Windows Media Center will download the TV options available for your region. Once this section completes, click the Next button to proceed.

It is recommended that you use the "Configure my TV signal automatically" selection, which will load the most common default settings available for your TV settings. You do have the option to configure your TV signal manually, but you will have to have specific information to provide to the wizard, including region and local information. Next, you are brought to the "Examining your TV signal setup" window. Windows Media Center scans your TV antenna signal to find the relevant TV information available to your hardware. Once this section completes, select the Next button to begin setting up your TV program guide.

You are presented with a menu selection asking you to agree to the licensing information provided to you. To proceed, you must select "I agree" and the Next button. Then enter your zip code in the text box provided, and click Next. Windows Media Center will download the guide information and show you a status of either Downloading or Download Complete. Once you see the Download Complete status, click the Next button to proceed. Congratulations, you have successfully installed and configured your TV signal and guide options.

Configuring your speakers

Use the Set Up Your Speakers option to configure your speakers within Windows Media Center. Click Next on the first screen of the wizard to proceed to the Speaker Connection Type window.

In this window, you need to select the type of connection you use to connect your speaker to the system. Table 25-5 lists the types of connections available for use in Windows Media Center.

Table 25-5. Cable connection types in Windows Media Center

Connector	Description
Mini-plug	A single stereo jack connected to your computer
Dual RCA	Two RCA connectors colored red and white
Single RCA	A single RCA connector colored yellow
Toslink	A single fiber-optic connector with a predominantly square connector and a shaft containing the filament for light connectivity on the end, usually colored white
HDMI/DisplayPort	An HDMI or DisplayPort connector that delivers high-definition video and up to 7.1 channels of surround sound in one cable
Built-in	Laptop-integrated speakers

After you have chosen the correct cable connection type for your system, click the Next button to proceed to the Speaker Setup window. Select the proper speaker configuration for Windows Media Center to test. Selections available include two speakers, 5.1 surround speakers, and 7.1 surround speakers. Table 25-6 provides more information concerning these configurations.

Table 25-6. Speaker selections available in Windows Media Center

Speaker setting	Description
Two speakers	Two individual speakers connected via a single cable to your system. The main speaker has the master volume, and the other connects to the main speaker.
5.1 surround sound	A subwoofer, center channel, and four satellite speakers connected to your system via a single connection managed through the subwoofer.
7.1 surround sound	A subwoofer, center channel, and six satellite speakers connected to your system via a single connector managed through the subwoofer.

Once you have selected the correct speaker type, click the Next button to proceed, and then click the Test button to test your settings. If you heard the sound provided by Windows Media Center, select the "I heard sound from all of my speakers" option. If you did not hear the sound, select the "I do not hear sound from all of my speakers" option, or click the Back button to change your speaker selection. If you continue having problems hearing sound from your speakers, refer to the section "Trouble-shooting Problems with Windows Media Center" on page 936 for more information on how to fix this issue.

Configuring your TV or monitor

Selecting the Configuring Your TV or Monitor option runs the Display Wizard. Click Next on the first screen to begin your configuration. You need to tell Windows Media Center whether your preferred display is connected to your system. Make sure you are watching the wizard from your preferred display to configure the correct settings. If you are viewing on your desired display, click the "Yes, I see the wizard on my preferred display" selection. If you are not, select "No, I want to use a different display" option. Click Next to proceed to the next screen, where you are asked to identify the correct display device connected to your system. Choices include Monitor, Built-in display, Flat panel, Television, and Projector. Table 25-7 provides information about each device type.

Table 25-7. Display types available in Windows Media Center

Display type	Description
Monitor	A single CRT-type monitor with an SVGA connector connected to your video card
Built-In Display	A laptop screen or all-in-one PC unit
Flat Panel	A flat-panel screen with a digital connector connected to your video card
Television	A television set connected to your system, usually with component, HDMI, or DVI cable
Projector	A device with a lens and separate lighting source used to project a picture onto a wall or screen, connected to your system with an SVGA connection, S-Video connection, HDMI connection, or additional connectors

Once you have selected the correct display type for use on your system, click the Next button to proceed. You need to tell Windows Media Center the connection type for the display. You have four options to choose from: Composite or S-Video; DVI, VGA, or DisplayPort; HDMI; and Component cable. Selecting the proper connection helps Windows Media Center optimize itself to your system by using the best settings for each type of cable and device connected to your system. If you have a digital connection such as HDMI, choose it over composite or S-Video.

Click next and then specify the width of your display. Only two formats are available: standard (4:3) and widescreen (16:9). Select the appropriate display ratio for your display and click Next. The next screen asks you to confirm your display resolution, and asks you to either keep or discard your current settings. Click the desired selection and then click the Next button. Once you have completed this task, you are finished setting up your display device.

Running the Windows Media Center Setup Wizard again

The next-to-last menu selection under Tasks→Settings is "Run Windows Media Center setup again." This selection will actually run the original Setup Wizard again, allowing you to reconfigure your system using the wizard. If you either did not initially run the wizard or did not feel comfortable going through the different setup menus, this option will help you add new hardware and change specific settings relevant to your system.

Before running the Setup Wizard again, Windows Media Center prompts you to confirm that you really want to do this. If you click Yes to continue, you will lose all current preferences and settings. If you click No, you will exit Setup.

Troubleshooting Problems with Windows Media Center

The options under Tasks→Settings→General offer the greatest flexibility in managing and troubleshooting Windows Media Center. This section provides detailed troubleshooting information with devices in Windows Media Center.

Troubleshooting with the Windows Media Center Setup Menu

Selecting Tasks→Settings→General→Windows Media Center Setup allows you to configure your options as you did during initial installation of the product. This enables you to set up your Internet connection using the same menu as the original installation wizard. Setting up your TV signal brings up the wizard to install the TV tuner card, which you need in order to watch TV and record desired shows. Using the Set Up Your Speakers option allows you to configure the sound within Windows Media Center, or change the settings previously input into the application during the initial installation, which may be necessary when you update your sound system or have trouble with sound working correctly in Windows Media Center.

Selecting Tasks→Settings→General→Extras Library Options allows you to control how applications control the media experience, access media information, and set the Windows Media Center Internet security settings. You also can edit programs and how they interact with Windows Media Center.

Selecting Tasks→Settings→General→Extras Library lists the different programs that can connect to Windows Media Center. Checking or unchecking a particular application allows or disallows the application to connect to Windows Media Center for content. These settings can help you diagnose problems with other applications and with Windows Media Center.

Selecting Tasks→Settings→General→Startup and Windows Behavior allows you to manage Windows Media Center startup behavior. You can have Windows Media Center start automatically during Windows startup, or leave it in the default mode, requiring you to start the program manually from the Start menu.

Selecting Tasks→Settings→General→Visual and Sound Effects allows you to manage transition animations and navigational sounds. You can also manage the Windows Media Center color scheme and contrast.

Selecting Tasks→Settings→General→Windows Media Setup→Configure Your TV or Monitor allows you to adjust your display settings within Windows Media Center for optimal viewing.

The Microsoft website offers additional information on troubleshooting Windows Media Center. Visit *http://www.microsoft.com/windows/windows-media-center/default .aspx* for more information. Many different websites and blogs versed in troubleshooting Windows Media Center problems exist on the Web and are easy to access using an online search engine.

Troubleshooting Windows Media Center Networking Issues

If you have problems with network settings and configuration during the Setup Wizard, this section describes how to overcome common obstacles and get your networking issues corrected. First, you need to know what type of network card you have installed in your system. Second, you need to have the latest driver from the manufacturer.

Once you have the items you need to find your way around Device Manager in Windows 7, you can open Device Manager by selecting the Start menu, right-clicking on the Computer icon, and selecting Manage. This opens Computer Management. In Computer Management, double-click the Device Manager node in the left pane. Then, in the right pane, click the + sign next to Network Adapters. This will show you the networking devices connected to your system. Once you have identified that a network card exists, right-click the appropriate icon and select Properties from the context menu.

Under the General tab listing, you'll see the device type, manufacturer, and location of the device. You also should see the Device Status listing, which should say "This device is working properly." If you do not see that the device is working properly, you need to click the Driver tab. The Driver tab has several buttons available for use. You need to click the "Update driver" button for this example. Once you have clicked this button, select "Browse my computer for driver software." Select the path to the driver you have for the network card and click the Next button. Windows 7 automatically installs the driver from the listing you gave and updates the driver on your system. Most of the time this will fix any problems you have with a network card.

If this procedure does not fix the problem, you may need to verify that the hardware actually works. You can do this by inserting a second network card, or running utilities available online. If you continue to have problems when you add a new card, you need to determine whether the slot in the motherboard is working correctly. Move the card into a new slot and see whether Windows 7 picks it up after you reboot. Make sure to turn off the system completely by unplugging the computer from the wall outlet before you attempt to remove or install any hardware devices. Chapter 5 provides additional information on device troubleshooting.

Troubleshooting TV Tuner and Video Capture Problems

If you have problems with your video card or video capture/tuner card during Windows Media Center configuration, check for known problems in Action Center and determine whether an updated driver is available as a solution. You can also have Windows run a check of your computer by clicking the "Check for solutions" link on the Maintenance panel in Action Center. If a driver is found, install it. Otherwise, you need to verify that you have the latest driver available from the manufacturer. You need to know the manufacturer of the card first, and then download the driver file from the company's website. Once you have retrieved the files, open Device Manager in Windows 7 and update the driver for the card, as discussed previously for network cards.

This procedure fixes the majority of issues you'll find with video cards. However, if you continue to have problems, you will need to verify that the card works correctly. Usually when you have video problems, you can identify them well before you load the operating system. If a video card fails to work correctly, you will not see any POST information from the system. If you are using a video capture or TV tuner card, this does not always stand true, however. If you have problems with these types of cards after updating the drivers in the operating system, you will need to move the card to a different slot to verify that the problem follows the card. If the card works in another slot, you need to check your motherboard for problems with the PCI bus. Make sure to turn off the system completely by unplugging the computer from the wall outlet before you attempt to remove or install any hardware devices. Chapter 5 provides additional information on device troubleshooting.

Troubleshooting Sound Problems

If you have problems with network settings and configuration during the Setup Wizard, this section describes how to overcome common obstacles and correct your sound issues. First, you need to know what type of sound card you have installed on your system. Second, you need to have the latest driver from the manufacturer. Once you have retrieved the files, you need to open Device Manager in Windows 7 and update the driver for the card, as discussed previously for network cards and video cards.

Most of the time this will fix any problems you have with a network card. If this procedure does not fix the problem, you may need to verify that the hardware actually works. You can do this by inserting a second sound card, or by running utilities available online. If you continue to have problems when you add a new card, you need to determine whether the slot in the motherboard is working correctly. Move the card into a new slot and see whether Windows 7 picks it up after you reboot. Make sure to turn off the system completely by unplugging the computer from the wall outlet before you attempt to remove or install any hardware devices. Chapter 5 provides additional information on device troubleshooting.

Index

Numbers

16-bit software, 122, 446
32- and 64-bit issues, 19, 105, 859
    FAT, 446
    installing to 64-bit, 118, 481
    Internet Explorer 8, 234
3D
    flip view, 44
    gaming, 66
    text and photos, 87

A

:: double-colon notation, 565
<< relative or abbreviated path, 197
>> expand button, 242
absolute path, 196
accelerators, 253
access permissions, 445
accessibility
    advanced options, 276
    Ease of Access center, 535
    internet options, 275
    keyboard options for, 540
    magnifier, 536
    narrator (text-to-speech), 538
    on-screen keyboard, 529, 537
accessories, 58
    Ease of Access, 535
    Journal, 531
    keyboard accessibility features, 540
    magnifier, 536
    Mobility Center, 521
    narrator (text-to-speech), 538
    on-screen keyboard, 529, 537

    Snipping Tool, 509
    Speech Recognition, 515
    Sticky Notes, 513
    Tablet PC Pen, 526
account name versus username, 725
account picture, 708
account type, 709
account, administrator (see administrator
        account)
account, user (see user accounts)
Action Center
    at log on, 12
    for resolving hardware problems, 179, 181,
        187
    for resolving software problems, 812
    notifications, 12, 47
    security and maintenance on, 595
activating Windows/Windows online, 17
activating with product key, 17
activation mode (speech recognition), 518
Active Directory Group Policy (see Group
        Policy)
Active Directory Group Policy Objects, 894
Active scripting settings, 269
ActiveX controls, 266, 269
ad hoc networks, 698
adapters
    display, 154
    networks, 157, 546, 548, 555, 557, 559
    USB, 146
    wireless networks, 157, 557, 695
Add Printer Wizard, 489
add-ons, 251
Address Bar, 196, 239
ADM, ADMX files, 887

Administrative Templates, 883, 887, 894
administrator account, 8, 727, 782
administrator LGPOs, 884
administrator options (Defender), 605
Advanced Performance Options, 101
advanced power settings, 38
Advanced Security Settings, 454
adware, 592, 594
Aero Glass, Windows, 26, 41, 68, 78, 80
album info, 303, 319
Album view, 292
All Programs menu, 58
all-user profiles, 557
allocation unit size, 744, 753
allowed items, 609
always available option, 499
analog video cameras, 350
animation
    adding to Live Video, 436
    controls, 99, 275
    title/credits, 420
    transition, 437, 926
antimalware (see malware)
Anytime Upgrade, Windows, 6, 866
Appearance and Personalization
        Troubleshooter, 813
appearance settings
    and performance, 65
    default, 25
    personalizing, 65
application access tokens, 112
applications, UAC-compliant versus legacy,
        112
archived files, 604
Archiving messages, 13
aspect ratio, 391, 422
attributes, file, 446
attributes, folder, 762
audio (see sound)
audit success/failure, 815
authentication methods, 625
Auto Volume Leveling, 306
automated backups, 823
Automatic Crash Recovery, 245
Automatic Download Options, 930
automatic private IP address, 564
automatic scanning, 600
automatic syncing, 326, 329
Automatic Update, 789

automatically fix file system errors, 799
automatically managing paging file size, 103
AutoMovie, 409, 435
AutoPlay, 113, 119, 301, 352, 356
Autorun, 112, 114

B

backdoors, 585
background message settings, 540
background services, 101
background video, 394
background, desktop, 82, 523
backup administrator account, 782
backup user profile, 781
Backup, Windows, 15, 836
backups, 819, 823, 836
balanced power plan, 38
basic disks, 735, 741, 742
basic permissions, 449, 450
batteries, 39, 141, 159, 522
Bayesian spam filtering, 643
BCD (Boot Configuration Data), 844
    data store, 876
    overview, 867
    using BCD Editor, 759, 871
    using Startup and Recovery, 869
    using System Configuration utility, 870
Bing, 240, 253
BIOS-based computers, 19, 548, 867
bit rates, audio, 313
blogging, 253
Bluetooth
    PAN (personal area network), 552
    printers, installing, 485
Boot Configuration Data (BCD) (see BCD (Boot
        Configuration Data))
boot environment
    Boot Loader, Windows, 871
    Boot Manager, Windows, 18, 842, 871,
        876
    boot options, 841
    Boot Sector Configurator, Windows, 879
    changing boot sequence, 879
    changing display order, 878
    repairing boot volume, 759
    restoring, 853
brightness, 309, 360, 438, 522
Broadband (PPPoE), 11
broadband connections, 684

browser proxy settings, 688
browsing advanced options, 275, 276
browsing history
    AutoComplete settings, 258
    clearing, 261
    cookies, 259, 286
    history list, 257
    temporary files, 255
browsing sessions, 246
bubbles screensaver, 86
Burn a Disc Wizard, 370, 372
burning, 379
    (see also DVD Maker, Windows)
    audio CDs, 322, 923
    data CDs and DVDs, 324, 370, 923
    region code and, 155
    video DVDs, 380–400, 923

C

cables
    Firewire, 145
    Media Center, 900, 934
    network, 546, 549
    parallel, 479
    SATA versus PATA, 142
    serial, 479
    USB, 144
    video, 350
caching, data, 106
Calculator, enhancements, 58
Calendar gadget, 51
calendar, searches using, 214
camera angles, 303
camera pictures, searching by model, 213
cameras, 195
    (see also pictures)
    analog video, 350
    digital picture, 349
    digital video/cell phone, 351
Caret Browsing, 244
cascade windows, 27
Cascading Style Sheets (CSS), 245
CD formats, 371
CDFS (CD File System), 372
CDs (audio)
    burning, 322, 370, 923
    playing from drive, 304
    ripping, 292, 312, 318
CDs (data), 324, 370, 923

cell phone cameras, 351
Certificate Export Wizard, 768
certificates, 613, 648, 765
change product key, 17
Change User Account Control settings, 14
Check This Website, 265
classful networks, 562
click-on keys, 538
clock, 159, 172
Clock gadget, 52
close programs to prevent information loss,
    811
closed captioning, 303
cluster size, 744
CMOS battery, 159
codec, audio, 313
color
    images, 360, 361
    inversion, 537
    Media Center, 926
Color, Windows, 80, 94, 96, 125
COM ports, 495
common folders and features (Start menu), 30,
    31
compatibility issues
    avoiding, 116
    examples, 117
    hardware, 147, 148
    running as administrator, 129
    running in compatibility mode, 129
    running Program Compatibility Wizard,
        124
    setting options manually, 128
Compatibility View, 244
component manifest files, 147
compression
    drives/disks, 760
    files/folders, 746, 753, 762
Computer Management, 610, 695, 814
Computer Name, 772
Connect Now, Windows (WCN), 550, 700
consent prompting, 72
context menus, enabling, 60
contrast, images, 360
contrast, Media Center, 926
Control Panel, 60
control tile, 521
controller cards, 142, 144
cookies, 259, 286

copy protecting music, 317
CPU Meter gadget, 53
crash (see recovery)
crash dump, 740
credentials, 72, 472
cropping images, 361
cross-fading, 306
cross-site scripting filter, 245
CSS (Cascading Style Sheets), 245
currency, 55, 172
cursors
   blink rate, 165
   pen, 527
custom size (paging files), 103
Customer Experience Improvement Program,
   15
Customize Start Menu, 36

D

data discs, burning, 324, 371–377
Data Execution Prevention (DEP), 104
date and time, 600
   (see also scheduling)
   Calendar gadget, 51
   computer, 174
   Date Taken (pictures/video), 337
   Daylight Saving Time, 174
   history list, 236, 255, 261
   regional, 172
   searching by, 214
   selecting pictures/video by, 385
debugging information, 785, 875
default media player, 285, 287
default operating system, 876
default printer, 484, 489
default programs, 129
default timeout, changing, 877
defaults, 500
Defender, Windows
   configuring, 598
   overview, 597
   running scans in, 607
   tools, 608
   troubleshooting, 610
   "Windows Defender is turned off", 610
Defragmenter, 799
delay, repeat, 165
denial-of-service attacks, 585
DEP (Data Execution Prevention), 104

Descriptive Tags, 338
desktop
   background, 82, 523
   customizing, 25, 76
   gadgets, 49–57
   navigating, 199
   Peeking at, 47
   secure desktop, 14, 72
device drivers, 13
   (see also drivers, hardware)
   and Windows 7 installation process, 478
   disabling, removing, uninstalling, 185
   how they are updated, 149
   how they are validated, 148
   installing new, 179
   maintaining, 182
   where they are stored, 146
Device Manager, 151
   viewing and managing with, 161, 188, 695
   viewing installed hardware, 152
diagnostics, 809–818
dial-up
   configuring connection properties, 560,
     678
   configuring dialing rules, 674
   creating a connection, 12, 672
dictation tool, 519
dictionary scanning, 590
digital cameras, 349
digital certificates, 648
digital signatures, 148, 163
digital video/cell phone cameras, 351
direct memory access (DMA), 153
DirectX, 68, 71
disabling versus removing device, 186
disabling, reasons for, 473
Disc Close on Eject, 854
discovery, network, 465, 488, 557, 569
discussion groups, 633
Disk Cleanup, 794
disk images, 19
disks and drives, 153, 199
   and multiple LGPOs, 889
   checking for errors, 797
   cleanup of, 794
   compressing, 760
   configuring, 735
   Disk Management for, 736–740, 741
   expanding, 761

installing and initializing new, 740
letters designating, 744, 754
optimizing performance of, 799
preparing for use, 743
system images, 823, 829, 831, 843, 845
system repair disc, 831
display adapters, 154
display order, 878
DMA (direct memory access), 153
DNS server addresses, 569, 579
document review, 518
Dolby Digital settings, 309
domain name antispoofing, 255
domains
   defined, 571
   enabling account, 774
   logging into, 705, 706
   managing security in, 597
   managing UAC in, 75
   managing user accounts in, 713
   no parental controls in, 705
DOSBox emulator, 122
double-colon notation (::), 565
double-tapping, 526
download parallelization, 246
drafts of faxes, 506
dragging and dropping, enabling, 60
driver software
   browsing computer for driver software, 184
   deleting, 187, 189
   installation, 181
   Update Driver Software Wizard, 183
driver store, 146
drivers, hardware, 13, 146
   (see also device drivers)
   keyboard, 165
   monitor/graphics card, 97
   mouse, 169
   printer, 500
drives (see disks and drives)
dump files, 135, 740, 785
DVD
   aspect ratio, 391, 422
   drives, 154
   formats, 371, 386
   menu, 302, 392
DVD Maker, Windows
   burning and playback options, 389

customizing slideshow and adding
     soundtrack, 395
customizing the menu, 392
encoding, 397
files supported, 380
opening and burning saved projects, 400
overview, 380
play order, 387
previewing and finishing project, 397
selecting pictures/videos for, 383
versus Movie Maker, 379
dynamic disks, 735, 741, 742
dynamic IP address, 564

E

Ease of Access tools, 58, 535
Easy Transfer, Windows, 5, 15
effective permissions, 449, 460
EFI (Extensible Firmware Interface), 867
EFI-based computers, 19, 867
EFS (Encrypting File System), 765
ejection, ReadyBoost device, 109
elevation, 72, 112
email, 631
   (see also Live Mail, Windows)
   audio alerts, 641
   forward scan as, 505
   global defaults for, 132
   junk, 635, 643
   pictures, 369
   sending snip as, 512
   videos, 370
EMS (Emergency Management Services), 875
encoding
   DVD Maker, 397
   Live Movie Maker, 441
   Media Audio, 312–316
   MIME, 574
   Movie Maker, 424
Encrypting File System (EFS), 765
encryption
   backing up keys, 767
   customizing, 624
   files and folders, 765
   files and folders, overview, 765
   indexing files, 228
   keys, 765, 769
   removing from files/folders, 766
   sharing files, 766

transport and tunneling, 572
end credits (Movie Maker), 420
energy consumption, 22
Enterprise edition, 4
environment variables, 31, 782
erasing (Pen), 526
Error Recovery, Windows, 839, 840
eSATA (External Serial ATA), 144, 180, 185
Ethernet, 546, 549, 689
Ethernet card, 157, 692
event logs, 231, 814
Event Viewer, 814
exceptions
    cookies, 260
    File and Printer Sharing, 468
    firewall, 612, 616
excluded files and folders, 603
expansion
    files/folders, 761, 764
Experience Index, Windows
    during installation, 16, 65
    improving your score, 69
    printing your score, 69
    re-running assessment, 13, 66, 69
    understanding your score, 67
    viewing your score, 66, 69
experience levels, 78
explicit consent, 259
Explorer, Windows, 234
    (see also Internet Explorer 8)
    Address Bar, 196, 239
    folder views, 203–208
    overview, 193
express settings, 285
extender, Media Center, 924
extending/shrinking volumes, 749
Extensible Firmware Interface (EFI), 19
extensions, default associations for, 129
external display (control tiles), 521
external hard disks, 740
External Serial ATA (eSATA), 144, 180, 185
extracting zipped files, 97, 120
Extras Library, 921

F

Face Detection, 346
fade and reveal (Movie Maker), 409
fail count, 818
failed resume recovery, 831

fast forward, 307
FAT (File Allocation Table), 446
fault tolerance, 738
Favorites Center/Bar (Internet Explorer 8), 236,
    244
fax machines
    changing drivers for, 497
    changing ports for, 495
    forwarding scans, 505
    installing network-attached, 488
    installing physically attached, 478
    managing faxed documents, 505
    managing jobs for, 501–507
    manual installation of, 482
    overview, 477
    receiving faxes automatically, 507
    scheduling and prioritization for, 499
    sharing, 491
features, adding/removing, 137, 284
Feed Headlines gadget, 51
File Allocation Table (FAT), 446
file and printer sharing, 466, 468, 491
file formats for
    background images for wallpaper, 82
    CD/DVD, 371
    Contacts, 708
    device drivers, 147
    DVD Maker, 380
    DVD Maker project, 397, 400
    faxes, 507
    Live Mail, 635
    Live Movie Maker, 428, 441
    Live Photo Gallery, 350, 351
    Media Player 12, 293, 294, 296
    Movie Maker, 401, 422, 423, 424
    screen savers Surface Styles, 88
    searches, 222
    snips, 511
    sound scheme, 91
    Theme, 94
    user account pictures, 715
FILE port, 495
files
    access permissions, 445
    attributes, 446
    encryption, 765
    expanding, 764
    names, long and short, 122
    sharing encrypted, 766

sharing permissions, 445
size, searching by, 217
type, searching by, 218
filesystem, 446
Filter Keys feature, 540
filters, 214, 218, 226, 340
fine-tuning
    application performance, 101
    virtual memory, 101–104
    visual effects, 99
Firewall, Windows
    alerts, 15
    blocking printer connection, 489
    configuring Advanced, 618
    configuring Basic, 614
    enabling/disabling, 615, 689
    exceptions, 612, 616
    features and improvements, 612
    hardware (router), 569
    network versus Windows, 547, 570
    troubleshooting Advanced, 627
    troubleshooting Basic, 617
firewalls
    hardware (router), 12
FireWire (IEEE 1394), 144, 145, 156, 180, 185
firmware, 867
fit to music (Live Video), 439
flash devices (see USB (Universal Serial Bus)
    devices)
flicking (Pen), 527
flip and slide (Movie Maker), 410
flip view, 44
folders, 122
    (see also files)
    display, 195
    optimizing views for, 206
    set current view as default, 208
    setting options for, 203
    sharing, 470
folders, system
    libraries (grouped personal and public), 34,
        223
    personal (user data), 32, 198, 398
    public (shared data), 32
force restart or shutdown, 831
foreground video, 395
forwarding faxes, 505
FQDN (Fully Qualified Domain Name), 772
fragmentation, 101, 799

frame advance, 307
Full Screen option, 303
Fully Qualified Domain Name (FQDN), 772

G

Gadget Gallery, 50–57
games
    controllers, 158
    improving performance of, 69
    parental controls, 729, 730
    rating systems, 729, 731
Genuine Advantage, Windows, 598
geographical settings (see regional settings)
GIANT Company Software, 597
GPMC (Group Policy Management Console),
    885
GPOE (Group Policy Object Editor), 885
graphic equalizer control, 306
graphics memory, 83
graphics/video cards
    and desktop background, 83
    for gaming performance, 68
    for Media Center, 896
    managing, 158
    obtaining correct driver, 97
group accounts, 706
    access permissions, 723
    adding/removing members, 726
    creating, 723
    deleting, 726
    renaming, 726
Group Policy
    Active Directory versus Local, 883
    and Internet Explorer 8, 238
    and Network Location Awareness, 885
    Client service, 884
    editing, 888
    improving management of, 885
    LGPOs, 884
    managing firewall using, 612
Group Policy Management Console (GPMC),
    885
Group Policy Object Editor (GPOE), 885
Guest accounts, 707
Guide option, 918
GUIDs (globally unique identifiers), 35, 867

H

HAL (hardware abstraction layer), 146, 147, 182

handwriting to text, 532

Hardware and Sound Troubleshooter, 813

hardware installation
  device drivers, 146–150, 179
  external hardware devices, 141, 143
  internal hardware devices, 141
  unconfigured devices, 177
  viewing settings, 777

Hardware Update Wizard, 162

headphones, 308

heuristic analysis, 591, 604

hibernation mode, 23, 37, 839, 875

hidden files, 447

high performance power plan, 38

highlight newly installed programs, 60

highlights movie (Movie Maker), 410

histograms, 361

history list, 236, 255, 261

Home Basic edition, 4, 26, 463

home networks, 545

home pages, configuring, 247, 632

Home Premium edition, 4, 379

homegroups, 9, 462, 467, 553, 776

hostname, 486, 490

hot keys for input languages, 172

Hotmail, 637

housekeeping tasks and performance, 85, 101

hover over keys, 538

HTTP (Hyper Text Transfer Protocol), 634, 638

HTTP 1.1 settings, 275, 278

hubs, 547

human interface devices, 156

Hyper Text Transfer Protocol (HTTP), 634, 638

I

ICMP (ping), 578, 617, 885

icons
  desktop, 27
  Location Indicator, 209
  notification area, 47
  size of, 31, 43, 61
  system, 49
  taskbar, 49

IEEE 1394 (FireWire), 144, 145, 156, 180, 185

IEEE 802.11 (Wi-Fi), 693

imaging devices, 156

IMAP4 (Internet Message Access Protocol 4), 633, 638

implicit consent, 260

in-place folder sharing, 461

in-place upgrade, 5

inbound connections, 621, 626

inbound packet filtering, 613

index settings, 228

indexing for faster searches
  adding/removing locations, 223
  including/excluding file types, 226
  optimizing file properties for, 229
  resolving problems in, 231

inheritance, 445, 449, 459

inherited permissions, 459

Initialize Disk dialog, 740

ink color (Pen), 512

InPrivate browsing sessions, 237, 243, 250

Install-Shield, Windows, 116

Installer, Windows, 116

IntelliType keyboard, 165

international domain name settings, 255, 275, 278

Internet
  access to home media, 290
  initial connection setup, 11, 933
  network connection to, 547
  radio on, 914
  setting advanced options, 275, 930
  TV on, 917

Internet Explorer 8, 255
  (see also browsing history)
  advanced options, 275
  configuring web pages as home pages, 247
  menu bar, 242
  new features, 234–238, 244
  status bar, 250
  toolbars, 238, 242
  web searches, 239

Internet Explorer Protected Mode (No Add-ons), 59, 234, 251

Internet Message Access Protocol 4 (IMAP4), 633, 638

Internet security zone, 267

Internet time, 176

interrupt requests (IRQ), 153

intranet, 266, 272
IP addresses, 486, 563, 569
IPSec (IP Security), 566, 572, 613, 622, 628
IPv4, 561, 567, 774
IPv6, 564, 567
IRQ (interrupt requests), 153
iTunes and iPod, Apple, 283, 310

J

Journal, Windows, 531
jumbogram, 566
jump lists, 45
junk email, 635, 643

K

key exchange, 622
key loggers, 585
keyboards, 156, 164–167
    ease of access options, 540
    language settings, 172
    on-screen mode, 529, 537
keys, encryption, 765, 769

L

L2TP (Layer 2 Tunneling Protocol), 571
LAN connection, 552, 688
language settings, 19, 172, 303
laptops
    accessories, 521
    and base score, 68
    and power management, 157
    connecting to projectors, 523
    Mobility Center, 521
    "When I close the lid" actions, 39
last known good configuration, 842
LGPO (Local Group Policy Objects), 884, 891
library/ies
    grouped personal and public, 34, 223
    media, 289, 309
    navigating, 201
    node options, 291
    pictures, 57, 294, 348
    recorded TV, 297
    video, 295, 348
Link-Layer Topology, 567, 569
linked library files (.dll), 147
Live Calendar, Windows
    agendas and to-do lists, 664

    creating and using, 657
    overview, 655
    scheduling appointments and meetings,
        663
    sharing with others, 658
    synchronizing, 637
    synchronizing with Google Calendar, 662
Live Contacts, Windows
    contact categories, 653
    creating contacts, 651
    importing/exporting contacts, 653
    information contained in, 650
    overview, 648
    synchronization, 636, 650
Live Essentials, Windows, 59, 89, 334, 379
Live Family Safety, Windows, 733
live filesystem, 376
Live Groups, Windows, 633
Live ID, Windows, 631
Live Mail, Windows
    changing security settings for, 646
    creating, sending, receiving email, 640
    Hotmail, 631, 636
    junk email, 643
    overview, 634
    phishing, 645
    set up and configuring, 637
    using, 634
Live Mobile, Windows, 633
Live Movie Maker, Windows, 336, 379
    adding a soundtrack, 438
    adding animations and visual effects, 436
    adding text overlays, 439
    creating a Live AutoMovie, 435
    creating and editing storyboard, 430
    opening and producing saved projects, 443
    overview, 427
    previewing and finishing, 441
    publishing, 441
Live Photo Gallery, Windows, 56, 89, 158,
        333
    (see also photos and video)
    basic controls, 334
    built-in CD/DVD burning, 370
    compatibility with Media Player, 333
    grouping and sorting, 339
    identifying people in, 346
    key features, 336
    ratings, tags, captions, 344

viewing pictures/videos in, 341
Live SkyDrive, Windows, 632
Live Spaces, Windows, 633
live thumbnails, 43
Live TV, Windows, 917
Live, Windows, 631
Local Group Policy (see Group Policy)
Local Group Policy Objects (LGPO), 884, 891
local intranet security zone, 266, 272
local user accounts
    adding/removing members, 726
    creating, 723
    deleting, 726
    renaming, 726
LocalService accounts, 707
LocalSystem accounts, 707
Location Indicator icon, 209
locked-down mode for Explorer, 234, 237
locking
    and screensaver, 85
    computer, 22, 37
    taskbar, 43
logging off, 22, 37
logging on
    Action Center icon, 12
    as another user, 21
    as local system account, 611
    first time, 8
    user versus administrator, 72
LPT ports, 495

M

magic packets option, 157
magnifier, 536
maintenance alerts, 15
maintenance, routine
    computer name and membership, 772
    configuring environment variables, 782
    configuring startup and recovery, 784
    configuring user profiles, 779
    hardware settings, 777
    homegroup, 776
    overview, 771
    scheduling of, 801–808
    system configuration, 772
    tools, 789–801
malware
    antimalware programs, 586
    avoiding, 14, 59, 74, 104, 243

overview, 584
    registry control and, 113
    scanning for, 607
Malware Protection Center, 610
mapping network drives, 199
mapping network infrastructure, 551
Master Boot Record (MBR), 867
MBR (Master Boot Record), 867
McAfee Security, 594, 793
MCE (Media Center Edition) (see Media Center
    Edition, Windows)
Media Audio Lossless, Windows, 315
Media Center, Windows
    About Windows Media Center menu, 931
    adding media to libraries, 902
    Automatic Download Options, 930
    burning disks in, 923
    configuring Internet connection, 930, 933
    configuring speakers, 934
    configuring TV or monitor, 935
    configuring TV signal, 933
    Extras Library, 921
    functionalities and requirements, 895
    installing, configuring with wizard, 897
    Movie Library, 915
    music functionalities and requirements,
        911
    Music Library, 912, 923
    Now Playing, 914
    optimizing, 931
    optimizing appearance of, 900
    Parental Controls, 927
    Picture Library, 903, 923
    Privacy, 932
    Recorded TV, 917, 923
    setting up libraries, 901
    setting up speakers, 900
    Setup, 932, 936
    sound cards for, 897
    sports, 919
    Startup and Window Behavior, 925
    troubleshooting, 936
    video cards for, 896
    Video Library, 909, 923
    Visual and Sound Effects, 926
media information, 286, 319, 921
Media Player, Windows
    building your music library, 309
    burning CDs/DVDs, 322

compatibility with Live Photo Gallery, 333
configuring for first use, 284
displaying media information, 286, 319
enhancing playback, 305
menus and toolbars, 287
navigating the music library, 291
navigating the video/TV libraries, 295
overview, 196, 283
playing audio CDs from drive, 304
playing library media, 298
playing video DVDs from drive, 301
playlists, 320
syncing media, 326
usage rights, 286
media streaming, 466
Memory Diagnostics, Windows, 811, 843
memory leaks, 811
memory protection, 104
Memory Tester, Windows, 875
memory-card reader, 349
menus, managing, 57
Message Store database, 635
metamorphic viruses, 591
mice and other pointing devices, 156
microphone settings, 171, 416, 516
Microsoft AntiSpyware, 597
Microsoft network diagnostics, 577
Microsoft Office, 789
Microsoft preinstalled games, 59
Microsoft SpyNet, 597, 608
Microsoft Update, 334, 789
MIME encoding, 574
mini-setup, 8
mirroring
    breaking/removing, 757
    creating/adding, 746, 759
    resynchronizing/repairing, 758
mismatch, paper size, 500
mobile phone access, 633
modem initial connection, 11
modularization, 19
monitoring folders, 310
monitors, 94, 125, 127
    Device Manager for, 157
    hide modes, 96
    multiple, 96
    USB/FireWire ports in, 144
    "Browse my computer for driver software",
        98

motherboard, 158, 867
mouse behavior
    and pointer schemes, 91
    open submenus with pause, 60
    optimizing, 167
    switching buttons, 168
    waking computer, 156
    with multiple monitors, 97
Mouse Keys feature, 540
Movie Library, 915
Movie Maker, Windows
    adding effects to video, 412
    adding narration, music, 416
    adding titles, credits, overlays, 419
    adding transitions to video, 414
    creating a storyboard, 404
    creating an AutoMovie, 409
    editing the storyboard, 406
    encoding settings for, 424
    opening and producing saved projects, 427
    overview, 401
    picture duration, 422
    previewing and finishing, 422
    publishing, 424
    setting video options, 421
    transitions, 410, 414, 422, 437
    versus Live Movie Maker, 379
MP3 audio format, 315, 326
MPLS (Multi-Protocol Label Switching), 571
MS-DOS and 16-bit software, 122
MSN info in gadgets, 55
multimedia (see Media Player, Windows)
multimedia advanced options, 275, 278
multiple bootable operating systems, 784
multiple LGPOs, 884, 889
multiple monitors, configuring, 96
Music Library, 912
music pane, 206
mute, 170, 288, 298, 301, 416, 418
My files (Computer, Documents, Pictures,
        etc.), 32, 193, 398
Mystify screensaver, 86

N

narration, adding, 416
Narrator (text-to-speech), 538
Navigation and Address toolbar, 196, 289,
        336
Navigation Pane, 194, 291, 335, 336

.NET Framework settings, 269, 270
Network and Internet Troubleshooter, 813
Network and Sharing Center
    creating broadband connections, 684
    creating dial-up connections, 672
    creating VPN connections, 684
    infrastructure, 551
    overview, 10, 669
Network Diagnostics, Windows, 574
network discovery, 465, 488, 557
network interface cards (NIC), 546
Network Location Awareness, 885
network projector, 524
networks
    adapters, 157, 546, 548, 555, 557, 559
    configuring protocols, 567
    connecting, 8, 11, 559, 691
    home or business, 462
    installing Ethernet routers, hubs, switches,
        549
    IPSec, 572
    IPv4, 561
    IPv6, 564
    location type, changing, 10
    Microsoft diagnostics for, 577
    navigating in Explorer, 197, 201
    Network and Sharing Center, 551
    Network Connections, 559
    Network Map, 558
    OSI Model, 573
    requirements for building a small, 546
    setting up wireless router or access point,
        550
    sharing, 462, 557
    TCP/IP, 561
    troubleshooting problems in, 555, 574–
        581
    VPN, 571
    work, 462
NetworkService accounts, 707
no-execute page-protection (NX), 105
nonadministrator LGPOs, 884
Norton Security, 594, 793
notification area
    Action Center icon, 12
    program notifications, 47
Now Playing, 288, 298, 301, 914
NSLookup command, 579
NTFS (NT File System)

and compression, 760
    converting FAT volume to, 744, 755
    overview, 446
NTSC video format, 389, 391, 421
nuisance software, 594
NX (no-execute page-protection), 105

O

Office Live, Microsoft, 633
old movie effect (Movie Maker), 410
on-screen keyboard, 529, 537
Online Crash Analysis, Microsoft, 811
online storage, 632
Online Store, 287
opacity settings (see transparency/
        translucency)
operating system reinstall, 831, 845
optimizing
    Aero Glass, Windows, 81
    disks and drives, 799
    folders, 206
    for faster searches, 229
    Media Center, 900, 931
    mouse behavior, 167
Options toolbar (media), 290
OSI (Open Systems Interconnection), 573
outbound connections, 621, 626
outbound packet filtering, 613
ownership permissions, 457

P

P3P (Platform for Privacy Preferences), 259
packet filtering, 613
PAE (Physical Address Extension), 105, 877
Page menu, 243
page order, 500
pages in history, 257
pages per sheet, 500
paging files, 101
PAL video format, 389, 391, 421
PAN (personal area network), 552
pan and zoom effects, 396
panoramic photos, 336
Parallel ATA (PATA) devices, 142
parallel cables, direct connection with, 479
parental controls
    application restrictions, 731
    configuring additional controls, 733

game rating system, 729
game restrictions, 730
Media Center and, 927
time restrictions, 729
turning on, 727
Windows Live Family Safety, 733
partitions
changing size of, 749
corrupted, 831
dismounting, 880
mirroring, 748
primary, 740
removing, 854
style of, 739
passwords, 9, 21
AutoComplete, 258
connecting to screensaver option, 85, 87
in Remote Assistance, 846
password-protected sharing, 465, 467, 723
protection on wakeup feature, 39
"Remember this password" setting, 11
user account, 710, 717
PATA (Parallel ATA) devices, 142
patches, software, 117
Path Selection list button, 197
Pause Printing option, 503
Peek function, 47, 99
peer-to-peer networking, 545, 571
Pen tool, 526
flicking, 527
tapping, 526
writing with, 528
People Tags, 337, 346
per-user profiles, 557
performance, 13
(see also Experience Index, Windows)
application, 101
balancing appearance and, 65
CPU Meter gadget, 53
desktop background and, 82
rating information, 13, 16
ReadyBoost, 106
virtual memory, 101
visual effects, 99
"Tell me if my device can perform faster",
161
permissions
and consent prompting, 72, 112
basic, 450

compatibility issues and, 126
effective, 449, 460
file access, 445
icon, 71
inherited, 459
NTFS, 449
ownership, 457
sharing, 445, 467
special, 453
personal (user data), 32, 198, 398
personalization settings
fine-tuning colors and experience level, 80
overview, 65
screensavers, 77, 85
sound, 77, 90, 169
phishing, 265, 645
phone number, 560
photos and video, 56, 389
(see also DVD Maker, Windows (video))
(see also Live Photo Gallery, Windows)
adding/removing media folders, 348
AutoPlay settings, 356
background and foreground video, 394
email videos, 370
emailing, 369
fixing pictures in, 359
getting your digital pictures, 349, 352
getting your videos, 350, 356
import settings, 358
importing pictures/videos, 356
sharing, 366
star ratings, 213, 340, 344, 466
tags for pictures/video, 337, 346, 356
text overlays (Live Video), 439
video controllers, 158
video formats, 391, 422
Video settings, 309
video timeline, 343
photos screensaver, 88
Physical Address Extension (PAE), 105, 877
Picture and Fax Viewer, Windows, 333
picture duration (Movie Maker), 422
Picture Library, 903
picture pane, 206
pictures
color, brightness, contrast, 360
display, 195
formats supported, 294, 296, 350, 351
in Media Center, 903

printing, 367
publishing, 366
red-eye, 363
rotate, 359
sharpening, noise, focus, 362
straighten/crop, 361
Undo/Redo changes, 364
pinging, 578, 617, 885
pinned programs, 41
Platform for Privacy Preferences (P3P), 259
play order, 387
playback speed, 307
Player ID, 286
playlists, 320
Plug and Play devices, 147, 179, 478
pointer schemes, 91
polymorphic viruses, 591
pop-ups, 592
pop-ups, blocking, 262
POP3 (Post Office Protocol 3), 633, 636, 638
ports
    for printers, scanners, fax machines, 482, 495
    USB/FireWire, 144, 145
Post Office Protocol 3 (POP3), 633, 636, 638
power button, 38
Power data (CMOS), 159
power options/plans, 23, 37
Power tab (USBs), 160
Power Users group, 111
power, saving, 38, 81, 157
PowerShell, Windows, 59
PPTP (Point-to-Point Tunneling Protocol), 571
Preinstallation Environment, Windows (Windows PE), 844
presentation mode, 522
preventive maintenance (see maintenance, routine)
previous versions of files, restoring, 821, 822, 834
Print Pictures options, 367
Print Preview options, 248
Print Processor, 501
print server, 478, 489
printers
    changing drivers for, 497
    changing ports for, 495
    disconnecting, 186

installing network-attached, 201, 488
installing physically attached, 478
installing wireless and Bluetooth, 485
managing jobs for, 501–504
manual installation of, 482
overview, 477
scheduling and prioritization for, 499
sharing, 466, 484, 491
printing
    pictures, 367
    "See what's printing", 501
    web pages, 248, 275, 279
privacy controls, 445, 586
private IP addresses, 564
Problem Reports and Solutions, 187
Processes tab, 134
product key, 17
Professional edition, 4
Program Cleanup, 797
Program Compatibility
    setting options manually, 128
    using the Assistant, 117, 119, 123
    using the Wizard, 117, 124
programmable keyboards, 165
programs list (Start menu), 30
Programs Troubleshooter, 813
projectors, 97, 523
proxy settings, 687
proxy settings, browser, 688
public (shared data), 32
public folder sharing, 461, 466
public IP addresses, 563
publishing
    Live Movie Maker, 441
    Live Photo Gallery, 336, 366
    Movie Maker, 424

Q

QoS (Quality of Service) Packet Scheduler, 567, 569
quadraphonic sound, 170
quarantined items, 609
queue, printer, 478, 500, 503
quick formatting, 753
Quiet Mode, 307

R

radio, 914

ratings
    star, 213, 340, 344
    TV/movie, 928
re-running the assessment, 13
reactivate disk, 757
reactivate volume, 758
ReadyBoost, Windows, 106, 400
real-time protection, 601
recent programs, number displayed, 30
recently used list, 30
Recommendation Wizard, 535
reconnecting at logon, 471
recorded TV, 35, 300, 917
recording, audio, 171
recovery
    from backup, 836, 845
    from failed resume, 839
    overview, 830
    using restore points, 831
recovery agent, 767
Recovery Environment, Windows (RE)
    recovering computer using, 843, 875
    safeguarding from corrupted, 844
Recycle Bin, 201, 365
red-eye, fixing in images, 363
reducing noise in images, 362
reference sheet (speech recognition), 519
refresh rate, 96
regional settings, 155, 172, 391
registry
    cleaners, 133
    Group Policy and, 883
    hand-editing, 587, 595
    safe mode and, 842
Remote Assistance, Windows, 785, 846
Remote Desktop, Windows, 787, 847
remote media files, 312
Remote tab, 785
rendering print jobs on client computers, 492
Report Unsafe Website, 265
rescanning disks, 757, 759
resolution, screen, 94
restart, 37
Restart Manager, 812
restart/shutdown issues, 838
restore points (see System Restore)
restoring previous versions, 834
restricted sites security zone, 267, 274
Results Pane, 194, 209

Resume Loader, Windows, 840
ribbon menu, 429
ribbons screensaver, 87
rights, usage (play/burn/sync), 286
ripping audio CDs, 292, 312, 318
roaming profile, 779
rolling back drivers, 184
rootkits, 585
rotating photos during import, 359
router, connecting with, 12, 549
RRAS (Routing and Remote Access Service),
    571
RSS (Really Simple Syndication) feeds, 51, 236,
    246
Run options versus Search box, 37
run without permission, 252

S

safe modes, 832, 842, 870
sandboxes, 591
SANS Internet Storm Center, 584
SATA (Series ATA) devices, 142
scan through keys, 538
scanners
    changing drivers for, 497
    changing ports for, 495
    forwarding images, 505
    installing network-attached, 488, 497
    installing physically attached, 478, 485
    managing jobs for, 501–505
    overview, 477
    scanning images with, 504
    scheduling and prioritization for, 499
    sharing, 491, 495
    "What is the name of your device?", 485
scanning for spyware/malware, 607
scenes button styles, 395
scheduling
    advanced tasks, 806
    automated backups, 823
    automatic scanning, 600
    basic tasks, 803
    defragmentation, 799
    troubleshooting the, 807
scratch-out gestures (Pen), 530
screen refresh rate, 96
screen resolution/orientation, 94, 95
screensavers, 77, 85
scrolling options, 168

SCSI (Small Computer System Interface)
    devices, 142
SCTP (Stream Control Transmission Protocol),
    573
search box
    Live Photo Gallery, 339
    options, 208, 210
    Options toolbar, 291
    Start menu, 30, 37, 39
search provider, setting, 240
Search service, Windows, 40
    indexing for faster searches, 223
    indexing problems in, 231
    overview, 40, 209
    save search options, 221
    search filters, 213
    search options, 210
search suggestions, 239, 241
SECAM, 391
sectors, bad, 799
secure desktop, 14, 72
Secure Mail, 648
security, 59
    (see also malware)
    advanced Internet settings, 275
    advanced options, 279
    restricting permission using zones, 265
security alerts, 15
security identifier (SID), 706
security levels, 265, 268
security zones
    configuring local intranet, 272
    configuring restricted sites, 274
    configuring trusted sites, 273
    individual security settings, 268
    levels, 266
    overview, 265
    setting the level, 268
Separator Page, 501
Serial ATA (SATA) devices, 142
serial cables, direct connection with, 479
Server Message Block (SMB), 468
service packs, 16
sessions, browsing, 246
Setup Information files (.inf), 147
Setup programs
    defined, 112
    working with, 114
setup, first time, 8

shared data
    accessing, 471
    enabling, 461
    folders offline, synchronizing, 472
    permissions, 445, 467
    specific people, 469
    wizard, 469
sharing permissions, 445
sharpening images, 362
shortcuts, 27, 121, 136, 195
Shrink button, 557
shrinking/extending volumes, 749
shuffling
    Media Player, 288
    music, 300
    priority order, 330
    slides, 57, 89
    wallpaper, 85
shut down (Start menu), 30, 37
shutting down, 22, 30, 838, 924
SID (security identifier), 706
Simple Mail Transfer Protocol (SMTP), 633
Size menu (video), 303
sleep button, 39
sleep mode, 22, 37, 839
Slide Show, 923
Slide Show gadget, 56
slideshow, 337
    adding music to, 396
    as screensaver, 86
    DVD Maker, 388, 395
    options, 88
    playing a, 342
    playing music during, 298
Small Computer System Interface (SCSI)
    devices, 142
small-business networks, 545
SmartScreen filters, 243, 265
SMB (Server Message Block), 468
SMTP (Simple Mail Transfer Protocol), 633
Snap function, 47
Snipping Tool, 58
    creating snips, 509
    editing and saving snips, 511
    setting options for, 512
software installation
    application setup, 115
    assigning default programs, 129
    AutoPlay, 113, 119

autorun, 114
making available to multiple users, 120
no Add/Remove Programs utility, 112, 137
performing the install, 119
reconfiguring, repairing, uninstalling, 132
user and administrator accounts and, 111
software, management, 479
Song List, 915
sound
audio file properties, 230
audio formats supported, 293
audio settings, 169, 410, 416
bit rates, 313
email alerts, 641
Music Library, 912
music pane, 206
personalization, 77, 90
setting up speakers, 170, 308, 900
troubleshooting, 938
sound, video, and game controllers, 158
soundtracks
DVD Maker (video), 396
Live Movie Maker, 438
slideshows, 396
source files (.sys), 147
space available, 103, 747
spam, 643
spanned drives, 736, 746
speakers, setting up, 170, 308, 900, 934
special permissions, 453
Speech Recognition, Windows, 59
configuring for first use, 516
dictation using, 519
overview, 515
speech reference card, 519
speed settings, 307
splitting video clips, 407
spoofing controls, 255
spooling, 478, 500
sports, 919
sports highlight (Movie Maker), 410
spyware
alerts, 15
antispyware programs, 594
defined, 592
SRS WOW effects, 308
Standard toolbar, 242
star ratings, 213, 340, 344, 466
start input panel gesture, 527

Start menu
adding features to, 36
common folder options, 35
overview, 29–31
Starter edition, 4
features of, 26
homegroup, 463
Snip not available on, 509
startup
and recovery, configuring, 784, 869
first time, 8
programs for automatic, 59, 135, 610
running speech recognition at, 519
Startup Repair (StR) tool, 840
static IP address, 564
Stationery (Journal), 534
stealth mode, 697
Sticky Keys feature, 540
Sticky Notes, 513
Stock gadget, 54
STOP error, 785
storage space, 828
Stream Control Transmission Protocol (SCTP),
573
streaming options, 290, 466
striped drives, 736, 746
subcontainers and objects, 458
subnet masks and prefixes, 570
Suggested Sites, 244, 246
surround sound, 170
switch users, 21, 37
switching mouse buttons, 168
synchronizing with Internet time, 176
syncing
folders offline, 472
media, 326, 924
status of file, 522
Synopsis screen, 915
System and Security Troubleshooter, 813
System Checkpoint, 820
system configuration
routine maintenance, 772
utility, 135, 870
system devices, 159
System Failure options, 785
system icons, 27
system images, 823, 829, 831, 843, 845
system properties, 199
System Protection, 821

configuring, 820
  previous versions of files, 821, 822, 834
System Repair disc, 841, 844
System Restore
  manual versus system restore points, 832
  operating system reinstall, 831, 845
  recovering after a crash, 830
  recovering using restore points, 831
  restore points, 116, 150, 604
  scheduling/maintaining automated
        backups, 823
  undo restore points, 832
System Restore and Shadow Copy Clean Up,
      797
System Services, troubleshooting, 816
System Tools, 59

T

Tablet PCs
  connecting to projectors, 523
  display orientation, 522
  Journal, 531
  Mobility Center, 521
  Pen, 526
Tabs page (Internet Explorer 8), 237
tags for pictures/video, 337, 346, 356
takeown command, 458
tapping (Pen), 527
Task Manager, 134
Task menu (Media Center), 924
Task Scheduler
  create advanced tasks, 806
  create basic tasks, 803
  overview, 801
  troubleshooting, 807
taskbar, 41
  behavior options, 43
  customizing buttons on, 41
  language bar, 172
  notification area, 47, 925
TCP/IP
  adding printer using, 486, 490
  networking with, 561
  ports, 495
television
  monitor, configuring, 935
  parental controls, 928
  recording, 917
  signal, 933

tuner problems, 938
templates
  administrative, 883, 887, 894
  predefined folder view, 206
temporary files, 794
text overlays (Live Video), 439
text prediction alternates, 530
themes, 77, 93, 127
thumbnails, 43, 290, 343
time zone, 174
timeline, video, 343
timeout value, changing, 877
title animation, 420
Toggle Keys feature, 540
Toolbars and Extensions, 251
Tools menu, 243
total paging file size, 102
tracert, 555, 617
trackball, 156
transitions
  animating, 437, 926
  between slides, 57, 396
  cross-fading, 306, 435
  Movie Maker, 410, 414, 422, 437
transparency/translucency
  compatibility issues, 127
  gadgets, 51
  in Aero Glass, 81
  memory issues, 81
  not available in all editions, 79
  Peeking at desktop, 47
transport encryption, 572
Trojans, 585
troubleshooters, built-in, 187, 555, 629, 812
troubleshooting and warnings, 13, 809, 849
  (see also diagnostics)
  (see also performance)
  account name not same as username, 725
  alerts, 12
  audio conflicts between Media Player,
        Windows 7, 308
  audio gap at start of video, 412
  Automatic Updates locks up, 793
  Basic Windows Firewall, 617
  changing monitor refresh rate, 96
  choosing format for videos, 425
  computer can't find network printer, 489
  corrupted partition, 841
  deleting LGPOs, 892

discovery protocols and security concerns, 569

email servers without password protection, 639

forcing a partition to dismount, 880

gaps, burn CD without, 323

grayed-out frames in Live Movie, 443

hardware, 187

indexing nontext-based file type, 229

installing controller cards, 112

insufficient storage space, 828

Internet Explorer 8, 280

list of common problems/resolutions, 849

Media Center audio, 938

Media Center networking issues, 937

Media Center setup, 936

Media Center TV and video, 938

Media Player not available, 284

network and printing, 555, 580

printer listed twice, 489, 504

printing continues after cancel, 503

Program Compatibility Assistant/Wizard, 117

recovery techniques, 830, 831

repairing failed uninstall, 133

spaces in video name, 424

System Services, 816

Task Scheduler, 807

turning off password protection for homegroup, 467

turning off Windows Firewall, 547, 570

undoing "always do this..." selections, 107

using built-in network/printing troubleshooters, 555

Windows Classic/Basic color/transparency limitations, 79

Windows Defender, 610

TruBass slider, 308

trusted sites security zone, 267, 273

tunneling encryption, 571, 572

turn off system protection, 822

turn Windows features on or off, 19

U

UAC (User Account Control) (see User Account Control (UAC))

UDF (Universal Disc Format), 372

UDP (User Datagram Protocol), 573

UEFI (Unified Extensible Firmware Interface), 867

Ultimate edition, 4, 379

unconfigured hardware devices, 177

uninstalling, 116, 132, 185

Universal Serial Bus (see USB (Universal Serial Bus) devices)

Unknown CD, 304

unpinning programs from taskbar, 41

unrated files, 466

unsigned ActiveX controls, 266

unsigned drivers, 149

Update, Windows

  and hardware diagnostics, 177

  and Microsoft Update, 789

  and Windows Live, 334

  checking for updates, 791

  configuring automatic updates, 790

  how it handles device drivers, 149, 180

  installing, 789

  removing updates, 793

  resolving problems with, 793

  restoring declined updates, 794

  selecting options, 8, 15

  viewing update history, 792

updates, hardware, 182

updates, software, 117

upgrading, 5, 864

URL handler, 254

URLs

  calendars online, 658

  detailed list of edition features, 6

  downloads from Microsoft, 234

  incoming email server, 638

  Internet time, 177

  large-sector disks, 746

  Live Essentials applications, 59

  magic packets, 157

  Media Center Privacy Statement, 932

  Media Center, troubleshooting, 937

  media database, 286

  Microsoft Support, 133, 849

  Office Live, 633

  outgoing email server, 638

  SANS Internet Storm Center, 584

  source for DOSBox, 122

  updates to this book, 860

  Windows Installer Cleanup utility, 133

  Windows Live Mobile, 633

Windows Live programs, 427, 631
Windows Virtual PC website, 123
usage rights, 286
USB (Universal Serial Bus) devices
    as password keys, 711
    Device Manager for hubs, 159
    distinguishing 1.0, 1.1, 2.0, 145
    installing/connecting, 180, 185
    ReadyBoost, 106
    removing, 185
    virtual ports, 495
    Y adapters, 146
use printer offline, 504
User Account Control (UAC)
    changing control settings, 14
    configuring and tuning, 74
    listed on startup screen, 21
    permissions, 71, 112
user accounts
    add or remove, 15
    changing names for others, 714
    changing picture for others, 715
    changing types for others, 716
    changing your name, 707
    changing your picture, 708
    changing your type, 709
    controlling how passwords are used, 721
    creating accounts for others, 713
    creating passwords for others, 717
    deleting local, 722
    enabling local, 720
    managing passwords for others, 718
    managing your password, 710
User Datagram Protocol (UDP), 573
user experience levels, 78
user interface, 25
user profiles, 25, 779
username versus account name, 725

V

video (see photos and video) (see pictures)
video cards (see graphics/video cards)
Video Library, 909
video pane, 206
view active networks, 10
View Magnifier icon (Internet Explorer 8), 251
Virtual Machine Based Rootkit (VMBR), 585
virtual machines for old programs, 122
virtual memory, 101

Virtual Private Network (VPN), 557, 571, 669, 684
viruses, 587
    (see also malware)
    antivirus programs, 590, 594
    defined, 587
Visual Effects, 99
visualizations (for audio playbacks), 305
VMBR (Virtual Machine Based Rootkit), 585
voice activation mode, 518
volume control
    computer master, 169
    laptop, 522
    laptop/Table PC, 523
    Media Player, 288, 298, 301, 306
    Movie Maker, 418
    tablet PC, 522
    Volume Mixer, 439
volumes
    assigning drive letters to, 754
    changing labels, 746, 755
    converting to NTFS, 755
    creating mirrored, spanned, striped, 746
    deleting, 756
    formatting, 753
    labels, 755
    shrinking or extending, 749
    troubleshooting, 757
    viewing details, 738
VPN (Virtual Private Network), 557, 571, 669, 684

W

waking the computer, 156, 157
wallpaper, 82
WAV audio, 316
WCN (Connect Now, Windows), 700
WCN (Windows Connect Now), 550
WDDM (Windows Display Driver Model), 68, 71, 154, 896
Weather gadget, 53
web searches, 239
Web Slices, 246
Wi-Fi networks, 546, 692
WIM (Windows Imaging Format) files, 19
windows
    color of, 77
    desktop display of, 26
    taskbar groupings of open, 41

Windows 3.0 and 3.1 virtual machine, 122
Windows 7
    editions, 3, 16, 859
    overview, 17–20
Windows 7 installation
    clean installs, 5, 863
    essential configuration tasks, 9–15
    installing previous version after, 880
    logging on and finalizing, 8
    overview, 862
    reinstalling, 831, 845
    reviewing and activating computer, 15
    upgrade, 864
Windows Basic experience level, 78
Windows Classic experience level, 78
Windows Display Driver Model (WDDM), 68,
    71, 154, 896
Windows domain, joining, 4
Windows features, table of, 137
Windows Imaging Format (.wim) files, 19
Windows Vista, 3, 112, 862, 868
Windows XP, differences with Windows 7, 3,
    111, 113, 121, 123, 595
wireless networks
    ad hoc, 698
    adapters for, 157, 557, 695
    configuring available/preferred, 699
    devices, 201, 694
    first time setup, 8, 11
    managing, 555, 692, 696
    printers, installing, 485
    routers/access points, 550, 700
    technologies, 693
Wise Install, Windows, 116
work network, 462
workgroup, 9
working offline, 244, 474
worms, 588
writing pad mode, 529

X

Xerox WorkCentre Pro Scanner, 491

Y

Y adapters for USB, 146
Yahoo, 637

Z

zipped files, 97, 120
zones
    local intranet, 272
    restricted sites, 274
    trusted sites, 268, 273
Zoom (Internet Explorer 8), 251
zoom key, 166

About the Author

William R. Stanek (*http://www.williamstanek.com*) has more than 20 years of hands-on experience with advanced programming and development. He is a leading technology expert, an award-winning author, and a pretty darn good instructional trainer. Over the years, his practical advice has helped millions of programmers, developers, and network engineers all over the world. He has written more than 100 books. Current or forthcoming books include *Active Directory Administrator's Pocket Consultant, Windows Group Policy Administrator's Pocket Consultant, Windows PowerShell 2.0 Administrator's Pocket Consultant*, and *Windows Server 2008 Inside Out*, all from Microsoft Press.

William has been involved in the commercial Internet community since 1991. His core business and technology experience comes from more than 11 years of military service. He has substantial experience in developing server technology, encryption, and Internet solutions. He has written many technical white papers and training courses on a wide variety of topics. He frequently serves as a subject-matter expert and consultant.

William has an M.S. with distinction in information systems and a B.S. in computer science, magna cum laude. He is proud to have served in the Persian Gulf War as a combat crew member on an electronic warfare aircraft. He flew on numerous combat missions into Iraq and was awarded nine medals for his wartime service, including one of the United States of America's highest flying honors, the air force's Distinguished Flying Cross.

William recently rediscovered his love of the great outdoors. When he's not writing, teaching, or making presentations, he can be found hiking, biking, backpacking, traveling, and/or trekking the great outdoors in search of adventure. Currently, he resides in the Pacific Northwest with his wife and children.

Follow William on Twitter at WilliamStanek (*http://twitter.com/williamstanek*).

Colophon

The animal on the cover of *Windows 7: The Definitive Guide* is an eland (*Taurotragus oryx*), a name derived from the Dutch word for moose. Native to the savannahs and arid plains of eastern and southern Africa, elands are the largest African bovids and the largest antelopes in the world. They stand about five feet high at the shoulder, and full-grown males (bulls) may weigh as much as 2,000 pounds. Both sexes are characterized by heavy, spiraling horns that extend up to three feet. Their coats are tan or reddish with accents of white; bulls have a tuft of black fur growing from their dewlap (the loose skin hanging from the neck) and a mat of fur on their foreheads that thickens with age.

The eland's diet consists mainly of foliage, though it also eats fruits, seeds, seedpods, and tuberous roots. It uses its long horns to move twigs and branches into reach. Elands feed for long periods of time to maintain their massive build. Both diurnal and nocturnal, they feed and sleep during the day and feed most of the night during cooler months, but sleep during the day and feed all night when the weather is hot. Though it has not adapted to desert conditions, the eland employs the same type of water conservation that desert-dwelling animals use. Its body temperature can rise as much as 13 degrees without the eland having to expend any energy to cool itself off.

Though the size and power of the male eland may discourage animal predators, female elands can be vulnerable to attacks from lions and spotted hyenas. Humans are a more pronounced threat, however, as the slowness and relative docility of the eland makes it easy to hunt, and it is valued for its rich milk, meat, and useful hide.

Elands are the animals most often depicted in early East African rock art. They also figure prominently into the mythology of tribes such as the Bushmen of southern Africa. In one famous myth, the wife of Cagn, the Bushmen's shape-shifting supreme god, gives birth to the first eland. Cagn's sons kill the young animal while hunting, angering their father. Cagn sprinkles the dead animal's blood and fat on the ground, and a multitude of elands emerge, which Cagn allows his people to hunt and eat. The Bushmen attribute the wildness of the eland to the fact that the first one was killed before it was ready to be hunted, and thus was spoiled.

The cover image is from Wood's *Animate Creation*. The cover font is Adobe ITC Garamond. The text font is Linotype Birka; the heading font is Adobe Myriad Condensed; and the code font is LucasFont's TheSansMonoCondensed.

Get even more for your money.

Join the O'Reilly Community, and register the O'Reilly books you own.It's free, and you'll get:

- 40% upgrade offer on O'Reilly books
- Membership discounts on books and events
- Free lifetime updates to electronic formats of books
- Multiple ebook formats, DRM FREE
- Participation in the O'Reilly community
- Newsletters
- Account management
- 100% Satisfaction Guarantee

Signing up is easy:

1. **Go to: oreilly.com/go/register**
2. **Create an O'Reilly login.**
3. **Provide your address.**
4. **Register your books.**

Note: English-language books only

To order books online:

oreilly.com/order_new

For questions about products or an order:

orders@oreilly.com

To sign up to get topic-specific email announcements and/or news about upcoming books, conferences, special offers, and new technologies:

elists@oreilly.com

For technical questions about book content:

booktech@oreilly.com

To submit new book proposals to our editors:

proposals@oreilly.com

Many O'Reilly books are available in PDF and several ebook formats. For more information:

oreilly.com/ebooks

O'REILLY®

Spreading the knowledge of innovators   **www.oreilly.com**

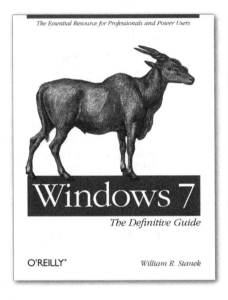